Ethiopia

EASTERN AFRICA SERIES

Women's Land Rights & Privatization in Eastern Africa
Edited by BIRGIT ENGLERT
& ELIZABETH DALEY

War & the Politics of Identity in Ethiopia: Making Enemies & Allies in the Horn of Africa
KJETIL TRONVOLL

Moving People in Ethiopia: Development, Displacement & the State
Edited by ALULA PANKHURST
& FRANÇOIS PIGUET

Living Terraces in Ethiopia: Konso Landscape, Culture & Development
ELIZABETH E. WATSON

Eritrea: A Dream Deferred
GAIM KIBREAB

Borders & Borderlands as Resources in the Horn of Africa
Edited by DEREJE FEYISSA
& MARKUS VIRGIL HOEHNE

After the Comprehensive Peace Agreement in Sudan
Edited by ELKE GRAWERT

Land, Governance, Conflict & the Nuba of Sudan
GUMA KUNDA KOMEY

Ethiopia: The Last Two Frontiers
JOHN MARKAKIS

Resurrecting Cannibals: Witchhunts, 'Pagans' & the Catholic Church in Western Uganda*
HEIKE BEHREND

Foundations of an African Civilisation: Aksum & the Northern Horn 1000 BC – AD 1300*
DAVID W. PHILLIPSON

* forthcoming

Ethiopia
The Last Two Frontiers

JOHN MARKAKIS

Emeritus Professor of History
University of Crete

JAMES CURREY

James Currey
www.jamescurrey.com
is an imprint of Boydell & Brewer Ltd
PO Box 9, Woodbridge, Suffolk IP12 3DF, UK
and of Boydell & Brewer Inc.
668 Mt Hope Avenue, Rochester, NY 14620, USA
www.boydellandbrewer.com

© John Markakis 2011
First published 2011

1 2 3 4 5 15 14 13 12 11

All Rights Reserved. Except as permitted under current legislation no part of this work may be photocopied, stored in a retrieval system, published, performed in public, adapted, broadcast, transmitted, recorded or reproduced in any form or by any means, without the prior permission of the copyright owner

The right of John Markakis to be identified as the author of this work has been asserted in accordance with sections 77 and 78 of the Copyright, Designs and Patents Act 1988

The publisher has no responsibility for the continued existence or accuracy of URLs for external or third-party internet websites referred to in this book, and does not guarantee that any content on such websites is, or will remain, accurate or appropriate.

British Library Cataloguing in Publication Data
Markakis, John.
Ethiopia : the last two frontiers. — (Eastern Africa series)
1. Ethiopia—History—1889-1974. 2. Ethiopia—History—1974- 3. Ethiopia—Politics and government—1889-1974.
4. Ethiopia—Politics and government—1974-1991.
5. Ethiopia—Politics and government—1991-
I. Title II. Series
963-dc22
ISBN 978-1-84701-033-9 (James Currey cloth)

Typeset in 10/11 pt Baskerville
by Kate Kirkwood, Cumbria, UK

Dedication

To all the people of Ethiopia
in the centre & the periphery, the high & the low lands

Contents

List of Maps & Tables

Maps

Tables

Preface

This book presents the gist of what I have learned about Ethiopia over several decades. Our acquaintance began in 1965 when I became fascinated with the quaint regime of Haile Selassie, and at the same time witnessed the rise of an impassioned political radicalism that put an end to the imperial era. The lowlands were below the horizon of my interests at the time. It was in the 1970s, while visiting refugee camps in the region filled with humanity fleeing the violence of war, that the seed for this work was planted in my mind. Many refugees were pastoralists who had no apparent connection with, nor clear understanding of, the political currents that swept them from their homes and landed them in these camps. I discovered that pastoralists were eager recruits in insurgent movements warring against regimes in Ethiopia, Sudan and Somalia, movements whose motives and goals had little to do with pastoralist concerns. I was intrigued by this apparent contradiction and set about to clarify it in my mind. This book is the result of that effort.

I have become familiar with Ethiopia's lowland periphery over the past two decades while working as a consultant for a variety of organisations with development and peacemaking projects in the region. I found myself drawn to an area little known in Ethiopia itself and scarcely at all abroad, where an ancient way of life is threatened with extinction. I was fortunate to work with the Ministry of Federal Affairs in 2005-2008; which gave me the opportunity to travel extensively in the borderlands and observe at close range the functioning of the federal system at the far ends of the state. Well meaning, hard working and experienced, the Ministry's staff provided an invaluable source of knowledge that I was privileged to draw upon. Special thanks are due to Dr. Sarah Vaughan, my colleague in the Ministry.

I was also able to consult with leaders of political parties within and outside Ethiopia. Among those whom I interviewed repeatedly and who deserve special thanks are Beyene Petros of the National Hadiya Democratic Organisation and the Southern Ethiopia Peoples' Democratic

Coalition; Merera Gudina of the Oromo National Congress; Abdilahi Mohammed Sadi, Mohammed S. Dolal, Abdirahman Mahdi and Mohammed A. Yassin of the Ogaden National Liberation Front; Sultan Mohammed Hadj Hassan Gababa of the Gerri clan; Taha Ali and Leenco Latta of the Oromo Liberation Front; Ali Mirah Hanfare of the Afar Liberation Front, Yusuf Yasin of the Afar National Liberation Front; Moohamooda Gas of the Afar Revolutionary Democratic Unity Front; Mohamud Dirir Geddi of the Ethiopian Somali Democratic League; Khadar Mualim, Abdirashid Dulune Raffle, Ahmed Shide and Jamal Ali of the Somali Peoples' Democratic Party.

Over the years I was befriended and helped by very many Ethiopian from all walks of life. With a characteristic penchant for political analysis, they contributed more than I can thank them for. I can only hope that the publication of this work offers some recompense, although I know many of them will disagree with its conclusions. To comment on politics is to court criticism and invite censure from those who think their particular cause is slighted in the telling of the story. I regret this, but have learned to accept it as a professional hazard.

Special thanks are due to friends and colleagues who took an interest in this work from the start, offering encouragement and thoughtful comments during the years it took to complete. David Turton shared his unrivalled knowledge of the Ethiopian lowlands and, more importantly, touched me with the empathy he feels for their people. Asmalash Beyene insisted that I maintain balance and objectivity, not easy in a work of political analysis. I trusted Martin Doornbos to guide me through the latest theoretical innovations in this field. Lionel Cliffe passed on a stream of relevant data that found its way into this work. John Young's comments were both insightful and encouraging. Mary Dyson read the manuscript with the insight drawn from a long and intimate knowledge of Ethiopia. My daughter Thalia took on the task of mapmaking, scanning, formatting and sundry other computer operations that are beyond me. Once more, my wife Judith generously allowed me the luxury of ample time for travelling and writing.

Acronyms

ALF	Afar Liberation Front
AETU	All Ethiopia Trade Union
AAPO	All Amhara Peoples Organisation
ANDM	Amhara National Democratic Movement
AEUP	All Ethiopia Unity Party
ANLM	Afar National Liberation Movement
APDO	Afar Peoples Democratic Organisation
ARDUF	Afar Revolutionary Democratic Unity Front
BGPDUF	Beni Shangul Gumuz Peoples Democratic Unity Front
BPLM	Berta Peoples Liberation Movement
CELU	Confederation of Ethiopian Labour Unions
COPWE	Commission for the Organisation of the Party of the Workers of Ethiopia
CUD	Coalition for Unity and Development
EBPDO	Ethiopian Berta Peoples Democratic Organisation
EDORM	Ethiopian Democratic Officers Revolutionary Movement
EDU	Ethiopian Democratic Union
EHRCO	Ethiopian Human Rights Council
ELF	Eritrean Liberation Front
EPDM	Ethiopian Peoples Democratic Movement
EPLF	Eritrean Peoples Liberation Front
EPRDF	Ethiopian Peoples Revolutionary Democratic Front
EPRP	Ethiopian Peoples Revolutionary Party
ESDL	Ethiopian Somali Democratic League
ESPDP	Ethiopian Somali Peoples Democratic Party
FDRE	Federal Democratic Republic of Ethiopia
FIDO	Front for Independent Democratic Oromia
GPDUP	Gambella Peoples Democratic Unity Party
GPLM	Gambella Peoples Liberation Movement
HNDO	Hadiya National Democratic Organisation
IFLO	Islamic Front for the Liberation of Oromia
ISEN	Institute for the Study of Ethiopian Nationalities
MEISONE	All Ethiopia Socialist Movement
NDRP	National Democratic Revolutionary Programme
NEB	National Elections Board
NRS	National Regional State of the Federal Democratic Republic of Ethiopia
NGO	Non-Governmental Organisation

ONLF	Ogaden National Liberation Front
OALF	Oromo Abo Liberation Front
OLF	Oromo Liberation Front
ONC	Oromo National Congress
OPDO	Oromo Peoples Democratic Organisation
PDO	Peoples Democratic Organisation.
PFDJ	Popular Front for Democracy and Justice
POMOA	Provisional Office for Mass Organisation
PMAC	Provisional Military Advisory Council
RRC	Relief and Rehabilitation Commission
SALF	Somali Abo Liberation Front
SEPDC	Southern Ethiopian Peoples Democratic Coalition
SEPDF	Southern Ethiopian Peoples Democratic Front
SLM	Sidama Liberation Movement
SNNPRS	Southern Nations, Nationalities and Peoples Regional State
SORDU	Southern Rangelands Development Unit
SPDP	Somali Peoples Democratic Party
SPLA/SPLM	Sudan Peoples Liberation Army/Movement
SYL	Somali Youth League
TLF	Tigray Liberation Front
TNO	Tigray National Organisation
TPLF	Tigray Peoples Liberation Front
UEDF	United Ethiopia Democratic Forces
UOPLF	United Oromo Peoples Liberation Front
WSLF	Western Somalia Liberation Front
WPE	Workers' Party of Ethiopia

Glossary

Abba Gaada	traditional Oromo title
Asrat	tax of one-tenth
Awraja	sub-province
Balabbat	person of substance/ traditional chief
Debub	south/southern regional state
Birked	cement water storage tank
Dergue	committee, the military regime (1975-1991)
Dejazmatch	traditional Ethiopian title
Ferenji	foreigner
Fitawrari	traditional Ethiopian title
Gaada	traditional Oromo institution
Gabbar	peasant/tax payer
Gim Gima	self-criticism
Gosa	tribe/clan
Gult	fiefdom
Gultegna	fief holder
Habesha	Christian highlander /Abyssinian
Kale Hiwot	Ethiopian Protestant Church
Kati	title of Sidama rulers
Kebele	rural and town dweller association
Kelad	unit of land measurement
Kenyazmatch	traditional Ethiopian title
Khida Aba	Afar traditional title
Kilil	regional state
Kwar	traditional Anywaa title/village chief
Mekane Yesus	Ethiopian Protestant Church
Neftegna	gun-man
Nyetch	traditional Anywaa title (king)
Pentes	members of Pentecostal Churches
Ras	traditional Ethiopian title
Rist	traditional landholding rights
Ristegna	landholder
Shanqila	black/slave
Sisso	one-third, land division
Tapath	Majangir ritual leader
Ugas	traditional Somali title
Woreda	administrative district
Woyane	1943 uprising in Tigray/TPLF
Zalan	pastoralist/nomad
Zamatcha	campaign/ expedition

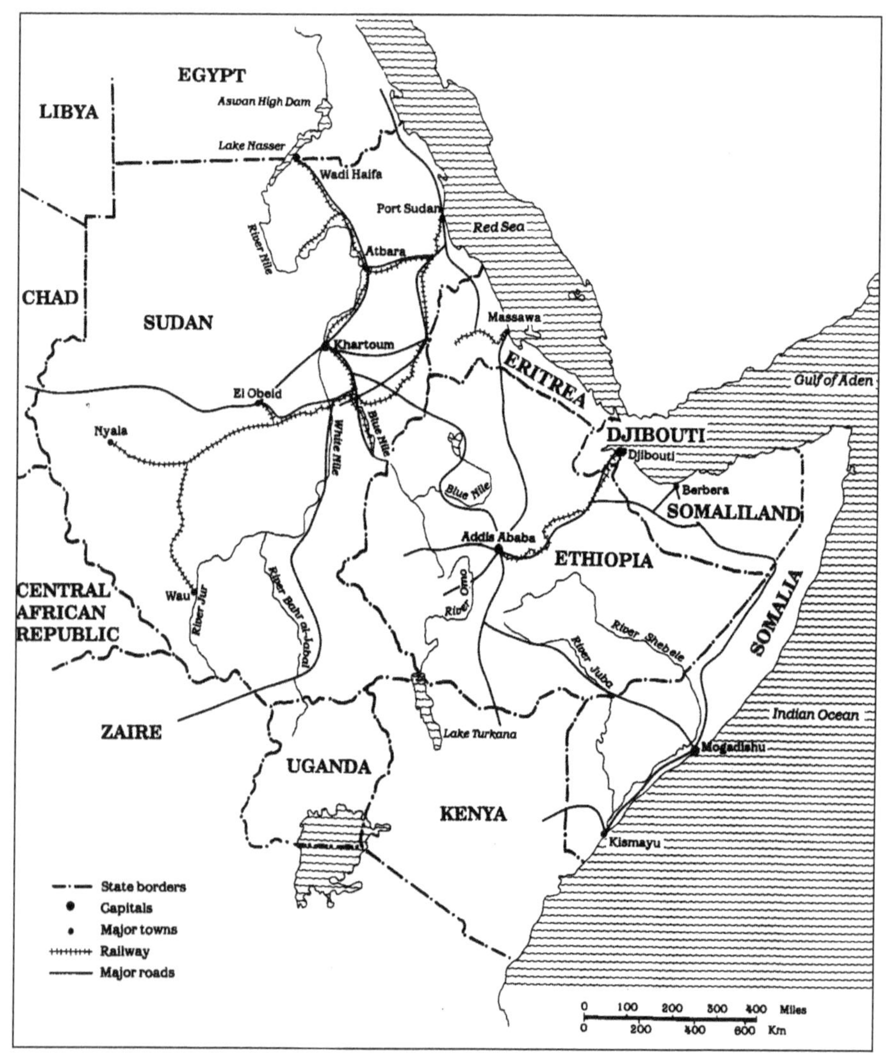

Map 1 The Horn of Africa
(Source: Tim Allen (ed.) *In Search of Cool Ground*, James Currey, 1996)

Introduction

This is the tale of a long drawn out struggle to forge a nation-state in Africa. Lasting over a century, it has made much progress, yet it is nowhere near an end. Waged against determined opposition, it has incited endless conflict and stained the pages of the country's history with the blood of generations. Today the struggle continues, and so does the bloodshed and the misery it brings. 'In a world that consists mainly of states … trying to become nation-states' (Claude 1986: 3) the story is not uncommon. In this world, where the pursuit of that exalted end justifies all means, bloodshed is not simply commonplace, it is inevitable. If there is a moral to this account of the Ethiopian story, it is not to raise the question whether the end justifies all means, but whether violence is the most effective means to that end in the 21st century.

To attempt to answer this question we must examine the process of nation-state building in this country in the context of African and world experience. Unfortunately, Africa is 'omitted from the scholarly literature on state creation and consolidation' (Herbst 2000: 20), the assumption being that the state in Africa emerged fully formed from the colonial womb. After decades of hopeful expectations for 'political development' and excitement over 'waves of democratisation' this literature now comprises the pathology of political life in the continent. The very existence of a functioning state in Africa is in doubt. 'It is a striking fact that, at the turn of the twentieth century, no large African country can be said to have consolidated control over its entire territory' (Herbst 2000: 254). Most often such states 'are states on paper and maps only. They are recognised internationally, but they often do not function as states' (Laremont 2005: 10).

We are obliged to turn to another part of the world, for whose experience historiography has much to say. In the mid-1960s, the Social Science Research Council in the United States launched a series of studies of early state formation in Western Europe aiming 'to generate insights relevant to today's state builders' (Ertman 1997: 2). Among the insights generated by the studies one was considered a seminal contribution. This concerned the role of war as the catalyst in the process of state building. 'War made the state, and the state made war', is the gist of it. Charles Tilly, the scholar credited with it, explains:

> In an idealized sequence, a great lord made war so effectively as to become dominant in a substantial territory, war making led to increased extraction of the means of war – men, arms, food, lodging, transportation, supplies, and/or the money to buy them – from the population within that territory. The building up of war-making capacity likewise increased the capacity to extract. The very activity of extraction, if successful, entailed the elimination, neutralization, or co-optation of the great lord's local rivals; thus, it led to state making. As a by-product, it created organization in the form of tax collection agencies, police forces, courts, exchequers, account keepers; thus it again led to state making. To a lesser extent, war making likewise led to state making through the expansion of military organization itself, as a standing army, war industries, supporting bureaucracies, and (rather later) schools grew up within the state apparatus… In the course of making war, extracting resources, and building up the state apparatus, the managers of states formed alliances with specific social classes. The members of those classes loaned resources, provided technical services, or helped ensure the compliance of the rest of the population, all in return for a measure of protection against their own rivals and enemies. As a result of these multiple strategic choices, a distinctive state apparatus grew up within each major section of Europe. (Tilly 1985: 183)

This analysis of state formation refers to the early modern history of Western Europe – 17th and 18th centuries. It is important to note that the concept of the 'nation' does not feature because it did not exist at the time. When it was introduced later as the nation-state, it involved a far more complex and difficult process, which not many modern states have managed successfully. Because state building in Western Europe is linked to the onset of modernity and technological progress, particularly in warfare, Tilly's insight has not been tested in Africa. The practice of warfare in pre-colonial Africa has not shed the 'primitive' label stamped on it by colonial historiography. It is not simply the crude technology and artless tactics that define it. It is also the absence of wider strategies and broader aims allegedly lacking in pre-colonial warfare in Africa, and the implication that it seldom served grand political designs or stimulated social change.[1] While fascinated by the colourful ritual and religious symbolism that attended 'tribal warfare', historians found the rest of it meaningless. 'African war was seen as less the mother of invention than an ongoing process of wanton destruction' brought to a blessed end by Western colonialism (Reid 2007: 232).

[1] This generalisation about Africa was challenged recently in a study of warfare in pre-colonial eastern Africa – the Great Lakes region and the Ethiopian Plateau – which concludes that warfare there had similar motives and objectives as elsewhere, and that 'war facilitated social, political, cultural and economic innovation, as well as causing great suffering' (Reid 2007: 235). Other studies have highlighted the role of warfare in the rise of pre-colonial states: the Hausa Fulani in West Africa, the Zulu in South Africa and the Mahdist state in the Sudan. What these cases have in common, of course, is that they did not survive imperialism, all except Ethiopia.

Neither is war credited with a role in shaping the state in post-colonial Africa. The modern state in the continent was created and its borders defined without the intervention of war. The absence of conflict over sovereignty and territory relieved African rulers of the need to pursue the centralisation and administrative integration of their states, while foreign aid balanced their inability to raise revenue through taxation (Herbst 2000: 113). There are some who attribute the failure of post-colonial state formation in the continent to the absence of war; an inverted test of Tilly's proposition. Convinced that state building in Africa can best succeed through war, there are even those who welcome the on-going violence in parts of the continent.[2]

The African paradigm notwithstanding, Ethiopia's experience conforms closely to the notion of war as the midwife in the birth of states. Warfare is the crimson thread that runs uninterruptedly through its long history, a tale 'of continual war with both internal and external enemies' (Bulatovich 2000: 100). Dating back to the 13th century AD, Ethiopia's royal chronicles recorded the martial achievements of its rulers, and more recently 'there was no time at which the empire as a whole could have been said to be at peace' (Clapham 2000: 5). These were not 'tribal' skirmishes, but involved large, well equipped armies. In the battle of Adwa (1896) the Ethiopians mustered a force of more than 100,000 to annihilate an Italian invading force of some 20,000. To field an army of this size required a degree of organization and tactical sophistication which, in this instance at least, out-performed a European force sent to colonise Ethiopia. Thanks to imported weaponry, Ethiopia's soldiers had enough modern firearms to match the invader's firepower. Unlike the rest of the continent, European imperialism met its match in this corner of Africa.

Ethiopia at the time was in the midst of its own expansion which turned the legendary Christian kingdom into a veritable empire. Completed within a few years after Adwa, this was the last and greatest stride in a centuries-long process of expansion that had seen the Christian kingdom's frontiers shift steadily southwards and the native people in its path subjugated and assimilated. Frequently halted and occasionally reversed, it is recorded in the royal chronicles, along with the endless wars that accompanied it. Halted for nearly three centuries – mid-16th to mid-19th – when the throne was submerged in a protracted struggle for supremacy and the kingdom itself dissolved into its provincial components – a period known as the Age of the Princes – the expansion resumed with great vigour in the second half of the 19th century. This was when the Age of the Princes concluded with the resurrection of the throne, and the unity of the Ethiopian state was restored. Undoubtedly, both events were encouraged by the appearance of foreign powers bent on conquest in the Horn of Africa. Subsequently, Ethiopia fought a series of wars to preserve its independence, and also competed successfully in the imperialist partition of the region. 'While rebuffing imperialism successfully in the north, Ethiopia managed to practice it in the south' (Erlich 1986: 4). Not a victim but a

[2] See Luttwak (1999).

participant in the 'scramble', Ethiopia doubled its territory and population in a burst of expansionist energy, and thereafter proudly styled itself the 'Ethiopian Empire'. The title was not a misnomer, since Ethiopia's rulers governed their new possessions more or less the same way and for similar ends as other imperial powers were doing.

The people who took pride in calling themselves Ethiopians were known also as Abyssinians (*Habesha*), a name commonly used by mapmakers and historians until well into the 20th century. When the kingdom became an empire, the name acquired political meaning: the builders and rulers of the empire were known as *Habesha*, regardless of ethnic origin. Today's ruling elite frown at the use of this name because it obstructs their effort to forge an inclusive Ethiopian national identity. The term is used here in its political connotation in order to distinguish the empire makers from the subjects of the empire, and not as the marker of a presumed ethnic identity.

The requirements of administering the population and exploiting the resources of its vastly expanded domain wrought fundamental change to the Christian kingdom, all of which falls within the process of state building described by Tilly. Its structure changed from a quasi-feudal form to a robust monarchical absolutism, and its administration was revamped in a quasi-bureaucratic pattern focused on extracting resources efficiently from a population cowed by a standing professional army. To rule the territories incorporated by the expansion, a complex system was devised that combined colonisation by transplanted Abyssinians and the co-optation of a subordinate indigenous elite.

From these raw beginnings, a process of state construction launched from the Abyssinian centre was pursued with increasing energy throughout the 20th century. Starting with the fairly simple task of administrative integration, the process widened to build a national economy and to provide the infrastructure it needed. Despite severe material constraints, considerable progress was made over the decades. In the second half of the 20th century, the architects of Ethiopia added national integration to their design. This was the heyday of African nationalism, and they were pursuing a universal goal. One could say they had little choice in the matter. 'Such is the dialectic of the political that the state seeks and must seek to foster the growth of a nation, indeed must posit its potential coming into being' (Friedrich, 1963: 551).

In Ethiopia's case, as in many others, the pursuit of national integration met stiff resistance within and outside the state's borders that came close to wrecking the project. Resistance came from territories incorporated in the imperial expansion, and from neighbouring states with their own nation-state building projects, which often overlapped and reinforced each other, making it impossible to insulate domestic issues from cross-border interference. The response of the state builders was twofold. Resort to force, the initial instinctive reaction, led to a steady growth of the military establishment and its gradual autonomy from the political authority, until finally the soldiers took over the running of the state. A parallel search went on for a formula that could give the state legitimacy and secure the loyalty of its subjects, and at the same time define a national identity broadly enough to represent a vastly heterogeneous population. After an aborted attempt at assimilating the entire population to the Abyssinian culture, resort was had to socialism and more recently to cultural pluralism and federalism. None of these addressed the fundamental political issue that continues to galvanise resistance: the assumed exclusive right of the Abyssinian elite to rule the state and plot the course leading to national integration.

*

Ethiopia is not alone in the region in its ambition to become a nation-state. In fact, all its neighbours in the Horn are pursuing this elusive goal. The fact that more often than not they work at cross purposes has turned the Horn into the most conflict ridden region of Africa. For half a century now, this corner of the continent has been a byword for conflict and poverty, two mutually reinforcing afflictions. The region holds the continental record for inter and intra-state wars; in Eritrea it boasts the only successful secession, and in Somalia the one truly failed state. The Horn is home to scores of 'national liberation' movements fighting for power within their own states, striving to join another state, or to build a state of their own. Indeed, the region is a chaotic laboratory for would-be state builders. During the same half century, the Horn experienced famine at a biblical level more than once, and a significant portion of its population now survives on food aid from abroad. War and famine have pushed massive waves of refugees across state borders and across the seas to other continents, while the number of internally displaced people cannot even be guessed at.

Conflict is not uncommon in Africa. What is distinctive about the Horn is the fact that major confrontations involve territoriality and sovereignty, issues seldom contested in other parts of the continent. Wisely or not, Africa's nationalist leaders accepted the colonial geopolitical dispensation and enshrined it in the charter of the Organisation of African Unity, ruling out disputes over territory and borders. Also accepted by the international community and guaranteed by the United Nations, this consensus has kept inter-state relations in Africa relatively free of such disputes.

There is no such consensus in the Horn, where decolonisation unleashed struggles over territory and sovereignty on several fronts. 'Almost all the states of the Horn of Africa have, at one time or another, staked claim on parts or the whole of a neighbouring country. The region is unique in Africa in this respect' (Leenco 2009; 4). Somalia's independence in 1960 led to clashes over territory with all its neighbours, and two years later a struggle for secession started in Eritrea that was to last nearly three decades. Civil war in the Sudan erupted even before that country's independence in 1954, and went on with a brief interruption for five decades, earning the dubious distinction of 'Africa's longest war'. With occasional intermissions and lulls in the fighting, most of these disputes are still simmering half a century later. In the meantime, new bones of contention have appeared. By the time the war in Southern Sudan reached a tenuous détente early this century, another conflict had broken in Darfur in Western Sudan. The collapse of the Somali Republic produced a second (*de facto*) secessionist state in Somaliland. Ethiopia and Eritrea resumed fighting in 1998, and both are heavily involved in the Somali civil war as well. Coveted by both Somalia and Ethiopia, the Djibouti enclave survived only by remaining a dependency of France.

Why did the colonial dispensation not survive in this corner of Africa? Part of the answer lies with Ethiopia, a country involved, directly or indirectly, in nearly all the conflicts in the region during the post-colonial era. 'There is a long history of state formation and conflict within the Horn of Africa, largely, though not exclusively, centred upon what is now the polity of Ethiopia' (Gilkes 1999: 4). When it came, decolonisation revealed a crucial difference between the Ethiopian and European brands of imperialism. Thanks to the advanced stage of its capitalist economy, Europe was able to retain ownership of its colonial assets and preserve control over Africa's natural resources. By contrast, in the mid-20th century Ethiopia's own economy had yet to move beyond subsistence, while the country's most valuable resources, especially fertile land, were found in the territories incorporated by the expansion. The exploitation of these resources was based on a system of accumulation that depended on coercion and closely resembled Western feudalism. This archaic mode of exploitation was labour intensive and required the involvement of a very large number of beneficiaries in the process. Accordingly, a commensurate number of people moved from the Abyssinian homeland in the northern plateau to the conquered territories in the south to control and administer them. Many more followed to take advantage of fertile land offered by the imperial state practically for free in order to expand its tax base and to exploit native labour in conditions of quasi-serfdom. Appropriately known as *neftegna* (gunmen), the northerners comprised a ruling class that was essential to the maintenance of the imperial state and its economy. It was large, armed and a pillar of the imperial state. To dispossess it required the sort of revolution that took place in Ethiopia in 1974.

Although it called Ethiopia an 'empire', the imperial regime did not regard the expansion as an imperialist venture. On the contrary, it saw it as the restoration of the *status quo ante*, the legitimate recovery of territories that Ethiopia had allegedly lost in times past. When decolonisation was redrawing the political map of Africa, Ethiopia's rulers were leisurely pursuing the integration of the 'recovered' territories into what they hoped would become a modern nation-state. There has been little time and even less resources for this immense task, and it remains incomplete and fiercely contested. Most of the issues involved in the tangled web that is the contemporary geopolitical situation in the Horn can be linked to Ethiopia's pursuit of the nation-state in the teeth of manifold opposition. This state has been compelled to fight persistent challenges to its territorial integrity, forfeiting in the process the prospects for socio-economic development and political stability. The aim of this study is to explore this process and weigh the results and consequences for the people of this country. The analytical perspective outlined below can usefully be applied to the study of its neighbours as well.

The centre/periphery perspective

The process of state formation is initiated and managed from an expanding centre of power that radiates outwards to annex territories along its geographical periphery, and then weaves an administrative network to incorporate them and capture their resources:

> Historically, states have arisen in response to the requirements of territorial control, surplus expropriation and external defense in relatively wealthy and densely populated areas. Almost invariably, they derive from a core zone in which the criteria for state formation are most clearly met and then expand into surrounding regions, until they are checked either by the countervailing power of rival states, or else the progressive weakening of the force that can be projected from the core, into poorer and less densely populated peripheries. (Clapham 2000: 10)

What distinguishes the centre from the periphery is not simply geography, though this is often a salient feature. The locus of power is the most significant indicator. Imperialism is founded on an uneven power relationship, 'a hierarchical system of political relationships with one power being much stronger than the other' (Lundestad 1990: 37), and a 'relationship of a hegemonial state to peoples or nations under its control' (Lichtheim 1971: 5).

What defines the centre is the monopoly of power and the hegemonic position it occupies in the state. 'Ultimately the notion of centre-periphery relations should not be based on geographical or cultural criteria, but primarily on a model of the structure and distribution of political power' (Abbink 2002: 157). What defines the periphery is its marginal position in the power structure of the state, or more precisely, its exclusion from state power. Normally, exclusion from power translates into lack of access to state resources, as well as the loss of native resources appropriated by the state and transferred to the centre. Equally important is the denigration of social and cultural accomplishments of societies in the periphery, and the expectation in the name of national integration that they should give place to the superior cultural accomplishments of the centre. Powerlessness, economic exploitation and cultural discrimination add up to a severe form of marginalisation, the defining feature of the periphery, the implications of which in Ethiopia are a major theme of this book.

Before setting out the analytical perspective, it is necessary to define what the terms centre and periphery refer to in this instance. Notionally the dividing line lies between population groups that are fully integrated into the structure of the state and the hierarchy of power that governs it, and those that are only partially integrated, or not all. Because we are dealing with a dynamic, multi-dimensional, fluid historical process where the dividing line separating centre from periphery is constantly shifting, drawing this line at any point in time and space is futile. It freezes a dynamic process at one point when, in fact, to the extent that integration proceeds the periphery recedes. Yet, because groups in the periphery respond differently, it does not recede symmetrically. 'Specific regions and communities could be defined as more or less peripheral, in accordance with their physical distance from the capital, their level of incorporation into the coercive and economic structures of government, and their degree of association with the legitimizing myths of nationhood' (Clapham 2002: 11).

On either side of the divide, the position of different population groups and classes on the integration/power scale varies, making it impossible to draw lines on the map to distinguish centre from periphery. For example, what we refer to as an 'auxiliary elite' in this study constitutes a class in the periphery enjoying a share of state power. Likewise, there is a world of difference on the power scale between the peasant class in the historical Abyssinian centre and the ruling elite of the same nationality. Consequently, reference to the 'centre' in this study is to the power elite and decision makers, who invariably find or create a subordinate elite to help them administer the periphery, and thus introduce class distinctions where they did not exist.

The fact that there are elite groups on both sides of the centre/periphery divide, does not mean they belong to the same ruling class, for the simple reason that the peripheral elites are creations of the centre and wholly dependent on it. The elite at the centre make decisions; the elite in the periphery implement them. Despite changes in the social composition of the elite at both ends over the past century, this feature of their relationship has not changed to this day. Furthermore, the fact that the mass of the people on both sides are dominated by elite groups does not erase the fact that they live in different worlds. Those who share the Abyssinian identity belong, psychologically at least, to the dominant nationality, and live relatively secure in the embrace of a culture defended by the state. It is this culture that the mass in the periphery is expected to embrace, willingly or not, in order for the nation-state project to be completed.

Lastly, given the massive in-country migration of peoples that took place over a century, defining centre and periphery in terms of geography represents a gross distortion in terms of demography. First, large numbers of Abyssinians from the north migrated to the south in the wake of the expansion at the turn of the past century, and were followed by a steady stream of their compatriots until the turn of this century. In the south, they formed a landholding ruling class that lived and intermingled with their subjects, and now their descendants comprise a significant part of the population in every part of the periphery, especially the towns. Second, during the same time, a reverse migration from the periphery brought masses of people to the geographic centre of the expanded state, the greater Addis Ababa region, where economic opportunities appeared. Some ethnic groups that found a particular niche in the emerging urban economy are now more numerous in the central region than in their homelands.

The approach followed in this study is to trace an outline of this process over the past century, examining three distinct phases, followed by a tentative assessment of the progress it appears to have made at each phase. The starting point in time is the last quarter of the 19th century, when the Abyssinians from the north overran the rest of the plateau and the lowland zone surrounding it. At this point, one can add a geographical reference by drawing a line on the map that joins the loop of the Blue Nile River with a line crossing Addis Ababa. Abyssinia lay to the north of it, and the bulk of the territories annexed by the expansion, that is the periphery, lay to the south. The second phase coincides with the rule of the military regime (1974-1991) at the end of which geographic references become blurred, and the third phase coincides with that of the incumbent regime since 1991, when things become even more complicated.

*

State-building histories are tales of conquest and domination celebrating the deeds of state builders and rulers: understandably so, since 'the initiative for establishing these polities came, in all cases, from the rulers – emperors, kings, or some members of a patrician ruling class' (Eisenstadt 1993: 13). The periphery features only as it appears in the path of the expansion to be overrun and incorporated into the expanding state, and little attention is paid to it afterwards. This 'centrist' perspective, according to one critic, 'overemphasizes determination by the center and underrates the active role of peripheral peoples' (Ferguson & Whitehead 1992: 4). Another critic calls it 'a presupposition of virtually unbridled state autonomy', as a result of which 'state-centred analysis in African studies concentrated almost exclusively on rulers' interests' (Boone 2003: 8, 16).

A more nuanced analysis of state formation dynamics has emerged lately in studies of so-called 'subaltern' groups. Until recently, this was solely the domain of social anthropology, a discipline that produced invaluable knowledge to which this study is heavily indebted. An earlier tendency to perceive subaltern groups in isolation meant that social anthropology often missed an important contextual dimension of its subject's existence and evolution, which is the centre/periphery linkage and interaction that shapes both sides of this relationship. Social anthropologists as well as political scientists now recognise that state construction is best understood as a dynamic relationship whose end product is negotiated rather than imposed. 'Center-provincial bargaining, rather than the unilateral choices of the center, is what drives the politics of national integration and determines how institutions distribute power,' adds this critic of the 'centrist' perspective (Boone 2003).

Following annexation, the periphery becomes a concern for the centre because it must be ruled, and the form of rule that emerges depends as much on the nature of the periphery as on the preferences of the centre. Empire builders 'find themselves obliged to administer the lands, goods and people they acquire; they become involved in extraction of resources, distribution of goods, services, and incomes and adjudication of disputes' (Tilly 1990: 20). Two sets of factors – internal and external – determine centre policy. Among the former is political geography, highlighted by Herbst (2000). Distance from the centre, topography and climate are factors crucially involved in determining the choice of instruments that rulers design to maintain control. These enter into a cost-benefit analysis they must make when they decide whether and how to invest in consolidation through the creation of administrative structures.

The political economy of the periphery also figures prominently in the cost-benefit analysis. Modes of production, population density, surplus availability, land tenure systems, and trade potential are among the factors that must be taken into account. Areas of low population density and no surplus, such as pastoralist regions, might not be considered worth investing in and are left outside the bounds of administrative arrangements. In Ethiopia, the differential impact of such factors accounts for the dramatic contrast in attained levels of integration between highland and lowland regions, a topic examined in detail in this work. Simply put, the imperial regime found the cost of integrating the lowlands prohibitive, because it could not be recovered by taxation or profits from trade. Consequently, the lowland pastoralist habitat was largely ignored, and remains to this day outside meaningful administrative control, mired in extreme poverty and endemic conflict, the high mark of failure in the state formation process.

Integration at certain levels – administration, economy – proceeded faster and farther in highland areas inhabited by agrarian societies, whose systems of social organisation and traditional authority lent themselves to the pattern of indirect rule and resource expropriation imposed after incorporation. Another variable is the degree of similarity and compatibility between the society and culture of state builders and those of their subjects. Sedentary agrarian societies across the Ethiopian plateau have much in common.[3] Similarity has not proved an unmixed blessing. Land being the highest value for all, it was fated to become the bone of everlasting contention, and a major obstacle in the path of nation-state formation to this day. Land's significance is assessed further in this study.

The centre/periphery interaction is a dynamic process that impacts and transforms both sides. The intimacy of this process is blurred when it is depicted with the two sides posed in confrontation. The effect of pressure on subject groups for integration and assimilation is obvious and acknowledged. If only because the history of states is written by their founders, the effect of this process on the centre itself is neither obvious nor acknowledged. Expansion transforms the centre by altering its geographic and modifying its demography. It changed Ethiopia from a relatively homogeneous nation to what an Italian scholar called a 'museo di popoli' (Cerulli 1933), turning the Abyssinians into a minority in their own state. By vastly expanding the scope of the economy and enriching it with new resources, it undermined the traditional Abyssinian social structure and system of government, opening the way for new social classes to emerge and compete for power in the centre. The contribution of the periphery to the emerging national culture is undeniable. Ethiopian culture today is quite different from the Abyssinian prototype. One has only to think of the status of Islam whose adherents were despised, discriminated and occasionally persecuted in the past.

Another feature of the centre/periphery interaction is the impact on the state itself, its structure, policies and methods of rule. 'The formation of the state itself has been to some extent a story of negotiation and compromise with such provincial circumstances' (James 2001: 249). As a rule, the initiative is attributed to those who make decisions in the centre. However, as noted earlier, the design of imperial rule is cut to fit the shape of the periphery; its geography, economy, society and culture. One can argue that decision makers in the centre react as often as they initiate, and the design of state structures, policies and methods owes as much as anything else to the exigencies of rule over the periphery. 'The challenge of integration may have been far more determinant of state structure, national political trajectories, and even agricultural development strategy' than most outsiders realized (Boone 2003: 344).

The weight of the periphery in the political history of Ethiopia is conspicuous in the contribution it made to the three regime changes that took place in the past century. Regime changes represent historical ruptures in the process of state building, they are caused by the stress of upholding centre hegemony by force, and are followed by significant modifications intended to ease the stress and move the integration process forward. Thus, the soldiers who deposed Emperor Haile Selassie adopted a rigid, statist form of socialism, while the insurgents of the Ethiopian Peoples' Revolutionary Democratic Front (EPRDF) who displaced the soldiers, reversed direction and turned to federalism. The role of the periphery features prominently both among the causes and the consequences of these ruptures. In order to avoid exaggeration on this point, it is important to emphasize the fact that ruptures and regime changes occur when the centre itself is politically divided and weakened, and its hegemony is vulnerable to challenges from the periphery. The imperial regime was fatally undermined by loss of legitimacy and authority at the very centre of the state. The knockout blow to the military regime came from Tigray, the archetypal Abyssinian province. And the rise to power at the centre in 1991 of the EPRDF added another discordant ingredient to an already volatile political situation that has deteriorated steadily since, presaging another rupture with unforeseeable consequences.

The modifications that follow regime change are intended to realign the centre/periphery relationship and ease the stress on the state without, however, relinquishing centre hegemony. This requires the presence and cooperation of a subordinate elite in helping to administer the periphery. If a genuine elite is not available in the periphery it must be created. The imperial regime was able to secure the collaboration of traditional authorities in the conquered lands and compensated them accordingly. This class was dispossessed by the 1974 Revolution along with the entire imperial establishment, and the military rulers produced an alternative peripheral elite in the form of a 'Marxist' cadre corps to staff the state

[3] The similarity is highlighted by Levine (1974).

apparatus. The cadre corps in turn was ousted by the EPRDF, which then produced its own auxiliary elite in the form of a class of 'regional intellectuals' to administer the periphery. In no instance was the hegemony of the centre diminished. 'Central rulers devolved authority and prerogative to localities, but local leaders often found that what they had been handed was an "empty envelope"' (Boone 2003: 317).

High and low land periphery

A clear distinction is made in this work between the high lands that are the natural extension of the Ethiopian plateau southwards, called here the 'highland periphery', and the lowland zone that drops abruptly from the escarpment and surrounds the plateau on all sides, called here the 'lowland periphery'. There is a world of difference between the two, and this difference is clearly reflected in their interaction with the centre over the past century. The process of integration proceeded at a different pace and made uneven progress over the two dissimilar terrains, making it necessary for us to treat them separately.

The highland periphery includes the region that lies roughly below the line that joins the Blue Nile River in the west with Addis Ababa in the east, sometimes called 'southern highlands'. Its role in the process of state building in Ethiopia was crucial in the past and will prove decisive in the future. Here, integration made significant progress, because conditions were favourable and the state made the greater effort. The heterogeneity of the region itself and the varied, asymmetrical experiences of its peoples in their interaction with the state make it difficult to be precise on this point by referring to specific regions or groups in the southern highlands. A degree of generalisation is unavoidable. This may be forgiven since it is not the purpose of this work to plot and measure accurately the progress of integration on the plateau. What can be done is to indicate the levels of integration that have made progress in this region in binding it to the centre.

Administrative integration comes first because it is a prerequisite for resource extraction. In its initial phase the state relied on the armed immigrants from the north, the *neftegna*, and the local chiefs who were incorporated into a system of indirect rule. Efficient as an instrument of control, it proved wasteful in raising revenue, and was scrapped after World War II in the reorganisation of the state under Emperor Haile Selassie. It was reorganised twice since – by the military regime (1974-1991) and by the Ethiopian Peoples EPRDF) since 1991 – each time with a view to raising its efficiency as an instrument of control and raising revenue. By the turn of the 21st century, a fairly dense administrative network covered the highlands, north and south, whose inhabitants were all subject to the same laws, rules and regulations, enforced by the police and judicial branches and, if need be, the military. Though uneven and ragged at places, the administrative coverage of the highland periphery is comprehensive.

Economic integration is another level where significant progress was achieved. It is a remarkable fact that the modern economy beginning to emerge in mid-20th century is located entirely outside the Abyssinian homeland in the north, and is concentrated in the geographic centre and the southern highland periphery. A number of factors determined its location. Key was the construction of the Addis Ababa–Djibouti railway along an eastern route, where a number of towns grew to form an industrial complex containing most of the country's modern economic establishment. The availability of land for the taking in the periphery, where the state claimed ownership rights and could enforce them against a subject population, was essential for the growth of a plantation economy that appeared almost overnight in the Awash River Valley, as was the presence of a large and docile labour force from the periphery. Yet another factor was the development of an export sector, based on coffee and *chat*, both products of the southern highlands.

Investment in transport and communication under the imperial regime was directed in areas of economic development where, in addition to the railway, all-weather roads as well as air transport linked the major towns. The emerging urban sector was a pole of attraction for traders, craftsmen and labourers from other parts of the plateau, both north and south. The towns also served as state administrative centres and provided opportunities for education, attracting civil servants, teachers and students from all parts of Ethiopia. Social services and amenities, such as hospitals, hotels, cinemas and sport clubs also drew people into them. The towns became melting pots where inter-ethnic intercourse flourished, reducing the cultural and social distance among peoples hailing from all parts of the plateau. Thus, under the imperial regime a degree of urbanisation and economic development began to transform the highland periphery, integrating it into an emerging national economy. By contrast, and for the reasons given above, the regime's Abyssinia base in the north languished, with a decaying agricultural economy whose deficiency was dramatically exposed in the famine of the early 1970s, a catastrophe that led to the regime's downfall.

Modernisation with the introduction of Western education and the concurrent spread of Amharigna as the language of instruction, state administration and commerce, was another big step on the path to integration. The language of the empire builders became the *lingua franca* of the country, at least as far as the urban sector was and still is concerned. This was reinforced with the banning of all other indigenous languages from being taught, printed, broadcast or spoken on public occasions. Proficiency in the official language was a requirement for state employment and the *sine qua non* for social mobility; thus the process of assimilation promoted by the imperial state came to be known as 'Amharisation'. As it turned out, modern education proved a double-edged weapon in the context of nation-state building. On the one hand, it brought the younger generation in the periphery within the ambit of the state, because it was trained mainly for state employment. On the other, it produced a politically restless intelligentsia that went on to challenge not only the authority of the imperial regime, but the legitimacy of the state itself.

This side effect of modernisation and social mobilisation was not anticipated by the theorists of political development, who had assumed that economic and social development transcends and dissolves cultural barriers, and promotes assimilation and national integration. According to one author, 'a decisive factor in national assimilation was found to be the process of social mobilisation which accompanies the growth of markets, industries, and towns, and eventually of literacy and mass communication' (Deutsch 1966: 188). This assumption was criticised by Connor, who argued that modernisation and social mobilisation in many instances raise ethnic profiles, strengthen ethnic identities and lead to the politicisation of ethnicity. Interestingly, he believed Ethiopia had been spared the politicisation of ethnicity until then precisely because it was a poorly integrated state (Connor 1973: 328). The situation changed soon and it nearly wrecked the state building project. A decade later, C. Young made this comment:

> The nation-building idea is likely to be most mischievous in center- periphery cultural polities. The historical association of the state with the core culture means that the nation is inevitably identified with the dominant group. The imperative of nation-building then means the imposition of the core culture upon the periphery. Given the higher levels of cultural consciousness now generally prevalent, this type of national integration strategy is likely to provoke a hostile counter-mobilization of the periphery. Burma, Iran, and Ethiopia are exemplary cases of this process. Nation-building as a moral cloak for intensified domination is a dangerous doctrine. (C. Young, 1982: 175)

The process of integration initiated under the imperial regime was expanded and invigorated under successor regimes, and so did the challenges it faced in the periphery. Despite the radical nature of the modifications that these regimes introduced in the centre/periphery relationship, neither relinquished the centre's monopoly of power, although both tried to disguise the fact by declaring war on other iniquitous divisions in society: between social classes for the soldiers, between nationalities for the EPRDF. The subterfuge was transparent and intensified opposition from the periphery.

Hegemonic rule is by definition authoritarian and often violent, and the instruments of violence – military, security and police – are among the most developed state institutions. It is no accident that Ethiopia built the largest army in black Africa during the second half of the 20th century. Since then, state authoritarianism backed by violence has blighted the lives of all Ethiopians. Regime change in 1991 raised their hopes for an end to violence and authoritarian rule, but these faded when hostilities with Somalia and Eritrea resumed, and domestic insurgencies reappeared in several parts of the periphery. At the end of the first decade of the 21st century, the incumbent regime in Addis Ababa is engaged in the same battles that exhausted its predecessors, impoverished the country, and blasted peoples' hopes for peace, democracy and an escape from dire poverty.

One of the last frontiers Ethiopia's rulers have to cross is to redress the imbalance of power that marginalises the majority of its people and is the cause of endless strife that holds them in bondage. This is a fundamental requirement in state building which, as C. Young observes, may be more important than nation building. 'The state which succeeds in demonstrating reasonable standards of probity, integrity, fairness, and effectiveness earns thereby the respect of its populace. As a valued collectivity, it may accumulate a reservoir of support, even without intense commitment to its national personality, which permits it to withstand the inevitable cultural tensions' (ibid: 180). The failure to cross this 'last frontier' makes it impossible to forge a system of government based on consensus and legitimacy, and to complete the process of nation-state building with political integration.

*

The second 'frontier' that has to be crossed is the lowland periphery, where the integration process has barely begun, and where it confronts greater obstacles. None of the issues mentioned above that concern the highland periphery apply to the vast lowland belt that encircles the highland massif and forms the last and least accessible fringe periphery of the state. A clear distinction can be drawn physically and otherwise between the highlands, both north and south, and the surrounding lowlands, and a line can be drawn on the map to trace the escarpment that marks the boundary between them. Vital differences in geomorphology, altitude, climate, flora and fauna endowment have shaped ways of life that are fundamentally different. No real effort was made to bridge the chasm until the coming of the 21st century. The lowlands remain a world on their own: a 'fringe periphery' according to one anthropologist (Donham 1986: 42) an 'outer periphery' according to another (Almagor 1986: 115).

The fundamental difference between high and low land is the material foundation that determines the ways humankind makes a living. The escarpment is the boundary between 'the desert and the sown' (Nelson 1973), between settled cultivation and mobile pastoralism, between the campsite and the village. The escarpment is also the boundary between different cultures built on these foundations, and the history of this cultural divide is filled with prejudice and hostility. Long before the making of the Ethiopian empire, Islam flooded the lowlands and has been at war with Abyssinian Christianity ever since, storing a treasure of enmity from which both sides draw inspiration to this day. This conflict defined the relationship of pastoralists with the highland peasant kingdom throughout the period covered in this work. Conflict remains an ever present factor in their interaction to this day; 'the hostile periphery' is another image of the lowlands (Almagor 2002: 115).

The Horn of Africa is home to the largest remaining concentration of mobile livestock producers in the world. Four states in the region – Sudan, Somalia, Ethiopia, Kenya – rank first, third, fifth and sixth respectively in the world in terms of pastoralist population size. Though never accurately counted, the estimated size of this population ranges from 6% in Kenya to

60% in Somalia. Vast expanses of land in the arid zone, comprising major portions of each state's territory – 52% in Ethiopia, 66% in Sudan, 70% in Eritrea, 72% in Kenya, 75% in Somalia, 100% in Djibouti – are pastoralist habitat.

Ethiopia shares borders with all the other states, and its portion of the lowland pastoralist zone is by far the biggest. It stretches in a great arc from Eritrea in the northeast to Sudan in the west, covering the borders with Djibouti, Somaliland, Somalia and Kenya along the way. Two of the country's federal states – Afar, Somali – are inhabited exclusively by pastoralists, as are sizable portions of three others – Oromia, Southern, Gambella. The pastoralist population of Ethiopia is roughly estimated at 12% of the total, and occupies 120 of the country's 550 administrative districts. Reputedly, Ethiopia has the largest livestock population in Africa, a significant portion of which is raised in the lowlands. The country's major rivers flow through this zone, which is also studded with a string of lakes. Most of Ethiopia's wild animal reserves are in the lowlands, which are also rich in genetic diversity. Finally, Ethiopia's main road and railway links to the sea through Djibouti cross the lowland zone.

This zone is also an arc of conflict. A glance at the map of the Horn shows that all state borders are drawn through the lowlands. Consequently, border conflicts are frequently fought in this zone, and there have been more of these in this corner of Africa than any other part of the continent. No regime in this region during the second half of the last century enjoyed sufficient legitimacy to avoid forceful political challenges. All faced armed opposition and, with the exception of Kenya, all were ultimately overthrown. Most of these political battles were staged and fought in the lowlands, which provide ideal terrain for guerrilla warfare, as well as proximity to borders across which rebels can find refuge and support.

The situation at the start of the 21st century remains unchanged. Past wars have not resolved border disputes, and politically motivated insurgency remains endemic. Interwoven with such broader conflicts are the perennial clashes among pastoralists over traditional resources such as pastures, water, livestock and access routes, and new ones such as control of major transport routes and contraband trade, as well as state dispensed subsidies and social services. The introduction of automatic weaponry in recent decades has raised violence in the lowlands to genocidal levels, and seriously hinders state efforts to secure administrative control of this region.

The administrative machinery of the state was introduced in the lowlands very late, is still very thin on the ground, and unable to perform any of its functions meaningfully. Life in the pastoralist domain still follows the traditional rhythm and is regulated by custom. Neither the civil nor the penal codes of the state have much currency here, every man is armed, no one pays taxes, and the people rely on themselves for security and on their traditional leaders for justice. Since conflict in the borderlands also concerns state security, the side of the state's profile most familiar to lowlanders is the military, whose exertions neither dampen conflict nor contribute to effective governance. Mired in poverty and distracted by conflict, the people subsist on the margins of the state, outside the national economy, cut off from highland society and culture, and at the whim of a political system whose periodic dramatic swings they scarcely comprehend.

Its dire condition notwithstanding, the fringe periphery is crucially important to the state. In the geopolitical scheme of things it forms a buffer against neighbours who have claims on its territory. The vast, inhospitable and facility-poor lowland terrain attenuates military threats from that direction. Conversely, control of the lowlands puts Ethiopia's forces within striking distance of its neighbours' territory, and most Ethiopian military bases are located in the lowlands. In the absence of links between pastoralist livestock production and highland markets, the contribution of the lowlands to the national economy was limited to a small plantation sector and gold mining until recently: this is now changing dramatically with the massive leasing of lowland territory to agri-business for the production of commercial crops and biofuels, and a concurrent intensive exploration for mineral sources of energy.

This study examines the process and prospects of nation-state building in Ethiopia as it confronts another frontier in the lowland periphery, a world little known to outsiders even in Ethiopia and, for that reason, neglected and unappreciated. And yet, existing in a unique and exceptionally challenging physical setting, its people have shown extraordinary creativity in fashioning ways to exploit nature's meagre endowment and to weave highly imaginative, intricate modes of social organisation and flamboyant patterns of culture. There is a huge variety of social and cultural creativity here: one need only to think of the linguistic wealth that exists. Yet, ignored and caught in turmoil of poverty and conflict, this precious cultural heritage is threatened with extinction. Bringing the pastoralist realm into the state without destroying it in the process is the second frontier that the process of nation-building in Ethiopia has to cross.

Structure of study

The centre/periphery interaction that concerns us is a binary process, and cannot be examined as long as one of the sides involved in it remains obscure, not to say invisible. The first part of this study (The Lowland Frontier) presents profiles of the groups that inhabit the Ethiopian lowlands – Afar, Somali, Borana, Anywaa, Nuer, Gumuz, Berta, and a dozen smaller communities found in the Omo Valley. This is to do no more than to bring them out of history's shadows, and accord them the recognition and respect their history and cultures merit. The profiles are drawn with data obtained from a wide variety of sources, written and oral, collected over several years, and are presented in the first three chapters of Part I (The Lowland Frontier) portrays the lowland communities in their present state. How they got here is examined in the parts that follow, dealing with the process of state formation in Ethiopia over the course of the 20th century.

The obvious point of departure for Part II (Building the State: The Imperial Model) is the expansion at the turn of the 19th century, when the present borders of the Ethiopian state were drawn and the parameters of the centre/periphery relationship were fixed. Chapter 4 (Winning an Empire) covers the reign of the empire's founder, Emperor Menelik II (1889-1913). It considers the pressures that propelled expansion and relates them to the consequences for the peoples found in its path. For those who lived on high land and were subjected to a regime of quasi-serfdom, the consequences were dramatic and left a lasting impact. By contrast, the lowlanders were least affected: exhausted by the time it reached them, the expansion wave accomplished little more than to deprive them of autonomy and envelop them in the imperial domain. Chapter 5 (Building the Imperial State, 1916-1974) spans the long reign of the architect of the imperial state, Emperor Haile Selassie. It focuses on the emergence of monarchical absolutism, and the gradual modernization-cum-bureaucratization of the antique state designed to serve the over-riding concern with strengthening state control in the periphery and appropriating the surplus produced in its economy. State construction was accompanied with the building of a formidable, by African standards, military and security apparatus, made necessary by the rise of rebellion in the periphery. During this time, the empire also achieved its last expansion through the annexation of Eritrea, an event that was to bear bitter fruit for Ethiopia subsequently. The experience of the peoples in the periphery under the imperial state is examined in Chapter 6 (Imperial Rule in the Periphery).

Part III (Rebuilding the State: The Socialist Model) begins with the upheaval that brought the soldiers to power in 1974. This was fuelled by simultaneous crises in the centre and the periphery and resulted in a historic rupture, a truly revolutionary event that swept away not only the political superstructure of the imperial regime but also destroyed its social foundations, leading the military regime along a path of radical social reform that no one had advocated or anticipated, let alone planned. Chapter 7 (The 1974 Revolution) treats the political upheaval that led to the overthrow of the imperial regime and the rise to power of the soldiers, who went on to deconstruct the imperial state and rebuild it on a pseudo-socialist model, with widespread social and economic consequences for the centre and the periphery. As its motto 'Ethiopia First' proclaimed, the regime made the defence of the state its main mission, and became entangled in multiple wars in the periphery, north and south, high and low lands. The soldiers built a garrison state where centralization reached new extremes, martial law became a permanent feature, and brutal, coercive force was the main instrument of government visited on all Ethiopians indiscriminately. These developments are examined in Chapter 8 (Building the Socialist State, 1974-1991), a period in which the state was able to reach the farthest corners of its domain and to penetrate deep into rural society. For the first time, the lowlands came into focus mainly due to security requirements, and as a result acquired the first transport and communication links with the highlands. The rupture of the revolution impacted significantly on the centre/periphery relationship, which became a major political issue. This part of the socialist model is discussed in Chapter 9 (The Socialist State in the Periphery).

Ultimately the military regime foundered as its predecessor did in a futile effort to suppress the numerous rebellions in the periphery. Its passing ushered in the fourth and current phase in nation-state building, which is the topic of Part IV (Rebuilding the State: The Federal Model). Understandably, the principal political concern of those who came to power in 1991 was the transformation of the centre-periphery linkage that had undermined their predecessors. The rebuilding of the state in a federal model marks a radical departure from the past and holds promise for the future. Were it to fail, the process of state formation would stall once more. This critical moment in the century-long process is examined in Chapter 10 (Building the Federal State, 1991-1995) and Chapter 11 (Ruling the Federal State, 1995-2010).

The centre/periphery interaction as restructured under 'multinational federalism' is examined in Part V (The Federal State in the Periphery), with a detailed examination of EPRDF policies and methods in its interaction with the lowland periphery. While it can be argued that this phase has not run its course and that it is too early to evaluate it, there are obvious continuities and changes that are reminders of the past and harbingers of the future. Chapters 12-14 take up the experience of the Afar, Somali, Borana, South Omo, Gambella and Beni Shangul Gumuz under multinational federalism.

Sources of study

It is a commonplace truth that state histories are written to celebrate the exploits of state builders and rulers. Ethiopian historiography has laboured under an additional burden, a claim to uniqueness. The basis for this claim has been summarised by the present author in an earlier work. It includes a long past reaching back to classical times, the preservation of an indigenous form of Christianity dating from the early Christian era, a rich, literate culture, renowned isolation on a mountainous massif, and a successful defence of the kingdom's independence against a series of enemies – African, Arab and European. Bowing to the prerogative of uniqueness, both lay and scholarly writings on Ethiopian politics generally eschew the conceptual tools and theoretical apparatus that govern inquiry into social processes in developing countries and discard the conventional standards and criteria normally applied to other African countries. With precious few exceptions, such writings are devoid of critical analysis (Markakis 1974: 13).

Ethiopia's past has fascinated historians, natives and foreigners alike, whose work, not surprisingly, has focused narrowly on the Abyssinian core. This is the rule since the royal chronicles first appeared centuries ago, and modern historians have followed suit. The strength of this historiography lies in description. If it can be said to have any theoretical orientation, it lies in the hero-worship tradition of Thomas Carlyle (1841) that inspired numerous encomiastic portraits of past leaders, especially of the last emperor, Haile Selassie, who himself produced a two volume autobiography.[4] In this tradition 'character analysis is deemed more important than social analysis', as noted by the Ethiopian historian, Bahru Zewde (1983: 2). Scholarly fascination with Ethiopia has its own history. It begins with German philologists and linguists who 'saw their work chiefly as a branch of Semitic studies' (Levine 2000: 19), and where 'the image of Ethiopia as a Semitic outpost has informed and inspired most of the best scholarship on Ethiopia to date' (Levine 2000: 12). For the generation of American, European and Israeli scholars that followed, Ethiopian Christianity was the focus of interest. The result was to buttress native claims of uniqueness with scholarly authority and, in effect, disengage Ethiopia from Africa and attach it to a mythical 'Christian Orient'. This so-called 'Great Tradition' school of Ethiopian historiography considered the 'Abyssinians proper, the carriers of the historical civilization of Semitized Ethiopia', as the true Ethiopians (Ullendorff 1965: 32).[5]

This 'by-product of cultural nationalism', as one historian has described it (Triulzi 2002: 280), shaped the perspective of various political scientists who proved susceptible to the appeal of ephemeral intellectual fashions that had little to do with Africa, let alone Ethiopia. Early on, guided by the pioneering work of Margery Perham (1948) – who, despite never having set foot in Ethiopia, produced a remarkably accurate description of the imperial state – they focused on 'institution building'. This perspective was superseded in the 1960s by the modernization 'paradigm', mesmerized by the awe inspiring personality of Haile Selassie, in whom it discovered a 'modernising autocrat' (Hess 1970).[6] Modernization itself was displaced by crude Marxism in the 1970s, a time of intellectual ferment as well as political torment in Ethiopia.[7] 'The Ethiopia it portrayed was the Ethiopia it imagined or hoped for the future', is an apt verdict on this episode (Triulzi 2002: 279).

It was inevitable that a revisionist historiography with a dissenting view would emerge. It appeared first with a mythical history of Eritrea intended to support the nationalist claim to independence (Jordan, 1998). Tigray

[4] For a representative sample see Gebre Selassie (1931), Asfa Yilma (1936), Mosley (1964), Rubenson (1966), Greenfield (1965), Abir (1968), Marcus, (1974, 1987), Zewde Gebre-Selassie (1975), Haile Selassie I (1976), Juniac (1979).

[5] For a discussion of this topic see Sorenson (1993). Teshale Tibebu offers an updated version of the Great Tradition yet, keenly conscious of its pitfalls, he proposes: 'Next time we write about Ethiopian history, let us start with Kaffa and end with Aksum' (1996: 181). For a concise, yet inclusive, review of Ethiopian historiography, see Crummey (1990).

[6] See also Lipsky 1962, Schwab (1972), Gilkes (1975), Keller (1988), Andargachew Tiruneh (1993).

[7] See Addis Hiwet (1975), Markakis & Nega Ayele (1978), Halliday & Molyneux (1981), Lefort (1983). The present author attempted a synthesis of these two frankly incompatible approaches in Markakis (1974).

nationalists followed with an attack on what they called 'great nation chauvinism' referring to the Amhara. Oromo nationalists soon joined the debate, daring to challenge the sacred article of faith in the Great Tradition, i.e., the preservation of Ethiopia's independence. 'The survival of Ethiopia's independence is perhaps due more to the ambitions of European powers cancelling each other out, than Ethiopian valour excelling that of the Ashantis, the Senegalese, the Zulus', is one scoffing comment (Leenco 1999: 150). According to others, Ethiopia was the 'invention' of European powers (Holcomb & Sisai Ibssa 1990).[8] A sceptical historian calls the dissenting approach 'ethnicised memory', and wonders whether its exponents are able 'to contribute a more balanced reappraisal of the past, or whether they have only reversed ... a paradigm of historiographical self-assurance and cultural "centrism" which marred the old state-centred official memory' (Triulzi 2002: 283).

The glaring focus of the Great Tradition on the centre cast the periphery into gloomy shadow. Its history remains largely unwritten, not to say unknown, since 'subaltern' studies have yet to gain respectability in this country. There are few scholarly works on the societies and cultures of the highland periphery, and hardly any of the lowlands. A partial exception are studies on the Oromo, a nation whose size, geographical spread and long-time political engagement in the heart of the Ethiopian state makes it impossible to ignore.[9] Nonetheless, being noticed was a mixed blessing for the Oromo, who are generally depicted as uncouth intruders who destabilised the Christian kingdom.

It is fair to say that 'Amharas and Tigrayans have their *history*, whereas other people have their anthropology' (Clapham 2002: 40). Social anthropologists found it worthwhile to study the people of the periphery, and have produced valuable monographs on which the present work relies heavily. The first generation of anthropologists treated their subject in isolation and without context, a 'holistic approach' (Triulzi 1984: 360) that missed the important dimension of its linkage with the centre. A second generation, whose ranks include a growing number of Ethiopians, has produced pioneering studies that focus squarely on this aspect, touching on the story that 'remains untold', and the history of those 'many others' who helped make 20th-century Ethiopia.[10]

[8] See Baxter et al., (1996), Asafa Jalata (1998, 2005).

[9] Among the early works on the Oromo, also called Galla in the past, are the following. Asme Giorgis (n.d.), de Salviak (1905), Bahrey (1954), Huntingford (1955), Haberland (1963), H.S. Lewis (1965), Knutsson (1967), Bartels (1983). For an extensive bibliography of works on the Oromo see the bibliography in Baxter et al., (1996).

[10] See Donham & James (1986), Kurimoto & Simonse (1998), James et al. (2002), Strecker & Lydall (2006). The centre-periphery perspective informs a study of religious persecution in Ethiopia under the military regime (Eide, 2000), and a work by the present author examines the rise of insurgent movements in the Horn of Africa (Markakis 1987). The formation of the Ethiopian state is the subject of critical analysis in several works by Leenco Lata (1999, 2004, 2009), and a study from an Oromo nationalist perspective refers to 'state formation' in is subtitle, but views the process solely as an Oromo-Abyssinian affair (Asafa Jalata 2005).

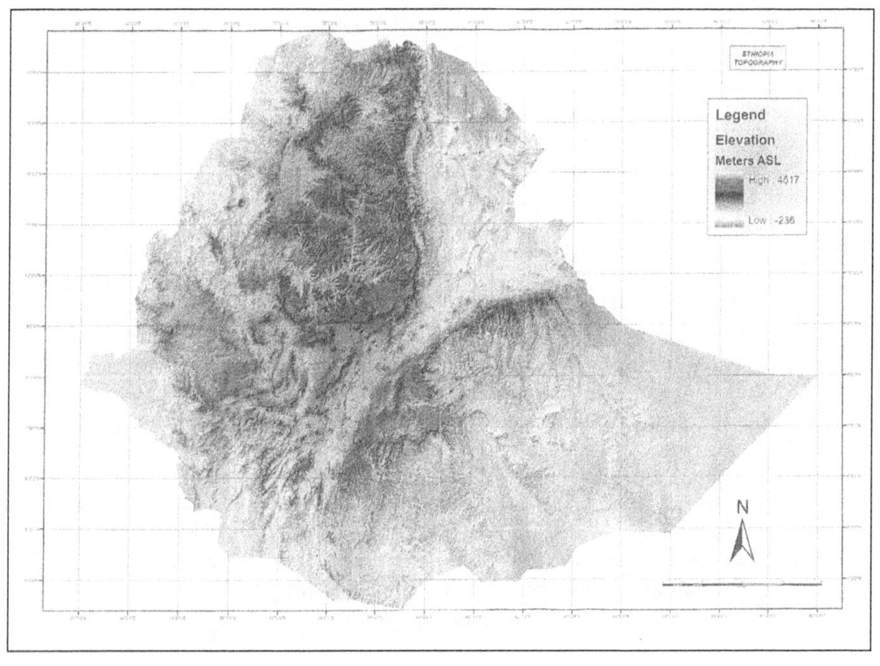

Map 2 Relief map of Ethiopia

Part I
The Lowland Frontier

1

High & Low Land

A Study in Contrast

'Ethiopia is a mountainous land' runs the typical introduction to the country, referring to the massive plateau at its centre that stands at an average elevation of 2000-2500m above sea level and boasts of peaks soaring above 4,000m. Yet this accounts for only half this state's domain of 1,127,127km^2. The hot and dry land below 1,500m the mountain folk call *kolla* and normally shun, makes up the other half. 'Ethiopia is a land of sharp contrasts' is another familiar rubric, which is nowhere more apt than in the multifaceted contrast between high and low land and the peoples who live there. The cool plateau and the hot lowlands that surround it are dramatically different physical environments and are host to societies with sharply different modes of livelihood and culture. Geography (distance, topography climate), demography and population density, political economy (modes of production, surplus availability, trade), and cultural variation feature among the differences. These are also variables that influence the process of state formation, because they determine the cost of integration of peripheral regions and the economic returns that can offset it. These variables are examined in this chapter.

The land

As it slices through the East African Plateau on its way to the Red Sea, the Great Rift, one of nature's extravagant creations, cleaves the Ethiopian massif into two uneven sections, usually referred to as the northern and southern plateaus. As far as the northern section, the Abyssinian homeland, is concerned, 'plateau' is a misleading description for a region studded with majestic peaks linked to each other not by valleys but by mountainous ranges. In this area, fifty-seven mountains rise above 3,000m and twenty above 4,000m. The plateau is a triangle inclining to the west and south. Water draining from the peaks cuts the surface into deep channels, and many rivers and countless streams plunge precipitously from the heights into deeply incised gorges, some of them hundreds of metres below the average surface level. Flat land is not plentiful on the northern plateau, and much of it is found on flat-topped mountains and hills called *amba*. Smaller than its northern counterpart, the southern plateau rises abruptly in a towering escarpment from the floor of the Rift Valley. Rugged, yet less tortuously dissected than the northern section, it is composed of a lot more flat and less eroded land.

'The water tower of East Africa' is yet another stereotypical description of Ethiopia, referring to the bounty of rainfall that flows from the highlands to the parched lowlands below. Both plateau sections have a typical highland tropical climate, with heavy rainfall in summer and autumn, and in some areas during winter as well. Precipitation in the highlands is normally plentiful. It is also the agent of catastrophic erosion when it falls with torrential force on the unprotected, tilled flanks of mountains and hills, carrying away the topsoil that is the Nile's gift to Egypt. An age-old erosion process has stripped the northern plateau bare, revealing the stony ribs of its mountains. Little water is retained on the plateau itself, where irrigation is not practised. The soil laden rivers make flood retreat and recession cultivation possible along their banks as they cross the arid lowlands. Rainfall in the arid zone is highly erratic and quite unreliable. Aridity occurs where rainfall is insufficient to replenish loss of moisture. According to this criterion, the entire coastal zone of the Horn is arid, as is all of Somaliland and Djibouti, southern Somalia save for the inter-riverain valley, three quarters of Eritrea and Kenya, and more than half of Sudan and Ethiopia. This means that crop cultivation using locally available technology cannot be relied on to sustain a sizeable human population in the lowland region.

Although it lies in the equatorial tropical zone, the Horn suffers from serious water deficiency, something it shares with the wider East African region which a scientist has described as one of the world's 'problem climates' (Trewartha, 1961). A pattern of recurring, severe drought afflicted the Horn region, highlands and lowlands alike, in the last quarter of the twentieth century. A rough collation of recorded incidents during the past century suggests major droughts have occurred every ten years. The trend has worsened in the last two decades of the century with nearly continuous drought, and scientific opinion concluded that a microclimatic phenomenon of long duration was evident in the Sudano-Sahelian zone and the Horn of Africa.

Due to the westward slope of the northern section of the plateau, the drainage system follows the same direction, with all but one of Ethiopia's major rivers flowing westwards. The only river in Ethiopia that flows eastwards is the Awash River, which follows the north-eastward course of the Great Rift before losing itself in swampy lakes near the Djibouti border. All the rivers cross the parched lowland periphery and are of paramount importance to the pastoralists who live there, providing dependable water and grazing during the driest part of the year. Access to this resource is a major cause of conflict in the lowlands among pastoralist communities. To some extent, surface water compensates for the shortage

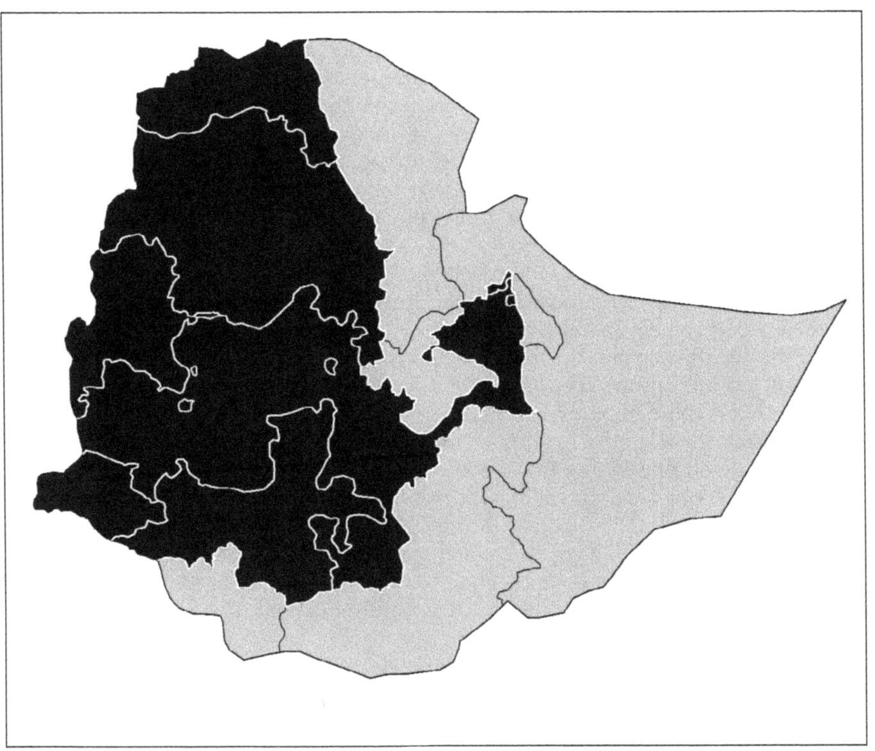

Map 3 Ethiopia: Cultivated & pastoralist terrain

of rainfall in parts of the lowlands, where it supports small scale cultivation on river banks and even large scale commercial production through mechanised irrigation. Promoted by the state and financed by foreign capital, the latter is now claiming huge tracts of land and is emerging as a serious threat to the pastoralist economy and way of life.

The people

The oldest group with a record of continuous occupation and cultivation in the Horn of Africa are the Abyssinian highlanders on the plateau north of the Blue Nile, whose production technology was linked to that of North Africa and the Middle East rather than to sub-Saharan Africa. Unique in sub-Saharan Africa, the use of the ox-drawn, steel-tipped plough is universal here in a relatively intensive system of cultivation, which raised the output per unit of labour above that reached by hoe and shifting cultivation methods prevailing elsewhere in the Horn. Abyssinian agriculture was highly efficient by African standards, producing surpluses to support a large and relatively densely settled population, a socially stratified society and a centralised state that dominated the entire region. Next to the riverain region of northern Sudan, the Ethiopian plateau is the most densely populated part of the Horn. Land was the scarce and most highly valued factor of production, also a unique situation in sub-Saharan Africa where labour was scarce and land abundant. Land remains the most valuable resource in Ethiopia, and is the object of perennial conflict and political controversy. Every regime that has ruled this country in the past century has sought to control and exploit this resource by manipulating the system of land tenure.

In the traditional Abyssinian system of land tenure, the right of access to land attached to membership in a kinship group and was called *rist*, or to a village, then called *diessa*. Rights of use were vested in individual family heads; a typical African compromise of collective and individual rights. So strong were the rights of *rist*, they were referred to as *atsme* (bone) *rist*. Only failure to pay tax could deprive a family of this right, or a successful challenge from another member of the kinship group claiming prior rights. *Rist* and *diessa* land could not be alienated outside the kinship group or the village, and land was not a market commodity, although it could be leased. This system afforded the peasantry secure tenure over specific plots of land that were valued more than life itself and were passed from generation to generation. The negative aspect of this system was land fragmentation that eventually dwarfed family holdings and forced people off the land.

Land also supported the state, whose rights were superimposed on the rights of the peasantry. The state claimed rights of tribute over all land, except those areas to which the Ethiopian Orthodox Church had rights. The obligation of tribute was attached to the land, not to persons; thus all land paid tribute, but not all persons did, and the entire burden fell on those who worked the land – the peasants. The state delegated its rights to tribute to a hierarchy of officialdom, ranging from the lowest district governor to the emperor himself, through the mechanism of a grant called *gult*. Granted by the emperor or other high official, *gult* entitled the holder (*gultegna*) to collect tribute from the land as compensation for the performance of his duties. Officials were not salaried, and were obliged to pass a portion of the tribute they collected upwards through the hierarchy until a portion of it reached the throne. *Gult* rights were attached to office and contingent upon service, but could also be granted hereditarily to members of the nobility and as a form of pension to lesser imperial servants.

In a real sense, agriculture in the northern plateau is the victim of its own earlier success. Steadily increasing human and animal population pressure forced the peasants to use methods that led to land degradation. Continuous cultivation and grazing stripped the earth of its natural cover, leaving it unprotected against the torrential rains that carry away the topsoil to the Nile. The evergreen forests that once covered the plateau were devastated by the need for firewood, fencing and building material, and the relentless pressure to open new land to cultivation. Lack of firewood forced the people to substitute cow dung, thus depriving land of its natural fertilizer. Population density led to continuous fragmentation of holdings, and the majority of peasants still to this day work parcels of land that keep diminishing in size, simultaneously reducing the efficiency of labour. The first landholding surveys, carried out in the 1960s, showed that two-thirds of holdings in three northern provinces were less than one hectare in size, and close to one half were less than half a hectare (Markakis 1974: 81). The line of cultivation descended steadily down the flanks of the plateau onto less suitable land with poor soils and unreliable climate. Steep slopes and ravines on the plateau came under the plough, exposing the land to rapid water and wind erosion. Good practices such as fallowing and terracing had to be restricted or abandoned and even crop rotation had to be curtailed. The result was monumental erosion that turned mountains into stony skeletons and valleys into grids of ever deepening gullies. The peasants are keenly aware of land degradation; '*merietu demquortal*' ('the land has reached menopause') they say, and '*merietu aynefesual*' ('the land has lost its eyes'), i.e., its most valuable part.

The staple item of the Abyssinian diet is *teff*, an indigenous cereal with high calcium and iron content. Cereal crop productivity in tropical regions is relatively poor compared to other regions, and *teff* has one of the lowest yields among cereal crops.[1] In Ethiopia only the southern plateau possesses deep soils with high organic material, while the western, central and northern highlands are seriously affected by problems of degradation (Kiflemariam Melake 1997: 626). Record numbers of cattle, goats and sheep are raised on the plateau and compete with humans for access to land.

Land hunger was the prime force that propelled the spectacular territorial expansion of the northern Christian kingdom in the late 19th century and led to the creation of the Ethiopian Empire. This expansion engulfed the bottom half of the northern plateau, below the bend of the Abbay (Blue Nile) River and south of Addis Ababa, an area that was relatively thinly populated and had preserved its pristine nature until that time. The region west of the Rift Valley enjoys the longest wet period in the highlands and retained a luxurious verdant cover and sizeable forests that teemed with big game. A typically African system of cultivation was practised here, based on the hoe and the production of *ensete*, a member of the banana family that stores carbohydrates in its edible stem. Crossing the Rift Valley, the expansion also engulfed the southern plateau in its entirety, a fertile and well-watered land where sorghum was the dominant crop. The historic role of the conquered territories was to host the excess population displaced from the north by land scarcity. In the wake of the conquest, a steady stream of northerners flowed into the highland territories to seize land and exploit the labour of the local population, both of which became the spoils of war.

The arid lowlands did not attract migrants from the north. They were and remain the habitat of mobile pastoralists. Pastoralist population data are based partly on guesswork, not least due to the difficulty of counting

[1] 8.8 quintals (one quintal=100kg) per hectare, compared to 14 quintals for sorghum and 15 for maize.

people on the move. It is generally believed that pastoralists have a lower population rate of growth then sedentary cultivators.[2] Pastoralism is not included as a category in the national census, consequently only approximate figures can be deduced from district population data. Pastoralists in Ethiopia are found in six out to nine federal states (*kilil*), and in 123 out of 550 administrative districts (*woreda*) that occupy some 60% of the country's land area. They belong to some 30 ethnic groups. Pastoralist herds in Ethiopia number an estimated 11 million cattle, 10 million sheep, 8 million goats, 2.5 million camels and just under a million equines, mainly donkeys (Sandford & Habtu 2002: 102).

Table 1 *Estimated Pastoralist Population in the Regional States (Kilil) of Ethiopia*

Region	Estimated Pastoralist Population	% of Total Pastoralist Population	% of Total Population
Somali	3,383,000	44	5.20
Oromia	2,577,000	33	3.96
Afar	1,100,000	16	1.69
Debub	559,000	7.1	0.86
Gambella	118,000	1.4	0.18
Beni Shangul Gumuz	37,000	0.5	0.05
Country Total	7,776,000	100	12

Source: *Kilil* Planning Bureaux (2000)

Occupying a distinct ecological niche, pastoralists have lived and thrived in this corner of Africa since 'God created the world' as they say, making the most out of nature's meagre endowment.[3] Directly dependent for survival on a scant natural resource base, they are obliged to be efficient managers of it, and theirs is the only surviving civilization that can claim to live in harmony with nature. Pastoralists do not control the environment through technology, they manipulate it with knowledge and skills accumulated with age, hence the principal role elders perform in pastoralist society and the high esteem they enjoy. The implementation of traditional pastoralist production strategies is premised on the double imperative of extensive use of land and unfettered freedom of movement. In order to provide for the varied foraging needs of different livestock species and to afford a margin of safety against the vagaries of the climate,

[2] Certain institutional arrangements and cultural practices are thought to wittingly contribute to it, including late marriage for men until they reach the proper age grade, abstention from sexual intercourse during a long breastfeeding period for infants, in addition to higher infant mortality and shorter life spans (Roth 1994: 63).

[3] Sudan, Somalia, Ethiopia and Kenya rank first, third, fifth and sixth respectively in the world in terms of pastoralist population size.

the herd must have access to dispersed, ecologically specialised and seasonally varied grazing lands and watering holes. The best protection against the unreliability of rainfall is freedom of movement over extensive territory, preferably containing a permanent water supply.

Movement is of the essence to the pastoralist way of life, and is the factor that differentiates this form of livestock production from those practised by farmers and ranchers. In the past, movement could cover great distances, such as the trek that brought the Somali from the tip of the Horn to within sight of the East African highlands, and the Oromo from the southern plateau to the gorge of the Blue Nile. There is no pastoralist group in the Horn whose oral tradition does not place its origins somewhere else than the place it now occupies. Such epic movements ended when the modern state appeared in the region, though smaller population shifts still take place regularly across state borders. The pattern of movement varies widely, ranging from the constant, irregular roaming of the nomad who eschews settled habitation, to the regular, seasonal sojourns of transhumance which permit a permanent abode. It was the violation of the double imperative of free movement and extensive use of land due to the loss of autonomy that set pastoralists on a collision course with the modern state, and their world on an irreversible path of decline that reduced the lowland communities to the level of powerlessness and abject poverty they occupy today.

Extensive use of land and freedom of movement over it also determines the pastoralist perspective of land rights. Theoretically, land and water are 'the gift of God', and all people have the right to use them. Private ownership rights are not recognized, unless labour is invested to improve resources. Access to improved water sources – wells, ponds, dams, tanks – is controlled by those who invest labour or money in them, and they can demand payment for water. In the constantly shifting spatial pattern of pastoralism, access to land is a perennial bone of contention, and never more so than at the present time, due to the marked shift to agro-pastoralism and worsening environmental conditions. While group claims over areas are recognized, they are vaguely defined in territorial terms, often overlap and, most importantly, shift over time: they are neither mapped nor registered. 'Pastoral boundaries were thus more ecological than physical, more flexible than fixed' (Mamdani 1996: 166). It is this flexibility that defies the state's attempt to measure, register, police and tax the lowlanders, and why 'throughout history the state has attempted to change pastoral domains into territories of fixed jurisdiction and boundaries' (Galaty & Johnson, 1990: 32). In this respect, the Ethiopian state has yet to succeed.

Despite their renowned self-sufficiency, pastoralists have always consumed foodstuffs they did not produce, such as grain, and used tools and weapons they did not manufacture themselves. To acquire them they exchange animals, hides and skins, dairy products, utensils, and decorations made from the flora and fauna of their habitat, with their sedentary neighbours. Such occasional involvement in trade does not alter the fact that pastoralist production is not designed to produce livestock for the market as its primary purpose. In subsistence oriented systems, exchange or trade is a complementary component rather than the main goal of production. To put it in the economist's terms: 'The objective of pastoral production is not to maximise returns per unit but overall household survival, in which case it makes more economic sense to keep large herds' (Muhereza 2004: 4). In contemporary economic logic based on the market principle, pastoralist practice is considered irrational. Livestock accumulation is doubly wasteful, since the surplus is not invested in alternative, more efficient forms of production, and it results in overstocking and ecological degradation that undermine the foundation of pastoralist production itself.

In the second half of the last century, the lowlands were hit by persistent drought that caused further decline in the traditional economy. Drought is a familiar visitor to pastoralists; its visits are named and remembered because they are accompanied by famine. However, the people have devised ways of coping with it. Drought need not lead to famine if traditional coping strategies are effective, but in the Ethiopian lowlands this is no longer the case, because the material base of pastoralism has been undermined beyond recovery. Crises have increased in frequency and intensity, and pastoralists are no longer able to overcome them by their own efforts. 'Pastoral production systems are a highly efficient response to an environment which began to disappear in the early twentieth century and has been disappearing at an accelerating rate every since' (Dyson-Hudson 1985: 173). Finding themselves in dire straits, pastoralists in the Horn respond with short-term 'survival strategies' 'that amount to no more than the plunder of existing resources to meet immediate needs: cutting down forests, abandoning practices that allowed seasonal pastures to rest, and grazing them across seasons instead' (Mamdani 1996: 166). Food aid is now indispensable to the survival of most communities in the lowlands. And in a situation of sustained crisis, conflict has become endemic, pitting herder communities against each other, against sedentary neighbours, and against the state that claims them as subjects.

*

The fact that the pastoralist economy is not governed by the laws of the market and does not produce taxable surplus has brought the pastoralists in direct confrontation with the state and the market, politicians and development experts alike. Recent concern with conflict in the arid zone has produced a two-pronged development strategy promoted by international aid agencies with the blessing of the state: agro-pastoralism. Its main thrust is to encourage settlement and cultivation, in the hope of ensuring food security in the lowlands. Herders traditionally rely on grain they get from cultivators to supplement their diet, and also try to produce it themselves where and when this is possible. Wherever the soil has enough moisture from rainfall they plant sorghum, the preferred crop because of its low water demand and short maturing period of three months; it takes six months on the highlands. Using a sharpened stick the herders also plant maize, beans, peanuts and watermelons. Despite the fact that climatic conditions and soil properties in the lowlands make it a hazardous enterprise, cultivation expanded steadily during the second half of the twentieth century, encouraged by the state and development agencies. A more substantial and regular form of cultivation is practised where bodies of surface water cross the arid region. The banks of large rivers, from the Awash in the east to the Baro in the west, have supported cultivation through flooding and recession irrigation for centuries. Small scale irrigated cultivation has expanded rapidly since the mid-1990s with the introduction of water pumps, which have provided pastoralists with an alternative livelihood.

The second prong of the development strategy is the commercialization of animal production through its integration in the market. Economic integration of high and low lands is a missing link, and there are many reasons for it. The most obvious is the poor state of transport and communications linking the two regions. The basic fact is that highland and lowland economies are not complementary. The highland market has neither the demand nor the purchasing power to attract livestock from the lowlands. Highlanders raise a huge livestock population of their own, and have no serious need for imports from the lowland periphery. Even if the need arises, the highland economy lacks the purchasing power to attract imports at appropriate prices.

Pastoralists have always traded when the need arises and the price is right. The lowlands are linked to a regional trade network that antedates colonialism and continues to flourish, because it follows the logic of the region's natural economy that strives to meet demand through the shortest route in order to minimise cost. At present, livestock surplus in the lowlands is channelled into the illegal cross-border market with a serious loss of revenue for the state. This anomaly has exercised the wits of administrators and development planners alike in their determination to reverse the direction of the trade towards the highlands. And while the administrators strain to disrupt cross-border trade by blocking its routes and harassing lowland traders, development planners are busy devising schemes to link lowland producers with markets on the highlands.

Despite their preoccupation with market mechanisms, planners ignore the obvious profit incentive that determines the direction of cross-border trade covering the entire lowland region of the Horn. In the last quarter of the 20th century, the livestock trade expanded spectacularly into the Arabian Peninsula which became a major importer of livestock from the Horn, the bulk coming from the south-eastern lowland periphery of Ethiopia. This market proved resilient and impervious to the obstacles placed in its path by state borders and custom controls, perennial insecurity, officialdom venality, and grossly inadequate transport and communication facilities. For several decades now, livestock from the lowland periphery in Ethiopia has crossed the narrow Red Sea, evading custom tariffs, export permits, health inspection and other impedimenta. These are intended to reverse the historical pattern and redirect trade towards the centre of the state, where it can be regulated, taxed and priced low for the benefit of townspeople and for export. Pastoralists are heavily involved in the illegal trade as producers, transporters, traders and labourers. A flood of smuggled manufactured products from Asia, second-hand clothing from Europe and America, and foodstuff from the Middle East flows in the opposite direction, turning the lowland periphery into an entrepôt of contraband commerce. By contrast, officially sanctioned trade among states in the Horn is negligible.

The Abyssinian core

Since it provides the template for Ethiopia's national identity, it is useful to outline the main features of Abyssinian society and culture whose roots lie in antiquity. The Aksumite Empire that flourished on the northernmost part of the plateau in classical times is considered the ancestor of Ethiopia. Christianity was introduced during the 4th century AD, and was preserved for centuries in isolation, the only place on the African continent, other than the Coptic Church in Egypt, where it managed to survive as a truly indigenous faith. Very little is known of Ethiopia's ancestors over the next millennium. Following the rise of Islam in Arabia, Muslim power flooded the Red Sea coast and the lowlands of the eastern Horn, forcing the Aksumites to retreat into their mountain stronghold. As Islam spread northwards towards Egypt, the Christian Kingdom became completely isolated from the outside world, a condition it was to endure until modern times. Aksum faded from the pages of history, and the fate of the Aksumites in the following centuries is scarcely known. Following the plateau contour and keeping to the heights, their descendants turned southwards and proceeded to subjugate and assimilate the autochthonous inhabitants. This southward movement was to become a fixed orientation for the second millennium.

The society that emerged from the fusion of Aksumite and Cushite elements comes into historical focus towards the end of the 13th century, thanks to the writings of its own clergy. It was then that a dynasty claiming a fanciful descent from King Solomon and the Queen of Sheba rose to power, and provided a religious foundation for an emerging Ethiopian national identity based on a celebrated Middle Eastern fable. The very name of this society derives from its faith. Its origins lay in ancient Greek references to Africans as 'Aethiopes' ('burnt faces'). In the Septuagint version of the Old Testament, the Hebrew name 'Cush' was translated into the Greek 'Ethiopia', and then adopted by the faithful on the northern plateau. It went without saying that a non-Christian could not be an Ethiopian, or an Ethiopian anything but a Christian. More or less contemporary chronicles appear from this time onwards to provide a narrative of the dynasty whose reign lasted, not without interruptions, until the demise of the imperial regime in 1974.

On the plateau, Islam was associated with trade from the beginning. The Red Sea ports were controlled by Muslims, who also dominated trade in the hinterland. Muslim traders performed missionary work as well, and gradual conversion produced the first Muslim communities within the Christian kingdom. Known as *Jabarti*, they dominated local and long distance trade. The Abyssinian nobility, whose social ethos prevented it from engaging in commerce, found their presence useful and the state gave them protection. Ethiopia's history was nearly brought to an end in the first half of the sixteenth century when a devastating invasion occurred, led by Imam Ahmed ibn Ibrahim al Ghazi (1506-43), better known as Gragn ('the left-handed'). Gragn set off from Harar with a mixed force of Afar and Somali warriors, and declared holy war against the highlanders. The Muslim onslaught proved irresistible and a large part of the kingdom was conquered. Religious fanaticism rendered the conflict exceedingly violent, and brought devastation to the Christian population, as well as mass conversion to Islam at the point of a sword.[4] This experience marked the Abyssinian psyche with an ever sensitive scar, and an abiding distrust of Islam and Muslims. Interestingly, this episode also witnessed the first external intervention in the Horn's internal conflicts. The Ottomans, who were then a dominant presence in the Red Sea, assisted Gragn with military hardware, while the Ethiopians were helped by the Portuguese in their ultimately successful struggle to repel the invaders.

Islam did not disappear from the northern plateau. In fact, the Muslim population there increased considerably afterwards. An observer in the early 17th century put it at one-third of the total population (Beckingham & Huntingford 1954: 55). By that time, their status in the Christian state was significantly degraded. They were barred from owning land in most areas, and from state office – except for that of market tax collector – everywhere. Periodically, imperial edicts ordered Muslims to live in segregated quarters, and even to convert to Christianity, none of which had an appreciable effect.[5] The social distance between the two faiths was maintained by taboos inhibiting social intercourse, such as a ban on Christians and Muslims eating together. Christians considered Muslims aliens in the kingdom. 'The sky has no pillar, the Muslim has no land', went a Tigray proverb. 'Instead of cleansing himself in the river, the Christian goes to the priest', is a *Jabarti* retort. When people quarrelled and severed relations, they were said to 'have become like Christian and Muslim'.

Abyssinian society and culture were pervaded and structured by religion. The world of the peasant was defined by the boundaries of his parish, and the church was the focus of social intercourse. The priest was easily the most important figure, and the ranks of the Abyssinian clergy were legion. The rhythm of rural life was determined by a church calendar that included innumerable holy and fasting days. Religion also provided the ideology and legitimacy of the state. Christianity was a pillar of the imperial dynasty, having provided it with a founding legend that joined faith, nation and throne in an indissoluble union with a mythical past and

[4] According to the chronicler, 'hardly one in ten retained his religion' (Conzelman 1895: 123).

[5] The last such decree was issued in 1878 by Emperor Yohannes and gave Muslims three years to join the Ethiopian Orthodox Church.

a prophetic future. The power of 'the Elect of God' – one of the emperor's many titles – came from God, therefore it was unlimited, unaccountable and unchallengeable, and its absolute nature was graphically depicted in many proverbs: 'When the King commands it, one is not allowed to bury one's own mother', and 'when asked to stop in the name of the King, water stops flowing.'

Between the *balager* (peasant) and the emperor lay an elaborate stratified social structure. Above the peasantry stood the local gentry that enforced the law and collected taxes, whose members bore minor titles and enjoyed modest privileges in lieu of salary. Jurisdiction and compensation – normally a percentage of the local tax – were stipulated in a grant known as *gult*, bestowed by the emperor or other high official on the person who was known as *gultegna*. Above the local gentry came the nobility (*makuannent*), men of blood and influence deserving important titles and privileges, governing districts and provinces. The highest rank of the nobility comprised the *mesafint*, princes of royal blood, some of whom bore the title of *negus* (king) and ruled provinces under the emperor, whose own title was *negusa negast* ('king of kings'). The ecclesiastical establishment, known as *kahinat*, constituted a parallel privileged hierarchy that rose from the simple village priest or monk, themselves no better off than the impoverished peasant, through tiers of clerical officialdom to the *Abuna*, the head of the Church, whose exalted position was second only to that of the emperor.

This stratified, highly authoritarian social system with its ranked allocation of authority, status and privilege, enjoyed spiritual legitimacy that ensured its acceptance by the peasant mass. According to the *Fetha Nagast*, an authoritative source of traditional law, 'where there is no authority there is confusion and lack of order' and 'God has appointed these magistrates and given them authority. One who opposes the magistrate and rebels against him, he rebels against the ordinance of God, his Creator.'[6] Tradition sanctioned the privileges entailed in the *gult*, as the following two proverbs make clear. 'The rich man with his *gult*, the poor man with his *rist*', and '*gult* is for the great warrior, *rist* is for the weak.' A 'Portrait de l'ethiopien typique' drawn in 1966, assures us that the Ethiopian 'in his respect for those who are placed higher than he, he entertains always a sentiment that is quasi mystical, he accommodates himself with good grace and never transgresses' (Mahteme Selassie 1966: 6).

The peasant was also called *gabbar*, a term derived from the word *gibr* meaning tribute and denoting the status of one who pays it. Taxation in Abyssinia was comprehensive, multiple, very burdensome, and the peasantry was taxed to the limit of its capacity. Taxes were levied on everything that grew or lived on land, and fees were levied on many forms of normal activity engaged in by the peasantry. Furthermore, the peasantry was compelled to provide corvée labour for various purposes and for a hierarchy of

[6] Dating from the 15th century, the *Fetha Nagast* includes sections on canon, property, family and criminal law, as well as a section on kings. An English translation was prepared by the Faculty of Law of Haile Seaside I University by Paulos Tzadua (no date), and the quotations here are from that manuscript (p. 447/496).

privileged ranks. The tribute exacted from the *gabbar* in taxes, fees and labour service was appropriated by the various levels of the ruling class, both secular and ecclesiastical, in lieu of salary. Tradition rationalised this burden in the following words: 'And for our spiritual and corporal benefits which are derived from the King, let us give him tribute and presents in payment for them, and this tribute is in order to provide the necessities which the magistrates of the law are in need of, since they leave their own interest and they care for the public welfare' (*Fetha Nagast*: 497-98).

Within the boundaries of the kingdom, Ethiopian society preserved a host of parochial identities based on territorial divisions, regional loyalties and local interests; referred to by this author in an earlier work as 'provincialism' (Markakis, 1974). At ground level, the reference point for a person's identity was the parish or village. At a higher level, it was one of the provinces that made up the Christian kingdom. These were clearly defined geographically, and served as administrative units ruled by the provincial nobility who often resisted the encroachment of imperial authority, while the more powerful provincial nobles were perennial candidates for the throne itself.

Amhara is a region whose name is linked with Amharigna, the language adopted by the imperial court in the 13th century and eventually became the official medium and *lingua franca* of the polyglot Ethiopian empire. Amharigna speakers inhabit all but one of the historical provinces of the kingdom, Tigray. In the imperial state during the 20th century, in cultural terms Amhara came to subsume Christian Abyssinian, and politically to signify imperial rule. Amharigna was the cutting edge of the cultural assimilation policy promoted by the imperial regime, a policy dubbed 'Amharisation'. The very process of assimilation itself, however, diffused and diluted the ethnic content of this term, since those who were assimilated often claimed Amhara identity, that being, after all, the object of the exercise. Such blending gave rise to the question that featured in the political debates on federalism in the 1990s: is Amhara an ethnic group and who belongs to it? In the context of state building, the answer is properly framed in political rather than ethnic terms. As one writer put it, 'Amhara was a metaphor for power, Galla for the relative lack of it' (Teshale 2006: 45).

At present the Amhara regional state (*kilil*) encompasses all the Amharigna-speaking provinces of Ethiopia. On that basis, Amhara is categorised as a linguistic group with a territorially defined homeland.[7] According to the 2007 census, the number of Amharigna speakers in the country was 19.87 million (26.89% of the total), and the population of the Amhara federal state (*kilil*) 17.21 million (23.3% of the total). Some 3.5 million Amharigna speakers live outside their own regional state, most of them in the highland periphery.

[7] Alan Hoben describes the Amhara as 'a self conscious ethnic and linguistic group' (1973: 50). Tegegne Taka (1998) points out that Amharigna speakers have no myth of common ancestry, no particular homeland, no ethnic markers, but have a common language, culture and a sense of solidarity. He sees an Amhara ethnic identity emerging in the challenging context of ethnic federalism.

The historical distinctions among the provinces where Amharigna was spoken were largely effaced by socio-economic change in the course of the past century, and their political rivalries were rendered inconsequential in the process of centralization of state power. One facet of Ethiopian provincialism was not effaced but, on the contrary, was exacerbated during the same period, and came to represent the main political fault line within the centre in the last decade of the past century. This is the rivalry between the Amhara and Tigray branches of the Abyssinian family. Theirs is essentially a linguistic difference, with Amharigna and Tigrigna having evolved separately from ancient Geez, the Aksumite tongue. Tigrigna is spoken by the people who live north of the Takkaze River in the province of the same name and on the highlands of Eritrea. According to the 2007 census there were 4.5 million Tigrigna speakers in Ethiopia. Occupying the region that comprised the core of the Aksumite empire, including its capital Aksum, and speaking a language considered the closest derivative of Geez, Tigray provincialism thrives in the conviction that it represents purity and continuity in Ethiopian culture, in contrast to the Amhara whom the Tigray are apt to refer contemptuously as 'half-Oromo'.

Provincialism reached a peak in the so-called 'Age of Princes' that lasted from the mid-18th to the mid-19th centuries. During this time, the state dissolved into its provincial components, which in turn became involved in an endless and ultimately inconclusive struggle for supremacy. The eclipse of the monarchy was followed by the rise of numerous provincial dynasties which competed fiercely for national ascendancy, plunging the country into endemic conflict waged on many fronts simultaneously. The Age of Princes came to a close with the rise of a man lacking dynastic credentials but endowed with unusual ability. Within a decade, he managed to subdue all the provincial contenders and claimed the throne as Emperor Tewodros (1855-1867). He is justly credited with having laid the foundations of the modern state of Ethiopia.

The highland periphery

Abyssinia's borders were never clearly defined. They fluctuated according to the waxing and waning of imperial power and the ambition and energy of the throne's occupants. Expansion southwards was a historical trend and there were good economic reasons for it. The imperial regime 'depended on expansion of the frontier to develop new patrimonies and sources of revenue' (McCann 1987: 18). In times of upsurge, Ethiopian power reached far to the south to impose tribute on local rulers and introduce Orthodox Christianity to their subjects, only to recede afterwards. Retreat and contraction of the borders was one result of the Muslim onslaught in the 16th century. It was the arrival of the Oromo soon afterwards that invested the Christian kingdom and fixed its southern borders for more than two centuries.

Before the coming of the Oromo, the bulk of the territory south of the Blue Nile River was occupied by peoples known as the Sidama. The name refers to a family of languages spoken by the natives of this region, while Sidamo is the name of one distinct group that lives south of Lake Awasa. Sedentary hoe and shifting cultivation was the dominant mode of production among the people here, who lived in a number of petty states ruled by hereditary monarchies, some of which had long histories and survived until the days of Menelik. Called *Kati* or *Moti*, some Sidama kings ruled powerful, centralised states, while others were merely ritual figures. History was not kind to the Sidama, placing them early on in the path of a massive Oromo migration northwards and again later squarely on the route of the equally massive Ethiopian expansion southwards.

What caused the Oromo pastoralists to move *en masse* from the lowlands of Bale onto the plateau is not clear. It might have been, as one Oromo historian assumes, the lure of a lush land that had been depopulated by the violence of the Muslim jihad in the 16th century and left unprotected by the exhausted Christian kingdom (Mohammed Hassen 1990: 20). Overrunning the western region north of the Gibe River, the Oromo subjugated the Sidama and set up a number of political entities known as the Gibe States. The assimilation of the native population that followed was so thorough that today the Sidama are no longer a distinct presence in this region. According to an Oromo historian, 'the Oromo genius for assimilation quickly claimed any non-Oromo, defeated or otherwise' (Mohammed Hassen 1990: 21). Interestingly, the 'Oromisation' of the Sidama is celebrated by Oromo nationalists who, on the other hand, fulminate against 'Amharisation'. 'The Oromo conquest and settlement were qualitatively different from the process of Ethiopian colonialism which took place within the context of a racist and capitalist world-economy. Reflecting values inherent in the *gaada* system, the Oromo structurally and successfully assimilated and integrated the conquered minorities' (Asafa Jalata 2005: 21). No doubt, when they come to write their own history, the Sidama will take a different view.

In the region south and east of the Gojeb and Omo rivers, the Sidama managed to repel the Oromo and retain control of the territory they occupy today. Among the most important states there was Hadya in the eastern part of this region, whose history went back to the 14th century and Ethiopia's wars with its Muslim neighbours, of which Hadya was one. Hadya paid tribute to the Christian emperor, as did Kambata immediately to the south. Also to the south, Wolamo had had its own monarchy since the 15th century, and a number of petty Sidama kingdoms existed further south, the most important of which were Kullo Konta, Konta, Gofa and Gamo. The best known Sidama kingdom in the southwest was Kaffa, whose territory lay west of the Omo River and immediately south of the Gojeb River. The genealogy of the Kaffa monarchy went back to the 14th century. Wedged between the Gibe and Omo rivers north of Kaffa was another Sidama kingdom, Janjero. The 2007 census listed 2.97 million Sidama speakers (4% of the total population of Ethiopia).

North of the Sidama, between the Awash and Omo rivers and Lake Awasa, live the Gurage people. They appear in Ethiopian history in the 14th century and often came under Ethiopian suzerainty, but were not completely incorporated until the days of Menelik. Distinguished by their Semitic tongue in the midst of Oromo and Sidama speakers, the Gurage are subdivided into numerous sections, seven of which form a confederation known as the Sabat Bet, or Seven Houses. Gurage political organization was extensively segmented, lacking integration above the district level, and political authority was highly diffused. Diversity among the Gurage is reflected in their language which spawned numerous dialects, and in the coexistence among them of Christianity, Islam and traditional faiths. In the 2007 census the Gurage numbered 1.8 million (2.5% of the total).

The Oromo were a nation of mobile pastoralists whose original home was in the Bale lowlands of the southern plateau. Taking advantage of the decline of Muslim power and Christian disarray following Gragn's wars, their migration carried them from the lowlands of the Horn to the highlands on both sides of the Rift Valley where they settled. The northern limits of the Oromo migration reached the borders of Tigray on the east, but the bulk of this nation settled in territories south of the Abbay River in the west and south of Shoa province. Thus, by the beginning of the 17th century, the borders of Ethiopia were fixed and remained so until the expansion in the late 19th century.

The Oromo subjugated and largely assimilated the indigenous inhabitants of the areas they occupied. Distinction between Oromo proper (*borana*) and assimilated (*garba*) is still alive: 'saglan borana, sagaltama garba' ('nine are the pure Oromo, and ninety are the assimilated') according to a local saying. At the same time the Oromo were in turn strongly influenced by the cultures of the people they conquered. By and large, they abandoned mobile pastoralism and turned to cultivation of local crops. In the Gibe River region they exchanged the traditional Gaada system of government for the monarchical system of the Sidama. The change to cultivation and monarchical rule destroyed the egalitarian and democratic values of traditional Oromo society. These were preserved only among the clans that remained in the lowlands, mainly the Borana, Guji, Arsi and Gabbra.

The Oromo who came into closest contact with Ethiopia, in Wolo and southern Shoa, converted to Christianity and adopted the Amharigna tongue. On the other hand, Islam made great inroads in the kingdoms of the Gibe River region and among the Arsi and Bale Oromo on the southern plateau who interacted with the Afar, Somali and Adari. The result was a wide ranging process of differentiation that transformed what was once a culturally homogeneous pastoral society, into a widely dispersed nation comprising groups with distinct social, economic and cultural systems, a diversity with significant political implications for the future of this nation. Today, Oromo are found in all parts of Ethiopia as well as in northern Kenya. The 2007 census in Ethiopia listed 25.5 million Oromo speakers (the largest linguistic group with 34, 5% of the total). The Oromia regional state is the most populous with 27.16 million inhabitants and the rate of population growth in Oromia was 2.9% ; higher than the national rate of 2.6%.

In the historiography of the Great Tradition, the coming of the Oromo, or Galla as the Ethiopians called them, is invariably termed an 'invasion' of what presumably was Abyssinian territory. 'While Ethiopia was rent by civil war, the Galla entered unobstructed, as if into No-Man's-Land', wrote a pioneer Ethiopian historian.[8] A revisionist approach from an Oromo nationalist perspective reverses the historical process. In the 16th century, 'the Oromo were actively recapturing their territories and rolling back the Christian and Muslim empires', is a typical version (Asafa Jalata 1993: 18). In the Great Tradition, the appearance of the Oromo is depicted as a cataclysmic event that blighted Abyssinian society and darkened its cultural horizon. 'The Gallas had nothing to contribute to the civilization of Ethiopia; they possessed no material or intellectual culture, and their social organization was at a far lower stage of development than that of the population among whom they settled', is the verdict of one foreign scholar (Ullendorf 1965: 76). Abyssinians themselves professed a cultural disdain for the Oromo, expressed in a wealth of derogatory sayings.[9] The segmented structure of the Oromo nation that divided it into numerous independent segments given to inter-clan warfare ensured that, despite their numbers and momentum, the Oromo did not seriously endanger the existence of the Ethiopian state. 'If God had not blinded them', wrote the Jesuit Manoel de Almeida, who visited Ethiopia in the 1620s, 'and willed that certain families or tribes among them should be at war with one another constantly, there would not have been an inch of land in the empire, of which they were not the masters' (1954: 135).

The lowland periphery

Inhabiting the same physical environment, societies on the highland periphery have a good deal in common with the Ethiopians who became their overlords. On the other hand, the contrast between high and low land could not have been greater or more vexing for the empire builders. 'A landless man is not human', claimed the Abyssinians, who found the wandering pastoralist way of life repulsive. Their name for the footloose herders, '*Zalan*', signifies coarseness, aggressiveness, as well as material and cultural impoverishment. The historians of the Great Tradition agreed. Noting that Islam, rather than Christianity, made progress among the lowlanders, one of them could not resist this snide comment: 'Perhaps its [Islam's] simple and clear cut theology makes a special appeal to the less sophisticated peoples in the hot and arid regions, with little or no civilization of their own' (Ullendorf 1965: 114). Of course, such perceptions are inevitably biased. While the material accomplishments of pastoralism are limited, its cultural inventiveness knows no bounds. Given the challenging nature of the environment in which it survives, pastoralism requires 'complex and specific forms of social organization, both for

[8] Atsme Giyorgis cited in Bahru Zewde (2002: 144).

[9] See J. Hultin, (1996).

production and for mutual protection in the face of a large variety of potential disasters' (Raikes 1981: 27). Even so, pastoralist systems are more than simple responses to the ecological possibilities of their habitat. They represent complex ways of life and fascinating illustrations of human creativity.

Two basic overlapping principles of social organization are found in the lowlands. One is based on blood kinship and takes the form of the patrilineal descent group commonly referred to as the clan, whose members claim descent from a common male ancestor. The clan provides its members with their primary identity, a network of solidarity and security, and a structure of authority vested in clan chiefs and elders. The clan welds its members into a corporate body that acts on their behalf in all matters and commands their absolute loyalty. In this system of social organization, there are many gradations in the depth of clan kinship within which an individual can identify and act. The smallest group is the primary lineage, with a depth of only a few generations, whose members form the most tightly knit unit. Secondary lineages – sub-clans – with a depth of many generations, encompass many primary lineages, and so on with major clans and clan families. Each level bears the name of its founder and has its customary leaders, as well as a vaguely defined territory to claim as its own. The level at which collective action takes place depends on the issue at stake. Groups of the same genealogical level may act together, or may be pitted against each other. Segmentation is a salient feature of this system, whereby ethnic groups and clans subdivide into smaller units each having autonomy to manage its affairs, while paying nominal obeisance to higher levels. Social segmentation is imposed by nature, since rainfall is sparse, erratic and unreliable and pasture is insufficient to feed large congregations of people and animals.

The second principle of social organization in the lowlands is the age-grade system that very often coexists with the clan system. This is both a structure of authority and a military organization. The enormous variety of forms of age-grade systems and their distribution across linguistic and ethnic boundaries has fascinated social anthropologists. With their penchant for precision, they have identified and distinguished many types, which they variously, and for the layman confusingly, label either as *age-sets* or *age-classes* (meaning groups of men of roughly the same age), or as *age-grades* and *generation sets* (meaning stages in the male life cycle).

In the age-grade system, males who reach a certain age are initiated into a set with its own name. Since initiations are held every few years and are often delayed for some reason, the age spread within a set can be considerable. With time, the set moves from one grade to the next – from boyhood to warrior to adulthood to senior to elder – each having its own functions, responsibilities and share of authority. The most important grades are the warriors whose responsibility is defence and raiding, and the seniors who are the decision makers. Age-grade systems provide a structure of authority to balance to the need of a pastoral society for household autonomy and economic self sufficiency. The age-grade system cuts across kinship and territorial cleavages, widening the scope for corporate unity and collective action. It bonds age mates and gives elders influence over younger men.

Pastoralist society is rigidly gender segregated. Gender disparity is proclaimed in a wealth of caustic proverbs. 'Women can grow tall, but without wisdom', and 'the leadership of a woman makes water flow upwards', are Oromo contributions. Here they see eye-to-eye with highlanders: 'A woman and a donkey can't be kept straight without the stick', is an Amhara equivalent. The preference for male children is universal among pastoralists. 'People desire a son as they desire rain', say the Afar, and the Somali add that 'one boy is worth four girls'. A Somali poem expresses the mother's feelings when a daughter is born:

> Where were you born?
> Why did you arrive at dusk?
> In your place a boy
> Would have been welcome
> (Gardner & El Bushra 2004: 1)

Tragically, this leads to exposure of newborn girls to die, reduced feeding for female children, and an overall reduced female lifespan that accounts for a shortage of females in the lowlands of as much as five per cent.

Reflecting the segmentation of pastoralist society, political authority is diffuse, non-hierarchical, and democratic to an extent that outsiders consider anarchic. Mobile pastoralists the world over have seldom created states, more often they have acquired them through conquest (Khazanov 1983: 295). They never did either in the Horn. Many reasons are cited for the absence of political superstructures in pastoralist societies, including low population density, high mobility, lack of surplus, marginal role of trade, absence of towns, and self-reliance in defence. One school of thought maintains that the pastoralist mode of production neither needs or can afford state institutions (Barth 1973: 12). Another calls it a 'low investment in politics', a form of organizational flexibility appropriate to dynamic, poorly predictable conditions (Dyson-Hudson 1985: 169).

The absence of formal state structures creates the impression of anarchy. A common view among outsiders of pastoralist society is of a world where a permanent state of warfare reigns, while neighbouring cultivators live in terror of nomad raids. Innumerable studies by social anthropologists have shown that this is not the case. Pastoralist societies are not without government – institutions, laws, leaders – otherwise they could not exist as communities. Customary law is precise, comprehensive, and efficient because it is known and respected by all members of the community. When interpretation and enforcement is required, it is the task of the elders, who also mete out punishment for violations. Arrived at by consensus, elders' decisions are unchallengeable. Pastoralist communities also have clearly defined structures of leadership, although authority is limited in scope and exercised only in conjunction with the elders. This is a simple, non-hierarchical, non-coercive, fully representative form of governance which, moreover, does not cost the pastoralists financially. Taxation was unknown to them, and they did not take it kindly when it was imposed by the state. The traditional system of authority may have suited pastoralists in the past, when they lived in a state of rough equilibrium with their sedentary neighbours in the Horn. However, social segmentation and political diffusion provided a weak base from which to launch a successful defence against the expansion of centralized states with a strong peasant base, or to resist the suppression and depredation of the pastoralist habitat in the years that followed.

Conflict in the pastoralist zone

Conflict is a familiar feature of life in the pastoralist zone, and has earned its inhabitants a fearsome reputation for their 'warlike' and 'rebellious' nature. It is understandable that highlanders, who believe that 'a good neighbour is one who does not shift land boundaries', would find the pastoralist disregard of territoriality abhorrent. This belies the fact that a symbiotic relationship sustained by cultural ties, trade, inter-marriage, political and military alliances is not uncommon among pastoralists and between them and cultivators, as well as the fact that all pastoralist societies have well defined customary principles and procedures of conflict management. These work well in instances of intra-group conflict and are relied upon to this day by the lowlanders in keeping the peace within their communities. By contrast, conflict between different communities is difficult to manage. Accords between unrelated groups are often made but are difficult to enforce, except by resorting to more conflict.

The founding principle of justice among pastoralists is to the restoration of peace through the restitution of stolen goods and compensation for lost lives, not to retribution through the deprivation of life, liberty or property, as is the case in Western legal philosophy on which the modern Ethiopian legal system is modelled. The practice of compensation through blood payment was not unknown on the plateau. It was sanctioned in the 1930 Penal Code (Art. 404), but was outlawed by the 1957 Penal Code, which ruled that 'any homicide, whether committed intentionally or by negligence, shall be punished by lawful judicial process.' (Art. 521) From a pastoralist viewpoint the result of taking a life in punishment leaves two families without a head and a burden to their kin, while compensation paid to the victim's kinsmen lightens the burden of supporting his family. Compensation for a man's life, as much as 100 camels – a woman's life is worth half of that – is beyond the means of most households, and is met by contributions from all households in the guilty party's community. Likewise, compensation is shared among the households in the victim's group.

The perennial cause of conflict among pastoralists is the struggle for resources essential for their mode of production: pastureland, sources of water, and the routes that lead to them. Since this mode of production has not changed, these remain the main cause of conflict in the lowlands. Domestic matters such as dowry, adultery, divorce, inheritance, civil disputes involving individuals and households, and crimes of violence involving injury and death, are causes of strife within a community. This is an area where custom rules and elders wield undisputed authority. Tradition still hold sway throughout the lowlands, where state law is little known and state legal institutions have only recently made an appearance. It is preferred by the people for whom the legal principles and procedures of state courts are alien and incomprehensible, as well as distant, protracted and expensive. The representatives of the state itself not only tolerate this disregard of official legal codes, but encourage the practice by urging parties in dispute to follow the traditional process.

While traditional mechanisms are still effective in managing intra-community disputes, inter-community conflict is far more difficult to resolve because shared resolution mechanisms seldom exist at this level. Inter-community conflict has intensified significantly in recent years because lowland resources are shrinking due to the increase in both the human and animal population, the intrusion of cultivation and climate change. Livestock theft is a common cause of inter-community conflict, where the goal is economic, namely to replace livestock lost to drought, disease or enemy raids, and to discharge social obligations such as dowry payment. Young men also indulge in this activity to prove their manhood and gain a reputation for bravery and social status. Raiding often results in violence and homicide. In the past it was a community concern, regulated and conducted with the approval of the elders. Women and children were not harmed, and the target community was not left destitute without animals. Nowadays, livestock theft is often carried out without the knowledge or approval of the elders, and the scale of violence has risen dramatically due to the introduction of automatic weaponry, causing large number of casualties that now routinely include women and children.

Although isolated, pastoralist communities are not untouched by trends that are fast changing the world outside the periphery. Certain trends impinge directly in the pastoralist zone and introduce new resources unrelated to livestock production, for example, transport routes. The sole railway line and major road arteries in Ethiopia cross the lowlands. Towns and hamlets providing services to the transport industry appear along these routes, and trade, legitimate or contraband, moves by the same means. Urban congregations attract additional resources from the state, such as education, health and veterinary facilities, abattoirs, and off-range employment opportunities for impoverished pastoralists. All these represent new resources worth fighting over.

Another type of conflict arose in the lowland periphery during the second half of the past century and continues to wreak havoc in the region. This is a political struggle fought under various banners – nationalist, ethnic, regional, religious – where the ambition is to wrest state power, or to create new states, or to secede from one state and join another. Such conflicts have different origins and leadership, and goals that are not necessarily related to pastoralist concerns. Nevertheless, pastoralists are enthusiastic recruits in the insurgencies that appear in the lowlands. Often they join opportunistically to get weapons for use in their own parochial confrontations. At other times, they respond to the appeal of ethnic or religious solidarity.

Summary

The sharp, manifold contrasts between high and low lands depicted in this chapter provides the setting in which the process of state building unfolded. The depiction is necessary because the setting has conditioned, not to say determined, the direction of the process, the methods used and the progress it made. Nature itself and its capricious bequests are critical aspects of the setting, and a distinction is made between two sections of the periphery, high and low lands. The highland periphery shares the same physical environment with the Abyssinian homeland, its agrarian economy provided a sound basis for the surplus extraction system devised by the imperial state, and the indigenous cultures and authority systems loaned themselves to the indirect system of imperial rule imposed on them. As a result, the interaction between the centre/highland periphery proceeded relatively smoothly, and the process of integration that underlay state building progressed faster and farther in this region.

By contrast, nature in the lowland periphery posed every imaginable obstruction to integration. It created immense obstacles to transportation and communication that have yet to be overcome, and presented mortal hazards to the health and welfare of highlanders who have ventured there; as a result, very few have done so. The pastoralist economy did not lend itself easily to surplus extraction, while the peripatetic mode of life and independent ways of the herders defied efforts to control them. Consequently, the process of integration halted at the edge of the escarpment for nearly a century, and resumed only at the turn of the 21st century.

2

Afar & Somali

The focus of this study is on the lowland periphery because its part in the story is little known and, even more significantly, because this region poses a critical test for the nation-state building project. Obviously, a similar treatment for the highland periphery is essential for a comprehensive treatment of this topic. However, the large number of societies involved, the variety and wealth of their cultures, the diversity of their interaction with the centre, and the uneven degree of their respective integration in the nation-state make this a formidable enterprise well beyond the scope of the present book. Moreover, some of the most important groups in the highland periphery have already been the subject of study, and their interaction with the centre is documented, to a varied extent. This is true of the Oromo, Gurage, Sidama, Hadya, Kambata and Adari. Even so, a great deal more needs to be done and will be done by their own scholars.

Chapters 2, 3, and 4 draw the profiles of lowland communities in order to bring them out of history's shadows and to cast them as actors in the Ethiopian drama of state building. The profiles highlight the distinctiveness they have preserved to this day, but are now required to forfeit in the name of integration and the promise of development. A degree of indulgence is required of the reader who is asked to cross this ethnographic frontier; it is a small price to pay in order to appreciate fully the story that unfolds in this work. The order of presentation follows the lowland arc on the map from east to west. This chapter introduces the Afar and Somali peoples, who are the largest groups in terms of population, as well as in the size of the territory they inhabit in Ethiopia's lowland periphery.

The Afar

THE LAND

The land of the Afar includes the most striking terrain in Ethiopia. Outsiders who venture there reach for sensational terms to describe it without fear of exaggeration. 'Torrid' is often used, quite appropriate for a place that holds the record for the highest ever mean annual temperature recorded on earth (34C). 'Barren' is also an appropriate word for a land where two-thirds of the area are designated as 'bare.' 'Desert' is yet another for a territory amounting to more than one-tenth of the country's area and less than 2% of its population. In the Afar Depression, the end section of the Great Rift in Africa, where the land's surface sinks to 155m below sea level, the visitor encounters the most awesome spectacle staged by nature: sun baked deserts and salt flats, active volcanoes and molten lava lakes – the 'hell hole of creation' as it was put in an early unflattering description (Nesbitt 1935). Hundreds of minor earthquakes convulse the region each year. This is the birthplace of Lucy (Australopithecus Afarensis) some three million years ago, whose remnants were discovered in 1974.

The estimated size of the Afar *kilil* (regional state) is 100,860 square kilometres. Traversed by the great river trailing a green ribbon of vegetation along its banks, the Awash River Valley in the south is its other defining feature. The second longest (700km) river in Ethiopia and the major drainage system on the eastern side of the northern plateau, the Awash is the only river in Ethiopia that flows eastward. The Valley divides into three sections, only the last two of which lie within the Afar *kilil*. The Upper Valley runs from Koka Dam to Awash Station (mostly within Oromia *kilil*), the Middle Valley from Awash Station to Gewane town, and the Lower Valley from Gewane to Lake Abe, where the river loses itself in a maze of lakes and swamps.

The climate of the Great Rift is uniformly hot and dry, ranging from semi-arid to arid. According to local records, annual rainfall in the Middle Awash Valley during 1970-2003 had a mean rate of 558.4mm, while the annual precipitation deficiency rate for the period was above 95%, which means that twice as much rainfall was required for sustained plant growth (WARC 2003: 3). The rainfall pattern in Afar is highly erratic and drought is a regular visitor. The Afar distinguish between normal visitations of limited duration and damage called *Unda* (small), and prolonged ones that annihilate livestock and bring famine called *Kadda* (big). They recall several major droughts since the infamous *Daggahabe/Daggacabe* ('the cow pen emptied') of 1888-92; the *Quran Mali* ('so many people died, they were buried without Quranic ceremony') in 1928-33, the *Awursanat-li* ('people exchanged an ox for a meal in the highlands') in the 1940s, the *Qabbali/Geera-li* ('a time when there was no blood left') in the 1950s, the *Yaahun Daban* ('people disappeared into the blue') in the mid-1970s, and the *Mermeris Daban* ('people wandered about to look for food') in the mid-1980s.

The Land Resource Inventory for the Afar *kilil* (1998-9) describes two-thirds of Afar territory as 'bare'. The Awash Valley has the best resources for livestock production. Wet season grazing and browsing is relatively easy here because of the availability of open rangeland, the free movement of livestock through the range, and the proximity of dry season pasture on the Awash River banks. The exceptional resources of this area made it the object of on-going violent contention between the Afar and their Somali neighbours. Vast, flat plains in the Middle Valley provide pasture during the wet season. East of the river, the Allighedi Plain stretches from the towns of Awash Arba to Gadamaitu, the Yangudirasa Plain from Gewane to Undorfo, and the Koroba Plain from Undorfo to Adaitu. Known as *Badhu*, this semi-arid zone with 300-500mm precipitation is seasonally covered with grass, evergreen bush, succulent shrub and six different types of acacia.

The Awash River has several tributaries along its meandering course used for cultivation and livestock production, and there are a few other bodies of surface water in the region with the same potential. Golina, Logia, Mille, Lodi, Chaleka, Borkena, Jara, Arsu, Kebena and Kesem rivers are tributaries of the Awash on the western side. On the eastern side, several rivers flow into the swamps of the Middle and Lower valleys: among them the Erer, Koraba, Dancago and Bordada rivers. There are also many lakes and hot and cold springs, most of them saline and unsuitable for irrigation or livestock watering.

THE PEOPLE

In the past the Afar were known by various names in the Horn: Adal, Adali, Oda'ali and Dankali among others. The Arab geographer Ibn Said visited the Afar coast in the 13th century and made it known as Dankalia, from the name of a northern Afar clan, the Ankal. According to him, the Afar occupied the Red Sea coast from Suakin in the north to Bab el Mandeb in the south.[1] In the late 19th century, the land and the people were apportioned among the emerging states of the Horn, and today the Afar live under three flags, Ethiopian, Eritrean, and Djiboutian. According to the 2007 census, 1.25 million of them live in Ethiopia. All are Muslim and overwhelmingly rural. Some 200,000 others, mostly Amhara, Oromo and Tigray, form the bulk of the urban population in the Valley. The census showed a striking gender disparity, with 786,338 males to 624,754 females. The influx of male highlanders in the towns partly accounted for this, but the gap is wider in rural areas and opens early. The rate for infant mortality for males was 107/1000, for females 133/1000. The under-five mortality rate was 150/1,000 for males and 206/1,000 for females. Gender disparity increased dramatically with age. There were more than twice as many males as females in the 65-69 age bracket in 2007, the result of the fact that the average life span for males was 53 years and for women 47 years.

Afar society shares the typical features of pastoralist communities throughout the Horn, that is, social segmentation and political diffusion. The founding principle of Afar society is blood kinship, and the building block of its social structure is the patrilineal descent group, or clan. It is estimated there are more than a hundred clan-families among the Afar. Each comprises a pyramidal structure of smaller lineage groups, each with its own identity, territory and leadership. *Dala*, at the bottom, is a group of extended families who trace their descent three to five generations from a

[1] Cited in Oberle (1971: 27).

common ancestor, and whose leader is known as *Dala Aba. Khida* is a cluster of several *Dala* who trace their descent through seven generations from a common ancestor, and whose leader is named *Khida Aba. Mela* comprises several *Khida* whose members trace their descent over many generations to an original ancestor. *Mela* is the largest unit with its own defined territory, within which resources such as pasture and water are shared. The *Mela* has its own leader, the *Makaban, and* several *Mela* make up a clan family. Clan kinship is the strongest social bond among the Afar, reflected in the following sayings: 'As one does not hesitate to ask help of his shoes, so one should not hesitate to make use of his clan', and 'one who has not been born among you will not suffer on your behalf' (Parker 1971). Afar clans are grouped into two broad categories known as *Asahimera* (red) and *Adohimera* (white), a distinction whose origin is unknown and whose meaning has been lost over time.

Afar society is integrated on the basis of kinship, economic cooperation and mutual help. The nuclear family (*Ko Budda*) lives in close proximity with related families in an extended family cluster (*Iniki Budda*). They move together, herd livestock collectively, share food and child care. The homestead (*Ganda Budda*) comprises several extended families that cooperate in labour. Men tend the herds, women construct huts (*Ari*) with mats woven from date palm leaves, collect wood, fetch water and go to market together. Strong bonds of solidarity are maintained through a system of mutual help that ensures no one suffers want, as long as there is enough to share within the community. In a recent study of the Wossema Afar the following are listed as common practice: *Irbu* is the contribution of animals to households who have lost their own due to raid, disease, flood, etc. *Malihato* is a similar contribution in money. *Dakath* is a version of the Islamic *zakat* (a tithe given in alms to the poor). *Hantila* is the giving of milch animals to others for their period of need, and *Kataisa* is the custom of exchanging animals to strengthen social ties and mutual support.

The Afar people have a well defined system of traditional authority in the *Makabantu*. Each kinship segment has a recognised head (*Aba*), who is chosen partly through inheritance and partly for his personal qualities. *Kidha Aba*, the sub-clan chief, is the one who is most closely involved in the affairs of the community. Even so, he is more of an arbiter of internal disputes and the community's representative in external dealings, than a powerful chief in his own right. Like most pastoralist societies, the Afar are egalitarian and averse to hierarchy. 'The Afar like a brave man, but will not let him become a despot', is a traditional saying. 'A cow's tail is equidistant from both legs', is another, signifying equality among all members of a group. The chiefs at each level work in councils (*Mablo, Edola/Idola*) that include all subordinate chiefs and community elders. These are the highest decision-making bodies in matters of social control, resource allocation and defence, and their actions are guided by the customary law, *Maada*, that has ruled Afar society for centuries.

Customary law and the elders' decisions are enforced by the *fimaa*, a formally organised group of young men who are circumcised at the same time. To a degree, *fimaa* resembles the age-grade groups of other East

African pastoralist societies. Responsible for internal policing, the *fimaa's* role is to apply sanctions and it may use any means to fulfil its duty, including violence. It is also responsible for defending the community against enemy raids and the land against intruders. The *fimaa* is led by the *Fimaa-Aba* who wields considerable authority and can act on his own, if need be, without prior elder decision.

The Afar embraced Islam in the 14th century and this may have been a factor in the appearance of more centralised and hierarchical forms of government in the sultanates of Tadjura, Raheita, Biru, Gobhat and Aussa, whose rulers were called Amoyto in the south and Dardar in the north, but are commonly referred to as sultans. These sultanates appear in Ethiopian history during the reign of Emperor Amda Seyon (1312-1342), who fought many battles in the eastern lowlands in his attempts to subdue the Afar. Emperor Eskender (1478-1494) fell in battle against the Afar in the lowlands, and Afar were part of Gragn's army when it invaded the northern highlands. Aussa Sultanate was a vassal of the Adal Emirate based in Harar, from where Gragn set off in 1540. Not long afterwards, Oromo pressure forced the Adal Sultan to move his seat to Aussa, where his descendants were to rule for a century. The Adal dynasty was followed by an interlude of four Yemeni sultans, before an Afar named Kaddafo seized power and founded a native dynasty that governed the fertile region of the Awash River inland delta until 1975.[2] The other sultanates were dismantled in the imperialist scramble and the land of the Afar was divided between Italy, France and Ethiopia. Only Aussa retained its integrity and a degree of autonomy within Ethiopia until the demise of the imperial regime in 1974.

*

Afar pastoralists are mobile but not nomadic. Movement is spontaneous, dictated by seasonal change and the search for pasture and water, and in the Awash Valley, the river provides both during the dry season. Movement there seldom exceeds 50km, and ranges between the settled homestead (*homa*) to the mobile camp (*magida*). Women, children and old people live at the homestead and look after small stock and lactating animals. Men accompany the herd whose movements are dictated primarily by their need to forage and occasionally by flooding. To avoid this, the homestead moves seasonally from low lying ground (*kelo*) to high (*alta*) pasture. The homestead may be forced to move also by vermin and insect infestation.

Cattle are raised primarily for milk and its by-products, and an estimated three million head are the mainstay of the Afar economy. Camels are highly valued – 'my lover is like a Harar she-camel', goes an Afar love

[2] The dynastic line is Kaddafo Hanfare Aodahis (1754-1768); Mahammad Kaddafo (1768-1798); Aodahis Mahammad Kaddafo (1798-1831); Hanfare Aodahis Mahhamad (1832-1861); Mahhamad Hanfare Aodahis (1861-1902); Mahhamad Aodahis Hanfare; Ali Mirah Mahammad Hanfare, Hanfare Mahammad Hanfare, Yayio Mahammad Hanfare (1912-1927); Mahammad Yayio Mahammad (1927-1944); Ali Mira Hanfare Aodahis (1944-). See Aramis (2005).

song – and there are an estimated 870,000 of them in the Afar *kilil*. Sheep and goats are sources of milk, meat, butter and cash. Goats are valued for their high rate of reproduction – as high as 48% per annum – for their resistance to drought, and their easy conversion to cash. The donkey is the beast of burden known as 'the servant of women'. Pastoralists normally do not abuse the environment on which they depend for their livelihood, and the Afar are no exception. Community resource management is part of their tradition. Tree cutting is not allowed, except for hut construction and even then the whole tree is not taken. Afar are not keen hunters of wild animals: as they say, 'we eat only what God kills.'

As in most pastoralist societies, the Afar traditional land tenure system is flexible. Unlike other pastoralist societies, however, it does not ordain congruence between clan and territory. Segments of one clan can be found dispersed in several parts of the region, sharing territory with segments of other clans. Claims to specific tracts of land are raised at the sub-clan (*Khida*) and lineage (*Dala*) levels. Unless it creates a shortage for the resident community, these do not exclude other clans or lineages from crossing or grazing. Claims tend to be more clearly defined and more exclusive depending on the value of the land, the presence of water in it, and the density of livestock population in the vicinity. For example, in the Amibara and Gewane districts of the Middle Valley, the flood-fed land and wet-season pasturelands are subdivided into *Khida* territories, and each territory is separated from its neighbours by natural boundary marks such as trees and water points. With the introduction of cultivation in recent times and the consequent rise in the value of land, claims to it have hardened, becoming a source of conflict between *Khida*.

Cultivation is not unknown to the Afar. In the Awash River Delta, they tilled the land intensively through irrigation, blending cultivation with livestock herding in a self-sufficient system of agro-pastoralism. With its plentiful and reliable supply of river water, the Delta was cultivated for centuries. At one time, cotton, maize and sorghum produced here were marketed as far as Assab and Djibouti. The area produced enough surplus to support the emergence of a centralised, hierarchical form of government in the form of the Aussa Sultanate founded by the Moodayto clan that settled here in the mid-17th century. Because of its high value, this part of the Delta is closed to non-Moodayto clans, and the land is parcelled into a large number of clearly demarcated *Kidha* territories. 'There is now not one piece of land in the whole Lower Awash area that does not have an Afar *Kidha* ownership tag on it', a visitor noted (Cossins 1973: 21). Over the first decade of this century, this oasis of traditional agriculture is due to be overrun by the expansion of commercial cultivation.

The Afar economy relies mainly on the produce of livestock, supplemented with grain grown in the Delta and the surrounding Oromo region. Dependence on grain has increased significantly in recent times, as the livestock economy has weakened due to the intrusion of commercial cultivation and adverse climatic trends. Grain consumption becomes critical during periods of drought, an increasingly common phenomenon in the Afar region. In the 2002-2003 drought, the Afar lost 87% of their cattle, 85% of their camels, and 85% of their small stock. Their economy is no longer self-sufficient even at subsistence level. Inputs of food aid that began during the famine of the 1970s have grown steadily and are now essential to meet the basic needs of the population. With the exception of a couple of years in the mid-1990s, the number of people requiring food aid in the past two decades has run consistently in the hundreds of thousands.

In contrast to their Somali neighbours, the Afar approach to livestock trade remains traditional, which means they engage in the market not for profit, but only to satisfy household needs. A study carried out in 1970 noted: 'The Afar are not interested in increasing annual returns from their herds or their surplus by improving herd quality. They sell only old or poor quality animals.' (Negussie Tilahun 1983: 4) They also sell small stock, kid skins, rope and mats, and buy grain, clothing, honey, chat, pepper, tobacco, cigarettes, spices, coffee, gourds, beads, sandals, livestock medicines and sugar. Occasionally they may sell large animals to buy firearms and ammunition. This does not signify commercialisation, but simply a changing pattern of consumption. The Afar trade mostly locally in what are called primary markets that take place weekly in various locations within their region. Relatively few Afar work as traders, a profession monopolised by highlanders.

Several factors account for the Afar's avoidance of the market, one of them being the geopolitical pattern that divided the Afar among three states – Ethiopia, Eritrea, Djibouti – and cut them off from their natural trade outlets on the Red Sea coast. Another is the difficult nature of the terrain on the escarpment, which the Afar must climb in order to reach markets on the highlands. Yet another is the perennial conflicts that mar relations with their neighbours and inhibit Afar participation in regional markets. 'Most of the cross regional markets are closed to the Afar pastoralists due to ethnic conflicts' (WARC 2003: 11). Finally, the extremely low rate of urbanisation among the Afar is in itself an impediment to participation in trade. 'There is no trend among the Afar in adopting the urban ways of life in *toto*', noted one report (Ethiopian Red Cross 1988: 47) Underlying and defining all these obstacles, of course, is the decline of the Afar pastoralist economy.

Salt found in the Afar Depression is highly valued in the northern highlands where it is scarce. Mined by the local peoples, it was in the past sold to traders mainly from Tigray to be transported by camel caravan to markets on the plateau. Its price rose with distance, and in the extreme west of the empire, one slave could be bought for one block of salt. The Afar also controlled the caravan trade that carried it across the Red Sea from the port of Baylum some forty kilometres from Assab. The recent opening of a motor road has stimulated commercial interest in this product, and the Ethiopian government has launched plans to develop it with the participation of private capital. If history repeats itself, the Afar are likely to lose both the salt and the land that holds it.

Conflict and peacemaking in Afar

In common with most pastoralist societies, the Afar cultivate the warrior ethos. The custom whereby young men attain manhood status by killing is known as *digif*, and such deeds are celebrated in song. 'I made war in four villages. I am the Sultan's right arm. Of my victims I report those who were proud. I have drunk their blood', boasts one warrior. Another complains: 'I killed ninety nine men but I did not kill the one who would have made it one hundred. That is what disappoints me.' 'No man may wear a coloured loin cloth, a comb or feather in his hair, nor decorate his knife with brass or silver until he has killed at least once', wrote an early visitor (Thesiger 1935: 3).

Conflict among Afar clans for natural resources and control of trade routes is a constant theme of their oral history, which also records incessant power struggles among the five Sultanates. Though Afar ideology stresses the collective aspect of land tenure, land has become the cause of frequent conflict among clans. 'We love each other, but we will quarrel with each other if it comes to land', is an Afar saying. The return in the 1990s of floodland taken by the military regime in the 1980s for state farms was the cause of much intra-Afar conflict. Like all pastoralists, the Afar have a history of shifting territories, and enter into no end of arguments over who are the original inhabitants (*suget*) of a territory and who are the latecomers (*yemete*). Normally academic, such disputes can turn violent in times of stress, or when the value of the land in question rises, for instance though the provision of water for irrigated pasture or cultivation. The forming of defensive clan alliances called *dalla-k-ballis* testifies to the tradition of inter-clan rivalry and conflict. Clan pairs have twin names, such as Afke-k-Maad, Arapta-k-Assabakari. Normally, both sides of a pair belong to the same clan family and occupy the same or neighbouring territories. Each clan in a pair retains its autonomy and leadership, but together they present a common front in interaction with other clans.

Like all pastoralist societies, the Afar have a well defined process of conflict resolution based on customary law (*Maada*), interpreted and applied by community leaders. The founding principle of justice is to make peace (*billi arri*), and the procedure followed is straightforward. When a crime is committed, the elders meet in council (*edola*) and ask for time to consider the matter. The victim's family is not supposed to retaliate while they do so, and the killer's family sacrifices a camel to feed the elders. At the end of the stated period, both parties are brought before the *edola* to hear the elders' decision and learn the amount of compensation to be paid by the killer's family. The senior *Khida Aba* announces the decision known as *fatha*, which is irreversible and is enforced by the *fimaa*. Another animal is then slaughtered for the elders to feast.

This traditional system of justice, blood payment included, is still prevalent among the Afar. The *kilil* officials themselves not only tolerate the setting aside of state legal codes, but encourage the practice by urging parties in dispute to follow the traditional process. 'Afar kill Afar all the time. We do not interfere' commented a local official.[3] According to one report, 'experience has demonstrated that decisions by state courts were not generally successful or effective in resolving conflicts or restoring peace in the manner achieved by the Afar traditional system' (Kelemework n.d.: 61). Occasionally, the two institutions work together, for example when the police apprehend a suspect and keep him in prison for his own protection until the case is decided by the elders.

Afar relations with their neighbours have never been easy. In the past their attitude towards strangers was notoriously aggressive and their reputation for violence fearsome. 'Inhospitable' was another familiar epithet for the Afar. Few outsiders crossed their land and lived to talk about it, and those who did depicted its inhabitants in lurid colours. 'Suspicious, treacherous, and bloodthirsty', was one such (Trimingham 1952: 172). 'The Danakils kill any stranger at sight. The taking of life has become a habit of their nature', was another (Nesbitt 1934: 79). Highlanders avoided the scorched land below, and when they met with the Afar on the escarpment bloodshed was likely. To this day, the Afar are seen as strange and unapproachable by their neighbours on the highlands. 'The Afar have always been a mystery. Their system remains enigmatic to this day', was the comment of an experienced observer in 1881 (Cossins 1981: 14).

Things have changed little since then. Afar relations with their neighbours in Ethiopia remain fraught with a history of hostility and ongoing disputes over territory. A particularly serious quarrel with their Somali neighbours has lasted for decades, defeating efforts by three successive regimes in Addis Ababa to resolve it. (See Chapters 7, 10, 14.) Bad neighbour relations perpetuate the isolation and ingrained conservatism of the Afar people. Conflict at this level is very difficult to resolve. The Afar have no tradition of concluding agreements regulating conflict with outsiders, nor are they easily coerced by the state to keep the peace.

The Somali

THE LAND

The Somali *kilil* occupies a diverse terrain with five distinct sections. The bulk of it is a sloping plain that stretches south-eastwards from the southern plateau towards Somalia and the Indian Ocean. The central and western sections of the plain, historically known as the Ogaden, are encircled on the northwest by the southern plateau which intrudes and dissects them with water draining declivities. By contrast, the eastern triangle of the region, known as the Haud, is flat and featureless. The northern part of the *kilil* (Shinile Zone) lies in the Great Rift Valley, and is linked to the plain through a narrow, elevated land corridor (Jijiga Zone)

[3] Dulecha district administrator, interviewed in November 2004.

on the eastern edge of the plateau. With an elevation reaching up to 1600m, Jijiga Zone is the northern summit of the plain that falls gently to around 500m as it reaches the border with Somalia.

The climate of the southeast plain is similarly diverse. The northwest corner, including the Jijiga corridor, has an elevation of 1400m-1600m and rainfall up to 600mm. Cultivation is possible here and has been practised for decades. The rest of the plain receives an average rainfall of less than 500mm, and is classified as semi-arid. Some 80% of the Somali *kilil* falls in this category. Precipitation determines a pattern of vegetation that is generally sparse and whose density decreases from northwest to southeast. Shrub, bush and grass are the dominant species, as well as a large variety of acacia, gum, incense and myrrh plants. While these are often permanent, they cannot endure continued grazing or browsing. Consequently, grazing systems must be based on movement of the nomadic or transhumance type. Movement is made all the more necessary and irregular by the erratic pattern of rainfall in the arid zone. Drought is a familiar visitor often accompanied by famine that people recall with poignant names, such as '*tolkay jab*' ('killer of my kindred') in 1975-78, and '*waan madhanay*' ('we are finished') in 1984-86.[4] Estimated losses in the 1999-2000 drought amounted to 60% of cattle, 25% of camels and 30% of flock animals. If the price of livestock is taken into account, livestock producers lose fortunes in market terms, while cultivators lose only one season's crop. Moreover, cultivators can recover completely within one season, while rebuilding a herd takes years.

Although direct rainfall in the Somali plain is scant, the region draws much of the rainwater that falls on the highlands. Its western half forms the drainage basin for the southern plateau, and is crossed by several major rivers and many seasonal streams and culverts. These are the mainstay of pastoralism, providing reliable sources of water and grassy plains for livestock, and also sustain cultivation along their courses based on flooding, gravity and pump irrigation. They also determine the pattern of population settlement, with most towns and hamlets sited on or near them. The Webi Shebeli is the longest river in Ethiopia with a catchment area of 205,000km^2. Rising in the Harar mountains, it flows for 1,340kms to the Somalia border, then continues eastward for another 660kms, before veering southwards to disappear into swamps near the Indian Ocean. Alluvial flats three to five kilometres wide begin at Ime and flank the river for the rest of its course.

The Genale River in the southwest begins in the Arsi highlands, and flows for 480kms inside Ethiopia to reach the border, where it joins the Dawa River to become the Juba River inside Somalia, then flows for another 1658kms until it reaches the sea near Kisimayo. The Weyeb is a seasonal river that also rises in the Arsi highlands and joins the Genale near the border. Several seasonal rivers flow in the northeast corner of the region. Shinile Zone has one perennial river, the Ere, and several seasonal

[4] Reported incidents of drought occurred in this region in 1910-11, 1920-21, 1925-31, 1935-37, 1950-51, 1962-65, 1967-68, 1975-8, 1982-84, 1991-2, 1998-9, 2000-3.

streams. Two seasonal rivers, the Jerer and the Fafan, cross the Jijiga plain and flow parallel for about 150kms before merging in an often unsuccessful effort to reach the Webi Shebeli. The Dakota, another seasonal river, manages to join the Webi Shebeli.

The Haud is a distinctive and highly prized land, and a bone of contention that will feature later in this work. A broad, undulating plain, it stretches parallel to the Somaliland border some sixty kilometres deep, and offers some of the best grazing land despite the lack of rainfall for more than half the year. The Haud receives 150-200mm of rain annually, has no permanent water sources and a very low water table that makes it very difficult to reach underground water. As its name indicates (*haud* means 'bushy'), it has a thick vegetation cover of bush and woodland and ample wet season grazing areas. In past the Haud was used only seasonally and was vacated during the dry season, thus giving vegetation time to recover.

The face of the Haud began to change in the mid-20th century with the introduction of the *birkad,* the cement-lined water tank that stores rainwater, or is filled with water brought from elsewhere. The *birkad* made it possible for herds to prolong their stay, and eventually to remain in the Haud throughout the year. The result is livestock congestion and overgrazing, soil erosion and environmental degradation that are now obvious to the naked eye. The appearance of human settlements where none existed before was another change. *Birkad* are build in clusters around which other enterprises emerge, such as teahouses, livestock trading and chat selling. These changes result in crowding and provoke disputes among the clans that use the Haud, particularly between the Ogaden and the Ishaq who have been involved in a violent confrontation that flares up intermittently to this day.

THE PEOPLE

At 4.5 million in 2007, the Somali population of Ethiopia represents roughly one-third of the widely dispersed Somali nation in the Horn, and equals half the estimated population of Somalia itself. The territory inhabited by them in Ethiopia (279,252km^2) is nearly half as large as the territory of the Somali Republic (638,000km^2). The Somali are the third largest nationality in Ethiopia (6.2% of the total), outnumbering the Tigray, and the Somali *kilil* is the second largest in area (after Oromia), covering about one-quarter of Ethiopia's 1.2 million km^2. The Somali *kilil* lists 67 towns, of which less than half had a population of more than 5,000 inhabitants. With some 125,000, inhabitants, Jijiga was by far the largest town, followed by Gode with about 45,000. The population is quite homogeneous and solidly Muslim. Typical of pastoralist societies, females account for 44.4% of the total, compared with 49.5% for the country as a whole.

Kinship (*tol*), the foundation of Somali society, is quite different from territoriality (*agar*), the pillar of highland peasant society. This difference is strongly reflected in the culture and authority systems of the two groups, and is often the cause of misunderstanding and tension in their relationship. More significantly, it greatly complicates the interaction of an egalitarian Somali society with a state rooted in the authoritarian political culture of the Ethiopian highlands. The cornerstone of Somali social organisation is the patrilineal descent group (*higto*) traced from a common ancestor over several generations. It is a vertical, exclusive, and highly segmented social structure that divides people into sections (clans) often named after the common ancestor (*xigaalo*). Every Somali is born into a clan and derives his identity from it. The clan 'represents the social division of people into corporate political groups. By reference to his ancestors, a man's relations with others are defined, and his position in Somali society as a whole is determined' (Lewis, 1961: 2). Somali society has not produced corporate structures to supersede the clan, therefore, clannishness as the mode of social and political behaviour remains of the essence. Given the propensity of this social system to segmentation, its members' political behaviour is highly volatile. The level at which one's identity is asserted and one's political position is determined depends on the context. It may be the lowest, most immediate kinship level (primary lineage), or higher levels, sub-clan, clan and family of clans. As the proverb ordains: 'to protect yourself from your son, rely on your brother; for protection from your brother, rely on your son' (Mohammed Abdi Mohammed 1997: 854).

Clan composition is not constant. Descent groups are inherently unstable, combining and breaking apart as they respond to changing circumstances. 'Somali society is a dynamic one, breaking up and rebuilding constantly, depending on the times, the circumstances, and the needs of the various communities' (Mohammed Abdi Mohammed 1997: 152). Clan segments alter their status and function in accordance with demographic growth, so lineages become sub-clans, while sub-clans become clans. A descent group may separate from the mother group and become a clan by itself, merge with others to form a new clan, join an existing clan, or become the client of another. A weak group may join a strong one in a merger called *sheegat*, whereby members of the weak group adopt the genealogy of the strong as their own, according to the saying 'either be a mountain, or lean against one.' All these permutations are common practice. The very terminology associated with kinship and clan in Somali culture is ambiguous. The various terms for clan (*qabil, jilib, reer, laf, golo*) have no precise genealogical definition.

Such fluidity allows the individual to manipulate clanship to suit circumstances. 'By tracing back the father's line to specific apical ancestors, every Somali was able to evoke numerous patrilineal units, some more restricted, some more expansive' (Schlee 2002: 259). In other words, one can pick the point of reference for his identity by choosing the depth – the ancestor (*higaalo*) – and thus the groups he wishes to identify with, in order to suit the circumstances. This can be done by individuals as well as groups to position themselves against others. The implication is that the identity of the relevant segment in a given situation depends to a significant extent on the situation itself. As the situation changes, the identities and group positions shift, and today's allies can become tomorrow's enemies and vice versa.[5]

[5] 'Every point of lineage segmentation – every ancestor in the genealogies – is at least potentially an axis of political division and unity' (Lewis 1994: 84).

The ease of clanship manipulation and the extreme volatility of Somali political behaviour baffle outsiders, Ethiopian officialdom included.

Such volatility is reflected in the nature of the traditional Somali political system, which lacks hierarchy and effective authority beyond the primary lineage level. While there are offices at various clan levels, variously titled *Suldaan*, *Ugaas*, *Garaad*, or *Bokor*, their holders enjoy only nominal authority. Decisions at every level are made in a council (*shir*), in which every adult male has the right to speak, and whose decisions are final. *Shir* decisions are shaped by an unwritten code of conduct (*heer*) that is constantly reinterpreted and adopted to changing circumstance. The Islamic religious code (*rumeysi*) overlaps and reinforces the *heer* and the clan code ((*dhaqan*). The latter comprises distinct categories, such as rules for the punishment of crimes, work, marriage and property, war and peace that are common to most clans. Infractions of the rules and consequent disputes are brought before a tribunal of elders, the *guurti,* whose decisions are final. Men of religion (*wadad*) also play a role in adjudicating matrimonial and inheritance disputes and assess damages for injury. These codes are native and ancient and do not require enforcing institutions. By contrast, state law (*dawlad*) is new and alien, and has yet to gain acceptance by the Somali people.

The institution of *diya* exemplifies the enduring significance and vitality of customary law in contemporary Somali society. *Diya*, also called *mag*, is recognised by the Islamic legal system, as long as it does not conflict with the *Sharia*. The primary lineage with a span of up to ten generations is the largest, clearly defined, exogamous unit, and the most important in clan relations. Within each lineage, a segment with a span of up to eight generations is designated the *diya* group whose male members are linked in a pact of mutual aid towards outsiders. The *diya*'s main function is to provide blood payment when one of its members harms an outsider, and to exact similar payment or revenge when one of its own members is harmed by an outsider. Payment and compensation are shared collectively within the *diya* group. The often cited payment of 100 camels for the life of a man and 50 camels for the life of a woman is an ideal case. In reality, the amount varies widely among groups and is modified to suit local conditions.

The endurance of the clan as the foundation of Somali social and political organisation is the subject of heated debate among social scientists. Established and staunchly defended over half a century by I.M. Lewis, the dominant view sees the clan as the eternal and immutable bedrock of Somali society, and insists that today 'the clan is basically the same phenomenon that it was in the 1890s' (1994: 233). Lewis' critics consider this an outdated view that fails to take into account changes that have affected Somali society in the past century. Rather than immutable, the critics argue, clan is a flexible construct shaped by circumstance. 'The starting point for analyzing clan differentiation in Somalia must be the larger political and historical contexts in which it is located' (Little 2003: 46). Which ever view one holds, it follows that clan is a critical variable that must be taken into account in any attempt to fathom Somali political behaviour.

The broadest distinction of the Somali nation is between the Samali and the Sab branches, which trace their genealogy to ancestors by the same names. The Samali are nomadic pastoralists who occupy the centre, north and east, while the Sab are descendants of pastoralists who moved south-westwards to better watered terrain, and took up cultivation alongside the indigenous Bantu people. Having preserved their nomad tradition and culture, the Samali have pretensions to superiority over the Sab and look down on them for tilling the land and mingling with the Bantu. By far the larger of the two branches, the Samali are divided into two main sections, Darod and Irir, and they in turn are divided into clan families. Much the larger of the two, the Darod is also the most widely spread and politically powerful.

Darod clans are predominant in Ethiopia, of whom the Ogaden is the largest and politically most important. Ogaden branches are found also across the border in southern Somalia and the north-eastern province of Kenya, while some Ogaden clans, such as the Mohammed Zubeir, Aulihan and Digodia, straddle the Ethiopia-Somalia-Kenya borders. The Somali inhabited territory annexed by Ethiopia at the turn of the 20th century became known as the Ogaden after this clan, despite the fact that all Somali clans are represented in its population, and it has entered the pages of modern history through maps and international agreements under this name. Ogaden clansmen are congregated in six of the *kilil*'s nine zones – Fik, Gode, Danan, Korahe, Afder, Degehabur – and claim to have an overall majority of its population. This claim is rejected by other Darod clans, for example the Dulbahante and Warsangeli who straddle the eastern Somalia-Ethiopia border, the Marehan who likewise straddle the south-eastern section of this border, and most strenuously by the Ishaq clan of the Irir clan family – the dominant clan in Somaliland – which has a strong presence in the Haud and the Jijiga plain inside Ethiopia. The issue has gained added prominence since the turn of the century due to the activities of the Ogaden National Liberation Front (ONLF) whose goal is secession (see Chapter 14).

*

In the past, the Somali were highly mobile nomadic pastoralists who ranged widely with their livestock throughout the Horn, constantly shifting territory in search of green pasture. Initially devoted to camel raising, they added cattle to their herds as they moved south-westwards, as well as goats and sheep on the higher elevations. The one-humped camel is the preferred animal, and it is estimated that Somali camel herds in the Horn form the largest dromedary population in the world. According to a Somali poem, 'One pays creditors and others with goats, sheep and cattle, but one keeps camels as insurance for life.'[6] The camel is preferred because of its many uses, adaptability, greater mobility, eclectic feeding habits, endurance in hot climates, selective browsing behaviour, longer lactation

[6] Cited in Dolal (2000: 88).

period, greater volume of milk per lactation, and resistance to disease and drought. The most important camel product is milk rich in vitamin C, a vital ingredient where fruit and vegetables are not available. The Somali also keep a large number of sheep and goats. As another saying has it, 'to set up a household you need a minimum of forty goats before four children.'

Water is the limiting factor in the nomad economy. The most dependable source of water are wells (*ella*), up to thirty metres in depth and one meter in diameter, dug by hand along stream banks in a linear arrangement for several kilometres. They fill with floodwaters and must be cleaned before use. Wells are also dug in flood plains in a circular pattern over one kilometre in diameter. These may be stone lined and capped and need little maintenance. Earth dams and ponds, natural (*balleys*) or man-made (*harr*) sited in drainage lines provide seasonal water. These are open to animals as well as humans, and are not cleaned or maintained. *Haffir* dams are bigger than earth dams, and have silt traps or sedimentation basins. They are fenced, not accessible to animals and contain only clean water. The labour involved in digging and maintaining man-made water sources entitles lineages to claim ownership and to charge for water.

As is common in the pastoralist milieu, in theory, land is common property. 'Land is the gift of God, and man has only the use of it', the Somali say. In practice however land is the object of bitter, endemic conflict throughout the lowlands. Among the Somali, there is recognition of territorial boundaries (*deegaan*) that separate the main clan families which, however, are not permanently fixed and are often contested. One example is the long feud over the Haud between the Ogaden and the Ishaq. Large clans and sub-clans also tend to have proprietary interests over territories they inhabit, and often have to defend them against incursion by other clans of the same family. Disputes over land are common among branches of the Ogaden clan family. The deciding factor in most cases is not the degree of kinship, but the degree of need. In normal times, passage and grazing will be allowed by agreement between clans. Conflict will break out if the outsiders violate the agreement, or are suspected of intending to settle permanently. Rights over man-made water sources are defended and provoke conflict if violated. Only primary lineages, the Somali say, 'never fight over water or grazing'. Certain developments in recent decades are undermining the traditional liberal pastoralist notions of land tenure and have raised the frequency and intensity of communal strife. These are related to the changes brought about by the proliferation of *birkad*, and the related trends of sedenterisation, land enclosure and privatisation which will be discussed in later chapters.

The Somali have a history of involvement in local trade, barter of livestock products for grain with sedentary neighbours, and long-distance trade in luxury goods such as ivory, animal skins, myrrh and frankincense, civet oil and ostrich feathers. In the past they were engaged as guides, guards and transporters in the caravan trade that linked the hinterland with the towns of the Red Sea coast – Djibouti, Zeyla, Berbera, and the

Indian Ocean – Mogadisho, Merca, Brava. Integrated into an international network linking three continents, these towns obtained many of the trade goods from the pastoralist hinterland.

Trade followed the dictates of the natural economy of the region and the logic of the market, linking points of supply and demand over the shortest distance and lowest transport cost. It also followed closely the pattern of clan networks that facilitated communication and offered protection. The geopolitical pattern that emerged in the Horn of Africa in the 20th century went against the logic of the natural economy of the region and had disastrous consequences for trade. Colonial and Ethiopian borders were drawn through the pastoralist lowland that was considered a no-man's land. Initially these borders had only a notional existence and did not seriously inconvenience pastoralists, or interfere with trade. Later on, concern with market control, smuggling, poaching, banditry and livestock disease led the states to begin tightening border controls, a process that has yet to be completed. The intention was and remains to reverse the traditional pattern of regional trade that follows the shortest routes to the nearest market, because these routes lead across the nearest border. The goal is to redirect trade towards the centre of each state, where it can be regulated, taxed and priced low for the benefit of townspeople and for export.

Sealing borders has proved beyond the means of any state in the Horn, and today cross-border trade is flourishing. It was greatly boosted in past decades by the opening of a major market for livestock across the Red Sea, and a related demand in the Horn for cheap manufactured products from Asia and elsewhere. What has changed is its status, for the trade now is illegal, evading regulation, taxation, inspection and sundry other exactions imposed by the state; impediments that have hamstrung legal interstate trade in the Horn. The scope of contraband trade includes Ethiopia, Djibouti, Somaliland, Somalia and northern Kenya, and extends across the Red Sea to reach the Arab Gulf, where the bulk of livestock exports from southeast Ethiopia end up and from where most of the imports come in transit from Asia and Europe.

Not all Somali are pastoralists. The flat Jijiga plain in the north of the Somali *kilil* has a history of settled cultivation. Cultivators have always lived off the land in the Shebeli–Juba Valley, where both irrigated and rainfed farming is practised. Somali who settled in this region adopted a sedentary mode of existence and became estranged from the pastoralist milieu. The Sab, as the sedentary people of southern Somalia are called, are distinguished from the other Somali by their language, their agricultural way of life, loss of genealogical continuity and weak attachment to lineage and clan, all grounds for the low esteem in which they are held by the pastoralists. Sab are also found within Ethiopia, living in villages and cultivating land along the banks of the large rivers that cross their territory.

Cultivation is widely practised in Gode Zone along both banks of the Webi Shebeli River, from Imi to the Somalia border. The people of this area are called *beerley* ('farmers'), and most of them practise controlled flood-recession using canals. Plots are cultivated up to seven kilometres from the riverbed. Production depends largely on the amount of rainfall on the mountains to the north that determines river water levels. The main crop is maize and is marketed in Hiran and Bakool in Somalia. Other irrigated crops include sesame, cowpeas, vegetables and fruit.

Riverain farming based on pump irrigation is practised also in Liben Zone along the Genale and Dawa rivers. The farming population here belongs mainly to the Digodia and Garimaro clans. Conversion to cultivation is of recent origin; most of the farmers were pastoralists a generation ago. The introduction of pump irrigation made cultivation a viable and preferred alternative to their precarious existence as marginal pastoralists. Maize is the main crop grown for food, while vegetables and fruit are grown as cash crops. The market for this produce is Dollo Ado, from where traders forward it to Mandera in Kenya. The majority of pump owners are people who fled the civil war in Somalia after the fall of the Siad Barre regime in 1991. Some of them are returnees who fled from Ethiopia during the war with Somalia in the late 1970s and took up farming in the south. They imported pumps to Ethiopia and leased land from the local communities.

Conflict and resolution in Somali

In the words of an elder, conflict among the Somali 'is everyday business'.[7] One survey listed twenty-one major incidents in the *kilil* during 1995-1999 with a total of over one thousand casualties.[8] The causes are the same as elsewhere in the pastoralist habitat of the Horn. Among the instances cited in the survey were a conflict between two sections of the Galimey clan in Gode Zone over farm land that lasted twelve months and left sixty dead; a clash between the Gasar and Bajimal clans in Kelafo over the deviation of an irrigation channel that lasted six months and left thirty eight dead; and a violent dispute between the Awdwak and Bah Gerri over a hand dug well that also lasted six months, with the cost of twenty lives. Normally, clan conflict is local, limited, transient and susceptible to management through traditional methods applied by elders. Although the impact on local society and economy can be severe, it is seldom lasting. Nevertheless, there are numerous cases of conflicts between large and powerful clans that have proved intractable despite the efforts of elders, local authorities and the central government.

Although traditional resource competition – over pastureland, water and access routes – remains the root cause of conflict, not all the contested resources are traditional. The shift to agro-pastoralism has raised the value of cultivable land and water for irrigation, making both major causes of conflict among clans. 'Somalis have always fought. There is nothing new in this. What is new is the injection of new resources or land use arrangements to fight about' (Hogg 1997: 121). New resources have

[7] Quoted in Ahmed Shide (n.d.: 16).

[8] Ogaden Welfare Society Proceedings. (Addis Ababa, 1999).

appeared in the lowlands that are not related to the livestock economy, such as transport routes and contraband trade. Furthermore, federalism has introduced another valuable resource in the form of subsidies from the federal government, and made control of local administrative office the object of fierce competition among clans. In 2000, two closely related Ogaden sub-clans, Rer Abdille and Ugas Koshin, fought for control of the Garbo district administration. Dozens of people were killed and much property was destroyed, before peace was restored with the intervention of the *kilil* government.

Conflict in the Somali region is further compounded and exacerbated by the impact of wider political struggles into which pastoralists are often drawn. For several decades now, the southeast has been a battleground for Ethiopia and Somalia, and the staging ground for insurgent movements warring against both. These movements depend on pastoralist manpower and logistical support, and in turn provide arms to the herders and are drawn into local disputes. The result is to raise the scale of violence and the destructiveness of conflict, and to compound the problem of peace-keeping. A typical example involved two sections of the Ishaq clan in the Haud. The construction of thousands of *birkad* in Harshin district, home of the Habr Awal/Ishaq clan, led to spreading sedenterisation and restricted livestock movement in an area previously visited only during the rainy season. Cultivation soon followed, and was taken up by two Habr Awal/Ishaq sections, the Rer Liban and the Rer Samatar, leading to land enclosure and disputes between the two kindred clans. When violence broke out between them in the early 1990s, each sought support from rival political factions across the border in Somaliland. The smaller and weaker Rer Liban received support from the government of Ibrahim Egal there, while the larger and more powerful Rer Samatar was assisted by those in opposition to Egal. Many lives and much property were lost as a result. The most extreme case of this sort case involves the Ishaq and the Ogaden, which is treated in later chapters.

Somali society has a traditional system of conflict mediation that functions effectively to this day. It is based on customary law (*xeer*), a set of rules and obligations developed to maintain peaceful relations between clans. *Xeer* has never been fully codified and remains an oral law passed down from generation to generation. Since it is open to interpretation by elders, it has developed local variations pertaining to specific clans and areas. Certain of its principles, however, are considered universal and immutable among all Somali. Among these are the following: 1) Collective payment of *diya* compensation for death, injury, theft, rape and defamation; 2) Sparing the lives of women, children, elderly, religious men, poets and guests, and entering peace negotiations in good faith; 3) Respect for family obligations, including payment of dowry, the right of the brother of a dead husband to inherit the widow of the deceased, the right of a widower to marry a deceased wife's sister, penalties for eloping, financial support for newlyweds and married female relatives; 4) Respect for resource utilisation regulations regarding water, pasture and other natural resources, and donation or loan of livestock to the poor (Le Sage 2005: 16).

Inter-clan relations are regulated by formal agreements known as *biri-ma-geydo* ('spared from the spear') that set out rules for mediation, compensation and resolution. No such rules or agreements exist to manage conflict with other nationalities, and Somali relations with many of their neighbours are volatile (see Chapters 13, 14).

Summary

Outsiders have vague, monochromatic perceptions of lowlanders, whom they perceive as archetypal stateless nomads attached to an austere traditional way of life, aloof, lawless, and strongly opposed to change. There is some truth in this, but it is not the whole truth. The Afar and Somali have histories that are older than those of many nations, and a record of independence and self-government that lasted until the era of Western imperialism. Despite nature's niggardly endowment of their environment, they devised ways to survive, if not to prosper, in it. They exploit its meagre resources by making the most economic use of them, and have been self sufficient until recent misfortunes have overtaken them.

The traditional systems of authority that prevail among pastoralists reflect the imperatives of the pastoralist mode of production and the corresponding forms of social organisation. They are highly decentralised, diffuse and egalitarian, to an extent that they are nearly invisible to outsiders who perceive the lowlanders as anarchists. Such social organisation served the pastoralists well until they were subjugated and incorporated into aspiring nation-states. The fact that pastoralist societies did not produce structures to transcend the clan level means that the concept of the nation-state does not have the same meaning for them as is has for others. This is a critical variable in their troubled interaction with the state, and is an issue that will be taken up later in this work.

One could argue that the endurance of the clan as the pillar of Somali society owes much to the imperialist dismemberment of that nation which has hindered its political consolidation on a national level. During the colonial era, the clan remained the sole representative and protector of its members' interests, continuing to perform its traditional role in a changing environment and in engagement with an alien state. It provided a network of social and political solidarity across the multiple political and administrative barriers raised by imperialism. Thanks to this network, a Somali could traverse the Horn region from one end to the other, crossing borders with ease to trade, pray, study, marry and otherwise interact safely with clan kinsmen. In short, the clan served the interests of the Somali people during that period, and that is the main reason why it has survived.

The geopolitical fragmentation of the Horn has not been repaired. The number of states remains the same, only their rulers have changed, while the divisions of the Somali body politic have deepened and widened, causing the collapse of the Somali Republic. It is hardly remarkable that in these conditions the clan remains the centre pillar of Somali society and retains the loyalty of the people. On the other hand, clan supremacy complicates the relationship of the Ethiopian state with its Somali subjects, and poses a challenge to the process of integration in a way that the country's rulers find incomprehensible.

3

Borana, South Omo, Gambella, & Beni Shangul Gumuz

This chapter presents the profiles of communities that make their home in the south-western lowlands. An extraordinarily diverse collection, they defy categorisation under conventional criteria and none is offered here. They range from small to miniscule, and inhabit a veritable beehive of human creativity in a seemingly pristine physical setting, a magnet for anthropologists, some of whom have devoted their professional lifetime to providing us with what we know about these people. Sharing an ecological niche and living in physical proximity, they interact in many ways and have common historical experiences. Even so, they defend their distinct identities and cultural integrity with tenacity in the face of an onslaught from many sides to 'civilise' and integrate them into the state that claims them as subjects.

Oromo pastoralists: Borana, Guji, Gabbra

THE BORANA

The Oromo nation is the largest in Ethiopia, and together with its branches in northern Kenya the largest in the Horn. In Ethiopia it occupies by the far the biggest territory on the plateau and a fair stretch of the southern lowlands bordering on Kenya. Historians trace the original Oromo homeland to Mada Walabu on the Genale River in southern Bale, from where they set out in the late 17th century on a historic migration that dispersed branches of the nation throughout the southern and northern plateaux. The Borana branch headed south-westwards to settle in the territory flanked by the rivers Genale, Segen and Tana, while the Guji settled to the north on elevated terrain between the Genale River and the Great Rift. Borana also live in Isiolo, Marsabit and Moyale districts of northern Kenya. By virtue of its size and geographic dispersal, the Oromo nation is also the most diversified, with many branches having evolved from the prototype Oromo pastoral society. Its various branches were differentially exposed to the integration project of the Ethiopian state and responded in various ways. As a result, some Oromo groups in the highland periphery are fairly well integrated in the national economy and dominant culture. By contrast, Oromo communities in the lowland periphery, especially the pastoralists, are among the least integrated. Three of them – Borana, Guji, Gabbra – are introduced below.

Historically, Boranaland comprised a vast, compact territory at the centre of the lowland periphery, stretching from the southern flanks of the plateau to the Tana River in northern Kenya, some 600kms south of the Ethiopia-Kenya border, and from the Genale River in the east to the Great Rift in the west. The Borana Zone of the Oromia *kilil* represents the core of this territory – from the Dawa River in the east to the Segen River in west, and from the Kenya border in the south to the border with Guji Zone – encompassing 69,373km^2. With a population in 2007 that includes Guji, Gabbra and some Somali, approaching one million in number, it is the largest zone in Oromia *kilil.*

Boranaland has a bimodal rain pattern. The rate of precipitation follows elevation, with the highest and most reliable rate upland, decreasing in volume and reliability as it moves southwards to the lowlands. There are striking differences between the northern and southern sections due to difference in elevation and climate. The northern third, now almost all of it in Guji Zone, is covered with coniferous and broadleaf forest. Woodland and savannah interspersed with vast grasslands cover the southern section of the zone, with arid steppe in the southwest (Teltele) and southeast (Dire, Arero, Liben) districts. Bush encroachment has made serious inroads in recent years, and is estimated to cover as much as 40% of the land. A ban on bush burning imposed by the state is considered the main cause. In comparison to neighbouring lowland regions, Boranaland is privileged in terms of water and pasture availability. Clusters of man-made, deep, permanent wells (*ellaa*) found throughout the region are the main sources of water. These wells are also signposts of Borana territory and the object of contention with intruding neighbours. Another permanent source of water is provided by the Dawa and Segen rivers at opposite ends of the zone.

Borana society has two exogamous moieties, Sabo and Gona, subdivided into clans (*gossa*), of which Sabo has five and Gona twelve, themselves further split into sub-clans called *mana* ('house') and *balbala* ('door'). The moieties are evenly balanced in population size, evenly distributed over the region, and the clans live interspersed throughout the territory. The Borana live in villages and have a territorial perception of identity. Villages (*olla*) are grouped in localities known as *ardha* that in turn form clusters called *deda*, themselves grouped in territorially defined units or *madda*, whose name derives from the word meaning a permanent source of water. Each level is governed by elders (*jallabba*) headed by a senior elder (*Abba*). Villages within a *deda* cooperate in the management of resources, particularly wet and dry season pasturage, a practice supervised by an *Abba Deda*. The *Madda* controls rights of access to land and water and defines the responsibilities of herd owners.

Having settled farthest south from the highlands, the Borana were least influenced by Ethiopian culture and Orthodox Christianity. Until recently, they also resisted the spread of Islam in their region. Most important, they preserved the traditional pastoralist economy, making few concessions to the expansion of cultivation, again until recently. As a result, the traditional culture *(Aaadaa Boorana)* and way of life of the Borana changed least of all the Oromo communities in the Horn, and enjoy an aura of authenticity and respect among them. 'To this day, Borana signifies to Oromo speakers a "cultural and linguistic purity" which is more apparent than real', according to the historian Mohammed Hassen (1994: 6).

The traditional system of governance *Gaada* that still lingers among the Borana is widely admired for its elaborate design and democratic ethos, and has become an icon of contemporary Oromo nationalism. It is based on communal decision-making in popular assemblies named *kora*, and on the age-grade system known as *Gaada*. Decisions at every community level (*olla, deda, madda, gossa*) are made in assemblies through consensus and with reference to customary law (*Aaadaa Borana)*. Customary law is made, interpreted and revised in these assemblies. Failure to reach consensus moves the issue to a higher level, yet no decision is made by edict. The highest communal assembly is the *Gumi Gayoo*, held every eight years – the fourth year of a *Gaada* – at Gayoo, one of the nine wells in Dire district. The most recent *Gumi Gayoo* was held there in July 2009.

The functions of government are invested in the *Gaada* age-grade system, in which men of similar age pass through a series of grades (*luba*) that succeed each other every eight years. Each grade in turn assumes military, economic, political and ritual responsibilities (Asmarom 1973: 8). The leadership includes the *Abba Gaada* ('father of the *Gaada*'), who is the central authority and supreme political leader, the *Abba Dula* ('father of war'), the *Abba Sera* ('father of the law'), and the *Abba Bokku* (keeper of the wooden sceptre, a symbol of authority worn by the *Abba Gaada* during assembly meetings). The current *Abba Gaada*, a 36-year-old herder, was chosen in 2009.

The *Qallu* institution represents spiritual authority and is the pillar of Borana religion. The *Qallu* is the prophet of the nation and the interlocutor of the god *Waqa* who controls fertility, peace and rain. Each of the two Borana moieties has its own *Qallu*, whose sanctity and moral authority is recognised beyond the borders of Boranaland. Leaders of other Oromo branches come to seek the blessing of the Borana *Qallu* (Bartels 1983).

Borana culture validates and celebrates the Peace of the Borana (*nagaa boorana*). Those who live within its purview enjoy its protection, for it forbids Borana from killing each other, and guarantees peaceful resolution of conflict between individuals, families and communities. Disputes are brought for resolution to the appropriate assembly, whose decisions hold unless taken on appeal to a higher level. Decision-making is a male prerogative; women do not participate in assemblies. According to a Borana saying, 'women's authority destroys the very people over whom it is exercised' (Asmarom, 2001: 255). The Peace of the Borana preserves order and resolves internal conflict, but does not apply to outsiders who 'live in the land where the customs and laws of fools apply'. Borana relations with their neighbours are marked by aggression and violence. Indeed, making war (*butta*) was an integral function of the *gaada* system, undertaken at least once every eight years when a new age-grade (*luba*) came to power. Custom required that it made war against outsiders. Borana culture extols martial values and warrior prowess. Epic poems (*farsa*) celebrate famous warriors, and boasting songs (*gerarsa*) praise their deeds: 'I have descended to the narrow valley and I have pulled down the horsemen. The beautiful girls will adorn my comb. My friends will kiss my mouth. The children will say to me, "You have killed well"' (ibid.: 1994: 12). A killer decorates himself with ivory armbands (*harbor*), ivory rings (*qube*), and a shaved head with one remaining lock (*gutu*).

The success of the Borana traditional politico-military system is evident in the hegemony they exercised over a wide region in the pre-colonial period. They were able to defend the borders of their territory and to control entry into it by outsiders who, in many cases, became their clients with subordinate status. Assimilation, fully or partial, was a result of this relationship, and the Peace of the Borana was extended to outsiders who accepted their customs and laws (*aaddaa seera boorana*), adopted Borana as a second language, and were to various degrees assimilated without, however, losing their original identity. This was the case with a number of pastoralist groups, or segments of groups, such as the Gerri, Ajuran, Rendile, Gabbra and Sakuye. Thus, a socio-cultural mix emerged at the interface between these groups and their Borana hosts. None thought of themselves in wider terms, such as Somali or Oromo, for these political identities came into being later to fuel new conflict.

The Borana raise cattle, sheep and goats. The production unit is the household (*warra*) headed by the *Abba Warra*. It adheres to the usual division between the mobile satellite camp (*fora*) and the village camp (*warra*) for lactating animals. Villages are fairly stable, staying in one location unless forced to move. Transhumant moves are over short distances. 'Borana herd management practice is designed to reduce as much as possible the need to move' and 'allows a relatively sedentary kind of pastoralism to emerge' (Hogg 1993: 70-72). Most Borana spend their lives within one *madda*. There were no clan or other territorial boundaries in the past, and all Borana had right of access to land throughout the territory. Access to wells was likewise free, though regulated by an official called *Abba Ella*. Every village had enclosed land (*Kaloo*) reserved for calves and other uses. Nowadays this term has come to refer to private land enclosure, something unknown in the past that has become widespread and has contributed to the reduction of available pasture. In common with other pastoralist communities in the lowland periphery and for the same reasons, agro-pastoralism is spreading among the Borana as a way of coping with adversity.

Before the Ethiopian conquest, the Borana participated in regional trade through the mediation of their Somali neighbours, whom they call *Warr dasse* ('People of the mats') because their tents were made of mats, unlike the grass huts (*man buyyo*) of the Borana. Gerri and Ajuran traders brought goods from the coast – white cloth (*banardiri*) worn by Borana women, household goods, beads and cowries – which they exchanged for livestock, rhino horn, myrrh and salt. Known as *safar goolo* from the hide bags in which they carried the cloth, the *War dasse* traders established clientelist relationships (*sheegat, tiriso*) with influential Borana families and clans, from whom they received protection and to whom they gave presents.

THE GUJI

Guji Zone had a population of 1.4 million in 2007 that included Borana, Gabbra and a few Somali, and Guji were found in large numbers also in neighbouring Borana Zone. Known also as Jem Jem and Jem Jamptu by their neighbours, the Guji are a cluster of four distinct and independent segments – Uraga, Mati, Hoku, Alabdu. Their social organisation resembles the Borana, with two exogamous moieties – Kontoma, Daritu – subdivided into clans. Each clan is also divided into sections called *mana* ('house'), and these in turn are further sub-divided into patrilineal descent groups. Their political system is patterned on the *gaada*, with each of the four segments having its own separate *gaada* structure and leadership. Each segment has its own territory as well, but they cooperate closely, particularly in war against outsiders.

Originally mobile pastoralists, the Guji turned to cultivation on highland terrain. Sedenterisation followed the rinderpest epidemic of 1886 that wiped out their herds, and accelerated after the Ethiopian conquest of the region soon afterwards. Since they occupy land on various altitudes and in various ecological settings, theirs is a mixed economy combining cultivation with livestock-raising, bee-keeping, timber production and charcoal-making. In lower altitudes, in savannah land and in the Great Rift, the Guji subsist mainly on livestock production. In middle altitudes with lush vegetation they mix livestock with cultivation, and higher up where there is adequate rain they are entirely sedentary and cultivate barley, coffee and chat.

Despite the prevalence of cultivation, the pastoralist ethic remains strong among them. 'While cultivation is more important to Guji than they admit, animal husbandry was and still is their favourite economic activity' (Tadesse Berisso 2002: 119). Upland Guji send animals to kinsmen in the lowlands to keep, because 'people who don't own cattle are not considered proper Guji' (Baxter 1991: 9). Along with their attachment to livestock, the Guji also retain the pastoralist warrior ethos. 'The killing of an enemy man and/or a big game animal is still highly honoured among the Guji, and they are ready to do so whenever they get the opportunity' (Tadesse Berisso 1994: 309). Intra-Guji conflict is settled through an effective resolution mechanism called '*gondoro*,' still used by pastoralists, while farmers are increasingly inclined to take their disputes to state courts.

Historically, the Guji fought with all their neighbours – Arsi, Sidama, Burji, and Borana – indiscriminately.[1] Their *gaada* system ordained that a major war (*dula*) be waged against one of them every eight years. The Guji, Borana and Arsi, all three of the Oromo, are traditional enemies. They refer to themselves as *Siddi Saddin*, meaning 'three enemies against each other', and rate killing each other the highest honour *(akaku)*. The killer smears his hair with butter for two years, sings special songs, and is greatly honoured. Killing members of other groups does not rate as highly. Alliances among the three are not ruled out: in recent years the Guji fought with the Sidama against the Arsi, and with the Arsi and Borana against the Gerri. A relatively long period of peaceful relations with the Borana ended suddenly in the first decade of the 21st century with large-scale fighting over territory (see Chapter 14). A third Oromo group, the Gabbra, were caught in the middle of this conflict and suffered grievously.

THE GABBRA

The Gabbra are a small group of cattle herders whose home is an expanse of land east of Lake Turkana in Kenya's Marsabit district. A Gabbra section is also found in Isiolo district along the banks of the Waso Nyiro River, making a total of some 50,000 Gabbra in Kenya. Known as Warra Gaalaa (camel people), the Gabbra are nomads who range widely from the Ghalbi Desert in northern Kenya to Mega district in Borana zone, where about 10,000 of them have congregated. A small group has settled in Surupta, south of the town of Hagere Mariam, on the boundary dividing Guji and Borana zones.

Gabbra society is divided into two sections, the Gabbra Malbe, most of who live in northern Kenya, and the Gabbra Migo, most of who live in southern Ethiopia. Combined, they have twenty-four clans. This community is a prime example of identity ambivalence common among minor groups historically squeezed between the Somali and Oromo. They tend to take on the cultural colouring of one of the two dominant groups, but intermarry with both – without, however, losing the sense of their own distinct identity. The Gabbra are Muslims and have much in common with the Somali, including the collapsible dome huts they carry around on their camels. They also have much in common with the Borana, including their language and the age-grade system called Diqo that resembles the *gaada*.

The Borana and the Guji have always considered the Gabbra as fellow Oromo, albeit an inferior branch. A Borana meeting a Gabbra on the road would place the end of his stick on the latter's foot and lean

[1] Hinnant (1972) describes the mutually negative attitudes cultivated by the Guji and their neighbours.

against it to assert superiority. The Gabbra accepted their inferior status in the past, but are no longer willing to do so. Encouraged by the status accorded to ethnicity under federalism in Ethiopia, 'they want to be equal with us', sneer the Borana and Guji. The Somali also claim the Gabbra as their own and have found Gabbra leaders who agree.

In the 1990s, the Gabbra were required to assume a political identity. Since the territory over which they roam was partitioned between the Oromo and Somali *kilil*, they had to decide which one to join. This being a political choice, the Gabbra responded opportunistically. Some opted for Oromo and others for Somali identity, based on a calculation of immediate benefit. They attached no more importance to this choice than to another that they have so far evaded: the choice between Ethiopian or Kenyan citizenship. Things went wrong for the Gabbra who settled on the Borana-Guji boundary with their camels, when they made bold to demand their own administrative district and territory. This sparked a violent response by the Guji and Borana, discussed further in Chapter 14.

South Omo

The Southern Nations, Nationalities and Peoples *kilil*, conveniently referred to as Debub ('South'), with a population at the last count (2007) exceeding 15 million, is a grand mosaic of some fifty ethnic groups. A dozen of them live in the South Omo Zone in a highly variegated and continuously changing physical setting that provides life-sustaining niches for communities of modest size. The north-central portion of the zone – Bako Gazar and Gelila districts – forms the tail end of the northern plateau with an elevation of 1000m-1500m, and a tropical climate with precipitation rates that reach 1200mm. Elevation drops sharply south-westwards to less than 500m in the Omo River Valley, where precipitation likewise falls below 600mm. The climate in the south and west, where evaporation exceeds precipitation, is arid, yet tempered to some extent by the abundance of surface water drained from the plateau by many rivers, among which the Omo and Mago are the mightiest.

This is a transition zone between ecologically and culturally contrasting terrains, the sodden savannah of Southern Sudan to the west, the arid steppe of northern Kenya to the south, and the humid Ethiopian highlands to the north. A varied topography and climate offer 'strikingly different environments, and the transition of one zone to the other over a distance of only a few kilometres is as noticeable in temperature, vegetation and crops as in culture' (Abbink 2000: 533). On the upland to the north they have adapted to rainfed cultivation, with two planting rounds annually to coincide with the big and small rains. Lower down they rely on a mixed agro-pastoralist system. Land is ample, but rainfall is low and erratic. Given good rain, they plant sorghum that ripens in ten weeks and is harvested in twelve. They clear land in the bush with machetes, use hoes to loosen the earth and digging sticks to plant. The land is used for some years, and is left fallow for some more before they return to it.

The Omo River sustains several communities living along its banks, or commuting between the river and the interior.[2] In its 760km long course, the Omo is fed by the Gibe, Mago and Gojeb tributaries, and drops 2,000m from its highland source to its final destination in Lake Turkana. Wetlands in the lower Omo delta support flood retreat cultivation that shifts with the river's whims. The Omo River is filled with fish, and the wooded bushland that flanks it up to ten kilometres on both sides provides honey and game, but is infested with *tse tse* that excludes livestock, which is the mainstay of the Omotic communities away from the river in the lower valley. The frequent change of channel direction in the Omo Delta, as well as the periodic rise and fall in the river's flow, are facts of life to which the communities depending on the area's resources are obliged to adapt.

The oral history of the Bashada, a tiny group of hunter-gatherers and potters, offers a poignant, if bleak, illustration of this process. Forced by drought to leave their land, their forebears set off in search of water. On the way, a cow was lost, but was found some days later in good health. Reasoning that the animal had found water, half of the group followed it to the Omo River, where they settled and became known as Karo ('fish eaters'). Too fatigued to follow, the rest settled where they were and became known as Bashada ('the exhausted ones').

South Omo's collection of mini-groups and micro-cultures has exercised the anthropologist imagination with two queries: first, the reason for such spectacular diversity, and second, how to account for the tenacity with which groups cling to and defend their distinct identities. What can possibly explain the Arbore taboo on honey collection, a product they themselves consume but have to buy from their Hamar neighbours? Obviously, such markers of exclusiveness are designed to maintain group distance and segregation. Among the dynamics of group formation and fragmentation is the drying out of the Omo Delta in recent times. The evidence includes a 25-metre drop in the level of Lake Turkana from the 1890s to the 1970s (Butzer 1971), and satellite imagery since the 1970s, confirming that the process is continuing. It is assumed that the resulting pressure on resources discourages group aggregation. Another presumed factor is the convergence of three major African language families – Cushitic (Dassanetch), Omotic (Hamar, Aari, Dizzi) and Nilo-Saharan (Mursi, Surma, Nyangatom) – in a relatively small area. One result of this extraordinary linguistic diversity is to produce and sustain cultural boundaries between communities living in proximity and interacting over a very long time. Finally, because South Omo did not come within the scope of the state building project and integrationist pressure until the beginning of this century, the social and cultural fluidity that characterises this region was allowed to continue unimpeded until recent times.

[2] '*Omo-riate*', ('Omo is my meal') is the name of the main Dassanetch settlement.

It has been suggested that conflict itself may perform the same function, that is, to maintain boundaries between groups.[3] According to one scholar, the Mursi do not fight with their neighours because they are separate groups, but rather the reverse: they fight in order to remain separate (Turton, 1994: 23). A colleague agrees that what outsiders often see as mindless exercise to which the lowlanders are addicted, 'is a "creative" or at least "constituent" force in social relations' (Abbink 2000: xii). If that is the case, then there is something seriously askew with conventional conflict resolution theories, in which the basic approach is to reduce distance between groups and promote mutual understanding. Sketchy profiles of the communities that live in South Omo are offered below, ordered by population size as registered in the 2007 census (shown in brackets).

*

The Aari (283,000) is the northernmost Omotic community, living in Bako Gazar district on the elevated northern part of South Omo, where they practise rain fed cultivation, producing ensete, sorghum, maize, vegetables, coffee and cardamom. They also keep sheep on high ground and cattle below. Their community is organised in territorially defined clans that were in the past ruled by a king. The fact that their language, Araf, has five dialects, illustrates the extent of fragmentation in the region. In the past, the clans were frequently at war with each other over territory, and as a result the Aari developed 'a culture of bellicosity and a cult of masculinity' (Naty 1994: 60).

The Maale (98,000) occupy territory between Jinka town and the Woito River. It includes highland in the centre and north and lowland in the southeast. Slash-and-burn cultivation is the main line of production on higher ground, with two planting seasons coinciding with the big and small rains cycle. Sorghum, corn, finger millet and teff are produced. In the lower and drier land, cattle-raising is more important, but fields are also planted once a year for the big rains. The Maale from the lowland exchange livestock for grain with their kinsmen on higher ground.

Maale social organisation combines kinship with territoriality. Their territory is divided into four regions, each of them sub-divided into chiefdoms, of which there are a total of thirteen. Each of the latter is headed by a chief *(goda)* and his deputies *(gatta)*. Traditionally, a king (*kati*) was the supreme Maale authority, a figure of divine powers who maintained the fertility and prosperity of his subjects, 'the ripening of crops, the fecundity of women, the reproduction of cattle and goats' (Donham 1999: 38). The king remained in his ancestral home while the chiefs collected tribute in the form of labour and kind from the people. Their fields were cultivated by their subjects under the supervision of the *gatta*, who also collected tribute in livestock and honey for the king and

[3] The insights contained in the last two paragraphs were contributed by David Turton in a private communication.

chiefs. The warrior ethos is highly developed among the Maale, and as usual is linked to raiding. 'No more masculinizing acts existed in Maale…than raiding cattle from enemy peoples, killing a large animal like a lion or buffalo, or killing an enemy' (ibid.: 1999: 119).

The Dassanetch (48,000), also known as the Geleb, inhabit the northern shore of Lake Turkana. The Omo River crosses the zone in the west, inundating it regularly and permitting bank cultivation. When the waters recede, the people congregate on the banks. Away from the river and the tse tse plague, they keep cattle and smallstock. The Dassanetch are grouped into eight clans, each inhabiting separate territory and living independently of the others. Inkabelo, the largest clan, accounts for about half the total Dassanetch population, and occupies the largest stretch of land along both banks of the Omo. The other clans occupy land on one side of the river only. Each clan is divided into exogamous sections whose members live dispersed and do not display significant solidarity. Each clan has its own age-grade system with six named grades. Authority is vested in the senior grade, and is exercised by an elected group of some thirty of its members known as *ara* ('bulls') (Almagor, 1978).

The Hamar (46,000) are the southernmost group of the Omotic peoples. Their system of social organisation has a combination of kinship and territorial features. Kinship is represented by two moities comprising twenty four clans, each divided territorially into two main sections and twenty four sub-sections. The Hamar live in settlements of ten to thirty households, each sited near a source of water and of fields for cultivation and pasture. Their system of authority is described by an anthropologist: 'The Hamar have hereditary ritual leaders *(bitá)*. They also select political spokesmen (*ayo*), leaders for war *(djilo)*, guardians of grazing and cultivated land (*kogo, gudili*), but the basic agents of politics are the married men (*donza*)' (Strecker 2006: 39). Public meetings (*osh*) of married men, held at various levels of inclusiveness – from the homestead to the entire Hamar community – are where matters of common interest are debated.

The Hamar are agro-pastoralists who practise slash-and-burn cultivation to produce maize, sorghum and beans. They raise cattle and small stock, and are particularly dependent on goats. 'People with goats are like ropes or leather straps. Their life is well secured, it will not snap', they say. Goat herding does not require the cooperation of large groups, and the Hamar are known for their individualism and resistance to authority. Hamar men are also keen hunters and livestock raiders. Strecker also notes: 'In Hamar a man should prove himself before he marries by hunting dangerous game and/or killing an enemy' (ibid.: 135). Those who distinguish themselves are ritually anointed. The man who kills a hyena shaves off his hair and smears white paint on his forehead. He who kills an elephant, lion or leopard smears red ochre on his forehead and sticks a feather in his hair. Raiding is an integral feature of Hamar society, and their Borana neighbours across the Segen River are a favourite target. Although only the width of the river separates them, the two speak different languages and are mortal enemies. A Hamar song boasts:

> *When we have lost our cattle, our mothers' brothers and fathers call out:*
> *Hey children! Yo! Have you lost your cattle?*
> *We have lost them.*
> *Do you see the mountains over there? Do you see the Borana mountains?*
> *Those are not clouds, they are cattle. If you go there you will collect cattle.*
> (ibid.: page 135)

The Bana (25,600) live between the Woito and Omo rivers. They are agro-pastoralists, inhabiting diverse environments stretching from mountainous cool terrain around Kako town to hot savannah near Dimeka. Their main settlement, Kay Afar, stands at 1,500m. Unusual in this area, the Bana use the ox-drawn plough. They also keep livestock, produce honey and hunt in the Mago Park. Territorially they are organised in two chiefdoms (*bitta*), sub-divided into sections (*kogo bitta*). In terms of kinship, they are divided into two exogamous moities, Binna and Galabu, each comprising a number of clans. They also have an elementary age-grade system, with males progressing from boyhood (*naasi*), to uninitiated (*ukuli*), to unmarried (*maz*), and to married adult (*donza*). Bull jumping is the main initiation ritual.

The Nyangatom (22,000), also called Bume in South Omo and Dogiro in Kenya, have an elaborate age-grade system that divides males into generation-classes graded according to seniority, with each generation in turn divided into age-grades comprising males of roughly the same age that are likewise graded. Junior generations, or 'Sons of the Country', advance in time to become 'Fathers of the Country' and exercise decision-making power. When an anthropologist visited the Nyangatom in the 1970s they had five generation-classes named Mountains, Elephants, Ostriches, Antelopes and Buffaloes. The Ostriches were the 'Sons of the Country', the Elephants were the 'Fathers of the Country', and the senior age-grade within the Elephant generation were the supreme rulers (Tornay 1981, 1989).

The Tsemay (20,000) territory includes lowland on the western side of the Woito River and upland further westwards. They are agro-pastoralists who depend mainly on cultivation, working both the rain fed land higher up and flood retreat land on the Woito River. The river floods twice annually and flood land is redistributed each time, a task carried out by their elders (*mura*). The Tsemay were the main suppliers of honey to the area markets until deforestation and pesticide spraying from the air in a plantation nearby killed off the source. They are grouped in seven clans that live in sixteen villages, and have an age-grade system with four grades. The Tsemay are affiliated with the Arbore, Hamar and Bana through marital exchange. However, the exchange is one way. Arbore men marry Tsemay women, but not the reverse. Consequently, there is considerable ethnic convergence and cohabitation in the area, as shown in the composition of the village of the main Tsemay chief, where one-third of its households were Arbore

(Yukio 1994). Tsemay relations with their neighbours are convoluted. They are allies of the Arbore and the Bana, but also of the Hamar who are enemies of the Arbore. In turn, the Arbore are allies of the Borana who are enemies of the Tsemay.

The Mursi (7,500) live in the lower Omo Valley north of Lake Turkana in an area bound by three rivers, Mago, Omo and Mara. They are a good example of the frequent location shifting that is noted in this region. They are said to have come from the west in two movements. The first brought them to the Omo River some 150 years ago, and the second to the Mara River in the 1920s. One other section moved northwards to higher land quite recently. They are divided into three territorial sections – Ariholi, Gongulobibi and Dola – each of them with its own age-grade system through which males move from boyhood (*lusi*) to adulthood (*hiri*). The Mursi cultivate flood retreat and rain fed land, planting sorghum, and keep cattle ten to twenty kilometres east of the tse tse infested banks of the Omo. Although on average they own very few animals and depend on cultivation for most of their food, their culture 'elevates cattle to a position of supreme symbolic importance' (Turton 1985: 334). However, neither livestock nor cultivation 'is sufficient in itself, nor even in combination, to provide a regular and reliable subsistence' for them (ibid.: 333).

The Mursi share the warrior ethos of all pastoralists. 'The age organisation of the Mursi turns men, ritually, not only into adults, but also into killers, ready – and indeed eager – to show towards non-Mursi the very antithesis of that peaceful sociability which they are required to show towards Mursi' (Turton, 2002: 179). Having killed an enemy, a Mursi man cuts a horseshoe shaped mark into the skin of his arm representing the spirit of his victim. Raiding offers the best opportunity to display valour, and is often exercised at the expense of their preferred enemies, the Nyangatom and the Bodi. Due to various setbacks, no age-grade was initiated from 1961 to 1991, when a new one was formed with an age range of fifteen to forty-five years. Two months later, the new age-grade attacked the Nyangatom, inflicting heavy casualties.

The Bodi (8,000) are an Omotic group whose blurred identity has tested anthropologists' mettle. Linguistically, they belong to the Surmi language group, and comprise two distinct clans that call themselves Mela and Chirim respectively. However, they are known as Bodi by their neighbours, although they themselves do not use this name. The Mela are divided into two territorial sections, Hana and Gura, each with its own chief (*komorut*) and separate territory. Hana and Gura in turn are subdivided into clans (Fukui, 1994). The Bodi have no corporate structures or political solidarity, and the various sections often clash with each other. The Mela also fight with their neighbours, the Mursi and the Hamar. They have peacemaking agreements with the Mursi and do not harm women and children, but they do not extend the same courtesy to the Hamar.

The Arbore (6,000), also called Hor, inhabit the delta of the Woito River before it ends in the salt flats of Lake Stephanie. Some Arbore live in Teltele, across the Segen River in Borana, where they are known as Wata Wendo and are considered by the Borana as part of their own community. Agro-pastoralism, in flood retreat land in the fertile delta of the Woito River, is their main productive activity. Land is communally owned and annually redistributed, and sorghum is the main crop. The language and culture of the Arbore are related to the Borana, whose language they also speak. They are similarly related to the Konso, whose language and Borana are mutually intelligible (Wolde Gossa Tadesse 2002: 130). Arbore social structure combines kinship and territorial principles with the age-grade system. Most of them live in four main villages, bonded in two pairs called Marle and Arbore. Their clan organisation has four territorial sections – Gandarab, Kulam, Murale, Egude – each with its own ritual leader (*gawot*), secular leader (*kernet*), distributors of flood land (*mura*), and councillors (*jaldab*) who comprise the senior age-grade (*berr*).

Like all their neighbours, the Arbore place high value on fighting. Their favourite enemies – because they have 'sweet blood' – are the Maale and Samburu. By killing someone of 'sweet blood', the warrior gains the power and fertility of the victim, and the latter's severed genitals are displayed as the symbol of power that will multiply cattle and children. 'Once a man kills a Maale and anoints his body with the blood of his victim, he will become rich in cattle, he will have many children. Arbore land will live in peace and there will be no famine', they believe (Wolde Gossa Tadesse 1997: 674).

The Kwegu (1,500) live in widely dispersed settlements along the Omo River. Inhabiting tse tse infested territory, they keep no livestock. They live by cultivating flood land, fishing, hunting and collecting honey, a valuable trade product used for making the mead liquor *tej*. Anthropologists have been hard put to pin down this small group with its opaque identity and many names. According to one, the Kwegu are in fact three distinct groups. One is associated with the Mursi, who call them Nyidi, another with the Bodi who call them Idinitt, and a third with the Kara who call them Muguji (Hiroshi, 2002: 180). Kwegu have their own language, but also speak the languages of the groups they are associated with.

Gambella

Jutting out into the southern Sudanese flood plain, Gambella is among the most remote of Ethiopia's far flung nether regions: 800kms from Addis Ababa. Its size – 25,000km^2 – makes it the second smallest (after Harar) of the federation's nine regional states. Located in the south-western corner of the country, where the northern plateau drops abruptly from heights over 2,000m to a flat plain at 500m, Gambella has a very hot climate with an annual average temperature reaching 37°C. Unlike most lowlands, however, it has an average annual rainfall of 800mm, sufficient for many crops. Dense tropical forest covers the elevated western edge, and savannah forest, grasslands and marshlands cover the lowland plain as far as the border with Sudan.

Also unlike much of the lowland belt around the Ethiopian massif, Gambella has an abundant and well distributed surface water system. The northern plateau slopes westward and Gambella is part of its drainage system, so it is crossed by several large rivers and innumerable streams that flow into the Sobat River in the Sudan and thence to the White Nile. The Gambella plain is part of the Sudd hydraulic complex; large parts of it are seasonally flooded, between June and November, and perennial marshes cover substantial areas. The rivers Baro, Akobo, Gilo and Alwero traverse the plain, and are a major natural resource on which Gambella's people depend for transportation and fishing. The flood regime provides irrigation and dry season livestock pasture.

The 2007 census recorded a population of 307,000, making Gambella the second smallest state after Harar. Its population is ethnically heterogeneous, comprising two major indigenous groups – Anywaa and Nuer – and three minor ones – Majangir, Opo, and Komo – as well as a sizeable immigrant community of highlanders. With a population of some 65,000, the Anywaa are spread comfortably over eight of the *kilil*'s nine districts covering some 70% of its land.[4] The Nuer, who are latecomers from Southern Sudan, number 148,000. They are squeezed into three districts, and are continually struggling to expand into their neighbours' territory. Highlander immigrants are a collection from many nationalities on both the north and south highlands with a combined population that surpasses that of the Anywaa.

THE ANYWAA

A pioneer anthropologist who visited the Anywaa in 1935 found them living in villages of a few hundred souls each, situated at some distance from each other, economically self-sufficient and politically autonomous. He noted: 'the village is the largest political and economic unit in Anuakland' (Evans-Pritchard 1940: 25). He found such segmentation unusual for an agricultural society, and attributed it to the ecology of the flood plain whose swamps, rivers and innumerable watercourses inhibit movement and interaction. The Anywaa are divided into twelve clans, but their village settlements are not clan based, although in some of them one clan may be dominant. Like most sedentary communities, the Anywaa have a strong sense of territoriality, that is, self identification with areas of land, and proprietorship, that is ownership of land. 'Anuak are strongly attached to the sites where their ancestors lived and often have tenaciously occupied them in the face of extermination' (ibid.: 37).

Evans Pritchard found the political system of the Anywaa 'very peculiar' (ibid.: 38). It was based on autonomous villages ruled by one of two types of leadership: *Nyech* (kingship) and *Kwar* (headmanship). Every village had a lineage from which the headman was chosen. Kings had a more exclusive line of descent from two exogamous royal lineages, and rose to their position through formal investiture and the possession of

[4] Anywaa also live across the border in the Upper Nile province of Southern Sudan. Their number there was estimated at 25,000 (Kurimoto 1997).

royal emblems, such as bead necklaces, ceremonial spears and stools. Otherwise, there was little difference in terms of authority or functions between a king and a headman. Both were expected to look after the safety and economic welfare of their villages, and to share their wealth by patronising the poor, helping young men marry and sponsoring village feasts. If either failed in their duties, they could be removed by the villagers and sent into exile, a process known as *agem*.

A strong sense of ethnic identity and purity is characteristic of the Anywaa. An unmistakeable marker of their identity is the practice (*naak*) of teeth excision.[5] For a person to claim pure Anywaa identity, both his parents must be Anywaa, a tradition that discourages inter-ethnic marriages. Children of mixed ethnic background are referred to as *jur* ('foreigner'). While this serves to maintain strong ethnic boundaries, it also limits the Anywaa's capacity for population growth. A feature of Anywaa society that distinguished them in the past from their pastoralist neighbours was the role that glass beads necklaces (*dimui*) played in their culture. *Dimui* could neither be duplicated nor replaced, and scarcity endowed them with great value. Traditionally, *dimui* was the medium through which important social transactions, such as bridewealth, blood payment and ransom, were carried out. *Dimui* were accumulated by the elders who received them as dowry for their daughters when they married and passed on to their sons to give to their fathers in law when they married.

The Anywaa were pastoralists who turned to cultivation at some point to plant maize and sorghum, fruit and vegetables on the river-banks. Hoe cultivation is productive on fertile alluvial riverain land, where both rainfed and moisture cultivation is possible; the former in the dry season and the latter during the wet. Fishing is also important to the household economy. The mythical Anywaa ancestor *Ocwudho* is portrayed holding a fishing spear (*kaak*). Due to tse tse infestation, the Anywaa own few animals.

Conflict among Anywaa villages was endemic in the past. Villages on high ground were protected by stockades and those on river banks by moats and enormous reed beds. Inter-village conflict could be sparked by quarrels between individuals and families from different villages, raiding for livestock and grain, or attempts by ambitious *nyieya* to impose their authority on their neighbours. Since there was no shortage of land, territory was not a common cause of inter-village conflict. Clusters of villages sharing a territory and the same ecological niche could band together for defence against outsiders. Traditional conflict resolution in the Anywaa villages was performed by the *nyieya* and the *kwaro* in whose house a killer sought refuge from retaliation at first instance. The village head sent presents to the victim's family and, if they were accepted, mediation could proceed. The next step was negotiation for compensation in the form of *dimui*, cattle, money, or women. The final ceremony

[5] The canines are destroyed in infancy, and the four lower permanent incisors are removed at the age of ten.

included the sacrifice of a bull, and the blunting of spears – one from each family. If the king or headman refused to offer asylum, the killer was executed by the victim's relatives.

THE NUER

The Nuer, who call themselves *Nath*, belong to the nation whose main body is found in Southern Sudan, where they are divided in three branches – western, central, eastern – referring to their geographical distribution. The recent history of the eastern Nuer is one of steady expansion eastwards in the Gambella plain, where the abundance of pastureland and permanent water sources are obvious attractions. At the beginning of the 19th century they were confined to the west of the Bahr Jebel River in Southern Sudan. By the end of that century they had flooded the Sobat basin and reached the Ethiopian border. By the early 20th century they had crossed the border and penetrated into Anywaa territory as far as the Baro River. By the turn of the 21st century, their number in Gambella *kilil* (148,000) was more than double that of the Anywaa. Nuer intrusion into Anywaa territory was accompanied by intermittent warfare that left an enduring tradition of hostility between the two communities (see Chapter 14).

Nuer social organisation is a classic example of the segmentation found among East African pastoralists, which is divided vertically according to lineage and horizontally according to age. The Nuer age-set system makes a simple distinction between men (*wut*) marked with facial scarification (*gar*) and unmarked boys (*dhol*).[6] A *wut* receives a spear to become a warrior, an ox to become a herder, and a woman to start a family. Nuer society is divided into clans that have a depth of ten to twelve generations and are serially subdivided into maximal, major, minor and minimal lineages, the last-mentioned having a depth of three to five generations (Evans-Pritchard, 1940: 248). The eastern Nuer are divided into two sections, Luo and Jikany. Nuer in Gambella are Jikany, most of whom live in the districts of Akobo, Jikaw and Lare, and are further divided into three sub-sections – Gaajak, Gaaguang, and Gaajok. The last are in turn sub-divided into five clans – Cie-reng, Cie-waw, Cie-nyejani, Cie-cany, and Thiang – found in Itang, Jikaw and Lare districts.

The Nuer belong to what anthropologists once labelled 'acephalous' ('headless') societies and 'tribes without rulers', because they lack hierarchical structures of authority or recognised leadership positions at any level of their segmented social structure, or indeed any semblance of a formal political process. The first anthropologist to study the Nuer called their society 'ordered anarchy' (ibid.: 181). This does not mean that they have no way of regulating social relations, but only that this process is not institutionalised but involves elders, spiritual leaders and charismatic personalities. Nuer elders command respect and are influential in community decision making. Influential also are those who

[6] Six parallel lines cut into a man's forehead to mark his initiation into manhood.

belong to large and powerful lineages, large herd owners, as well persons with character and ability for leadership known as *tut*. Nuer spiritual leaders ('prophets') also play a leading role in community decision making. They heal the sick, bless the men to prevent them from being killed in battle, help barren women to conceive, prevent the death of infants, guide communities to establish settlements, and put the curse on wild animals harmful to people and cattle.

The Nuer are devoted to cattle production, though it has been a long time since livestock products sufficed for their diet. Like most of their fellow pastoralists, they work the land, plant grain, and further supplement their diet with fishing, hunting and gathering. The Jikany Nuer year is divided into two seasons, passed in separate locations. The rainy season (May/June to November/December), is spent in settlements on high ground away from the rivers to escape the floods. At the beginning of the dry season, they move to camps along the major rivers, mostly inside Ethiopia, and stay there until the start of the wet season.

Conflict among Nuer is endemic and takes place at every level of their segmented social structure. It can occur over family affairs, such as marriage, divorce and inheritance, over natural resources, and over seniority, authority and power. Cattle theft is a perennial and endemic cause of it. In the dynamics of the segmented social system, conflict among individuals can escalate wildly. The spiral process is described as follows: If a man in one village kills a man in another village, the two villages would be forced into confrontation. If a man of one district kills a man of another district, then all the villages of the victim's district unite against all the villages of the killer's district (ibid.: 49). Traditional mechanisms for resolving disputes exist, but their effectiveness diminishes with genealogical and territorial distance.

At the centre of the peace making process is the so-called 'leopard skin' chief, in whose home a killer seeks sanctuary to escape retribution. The chief performs a ritual, cleansing the killer of his victim's blood, in case he and his relatives become polluted. Then he begins negotiations with the victim's family to see if they are amenable to compensation. If so, recompense in cattle is negotiated according to custom by the elders of both sides, and a reconciliation ceremony follows with the sacrifice of a bull and the blunting of spears. Prophets are involved in dispute mediation and the ritual sealing of peace agreements. They can also instigate conflict, particularly against outsiders who violate tradition. In the past, they were instrumental in fomenting opposition to the colonial administration, compelling the British to wage full scale war against them.

THE MAJANGIR

With a population of 22,000 in 2007, the Majangir, also known as Masengo, are the third largest indigenous group in Gambella. They inhabit the border region with Oromia and Southern regional states, and are found also in small numbers in these two *kilil*. In Gambella they congregate in Godere district, and are found in small numbers in Abobo and Gambella districts. Theirs is a thickly forested land on the south-western edge of the plateau that stretches from Dembidolo in Oromia to the Baro River and the Tepi and Yeki district in the Southern *kilil*, an area with an elevation ranging between 2,000 and 3,500ft and abundant precipitation.

The Majangir language belongs to the Surmic cluster of south-western Ethiopia and Southern Sudan, and differs from the Cushitic and Nilotic tongues of their neighbours. Their social organisation is one of stark simplicity. 'There are no rulers or "chiefs" or even councils of elders. There are no lineage heads. There are no lineages. No age-set system exists. Villages do not exist. Organised, corporate local groups are absent', marvelled the first anthropologist to study them (Stauder 1971: 6). Although the Majangir lack corporate lineage organisation, they do have forty exogamous clans (*komwoyir*), albeit without chiefs or other figures of authority. Ritual leaders (*tapath*) wield influence among them, but occupy no formal office. They exercise informal leadership based on age, experience, skill, personal charisma and social contacts. The *tapath* organise communal activities, offer ritual protection from violence, mediate disputes, divine the future and cure illness.

Separated from their neighbours by large tracts of forest, the Majangir lived in splendid isolation until the mid-1960s, when it took the anthropologist a trek of two and a half days from Gambella town to reach them (ibid.: 4). Although they were occasionally raided by their neighbours and taken as slaves, they did not experience serious incursions into their habitat and no land shortages. Their response to enemy raids was to flee and hide; resistance was seldom attempted. Consequently, they never organised collectively to defend their territory, and lived in dispersed homesteads, moving periodically to facilitate shifting cultivation. Crossed by many watercourses, the Majangir sanctuary of thick forest has always been unsuitable for regular cultivation or livestock herding because of tse tse infestation. The traditional economy involves hunting, gathering, fishing and cultivation of maize, sorghum, sesame and vegetables, as well as honey production. The traditional way of settling internal disputes is the simplest and most effective: when a confrontation threatens, one of the parties moves away.

Two small groups complete the indigenous ethnic profile of Gambella. The Komo, with a population of some 8,000 live dispersed in Gambella district. Komo also live in Beni Shangul Gumuz. The Opo number less than 1,000 and occupy one village in Itang district with a few settlements in Akobo and Jikaw districts. Probably due to their insignificant size, no anthropologist has chosen to study them and little is known about them

THE HIGHLANDERS

Immigrants from the Highlands attracted to Gambella by economic opportunities make up the third largest population group. Numbering 25,000, Amharigna-speakers are the most numerous, having arrived first with the imperial expansion as soldiers and administrators. Numbering 15,000, Oromo are the second largest immigrant contingent, having established economic contact with the Anywaa long before the Ethiopian conquest, when the area was a centre for trade in slaves and ivory. More recently, Oromo with skills and education have found employment opportunities in Gambella that are scarce at home, as have some 4,000 natives of Tigray who form the third largest immigrant group. Peasants from the highland periphery – including Kambata, Kaffa, Sidama, and Mocha – were brought to Gambella as settlers in the 1980s. Known locally as *Kambathee*, they numbered over 25,000 in 2007. Gurage and Hadiya were attracted to the region by trade opportunities created by the international aid regime and linked to the refugee and resettlement schemes of the 1980s.

Gambella exhibits in amplified form certain trends set in motion under imperial rule that have in time produced disparities between ethnic groups and acrimonious rivalry among them. The massive Nuer influx and consequent displacement of the Anywaa set these two kindred groups at each other's throats throughout the period covered in this work. The highlanders dominate the modern sector of the region's economy as well as the state administration where they perform clerical and technical tasks. The great variety of their ethnic composition notwithstanding, the *galaa* ('red skins', as the highlander immigrants are labelled), are seen as a compact, dominant group exploiting local resources. Their presence is increasingly resented by the emerging indigenous elite, and a series of violent incidents in recent years has created an explosive political situation (see Chapter 14).

Beni Shangul Gumuz

The Beni Shangul Gumuz *kilil* occupies the sloping terrain of the western escarpment covering some 80,00km^2. The landscape is spectacularly broken, rugged and uneven, with elevations reaching 2,700m in the east and descending to 550m in the west. Several mountains rise to great heights overlooking valleys lying in deep depressions. All three climatic zones are found here, from torrid *qolla* to frigid *dega*, with the former by far the most prevalent. The precipitation pattern changes accordingly, from a high of 1,500mm on the highland to 600mm on the plain. Over half of the region is covered with forest, including bamboo, eucalyptus, rubber, incense and gum and other indigenous tree species. The region is dissected by many rivers that drain the plateau and cut wide, deep gorges in the process. The mightiest of them, the Abbay (Blue Nile) River, dissects the region with a huge gorge, and is flanked by the Didesa, Dabus and Angir rivers to the south, and the Dinder and Beles rivers to the north. Unnavigable and turbulent, great obstacles to transport, communication and group interaction, these rivers have much to do with the ethnographic diversity of the region.

Indigenous modes of livelihood follow traditional subsistence patterns. Shifting cultivation using hand tools is relied upon to produce maize and sorghum, as well as sesame, haricot beans and *noog* (oil seed plant).

Hunting, fishing and beekeeping are supplementary activities. Tse tse infestation limits livestock production in most areas. Plough cultivation is practised by Abyssinian peasants who have moved down the western escarpment in large numbers over the past century, and by Oromo farmers who have moved northward from Wollega into the Didesa River Valley. This gradual and spontaneous immigration was overtaken by the abrupt, massive intrusion of impoverished peasants from many parts of the plateau, caused by a forced resettlement programme under the military regime of the 1980s.

The migration of highlanders to the lowlands changed the ethnographic profile of a region that had historically formed a buffer zone and a trade entrepôt between Christian Abyssinia and Muslim Sudan. Gold was the mainstay of trade and source of power of local leaders; the means whereby they secured the protection of rulers in Sudan and Abyssinia. The region was the hunting ground for slavers from both sides, whose raids tore the fabric of indigenous communities, fragmenting and dispersing the people to find refuge in inaccessible malaria-ridden depressions and mountaintops, from where they emerged only recently to confront a perplexing world.

THE BERTA

The mixing of the Sudanese with indigenous people left an ethnic blend called Berta who, with 173,000 members in 2007, represent the largest indigenous community in this state. The Berta are concentrated in Assosa Zone, bordering the Sudan. Situated on a plateau with an elevation exceeding 1,500m, the zone is crossed by several tributaries of the Blue Nile River, and has several mountains that rise to 2,550m. Assosa is known for its bamboo forests stretching south of Assosa town to Bambasi. Bamboo is important in the livelihood of the Berta, used for house and bridge construction, furniture making, spears, animal feed, and feeding humans in times of famine. Like the other native communities, the Berta are subsistence cultivators using shifting agriculture methods to produce the grain and vegetables that comprise their diet.

The Berta ethnic identity emerged from the ebb and flow of struggles to control the trade in gold and slaves at the interface between Sudan and Ethiopia. The gold is alluvial and available mainly in the rainy season. Panning requires intensive labour provided by slaves taken from the indigenous Gumuz community. In the Sudanese idiom, 'berta' means 'slave'; and that may, or may not, be the origin of the group's name. The frontier area was called Bela Shangul, and that may, or may not, be linked to the Amharigna word '*shanqila*' for negro/slave. The local ruling dynasties were Arabic-speaking Muslims, who claimed kinship ties with the Sudanese Funj rulers and who styled themselves Shaikhs. When the Funj era came to an end with the Turko-Egyptian occupation in 1821, the local ruling houses in the borderland were supplanted by a new ruling class (known as Watawit), made rich and powerful through trade, and whose descendants are today the aristocracy of Berta society, while their predecessors, known as Jabalawin, hold second rank. The bottom of the social scale in this stratified society is occupied by a miscellaneous class formed by the descendants of slaves, poor peasants and pastoralists who produce the food consumed in the region and still pan for gold. The Watawit and Jabalawin despise them and still call them '*abid*' ('slave').

THE GUMUZ

Metekel Zone north of the loop formed by the Blue Nile River is the home of the Gumuz people who also live in Kamashi Zone and numbered 160,000 in 2007. Something of a vast bowl surrounded on its eastern and northern rim by spectacular mountains and to the south by the river, Metekel is mostly hot lowland with undulating plains and thick tropical forest that receives heavy rainfall. The average altitude rises from less than 600m in the west to 2,731m in the east. Classified as forested land, the bulk of it is sparsely inhabited by peasants practising shifting cultivation.

Outsiders have called the Gumuz many names, all of them derogatory, of which '*shanqila*' (slave) is the most common. The name Gumuz is of recent origin. In Metekel the people use the name Bega for themselves and Shuwa for the highlanders. The highlanders are also called '*qay*' (red) in contrast to '*gumz*' (black). In the past the Gumuz inhabited a vast region from Guba on the Sudan border to the heights of western Gojjam. The chiefdom of Guba was a Gumuz centre and contact point with the Sudanese states of Funj and Sennar. Historically, the entire area was a buffer zone between Ethiopia and Sudan, known to the highlanders as the 'land of the Arabs'. In recent times, the Gumuz came under pressure from the Muslims in the west and the Christians in the east, gradually losing territory to both, and were forced to move southwards across the Blue Nile River. Under Egyptian and Mahdiya rule in the Sudan, the borderland was attacked and plundered repeatedly but was never conquered. The Gumuz reaction was to disperse and hide in the interior. 'Easy retreat, mobility and inaccessibility through dispersion and bad communications have been the means of self-preservation of (Gumuz) communities in living memory' (James 1986: 35).

Oppression and dispersion prevented this sedentary community from evolving beyond the clan level, which remains the pillar of Gumuz society and determines the identity of its members. Clans have defined territories within which their members live in dispersed settlements. Gumuz society is egalitarian, lacking social or political hierarchies, and the role of community elders (*ganza*) is decisive in all aspects of everyday life. The elders are responsible for administration, justice, and the settlement of disputes. 'Once conflict occurs, they resolve it in a compromising way such that neither of the conflicting parties will be a total winner or a total loser,' notes one anthropologist (Wolde Selassie Abboute 2004: 72). The Gumuz cling to their traditional faith, except in Guba where they came under Islamic influence. More recently they have been the target for proselytisation by foreign evangelists (see chapter 14).

THE SHINASHA

With a population of 51,000 in 2007, the Shinasha are the third largest indigenous community and live in Metekel Zone. Their little known history is not unlike that of the Gumuz in its travails. It is believed they once lived south of the Blue Nile River until Oromo pressure forced many of them to move north of the river in Bulen and Wembera districts, where most of them live today. Those who remained south of the river were fully assimilated by the Oromo, while in Metekel Zone they were partly assimilated by the Agaw, whose language they use to such an extent that their own is in danger of extinction. They do retain their traditions and sense of identity, albeit under various names, such as Gonga and Boro. Their mode of livelihood is the same as the Gumuz. The Agaw are the third indigenous group in Metekel who, according to their tradition, are said to have come from Seqota Lasta in the north. Today they occupy the fertile lands of Dengur, Belaya, Gwangwa, Mandura, Debati and Wembera districts. Mao and Komo are the last two indigenous communities with a combined population of some 19,000 in Assosa Zone.

THE HIGHLANDERS

For centuries now, land scarcity on the plateau has forced Abyssinian peasants to move to lower elevations on land sparsely populated by the indigenous Gumuz. The process was described by a European traveller in the 1880s:

> ...each time a strip of land is annexed a certain number of families are told off out of overpopulated Godsham (Gojjam) to settle as colonists in new territory. They are judiciously not allowed to herd together in separate villages, but distributed all over the country, so that even the most insignificant negro hamlet shall have its one or two Abyssinian houses... Not much persuasion is needed to induce these people to leave their native country, where every inch of land is private property, for the half-desert negro-lands where any amount of as good as virgin soil can be had for the taking.[7]

An additional push factor was the proscription on land ownership imposed on the Muslim population in the Abyssinian provinces; it impelled them to seek land in areas where the *rist* system did not apply. There were significant Amharigna-speaking (largely Muslim) settlements in Guangua, Mandura and Debati districts in Metekel before the 1980s resettlement programme. The Gumuz were relentlessly pushed westward to lower and less fertile land and a good number of them crossed the Blue Nile River to join kinsmen in what is now Kamashi Zone. The descent of land-hungry highlanders was reinforced by the resettlement programme that brought in a large number of them at one fell swoop. The result is that today the Amhara with 142,000 make up 22% of the population of the Beni Shangul Gumuz *kilil*, whose entire population in 2007 was 670,000.

Numbering 89,000 in 2007, the Oromo are another significant popu-

[7] Schuiver cited in James (1986: 124).

lation segment in Metekel Zone, specifically in Wembera and Debati districts. Following the Ethiopian conquest of Wollega in 1882, land expropriation and oppressive rule forced Oromo peasants to move north across the Blue Nile River to areas where imperial rule had not yet hardened. Even after this annexation, Wembera and Debati districts continued to be ruled by local Oromo chiefs who encouraged Oromo settlement there. The migrants took control of higher terrain, confining the Gumuz and the Shinasha to the low lying areas.

SYNOPSIS

The demography of Beni Shangul Gumuz exemplifies many of the oddities inherent in the Ethiopian design of federalism, or the lack of it. There is no obvious rationale, geographic, ethnic, economic, political, or other, for the formation of this unit of the federation. It would seem that it was invented simply to collect several groups that did not fit anywhere else. It also seems to have gone unnoticed by the designers that their creation included sizable highlander communities forced to move down the escarpment by land scarcity higher up, and that these impoverished people took land claimed by the even more deprived indigenous communities. The result is that the highlander and lowlander cultivators are in direct confrontation over land, with predictably troubling consequences (see Chapter 14).

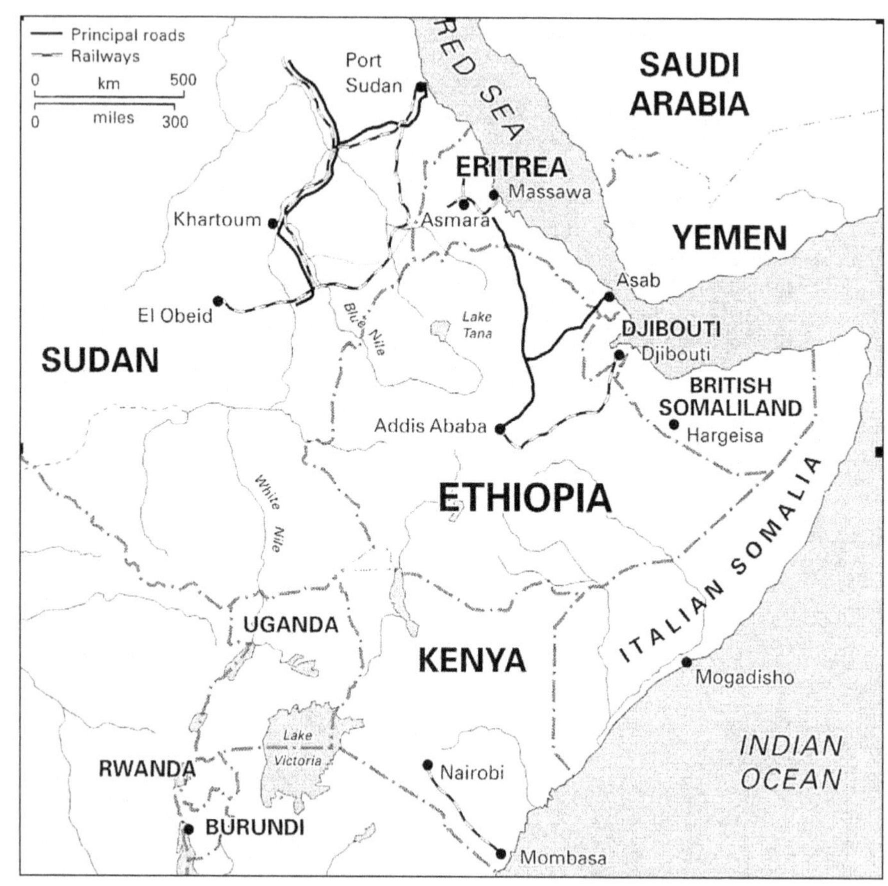

Map 4 Colonial map of the Horn of Africa

Part II
Building the State: The Imperial Model

4

Winning an Empire

Empire building in this corner of Africa follows the classic pattern of expansion from a dynamic core state whose energy spills over its borders to conquer neighbouring lands, from which it draws resources and additional strength for further conquests abroad. The core state in this tale is Shoa, the southernmost Abyssinian province, and the following pages recount the initial phase when the foundations of the imperial state were put in place. Building an empire is a monumental feat of construction, justly celebrated in history. It is also a deed of enormous destruction for those who are swept aside in its path, a part of the story imperial histories mostly ignore. This chapter treats both aspects.

The Shoa phase

The period of civil strife known in Ethiopian history as the Age of Princes lasted until the middle of the 19th century. The man who ended it and restored the authority of the imperial throne was an upstart genius who emerged the winner in the provincial elimination contest, and had himself crowned Emperor Tewodros (1855-1868).[1] During a brief but eventful reign, he strove to subdue the Ethiopian nobility and clergy and to set the foundations of a powerful monarchy. He was succeeded by the ruler of Tigray province, who was crowned Emperor Yohannes IV (1872-1889), the only native son of this province to sit on the imperial throne in modern times.[2] During his reign, Yohannes was preoccupied with external threats that appeared from the north. The opening of the Suez Canal in 1869 had restored the Red Sea to world prominence, leading to a struggle for control of the coast. Towering over the Red Sea littoral, the Ethiopian plateau was emerging from its long isolation

[1] For a history of Tewodros see Rubenson (1966).
[2] For the history of Yohannes see Zewde Gebre Selassie (1975).

at this time to become a focus in the contest that ensued. Having landed in Massawa in 1885, the Italians had already moved onto the edge of the northern plateau to establish the colony they named Eritrea. At the same time, the Mahdist forces in the Sudan were spilling into Ethiopian territory in the west, and Yohannes was to lose his life fighting against them.

The imperial throne now passed to the most powerful of the provincial rulers, Menelik of Shoa, whose reign (1889-1913) is a milestone in Ethiopian history.[3] It marks the full restoration of imperial authority in the Christian kingdom, its vast territorial expansion and transformation into an empire, and the planting of the seeds for its development into a modern state. The southernmost province of Ethiopia, Shoa was the most exposed to the Oromo migration on the northern plateau. Oromo tribes had settled early in the southern districts and gradually penetrated into Shoa's centre, bringing Islam with them. In the 1840s, Shoa province had a population of 2.5 million, of which one million were Amharigna-speaking Christians and the rest Oromo and Afar Muslims (Darkwah 1975: 29). Ruling the only province to remain aloof from the civil wars during the Age of Princes, Shoa's dynasty was able to secure and expand a power base that enabled it ultimately to seize the imperial throne.

Once the rulers of Shoa had consolidated their power at home, they began to expand their domain by incorporating the adjoining Oromo districts. 'By 1837 it had become customary for the king of Shoa to make each year an expedition against the Macha and other Galla to ensure the collection of tribute; and the lands of those who refused to pay were looted and devastated' (Huntingford 1993: 43). Sahle Selassie (1813-1847) already styled himself 'King of Shoa and the Oromo', and Shoa's population had reached five million by 1881 (Darkwah 1975: 108). Menelik succeeded to the throne of Shoa in 1865 and, while still formally a vassal of Emperor Yohannes, he resumed the campaign of expansion. Within four years (1882-1886), the western section of the northern plateau, from the Blue Nile River to Illubabor, was brought under Shoa control with 'little or no resistance' (Bahru Zewde 1991: 62). Crossing the Awash River and the Rift Valley, Shoa forces then invaded the southern plateau. Here they met fierce resistance from the Arsi Oromo and fighting did not end until 1886. The conquest of Arsi opened the way to the city-state of Harar, which fell in 1887.

After succeeding Yohannes on the imperial throne in 1889, Menelik was able to command forces from other Christian provinces. The tide of Abyssinian expansion southwards was interrupted briefly by an Italian invasion from the north in 1895, when their forces crossed the Mareb River from Eritrea to invade Tigray province. Supported by all his vassals, including contingents from three Oromo clans (Ahmed Hassan Omer 2002: 236), Menelik led a large peasant army to meet them. The battle of Adwa in 1896 was an unmitigated disaster for the Italians,

[3] See a biography of Menelik by Marcus (1974).

whose army was decimated. Surprisingly, the Ethiopians did not pursue the invaders to the sea. In a conciliatory gesture, Menelik allowed them to retain their colony in Eritrea, a gesture that was to have profound repercussions for Ethiopia's future.

The campaigns of expansion resumed immediately afterwards at a furious pace, and the subjugation of the entire plateau was completed with the occupation of the Oromo state of Jimma in 1897. The Ethiopian armies did not stop at the edge of the plateau. They descended the escarpment to the lowlands and advanced as far they could, until they were halted by political obstacles raised by the rival imperial powers, Britain and Italy. In the west, they took advantage of the disarray that followed the collapse of Mahdist rule in the Sudan in 1898, to seize the lowland fringe that is now the state of Beni Shangul Gumuz. In the southwest, they crossed the Gambella plain in 1898 to plant the Ethiopian flag in the Sobat River, and reached the northern shore of Lake Turkana the same year. In the south, they descended the slopes of the plateau to seize Boranaland, and then annexed the Ogaden in the southeast. By the time it was over, Ethiopia had secured the boundaries it has today.

Superior military power accounted for the swift success of Menelik's campaigns. In this respect, the Christian kingdom was far superior to any of its opponents. The military had always served as the pillar of state authority in Ethiopia. From the throne at the apex of the pyramid, to the provincial rulers and their subordinates in the districts, and to the *gultegna* who administered the countryside, all maintained bodies of armed men to enforce their authority. The largest and best equipped standing force was the emperor's own army (*chewa*) whose size varied according to imperial resources. A standing professional army, it consisted of trained soldiers – infantrymen, archers, horsemen, musketeers – many of them non-Abyssinian freemen and slaves. Provincial rulers maintained armies of retainers for their own purposes, and supplied them to the emperor's forces when they were commanded to do so.

Soldiering was a traditional profession in Ethiopia, open to anyone who aspired to escape the drudgery of peasant life by becoming a *matador* ('warrior'). In time of war, the standing army was reinforced by peasants who arrived in large numbers bringing their own weapons, mounts and supplies and, not infrequently, their wives to look after them. Soldiers received no payment or any form of support. They 'ate the land' as it was said, and were a scourge to the rural population. At Adwa, Menelik led a force of 100,000 against an invading Italian army of 20,000. At various times, Menelik fielded more than one army simultaneously, and had spare troops to garrison occupied territories.

No ruler in the path of the expansion was able to mobilise forces on a comparable level. This was partly because no group had developed political cohesion to the same degree as the Christians, who moreover proved adept in dividing and undermining their opponents. More often than not, they were able to exploit local rivalries and strike opportunistic alliances with local rulers, some of whom joined the invaders against their ethnic kinsmen. The Oromo were particularly vulnerable in this respect. From the very beginning, Shoa's armies included significant numbers of Oromo, and some of Menelik's ablest generals were themselves Oromo. In the course of the expansion, collaboration with Menelik was the rule among Oromo rulers.

Possession of firearms was another advantage. Imported from Europe, and crucial in fulfilling Ethiopia's expansion, they were, ironically, equally useful in obstructing European imperialist schemes in the Horn. Ethiopian leaders manipulated European rivalries in order to acquire modern weaponry. Britain, the most ambitious coloniser, placed Ethiopia under an arms embargo to keep it weak and pliable. France and Italy, however, thwarted British plans, allowing Menelik to obtain a sizeable arsenal from both. In preparation for the war with Italy, the Emperor imposed a special tax to finance the import of 100,000 carbines. All in all, it was estimated that Ethiopia possessed about 200,000 carbines when that war started.

In addition to manpower and weaponry, the Abyssinians had a decisive advantage in the organisational capacity of a centuries-old state, with a hierarchical structure of authority and clear lines of command serving both civil and military functions. The nomenclature of the structure included many military titles, such as *ras* (army commander), *fitawrari* (commander of the vanguard), *kenyazmatch* (commander of the right wing) and *grazmatch* (commander of the left wing). Automatically transposed for purposes of war, this structure was far superior to anything possessed by other states in the region. Yet Menelik's army had no wheeled transport and only beasts of burden to move supplies. There were no roads or bridges in his domain, and no means of communication faster than fleet footed messengers.

The capacity of the people who faced the Abyssinian onslaught to defend themselves varied considerably, but was nowhere adequate for the task. The possession of specialised military institutions depends on the ability of a state to produce the surplus needed for their maintenance. There were few such states in the Horn. The most significant were the five Oromo states in the Gibe River region, all of which, a historian tells us, were created by and for war. 'War made the Gibe kings, and all of them made war the prime business of their administration' (Mohammed Hassen 1990: 93). Supported by peasant taxation, their rulers maintained large bodies of armed men to enforce their authority and protect their wealth. The Sultan of Jimma had an army at the palace that 'acted as the heart of the war forces and as the king's retinue and bodyguard' (H.S. Lewis 1965: 102).

A similar trend towards political centralisation was apparent among the Oromo in the northwest, in the region of Wallega. Two political entities there, Nekempt Qellam and Leqa Qellam, were ruled by dynasties that had attained power 'through war, confiscation of land, collection of booty, tribute and market dues, and through the establishment of hereditary rights to ownership of property and political office' (Asafa Jalata 2005: 36). Even so, none of the Oromo states stood against the invaders from the north, nor did their rulers resist the temptation to collaborate with them. On the other hand, the invasion met with determined, even fierce resistance from Sidama rulers in Kambata, Wollayta, Gedeo, Kaffa and from the Adari of Harar. The arms trade had not penetrated the interior of the Horn before Ethiopian expansion, and none of the groups in its path possessed firearms in adequate numbers. They fought mostly with spears and daggers, bows and arrows, against rifles.

*

From the perspective of the Great Tradition, the 'expansion,' as it is invariably described, was the finale in the struggle for the 'reunification' of Ethiopia, a process began by Tewodros and completed by Menelik, that is, the recovery of lands that allegedly belonged to the Christian kingdom in the past and lost in the aftermath of Gragn's invasion. 'This region (Horn) had been under the control of the Emperors of Ethiopia from about the beginning of the Christian era until the revolt of the vassal king of Adal, Grany (Gragn), in the sixteenth century, and the subsequent invasion of the Horn by the Oromo and the Somali,' is a concise statement of this view (Getachew Haile 1986: 465), or, simply put: 'Menilek during his long years reign, restored and united most of the medieval territories of Ethiopia' (Teferra Haile Selassie 1997: 36). A foreign scholar makes the same point more subtly: 'Should the imperial expansion...be viewed basically as a subjugation of alien peoples or an in-gathering of peoples with deep historical affinities?' (Levine 2000: xxi). The Great Tradition endowed the 'lost lands' with truly vast proportions, and Ethiopian rulers made extravagant claims in this respect. Appropriately, it was Menelik who surpassed them all by announcing to the world his intention to 're-establish the ancient frontiers of Ethiopia up to Khartoum, and as far as Lake Nyanza with all the Galla'.[4]

Mundane motives were certainly involved. Most frequently cited are 'the green and lush Oromo lands and their boundless commodities (gold, civet, ivory, coffee) and prosperous market' (Addis Hiwet 1975: 4). The Horn had a flourishing regional commerce with a network that criss-crossed the region; professional traders such as the Ethiopian *Jabarti*, the Sudanese *Jallaba* and the Somali *Safar*, carried on a far-flung caravan trade. The principal goods were slaves, gold, ivory, civet and coffee from the southwest plateau; salt, myrrh, resins, ostrich feathers, and leopard and lion skins from the eastern lowlands. Shoa sat on the crossroads of the regional trade, and its rulers were not indifferent to its value. The northern highlands produced little for the regional market, and the Ethiopian economy ran a considerable trade deficit with its neighbours. Menelik imposed a trade monopoly on salt, gold dust and civet, collected a fee for every slave sold, and a market tax of 10% on all transactions. His avid interest in trade led one author to describe him as 'literally a merchant King' (Jesman 1958: 60).

[4] Rodd to Salisbury, 4 May 1897 (F.O. 1/32).

If the riches of the southwest were a pull factor, land hunger in Ethiopia was a push factor, the importance of which became clearer with the passage of time. There were no safety valves for growing population pressure on a land of declining quality. Urban growth was the missing link. Highland societies are not known for intensive urbanisation, and Ethiopia less so than most. None of the plateau's many rivers are navigable to this day and none hosted towns on their banks. The peasant-based subsistence economy did not reach the level of craft specialisation that correlates with urban growth, nor did the state, with its tradition of 'mobile capitals', or the Ethiopian Orthodox Church with its monastic ethos, create structures that required an urban base. The first town to emerge since the days of Aksum was Gondar, which served as the imperial capital from the mid-17th to the mid-18th centuries. After the decline of Gondar during the Age of Princes, it was not until the beginning of the 20th century that Ethiopia acquired a capital city, in Addis Ababa.

The great famine known as *Kefu Qan* ('Evil Days') that devastated the Horn in 1888-1892 was an exacerbating factor. It started as a livestock rinderpest epidemic set off in Massawa by infected cattle brought by the Italians, and swept like wildfire through the Horn. By 1890 it had reached Somalia. It killed about 90% of the cattle in Ethiopia by 1892, leaving the peasants unable to plough the fields (Mesfin W/M 1986: 33). Drought, locust, cholera and army worms followed in successive waves and a biblical famine ensued. 'The dead awaited the hyenas, and the living awaited death', wrote an observer,[5] and a historian concludes: 'The process of territorial expansion...was partly spurred on by this social catastrophe' (Bahru Zewde 1991: 71). The Oromo lands offered what today we would call a famine 'coping strategy' for the Ethiopians. According to a contemporary observer, 'while the poor died, the less weak went to the country of the Galla' (Asme Giorgis n.d.).

The intrusion of European imperialism in the region during the last quarter of the 19th century was a precipitating factor. The opening of the Suez Canal in 1869 had turned the Horn into a prime site of imperialist contention. By the time Menelik became emperor in 1889, European imperialism had already staked claim to the entire Red Sea coast and was poised to invade the interior. Ethiopia was surrounded by intruders whose predatory intentions were ill-concealed, and the need to head them off was undoubtedly a factor in stimulating Ethiopia's expansionism, particularly in its final stage. 'If Powers at a distance come forward to partition Africa between them, I do not intend to be an indifferent spectator', was the African monarch's warning to the European powers in 1891.[6] With Italy subdued and France confined to the Djibouti enclave, Britain and Ethiopia scrambled to seize what remained unclaimed in the Horn.

Ethiopian methods of dealing with enemies were based on guidance

[5] Quoted in R. Pankhurst (1964:44-45).
[6] Rodd to Salisbury, 4 May 1897.

offered in the compendium of customary law, *Fetha Nagast* (Law of the Kings):

> When you reach a city or land to fight against its inhabitants, offer them terms of peace. If they accept you and open their gates, the men who are there shall become subjects and give you tribute, but if they refuse the terms of peace and offer battle, go forward to assault and oppress them, since the Lord your God will make you master of them.[7]

Menelik and his generals followed this advice faithfully. The rulers of states in the path of the Abyssinian advance were offered the choice of submission and tributary status, in return for which they were allowed to retain their position, at least temporarily. Submission accompanied by conversion to Ethiopian Orthodox Christianity opened the doors to assimilation into the Abyssinian ruling class, and even links with the royal household. On the other hand, resistance invited the harshest retribution for defiant rulers and their peoples.

The furthest Oromo penetration in the northern plateau was in Wollo on the eastern edge of the northern plateau. Early converts to Islam, the Wollo Oromo were governed by two dynasties perennially feuding with each other, while also fending off Ethiopian attempts to subjugate them. They were the first to be brought to heel, when Yohannes and Menelik jointly campaigned against them in the 1870s and forced their rulers to become Christians. One of the latter, Mohammed Ali, was baptised as Mikael and made ruler of Wollo with the title of Ras. He also married Menelik's daughter and later saw his son Yasu named Menilek's heir, only to be deprived of the throne by the Shoa.

The most successful case of accommodation was Jimma, one of the five Oromo states in the Gibe River region. Jimma is the best known of the group, because it retained an identity of sorts under Ethiopian rule. Abba Jifar II, the Sultan of Jimma at the time of the invasion, counted himself the twenty-sixth ruler of his dynasty. Submitting peacefully, he further ingratiated himself by joining the conquerors in attacking his Sidama neighbours. In return, he was allowed to govern Jimma as a vassal until his death in 1932, reigning for a total of fifty-four years. The imperial government took over the administration of Jimma afterwards, but continued to appoint Abba Jiffar's descendants to the office of local governor until the demise of the imperial regime itself in 1974.

Ras Gobana, Menelik's ablest Oromo general, secured control of the other four Gibe states without fighting a single battle. Their rulers saw the wisdom of submitting peacefully, hoping to retain their positions under Ethiopian suzerainty. At first, their hopes seemed to be realised, as the conquerors appeared well disposed towards them. However, when rebellion spread among their subjects later, they were removed and ended their days in captivity in the dungeons of Abba Jiffar. With

[7] The *Fetha Nagast* ('Law of Kings') contains sections on canon, property, family and criminal law, as well as a section on kings (p. 501).

similar ease, Ras Gobana secured the submission of Nekempt Qellam and Leqa Qellam in Wallega, whose rulers joined the expedition that brought the lowlands of Beni Shangul into the Ethiopian domain. Baptised Gebre Eghziabher and raised to the rank of Dejazmatch, the son of the ruler of Leqa Qellam remained governor of his province until 1932. He was succeeded by a son until 1936, and a grandson until the 1950s. Some of his descendants married into the royal family, and Ras Gobana's own son married a daughter of Menelik.

The expansion met with stiffer resistance elsewhere. The campaign to conquer the Gurage, launched while Menelik was still king of Shoa, lasted nearly a decade. The first Shoa incursion was repelled in 1876 by a united Gurage force, with many casualties on both sides. Menelik then switched tactics, playing upon Gurage division, until he was able to secure the submission of all segments, except one, the Gumer. Led by a man called Darssano, the Gumer fought valiantly until they were defeated in 1886. When Darssano surrendered, he was baptised on the spot with Menelik acting as his godfather.

Having overcome Gurage resistance, Menelik's soldiers moved into Sidama territory. The first expedition was repulsed by a Sidama chieftain, Baalicha Worayo, and it took a second to capture and kill him. The conquest of Hadiya and Kambata was effortlessly completed by 1892. The Wolayta ruler, King Tona, chose to resist and engaged the Abyssinians in the bloodiest battles of the expansion. Menelik himself led an army against the king in 1894, joined by two Oromo vassals, Ras Mikael of Wollo and Abba Jiffar of Jimma. Vanquished, King Tona ended his days in chains in Addis Ababa. The same fate befell Gaki Sherocho, the ruler of Kaffa, who resisted an invading force joined by the ever obliging Abba Jiffar. Taken to Addis Ababa, Gaki is said to have berated Menelik: 'You think yourself a great king, but your claim bears no comparison to mine. Your crown was placed on your head by the hands of men. Mine came down to me straight from Heaven on high' (Perham 1969: 318).

When their turn came, the Arsi Oromo pastoralists on the heights of the southern plateau put up the fiercest resistance. Mobilising men from all the clans, they rebuffed an initial Shoa incursion across the Rift Valley in 1881. The Shoa returned the following year and a series of battles followed until the Arsi were beaten. The biggest prize in the southern plateau was Harar, the walled city-state with a history dating back at least to the 14th century, and a reputation as a centre of Islamic learning. Occupied by the Egyptians in 1875, it was vacated in 1882, leaving it open to attack that came only two years later. Invited to submit, its ruler Emir Abdulahi allegedly sent Menelik this answer: 'When you become a Muslim I will consider you my master' (Greenfield 1965: 100). Harar managed to repel the first attack, and Menelik himself led the second, taking the city in 1887. Emir Abdulahi made his submission and was appointed assistant to the Ethiopian governor.

The wages of conquest in the highlands

Abyssinian rule had diverse consequences for the peoples of the conquered regions, depending partly on the reception they gave the invaders and partly on the wealth of their countries. The conquered territories were divided into fiefdoms assigned to Menelik's victorious generals, many of them royal relatives, to govern and exploit. The ethos of the system was captured in the saying that they were given these territories 'to eat' (Cerulli 1933: 125). Resource expropriation was a priority, because it was the only way to compensate the soldiery and to replenish the imperial treasury. At first instance, this took the form of massive plunder. Human beings themselves were a major resource: they were enslaved and traded in markets that grew dramatically in the wake of the expansion. Two areas that put up the stiffest resistance, Kaffa in the southwest and Arsi in the southeast, were depopulated as a result. The Abyssinian ruling class and its allies acquired vast numbers of slaves and even exchanged them as presents. Menelik and his wife reportedly had 70,000 slaves and Aba Jiffar 10,000.[8] A slaving expedition (*razzia*) in the southwest, led in 1912 by Menelik's heir presumptive, Lij Yasu, netted some 40,000 Dizi slaves and trekked them to Addis Ababa, where only about half of them arrived alive (Bahru Zewde 1991: 93).

This practice was zealously imitated by officials and soldiers serving in the conquered territories. Their period of service was normally short, and whenever a governor was transferred, he stripped his fiefdom bare before departing. When the governor of Kaffa and Maji, Ras Wolde Giorgis, was transferred to Begemdir in 1910, his soldiers collected all the natives they could and took them north as slaves, along with livestock and other movable booty. This was repeated in 1922 when another governor, Dejazmatch Desta Birru, was recalled, and once more when his successor, Dejazmatch Mekuria, left with 50,000 sheep and his wife's 93 slaves. During 1925-1932, Maji had six governors. Departing governors taxed heavily and raided for slaves in order to take what wealth they could to their home areas. Local peoples struck back when they were able, often raiding each other for slaves, for that was the only way to get arms. Incoming governors then brutally crushed the rebellion, after which *gabbar* had nothing left, were unable to pay new taxes and were therefore forced to sell their children as slaves. This was a pattern repeated again and again between 1910 and 1936 (Garretson 2002: 217). It was estimated that the population of Maji province dropped from thousands before the invasion to a few hundred in 1925 (ibid.: 202).

Slavery became an international issue when Ethiopia applied for admission to the League of Nations in the early 1920s. It was admitted in 1923, after signing the Convention of St. Germain to suppress slavery

[8] R. Pankhurst (1968: 75); H.S. Lewis (2001: 66).

in all its forms. A proclamation issued for the occasion by Empress Zawditu and the Regent Ras Tafari (Haile Selassie's name before taking the throne) explained that 'the reasons why some men were declared slaves (in the past) was that certain nations were at war with us, and this had caused money to be spent which these nations had to repay by their labour and, moreover, that they should learn virtue by communication with Christians.'[9]

Slavery has not merited attention in the historiography of the Great Tradition, save as a trade factor. One historian claims that Menelik was 'strongly opposed to the trade' before going on to note its spectacular growth during his reign.[10] By contrast, slavery is a staple theme in revisionist historiography, where it is implausibly presented as an exclusively Abyssinian practice. 'The Ethiopian colonial expansion resulted in mass killings, destruction and expropriation of property, plundering, enslavement, and genocide' (Asafa Jalata 2005: 72). 'At the time she managed to subdue and started ruling over her neighbours, Ethiopia was a slave-owning medieval state' (Leenco Latta 1999: 156). Slavery in the Oromo states of the Gibe River region is downplayed as a minor derivative of the Abyssinian trade (Leenco Latta, 2004: 48-50).

Livestock was another valuable resource, especially following the wiping out of the herds by the rinderpest epidemic of the 1890s. Special expeditions were sent to move livestock in vast numbers from the lowlands, especially the Somali areas, to the northern highlands. The Arsi Oromo lost so much livestock they were compelled to take up cultivation, and at the same time espoused Islam. Ivory was another valuable commodity for which the southwest was known, and was hunted assiduously until the elephants disappeared from the region.

Those who thought submission the wiser course and joined hands with the conquerors against their neighbours were spared the worst depredations, and were obliged to pay tribute instead. A fixed tribute was imposed on six states that were left under the control of their traditional rulers – Jimma, Leqa Nekempt, Leqa Qellam, Beni Shangul, Guba, Aussa – and for some time they were spared the expropriation of land described below. In 1904, Abba Jiffar's tribute was assessed at 350,000 Maria Theresa dollars, 150 kilograms of gold, 20 richly caparisoned horses, 100 mule loads of wooden furniture, and a special gift of gold plates and silver cups for the emperor (Marcus 1975: 191). Wallega Qellam paid 1,000 measures of gold, plus ivory and honey. Tribute was raised by taxing the people, whose local leaders imposed additional taxes for their own treasuries. When the tribute imposed on Leqa Qellam was increased, its native ruler complained to Addis Ababa of having to double the tax on the people, as a result of which 'the poor suffer and groan' and fled from the region (Triulzi 2002: 62).

By far the most important resource in the conquered territories was

[9] 'Correspondence Respecting Abyssinian Raids and Incursions into British Territory', Abyssinia No. 1 (1925) (London, HMSO).

[10] R. Pankhurst (1968: 99).

the land: still in pristine condition, unaffected by erosion and thinly populated. Securing it for sustainable exploitation was no mean task for a state with a rudimentary fiscal system such as Ethiopia possessed. Nevertheless, it was accomplished in short order and with a minimum of turmoil. The time-honoured *gabbar-gultegna* system of the northern highlands was modified to maximise surplus extraction from the rural economy of the highland periphery. The basic principle was straightforward, focusing on the exploitation of the land and the labour of the subjugated population. Its design however was quite complex. Given the many different categories of claimants who lined up for a share of these resources, there was enormous variation in the arrangements made. Furthermore, many of the arrangements changed over time, so that when the system was being scrapped in the 1960s, no two sources agreed on its details.

The victorious army was the first to receive its share of the spoils of war. The process of distribution coincided and paralleled the setting up of a skeleton administration for the conquered territories. In its simplest form, this was a quasi-feudal arrangement, whereby landed fiefs were allocated to the army, from generals to simple soldiers. The fief covered an area of land whose size and value was determined by the number of *gabbar* (tiller) families settled on it. Land without *gabbar* to work on it was valueless. The size of the fief varied according to rank, and could range from entire districts and hundreds of *gabbar* families for high ranking nobles and members of the royal family, to plots with a few families for plain soldiers. Whole provinces were 'given' to victorious generals and nobles of Menelik's court 'to eat'. These were subdivided among their principal lieutenants, who in turn allotted portions to subordinate officers and soldiers in their command, until a full landlord hierarchy was established.

Depending upon length of service, a simple soldier could receive from one to three *gasha* of land (depending on quality, the size of a *gasha* varied from a minimum of 40 hectares to twice as much), and could exploit the labour of several *gabbar* households. This was a princely estate compared with the average peasant-holding in the north that did not exceed one hectare. Some of the fiefs were given in freehold as reward for past services, others were attached to office and on condition of continued service. In the first instance, soldier-landlords also functioned as administrators. Only they were allowed to carry arms and became known as '*neftegna*' ('gunmen'), a name that came to be widely applied subsequently to all northerners who settled in the periphery. The *neftegna-gabbar* nexus was the foundation of Ethiopian imperial rule. Except for the regions paying a fixed tribute, it was imposed on the conquered territories without delay.

The burden on the peasantry was oppressive. The *gabbar* had to surrender a portion of the land's produce to the landlord as tribute (*gibr*) – the amount varied between one-quarter (*erbo*) and one-third (*sisso*). In addition, the *gabbar* paid the *asrat* (tenth) tithe levied by Menelik in 1892. The *gabbar* was also obliged to provide the landlord with honey, meat, firewood, dried grass and other essentials. *Gabbar* labour was required for a variety of purposes: to cultivate the fields set aside for the landlords' kitchen (*hudad*); to grind the *neftegna*'s share of the grain produced in his fief and carry it to his house in town; to build his house, maintain his fences, care for his animals, and act as his porter, messenger and escort. Whether holding an official position or not, the *neftegna* exercised great power over the *gabbar*. He was responsible for maintaining law and order in his fief, for the collection of state taxes, for the performance of other obligations to the state, and for the administration of justice, in the course of which he imposed fines and collected fees that he kept for himself.

The situation in which the *gabbar* in the conquered region found himself differed significantly from that of the Abyssinian peasant who was also designated as *gabbar*. In the Abyssinian homeland, the term referred to the tributary status of the free peasant who had secure (*rist*) rights over his land. The peasant in the periphery who found himself on land expropriated by the state and allocated to others, lost whatever rights he had over such land, and was reduced to the status of a tenant 'quartered on the land of another' (Pankhurst 1968: 174). Furthermore, the burden imposed on the cultivator in the periphery was much heavier than that borne by the Abyssinian peasant, whose rights and obligations were prescribed and protected by traditional law and custom shared with his governor. The *gabbar* in the periphery had no recourse against an alien landholding class, and could not refuse a landlord demand. 'To accuse one Amhara before another Amhara is like trying to separate water from water', went a Kambata proverb, and another protested: 'A Kambata who cuts a tree is guiltier than an Amhara who has killed a man.'

The multiple exactions imposed on the *gabbar* by the landlords entailed a loss of a sizeable portion of household production, onerous labour service and manifold other impositions. The primary economic effect was a depression in the peasant standard of living. Since the local economy was based exclusively on subsistence agriculture, and trade was narrowly restricted to the local level, the impact of the depression was muted and had no wider economic repercussions. Most important, since land was useless without the means to exploit it, the landlords rarely evicted the cultivators, and there was no mass displacement or a sudden appearance of an indigenous landless class. Finally, the precise nature of the loss suffered by the peasantry was concealed behind the feudal facade of overlapping forms of landholding rights, and did not become clear until the twilight of the imperial regime when an aborted move was made to adopt the Western model of private property.

The loss of independence and the many deprivations it entailed left a scar in the psyche of the subjugated peoples. A Wolamo saying sums up their feelings: 'Menelik gave the land to the Amhara, and other people to the birds', meaning the loss of land reduced people to corpses to be eaten by predators. An Oromo song from Wallega lamented:

Boys of the region, what have we done to our region?
We farmed and filled the grain store, and couldn't say "The wealth is ours."
We killed and brought trophies, and couldn't say "See, here is my trophy."[11]

The *gabbar* lamented their loss and excoriated the *neftegna*, whom they depicted with unanimity as grasping and devious. 'An ordinary person is born with crossed hands, an Amhara is born with outstretched hands', said the Adari of Harar. 'The Amhara and the wolf count sheep they haven't raised', added the Wolamo.

The wages of conquest in the lowlands

A century ago, the vast lowland expanse that encircles the plateau was an alien world to highlanders, the world of pastoralism and Islam both despised in equal measure. There was nothing to entice the highlander to descend from the cool heights to the parched, arid and disease afflicted nether lands, the domain of people with an intimidating reputation for savagery. In contrast to the highland periphery, there was no migration of northern highlanders to the lowland zone after the expansion. The lack of cultivable land and settled population to play the role of *gabbar* ruled out the appearance of an immigrant landlord class to play the role of *neftegna*. A third missing link was the lack of a dependable local elite to play the role of *balabbat* (for the meaning of *balabbat* see Chapter 5). As described in previous chapters, political authority in pastoralist communities was decentralised, fragmented and levelled, precluding the rise of powerful leaders that could be relied upon to play the role of a subordinate elite in the imperial system effectively. Finally, there was little land in the arid zone for cultivation and no surplus in the pastoralist economy with which to compensate for a local elite. The paltry stipends and petty titles offered them were not enough to buy genuine collaboration from pastoralist chiefs and elders.

The imperialist scramble for outposts on the Red Sea fragmented the Afar nation, dividing its people under three flags – Ethiopian, Italian, French – a burden they bear to this day, albeit under flags of different colours. Of the five Afar sultanates only Aussa survived and was to enjoy an unusual degree of autonomy under Ethiopian rule. The others faded away, leaving scarcely a trace of their existence. The Afar Depression was a *terra incognita* and little was known of its inhabitants who had a fearsome reputation for xenophobia. It took a foolhardy person to attempt its crossing, and such a man was Werner Munzinger, a Swiss adventurer in the pay of Egypt, who set off from Tajura in 1875 with a force of 350 men on his way to Shoa. His party was attacked in Aussa and nearly all of them perished. When Italy arrived on the scene, it tried to inveigle the Afar chiefs in its machinations against Ethiopia. The Italian agent, Count Antonelli, had better luck than Munzinger. In 1883, he signed a treaty of friendship and commerce with Sultan Mohammed

[11] Cited in Triulzi (1977: 180).

Hanfare of Aussa, and a second treaty in 1888 with Sultan Ali Mirah Hanfare I. This prompted Addis Ababa to send an army in 1895 that engaged and defeated the Aussa forces in the battle of Anudo near Tendaho. Having administered this lesson, the Ethiopians returned to the highlands, leaving the Afar much to their own devices. Addis Ababa asserted sovereignty over the Afar Depression as far as the Italian and French colonial borders, but did nothing to establish a presence there.

Having taken Harar on the easternmost heights of the southern plateau in 1987, Menelik's generals could see the vast lowland plain stretching south to the Indian Ocean and east to the Red Sea. Thinly populated by roving Afar and Somali nomads, the region was already in the sights of three European imperialist powers – Britain, France, and Italy – busily negotiating agreements with local chieftains. The Ethiopian army followed high ground eastwards building forts along the way, until it reached Jijiga, 105kms from Harar in 1891. A fort was built there to control the strategic Kara Mara pass through the Gurez mountain range that leads to the ports of Berbera and Zeila on the Red Sea. The immediate goal was to control the caravan trade that linked the Harar region with the Red Sea. Jijiga was already 'the tax collection station for all caravans using this route' (Wellby 1901: 19). The trade was taxed by the Bartire Somali clan, whose chief collected tolls seated under a tree (Burton 1856 192-3).

Although the invasion of the Somali homeland met little initial resistance, the occupation soon faced fierce opposition that had severe consequences for the Somali people and their relationship with the Ethiopians. The latter hardly had time to settle there when Jijiga came under attack in May 1900 by a force of 6,000 under Sayyid Mohammed Abdulah Hassan. This was the opening act of a war that would last two decades, a period during which Jijiga served as the staging ground for successive campaigns against the insurgency led by a religious leader, whom his enemies mockingly dubbed the 'Mad Mullah'. Britain and Italy now found common ground with Ethiopia, and conducted joint military operations against the 'Dervishes', as the Somali rebels were called.[12] Like other visionaries before and after him, the Sayyid looked to Islam to transcend the centrifugal force of clannism and forge unity among the squabbling Somali branches. 'I am not of this or that tribe', he proclaimed, and initially commanded broad support among the people. Ultimately however, he became enmeshed in the tenacious web of clannishness, and came to rely increasingly on his own clan kinsmen. The Sayyid belonged to the Bah Gheri section of the Dolbahanta clan and was related through his mother to the Ogaden. Many of his followers were Ogaden, and much of the fighting took place in their region, whose people suffered the consequences. The expeditions against the rebels were occasions for mass looting of livestock. In 1903 for instance, 50,000 animals were brought to Jijiga and sent on to Harar

[12] For the story of Sayyid Mohammed Abdullah Hassan (1864-1921) see Said S. Samatar (1982).

(Jennings 1905: 81). Other Somali clans kept out of the war, and some fought against the rebels on the side of the occupiers. Prominent among the latter were the Ishaq, whom the British called 'friendlies', and who saw an opportunity to inflict damage on the Ogaden, their rivals for control of the Haud.

Despite combined British-Ethiopian efforts in the first decade of the 20th century, the Dervish rebellion gathered momentum and reclaimed control of large portions of the contested region. In 1910 the British decided to cut their losses and withdrew from the interior of the Somali Protectorate, hanging on to the coast while they were engaged in Europe during World War I. When that conflict was over, they attacked the rebels from the air, routed them from their strongholds, and the rebellion collapsed in 1920. The Sayyid evaded capture and is believed to have died in 1921 of natural causes somewhere in the Ogaden.

*

Borana hegemony in the south ended when Menelik's soldiers appeared during the *gaada* of Liiban Jaldeesa (1891-1899). An initial attempt to resist was heavily defeated at the battle of Dildil Daraa near Neghele in 1897. Overawed by the lethal efficiency of the invaders' firearms, the Borana chose to submit. Their country was given to the victorious general, Fitawrari Habta Giorgis 'to eat' until 1924, then passed to Ras Desta Damtew, who administered it through a hierarchy of appointed Borana *balabbat*. The top *balabbat* position was shared by the *Qallu* of the two Borana moieties, Gedo Jillo and Guyo Anna of the Sabho and Gona moieties respectively. This was a violation of Borana custom, because these purely religious posts had now become contaminated with secular power, and also made hereditary, remaining with the families of the *Qallu* until 1975. Both the accretion of political power to the *Qallu* and the introduction of the hereditary principle contradicted the *gaada* system of governance and were the first steps in its decline. The drawing of the border between Ethiopia and Kenya in 1903 was a major blow to Borana power. Dividing the people between two states, it put them at a disadvantage vis-à-vis rival ethnic groups on both sides of the border.

Because the Borana had submitted, the *neftegna-gabbar* system was not imposed in their country. The people were required to pay tribute to Ethiopian governors in livestock, honey, myrrh, incense and labour. Few highlanders came to settle in the region, and those who did preferred the higher elevations in the northern part of Boranaland where cultivation is possible; they brought Konso and Burji to work their farms.

Donalson Smith, an American adventurer, appeared in Lake Chew Bahir in South Omo in 1895 with a Somali escort, and asked to buy livestock from the Arbore. When they refused, he attacked one of their villages and looted animals. Arbore tradition recalls their first encounter with firearms: 'The man was white like cattle, and had a red firing stick...When the fighters approached, guns were fired. Since they had not known guns, they thought drums were beaten. Then they found that some were shot in the leg, others were shot in the belly, and saw them dragging intestines' (Yukio 2006: 189). Two years later, Fitawrari Habta Giorgis arrived in Borana with his soldiers. From there he sent messengers to the Arbore asking them to bring their *Gawot* and elders to submit. Despite their recent bitter experience with 'firing sticks' the Arbore chose defiance, and the Gawot Gino Kooka had the messengers speared to death. Habta Giorgis' reprisal was savage. All four Arbore villages were burned to the ground, the men massacred and the women and children taken as slaves. Arbore tradition recalls this calamity: 'Menelik's army swarmed over Arbore land. Hyenas ate the dead as well as the living' (Wolde Gossa Tadesse 2006: 297).

Further west, the initial thrust into the South Omo region met with stiff resistance. A force led by N. Leontief, a Russian mercenary, that had moved along both sides of the Omo River in 1898 was attacked and lost over two hundred soldiers (Leontief 1900: 15). Another force commanded by Ras Wolde Giorgis was more successful. The invaders also found indigenous communities ready to join the attack on their neighbours. The Maale had lost land to the Aari earlier, and now joined Wolde Giorgis' attack on their neighbours. Travellers noted the looting that followed. One of them mentions a raid in Lake Rudolf that netted 'between 30,000 and 40,000 heads of stock, as well as a great many slaves' (Brooke 1905: 528).

The *negtegna-gabbar* system was imposed in the higher elevations of South Omo, where settled indigenous communities worked the land. Despite their collaboration, the Maale were not exempted. A garrison was installed in Bako, and the officers and soldiers were allotted fiefs for their maintenance. Ranking officers were given entire villages, while simple soldiers rated several *gabbar* families. The Maale *kati* became *balabbat* of his people, and the twelve Maale chiefs were recognised as village heads. The lot of the Aari was worse. They found the *gabbar* burden so heavy that many preferred to become outright tenants (*chisenya*), because as such they paid tribute only on the land they cultivated, while the *gabbar* paid on all the land they held.

Keeping European imperialism far from the plateau was the first imperative of Ethiopian foreign policy. Direct access to the lucrative trade in slaves and ivory originating in Gambella and passing through Leqa Qellam was the second. Ethiopia did not have a free hand in the territorial carve-up of this region. Here, as elsewhere, it faced the two European imperialist powers, Britain and France, which were engaged in a reckless race for territorial annexation that brought them to the brink of war in the so-called Fashoda Incident in 1898. The Ethiopians became involved when they sent a force from Gore to accompany the French on their way to Fashoda. When it reached the confluence of the rivers Sobat and Nile, it planted the Ethiopian flag and returned to its highland base. On its way to Fashoda, the British force captured Khartoum and put an end to the Mahdiya state in the Sudan, while the confrontation at Fashoda led to a French withdrawal from the area. It remained for Britain to come to terms with Ethiopia, and an agreement was sealed in 1902 that fixed the border. According to its terms, the majority of the Nuer, save for a section of the Jikany, found themselves in the Sudan, and all the Anywaa, except for those in the districts of Adongo and Akobo, in Ethiopia.

It was British policy to develop indigenous resources for trade. There was potential for coffee and rubber production in Gambella, and the Baro River offered transportation that took seven days to reach the centre of Sudan. The British convinced Menelik to allow them to establish an inland port in Gambella under their own administration, a stipulation that became part of the 1902 boundary agreement. Inaugurated as a free port in 1907, Gambella became an important entrepôt for Ethiopia's foreign trade. The Agreement expired upon Sudan's independence in 1956.

The immediate consequences of subjugation for the Anywaa were awesome. A traveller who visited the area in 1899-1901 found them in dire straits, 'pillaged by the Galla and Abyssinians' (Austin 1902: 14). The Nuer incursion that had begun in a massive way earlier, when the Anywaa abandoned the lowest reaches of their land to escape Mahdist raids, was now a mortal threat. A historian noted: 'The Nuer left the Anywaa shattered. Many had died opposing the Nuer advance. Others had perished from the famine which followed, and all suffered the loss of cattle. At the end of the century the Anywaa appeared near extinction' (Collins 1971: 203).

What saved them from extinction were firearms supplied by the Oromo in Gore and Dembidolo in exchange for ivory. Firearms strengthened the position of the Anywaa traditional leaders, enabling them to consolidate their authority over their villages. Nuer-inhabited areas were remote from the corridors of trade with the highlands, and they lagged behind the Anywaa in acquiring firearms. Moreover, unlike Ethiopian controlled territories where guns were traded freely, the British colonial government across the border exerted itself from the start to ban the trade and disarm the Nuer. It was also determined to tax them, and this caused no end of trouble along the border, because both governments claimed the right to tax herders who wandered across the frontier. It was agreed later that the Anywaa were Ethiopian subjects and the Nuer were Sudanese, and should be taxed accordingly.

Menelik's circular to the foreign powers in 1891 claimed an immense territory lying between the 2nd and 14th latitudes north and west of the White Nile, a useful buffer zone between his domain and the Sudan then under Mahdiya rule. After the battle of Adwa in 1896, he moved to put part of this area under Ethiopian control, in preparation for the anticipated confrontation with the British, who were to return to power in Khartoum within two years. Menelik sent Ras Makonnen with an army estimated at 80,000, accompanied by the Oromo rulers of Wallega, Gebre Egzhiabher and Jote Tullu, to secure control of the western lowland. Of the four sheikhdoms in that area, only Bela Shangul under Sheikh Abd al-Rahman Khojali resisted the invaders, but without success, while Assosa under Sheikh Khojali al-Hassan joined forces with them.

Keen to occupy the gold-producing area and to cut out the Oromo middlemen, Menelik set up small garrisons in Beni Shangul. Isolation and the climate demoralised the highlander troops; some died and others deserted. The area lapsed into anarchy, and in 1903 it was turned over to the ruler of Leqa Qellam, Gebre Egziabher. At the same time, the traditional rulers of Bela Shangul, Assosa and Komosha were imprisoned in Addis Ababa. Only Guba was assigned tributary status under its own Sheikh. This arrangement did not last long either. Released five years later, the three Sheikhs were reinstalled in their sheikhdoms as *balabbat* with a large degree of autonomy, for which they had to pay Addis Ababa dearly in tribute.

What followed was an orgy of slave trading, fuelled by increased demand in the Ethiopian highlands and the markets in eastern Sudan. Sheikh Khojali al-Hassan of Assosa was the principal trader specialising in breeding child slaves, with branches in the Sudan managed by his wives and sons. Consignments of slaves were sent to Addis Ababa regularly. In a letter to Sheikh Khojali, Empress Menen, Haile Selassie's wife, asked for 600 slaves between seven and thirteen years of age (Abdussamad 1999).

Summary

The making of the Ethiopian empire is not a unique phenomenon, either in time or in place. It was the time of modern imperialism, a global phenomenon, whose disturbing impact was felt early and directly in this corner of Africa and acted as a catalyst for the Ethiopian expansion. Nor was it the only native instance of its kind in Africa at this time. Egypt in the north, the Mahdiya in the Sudan, the Fulani in the west, and the Zulu in the south went through similar contemporary events. The crucial difference is that Ethiopia succeeded while the others failed. One of the immediate consequences of the Ethiopian expansion was the dismantling of indigenous states that vanished from the face of the earth along with their history. In this respect, the impact of Ethiopian imperialism was the same as that of the European onslaught elsewhere in Africa: the obliteration of indigenous polities and the interruption of autonomous indigenous political development

Nor were the motives that drove Ethiopian empire builders exceptional. Land hunger was an enduring, compelling reason for the expansion. Accordingly, control of land became the organising principle of imperial rule, translating into subjugation and exploitation of the rural producer – again a familiar feature in world history. Tilly's comment with reference to Western Europe is apt: 'With predominantly peasant populations, the great bulk of the resources of any kind which might be pried loose for governmental use were embedded in agriculture' (1975: 396).

Founding the imperial edifice on a system of land tenure imposed and maintained by force proved to be a structural flaw, that is, the fateful conjunction of ethnic and class divisions in the iniquitous *neftegna-*

gabbar coupling. The great majority of the *neftegna* were Christian, Amharigna and Tigrigna-speaking Abyssinians, a distinct nation in a region inhabited by many other groups, speaking various languages and adhering to Islam and traditional faiths. The distinctiveness of the Abyssinian identity was accentuated by a monopoly of political power, economic privilege and superior social status. All Abyssinians who settled in the highland periphery became landlords on expropriated land and exploited the labour of the indigenous peasantry. The relationship between them was that of master and servant, landlord and tenant, tax-collector and tax-payer. This conjunction made for a potentially explosive outcome that took only a few decades to mature.

5

Building the Imperial State
1916–1974

The conquest of the Ethiopian empire took the last quarter of the 20th century. Building a state capable of ruling it took twice as long. In fact, building did not begin in earnest until the end of World War II. The intervening period was consumed in a struggle for power at the centre that ended with the accession of Haile Selassie to the throne in 1930. Soon afterwards Ethiopia was attacked for a second time by Italy and had a brief taste of European colonial rule (1935-1941). The Italian interlude was a mini-rupture that separated the struggle for power at the centre before 1935 from the centralisation of power and its application to state-building, under the guidance of an absolute monarch, after 1941.

The centre divided: 1913–1930

Emperor Menelik fell ill in 1906 and was gradually incapacitated until his death in 1913. Despite several marriages and many illegitimate offspring, Menelik had no direct male heir and only one living daughter, Zawditu. An older daughter had married King Mikael, the Wollo Oromo ruler who had been forced to become a Christian, and in 1908 the male issue of this marriage, Lij Yasu, a mere boy of thirteen was named heir to the imperial throne. His accession would have meant the passing of the throne to an Oromo dynasty, threatening the political hegemony of the Shoa nobility and the privileges it had accumulated under Menelik. A conspiracy was hatched to prevent this from happening, and Lij Yasue never succeeded to the throne. The guiding spirit of the conspiracy was a young Shoa noble, twenty four years of age, named Ras Tafari Makonnen. A scion of the Shoa nobility, he had good credentials for the role, but was obliged to bide his time, while Menelik's daughter, Zawditu, was enthroned. Ras Tafari was named Regent and heir to Zawditu. It was a crude division of power, undermined further by the distrust that marked relations between the rivals at the top. Virile provincialism reclaimed Ethiopia during the next ten years, with powerful provincial satraps plundering the periphery and ignoring the government in Addis Ababa.

The power gridlock was broken in 1926, when a formidable obstacle represented by the Minister of War, Fitawrari Habte Giorgis, was removed by his death. The old warlord's army of some 16,000 men passed into the service of the Regent, as well as vast estates, stores of weapons and other sources of wealth. Thus reinforced, Tafari moved against his rivals. Over the next few years, the most powerful provincial lords were shorn of their power and possessions by a mixture of guile and force. Having thwarted an attempt, abetted by Zauditu, to remove him in 1928 he forced the cowed Empress to name him *Negus* (King), putting control of government affairs entirely in his hands. Zawditu died in 1930, and Tafari became King of Kings at thirty-seven years of age, taking the throne-name Haile Selassie ('Power of the Trinity'). The taming of the provincial lords was completed the same year when, following the death of Abba Jiffar, Jimma lost its administrative autonomy. The same fate had earlier befallen the traditional rulers of Wallega and Beni Shangul. Thus, the struggle for succession ended seventeen years after Menelik's death.

Imperial foundations

Ethiopia acquired its first constitution in 1931. An early monument to the kind of formalism that was to become a noted trait of governance in this country ever since, it was intended to create a modern facade for the absolute monarchy that Haile Selassie was fashioning, and to improve Ethiopia's none too bright image abroad. The gist was contained in the article that stated simply: 'In the Ethiopian Empire supreme power rests in the hands of the Emperor', whose person was declared 'sacred', his dignity 'inviolable', and his power 'indisputable'. Thus, a modern instrument designed to limit a ruler's power was enlisted by a traditional ruler in pursuit of absolute power.

With his country ringed with European colonies, and his capital crowded with foreign diplomats, concession seekers, merchants and adventurers of all sorts, Haile Selassie was forced to employ foreign advisors, none of who were fully trusted by the Ethiopians. It was through them that he was able to introduce such innovations as a national currency, a state bank, a postal, telephone and telegraph system, and the training of Ethiopian soldiers in the use of modern weapons. In the early 1930s, the central government was revamped. New ministries were added, the customs service was reorganised, new tax regulations were introduced, and a new currency was issued in 1933. Road building and other public works began to change the rustic image of Addis Ababa, motor cars made their appearance in the capital's streets, and a police force was assembled.

The state's need for trained administrators was keenly felt. Before this time, education was the function of the Church, which ran an elementary system serving its own needs. In 1925, Regent Tafari Makonnen opened a school named after him for the sons of the nobility and six years later his wife Menen sponsored a school named after her for girls. A school for the children of *balabbat* called Medhane Alem was founded in the capital, and other schools were sponsored by local notables in provincial towns. A Department of Education was founded in 1909 and raised to ministry level in 1930. All told, some thirteen schools existed before the Italian invasion, offering primary education to a few hundred students. During Menelik's reign, a handful of Ethiopians had managed to make their way abroad, returning with degrees and a command of foreign languages. Haile Selassie sought them out and appointed them to responsible posts. They formed an alternative source of recruitment for the state, enabling Haile Selassie to balance the influence of the traditional Abyssinian elite without creating a threat to his own power. The nobility at that time had little interest in modern education, consequently the majority of the first generation of educated Ethiopians had humble social origins and owed their rise to their own efforts and royal favour. The emperor 'raised them from the dust', the people said.

The system of administration designed for the annexed regions conformed to the time-honoured arrangement linking the dominant elite in the centre with a subordinate elite in the periphery. 'Rulers of empires generally sought to co-opt regional and local powerholders without utterly transforming their bases of power, and to create a distinctive corps of royal servants ... whose fate depended on that of the crown' (Tilly 1990: 24). The administrative structure at the periphery rested on the traditional leadership of local communities. Indigenous authority hierarchies were preserved, mostly in truncated form, to facilitate the administration of the new provinces under Ethiopian governors. The subordinate elite, known as the *balabbatnet* constituted a hierarchy of its own; its contribution to imperial rule was indispensable.

Balabbat is an Amharigna term referring to persons with hereditary *rist* tenure rights to land, and denoted a certain social standing in Abyssinian rural society. In the periphery the *balabbat* was a person of traditional standing, elder or chief, who was strictly subordinate to the lowest *neftegna* in the area. His role was twofold. He acted as the agent of the state vis-à-vis his people, and as their representatives vis-à-vis the state, 'serving as both objects of central policies of domination and as subjects in their implementation and execution' (Motyl 1999: 119). The *balabbat* was responsible for maintaining law and order, reporting crimes and apprehending perpetrators, hearing disputes and administering traditional justice, as well as assessing and collecting taxes. He was compensated for his services with rights over land and labour service, and retained a share – usually a tenth – of the state tax they collected from his people. The alliance of the centre and peripheral elite served both sides well. The *balabbatnet* facilitated the extraction and transfer of resources from periphery to centre, and also enriched its members in the process.

*

The power struggle at the centre that preoccupied the ruling class notwithstanding, resource capture in the periphery remained a paramount concern and inspired attempts to improve the extraction process. Land in the highland periphery was divided between the state and the subject people according to the so-called *sisso* (one-third) principle. In theory, all land was divided into three equal portions, two of which passed to the state and the third left to the indigenous population, although such symmetry was seldom realised in practice. The two-thirds appropriated by the state became its property to dispose of at will. A large portion of it passed – *gratis* or for token payment – to northerners who came to settle on condition that they pay the *asrat* tax. The bulk of it was allocated in the form of *gult* for the maintenance of state servants who administered the conquered territories in lieu of salary and pension. Attached to office and contingent on service, this land was generally known as *maderia* (literally 'to spend the night'). Land was granted to Christian churches and clergy, members of the nobility and royal family, while other lands were reserved for the imperial palace. The *balabbat* were given a share as personal property (*balabbat meurt*) on which they paid nominal tax. Furthermore, they were granted *gult* rights over portions of land not expropriated by the state (*sisso gult*), which meant that they enjoyed the same privileges as the *neftegna* over their own people who worked that land.

It did not take long for the flaws of the haphazardly imposed *neftegna-gabbar* system to show. A major flaw was the multiplicity of layers of beneficiaries interposed between the taxpayer and the state treasury, and the filtering out of revenue at each level, allowing a small portion of the total to reach Addis Ababa. A technical problem was the absence of standards of measurement for a uniform tax assessment. While the land grants were evaluated in terms of the number of *gabbar* families living on the land, there was no measurement for the size of the land itself or the value of the produce. This resulted in gross underestimation of the *asrat* tax on the part of the landholders. Now a different arrangement was made to eliminate some of the intermediaries, and at the same time rationalise the method of taxation. Known as *kelad*, this system was put into effect throughout the highland periphery in the 1910s and 1920s. The instrument of measurement was a length of rope or leather thong called the *kelad*. The unit of measurement was the *gasha*, whose dimensions varied according to the location and quality of land. The ruling principle was to assess a fixed tax for each unit of land to be paid directly to the state treasury. Not all land in the periphery was measured by the *kelad*. Unmeasured land was assessed in terms of *kutre gabbar* units, whose tax liability was based on the number of *gabbar* families, ownership of animals and soil quality.

Certain measures were decreed subsequently to lighten the peasant load. *Gabbar* labour was restricted to periods of agricultural recession, and the honey tax was abolished. Labour on land reserved for the Palace (*hudad*) was reduced, and the *gabbar* were given the option of money payment. A circular warned officials not to abuse the *gabbar*. 'Don't go near his doorway and never dare to ask him to carry, or till, or fence, or offer you gifts, or transport the grain for you' (Haile Larebo 2006: 49). Tax receipts were introduced in 1929, and tax payment in money was introduced in 1934. In 1935, just before the Italian invasion, the tax per *gasha* was fixed at thirty Maria Theresa dollars, and all other exactions were abolished.

The government was quick to recognise trade as a major source of revenue, and took measures to tap it. A Ministry of Commerce and Customs created by Menelik had branches in several provincial centres, but its work was hampered by the multiple internal taxes on trade imposed by provincial governors. His advisers urged Haile Selassie to abolish these feudal constraints and to centralise the process of customs collection. When young, educated tax officials (*nagad ras*) were appointed and given salaries rather than a percentage of the collection, the result was 'astonishing' (Marcus 1987: 42).

Equally significant was the development of domestic trade. The appearance of garrison towns (*ketema*) that served as military and administrative centres throughout the highland periphery provided the demand and the infrastructure for it. In these towns, the ruling class of *neftegna*, soldiers, clergymen and landlords congregated, representatives of a market demand exceeding the scope of the traditional rural markets operating on barter. These towns provided not only demand but permanent market places with stalls, shops and warehouses, as well as professional traders and monetised transactions.

The construction of the Djibouti-Addis Ababa railway – begun in 1897 and completed in 1917 – gave a great boost to foreign trade. The link to the sea marked the start of an export trade in hides, skins and coffee that has remained a staple feature of Ethiopia's foreign commerce to this day. The first step towards weaving a communications network to link the far flung provinces of the empire was taken by Menelik, who insisted that a telegraph line accompany the rail line from Djibouti to Addis Ababa. Soon, it was combined with a telephone link. In 1933, a radio station was inaugurated, a school for radio operators opened, and a Ministry of Posts, Telegraphs and Telephones was founded. Radio broadcasting began a few days before the Italian invasion, in time to carry Haile Selassie's futile appeal to the world, on 13 September, 1935, to come to his aid.

Italian occupation (1936–1941)

Mussolini's regime in Italy revived that nation's ambitions for expansion in the Horn of Africa, and after a campaign of provocation on the ground and vilification of Ethiopia internationally, it launched a two pronged invasion from Eritrea in the north and Somalia in the southeast. The Italians committed more than one-quarter of a million of their own soldiers, plus a large number of auxiliaries from Eritrea and Somalia. The number of Ethiopians who responded to the Emperor's call on 2 October 1936 was greater:

> Everyone will now be mobilized and all boys old enough to carry a spear will be sent to Addis Ababa. Married men will take their wives to carry food and cook. Those without wives will take any woman without a husband. Women

> with small babies need not go. The blind, those who cannot carry a spear, are exempted. Anyone found at home after receipt of this order will be hanged. (Nelson & Kaplan 1981: 243)

Determined not to repeat the fiasco of Adwa, the Italians waged a ruthless campaign using aircraft and mustard gas. The Ethiopians fought bravely but in vain. Haile Selassie went abroad, and in May 1936 made a dramatic appearance before the League of Nations in Geneva to deliver a memorable and prophetic speech pointing out to his cynical audience the inevitable and universal consequences of their timidity. This performance gained the diminutive ruler world-wide recognition and a store of sympathy that proved inexhaustible.

Inside Ethiopia, a resistance movement soon became a major problem for the Italians. Collaboration with the invader was also not unknown. As was to be expected, the most prominent collaborators were to be found among the enemies of the Shoa regime. Released from prison, Ras Hailu was restored to the governorship of Gojjam. One Tigray lord and imperial son-in-law, Haile Selassie Gugsa, assisted the invaders, and another, Ras Seyoum Mangasha, apparently came to an understanding with them and was allowed to keep his position.

Not surprisingly, the abrupt collapse of Ethiopian rule in the periphery gave vent to acts of revenge and hopes of emancipation among the subject peoples. The Guji rejoiced with a song: 'We were jailed and released by Atala (a Guji balabbat); we were jailed and bitten by Habasha; now it's our time, we have the opportunity to retaliate against them' (Tadesse Berisso, 2006: 215). When the Italians arrived, a Selti chieftain named Sugato Zayni greeted them saying: 'When a government comes, I welcome it, when it leaves I say farewell, like to a guest' (Bustorf 1997: 6). There were many such incidents in the highland periphery. A Wollo Oromo chieftain, Amedi Ali, was made *ras* by the Italians in 1939. Abba Jiffar and some forty other Oromo dignitaries were taken to Rome in May 1938 to meet Mussolini. Another traditional figure who courted Italian favour was Emir Sufian Abdulahi of Harar. Other Oromo fought against the invader.

After the Emperor's flight abroad and before the Italians arrived in the southwest, an attempt was made to forestall Italian occupation by placing this Oromo region under British protection. Petitions signed by leading Oromo chiefs in Wallega, Jimma and Illubabor were submitted to the British Consul at Gore, proposing the formation of a Western Oromo Confederation to be ruled by Britain under a mandate from the League of Nations. The Consul reported to London:

> The Galla provinces have disarmed the Amhara officials and soldiers in their areas and the Galla hereditary chiefs have assumed control of the government in their areas. All Galla chiefs have sent seals and signatures and delegations asking the League of Nations to place the provinces of Western Abyssinia under British mandate.[1]

An Oromo delegation met British officials in Gambella on 8 June 1936. It

[1] F.O. 371, 20206, HN 09582. 24 June 1936.

carried a similar appeal signed by the traditional rulers of Leqa Nekempt, Leqa Qellam, Jimma and Beni Shangul.[2] Britain did not respond.

Initially, the Italians confiscated the land holdings of the Ethiopian royal family, the grand nobility and those who led the resistance against them, declaring them state domain. The Ethiopian Orthodox Church was allowed to retain its vast landholdings in return for a promise of cooperation (Haile Larebo 2006: 242). Italian propaganda against Ethiopia had made the *gabbar* system its focus and its abolition a priority. Finally, they freed all the slaves. All in all, the Italian interlude brought welcome relief from the burden of Ethiopian rule to the people of the periphery, something that made its restoration in 1941 all the more unwelcome. Nevertheless, despite the Italians' systematic attempt to foment dissension by courting the Muslim population, they failed to gain the active support of that or any other section of Ethiopia's population.[3]

Brief though it was, the Italian occupation unwittingly made a significant contribution to the project of state-building. The Italians invested heavily in road construction over terrain so difficult that it had prevented the use of the wheel until then. Using native labour, the Italians constructed 3,200km of metalled and tarred roads with innumerable bridges within twenty-four months, and completed 6,400km of all-weather road before they left. Urbanisation also made progress during a period that saw the proliferation of provincial towns linked by the new road network, and the introduction of an elementary form of urban architecture in stone and brick to replace the traditional wattle.

Another aspect of the Italian episode was that it facilitated the process of centralisation of state power after liberation. The war and occupation accelerated the disintegration of an already crumbling quasi-feudal system, whose capacity was stretched to the limit by the expansion. The Abyssinian traditional elite that had strenuously opposed the rise of monarchical absolutism was gravely weakened; many of its leading figures had been killed or compromised by collaboration with the enemy. The violence of that episode decimated and uprooted the ruling class in the periphery, as most of the *neftegna* abandoned their landholdings for the duration of the occupation. The experience of this class during the Italian occupation sharpened an awareness of its vulnerability in the midst of a hostile *gabbar* population, and made it much more accepting of tightened central government authority than it had been previously.

Integrating the periphery

The Italians were ousted from Ethiopia by a two-pronged British attack; from the south via Kenya and the west via Sudan. An Ethiopian contin-

[2] Habte Mariam of Leqa Nekempt, Yohannes Joti and Hosana Joti of Leqa Qellam, Abba Jiffar of Jimma and Sheikh Khojali of Gubba.

[3] Non-Abyssinians were given special consideration. Islam was promoted, Quranic schools and mosques received grants, Islamic law and courts were given official status, and Arabic was made an official language in the non-Amharigna-speaking provinces.

gent accompanied them from Sudan, and in May 1941 Haile Selassie made a liberator's triumphant entry into Addis Ababa. He faced no opposition on reclaiming the throne and was soon able to gather the reins of power in his hands once more. Those who led the resistance against the Italians were rewarded with titles, appointments and land grants. Prominent collaborators were punished. The most serious challenge to the Amhara regime came from the Abyssinian heartland, the province of Tigray, where the provincial dynasty was tainted by its collaboration with the enemy. After liberation, the province was put under Shoa governors and garrisoned with government soldiers who 'ate' the land. The result was a spontaneous rebellion that brought Tigray nobles and peasants together in fierce battles against government troops lasting several months in 1943. The rebellion was finally put down with great force and heavy rebel casualties, adding fresh fuel to the store of Tigray resentment against the Amhara regime.

Reforming the provincial administration to gain effective control of a periphery unsettled by the Italian occupation was a priority. The geographic pattern was changed. Some thirty-four provincial units existed before the Italian interlude. The administrative map was redrawn afterwards, with these units integrated into twelve large provinces: Tigray, Begemdir and Semien, Wollo, Gojjam, Wallega, Shoa, Arsi, Sidamo, Kaffa, Gemu Gofa, Illubabor and Hararge. Later, Hararge was split to create Bale province, and the annexation of Eritrea in 1962 brought the number of provinces to fourteen. The provinces (*Teklay Ghizat*) were divided into sub-provinces (*Awraja Ghizat*), in turn divided into districts (*Woreda Ghizat*), and further sub-divided into sub-districts (*Mikitil Woreda*); the last were abolished later. A serious handicap in the process of periphery integration was lack of reform in the recruitment of provincial officialdom. Although the Abyssinian nobility's prerogative to state office was somewhat circumscribed, provincial administration remained its preserve. The paramount criterion being loyalty to the Emperor, provincial officials as a rule had neither modern education nor any other relevant qualifications. They were not expected to display any accomplishments in office, other than collect taxes efficiently and maintain what the government called 'calmness' (*tseteta*) loosely translated as 'security'.

In 1942 the provincial administration was brought under the jurisdiction of the Ministry of Interior, and a list of regulations was issued to control its activities. The most important change was the granting of salaries to provincial officials for the first time in Ethiopian history. In turn, they were forbidden to impose taxes or dues other than those fixed by law, to collect money from the people, or accept gifts in any form. Thus, many extractions that accompanied landholding rights attached to state office were eliminated, bringing a measure of relief to the *gabbar*. Army generals were put in charge of the police, security and prisons in each province, and tax collectors (*bejirond*) were sent to represent the Ministry of Finance. The Ministry of Justice also set up its own provincial network, thus completing the holy trinity – tax collector, policeman, judge – of state representatives in the countryside. Remarkably, the regulations issued in 1942 were the sole innovation in the sphere of provincial administration until the end of the imperial era. 'The system at most maintains order and collects taxes' was one assessment (Cohen & Weintraub 1975: 91). The criteria for recruitment of provincial officials were not improved, and they continued to regard appointment as licence to accumulate wealth at the expense of the people they governed. After the attempted coup d'état in 1961, the Ministry of Interior repeatedly cautioned provincial officials to refrain from abusing their authority, and to treat people as citizens rather than subjects.[4]

Reforming the centre

In the second phase of his reign, Haile Selassie was able to recruit a group of younger, educated men of humble social background to positions of power in the central government: men he had chosen himself, whose careers had unfolded under his personal aegis, and who depended upon him exclusively for their position. They formed a corps of imperial retainers and functioned as the physical extension of the imperial person himself. People from Shoa remained predominant in the higher ranks.[5] Muslims neither sought, nor were sought, for membership in the corps of imperial retainers who transformed the central government through a process of modernisation-cum-centralisation. The first decree issued in 1943 reorganised and expanded the ministerial system, defining the functions and powers of ministers, and a Council of Ministers was established headed by a Prime Minister. Vis-à-vis the Emperor, they were given essentially advisory powers, which suited Haile Selassie's inordinate concern for his own power and characterised his style of rule. As a foreign adviser to the regime put it, the intention 'was not to liberalize government but to centralize it' (Spencer 1984: 131).

Imposing a uniform legal system throughout the state is a key element in the process of centre/periphery integration. A Codification Commission composed of foreigners and Ethiopians drafted a series of codes – Civil, Commercial, Maritime, Criminal Procedure, Civil Procedure – and revised the 1930 Penal Code. The Civil Code avoided giving offence to Abyssinian customs by opting, as its main author stated, 'pour une solution transactionelle' (David 1967: 5). Thus, though monogamy was upheld, customary marriage – which could be polygamous – was not prohibited, and a third alternative, civil marriage, was offered. There was less concern for the customary practices of non-Christians. Certain provisions relating to marriage, divorce, minimum age, and family property ran contrary to Muslim religious law and practice. The drafting committee consulted

[4] *Journal of the Ministry of Interior.* (1963) Year 2, No. 2. (Amharigna).

[5] One study estimated that 62% of those appointed to vice-ministerial and ministerial posts were natives of Shoa (Clapham 1969: 77). According to an Oromo who made it to the top, Haile Selassie's closest aides 'had determined and striven to reserve all the key positions, if not all the power, of the state for natives of Shoa as a monopoly' (Emmanuel Abraham 1995: 178).

Christian Church leaders and others versed in Abyssinian culture, but Muslims were not asked to express an opinion on the draft code. 'The Civil Code was made for the more advanced populations of Ethiopia and Eritrea', explained its principal author. 'Its application in other regions is not excluded, but cannot be envisaged in the near future' (ibid.: 679). However, the revised Penal Code followed the example of the old one that exempted Muslims from the penalties for bigamy.

The same evasiveness kept the Muslim courts in juridical limbo. These were first formally recognised by the Italians, and the imperial government followed suit in 1942, extending recognition to the *Kadi* courts, and a Sharia court of appeal was established in Addis Ababa. In 1944 the structure was enlarged with the addition of *Naiba* courts, and was brought under the Ministry of Justice. However, the revised Penal Code expressly outlawed customary institutions and appeared to nullify the Muslim courts, while the Courts Proclamation of 1962 and the later Civil Procedure Code of 1965 did not even mention them. Muslims petitioned the Emperor and questions were asked in Parliament. They were reassured that the Muslim courts could function informally, but no further mention was made of them officially.

The 1931 Constitution was revised in 1955, on the occasion of the twenty-fifth anniversary of Haile Selassie's coronation. The basic motives for the revision were the same ones that had inspired the constitutional exercise in 1931, namely, legitimisation of monarchical absolute rule and concern for Ethiopia's image abroad. Other African states, soon to become independent, were adopting constitutions of the most advanced kind. Eritrea, with which Ethiopia had formed a federal union, already possessed a modern constitution. Far from threatening the authority of the throne, the revision greatly reinforced it. The emperor was vested not only with 'supreme power' but with the 'sovereignty of the Empire', a provision that had clear implications for Eritrea's relationship with Addis Ababa. The usual list of freedoms and rights of the people were also included in what amounted to a grand exercise in formalism. Few Ethiopians took the constitution seriously, and the masses were unaware it existed. The introduction of elections for the Chamber of Deputies on the basis of universal adult suffrage was a purely cosmetic gesture, while the Senate remained an appointed chamber reserved for retired nobles and high officials. In theory, Parliament was entitled to play a role in initiating and approving legislation. In practice, legislative traffic was predictably one way, with Parliament's role being less than minimal. As it turned out, this was not an unmitigated loss, since the best known example of parliamentary initiative was the addition of flogging as a punishment in the Penal Code of 1957.

Land and the peasant

The expropriation of land in the highland periphery continued uninterrupted throughout this period, as did its distribution to individuals and groups. The war with Italy produced a large crop of candidates. A series of declarations in the early 1940s granted land to war veterans, widows and the orphans of fallen soldiers. In 1952 it was declared that all landless Ethiopians were entitled to half a *gasha* of land but few actually received any.[6] In 1958 all members of the armed forces and police became eligible for land grants of one *gasha* each, and the same entitlement was given to civil servants with five years of service. Throughout this period, those who held land in exchange for service to the state – civil or military – were allowed to convert part of it to private property, and in 1967 all military personnel were permitted to do so. As a result, *gabbar* settled on this land were converted to tenants.

In its persistent efforts to increase the flow of revenue from land, the regime imposed a series of new taxes on the rural sector. In 1942 it established a uniform rate of taxation payable in the newly issued official currency. At the same time, it abolished certain forms of tribute paid by the *gabbar* to the landlord, such as labour service, the provision of grass and firewood, and gifts on feast days and other occasions. Another innovation was the issuing of tax receipts by the tax collector. In 1944 a new tax schedule was set; all previous taxes were repealed and replaced by two new taxes, the *asrat* (now called 'tax in lieu of tithe') and the land tax, the rates of which differed among provinces – Shoa paying the lowest. Since the proclamation repealed 'any other taxes, services and fees heretofore payable', in some areas the *gabbar* on church land refused to fulfil their traditional obligations, obliging the government to issue another proclamation explaining that church land was exempted. In addition to the land tax and the tithe, two more taxes were levied on land, an education tax in 1947 and a health tax in 1959.

The combined tax burden fell on the shoulders of the peasants, who were forced to pay all four types of taxes according to the size and category of land they cultivated. The landlords not only escaped taxation on the tribute they collected from the *gabbar*, but also continued to appropriate part of the land tax they collected for the state. The Church collected and retained all the taxes paid by the peasantry with the exception of the health tax. In short, according to the convoluted taxation system that existed until 1967, the landlord class was not taxed either on its holdings or on the revenue derived from them. On the contrary, it continued to appropriate part of the land tax paid by the *gabbar*, though not as large a part as before. A final attempt to increase revenue from the land was made in an amendment to the income tax schedule in 1967. It abolished the tax in lieu of tithe (*asrat*) and replaced it with a graduated tax on agricultural income. Landlords now were to pay income tax for the first time.

The process of rationalising the expropriation of land in the periphery and making it irreversible started in the twilight of the imperial era and was halted by its closure in 1974. The intention was to make private property the only form of land tenure, a move urged on the regime by the

[6] According to a report based on government data, of the total land granted between 1952 and 1968, less than 5% went to landless peasants (See Markakis 1974: 349).

World Bank and other international institutions. To that end, a proclamation in 1967 abolished all forms of *gult* rights on land, and decreed that landlords and peasants pay tax directly to the state, thereby establishing private rights of ownership. Not all the intermediaries and privileges were eliminated. The Church retained its traditional privileges intact, and the *balabbat* and village chiefs (*Chika Shum*) who acted as tax collectors continued to retain their share.

The removal of the last feudal trappings surrounding property relationships began to reveal the massive and irremediable alienation of land in the highland periphery. A first intimation appeared in a series of land tenure surveys carried out by the Ministry of Land Reform and Administration in the 1960s that showed the extent of different forms of landholding in the various provinces. Completed before the final abolition of *gult*, they showed the extent of absentee ownership and its corollary, tenancy. In the highland periphery the findings were staggering. Tenancy exceeded 50% of holdings in three provinces and 40% in four others. By contrast, tenancy and absentee ownership were minor phenomena in the Abyssinian provinces. In their case, the surveys revealed a dismal pattern of land fragmentation and dwarf family holdings. Two-thirds of holdings in three northern provinces measured less than one hectare in size, and close to one-half less than half a hectare (Markakis 1974: 81). The Abyssinian peasantry was living on the edge of subsistence.

The regime's efforts to increase the flow of revenue from land during the postwar period failed miserably. Tax revenue from that source hardly changed between 1944 and 1967, and the contribution of agriculture to state revenue declined steadily for twenty-three years, reaching the point where the sector that employed about 87% of the population and produced about 65%of the gross domestic product contributed less than seven percent of the state's ordinary revenue.

Modernisation

In the postwar period the imperial regime exerted some effort to promote a modern sector in the economy relying on foreign investment. To compensate for the lack of conspicuous economic attraction, it enacted an Investment Code praised as 'one of Africa's most liberal'.[7] Foreign capital was invested in manufacturing for import substitution, and soon the country acquired a modest modern economic sector that was mostly foreign owned.[8] First allowed in 1962, labour union organisation spread quickly, and by the end of the decade it had enlisted more than 50,000 workers, the sum total employed in modern industry. Unprotected by the state, Ethiopian workers were harshly victimised. Employers were free to use any means to cut labour costs, and they used all the familiar ones and

[7] *New York Times*, 17 June 1967.

[8] The contribution of manufacturing to the GDP in 1969 was 4.6% (*Statistical Abstract* 1970: 125).

then some more. The result was a fledgling working class disgruntled and ripe for political radicalisation.

The location of the new sectors of economic activity was important for the process of integration. Nearly all the investment in manufacturing and commercial agriculture went to the periphery outside the Abyssinian homeland. There were sound economic and political reasons for it. Briefly put, this was where land could be appropriated without economic or political cost, where a cheap and docile labour force was readily available, combined with the feasibility of irrigation, the presence of coffee, and the regime's desire to enrich Shoa, its home base. Furthermore, it was also where the railway connection to Djibouti and the outside world ran, with the road to the port of Assab running almost parallel to it. A string of towns that emerged along its length of the railway from Addis Ababa to Dire Dawa hosted the entire industrial plant, save what was found in Eritrea. Nearly the whole of this was located in Oromo inhabited land. As far as agriculture was concerned, commercialisation was most impressively introduced in the eastern lowland periphery in the Awash Valley, where land and water were simply seized and the pastoralist inhabitants displaced. In the coffee producing region of the southern highland periphery, a start was made on modernising production and processing the berry that had previously been picked in the wild. In Eritrea, Italian investment went into the production of cotton, fruit and vegetables, and in the northwest, oil seeds were produced in the Humera border region.

Agriculture was the mainstay of the export trade. Coffee was the leading export, followed by skins and hides. However, exports consistently and increasingly fell behind imports, opening a yawning deficit gap that became a structural flaw in the country's economy and has been a permanent threat to its stability to this day. The regime took care to preserve certain lucrative trade monopolies – coffee, tobacco, petrol and cement for the state. Traditional agriculture throughout the rest of Ethiopia stagnated. Nothing was done to change its subsistence nature, or to raise food production for the domestic market. From 1963 to 1973, agriculture was allotted 4.2% of the state's combined ordinary and capital expenditure. With a high rate of population growth, food production per capita fell steadily, setting the stage for the shocking famines that swept the country in the last quarter of the 20th century.

Urbanisation was equally important for the process of integration. The official estimate of Ethiopia's urban population in 1970 was approximately 2.3 million, about 9.4% of the estimated total population.[9] Addis Ababa expanded rapidly as the main centre of economic activity, and its population reached the one million mark in the mid-1970s. A string of satellite towns along the railway line contained the rest of the country's industrial establishment and much of its urban growth. Most impressive was the growth of many old garrison towns on the highland periphery. A survey in the mid-1960s showed that out of twenty-three major towns, fourteen were

[9] Ethiopia had yet to carry out a population census and all figures are estimates. Given the fact that the definition of 'town' was based on a minimum population of 2,000, this particular estimate was more than a little exaggerated,

in that region. With the exception of a textile factory in the town of Bahir Dar on Lake Tana, no investment worth mentioning was made in the Abyssinian provincial capitals of the north, and they remained stagnant throughout this period. The annexation of Eritrea boosted the country's urban assets considerably, the most important being its capital Asmara and the two ports on the Red Sea, Massawa and Assab.

A striking feature of urban growth in the highland periphery was its ethnic and cultural diversity. It appeared that a majority in some towns and a near majority in most others were immigrants from the north. Most of these towns owed their origin to the administrative and military activities of the state, and the core of their original population consisted of Abyssinian officials, soldiers, landlords, settlers and clergy. A steady flow from the northern provinces reinforced this element, and most northerners on the highland periphery congregated in towns.[10] Most came as single males and mixed uninhibitedly with other groups, taking wives where they found them and fathering children who, in most cases, took the superior ethnic identity of their fathers. A second source of immigration into these towns was from the variegated population of the highland periphery itself, particularly groups specialising in trade, like the Gurage, and crafts, like the Dorze. The towns in the periphery became melting pots where ethnic identities were commingled and diluted, the foundations of a national economy were laid, and the Amharigna language, promoted by education and economic interaction, was the *lingua franca*. There was no counter-migration from the periphery to the Abyssinian provinces in the north, and the towns there remained placidly homogeneous.

Urban growth provided the context for yet another development impacting on the process of integration, that is, modern education. Starting after liberation in 1941, the imperial regime made a notable effort in this field. A Ministry of Education and Fine Arts was established soon afterwards, the first budget for education was adopted for the year 1943-44, and the first secondary school, named after Haile Selassie, opened at the same time. Expansion was slow but steady. In the two decades between 1950 and 1970, overall expansion was almost tenfold. Teacher training institutes were founded, a decision was taken to use English as the language of instruction beginning with the fifth grade – Amharigna was used in the first four grades – and secondary school teachers were hired from abroad. The aims of elementary education were defined in 1963-4 as 'loyalty, unity, citizenship, happiness, usefulness, productivity, and preparation for secondary education' (Tesfaye & Taylor 1976: 390).

Although enrolment increased, particularly at the primary level, it still represented a small percentage of the school age population. In 1969, enrolment at the primary level stood at 14.1%, and at the secondary level at 1.9% of the relevant age group. There was great gender disparity in enrolment, with female participation at less than one-third at the

[10] An official *Survey of Major Towns* carried out in the mid-1960s showed those who claimed Amharigna as their mother tongue exceeded one-third of the population in the towns of the highland periphery.

primary and less that one-fifth at the secondary level. There was marked disparity also on ethnic and religious lines. Abyssinians were privileged on two counts. Firstly, they were the most urbanised group, because the *neftegna* landlord class and state officials in the periphery congregated in towns where educational facilities were concentrated. Secondly, with the exception of the Tigray, they enjoyed the advantage of having Amharigna as their mother tongue. The results were seen in the composition of students passing the examination for entry to the country's sole university, founded in 1950 in Addis Ababa. In 1968, 60% of those who sat the examination were Amharigna-speakers, as was 55% of the entering class.

The educational policy of the imperial regime posed problems for Muslim communities and caused considerable resentment on their part. Quranic schools maintained by them received no state aid of any kind. The regime claimed that religious education was not the responsibility of the state, and that Quranic schools, as well as the traditional schools of the Orthodox Church, should be self-supporting. Muslims pointed out that Orthodox Church education was subsidised by state grants of land to churches and clergy, the tax exemption of Church property and income, and the retention by the Church of the education tax on its lands. Given the fact that many of the *gabbar* cultivating Church land in the periphery were Muslims, the education tax paid by them was in effect used to support Christian education.

A greater cause for resentment was the ban on the teaching of Arabic in state schools. Muslims deemed it essential; otherwise, they feared, the next generation of Muslims would be unable to read the documents that expound the tenets of their faith. The regime's policy on this subject, as in all matters pertaining to Islam, was never made explicit. An official memorandum issued in 1944, apparently inspired by British advisors attached to the government at the time, stated that Arabic would be taught in Muslim areas, and other indigenous languages would be used in the early stages of education. That remained a dead letter, and neither Arabic nor any indigenous languages were ever taught in state schools. Muslim communities maintained private elementary schools with a modernised curriculum and Arabic as the medium of instruction. A few of these were supervised by the Ministry of Education, and were assisted through the provision of teachers paid by the state for the teaching of Amharigna, English and modern subjects.

During the federation, Eritrea maintained a bilingual system of education, with Arabic and Tigrigna as the languages of instruction at the elementary level in Muslim and Christian communities respectively, and English as the language of instruction at the secondary level; Amharigna was taught as a subject. After the abolition of the federation in 1962, Amharigna was imposed as the language of instruction at the elementary level. Tigrigna was abolished fairly quickly, and the teaching of Arabic was phased out gradually by the simple means of not providing teachers for it.

The participation of Muslims in modern education under the imperial regime was very limited. The imposition of Amharigna, the ban on Arabic, the obligation to attend school on Friday, the widespread use of Christian clergy to teach religion thinly disguised as moral education, and the predominance of Christian teachers and administrators created the impression among Muslims that state education was designed to propagate the official religion of the state. At the very least, Muslims feared such education would alienate their children from the faith of their parents. Needless to say, very few Muslim girls entered the education process at all.

Militarisation

'Preparation for war has been the great state-building activity', according to Tilly (1975: 73) and the founding of a professional army is the first step in that process. It is also 'the bulkiest, riskiest, costliest, and perhaps the most influential enterprise of Western states throughout their modern history' (ibid.: 410). Haile Selassie began by forming a special unit specifically for his own protection, initially known as the Better Armed Unity (*Malafia Birat Yaj*) and later, the Imperial Bodyguard. In 1928, young Ethiopian graduates of local schools were sent to the St Cyr Military Academy in France. When they returned, they became instructors in the Holeta Military Training School founded in 1934. The first modern military training institution in Ethiopia, Holeta, selected its cadets from promising graduates of local schools. In 1935, a start was made towards establishing a modern police force for the capital with British assistance. Airplanes flown by foreign mercenaries completed the preparations the regime had time to make before the Italian attack in 1936.

After World War II the growth of the military proceeded further and faster than any of the developments discussed above, progressing far beyond the capacity of the domestic economy and native technology to maintain it. Militarisation in this remote corner of Africa was encouraged by the world superpower as a side show of the Cold War, and Ethiopia became dependent on foreign support quite early. The country came under British military administration before World War II ended, and a British Military Mission to Ethiopia began work in 1944. The relationship did not last. There was friction between the British, who preferred to keep their options concerning the future of the Horn open, and the Ethiopians who rightly suspected these options included designs on their territory. Britain was uncertain whether building up Ethiopia's military capacity was conducive to its own position as a colonial power in the Horn. At any rate, Britain lacked the means to meet Ethiopian demands for all types of assistance. The regime in Addis Ababa read the signs of the time correctly, and proceeded to attach itself to the rising superpower across the Atlantic.

United States involvement in Africa followed the retreat of European colonial rule. Among the first steps in that direction was the takeover of an Italian radio station near Asmara in Eritrea, where the Americans went on to establish a major communications base devoted to gathering intelligence worldwide. When the British military advisors left Ethiopia in 1951, they were replaced by Americans. In 1953, the two countries concluded agreements governing the lease of the Kagnew base in Asmara by the United States and the provision of military aid to Ethiopia.

From that time on, American aid fuelled a militarisation drive without parallel in sub-Saharan Africa. Initially it undertook to equip and train three Ethiopian army divisions of 6,000 men each. Upon gaining independence in 1960, Somalia also applied to the Americans for aid. Ethiopia not only managed to block the Somali bid but, exploiting Somalia's turn soon afterwards to the Soviet Union, secured additional aid from the United States to raise a fourth army division. The United States also provided airplanes for its client's Air Force and assistance for its fledgling navy. In the mid-1960s, Ethiopia's armed forces exceeded 40,000, and were by far the largest military establishment in sub-Saharan Africa at the time. In the latter part of the 1960s, a fifth division was formed, as well as paratroops and commando units trained by Israelis to fight the nationalist rebellion in Eritrea. A second military academy opened in Harar in 1957 staffed by Indian officers, followed by an Air Force academy staffed by Swedes and a Naval College in Massawa staffed by Norwegians.

Up to 1970, Ethiopia had received 60% of all American military aid to Africa. Starting in 1953, Military Assistance Advisory Groups (MAAG) were attached to all branches and training institutions of the Ethiopian armed forces, nearly 3,000 Ethiopian officers went to training courses in the United States, and a military mapping mission prepared the first detailed maps of the country using aerial photography. Even so, the Ethiopian state had to spend a sizeable portion of its meagre resources for defence and internal security. The share of the published budget for the ministries of Defence and Interior reached 40% of the total current expenditure in the 1960s.

Haile Selassie took great care in grooming the men who commanded the instruments of force, keeping them under close scrutiny. He did not adopt the American model of a unified supreme command for the armed services, reserving that role for himself. Special care was lavished on the Imperial Bodyguard Division, whose strength rose to some 10,000 men. It had its own training school and produced hand-picked officers, whose careers unfolded literally under the eyes of the Emperor. The Imperial Bodyguard was the best equipped unit in the Ethiopian army, and had facilities designed to monitor radio communications within the military establishment, as protection against conspiracies. Ironically, it was this coddled unit, led by its commander, which mutinied in 1960 and attempted to overthrow it founder and patron. The mutiny failed when the regular army opposed it.

The ethnic composition of the military was far more diverse than the civil branch of the state. Though relevant data are not available, it was generally believed that the ranks of the common soldiery included a large number of Oromo. The hierarchy also included Oromo officers, several of whom reached the rank of general, as did four Gurage officers. The bulk of the officer corps was of Abyssinian origin, and Muslims were conspicuously absent in it.

Living above its means militarily, Ethiopia became a dependant of the United States and a pawn in the Cold War. This had serious consequences for its standing in the region, where it was seen as an outpost of American imperialism and an ally of Israel. Consequently, Arab states such as Egypt, Syria, Iraq and Libya felt justified in their support of the Eritrean nationalists, as did Sudan and Somalia nearer to home. In this hostile regional climate, Ethiopia's age-old sense of isolation and siege mentality intensified, and it became routine for successive regimes in Addis Ababa to charge their Arab neighbours with plotting to dismember it. 'In the case of Ethiopia, the Arab objective appears to be a complete or partial disintegration of the Ethiopian state', was the comment of a prominent Ethiopian academic not long ago (Mesfin W/M 1999: 84).

Nation-building

If only because it feared rebellion, the ruling class became concerned with the political implications of ethnic and cultural heterogeneity among the subjects of the empire, and it was only natural that they should wish to replace such diversity with a homogeneous 'nation'. State builders have always feared 'the failure to homogenize increased the likelihood that a state...would fragment into its cultural subdivisions' (Tilly 1975: 44). Homogeneity and a shared national identity endow the state with legitimacy and reduce the need to use force as the instrument of rule. Striving for legitimacy, 'empires construct themselves around a specific culture that they intend to defend, promote, or possibly expand' (Badie 2000: 48). 'National integration' of the post-colonial state was the first political task undertaken in Africa, a choice condemned by a far-sighted historian as the 'curse' of modern Africa and 'the black man's burden' (Davidson 1982). Saddling itself with this burden, Ethiopia has been heavily encumbered by it ever since.

It was taken for granted that integration meant assimilation and Ethiopia was to become Abyssinia *writ large*. This was succinctly stated by a member of the first generation of Ethiopians educated abroad:

> The policy of assimilation should be at the top of our reforms; for without the union of the Amhara and Galla, it is impossible to visualize the future with certainty or enthusiasm...It is for the Galla to become Amhara (not the other way round); for the latter posses a written language, a superior religion and superior customs and mores.[11]

Language, the emblem of culture, is the cutting edge in the process of homogenisation. 'Cultural and linguistic unification is accompanied by the imposition of the dominant language and culture as legitimate, and by the rejection of all other languages into indignity' (Bourdieu 1994: 17). Traditionally known as *lesane negus* ('the King's language'), Amharigna was the main tool in the assimilation process inevitably dubbed 'amharisation'. A Ministry of Education report in 1955 declared: 'the promotion of Amharic at the various levels...is an important task that is fundamental to national

[11] Cited in Bahru Zewde (2002: 132-133).

integration.'[12] To smooth the path of the preferred official medium, the regime sought to eradicate all other indigenous languages, including Tigrigna. Amharigna was named the official language of the state in the 1955 Constitution but, long before that, no vernacular was allowed to be printed, broadcast, taught, or spoken on public occasions. Private schools were permitted to use foreign languages as long as they taught Amharigna as a subject, but no school could use an indigenous language, or teach it as a subject. Proficiency in the official language was required for entry to the University, although its language of instruction was English.

The exclusiveness afforded to the official language was reflected in the ethnic composition of university students. In the entering class of 1968, Amharigna-speakers accounted for 55.5%, Tigrigna-speakers (including Eritreans) for 23.5%, Oromo-speakers for 10.4%, and Gurage-speakers for 2.3% (Cooper & King 1976: 273). A survey in the same year of students who sat for the Ethiopian School Leaving Certificate examination upon completing secondary level showed 60% Amharigna-speakers speakers and 22% Tigrigna-speakers, including Eritreans (Langmuir & Getachew 1968). Needless to say, the blanket ban on languages other than the official one stymied the study of the language, history and culture of subordinate groups.

To the outside world, the imperial regime presented Ethiopia as an ancient society welded in unity by its history and devotion to the Christian faith. Addressing the United States Congress in 1954, Haile Selassie described his realm as the 'largest Christian state in the Middle East'.[13] On the subject of religion, the regime's policy was ostensibly based on a statement attributed to the Emperor: to wit, 'religion is personal, the state is for all', despite the glaring fact that the Ethiopian Orthodox Church was the official state church, the owner of immense wealth and beneficiary of state largesse. The pursuit of homogeneity reached a peak when the regime began to 'abyssinianise' place names in the periphery. For instance, the Oromo towns of Adama and Wolliso in southern Shoa became Nazareth and Ghion (Zion) respectively.

The Ethiopian Church lacked missionary zeal and did little to spread the faith in the periphery, where it was part of the *neftegna* ruling class and resented by the *gabbar*. In the wake of the conquest, traditional rulers in the periphery who converted to Christianity sometimes brought their people to mass conversion ceremonies, where all men were baptised with the name Gebre Maryam (servant of Mary) or Wolde Maryam (son of Mary), and women took the name Wolete Maryam (daughter of Mary). No campaign was launched afterwards to promote the official creed. It was taken for granted that it would spread naturally as a result of the advantages – social, economic, political – that it offered to its adherents.

[12] Cited in Paulos Milkias (2006: 54).

[13] In a 1962 publication, *Image of Ethiopia*, prepared by the Ministry of Information in English, Islam appears only as a historical threat to Ethiopia. Another publication, *Harar*, prepared by the Ethiopian Tourism Organisation (n.d.), described the overwhelmingly Muslim province of Harar without once mentioning Islam.

Imperial overreach: the annexation of Eritrea

An opportunity to expand the imperial domain presented itself in the 1950s, when the future of Italy's former colonies in Africa – Libya, Somalia, Eritrea – was being decided by the Great Powers. Eritrea's territory comprises the northern corner of the Ethiopian plateau and a large lowland belt encircling it from the Red Sea on the east to the Sudan border on the west and north. The bulk of the Eritrean highland is a geographical extension of Tigray province in Ethiopia, and is inhabited mainly by Tigrigna-speaking Orthodox Christians. The foothills and lowland plains are home to several pastoralist groups, who are Muslim and speak different languages from those found on the plateau. Muslims also dwell on the highland. Eritrean Muslims used to have close contacts with fellow Muslims in the Sudan and across the Red Sea in Arabia. Massawa was a prime port since ancient times, coveted by every power that sought to control the Red Sea. In recent centuries, the coastal zone and Massawa itself have passed successively under the control of Arabs, Ottomans, Egyptians and Italians. In 1941 Eritrea came under British military control, and for the rest of the decade its future was contested locally and abroad.

Given the fact that it included two major ports on the Red Sea, the temptation for Addis Ababa to claim Eritrea was simply irresistible. It was also historically compelling: from the Abyssinian perspective Eritrea is a part of the motherland that was lost in recent times. In a message to the United Nations General Assembly in 1949, Haile Selassie declared: 'Time and time again, it has been clearly demonstrated that these provinces formed an integral part of Ethiopia, but were torn away from her by force of aggression.'[14] The opportunity to annex Eritrea was eagerly grasped, and the consequences proved fateful for the imperial regime and its successors. While the Great Powers argued, the Eritrean people defined the issue for themselves mainly along ethno-religious lines. Generally, Christian Eritreans, who constituted approximately half the population, supported Addis Ababa's bid for 'unification'. However their enthusiasm was tempered by Tigray hostility towards the Amhara dynasty in Ethiopia, and the knowledge that their own language was suppressed there. A small minority of Christians openly opposed Ethiopia's embrace. Unsurprisingly, the Muslims of Eritrea, who made up the other half of the population, were against joining the Christian Empire and preferred independence.

A compromise was worked out by the United Nations in 1950, giving Eritrea self-government in a federation with Ethiopia. For the first time in its modern history, the country now had access to the sea. Eritrea adopted a model constitution that accorded parity to the two religious communities in every sphere of public life. Political parties, elections, a free press, and a viable labour movement made it an unsettling contrast to the rest of the

[14] Cited in Marcus (1987: 137).

imperial domain, and was one of the motives behind the cosmetic revision of Ethiopia's constitution in 1955. It was also a glaring contradiction to the centralisation drive pursued by the imperial regime, and no sooner had the federal agreement been signed than Addis Ababa set about undermining it. Working through an accommodating clique of Christian politicians in control of Eritrea's government, Addis Ababa subverted the fragile political arrangement. Complex manoeuvres and the exercise of *force majeure* over a decade culminated in the arbitrary revocation of Eritrea's special status in 1959, and its incorporation into the imperial state in 1962.

The loss of self-government shattered the delicate compromise achieved with great difficulty in 1950. Eritrean Muslims found the balance of power turned heavily against them. Islam was relegated to unofficial status, and Arabic was eliminated from the public school system, as was Tigrigna. Parity in state employment was lost, and Muslims were supplanted by Addis Ababa's appointees. As a result of the successive departures of Italian and British administrations, the local economy had deflated, the growth of the capital city Asmara was stunted and smaller towns deteriorated rapidly. Unemployment became rife, forcing Christian Eritreans to migrate to other parts of Ethiopia to seek employment, while Muslims likewise crossed the borders to Sudan and the Red Sea.

The long list of 'liberation fronts' in the history of the Horn is headed by the Eritrean Liberation Front (ELF) formed in 1961. Its leadership came from the Muslim urban community and support came from certain Arab states and Somalia. The rebellion escalated significantly during the 1960s, forcing Addis Ababa to maintain a large military presence in the province, which made little progress in stemming the growth of the insurgency. A series of bombings and highjackings of Ethiopian Airlines aircraft in 1969 won the ELF international attention, and forced the regime in Addis Ababa to acknowledge its existence and put Eritrea under military rule. The preamble to the martial law decree summarised the centre's perception of challenges from the periphery, something that has not changed to this day. It began: 'Whereas, certain foreign governments have, within their respective territories, organised and trained bandits, supplied these bandits with modern arms, money and para-military personnel, and supported them to infiltrate the territory of Ethiopia, for the purpose of undermining the territorial integrity of Ethiopia…'[15]

Christian participation in the rebellion was initially limited and highly selective. It came from the generation of students and recent graduates infused with the political radicalism that produced the radical student movement in Ethiopia in the 1960s – the vanguard of the 1974 revolution. The position of the Christian radicals in the Muslim dominated movement was anomalous, and soon brought them into conflict with the conservative ELF leadership. In 1970, the radicals, most of them Christians, left to form what eventually became known as the Eritrean Peoples Liberation Front (EPLF). Adopting a secular class ideology, the EPLF opened up new vistas for the nationalist movement, gaining support from the Christian

[15] Order No. 66 of 1970.

community, whose role had thus far been limited by the Muslim identification of the ELF. An internecine struggle broke out when the ELF tried to eliminate its rival by force. This reached a decisive stage in 1972-1974, the outcome demonstrating the younger movement's viability as a fighting force.

The annexation of Eritrea was an instance of imperial overreach that failed. The main reason for this failure was the absence of a reliable, subordinate Eritrean elite to assist Addis Ababa in administering the latest addition to the empire. As noted earlier, the centre/periphery interaction requires the collaboration of a subordinate elite with social status and political authority within its own community. The faction in Eritrea that made common cause with the imperial regime did not meet these requirements. The 'Unionists', as they were called, were nearly all highlander Christians linked to the Orthodox Church. They lacked social status in their own community; whatever authority they acquired was owed to their link with Addis Ababa, and they lost even that after the forced annexation of Eritrea. The Muslim community of Eritrea – half of the population – was simply ignored by Addis Ababa, as if it did not exist.

Summary

The structural consolidation of the Ethiopian empire followed guidelines familiar in similar enterprises throughout history. Linking the dominant elite at the centre with a subordinate elite in the periphery is the basic structural component and defining feature of imperial rule. It has three characteristics: 'a distinct core elite and distinct peripheral elites; relations of dominance between the core elite and the peripheral elites; and a hub like [sic] structure to these relations' (Motyl 1999: 133). 'Hub-like' means that there is no direct interaction among peripheral elites and regions, who interact only with and through the centre. The structure resembles a wheel with spokes but without a connecting rim. The first step in state-building is to secure control of the periphery through an administrative network that is cheap and effective: the *neftegna-gabbar* arrangement backed by the *balabbatnet* was Ethiopia's choice. Since it was funded entirely by the subject population, it was cheap. Effectiveness is judged by the efficiency with which resources are transferred from the periphery to the centre. Reforms to make the system cost effective were to follow, and it worked tolerably well in the highland periphery.

The quasi-feudal Abyssinian state that Haile Selassie inherited was far from centralised. The foundations of absolute monarchical rule were gradually put in place afterwards, making it possible to say, as in the proverb: 'in the name of the King, water stops flowing', and for an admiring subject to boast:

> The power of the Emperor of Ethiopia over the land under his jurisdiction is very wide and unlimited. He interferes both in spiritual and secular matters. By his power he can appoint, dismiss, give, take, imprison, release, kill and execute. He does these things as well as many others. The people, big and small alike,

> accept his orders with pleasure and without excuses assuming that he is the representative of God. (Mahteme Selassie 1966:58)

It was at this time also that the goal of national integration was added to the state-building project, and assimilation was chosen as the method of achieving it.

Unfortunately, the process of nation state-building was caught in a time warp. By the time the structure of the imperial state was completed and absolute monarchical rule was perfected in Ethiopia, empires and absolute monarchs had become obsolete phenomena worldwide, and the pursuit of national integration via forced assimilation had proved to be counter-productive.

6

Imperial Rule in the Periphery

Controlling the periphery, exploiting its resources and binding it closer to the centre preoccupied the imperial regime throughout its reign. It shaped nearly all the important policies it formulated and consumed most of its energy and resources, economic, military and political. By contrast, the Abyssinian provinces in the north were ignored and stagnated as a result. The focus of the regime's efforts was on the highland periphery, where a measure of success was achieved, as noted in the first part of this chapter. Little progress was seen in the lowland periphery, where the regime became involved in debilitating struggles to suppress secessionist rebellions. The rest of this chapter looks at these developments in the various lowland regions and the impact on the people living there.

Imperial rule in the highland periphery

As already noted, any attempt to assess the progress of the state building project made on the highland periphery is subject to so many caveats that one may well question if an assessment is worth attempting. However, it is impossible to ignore the trends that affected this region under imperial rule, because they determined the course of the centre/periphery interaction that followed under successive regimes. If one had to assign priority to these trends, the development of the national economy was most important factor in binding the highland periphery to the centre. Although it was not deliberate, the eventual location of this sector outside the Abyssinian homeland was crucial. The shift of the state's centre of economic gravity southwards involved people of diverse ethnic origins. Non-Abyssinians dominated trade, transport and construction, both as owners and employees, and provided the bulk of skilled and unskilled labour in the service sector, in manufacturing and commercial cultivation. Most of them lived in towns, where Amharigna was essential for communication and where their children were schooled. Inevitably, they came to see their own

Map 5 Imperial provinces

welfare as rooted in the national economy and in the state that controlled it. In sum, they were caught in a socioeconomic nexus woven by and dependent on the Ethiopian state. Such life-defining associations can be the first step towards national integration. People 'become nationalists through genuine objective, practical necessity however obscurely recognized' (Gellner 1964: 173). This was even truer of those engaged directly with the state in civil or military posts. While control of the state service and the military remained firmly in Abyssinian hands, others, particularly Oromo, were recruited through the education system and were to be found at all levels, even though non-Abyssinian representation at the top remained token.

A process of manifold social differentiation accompanied economic development and urbanisation, affecting communities in the highland periphery and influencing how 'people perceive necessity' and react politically. A widening urban-rural divide was one dimension with obvious impact, since the rural mass was little affected by the trends that were promoting integration among the townspeople. An emerging class division within the urban sector was another. In this respect it was the people involved in the various branches of the modern economy – trade, services, manufacturing, crafts, and transportation – that most felt the pull of the centre.

Another product of social differentiation was the emerging intelligentsia, whose social position was ill-defined and whose political orientation was ambivalent. Urbanisation was pulling this class away from its native ground towards the centre, and modern education was preparing it for state employment, further distancing it from its own culture. The future of this class was uncertain, since advancement was premised on assimilation in the dominant culture. Caught in this transitory and precarious position, the political orientation of the intelligentsia in the periphery was understandably ambivalent and vacillating, and to a significant extent remains so to this day. This class provided the auxiliary peripheral elite for succeeding regimes, but challenges to cultural assimilation and centre political domination also came out of it, obliging regimes to modify their relationship with the periphery in a radical way.

The appearance of other Christian sects to compete with Orthodox Christianity in its own domain introduced yet another dimension to the process of social differentiation in the highland periphery. Christianity, in its various Protestant versions, was zealously promulgated by foreign missionaries who arrived on the plateau very early, having reached Eritrea with the Italian colonisers, and moved southwest to Wallega before the Ethiopians themselves arrived there. According to its historian, 'the Evangelical movement from the very beginning of its history in Ethiopia identified itself with the periphery' (Eide 2000: 12). One result, according to Eide, was that people in the periphery 'gained a sense of worth and pride in their cultural identity' (ibid.); a strange conclusion indeed, since acculturation was the missionary goal. The imperial regime allowed missionaries to work outside the Abyssinian homeland, and sought to use them to spread Amharigna in the periphery.[1] Nevertheless, missionaries were pioneers in the use of vernacular languages for religious and secular education in Ethiopia. They translated the Bible into indigenous languages using the Geez alphabet shared by Amharigna and Tigrigna. This had an ambivalent effect. On the one hand, it spread familiarity with the alphabet of the dominant language among subordinate groups, and on the other, the appearance of a shared language in written form was a catalyst in stirring consciousness of their own ethnic identity and solidarity. It was no

[1] They were ordered to use this language in their schools, an order they were forced to circumvent because their pupils had no knowledge of Amharigna. In December 1933, the government newspaper *Berhanena Selam* criticised the missionaries for using indigenous languages 'since it creates obstacles to unity'. It was government policy, it stated, 'to have all the people in the country speak Amharigna. With language unity there is also unity of ideas.' This would facilitate mutual understanding and intermarriage. 'Thus the border peoples and the central inhabitants will become related.' Cited in Marcus (1987: 137)

accident that the seed of Oromo nationalism took root in the minds of missionary-educated youth.

Imperial rule in the lowlands

State building lagged far behind in the lowlands and integration made little progress there. Simply put, the imperial regime found the cost of integrating the lowlands uneconomical. As a British colonial official referring to the Northern Frontier District of Kenya reasoned, 'it is useless to put schemes of expenditure in an area which is costing...a great deal and yielding practically no revenue.'[2] After the massive looting of livestock by the invading armies, lowland resources proved impossible to extract by orthodox methods. Periodic forays that differed little from livestock raids were relied upon in consequence, and did little to win pastoralist acceptance of Ethiopian rule. In other respects the nomads were left to their own devices, and no attempt was made to 'civilise' them. The state kept a low profile in the pastoralist habitat. Officials stayed on the heights and seldom ventured below, and only an occasional post manned by disgruntled policemen and soldiers showed the Ethiopian flag. An observer noted: 'The country to the south and southeast was not effectively occupied by the Abyssinians because they could not live in the plains, and the way the country was dominated was from posts in the highlands, whence demands for tribute were made, and if refused, were followed by a raid.'[3] Another added: 'The Abyssinian chiefs will never go into the low country, except for a raid, with such a quick and valuable profit in sight as will compensate them for the risk of fever.'[4] Few highlanders came to make their home in the area and, as a result, even basic infrastructural facilities did not appear. Urbanisation was limited to a couple of garrison towns, and modern education facilities were not forthcoming until the 1950s, and then only at the elementary level and very sparsely.

An attempt to replicate the *balabbatnet* model by creating a reliable subordinate elite in the lowlands failed. Elders and chiefs were recognised as representatives of their clans and were expected to see that they followed government orders. Since they could not be compensated for their services with grants of land, they were given stipends. Occasionally they were appointed deputies or advisors to local governors, and sometimes were awarded traditional Abyssinian titles. Unlike their counterparts on the highland periphery, the pastoralist leadership proved of little help to the imperial administration. Chiefs and elders could not compel the nomads to follow government regulations, especially in the absence of a state infrastructure to bolster their authority, nor was the compensation they received enough of an inducement for them to alienate their communities.

Because land in the arid lowlands was not a resource coveted by highlanders, it was not parcelled out in the *neftegna-gabbar* formula, nor

[2] Cited in Markakis (1987: 31)
[3] Cited in Getachew Kassa (1983: 34)
[4] Cited in Barnes (2000: 65)

measured according to the *kelad*. Its status remained legally ambiguous, leaving it open to seizure by the state or by individuals in the future. Rights to land derived from taxation paid by the cultivators. Since pastoralists did not pay land tax, they were deemed to have no tenure rights to land, a point reiterated in legislation. According to the 1948 Proclamation on Civil Matters, the right of possession required 'continuous, uninterrupted, peaceful and public' possession for twelve years. According to the 1955 Constitution: 'All property not held and possessed in the name of any person, natural or legal, including all land in escheat, and all abandoned properties, whether real or personal, as well as all products of the subsoil, all forests and all grazing lands, water resources, lakes and territorial waters, are State Domain' (Art.130). And according to the Civil Code of 1960: 'Immovable assets in Ethiopia which are vacant and without a master shall be the property of the state' (Art. 1194). Two issues that concerned pastoralists – what constitutes possession, and whether payment of the livestock tax established the right of possession – remained unresolved. In the twilight of the imperial era, a legal advisor to the Ministry of Land Reform and Administration found the legal situation 'complex, indeed confused', and correctly predicted that 'in such circumstances the considerable weight given by the courts to Government arguments on basic issues of legal policy might result in holding in the Government's favour' (Bruce, 1972: 19).

In 1950 the government imposed a '*zelan*' (nomad) tax at the rate of 0.50 birr per camel, 0.25 per cattle, horse, mule, donkey, and 0.05 per goat and sheep. Sparsely manned police posts and finance offices were set up in the outlying areas, and local officials were put under great pressure to collect taxes – no mean task given the scarce resources at their disposal, and the reluctance of the pastoralists to pay up. It was during this period that firearms became available in the pastoralist habitat. They were first seen in the lowlands when Ethiopian troops arrived to plant the imperial flag and set up garrisons. The natives were duly impressed with their lethal power, and rifles soon became the most valuable nomad household asset and every man's indispensable accessory. Then, because girls would not deign to look at a man who still carried a spear, firearms were incorporated into the payment of bridewealth. A harassed official in Geleb *awraja* in South Omo complained to the Governor General of Kaffa province in 1957:

> You see only three or four policemen in every police station as our district is very vast, and most of its inhabitants are pastoralists who move from place to place with their herds of cattle…I explained to them that people are considered loyal to their government only when they are paying the tax levied on them...As long as they have firearms these people will not willingly pay their tax, so one thing is clear, they should be disarmed...Otherwise, they don't show the slightest interest in paying either the outstanding or the current tax…I wanted to use force against them in order to make them pay...but it would have been meaningless, since they possess more firearms than the police force of the woreda possesses.[5]

[5] Report from the Governor of Maji Awraja to the Governor-General of Kaffa Province. No. 3647/13/123 (8 May 1957).

The Afar

There was no sign of the imperial state in Ethiopia's share of Afar territory, and the nearest administrative post was in the town of Dessie on the escarpment, where the governor of the region had his headquarters. A traveller who crossed the Afar land from south to north unscathed in 1934 remarked: 'Although the Danakil country belongs to Abyssinia, the agents of the Government are unable to penetrate into its deserts, except at the fringes' (Nesbitt 1935: 71). The coming of the Italians stirred things somewhat. Their approaches to Sultan Yayo were not repulsed, and he acquired a reputation for being 'favourable' to the Italians, something he was to pay for later. His successor, Sultan Dada Mohammed Yayo proved likewise susceptible to Italian blandishments, and welcomed them to his capital.

During the Italian occupation, the Afar territory in Ethiopia was added to Eritrea. The occupation proved disastrous for the Afar, who found themselves under sustained attack by the Issa Somali and were forced to abandon territory they had occupied for centuries. The recorded history of this confrontation goes back over a century, when the battlefront was on the Erer River north of Dire Dawa in Ethiopia and in Djibouti south of Tadjura Bay. A traveller to Harar at the close of the 19th century placed this town at the interface between the rivals, noting: 'Herrer est sur le territoire dankali; c'est une sorte de point très neutre, sur la frontière des Danakil des Issah et des Oromo' (Borelli 1890: 77). ['Harar is in Danakil (Afar) territory: it is a sort of neutral point on the frontier between the Danakil, the Issa and Oromo.'] Three decades later, the Issa had pushed the boundary northwards to the newly-founded railway town of Dire Dawa. The construction of the Addis Ababa-Djibouti railway facilitated Issa expansion. To gain safe passage, the construction company hired Issa clansmen as transporters, workers and guards, who later settled in the region crossed by the railway that now lay within the Somali regional state. According to a historian, the French company supported the Issa against their rivals: 'L'administration les soutenait a cette époque dans leurs differences avec le voisin Danakil' (Oberle 1971:97). ('In that period, the administration supported them in their disputes with their Afar neighbours.') In the 1930s, the Afar-Issa front had moved to the Erer River valley, the most valuable territory east of the Awash River. The Italians, whose forces included a large number of Somali auxiliaries from their colony in the south, considered their kinsmen in Ethiopia as allies. In the face of relentless Issa pressure, the Afar retreated to the Alligedhi Plain east of the Awash River, where the battle line is drawn today.

Having consolidated its authority in the centre after the expulsion of the Italians, the imperial regime moved to settle accounts with the Sultan of Aussa, Dada Mohammed Yayo, who had welcomed them in 1936. Holder of the Aussa throne since 1927, Dada had a fearsome reputation, having done away with several of his eleven brothers. An Ethiopian army was sent to Aussa in 1944 to depose him and bring him to Addis Ababa, where he later died. Addis Ababa chose his nephew Ali Mirah, whose father had died in Dada's prison, to succeed him. Only twenty-two years old at the time, Ali Mirah was the thirteenth of his line to sit on the throne of Aussa. He ruled the Aussa Sultanate with little interference from Addis Ababa, and was the longest surviving traditional ruler in the entire lowland periphery. The Sultanate delivered a tribute of 2,000 litres of ghee annually in lieu of taxes. Ali Mirah was treated with deference by the Ethiopians, and was trusted by Haile Sellassie to whom he had easy access. He was regarded as the representative of all Afar, a gross exaggeration of his position, and was given the exalted Abyssinian title of *Betwoded* ('beloved'). In turn, he proved himself to be the model subordinate of imperial rule and profited greatly from it: he lives to enjoy his good fortune to this day.

An alternative Afar leadership was being hatched at the same time. A tiny fishing village named Tio, between Massawa and Assab, was to play an important role in Afar political affairs as an antipode to Aussa. Tio's youngsters got a head start in education from an elementary school opened by the Italians who had an administrative post in the village, and the Protestant Red Sea mission opened its own school there in the 1950s. A few students went on to a Muslim school in the port of Arkiko, near Massawa, where one of the teachers was Osman Saleh Sabbe, a pioneer Eritrean nationalist and one of the founders of the Eritrean Liberation Front. A few others were sent to the *Balabbat* School in Addis Ababa. Tio was the base of Yassin Mohamooda, a politically active elder who sided with Addis Ababa in the contest over the future of Eritrea. Like most politically conscious Afar, Yasin's true goal was to have all his kinsmen within one state, and he supported the Eritrean unionists for that reason. A grateful imperial regime awarded him the title of *Fitwarari*. After the annexation of Eritrea in 1962 however, instead of achieving unification the Afar were parcelled among five Ethiopian provinces.

*

The isolation and virtual autonomy of the Afar region came to an abrupt end with the coming of commercial agriculture in the Awash River Valley. Chosen because it offered optimum conditions for this enterprise, the valley became the site of the first ever development scheme in Ethiopia. The flat terrain crossed by the great river is an ideal site. It is further recommended by the availability of rail transport, and its proximity to the area of industrial concentration that extends along the railway line below Addis Ababa. The imperial government took the trouble to inform Sultan Ali Mirah, and did so in a manner that perfectly illustrates the nature of the relationship between the centre and peripheral elite. The Afar Sultan was summoned to a meeting of cabinet members and representatives of Mitchell Cotts, a British firm with extensive interests in Africa, to be informed of its plans to plant cotton in the Middle Awash Valley. 'In the Emperor's name we demand that you welcome the Mitchell Cotts people who will develop the land and make agriculture', he was told. 'I will not give Afar land to the *ferengi* ('foreigners'). You'll have to take it by force,' was the Sultan's impulsive reply. The meeting broke up. Makonnen Habtewold, an eminent courtier and imperial confidant, proposed they meet again the following morning. Taking Ali Mirah aside he tried to make him change his mind, but the Sultan was adamant. The following morning, on their way to the second meeting, Makonnen issued Ali Mirah with a blunt warning: 'Don't repeat what you said yesterday. It will go better today if we reconsider our position.' ('Il vaut mieux aujourd'hui que nous assouplissons notre position.') Having thought about it overnight, Ali Mirah consented: 'Tell them I accept. I will not open my mouth' (Aramis 2005: 74-75).

This was not the first intrusion of commercial cultivation in the Awash Valley. The pioneer project was founded in 1951 in the Upper Awash Valley by a Dutch firm with colonial experience. The Handels Verenigins Amsterdam (HVA) was given some 6,000ha in the Wonji Plain at a nominal price to establish a sugarcane plantation and processing factory. The company was granted complete exemption from taxation on all goods it imported, including fuel, and a virtual monopoly of the domestic market through the imposition of a high tariff on imported sugar. A police unit was stationed permanently on the Wonji Sugar Estate grounds to ensure a docile work force. The displacement of pastoralists from their land commenced when the local Gilo Oromo herders were forced out of the Wonji plain due to land clearing for the plantation.

In 1962, Addis Ababa set up the Awash Valley Authority (AVA) to promote commercial agriculture in the Middle and Lower valleys. Its charter gave it authority to manage the area's resources as it saw fit, and it proceeded to dispose of it by granting leases to investors. By 1971, 31,000ha were under cultivation in the Lower Valley, half the estimated irrigable area. In 1975, a total of 33 enterprises operated under AVA auspices. Twenty of these were private, the rest were joint ventures of foreign firms with the Ethiopian government. The total area under irrigation covered more than 60,000ha, equivalent to over one-quarter of the estimated 200,000ha of potentially cultivable land, and cotton occupied 87% of it. The Afar people were perplexed and they expressed this feeling in song:

> They are taking our soil; we don't know why;
> They are digging our land; we don't know why;
> Motorcars overwhelm our animals;
> Foreign languages overwhelm our language.[6]

AVA's authority went unchallenged in the Upper and Middle Valleys. In the Lower Valley however it encountered the opposition of the Aussa Sultanate, where agro-pastoralist Afar communities were keenly aware of the land's value and the danger of losing it. The AVA met its match in the

[6] Provided by Abhallah Abdo Adou. Personal communication to the author.

person of Ali Mirah, whom one observer described at the time as 'a man of many parts; holy man, large farmer, innovator, businessman entrepreneur, educator planner, leader and judge' (Cossins 1973: 34). Almost overnight, the Sultanate turned itself into a highly profitable enterprise by establishing its own plantations, wherever possible in the path of potential expansion by foreign investors. An admiring observer marvelled how 'in a metamorphosis of startling rapidity and foresight, an ancient and tradition bound subsistence autocracy has adapted to the needs of a modern surplus money oriented economy' (ibid.: 4) According to the first report (November 1972) issued by the Aussa Farmers' Association, land under Afar control represented 22% of the total cultivated in the Lower Valley. When world cotton prices doubled in the early 1970s, profits rose to an incredible 67% of the value of production, and the small group of Afar investors were hard put to spend their newly-gained wealth. It did not last long. The nationalisation of their holdings by the 1975 Land Reform Act nipped the emergence of an Afar landed gentry in the bud.

*

The intrusion of commercial agriculture was an unmitigated disaster for Afar pastoralism. Serious damage to livestock production was caused by the loss of vast areas of fertile grazing land on the eastern side of the Awash River. Displaced herders moved into the territories of kindred clans, others were pushed southwards closer to the Issa, and the rest struggled to survive in much reduced circumstances. Needless to say, there was no compensation for this loss. It caused overload in the remaining grazing areas, with overstocking and overgrazing as the result. Even more damaging was the blocking of livestock access to the Awash River by plantations that multiplied along its eastern flank. Farms were established across major access routes to the river, obliging the herders to trek great distances to find access, or forcing them to invade these properties, causing damage to fencing, crops and irrigation canals, while their own animals drowned in the muddy canals. Such incidents became routine and poisoned relations between planters and herders.

The taming of the Awash River with hydroelectric dams in the Upper Valley, and the manipulation of its flow for plantation irrigation in the Middle and Lower valleys, had a lasting impact on the moisture and vegetation regimes throughout the region. The dams reduced flooding and distorted its pattern, affecting pasture growth throughout the Valley. Irrigated cultivation on a massive scale had serious health implications. The herbicides and biocides used in the plantations contaminated canal water that was used by people and animals. Plantation crop residue and the weeds foraged by animals were likewise contaminated. Malaria, called *Dahanaso* ('milk sickness') because it comes with the rains when animals give lots of milk, became a serious health problem in the Afar region, and is now the leading cause of death (36.2%). [7]

[7] Central Statistical Authority (2003: 318).

There was no obvious compensation for the Afar. The scale on which the plantation economy operated was far beyond the scope of the local economy, and there was no possibility of effecting linkages between them. The plantation system of sugar and cotton production was not in any way complementary to the economy of mobile pastoralism, and did not create labour opportunities for the local population. Few, if any Afar, had the skills or education for better paid jobs, and most lacked the motivation for low-paid, seasonal work. The former employment went to qualified highlanders, and the latter to destitute Oromo peasants from Wolo and Shoa, who did the seasonal weeding and cotton picking for pitiful wages. Finally, commercial production was devoted mainly to export, ignoring the growing needs of the region and the country for increased food production.

The plantation economy brought with it the first signs of urbanisation in the Awash Valley. Urban facilities made a modest appearance in Asayita, the old capital of Aussa. In 1973, the town had two secondary schools – one maintained by the government, the other by the Sultanate, branches of several banks, a Seven Day Adventist mission, and a bus service to Assab. A string of towns – Mille, Adaitu, Gadamaitu – began as camps for the construction company that built the road from Awash Station to Mille in the early 1970s. Other than Asayita and Gewane, however, Afar were not attracted to the towns. All other emerging townships in the Middle and Lower valleys were dominated by highlander shopkeepers and Oromo labourers.

The introduction of a new mode of production based on profit inevitably affected the status of land that was traditionally shared equally by all members of the *Khida*. Land had become a market factor to be parcelled, enclosed, and otherwise disposed of by its owners. Renting of land to private investors, Afar and non-Afar, became common practice during this period, and was handled by the *Kidha* elders who collected rent and distributed it among their clansmen. As land came to acquire market value, Afar perceptions of it began to change. Claims to land became more exclusive, and conflicts over land between neighbouring *Kidha* became more frequent. The prevailing legal ambiguity over land rights in the pastoralist habitat was further muddled. The AVA claimed ownership based on state law, and the Afar claimed it on the basis of tradition and possession. The AVA gave concessions and the *Khida* rented land to outsiders, from which the Afar were excluded. The Sultan's Office cultivated vast areas with unspecified rights over the land. 'The present almost unique situation where large farmers are more or less the tenants of a large number of *Kidha* ownership group members is probably only a transitional stage' an observer remarked hopefully at the time (Cossins, 1973:80). In fact, the situation is little different today (see Chapter 13).

The decline of the local economy was tragically revealed in the catastrophic drought and famine of 1973-74, known as *Unda Abar* ('Great Famine'). The Afar lost the bulk of their cattle. Isolated in a territory of which a large part was still *terra incognita*, they died in the thousands without aid ever reaching them. 'There are no exact figures for how many Afar died during the drought and famine of 1973-4. Estimates vary and reach as high as 30 per cent' (Helland 1978: 25). 'This destruction of both livestock and grazing areas is of such magnitude and persistence, that the ability of Afar society to survive as significant pastoralists is endangered,' was the dire verdict of a well-informed observer (Cossins 1981: 11, 24).

Loss of land and displacement fuelled conflict over diminishing resources between the Afar and their neighbours. On the approaches to the escarpment of the northern plateau, Afar clashed with the Karrayu Oromo, who themselves had been devastated by the sugarcane plantations on the Metahara plain. Before the introduction of sugar cultivation, the size of the Karrayu territory was estimated at 150,000ha: by 1963 it had been reduced to 60,000ha, and was no more than 40km wide at any point.[8]

On the opposite side of the Valley, the struggle to contain Issa Somali incursions intensified. Afar-Issa clashes in the area crossed by the railway forced Addis Ababa to intervene, and it repeatedly tried to demarcate the area to separate the two groups, but in vain. At first it sought to hold the line on the Erer River. In renewed fighting in 1963, the Issa inflicted a heavy defeat on their rivals and crossed the line. A series of meetings were held in the following years, resolutions were passed and promises were made to pay for a peace settlement. The largest meeting was held in Addis Ababa in 1965, where a decision was taken to forbid the warriors to adorn themselves with the sexual organs of slain enemies.

Responding to the lure of tourism, the government proceeded at the same time to designate vast tracts of land in the Awash Valley for national parks, game reserves and protected areas. The entire surface area set aside for wildlife protection covered no less than 35% of the Afar *kilil* land surface (UNDP 2003: 2). The stated purpose of designating protected areas was to 'exclude human interests in the form of grazing, farming, mining' (ibid.: i).

The Somali

Save in the relatively fertile Jijiga plain, few Abyssinians came to settle in the Ogaden. Few army garrisons were set up there to give birth to towns, though Jijiga in the northeast and Moyale in the southwest did develop into administrative and economic centres, and the same was true to a lesser extent for Degehabur and Kebridehar. Both grew into sizeable settlements around wells on the Jerer and Fafan rivers. 'In the late twenties, it was estimated that the vast Ogaden "wilderness" was garrisoned by no more than 50-60 soldiers' (Barnes 2000: 120). Somali elders with titles such as Sultan, Ugas, Garad, Damin and Malaq were recognised as *balabbat* and received handouts. The settlement in Jijiga grew apace during this period, and the government sought to boost its potential as a trade centre by appointing merchants as governors. In 1932, a rough, 100km road was cut to link Jijiga to Harar.

[8] For the story of the Karrayu, see Ayele Gebre (2001).

This period saw the rivalry between the Ishaq and Ogaden clans over the Haud pastures turn violent. The resources of the Somaliland Protectorate were insufficient for the needs of its pastoralist population, and Ishaq rights to use the Haud during the wet season were recognised in various treaties concluded between Ethiopia and Britain. The Ogaden clan grew increasingly resentful of what it considered Ishaq intrusion in its own territory, and violent clashes between the two were frequent. Not surprisingly, in the rebellion led by Sayyid Mohammed Abdille Hassan, these two joined opposite sides. The Sayyid belonged to the Bah Gerri/ Ogaden clan and his fighting force consisted mainly of Ogaden clansmen. By contrast, the Ishaq were recruited by the British to fight against him. When Haile Selassie came to Harar in 1935 to rally the Somali against the impending Italian attack, he listened to Ogaden complaints. 'If it is wished that the Somali become sincere friends of the Abyssinians,' a youthful Ogaden leader, Makhtal Dahir, told the Emperor, 'then the English subjects should be obliged to move out of the Ogaden immediately.'[9]

As Fascist intentions became increasingly clear, Addis Ababa's attention was drawn to the southeast. The completion of a hard surfaced road from Mogadisho to the Ethiopian border, the recruitment of Somali auxiliaries known as *Banda*, and the increased traffic of Italians ships crossing the Suez Canal laden with soldiers and arms headed for Eritrea and Somalia left little doubt on this score.[10] Haile Selassie himself came to Harar the same year and summoned the Somali notables to a meeting lasting a whole night. He began by telling them he was the leader of all the black people in the Horn. Admitting conditions in their region were not good, he absolved himself by saying 'all this is not my fault', blaming local officials instead. He then made a series of promises for reform, and asked the nomad leaders to help the Ethiopian army defend their country against the whites. In their response, the Somali elders did not mince their words. Why should they fight the Italians, one asked, when it was the Ethiopians who called them dogs, abused their women and killed their animals? Another derided the Abyssinian titles bestowed on them since, as he said, everyone knew that the lowest Abyssinian official had more authority than the highest ranking Somali. The Emperor went on to Jijiga to address another meeting, where he declared: 'Keep in mind that the black man is always black and the black Christian and the Black Muslim are brothers.'[11] In the event, his Somali subjects showed little enthusiasm for either side in the war that broke out soon afterwards.

The Italians abolished taxation, returned land that had been taken by highlanders in Jijiga, and generally favoured the Muslim population and Islam. One of their construction feats was to connect the Harar-Jijiga road with Mogadisho 1,197km to the south. With the expulsion of the Italians in 1941, the entire southeast region of Ethiopia came under British military

[9] Cited in Markakis (1990:172).
[10] Ethiopia had an agent in the Canal, a Greek employee named Petridis who kept Addis Ababa informed.
[11] Cited in Markakis (1990:172)

administration, which was responsible also for the former Italian colony in the south and the British Somaliland Protectorate in the northeast. A belt of land alongside the railway line to Djibouti – called the Preserved Area – also came under British administration. Thus, all the Somali lands remained administratively united, as they had been under the Italians, and the people were free to move and trade without border restrictions.

It was during this time that the Ishaq and other clans from the Somaliland Protectorate took advantage of British protection to move *en masse* into the Haud in Ethiopia. This move was partly forced by livestock congestion, overgrazing and ecological deterioration in Somaliland itself. Up to half its population moved with their herds across the border annually and stayed in the Haud for up to nine months, initiating a process of ecological decline that continues to this day, and exacerbating an already tense relationship with the Ogaden clan in Ethiopia. The spreading of cultivation on the Jijiga plateau was another source of clan strife in this region. Several clans were converting to settled cultivation and living in permanent village sites near their farms. Grain cultivation in the Jijiga plain was introduced initially around Islamic religious settlements, and was encouraged by the demand for grain from the town's growing population. Production boomed in the 1930s under the Italians and in the 1940s under the British, when taxation was minimal or nil. When the Ethiopians resumed control in 1948, they reimposed taxation, but also encouraged cultivation in order to boost tax revenue. A visitor to the Jijiga plain in 1971 observed:

> The spread of cultivation is almost equally dramatic in its effect on the pattern of Somali pastoral life. People are turning to farming and in doing so are leaving a centuries' old established life style. Their reasons are complex and their feelings mixed, but the fact that it is an increasing trend bears import for any livestock development scheme. (Cossins 1971: 2)

*

The rise of Somali nationalism opened a new chapter in the relationship of the imperial state with its Somali subjects. Two Somali nationalist organisations emerged across the border in the 1940s; the Somali Youth League (SYL) in Somalia and the Somali National League (SNL) in Somaliland. The British, who encouraged the formation of the SYL in Mogadisho in 1943, allowed it to open an office in Jijiga. Another office opened in the city of Harar, where the Ethiopian authorities had not yet awakened to the import of Somali nationalism. Awakening came with the disturbances that followed the announcement of the Bevin Plan, which proposed the unification of all Somali territories. A transparent bid by Britain to bring all Somali under its rule, it was opposed by all the other powers. Nevertheless, it inspired pan-Somali nationalism, whose motto became 'Be United in the Name of God'. Alerted to the looming threat from the southeast, Addis Ababa demanded that the British restrain SYL agitation in Jijiga. Just before the restoration of Ethiopian control in 1948, this provoked a riot in the town that was put down by the British with the loss of some twenty Somali lives.

Initially the call of Somali nationalism appeared to find little echo among the Somali in Ethiopia. The restoration of Ethiopian rule in 1948 did not provoke widespread opposition, and while some people fled across the border to Somalia, the rest acquiesced to the change of regime.[12] Such acquiescence led one observer to conclude that the Ogaden clans were 'less influenced by Somali nationalism' than their kinsmen across the borders (Touval 1963: 134). This was to change soon and dramatically so.

Trouble began with the birth of the Somali Republic in 1960. Imperialism had dismembered this nation of nomads into five pieces parcelled among Britain, Italy, France and Ethiopia. The Somali Republic joined only two of the five fragments; the Italian colony and the British protectorate. Not surprisingly, *Soomaliyen* (Somali unification) became the categorical imperative of Somali nationalism, and the new state was born with a ready-made cause for serious conflict with all its neighbours. Its flag was graced with a five-pointed star representing all five Somali inhabited regions, its constitution extended full citizenship to all people of Somali blood, and it joined the OAU while refusing to sign the article endorsing the colonial borders. A map drawn in Mogadisho showed a *terra irridenta* of some 600,000km^2, only slightly less than the size of the Somali Republic itself (638,000km^2). No wonder that Mogadisho became the sponsor of irredentist movements in Ethiopia, Kenya and Djibouti in the 1960s, and plunged the Horn into its first round of post-colonial strife.

Sufficiently warned, the imperial regime sought to take preventive measures. Haile Selassie visited the south-eastern region once more. Speaking in Kebridehar, he told the Somali: 'All of you are by race, colour, blood and custom members of the great Ethiopian family', and advised them to learn Amharigna, promising them schools and development projects (Markakis 1987: 174). The Somali elders handed him petitions asking for clinics, waterholes, roads, etc. In 1957, eight million Ethiopian birr was allocated for this purpose, and elementary schools opened in four district capitals. The medium of instruction was Amharigna, a language quite unknown in the region. The elders also asked for government jobs. 'From private to general, from doorman to minister, not a single Somali', they complained. (ibid.: 175)

The elders also asked for the appointment of local people to administrative posts, pointing out this had become practice in the Somali lands still under British and Italian Mandate rule. Hoping to buy their loyalty with state salaries, the government made a series of appointments at the beginning of the 1960s. Three of the four *awraja* and some twenty-three *woreda* were put under Somali governors, and several more were appointed advisors to the provincial administration. Abdurahman Sheikh Abdi, a nephew of the rebel Sayyid Mohamed Abdille Hassan, was later made Vice-Minister of the Interior. At the same time, Addis Ababa moved to strengthen its control in the south-eastern lowlands. An Ogaden Administrative Region with Kebridehar as its capital was established, with four

[12] Makhtal Dahir, who took to the bush to fight the Ethiopians for the next couple of years, was an exception.

awraja – Kebridehar, Degehabur, Kelafo and Warder. In 1956, the territory west of the Webi Shebeli River was sliced off and incorporated in a newly created Bale province.

Rising tension in the wake of Somalia's independence in July 1960 led to an ugly incident one month later. In the beginning of August, Issa clansmen attacked a train on the Addis Ababa-Djibouti line near the town of Aishia killing a Frenchman. An important link in the Zeila-Harar trade route, Aishia is an Issa cultural centre and the birthplace of the clan founders. A few days later a unit of the Imperial Bodyguard arrived by train and began killing nomads indiscriminately outside the town. The next day the massacre moved inside the town with men being targeted, and was followed by mass looting. The survivors fled to Djibouti and northern Somalia, and the town never recovered from this blow.

By this time, the call of pan-Somali nationalism was growing louder. Radio Mogadisho sounded the call to arms for the liberation of the unredeemed Somali lands. Songs described as 'incitement to violence', played a key role. 'I shall not feel well until we go to war to unite the Somali', went one of them (Legum 1963: 505). Young Somali from Ethiopia who visited Somaliland and Somalia to trade or attend school were most susceptible to the call, and began to dream of rebelling against '*Habasha*' rule. Two groups were formed inside Ethiopia to prepare for the coming struggle – Nasrullah (from Nassir Allah, 'God's Grace') and the Ogaden Company for Trade and Industry. Nasrullah branches were formed in the four *awraja* capitals, young men were recruited, contact was made with Ogaden clan notables who had taken refuge in Mogadisho and Hargeisa since 1948, and a leadership was elected in Mogadisho in June 1960. The Ogaden Company for Trade and Industry had branches in the same four *awraja* capitals, where it carried out legitimate commerce that provided cover for subversive activities. The intention was to stockpile weapons and supplies in the Company's warehouses in various parts of the region. These were long-range plans and did not anticipate an imminent clash. When this happened, the conspirators were caught unprepared. As a result, the Somali went to war woefully short of weapons and supplies.

The precipitating factor was a classic *casus belli* in this setting: an attempt to tax the nomads. No effort had been made to collect the livestock tax in the postwar years, and a market tax to which the herders were liable was easily evaded by carrying out transactions in the bush. This state of affairs seemed fair as long as the state provided no services for them. Following the initial allocation for education, it now seemed proper to raise revenue for development in the Somali territory. In February 1963 it was decided to impose a head tax, and the elders were ordered to collect it, sending a wave of mutinous excitement across the region.

Shortly afterwards, at a meeting of some two dozen Nasrullah members outside Kebridehar was called to discuss ways of acquiring weapons. It was agreed the nearest source was the Ethiopian police posts that were thinly spread in the vast province. The meeting was betrayed, and most of the participants were arrested when they returned to town. A few avoided capture and made their way to Kelafo, where two of them attacked the policemen guarding the bridge on the Shebeli River, killing three of them. This was the first blood drawn in yet another round of carnage between Ethiopians and Somali. When the Ogaden governor issued an ultimatum to the recently appointed Somali local officials to produce the killers, most of them fled to Somalia, followed by conspirators and elders.

They gathered in Mogadisho and took counsel with government leaders in the Somali Republic. For the latter, the clash came at an awkward time. On the eve of Kenya's independence in 1963, Somalia was caught in a wrangle with Britain and the Kenyans over the fate of the Northern Frontier District with its Somali population. In the course of the dispute, Mogadisho broke relations with Britain, made an enemy of Kenya, and caused the Western powers to scale down their offers of economic and military aid to Mogadisho. An approach to the Soviet Union for aid proved more rewarding, but the benefit of military assistance from that quarter was not felt for another year. In these circumstances, starting a war against vastly superior Ethiopian forces hardly seemed advisable. Nonetheless, given the overweening appeal of pan-Somali unification, the government, dominated by the Somali Youth League, could not refuse its support to the Ogaden rebels. 'No politician in Somalia can suspend his preoccupation with the problem [of unification]', acknowledged Adam Abdullah Osman, the country's first president.[13]

In June 1963 about three hundred men – elders, religious notables, young warriors – gathered in Hodayo, a watering place north of Warder, to plan and choose a leadership. Overall command was entrusted to Makhtal Garad Dahir, senior elder of the Rer Ishak/Ogaden, a red-bearded giant with a reputation to match.[14] Several other prominent elders were chosen for positions of leadership, and the Ogaden was divided into four operational sectors, commanded by natives of each area. The rebels' number was small, their weapons few and ancient. Ill-prepared to confront the Ethiopians, they decided to avoid engagement and concentrate instead on recruitment, training and weapon procurement. Unwisely, they left Hodayo as a group and moved west towards Ime – a move detected and intercepted by the Ethiopians. As a result, the first clash occurred only three days later at Garasbur, south-west of Degehabur.

Isolated clashes occurred throughout the Ogaden during the next three months. The rebels attacked outlying posts manned by policemen armed with antiquated Enfield 303 rifles, and forced the government to abandon them, thereby gaining control over large parts of the contested region. The

[13] Cited in Bayne (1965: 149)

[14] Born in 1907, the son of the chief of the Rer Ishaq, Makhtal became chief himself in 1928, after his father and an older brother died in clan clashes. Subsequently, he was imprisoned in every state of the Horn. He redeemed himself with the Ethiopians by fighting on their side against the Italians, but fell out with them when he joined the Somali Youth League in the 1940s. He was arrested the same year by the authorities in Kenya and handed to the Ethiopians, who promptly sentenced him to death in Jijiga in 1949. Haile Selassie granted him a reprieve and kept him in prison in Addis Ababa until 1958. Returning to the Ogaden in 1962, he was appointed sub-district governor in Degehabur and given the title of *Dejazmatch*.

Ethiopians instead reinforced their hold on the main administrative centres, from where the army ventured out on lorries for daily sorties, while the guerrillas moved about freely under cover of darkness. Ambushing army convoys became their favourite tactic, and the means of obtaining the American M1 rifles used by Ethiopian soldiers. According to an agreement reached at Hodayo, the rebel leadership reassembled three months later at Higlole, another watering place between Kebridehar and Kelafo. With the Ethiopians stalking him, Makhtal Dahir was unable to come and made his way to Mogadisho instead. The guerrilla ranks had multiplied tenfold in this period and their number now was estimated at 3,000. The need for weapons had become acute, and a delegation was dispatched to Mogadisho to acquire them. It returned with 180 rifles of pre-war Italian vintage that belonged to the Somali army, the first instalment of 1,500 rifles obtained from this source during the course of the rebellion.

The rebels stepped up their attacks in the autumn of 1963, when Ethiopian forces were ambushed on many occasions in various parts of the Ogaden. Army reliance on motor transport and the scarcity of available routes made it vulnerable to this tactic. Most of the action took place in the northern sector, where the presence of government forces was greatest, but it was sporadic and localised, lacking coordination and overall direction. An organisational structure was never established, and Makhtal Dahir was never able to exercise overall command. Nor was the rebellion able to rise above the limitations of the pastoralist milieu in order to create the foundation for a protracted struggle. It remained wholly dependent on the Somali Republic, though it was not at this stage a tool of its government. Ethiopian control of the Ogaden was not seriously threatened. The guerrillas had neither the organisation nor the material resources to wrest control of the region from the Ethiopian army, which was on its way to becoming the largest force in sub-Saharan Africa, with an establishment of 40,000 men. Ethiopian control could be seriously threatened only if the Somali Republic chose to commit its own forces to the battle. The likelihood of this happening appeared to increase towards the end of the year with the announcement of a pact concluded with the Soviet Union, in which the latter undertook to equip a Somali army of some 20,000.

The announcement came in November 1963, and Addis Ababa decided to move before the Somali had a chance to build up their forces, which, at that time, were less than one-fifth the size of the Ethiopian army. It moved army units to various strategic points along the 1,600 km border with Somalia and, in mid-January 1964, launched ground and air attacks on Somali border posts and nearby towns. The Somali government moved its own army to the border and proclaimed a state of emergency. During the first three months of 1964, heavy fighting took place at several border points, particularly at Tug Wajale in the north, 65km from Jijiga and at Ferfer and Dollo in the south. Ethiopia made intimidating use of its superiority in the air with raids against Somali towns, including Hargeisa.

Strenuous propaganda and diplomatic activity accompanied the action on the ground. The Organisation of African Unity held emergency sessions and became involved in mediation efforts. The Soviet Union appealed for moderation and sent its deputy foreign minister to Addis Ababa and Mogadisho at the beginning of March. The United States reiterated its opposition to Somalia's territorial claims, and put pressure on its government to end its support of the rebellion. Somalia's challenge to the colonial borders found no support among the African states, and even Egypt refrained from backing Mogadisho.

March 1964 was election month in the Somali Republic. Despite the defiant slogan: 'With one hand we fight, with the other we vote', it was obvious that Mogadisho could not continue the confrontation. The outgoing government of Abdirashid Ali Sharmarke began negotiations with the Ethiopians, and a cease-fire was agreed upon on 6 March. It fell to the new government of Abdirazak Hadj Hussein to persuade the Ogaden clansmen to give up the struggle. This task was entrusted to the commander of the police, General Mohammed Abshir, who instructed the Ogaden elders in Mogadisho not to return to their homeland. They asked to talk to the Prime Minister, who told them bluntly that the security of the Somali Republic was at stake, and that they could expect no more help. To sweeten the pill, the Ogaden notables were offered pensions and houses, and younger men were offered state employment, or a chance for education.[15]

Following the failure of the rebellion, military rule was imposed in the Somali region of Ethiopia, and the army was given a free hand to deal with subversion. Few Somali were considered trustworthy, few were given state posts, and those who accepted them were viewed by the people as collaborators. Away from the few towns that served as administrative centres and military garrisons, a visitor to the area noted that 'civil government is very thin on the ground in the Ogaden, especially outside the *awraja* capitals' (Cossins 1971: 2). An uneasy peace reigned in the troubled province for some years. 'The peace however is transient. The fabric of this society has been torn and a lifestyle is gradually seeping away' the same visitor concluded (ibid.: 1).

Although it failed, the uprising inflamed the Somali nationalist imagination and whetted an appetite for greater efforts in the future. The slogan 'Somali Hanolato, Ethiopia Hadhimato' ('Long Live Somalia, Death to Ethiopia') was on everyone lips, and popular songs lamented the loss of the Ogaden:

> The Ogaden has been taken by force
> And its people are under the Amhara yoke
> They are out kith and kin
> Who are subject to enslavement
> To have our revenge
> Oh! All of you cry unity
> And strengthen it. [16]

[15] Prime Minister Abdirashid Sharmarke confided to the American ambassador: 'it costs us from 200 to 800 shillings a month to pay off the liberation fighters. Sultans cost 1,500 to 2,000 shillings a month' (Thurston, 1978: 14).

[16] Mohamed Abdillahi Rirash in personal communication to the author.

The Borana

The Borana was another community that came under persistent Somali expansionist pressure on both sides of the Ethiopia-Kenya border. The Somali spearhead in Ethiopia was the Gerri clan, onetime clients of the Borana, who now raised claims on their patrons' land. Addis Ababa tried in vain to mediate, calling their elders to Addis Ababa in 1907, along with British border officials, to settle the conflicting claims. In 1930 the bulk of the Gerri from Kenya crossed into Ethiopia to avoid a newly introduced poll tax, putting renewed pressure on the Borana, and prompting yet another futile attempt by Addis Ababa in 1932 to demarcate a boundary between them. The Somali push made significant headway during the Italian occupation when Boranaland was ruled from Mogadisho as part of Italian Somalia. At that time, the Gerri began moving on Borana wells, setting a pattern of intermittent clashes between the two groups that continues to this day. The restoration of Ethiopian rule did not reverse the situation. In the years that followed, the records of Sidamo Province where Borana was an *awraja* were filled with reports of violent clashes between the two neighbours.

Across the border inside the Northern Frontier District of Kenya (NFD), the Somali had reached the Dollo confluence of the Genale and Dorya rivers in the north and the Tana River in the south. To contain them, the colonial administration in 1910 drew the so-called Galla-Somali line between the Borana dominated districts of Moyale, Marsabit and Isiolo and the Somali districts of Mandera, Wajir and Garisa. The British did not bring the NFD under control until the 1920s and then only after a prolonged struggle with the Somali clans, among whom the Ogaden proved the most resistant. Subsequently, the NFD was declared a Closed District in 1926 and a Special District in 1934, perpetuating its isolation from the rest of the colony.

The rebellion that broke out in the Ogaden in 1963 spread like wildfire westwards across the Webi Shebeli River into the adjoining Bale province, and from there across the Genale River into southern Sidamo province. Bale is shared by Oromo and Somali clans. Its lowland portion to the south is a demographic extension of the Ogaden and the home of Somali clans that straddle the Kenya border. The northern, elevated portion of the province is the home of the Arsi Oromo, former pastoralists who converted to cultivation and espoused Islam after their subjugation by the Ethiopians. The highland part of the province proved attractive to Abyssinian *neftegna* who settled on expropriated land, reducing many Arsi to *gabbar* status. Some Arsi clans retained the pastoralist vocation by moving down to the southern lowlands where they mingled with the Somali. Since the latter were moving westwards, they did not clash with the Arsi as they did with the Borana in the west, and relations between them were good enough to bring them together in the rebellion against

Ethiopian rule. The Arsi Oromo generally, and the Rayitu clan in particular, identified with their Somali coreligionists rather than their Oromo kinsmen, the Borana. It was said of them that 'they no longer regard themselves as Arussi or Oromo since these names to them imply paganism, but as members of the Muslim world' (Haberland 1963: 783).

The Arsi Oromo in Bale had good reasons for siding with their Somali coreligionists. Among the first measures taken by the restored imperial administration in Bale was to impose the *kelad* land measurement and *sisso* expropriation in order to boost tax revenue. The governor-general of Bale at the time, Worku Inquo Selassie, was an archetypal Abyssinian provincial satrap whose actions helped fan the flames of rebellion. In addition to the legal exactions of the state and those imposed by the *neftegna*, the population suffered from massive extortion at the hands of officialdom, whose venality reached an apogee in this province and affronted even their colleagues in the Ministry of Interior (Gebru Tareke 1977). Bale held the record among all provinces for land confiscated due to tax default and political offences. There was precious little return for such impositions. There was no sign of development in the province, no towns, no roads, no communication facilities, not even electricity or a postal service. In the fields of education and health, Bale was the worst served of all the provinces.

Until the middle of the 20th century, the Ethiopian state kept a very low profile in Boranaland, maintaining what an anthropologist called an 'attitude of benign neglect' and minimum interference in peoples' lives' (Helland 2002: 52), leaving the Borana to deal with their aggressive Somali neighbours. With the rising spectre of Somali nationalism in the late 1950s, Addis Ababa became wary of the footloose and unruly Somali *zelan*, whose reputation on the highlands had never been high. A local official in Bale warned

> It must be known that these people cannot be faithful citizens of the Empire and cannot be trusted, because they are deceitful, spread rumours, and when they find the opportunity they side with the stronger side, adjusting their political position and views. And when this is not possible, they pillage and rob the peaceful population.'[17]

The imperial government was now prepared to listen to Borana complains favourably, and took measures to halt Somali expansion into southern Sidamo province. In 1959, Addis Ababa acceded to Borana demands to declare the region west of the Genale River Borana *rist*, and to withdraw recognition from the Somali *balabbat*. It also distributed weapons to the Borana and Guji Oromo, which they promptly put to use attacking the Somali.

In 1963, several bands of Somali and Arsi men trekked to Mogadisho to ask for help. The government there had little of substance to offer, but it did provide them with antiquated Italian rifles and training at an army camp at Belet How on the border. They returned to Ethiopia in two groups, one heading for Sidamo and the other for Bale. On arrival, they

[17] Cited in Markakis (1987: 195).

split into clan units and headed for their home districts. The Gerri chief, Alio Gababa, was the main leader in Sidamo. One Arsi group in Bale was led by Hadj Ishaq Dadi, and another by a young Rayitu Arsi named Wako Gutu Usu, whose deputy was Mohammed Ali Rube, the son of the local Ajuran Somali chief.[18] Immediately upon returning to Sidamo, the Somali fell on the Borana and Guji, who in turn appealed to Addis Ababa for help. The government now decided to finally halt the Somali drift westwards by drawing a line, as the British had done in the NFD. That line was the Genale River, which all Somali in Sidamo were now ordered to cross and to return to Bale, where many joined the rebels. The rebellion spread to the El Kere district among the Aulihan Ogaden, and was also joined by peasants in Wabe district. Only one district, Fasil in southern Bale, remained peaceful.

The Ethiopian army was already committed in Eritrea and the Ogaden, and the brunt of the counter-insurgency effort there was borne by the provincial administration, whose forces included the police, Territorial Army, rural guards and volunteers from the local *neftegna* community. With the exception of the police and Territorial Army, the rest were unpaid and were expected to compensate themselves by plundering the rebel communities. Understandably, their forays often became looting expeditions. 'There is no other way', the governor general, Worku Inquo Selassie, wrote to Haile Selassie, 'but to mete out punishment commensurate with its [nomad population] faults.'[19] The ill-assorted and untrained forces who were led, feudal fashion, by provincial administrators, were unequal to the task and soon lost control of the countryside. By the end of 1966, when the government was compelled to commit the army, the rebels controlled southern Bale and south-eastern Sidamo, and were threatening the northern districts in both provinces.

This was no mean achievement for a movement without central organisation or leadership, or even a degree of coordination. In fact, the various bands had no direct contact with each other; nor was there any semblance of political orientation and goals. A rare announcement issued in the name of Wako Gutu appealed to people 'to remember that since the enemy occupied your country in 1885-1891, you have been robbed of your land and property, your history destroyed and your dignity violated.'[20] Religion was the closest the rebels came to ideology, with Muslims everywhere urged to rise against the *kaffir* ('infidel') Ethiopians. In this vacuum, the aspirations of Somali nationalism provided a frame of reference, and the Arsi leaders raised no objection to the goal set by Mogadisho: the liberation of Somali Galded (western Somalia). Wako Gutu lent credence to this by using a stamp designating himself 'General of Western Somalia'.

[18] Wako was born in 1924 in Mada Walabu, Bale, in a family of 19 children. He is said to have fathered 49 children himself, 34 of which survived him. The dominant clan in Arsi, the Rayitu are agropastoralists who live intermingled with the Ajuran and Gurrah Somali clans with whom they intermarry.

[19] Quoted in Gebru Tareke (1977: 311).

[20] Cited in Gebru Tareke (1977: Appendix IIA).

This was also an opportune position to take, since the rebels continued to depend of Mogadisho for supplies, whose quality improved in the second half of the 1960s.[21]

Having reinforced itself, the Ethiopian army took over at the end of 1966. The weakest flank of the rebellion was in Sidamo, where the soldiers, joined by Borana and Guji warriors, had little trouble scattering the Digodia and Gerri bands within a few months. Fighting in Bale was to last for three more years. Two Oromo generals, Wolde Selassie Bereka and Jagama Kello, were appointed provincial governor-general and military commander respectively. If the choice was intended to sow division in the rebel ranks by courting Oromo ethnic sentiment, it did not work. It took heavy fighting on the Arsi highlands and aerial bombardment to bring the rebels to heel. A change of foreign policy in Mogadisho with the coming to power in 1967 of Ibrahim Egal sealed their fate. Egal initiated a process of regional rapprochement and cut off supplies to Somali insurgents in Ethiopia and Kenya. Wako Gutu was the last to surrender in March 1970. The Borana in Ethiopia now recovered control of their traditional territory in Dire and Liben districts west of the Genale Dorya River and, most important, the complex of wells at Melka Gubba.

The Borana in Kenya's NFD were caught in the middle of the Somali uprising in this area during the 1960s and suffered grievously. Numbering about 58,000 in 1960, the Borana dominated the three western districts of Moyale, Marsabit and Isiolo. Numbering about 275,000 in 1960, the Somali inhabited the eastern part of the NFD (now the North-Eastern Province) comprising the districts of Mandera, Wajir and Garisa. Most of them belonged to the Darod branch, and more than half to Ogaden clans. The call of Somali unification was raised by local organisations demanding the incorporation of the NFD into the Somali Republic. As in Bale across the border, faith outweighed ethnicity, and other Muslims in the NFD, including Borana, sided with the Somali in support of secession. Non-Muslims generally were against it, and sided with the Kenyan nationalist parties that fought the secession to the end.

Following the same path taken by their kinsmen in Ogaden, Bale and Sidamo, young Somali from the NFD trekked to Mogadisho to seek assistance for an attempt to wrest the NFD from Kenya, before the fledgling state was able to establish itself in that region. The rebellion, dubbed the 'Shifta War', broke out in mid-1963, confronting the government of Jomo Kenyatta with a major crisis, as it proclaimed Kenya's independence in December of that year. The rebellion lasted nearly four years and was fought guerrilla style, which meant that civilians paid the heaviest price. Mogadisho provided assistance to the rebels, while the British supplied and advised the Kenyans. In 1966, a programme of forced settlement and regimentation of the nomads was instituted, and about one-quarter of the

[21] Radio Mogadisho started an Oromo language programme that featured music and propaganda. A song 'Bilisummaan Aannani' ('Liberation is Milk') became a hit in Ethiopia (Leenco, 1999: 176). When an Afar language programme was added, Addis Ababa was forced to initiate programmes in both languages in its own radio station.

NFD's population was settled in fifteen strategic hamlets encircled with barbed wire and thorn bush fences. A 32km wide zone around villages was marked for grazing; beyond it was a free shooting area. The result was the annihilation of livestock due to the disappearance of pasturage around the camps, the spread of epidemic disease, and confiscation by the police and soldiers. Worse hit were the Muslim Borana in Isiolo who had sided with the rebels. They lost all their livestock when they were interred in camps, a disaster they recall as '*Gaaf Daaba*' ('Time to Stop'), and from which they never quite recovered. The end came in 1967 when the Egal government in Mogadisho changed policy and ceased to supply them.[22]

South Omo

Little is known of events in this part of the lowland periphery during the first three decades of imperial rule. Neither travellers nor anthropologists ventured there to leave a record. Evidence from indigenous oral history suggests it was a period of instability and population shifts, as the people resisted the plunder of their properties by the new rulers on one hand and, on the other, plundered each other. Impressed by the firepower of the *neftegna*, the Hamar named them *kushumba* ('horn'). Much later, an anthropologist recorded one Hamar recalling how his father lamented the loss of livestock: 'The foreigners, they are smallpox, they are diarrhoea, they are fire', the father had said, adding how the Hamar finally sued for peace by sending a lion cub to Haile Selassie (Strecker 2006: 154). Ethiopian garrisons were established in Bako and Gidole on the heights overlooking South Omo, and a small number of highlanders came to settle among sedentary communities, where they acquired land and *gabbar* to work it. Understandably, the latter resented the burden imposed on them. The Aari described their situation as '*set homenal*' ('becoming women') and '*beg homenal*' ('becoming sheep') (Naty 1994: 62). The Italians occupied South Omo briefly during 1938-1940, leaving stores of weapons when they departed.

In the post-1941 administrative reorganisation, South Omo became an *awraja* in Gemu Gofa province, with Jinka as its capital. The life of administrators stationed in the lowlands was an unenviable one. Posting there was considered punishment. 'Amelu kekefa lakew Gemu Gofa' ('If someone misbehaves, send him to Gemu Gofa') people said. Living conditions were primitive. 'I am now found under the shade of trees as usual,' wrote one *woreda* governor, complaining of not having even a hut for his office and asking for transfer. His request was backed by his superior, the *awraja* governor, who also made a sensible suggestion that 'people who are of the same culture and know the reality be appointed' to such posts.[23] Police and military stations were set up after 1941 in some places, remote, isolated,

[22] For the full story of this conflict see Nene Mburu (2005).

[23] Letter to Maji Awraja Governor from the Governor of Geleb Woreda. No. 341/6149 (10 September1949).

and scarcely sufficient to uphold the authority of the state. The logistics of maintaining these outposts were a serious problem. One that was planted among the Dassanetch in the southeast border had to be supplied by truck from Jinka, and was cut off by floods for several months each year. Soldiers' morale was low; drunkenness and suicide were common among them (Almagor 2002). These solitary outposts were the closest most people in South Omo came to a sign of the state's existence.

The function of this thin police presence was to back up the administrators in their main task, tax collection. It was easier to enforce in the higher reaches of the region, among the Maale and the Aari, where cultivation was practised, *neftegna* had settled, and the *balabbat* were able to facilitate this task. Lower down, in the pastoralist habitat where the population outgunned the state's representatives, it was a frustrating chore and seldom worth the effort. As late as 1957, an *awraja* governor complained that he had no clue about the livestock holdings of the Surma on which to base their tax liabilities, and he had to take their word for it.[24] Understandably so, since he had a force of 150 to police a community armed with an estimated 2,300 firearms.

It was inevitable that the incessant demand for taxes, for which the state offered no obvious return, would colour the perception and attitude of the people towards its representatives. The Arbore called the Ethiopians 'Sidam' and held very negative opinions of them:

> The Sidam do not raise cattle but like meat very much. They consume cattle other people have raised. They do not like to carry their own belongings while travelling and do not cook their own food, but make others carry and cook for them. They love taking bribes, other people's possessions and rifles. They like wearing clothes. They are to be avoided'. (Wolde Gossa Tadesse 2002; 154)

The Aari who had collaborated with the Italians were harshly punished by returning *neftegna*, a time they remember as '*aushtra dagnia*' ('justice by the gun').[25] The *neftegna* regarded themselves as socially superior and disdained the natives. They would not eat or drink with them, and would not join the Aari working parties. The Maale, among whom a sizable *neftegna* presence was established, were most affected during this period. The appropriation of land by the *neftegna* and the Maale *balabbat* led to scarcity for the rest of the people and was strongly resented. By the late 1960s, a social division was emerging, with the *neftegna* and *balabbat* landowners in one class and the erstwhile *gabbar*, now tenants or holders of dwarf plots, in another. These underlying class tensions came to the surface during the 1974 Revolution.

What an anthropologist terms 'a form of mutual exclusion' characterised the interaction between highlanders and pastoralists in South Omo (Almagor 2002: 96). Social relations between them were confounded by superstition and misapprehension, as shown in the report by one official written in 1957:

[24] Report to the Governor-General of Kaffa Province from the Governor of Maji Awraja. No. 3647/13/123. (8 May 1957).

[25] *Aushtra* refers to the Austrian Mannlicher rifle.

> The men don't put on clothes and they go about naked. When they go naked, it is difficult to identify them as human beings...The land is good enough to cultivate cotton. If they took the initiative to cultivate the land and grow cotton, they could sell the surplus in Jimma and not use all of it for themselves. They could put on clothes made of cotton instead of going naked. But they don't do this, because they prefer to spend their time beating each other with a stick rather than work in the fields. They have a lot of cattle...If they sold butter they could pay the outstanding tax ...They don't do this, instead they drink full cream with blood.[26]

The Abyssinians' scorn for the *zelan* did not endear them to the natives. 'They do not love animals and do not like people who raise and live with animals', said the Arbore (Tadesse Gossa Wolde 2002: 54). The Dassanetch called the Ethiopians 'Ochumba' ('stranger with cloth'), and their own *balabbat 'kansitch ochumba'* ('leader for the foreigners'), and were horrified by the Abyssinian habit of eating raw meat and drinking *tej* (honey wine). On their part, the soldiers called the Dassanetch *'baria'* ('slaves'); 'women' because they wore necklaces and arm bands; 'cannibals' because they bled and drank cattle blood in the dry season, and despised them because they were not Christians (Almagor 2002: 107). By 1970, the Dassanetch did not speak Amharigna or practice any of the so-called 'Amharic' customs. They had been 'institutionalized at a relatively low – and finally hostile – level of interaction' wrote one anthropologist (ibid.: 97), a conclusion that applied to most aboriginal pastoralist groups on the fringe.

South Omo was little touched by the state's integration efforts, and that was only in the higher elevations where highlanders had come to settle, and new agricultural products – teff, coffee, cardamom – were introduced and marketed. This helped the growth of Jinka, the only town in South Omo that was founded as a garrison town and survived as an administrative centre. At an elevation of around 1000m, Jinka has a milder climate, albeit still exposed to malaria, yellow fever and yaws that threatened the immigrants who came as civil servants, traders and policemen. State elementary schools for the children of the highlanders opened in Jinka and a few other large settlements, and Orthodox churches were founded to care for their spiritual needs.

During this period, foreign missions established a presence in South Omo. A Sudan Interior Mission (SIM) station was set up in Aari land in 1927, but had little success and was finally closed by the Italians. SIM trained indigenous missionaries from Wolayta remained in the area and continued to proselytise, founding another station in Bako in 1945 (Naty 2000). SIM returned that same year, began offering medical treatment and set up another station in Konso in 1952, where it made rapid progress. By contrast, a Swedish Mission that went to Nyangatom in 1972 with plans for education and health made no converts at all. The missionary approach was described by a Bashada man in South Omo:

[26] Report to the Governor-General of Kaffa Province from the Governor of Maji Awraja. No. 3647/13/123 (8 May 1957).

> 'Father' has brought us oil, and he showed us how to cook with it. He also showed us how to boil water and milk. He taught in his house. If you stayed here for a few days he would afterwards give you a cloth. He would also give coffee, or salt, everything. And he took you home in his car. The Ethiopian government simply says 'pay taxes'.[27]

Conflict in the pastoralist zone continued as before, only now it became increasingly lethal given the quantity and quality of firearms that became available. The collapse of the Ethiopian army in 1936 and the Italian army in 1941 released a large supply of rifles onto the local market and lowered the price to make the weapon affordable to pastoralist warriors. The collapse of higher authority – twice in that period – incited communities to settle scores with attacks on each other and waves of livestock raiding. Hostilities, as often as not, took place across borders. These were neither marked nor guarded; a cause of great frustration for the Ethiopian administrators who vainly complained to their superiors. As one reported:

> As we have noted earlier on many occasions the border is not identified properly. It is impossible to pursue offender who cross the line between one country and another having killed people and plundered cattle. There is no post or sign that indicates a borderline, so it is difficult to say whether a locality is in Ethiopia, Kenya or Sudan.[28]

Gambella

The first decades of Ethiopian rule in this remote region were marked by ceaseless conflict between the Anywaa and the Nuer. Thanks to rifles they acquired from Oromo highlanders in exchange for ivory, the Anywaa succeeded for a time in halting the Nuer intrusion. By the 1910s they were reported to have accumulated 25,000 weapons (Bahru 1987: 119). Access to firearms shifted the balance of power in their favour, and they launched continuous raids on the Jikany Nuer, taking slaves, stealing animals, and driving many of the people across the border into Sudan. The colonial administration there was understandably perturbed and determined to disarm the Anywaa. In 1912 it sent an expedition against the *nyieya* Akwei in the Adongo region inside Sudan, but despite their inferior weaponry, the Anywaa carried the day, inflicting heavy casualties on the enemy (Direje Feyisa 2003 :321). British pressure on Addis Ababa to cooperate fell on deaf ears. Mainly interested in the profits of the ivory trade, the Ethiopian government was inclined to tolerate the assertion of Anywaa power, even their unwillingness to pay tribute regularly, until they went too far.

Addis Ababa kept a representative in Gambella town to keep an eye on the British who administered the inland port. In 1913, the Anywaa killed this official, starting a confrontation with Addis Ababa that was to last for

[27] Cited by Epple (2005).

[28] Report to the Governor-General of Kaffa Province from the Governor of Maji Awraja. No. 3647/13/123 (8 May1957).

years. A force of five thousand men under the command of Jote Tullu's son was sent to punish them: it was repulsed by the Anywaa. Addis Ababa then entrusted Majid Aboud, a Syrian mercenary, to deal with them. Having failed for two years to persuade them to submit peacefully, Majid led a large force against them in 1916. This time, 'in a sordid feat of carnage, Majid asserted government authority' (Bahru 1987: 142). In 1931-32, the Anywaa resumed raiding the Jikany Nuer and the Murle inside the Sudan, escaping reprisals by retreating into Ethiopia. The British asked Addis Ababa to punish the Anywaa and make them pay compensation. Majid led two more campaigns against them without success; he himself was injured in battle in 1934. 'The Abyssinians have never administered the Anuak who lie within the Kingdom of Ethiopia – at least not in the sense understood by civilized peoples' was an anthropologist's verdict in 1940 (Evans Pritchard 1940: 13).

Across the border in Sudan, the stubborn refusal of the Nuer to disarm and pay taxes involved them in continuous clashes with the British, who went as far as to bomb the natives from the air in order to subdue them. This conflict was an additional push factor in the Nuer migration across the border into Gambella, where they found Ethiopian rule more flexible and, unlike the Anywaa, never challenged it directly. A bone of contention between the two imperial powers at this period was the right to tax the roaming Nuer herders who crossed the border seasonally. The British had long sought a grazing agreement to allow the Gaajak seasonal entry into Ethiopia, and it was finally concluded in 1935, just before the Italian invasion. The British claimed an exclusive right to tax the Gaajak, who regularly crossed the border into Gambella, and the Ethiopians countered with a similar claim. In 1931, Britain recognised Ethiopia's right to tax the Gaajak in their dry season camps, and the Ethiopians appointed a Gaajak *balabbat* to perform this task.

State control was strengthened after 1941, when police stations were established and finance offices set up to collect taxes now paid in money. It was staffed by highlanders most of who were repelled by the less benign features of indigenous culture, and shared the opinion reported by a governor of Gambella in 1954: 'In order to bring the people of Gambella into civilization (*silitane*) we need the establishment of modern schools together with religious teachers from the Orthodox Church.'[29] There were others, however, who recognised positive features, like the governor who made this report:

> In Anywaa culture lying, theft and deceit are non-existent. Among the Anywaa, if somebody is accused of homicide, the accused confesses and describes the details of how he killed the person. The Anywaa started learning lying and theft from those highlander vagabonds in Gambella town. When an Anywaa was asked why he stole or lied, he could reply I learned it from the *gaala*.[30]

These measures did not dampen Anywaa defiance, manifested in many

[29] Cited by Direje Fiseha (2003: 332).
[30] Ibid.: 333.

incidents throughout the 1950s. A veritable state of rebellion in the districts of Gog and Itang, with a series of raids against police stations, lasted until 1960, when it was put down by an army sent from Gore. In the 1960s, Anywaa resistance linked up with the rebellion across the border in Southern Sudan. The AK 47 rifles used by the Sudan army and the M 14 used by the Anya-nya rebels found their way into Gambella. By contrast, the Nuer avoided confrontation with the Ethiopian state, whose local officials were still concerned with winning Nuer loyalty in competition with the British, and bestowed imperial titles to Nuer *balabbat* in the 1950s and 1960s. The Nuer were themselves heavily involved in the Anya-nya rebellion, and equally well equipped with weaponry from that source.

Anywaa restlessness inside the border and its potential links with the civil war in southern Sudan worried Addis Ababa enough to set up a Gambella Security Group to investigate. The Group reported in 1963:

> Before a second Ogaden is created in Western Ethiopia, we should nip the political developments in the Gambella region in the bud. This entails various mechanisms. For one, the armed force in the region needs to be strengthened (from the current 404 to 797 people); a development package needs to be carried out, such as health facilities, schools, roads, motor boats, occasional flights (to Tiergol). In order to ensure the loyalty of the balabbat, they need to be salaried, like their fellow officials in the Sudan; occasional visits should be organised to bring them to Addis Ababa and show them some big factories in order to impress them by the grandeurs of imperial power. Besides, to make them similar with the Ethiopian people, evangelists and teachers from the Orthodox Church should be sent, and the activities of the missionaries (the American Presbyterians who sympathise with the rebels) should be regulated.[31]

The Sudanese civil war has had a manifold impact on Ethiopia since the early 1960s. It proved a source of modern weaponry that remains inexhaustible to this day, and has resulted in the bizarre situation where the populace is far better armed than the police. The storm raised by the civil war in the Sudan drove successive waves of refugees across the 1,605km border into Ethiopia, with serious demographic, economic and political consequences. By 1969 there were 20,000 refugees in Gambella. Most of them were Nuer, whose influx changed the demographic balance in Gambella in their favour, and set the scene for the confrontation with the Anywaa which is discussed in later chapters, (9 and 12). The appearance of refugees in growing numbers was followed by the arrival of international agencies concerned with their welfare, also in growing numbers. The agreement that established the Gambella free trading zone lapsed with Sudan's independence, and the region's economy deflated like a pricked balloon, since no alternative economic enterprise had emerged. In time, a refugee based economy involving aid emerged, leading to a long term dependence on this source as the only supplement to the declining local subsistence economy.

Modern education had a late and slow start in this region. The first state elementary schools did not appear until the 1940s and the first

[31] Ibid.: 445-6.

secondary school not until 1972. Refugee care included education, and it was in the camps that modern education made its appearance in Gambella region. Education was also the incentive offered by another newcomer to the region, the missionary. First on the scene was the American Presbyterian Mission (APM), one of several organisations active in southern Sudan under British rule. The APM first appeared among the Anywaa inside Sudan in the late 1930s, and in 1952 was given permission to establish itself in Akado, an Anywaa village on the Baro River inside Ethiopia. A second mission was established in the Pinyudo area on the Gilo River in 1962, and by 1964 the American missionaries had reached the remote Majangir community in the forest. They set up clinics and schools, built runways for their light airplanes, learned local languages, translated the Bible and trained local clerics.

Beni Shangul Gumuz

What little is known of this period pertains mostly to the two sheikhdoms of Gubba and Assosa that were administered by their native rulers as Abyssinian vassals. Initially, Gubba came under the authority of the governor of Qwarra in Gojjam who collected tribute and trade taxes. In 1925 the overlordship and the resources were transferred to Addis Ababa. Gubba flourished for a time as a market for gold, ivory, slaves, beeswax, honey and cattle of local origin, guns and coffee from the highlands, and cloth, grain, sesame and other agricultural products brought in by the Jallaba traders from the Sudan. Its ruler, Hamdan Abu Shok (1898-1938), was the biggest trader in the region and a regional figure important enough to be invited to Haile Selassie's coronation in 1935. He was not important enough, however, to avoid being taken hostage in Addis Ababa when he failed to pay tribute. At such times, Abyssinian troops were sent to collect it. According to a British intelligence report, 'The method…is simple in the extreme, soldiers are sent to each hut and the owner or occupier is asked for the tax (fifty piastres). Should he say he has not got it, his sheep are driven off.'[32]

The Assosa sheikhdom was overseen by the Oromo rulers in Nekempt. They collected tribute from Sheikh Hojele, who returned to power in 1909 when he was released from an Addis Ababa prison. He was jailed a second time in the 1920s, apparently because he would not give up the slave trade. Khojali and one of his sons, Almahdi Khojali, died during the Italian occupation. Another son, Alshafi Khojali survived and governed Assosa until 1970; two of his sons were district governors in the early 1970s.

Until the end of the imperial era, Metekel was an *awraja* of Gojjam province which was loosely administered from the provincial capital Debra Markos. Immigration of people from the central highlands continued unabated and unopposed during this period. The newcomers chose

[32] Cited in Garretson (1980: 202).

elevated areas with better soil to settle on. Plough cultivation needs flat, open fields, and they cleared the land of trees, which they used also for construction, fencing and fuel. The Gumuz retreated to low lying, remote areas within Metekel and across the Blue Nile, and their society turned ever more introverted and xenophobic. They were appalled by the highlanders' destruction of the forest and the wiping out of wild animals. The settlers, who always carried an axe on their shoulders, were said to cut even the tree 'under which they sit while defecating' (Wolde Selassie Abboute Deboch 2004: 116).

Summary

In the period after World War II, the patchwork structure that Haile Selassie had inherited was renovated to make the state a more efficient instrument of population control and resource extraction. At the same time, a parallel, multi-faceted process of socio-economic change intensified the interaction between centre and highland periphery, bringing them closer together and advancing the integration sought by the state. Change also sowed the seed for a countervailing trend against integration if that meant cultural assimilation and continued centre domination, a trend that was soon to mature into forceful opposition.

For the most part, the lowland periphery remained outside the scope of the changes described above. The development of commercial cultivation in the Awash Valley was a notable exception, and was managed without significant reaction from the Afar community. Violent opposition from the Somali occurred in the eastern lowlands, provoked by the state's initial attempt to strengthen its grip on this troublesome region. Equally important was the instigation of pan-Somali nationalism from across the border. Rebellion there and in Eritrea led to the build up of the military establishment, a weapon that was to strike the death blow to the imperial regime. Little changed during this period in the western lowlands at the other end of the empire. As an anthropologist saw it, the centre-periphery dynamics in that region 'remained stable for roughly three quarters of a century...The overall pattern of how Ethiopia "fits together" was not different in 1970 compared to 1900' (Donham 2002: 2).

Part III
Rebuilding the State: The Socialist Model

7

The 1974 Revolution

The fall of the imperial regime in 1974 was brought about by a revolution whose radical nature invited comparisons with the French, Russian and Chinese revolutions.[1] Like those historic events, the revolution in Ethiopia swept away the material and social foundations of an *ancien régime*, ruling out the possibility of restoration. Unlike them, it failed to produce a new social order; thus it proved barren. The upheaval divided the centre and created a political vacuum inviting intervention by the army, and a military regime ruled Ethiopia for the next seventeen years. The radicalism that inspired the revolution owed nothing to the soldiers. Its authors were the youthful urban intelligentsia, and its messengers were university and secondary school students. The 'Student Movement', as it became known, enlisted children fated to be devoured by the revolution they unleashed.

While radical Marxism was its avowed ideology, Ethiopian nationalism and a commitment to the nation-state project was the revolution's driving force. Students and soldiers alike were fervent nationalists committed to the preservation and consolidation of the state inherited from the Abyssinian empire builders and, like them, regarded centre hegemony as the cornerstone of the project. Nevertheless, they were aware that some policies of the imperial regime were proving counter-productive, and raised them to the top of the political agenda, obliging the successor regime to modify their aims. Consequently, the rupture caused by the 1974 Revolution marks an important turning point in the nation-state building project and the opening of a second phase under a new political order and fresh perspectives.

[1] It was acclaimed abroad as 'reminiscent...of the classic revolutions of Europe – France in 1789 and the February 1917 revolution in Russia' (Halliday & Molyneux 1981: 14). 'This one is real. It thus takes its place, not only with France and Russia, but with...China, North Korea, Cuba, Kampuchea, Vietnam' (Clapham (1988: 2).

The radical thesis

These perspectives were formulated in an intellectual climate saturated with radical ideological currents running through the post-colonial world in the second half of the 20th century. Until then, Ethiopians with modern education were a privileged class, and showed few signs of disenchantment with the paternalistic authoritarianism of Haile Selassie's government. This changed drastically as Ethiopia's economy entered a period of depression in the mid-1960s. In the preceding two decades, the slowly increasing output of the education system had been absorbed by an expanding state structure. Now the point of saturation was reached, austerity measures were in order and recruitment was seriously curtailed. Unemployment among the educated strata signified a contradiction of the first order, since it had always been argued that a shortage of skills was hampering the country's economic development.

In 1956, the editor of the Addis Ababa University College student paper requested articles on any topic 'except politics and religion'.[2] In 1968, an editorial in the student paper declared: 'the basic role of university students in our country is to make the masses conscious of the suffering they are enduring resignedly, due to a long socialisation process that inculcates in them respect for authority and hierarchy.'[3] An abrupt political awakening had transformed this generation within a few short years from complacent recipients of imperial beneficence to the nemesis of the imperial regime and the catalyst of the upheaval that caused its collapse. The 'Student Movement' drew inspiration from the extreme left of the Marxist ideological spectrum. Mao Zedung's treatise *On Contradictions* was its bible, and even Albania's quixotic despot, Enver Hojha, had his admirers here. Mao's disciples in Ethiopia came neither from the downtrodden peasant mass nor the minuscule working class. They were the offspring of the ruling elite, the *makuannent*, *gultegna*, *neftegna* and *balabbat;* the overwhelming majority were of Abyssinian origin, and lived in towns where educational facilities above the elementary level were available. Feverishly ideological, the town-bred radicals were little acquainted with conditions in the countryside. It was their self-deluding perception that the country was in the grip of a class struggle that could 'telescope' it from feudalism to socialism in one giant leap. Both past and future were seen through the prism of the class struggle, a point of view that conveniently dissolved ethnic and national divisions and contradictions and magnified social ones. While most African nationalists saw post-colonial society as classless and discounted the class struggle as the key to the future, Ethiopians saw the class struggle as the only path open to them. Such was the radical momentum that alternatives to 'scientific Marxism' were not mentioned, let alone considered.

[2] Cited in Markakis (1974: 358).
[3] Ibid.

The class perspective defined Ethiopian society as 'feudal,' and feudalism proved a versatile concept. It cast the imperial era neatly into the Marxist schema of historical materialism, gave the revolution impeccable class credentials and claimed historical justification for its deeds. The feudal tag was fixed not only to the founders of the imperial regime, but to the traditional elite (*balabbat*) of the periphery as well. The class struggle was to be waged in common, transcending the centre/periphery divide and forging unity among the oppressed masses. This perspective offered Ethiopian nationalists the comfort of imagining bonds of class solidarity spanning the centre/periphery divide where none existed. Feudalism was enlisted also against the threat of Eritrean secession. While the Ethiopian radicals recognised the Eritrean rebels as strategic allies in the fight against the imperial and later the military regimes, they never accepted the colonial thesis, arguing that feudalism historically had never been associated with colonialism; *ergo* Ethiopia could not have been feudal and colonialist at the same time. Neither did Ethiopian nationalists recognise the existence of an Eritrean nation, because in the Marxist schema the nation is a feature of bourgeois society and Eritrea had yet to reach that level. 'The transition from nationality to nation can be affected only through the abolition of feudal relations and the introduction of bourgeois relations. This did not take place in Eritrea', argued a leading radical (Andreas Eshete 1970: 15). The Ethiopians invoked class solidarity to exorcise the spell of secessionism. Ideology was a handy weapon and they used with abandon. While this might have seemed a clever exercise in ideological sophistry, it had dire consequences, since the argument was settled finally with bloodshed.

The radical movement in the centre thrived in the ideological arena, but operated in a political vacuum. It was not until two rival groups emerged in 1975 – the Ethiopian People's Revolutionary Party (EPRP) and the All-Ethiopia Socialist Movement (Amharigna acronym MEISONE) – that the movement produced the rudiments of organisation outside school grounds. While politically conscious workers may have sympathised with their aims, neither had links with organised labour, let alone the peasantry. This did not prevent them from styling themselves the 'vanguard' of the proletariat leading the revolution. As the EPRP organ *Democracia* explained, this dubious claim referred to its 'class representation, not its class base'. The party, it went on, was a Marxist-Leninist proletarian vanguard in its 'political position and the purity of its line'.[4] The radicals were not the only ones to claim the 'vanguard' role. The soldiers called themselves 'Workers in Uniform', and claimed to have inherited this role by historical necessity. As one member of the military junta put it in a public speech, 'workers in uniform are not confined to military duties alone, but have also to politicise, organise and arm the masses in line with programme of the National Democratic Revolution.'[5]

[4] Cited in Girma Negash (1982: 46).
[5] Ethiopian Herald (6 January 1977).

While the state inherited from the imperial regime was declared sacrosanct by the radicals, the same was not true of the 'nation'. The crudeness of the assimilation process carried out in the name of national integration could not be ignored. It was first raised indirectly in the late 1960s, a time when 'defining what "being an Ethiopian" means started to occupy the minds of mature students. They seemed to grab every opportunity to pose the question "Who is an Ethiopian?"' (Leenco Lata 1999: 161). A paper entitled 'Is Ethiopia one people or many peoples?' circulated in 1969, and a meeting was held soon afterwards in the University to debate the issue of '*Etiopiawi mano*?' ('Who is the Ethiopian?'). After a raucous session, it was resolved that the *gabbar* (peasant) is the real Ethiopian.

The taboo was broken resoundingly in a second paper titled 'On the Question of Nationalities in Ethiopia'.[6] The author, himself an Amhara, cut through the facade of what he called 'fake nationalism' by calling it 'Amharisation':

> To be a 'genuine Ethiopian', he wrote, 'one has to speak Amharic, to listen to Amharic music, to accept the Amhara-Tigre religion, Orthodox Christianity, and to wear the Amhara-Tigre shamma in international conferences. In some cases to be an 'Ethiopian', you will even have to change your name. In short, to be an Ethiopian, you will have to wear an Amhara mask.

Printed in the student newspaper, it prompted censorious editorials in the government press; one of which ominously quoted the proverb: 'a snake must be killed before it grows'. The outspoken president of the University student union was murdered at the end of the year. When the students seized his body for burial, a unit of the Imperial Bodyguard stormed the campus, shooting indiscriminately. This marked a turning point in the tactics of the radicals, who now turned to underground activity in preparation for an armed struggle against the regime. 'The nationality issue', as it was called following Soviet usage, was now firmly set at the top of the radical agenda.

The centre divided

The radical wave coincided with rising public discontent caused by the downturn in the economy in the second half of the 1960s, with inflation and urban unemployment as the result. The closing of the Suez Canal in 1967, and a parallel drop in the price of coffee, led to a decline in foreign trade and reduced state revenue from that source. The country's borrowing capacity was already badly strained, with debt servicing equal to 15.8% of export earnings. Inflation was spurred by converging domestic and international trends. Ethiopia's petroleum bill tripled in just one year, and the government was forced to increase the price of petrol by 50%. Unemployment soared, and hit the intelligentsia for the first time.

The famine of 1972-74 revealed a regime in a state of advanced decay, and still in thrall to an octogenarian autocrat incapable of assessing the

[6] The author was a leading radical named Wallelign Makonnen.

changes his own rule had wrought. This became obvious in the regime's lethal assumption that it could conceal the famine and spare itself embarrassment. The disaster was exposed by foreign media in 1973. Aid flowed in afterwards, but came too late to prevent the loss of some 100,000 lives. Demonstrating students alerted their countrymen to the ravages caused by what they branded the 'man-made famine'. The tragedy shredded the last vestiges of authority that the regime had in the urban sector, and also lost it peasant support in the north where the famine raged. After it was over, Haile Selassie visited the area and sought to exonerate himself by claiming, as Menelik had done once, that such disasters are the work of God.

The imperial regime's final year began in January 1974 with an army mutiny in the remote town of Neghele, the district capital of Borana. The apparent reasons were banal; lack of clean water, inadequate supply of food, and generally intolerable living conditions. An ominous aspect was the initiative taken by non-commissioned officers, who arrested their officers and held them hostage. One month later, taxi drivers went on strike in protest at the increase in the price of petrol. Schoolteachers joined them to demand higher salaries, and to condemn a plan to limit the expansion of the education system in order to match the limping pace of the economy. Schools closed down for the duration, allowing students to join clamorous demonstrations that became daily routine in the town. This coincided and dovetailed with an uprising in the armed forces that deprived the regime of its main instrument of control. Thus began what became known as the February Revolution.

To circumvent the regime's stranglehold on the means of communication, the radical activists introduced a new medium, the leaflet. It soon became the main means of communication in the urban sector, with many groups producing leaflets to publicise their grievances. The radicals used it not only to impart information and discredit the regime's concessions, but also to urge unity of action among the disparate groups and exhort them to raise the political stakes by challenging the existence of the regime itself. Special attention was paid to the soldiery. 'Ministers and Generals enrich themselves at the expense of the soldier', read one leaflet. 'Ethiopians rise! Crush the government that benefits only the few.'[7]

The Second Division in troubled Eritrea was the next to mutiny, and from then on mutiny spread like a virus through the ranks of the military, manifesting the same symptoms everywhere. The initiative was taken by the lower ranks and was directed against senior officers who soon lost control. Authority passed to committees (*dergue*) chosen in every unit, comprising plain soldiers, non-commissioned and junior officers. The social composition of the first two ranks rendered them susceptible to the radical message, because they were recruited from the peasantry, with a large portion coming from the highland periphery where land was a burning issue. Retired soldiers had no other means of subsistence, and despite promises of land for service, it was mostly officers who benefited.

[7] Cited in Markakis (1987: 86).

The ranks of the non-commissioned officers, who assumed leadership in the initial stages of the uprising, had been enriched recently with the recruitment of young men with a measure of modern education in the Air Force and specialist units. They also were inclined to the radical view.

Junior officers were mostly secondary school graduates who followed a four year course that included academic training in the Harar Military Academy. Founded in 1957, the Academy's oldest graduates had reached the rank of major in 1974. The social composition of this group was the same as that of the intelligentsia at large, and its members were highly sympathetic to the rebellious mood of the soldiery. Others came from the older training institution at Holeta, which recruited promising non-commissioned officers and put them through an abbreviated course of military training. Some of its oldest graduates had reached general rank in the 1960s. Untouched by the miasma of power and corruption of the senior officer corps, junior officers retained the trust of the soldiers and were able to participate in the movement from the outset. Eventually, they assumed a guiding role, and ultimately emerged as the dominant element in the successor regime.

While the hierarchy of the military establishment was being dismantled, the regime was buffeted by a series of strikes and demonstrations that kept it off balance. The teachers' strike continued, and in March the Confederation of Ethiopian Labour Unions (CELU) called a general strike that lasted a week. An avalanche of strikes followed in state and private enterprises, and protest demonstrations were staged by many groups, including the Orthodox clergy who called, *inter alia*, for the confiscation of bishops' property. Even more significant was the participation of Muslims. This politically passive community asserted itself in the biggest demonstration seen in the capital up till then, demanding an end to the discrimination practised by the state against Islam and the second class citizenship of its adherents.

Intimidated by the mounting assault, senior imperial retainers sought to remove themselves from the line of fire by resigning their cabinet posts. Endalkatchew Makonnen, the Oxford educated member of the royal nobility, was named Prime Minister to replace the man who had occupied that post in remarkable obscurity since 1957. His first move was to pacify the soldiers by purging the top of the military hierarchy and offering substantial increases in pay and allowances to other ranks. The statements of the new cabinet indicated a clear awareness of the threat that the split in the centre posed to the security of the state. The aim of 'safeguarding the unity of the nation and territorial integrity of the country', was a mantra repeated endlessly. The danger of losing control over the periphery was highlighted. 'It is incumbent on all of us that we should realize that our country faces at present serious difficulties. National security is one of them. Unless we are vigilant, the continuation of the present situation may weaken our positions on our sea coasts and borders', warned the new Prime Minister.[8] On the other hand, he seemed quite insensible to the

[8] Cited in Tefera Haile Selassie (1997: 108).

nature of the crisis that divided the centre. On the burning issue of land, he added: 'Government land grants will henceforth be made only to those who shall make their livelihood by working on the land. In order to solve the land shortage problem, the Government will undertake appropriate settlement schemes.'[9]

In some rural areas there were sporadic peasant attacks on prominent landlords, and many of them prudently removed themselves from the countryside. However, the peasantry was slow to awaken to the possibility of emancipation, and its part in the February Revolution was marginal. The primitive state of its existence, the weight of tradition pressing it down, the distance from the urban centres, the lack of communication can be said to account for it. Most important however was lack of leadership. The *balabbat* in the highland periphery, where one would have expected spontaneous rebellion, were beholden to the imperial state and showed no desire to challenge its authority. While astutely exploiting the political importance of the land issue, the radicals made no attempt to agitate and involve the peasantry.

Regime change

By late April 1974, the process of co-ordination among the mutinous elements in the armed forces had reached an advanced stage. A committee of elected representatives of most units was formed, named the Co-ordinating Committee of the Armed Forces, popularly known as the Dergue (Committee). Its first action, taken at the end of the month, was to arrest the members of the old cabinet that had resigned at the end of February. It did nothing for the next two months, while the government, led by Endalkatchew, tried desperately to weather the political storm. At the same time, the soldiers were being challenged by the radicals to take action against Haile Selassie himself. 'Who is more responsible than he?' asked *Democracia.*[10] At the end of July, Endalkatchew himself was arrested and replaced by Mikael Imru, another scion of the royal nobility. He was no more sensible of the nature of the crisis than his predecessor. 'Nothing that creates chaos in society will be attempted', he promised. As for land reform, he envisaged a policy that 'will suit both tenants and landowners'.

The time for reform had passed by now: revolution was in the air. The radicals were raising fundamental demands that could not be accommodated through reform. These were expressed in clear and concise form through a regular underground press that rapidly gained widespread circulation and formidable influence in the agitated urban milieu. Through these papers and pamphlets, the radicals fashioned a vocabulary to accommodate the semantic needs of the revolution. Since the official language had no word for revolution, they started by coining one – *Abyot,* from the Geez verb 'to refuse', or here, 'refuse to obey.' The oft-used label *adhari*

[9] Ibid.: 116.

[10] Cited in Markakis (1987:109).

('reactionary') was coined from the Geez verb meaning 'to walk backwards'. *Hibrette* (social) *sebawinet* (humane) became the word for 'socialism.' Neither did Amharigna have a word or concept for 'nation', and one – *beher* – was now coined.

As the Dergue moved cautiously towards the centre of power, the radicals awakened to the danger of a military dictatorship, and raised the alarm demanding the formation of a provisional 'Peoples Government'. 'Change is not to be given to the people from above, in the manner of Haile Selassie', they argued. 'It can come only from the popular struggle.'

The last act of the drama was preceded by a cunningly designed campaign to deprive the Emperor of the institutional appendages to the throne, such as the Ministry of Pen, his Special Chief of Staff and Special Security Branch. The palaces built for him in several parts of the country were confiscated, and the retainer corps that surrounded him was disbanded. A campaign of defamation against his person was waged, exposing the vast accumulation of landed, industrial and commercial properties held by himself and his family; these were nationalised. The night before the final scene, a searing film of the famine was shown on television, followed by scenes of the Emperor feeding choice chunks of meat to his dogs. The following day, 12 September 1974, a delegation of Dergue members read the act of deposal to Haile Selassie in his palace. Afterwards, the man who had ruled the country for 58 years, and owned a fleet of limousines, was bundled into a tiny Volkswagen car and taken to detention. He was kept in the Dergue's headquarters, where he was murdered nine months later.[11]

Renamed the Provisional Military Administrative Council (PMAC), the Dergue seized power without opposition, save for the vociferous protests of the radical pamphleteers who accused it of hi-jacking the revolution. The junta was a miscellaneous collection of more than one hundred individuals ranging in rank from plain soldier to major. Other than disenchantment with the imperial regime and a desire for change, most of them lacked ideological or political convictions. Aware of their shortcomings and anxious to overcome them, the soldiers turned to the radical camp for guidance and support, and began to engage prominent activists as advisers appointing many to high government posts. This approach sowed confusion in the radical camp that now split into three factions. The most resolute opposition was mobilised by the EPRP and went on to engage the military regime in a suicidal confrontation. By contrast, labouring under the illusion that it could ease the soldiers off the seat of power and replace them, MEISONE supported the new regime and helped it consolidate its power during the first couple of years. When its support was no longer needed, this faction met the same bloody fate as the EPRP.

The fratricidal struggle that engulfed the radical factions and the soldiers obscures the fact that they all were nationalists committed to the vision of the Ethiopian nation-state. The appeal of Marxism for Ethiopian nationalists derived from the solution it seemed to offer to the

[11] A medical charade was improvised to present his death as the result of natural causes.

'nationality issue', much dreaded because it harboured the spectre of secession. 'Scientific Marxism' offered a solution designed by Stalin himself and implemented in the Soviet Union, where it seemed to have satisfactorily passed the test with a formula combining cultural pluralism – 'national in form' with collectivism – 'socialist in content.' Though it failed to gain power, or even to survive as a political force, the radical movement left a legacy that is still to be reckoned with in Ethiopia. It dominated the political climate throughout the reign of the military regime and was shared by every side in the manifold conflicts that followed, including the assorted rebel movements that were led by veterans of the Student Movement and who ultimately toppled the regime. Those who came to power in Ethiopia in 1991 still cling to the same radical rhetoric.

Military rule as a solution to the impasse faced by the post-colonial state is nothing new. By the time the soldiers took over in Ethiopia, many African states were ruled by their colleagues. Nor was the invocation of socialism exceptional. Ethiopia's neighbours, Sudan and Somalia, had had military regimes committed to 'scientific Marxism' since 1969. Military intervention in Ethiopia was prompted by the obvious fact that centre control over the periphery was slipping and the territorial integrity of the state was threatened. As they saw it, the soldier's task was to reverse this trend, and they set about it with radical zeal, making *Andinet* (unity) and *Etiopia Tikdem (*Ethiopia First) their mottoes.

Like its predecessor, the military regime began as a collegiate affair with a large number participating in the making of major decisions. It had taken Haile Selassie many patient years to gather the reins of power in his own hands. In far more pressing circumstances, the power deadlock in the Dergue was broken quickly and ruthlessly. Through a series of murderous purges, the junta shrank quickly in size, until its evil genius, Major Mengistu Haile Mariam, emerged as supreme leader in February 1977. Thus, by the third anniversary of the Revolution, Ethiopia was again ruled by an autocrat – not yet forty years old – whose power exceeded even the limits reached by the last emperor, and who had far more effective means at his disposal to enforce it. His recklessness and ruthlessness were responsible for a series of ill-fated, blood-stained schemes, whose wreckage comprises the forlorn record of this regime.

Land to the tiller

The radical input was first manifested in a sweeping nationalisation of the economy the extent of which no one had recommended nor anticipated. The Dergue's 'Declaration on Ethiopian Socialism' in December 1974 was unambiguous: 'The entire economy shall be in the hands of the state.' Implementation began a month later, when banks, financial institutions and insurance companies were seized, followed by dozens of enterprises in various sectors. The main losers were foreign investors and the expatriate communities of Greeks, Italians, Arabs and Armenians long resident in the country. In February 1975, a 'Declaration on Economic Policy of Socialist Ethiopia' envisaged a three-tiered economy with state ownership of basic industries, resources and utilities; a joint state-private sector in mineral exploration, large construction and tourism; and a private sector in trade, transport, food processing, small manufacture and lesser enterprises. Foreign trade, the largest contributor to tax revenue, was also nationalised.

Land reform was widely expected. The radicals grasped clearly the fact that the greatest threat to the security of the Ethiopian state was the volatile conjunction of national and class divisions in the periphery, and were anxious to defuse it. With some political insight, the youthful activists launched their first public demonstration in the capital while Parliament was debating the 1966 agricultural income tax legislation. 'Land to the Tiller' (*meret merashu*) was their slogan, borrowed from the Chinese Communists. The soldiers were even more conscious of this threat, and willing to go further to meet it than the radicals anticipated. The Declaration on Ethiopian Socialism declared: 'The right to own land shall be restricted to those who work the land.'

Even so, on its introduction a few months later, the drastic nature of the reform was unanticipated. Its genesis is traced to a study carried out in a Swedish-sponsored rural development project in Arsi province, known as the Chilalo Agricultural Development Unit (CADU), where several university graduates were employed. According to the study, the maximum area of land an average family could cultivate was five hectares. Taking into account grazing requirements, and in order to allow efficient farmers to produce more, a proposal for reform recommended a maximum of ten hectares be allowed per family. The land was to be given to the tiller (*meret merashu*) in full ownership. State ownership was recommended only for large commercial farms. In the version decreed in March 1975, land was declared state property (*meret mengist*) and was seized without compensation. Land ownership and tenancy were abolished, a maximum of ten hectares per holding was set, and the sale and rent of land were prohibited, as was hired labour and land litigation. No mention was made of the Ethiopian Orthodox Church, and it was taken for granted that it was finally to be deprived of its ancient landholding privileges.

The 1975 Land Reform was an authentic revolutionary act, a landmark in the country's history symbolising a clear rupture with the past by wiping out the economic foundations of the *ancien régime*. The reform severed the link that had joined class and national divisions in a politically explosive blend, and had a greater impact on the centre/periphery relationship than any other event thereafter. The impact of the reform was felt mainly in the highland periphery, where it eliminated both the *neftegna* and *ballabat* classes, and proved wildly and enduringly popular. The *gabbar* suddenly discovered, as one of them put it to this author, that 'we are children of Adam also, and from now on will live like other men.' Predictably, the reform did not inspire commensurate enthusiasm in the northern provinces, where smallholding was the rule and large estates and tenancy the exception.

This sweeping nationalisation was completed in July 1975, when urban land and multiple housing were nationalised. Urban tenancy was, if anything, even more widespread than agricultural tenancy, and urban rent was a significant source of income for the former ruling class that was now deprived of it. However, many less privileged townsfolk supplemented their income by building and renting out the mud-plastered shacks that comprised the bulk of urban housing. Their nationalisation created a nightmare for town administrators who had to collect the petty rents and maintain the ramshackle structures, and also pay monthly compensation to former owners who had no other source of income. Unlike the rural sector, where expropriation did not create the anticipated drop in production, the urban housing sector went into a steep decline with a severe housing shortage as the result, from which it has yet to recover.

*

Restoring control over a periphery agitated by the political turmoil at the centre was a priority in re-building the state. The very first elucidation of *Etiopia Tikdem* in July 1974 included a pledge 'to modernise the existing provincial administration'. The imperial provinces (*teklay gizat*) were now renamed regions (*kifle ager*), and the imperial title *gazi* (governor) was dropped in favour of *astedadari* (administrator). The first step was to replace the imperial officialdom with new blood. Officials were drawn initially from the ranks of university and secondary school graduates, most of them veterans of the Student Movement, who found themselves sent to administer *awraja* and *woreda* in the periphery. Of a total 570 *woreda* governors, 340 were replaced, mainly by transfers of teachers from the Ministry of Education, and out of 102 *awraja* governors, 74 were replaced with university graduates.

The implementation of the land reform was the occasion for the first ever massive exodus of townsmen to the countryside, where they came face to face with the grim reality of peasant life. A student campaign for 'National Development through Cooperation, Enlightenment and Work,' was launched in December 1974 to bring the message of *Etiopia Tikdem* to the rural masses. Popularly known as *zamatcha,* it involved some 60,000 students and teachers and lasted for eighteen months, during which the process of education above the tenth grade was halted.

The land reform proclamation provided for the formation of peasant associations *(gabbar kebele)* to carry out land redistribution, to administer public property, and to organise cooperative schemes and development projects. While it was far from clear what status the *kebele* had in the government structure, the student campaigners were determined to turn it into a genuine instrument of local self-government, and set about this task with revolutionary zeal. They helped the peasants to organise and elect *kebele* leadership, and steered them towards self-assertion vis-à-vis the government and its local representatives. They instigated attacks against former landlords and agents of the imperial regime, and encouraged radical initiatives that violated government policies and laws, such as the refusal to pay rent for past years, the seizure of landlord movable property, and the occupation of state farms. Great pressure was brought on the Dergue to recognise the *kebele* as institutions of local government, and a decree issued in December 1975 granted them legal status 'to enable the peasantry to administer itself'. *Kebele* judicial tribunals were given jurisdiction to handle minor civil cases, property disputes and petty offences against the Penal Code. They also collected taxes for the state. Finally, the *kebele* were allowed to maintain armed defence squads with police functions.

For a time, the three pillars of the state – the tax collector, policeman, and judge – disappeared from the Ethiopian countryside. This was the high water mark of the revolutionary tide, but did not last long. Understandably, the regime did not share the *zamatcha* enthusiasm for peasant political emancipation. The alarm sounded when the campaigners raised the demand to 'Arm the Peasants'.' 'Today they get guns, tomorrow they refuse to pay taxes,' warned a member of the Dergue. By this time, the looming confrontation with the radicals had hardened the regime's attitude, and the *zamatch* unravelled amidst violent clashes with the students in the countryside. By mid-1976, the students had returned to the towns, and the staffing of the provincial administration changed once more. All the recently appointed officials were dismissed, transferred or resigned, to be replaced by army officers and members of the emerging corps of political cadres mass-produced by the regime. With their help, the state's administrative network became denser, wider and reached deeper into rural society than ever before. A purge in 1978 had removed the freely elected *kebele* leadership and replaced it with another vetted by the regime's agents. Accompanied by violence, this served as a warning to the peasants, and from then on the *kebele* functioned as adjuncts of the state administration. By 1987, there were some 20,000 *gabbar kebele* in Ethiopia. It was a huge effort to 'capture' the peasantry and it was effective for a time.

A similar fate was reserved for the urban dwellers *kebele* that were established to manage low cost housing and neighbourhood affairs. The first battle between rival radical factions was fought over control of some 300 of these in Addis Ababa. The EPRP sought with initial success to infiltrate the *kebele* in the capital, and placed its supporters in their elected leadership. Alerted by MEISONE, the Dergue ordered new elections in October 1976, in which former house owners and rentiers were not allowed to vote. Carried out under cadre supervision the elections secured the desired result. At the same time, the urban *kebele* jurisdiction was extended to include police functions and the recruitment of an armed militia. Politically reliable elements took over, and lumpen proletariat types were drafted into the militia to turn the *kebele* into instruments of urban mass control. They were relied upon to spy on, inform against and harass suspected dissidents. On every required occasion, they provided mass audiences by herding people together in 'spontaneous' demonstration and rallies. And when the battle against the radicals was joined, they were to play a murderous role.

*

State ownership of the economy empowered the Dergue to think in grandiose terms about reversing the declining trend in the country's economic fortunes. Coming to power in the wake of the 1974 famine, it gave priority to the agricultural sector where it experimented with a number of schemes. The land reform proclamation had envisaged the formation of consumer cooperatives, and since they provided consumer goods at reasonable prices they proved quite popular. A parallel scheme to establish collective farms proved far less attractive, even though taxes paid by their members were set at half the rate paid by the rest. A serious effort to increase agricultural production went into the development of a state farm sector using wage labour. It started with nationalised commercial farms to which more land was added. By the early 1980s, state farms occupied about 4% of all cultivated land, and consumed an average 80% of all the agricultural inputs provided by the state.

At the same time, the regime sought to increase revenue from the rural sector. In January 1976, the old system of agricultural taxation was revised, and a simpler schedule was introduced comprising a fee for the use of land and a tax on agricultural income. Initially the rates were set low, and collection was entrusted to the peasant *kebele*, which was allowed to keep 2% of the total collected. The rates were raised later, but the main mechanism of siphoning off the agricultural surplus was the state purchasing monopoly, the classic method of appropriating rural surplus through administrative means. An Agricultural Marketing Corporation was set up in 1977 with a purchasing monopoly on agricultural produce, and the peasants were forced to sell only to this agency at prices fixed by the state. Further state monopolies were set up to monopolise agricultural inputs; machinery, tools and other manufactured products.

The result was a steady decline in production, as peasants produced less and consumed more of what they produced, thus selling less to the state monopoly. Food production in 1978-1979 was 10% less than in 1977. On the fourth anniversary of the Revolution, Mengistu assailed peasant 'individualism', saying that 'to produce only what is sufficient for one's own family, to refuse to bring crops to the market until prices rise, and to under-produce in order to maintain prices at a very high level, all these are manifestations of individualistic and anti-socialist attitudes.' Food shortages became a permanent and worsening feature, accompanied by rising prices and futile state attempts to control them.

In the early 1980s, drought once again scorched the countryside. It hit the same blighted region of the north before the people had recovered from its visitation ten years earlier. This famine was ten times worse than the last. By 1984, ten of Ethiopia's fourteen provinces were affected, and one-third of its population faced starvation. There was no attempt to conceal the disaster this time. On the contrary, the Dergue appealed loudly for world help. When it arrived, however, the regime refused to help with transport to remote and inaccessible districts of the interior, or to launch the oft-used *zamatcha* to mobilise domestic aid for the stricken regions. Like Haile Selassie earlier, it pinned the blame for the famine on drought, and no one dared recall the slogan coined on the previous occasion: to wit 'drought is natural, famine is man- made'. The toll taken by this famine was estimated at one million souls.

The disaster prompted the regime to launch another ill-considered scheme. This was to move land hungry peasants from the north *en masse* to the south, i.e. from the centre to the periphery. Hardly an original idea, it had been the dream of Ethiopian rulers at least since Menelik. Resettlement had been considered by the imperial regime, when a pilot project was started in the 1950s and moved some 20,000 families by 1974. A Settlement Authority was founded in 1976 and was absorbed in a Relief and Rehabilitation Commission (RRC) in 1979. At the outset, resettlement proceeded gradually; about 100,000 people were moved by 1983. It was then, in the midst of famine, that a *zamatch* was unleashed with a characteristic propaganda barrage and unseemly haste to drain the worse affected areas of excess population. In a crash programme – more in the nature of evacuation than planned resettlement – the regime's cadre harassed people dazed by starvation with promises and threats. Some 700,000 were moved within two years (1984-5). They came mainly from Wollo (62.4%), Shoa (18.4%), Tigray (15.3%), and went to the lowlands of western Ethiopia and to parts of the south. Weakened by hunger, many perished on the way, and many others died from lack of basic facilities in the receiving areas. After the fall of the military regime in 1991 most resettlement sites were abandoned and little survived of that costly scheme.

This was the fate also of yet another Dergue project, villagisation. Many highlanders live in widely scattered homesteads near or inside their fields and far from roads. In the north, these are often perched on the flat tops of hills and mountains that discourage plans to link them with transport facilities and provide their inhabitants with the services of education and health. Inaccessibility is also a key reason for the high toll taken by famine. On the other hand, inaccessibility affords a decree of protection from interference by the state. One author described the imperial Ethiopian state as 'partially blind: it knew preciously little about its subjects' (Scott 1998: 2). In fact, the imperial administration was not certain even of the number, location and names of the country's districts (*woreda*) and sub-districts (*mikitil woreda*) (Markakis 1974: 349).

Villagisation began as a security project in Bale province during the 1977-8 war with Somalia, and was extended, for the same purpose, to Hararghe province in 1984, where one million households were moved into villages within months. Over the following years, it was decided to implement the programme nationally. A National Villagisation Coordinating Committee was formed, and another *zamatcha* was unleashed on the hapless Ethiopian peasantry. Bullied by their *kebele* leaders and local administrators, they were forced to dismantle their huts and use the material to build others in sites laid out grid fashion along roadsides. Detailed but flawed guidelines were issued for every aspect of the programme – from village size that proved too large, to house dimensions that proved too small – making no concession to the immense diversity of Ethiopia's countryside. Some villages were provided with social services, but agricultural production suffered. There were no economic gains from this upheaval, but then, this was not the intention. According to a high official, 'the main goal was the control of and regimentation of society, not development' (Dawit Wolde Giorgis 1989: 307).

By the time the villagisation programme was completed at the end of the decade, people were already abandoning the new villages, and almost all were abandoned after 1991; this being the peasants' final verdict. A song composed at the time shows that villagisation was the last straw:

> If land was distributed, I could bear it
> If debts were plenty, I could bear that too
> If I have to go to the war front, I can bear this also
> Asking me to tear down my own house
> Is definitely the puzzle of puzzles
> (Fekede Azeze 2002: 166)

The cadre and the state

The dispossession of the ruling class left a political vacuum in the centre that could not be filled by the 'workers in uniform' alone. Just as the imperial regime had brought into being a class of western educated retainers to govern the state from the centre, its successor regime fabricated a 'socialist' elite for the same purpose. The task was made easier by an education system that was now hugely expanded to meet the manpower needs of a bloated state. Western education was the trademark of this class, hastily garnished with a dose of raw Marxism provided in a special training centre. The economic base of the new class of '*guad*' ('comrades') was state office, not unlike the 'bourgeoisie of the public service' that had emerged with decolonisation everywhere in Africa. The state expanded prodigiously, spawning new ministries and agencies in the centre with branches in the provinces, and the number of civil servants rose from 109,322 in 1978 to 167,860 in 1983 (Clapham 1988: 124). Dozens of parastatal organisations were formed, some to manage the economy, others to erect a political facade for the military dictatorship, and others yet to regiment society through mass organisations in Soviet fashion.

The new class of state functionaries was markedly more heterogeneous ethnically than the retainers of the imperial regime. The Abyssinian element remained dominant, but was supplemented by expanding recruitment from the highland periphery, leavened with the beginnings of Muslim participation, and even a token representation from the lowland periphery. It was the military establishment that expanded most, and in the process became more representative of the country at large. Prominent in the new cadre class were the Oromo, who also figured in the ranks of the military and in the Dergue itself. The ethnic composition of the Dergue in turn was mixed, although the precise nature of it was never established.

The new peripheral elite had to be groomed to replace the *balabbat*. Unlike the imperial regime that simply co-opted the traditional elite in the conquered territories, the Dergue had to produce it from whatever material was available. This proved to be the first generation of educated youth in the periphery who had imbibed the radical ethic. The regime's apparent divergence from the Abyssinian model of the nation-state, its pronouncements on ethnic equality, cultural emancipation and, above all, its land reform, were powerful incentives for those who had come of age in the midst of the Revolution. They accepted the radical thesis that national contradictions could be resolved through the class struggle, and put their faith in the soldiers to see this through.

The introduction of *Etiopia Tikdem* made no mention of centre/periphery contradictions, but they were soon to be codified as the 'nationalities issue'. Only 'the abolition of certain traditional customs which may hamper the unity and progress of Ethiopia' could be taken as a hint of things to come. A further clarification issued on the day after Haile Selassie's deposal promised the 'abolition of discrimination on the basis of nationality, religion and income'. The soldiers were finding their way, and henceforth the 'equality of all nationalities in Ethiopia' was routinely affirmed, usually followed by a declaration of the 'absolute', 'inviolable' and 'eternal' unity of Ethiopia. *Etiopia Tikdem* meant 'the dignity of labour; the supremacy of the common good; the inviolability of Ethiopian unity'.[12] The declaration of Ethiopian Socialism began by averring that 'Ethiopia shall remain a united country, without ethnic, religious, linguistic and cultural differences.'

The clearest statement on the 'nationalities issue' came more than a year later with the Programme for the National Democratic Revolution (PNDR) in April 1976, the definitive statement of the regime's credo. This was the product of intense debate among radical factions that had thrown their lot in with the regime. They were assigned the task of drafting a programme that would meet the challenge of Eritrean nationalism in ideological terms, and they met it head on. The PNDR proclaimed the right to self-determination of all nationalities, avowed that no nationality would dominate another, declared the history, culture, language and religion of every nationality would have equal recognition in accordance with the 'spirit of socialism,' and went on to promise that 'each nationality will have regional autonomy to decide on matters concerning its internal affairs'(Art. 5). It envisaged 'a people's democratic republic' under the leadership of the proletariat acting in close alliance with peasantry and supported by the petty bourgeoisie, and foresaw the formation of a workers' political party. It was a decade before this last project materialised.

Having hoisted the standard of 'scientific Marxism' to the mast of the Revolution, the Dergue came under pressure from its radical allies and its Soviet patron to produce a 'workers' party'. Obviously reluctant, the regime took years of Byzantine scheming and manoeuvring to achieve it. Before doing so, it had to clear space by fighting off the radical opposition and its demand for a 'people's government'. A hesitant start was made when the Provisional Office for Mass Organisation Affairs (POMOA) was

[12] *Ethiopian Herald* (23 December 1975).

unveiled along with the PNDR. Its mandate was to mobilise support for the regime through the creation of mass organisations, and to produce a corps of cadre to manage them. The regime's first political initiative became the target of the radical opposition drawn together in the EPRP. Its mouthpiece, *Democracia*, levelled a barrage of strident criticism against POMOA and its supporters, calling them fascists and threatening a mass uprising. While the threat remained rhetorical, the Dergue shrugged off the criticism. However, as the urban economy went into a slump, with inflation and unemployment rising, the opposition's capacity for mischief grew and gave cause for concern. EPRP activists made contact with leaders of the Confederation of Ethiopian Labour Unions (CELU) in the hope of coordinating activities. Talk of socialism notwithstanding, Ethiopian workers had yet to see any benefit from the Revolution. Instead, CELU had come under attack by a regime intent on transforming the labour movement into a parastatal body, which it accomplished when CELU was violently disbanded in mid-1975, to be replaced by the All Ethiopia Trade Union (AETU).

The EPRP hastened the confrontation when it decided to plunge into urban guerrilla warfare, for which it was woefully unprepared. POMOA cadre became targets of assassination, followed by urban *kebele* officials and, in a botched attempt on his life on 25 September 1976, Colonel Mengistu himself. The regime's reaction was savage and indiscriminate. Mobilising POMOA's cadre, urban *kebele* militia, police, security and military units, it unleashed a murderous campaign officially branded the 'Red Terror'. House to house searches in the capital and other towns targeted suspect groups such as students and young teachers, who were arrested, tortured. Occasionally, 'revolutionary justice' was meted out with a bullet to the head.

The bloodshed shocked people in the towns, where streets were jammed with funeral processions. The shock waves were felt inside the Dergue itself, where one faction sought to curb Mengistu's power. It succeeded in installing General Tafari Bante at the head of the Provisional Military Advisory Council (PMAC), thus putting him directly in Mengistu's path. Less than one month later, the latter struck back with characteristic brutality. On the occasion of an official meeting, his henchmen detained and massacred five of his rivals, including Tafari Bante. In February 1977 Mengistu assumed the chairmanship of the PMAC and was henceforth acknowledged its undisputed master. It had taken less than three years for Ethiopia to revert to a personalised dictatorship.

*

Having toyed with the radicals in its camp for some years, the regime now dashed their hopes by deciding to form its own 'proletarian party'. In September 197, POMOA begat the Commission for the Organisation of the Ethiopian Workers Party (COPWE), the bulk of whose membership were soldiers. Four years later, COPWE begat the Workers Party of

Ethiopia (WPE), whose founding congress in September 1984 coincided with extravagant celebrations for the tenth anniversary of the Revolution, in the midst of the worst famine the country had experienced in living memory. WPE was simply a renaming of COPWE, with identical membership and leadership and with Colonel Mengistu as Secretary General. He took the opportunity to settle an old issue, declaring: 'Other than the Workers' Party of Ethiopia...there can be no other vanguard organization representing workers in revolutionary Ethiopia today.'

At last, after ten years, the Revolution had found its vanguard. Mengistu raised another outstanding issue that awaited resolution: 'Since the eruption of the revolution, there is not a single time when the revolutionary government has not considered the rights of nationalities', he declared. In fact, the Dergue was under pressure from its Soviet patron to create the institutional framework for a lasting settlement of the conflicts that were consuming the regime's energy and the country's meagre resources. In his report to the founding congress of the WPE, Mengistu explained 'the aim of the Workers' Party of Ethiopia concerning nationalities is that the democratic rights of each shall be recognised, and that they shall build their common prosperity together by co-ordinating their resources and ability in the spirit of brotherhood and equality.'

Ethiopia was a rarity among states in never having had a population census. The imperial regime made do with guesstimates that proved wildly off the mark. The Central Statistical Office estimate for the population in 1970 was 24.3 million with a growth rate of 2.5 per cent. The results of the first census, carried out in 1984, came as a shock. It reported a staggering 42.6 million people with a growth rate of 3 per cent.

The timely appearance of the census made the task of the Institute for the Study of Ethiopian Nationalities (ISEN), formed in 1984, easier. The idea for ISEN was taken from China, whose own Institute of Nationalities was visited by a Dergue delegation in 1975.[13] The Institute's task was to '(a) study the political, social, economic and cultural conditions of Ethiopian nationalities, and (b) conduct studies for a constitution, state structure and administrative set up on the basis of which a peoples' democratic republic could be established'. It was put under the wing of COPWE's own Bureau of Nationalities, and was staffed mostly by university teachers and civil servants with no affiliation to the regime. Few of them were enthusiastic, but none dared refuse when they were asked by Mengistu himself. The task of drawing Ethiopia's ethnic mosaic fell to the Institute's Cultural and Historical Affairs branch, particularly its Language unit, because mother tongue was taken as the sole criterion for the definition of nationality. After all, it was Stalin himself who wrote that 'a national community is inconceivable without a common language', and a 'community of language is one of the characteristics features of a nation' (1936: 5-6). With this imprimatur, an early ISEN report concluded optimistically: 'Since language is the indicator of a nationality's existence, the success of our building on the basis of equality

[13] Personal communication from the late Dr. Assefa Medhanie, a member of the delegation.

and respect for nationalities will depend on our vision of language' (August 1984).[14]

Relying heavily on the 1984 census which recorded data on ethnic languages, ISEN produced a list of 89 nationalities, although the census itself listed 91 groups. The Institute questioned the accuracy of its own list, the main reason being the confusion that reigned over nationality names. Many groups call themselves by one name; their neighbours call them by different names; the state knows them by yet another name, while anthropologists and linguists have yet others for them. Many groups are known by the names of their clans, and others by their religion. Often, it is unclear whether a name refers to a group, the area it inhabits, its language, or something else. Furthermore, groups that may share a language do not always consider themselves one nationality. ISEN produced brief ethnographic sketches, as well as maps showing group location and size by province, *awraja* and *woreda*. Given the resources at their disposal, this was no mean feat. Flaws notwithstanding, the work provided the material that also went into the design of the federal system in the 1990s.

It was made clear at the outset that the constitution would be based on the principles of Marxism/Leninism. 'The client state must bring its own political structures into alignment with those of the patron state' (Badie 2000: 26). The experience of socialist countries was relevant, especially those with federal structures: ISEN staff dutifully travelled to the Soviet Union, Yugoslavia and other Eastern European states to learn from their experience. Autonomy for nationalities was part of the Leninist legacy that had been repeatedly promised in Ethiopia. Addressing the founding congress of the WPE Mengistu had reiterated: 'Regional autonomy is the practical solution to the problem, in view of the objective conditions of our country.' What form of autonomy would entice Eritreans and other insurgents to renounce secession? When ISEN staff asked if autonomy implied federalism, the answer was negative. Self determination, another Leninist article of faith, was ruled out by Mengistu in the same address: 'This is not to say that nationalities will lose the right to self determination. What it means is that...the question cannot be raised in the form of secession, but it will be applied in the form of local self-determination.' ISEN prudently concurred: 'At this time, the idea of secession contradicts the interest of the whole Ethiopia, so revolutionaries will struggle in all fields against those who have secessionist positions, and will agitate and educate the people for unity based on equality.'

When it came to defining the criteria that would determine the unit of autonomy, ISEN faced a serious problem. A preliminary survey showed that out of 580 *woreda*, only about 30 were monolingual. Accordingly, mother tongue was rejected as the basis for drawing a regional map. The

[14] ISEN Basic Documents (handwritten, undated). All the documents mentioned here were found in the ISEN library located in a building afterwards occupied by the Ethiopian Elections Commission.

[15] Information on the ISEN drafting process came from interviews with former members, Assefa Medhanie, Eshetu Chole, Asmalash Beyene and Haile Wolde Mikael.

regime's often stated preference for economic development criteria was adopted instead. 'If there is a question of priority, the building of the economy will be first', were Mengistu's instructions, and the ISEN again concurred: 'The main criteria for the regional division are to satisfy the needs of the working people and to build the socialist economy.' A consensus finally emerged on the need to consider, in addition to language and culture, the physical infrastructure and economic conditions of nationalities, and their relative ability to self-manage development. Special committees were formed to work on thorny issues, drafts were circulated between the ISEN and the WPE, and Mengistu showed up several times to join the discussions and issue further instructions.[15] ISEN drafts generally favoured greater autonomy for the relatively more developed and politically stable highland regions, and less for peripheral ones lacking infrastructure. As it turned out, the final document gave more autonomy to peripheral regions where political problems were the worst.

The final draft, made public in March 1987, came as a surprise to the staff of the ISEN, for their work had been substantially modified by the regime's leading lights. The commitment to economic development notwithstanding, the scheme had been designed on blatantly political grounds. Nor was the nationality principle conspicuous in the regional profiles. Some regions were homogeneous, most were not, and none of the major nationalities got their own region. Ethiopia was divided into twenty administrative regions (*akakabi*) and five autonomous regions (*ras gez*). Three of the latter – Eritrea, Tigray, Ogaden – were in the throes of nationalist uprisings, and all three lost territory to other regions. Tigray, the other rebellious province in the north, lost three eastern districts to the Assab autonomous region. The Somali also paid the price of dissidence by being parcelled among four regions: Dire Dawa, Ogaden, Assab and Eastern Hararghe. The regions were required to establish their own administrative institutions before the system could become operative. None of these came to pass, of course. Even as the final touches were being applied to the constitutional façade, the military regime was nearing its end.

Summary

Undoubtedly a landmark in the modern history of Ethiopia, the 1974 Revolution left an ambiguous legacy. It hurried the demise of an obsolete system, and cleared the ground for a modern society and system of governance. Yet, it failed to lay the foundations of such a system. 'What makes a revolution is not the destruction of the old order, but the construction of the new one' (Clapham 1988: 6). This is a task of a different order, and it proved beyond the capacity of Ethiopia's revolutionaries. Lack of imagination may appear to be one reason for failure. The Ethiopian radicals set about the task armed with an ideology borrowed whole-cloth from abroad, and proceeded single-mindedly to try and turn a pre-modern society into a post-modern utopia, making no concession to time or place. They showed little understanding of their country's immense complexity, and even less capacity to innovate in order to deal with it. Appearances do not tell the whole story. The revolutionaries, in and out of uniform, were first and foremost nationalists committed to the defence of the state in the shape and form it had inherited from the imperial regime. If only because they believed it was essential for this purpose, this included the preservation of centre dominance over the rest of the country. The appeal of 'scientific Marxism' lay in the fact that it offered both an ideological defence and an institutional model for a state with a decentralised administrative structure but a rigidly centralised decision-making process.

Land reform proved a rare, lasting contribution of the Revolution. The reforms initiated during the last years of the imperial regime threatened to let the country's main resource slip out of state control. Nationalisation aborted this threat, enabling the regime to directly appropriate the agricultural surplus, and to freely allocate land as it saw fit. State ownership of land also facilitated population control, the quintessence of state building. The rebuilt state had a vastly wider, longer, deeper and firmer reach than its predecessor. For the first time in the country's history, it could be said that most of its subjects became aware of its presence and felt its impact.

8

Building the Socialist State

1974–1991

The annihilation of the radical factions in the centre was a Pyrrhic victory for the Dergue, because it shifted the focus of opposition to the periphery, where other nationalities emulated the Eritreans by launching their own 'national liberation' struggles. Among them were the Oromo, Sidama, Somali, Afar, Anywaa and Berta. The conflict in Eritrea widened to involve the Christian community, and the war there went on for fifteen more years to sap the strength of the regime in Addis Ababa. What sealed the regime's fate, however, was a rebellion that broke out in Tigray, deep in the Abyssinian heartland, which combined political radicalism with Ethiopian nationalism in an original and politically effective blend. With the radical banner kept aloft by the rebels in Eritrea and Tigray, the argument over national versus class contradictions was settled in favour of the former, and 'national self determination up to and including secession' now became the radical creed.

With 'national liberation' movements mushrooming, the state rebuilding project faced collapse. The embattled regime in Addis Ababa rallied the population to '*innat agar tirri*' ('call of the motherland') and mobilised the country's resources for total war. Turning Ethiopia into a garrison state, it unleashed a storm of violence that took a frightening toll in lives on all sides, laid rebel regions waste, forced millions to seek refuge abroad, crippled an already feeble economy and reduced the country to pauper status.

The call of the motherland

The expansion of the military began immediately and was soon to reach improbable levels for a country mired in abject poverty. The size of the armed forces expanded from five army divisions to thirty one, and is estimated to have reached half-a-million men and women under arms. The bulk of the soldiery was provided by the peasantry throughout the country, the highland periphery included, with the rural *kebele* instrumental in the recruitment process. Quotas were imposed on them and failure to meet them invited serious sanctions. The *kebele* were expected to clothe and pay the recruits, to plough their fields and maintain their families. Won over by the Land Reform and the regime's appeals to patriotism, initial peasant response was adequate to meet the needs of the military. In time, the regime's economic policies dissipated peasant support, and mounting battlefield casualties cooled their patriotism, forcing the Dergue in 1983 to impose compulsory military service of twenty four months on males between the ages of eighteen and thirty. In a press conference (14 February 1978), Colonel Mengistu envisaged raising a peasant militia of six million, and on a similar occasion ten years later (31 May 1988), he declared: 'We cannot view our country, our social and economic development, our freedom, our sovereignty and unity in isolation from arms.'

Ethiopia had no serious difficulty securing foreign support for this purpose. When the United States was put off by the Dergue's affectations of 'scientific Marxism', it was quickly replaced by the Soviet Union rushing to the aid of a 'fraternal country in transition to socialism'. Moscow had previously taken under its wing another 'fraternal country on the road to non-capitalist development' in the Horn. This was Somalia, ruled by a military junta that had seized power in 1969 and, quite improbably, committed this nation of nomads to 'scientific Marxism'. In return for its patronage, the Soviet Union took an option to set up a naval base in Berbera on the Red Sea. Although it never actually made use of it, it managed to alarm Washington, setting off the Cold War in this corner of Africa. The turmoil caused by the 1974 Revolution in Ethiopia provoked great excitement across the border in Somalia, especially among the multitude of refugees from Ethiopia, who now saw a God-given opportunity to liberate their homeland. The Siad Barre regime in Mogadisho came under great pressure from that quarter, and was pushed into action relying imprudently on continued Soviet material support and diplomatic backing. Despite a gross disadvantage in capacity – its army did not exceed 40,000 – Somalia launched an invasion of south-eastern Ethiopia in 1976 (see Chapter 9).

At this time, citing a newly found concern for human rights, Washington cut off aid to Ethiopia and the Dergue turned to Moscow. Apparently believing it could play both sides, the latter responded favourably, only to be expelled from Somalia unceremoniously by the enraged regime. Subsequently, a gigantic airlift was launched using Benghazi in Libya and Aden in South Yemen as stages, to bring one billion dollars worth of arms to Ethiopia in record time. Virtually every Soviet satellite, including South Yemen, was pressed into aiding Ethiopia, and a Cuban force of 15,000 arrived to help expel the Somali invader in 1978. The Cold War *pas de deux* was completed with a United States offer to arm Somalia with 'defensive weapons'.

Having undermined the imperial regime, the war in Eritrea went on to haunt its successor. At the same time as the radical factions were losing the fight in the centre, radicalism was agitating and invigorating the nationalist movement in Eritrea. The agitators were Christian Eritreans converted to Marxism while attending university in Addis Ababa, the birthplace of the Student Movement. Before long, they clashed with the conservative Muslim leadership of the Eritrean Liberation Front (ELF), and went on to set up a rival organisation, the Eritrean Peoples Liberation Front (EPLF). The impact on the secessionist movement was twofold. The fact that it was now led by Christians eased the conversion of that previously hesitant community to Eritrean nationalism, and brought an influx of recruits into the guerrilla army.[1] Among them were many students who reinforced the radical ethos of the new Front, infusing Eritrean nationalism with a strong dose of Marxism that became EPLF ideology. The ELF rejected its rival's radical posture, because it ran the risk of dividing Eritreans along class lines and weakening the momentum of the revolution.

Since the rebels in Eritrea had declared that only unconditional independence would satisfy them, the Dergue ignored them and addressed the Eritrean people instead. General Aman Andom, himself an Eritrean and newly appointed Chief of Staff, was chosen to make the overture. A highly respected officer, but not a member of the Dergue, Aman made his first tour of Eritrea at the end of August, addressing mass rallies in Tigrigna and Arabic to explain the nature and aims of the Revolution. He returned there in October, now as head of the Provisional Military Administrative Council, to admonish the people for failing to appreciate the changes taking place in Ethiopia. Since the oppressors of the people had been overthrown, 'who is the enemy of Eritrea now?' he asked. He ruled out political concessions, declaring 'the unity of Ethiopia and Eritrea is eternal', and threatened the rebels saying: 'We have formidable force. We have shunned from using it so far.'[2] However, when the Dergue decided to send the Bodyguard Division to Eritrea, Aman refused to sign the order, and the first act in the bloody power struggle within the regime followed. On 23 November, Aman was killed in a clash at his home with soldiers sent to arrest him. In a grisly sequel that night, a group of 59 prisoners comprising the political elite of the imperial regime were massacred by the soldiers.

As far as Eritrea was concerned, the die was now cast. The Dergue adopted the imperial regime's favoured line, to wit: the problem was caused by a handful of *shifta* (bandits) supported by Ethiopia's enemies in the Arab world. In his first public appearance, four days before the November massacre, the emerging strongman of the regime, Major Mengistu Haile Mariam, repeated this line verbatim, adding that the choice for Ethiopians was between 'unity or death'.[3] And in a press conference on 14 February 1978 he made a chilling prediction: 'If necessary the war will continue for generations to come, but the sovereignty, the honour and territorial integrity of Ethiopia will never be a subject of negotiation.'

[1] The five men of the EPLF who drafted the manifesto titled 'We and Our Objectives', were Christians and former students.
[2] *Ethiopian Herald* (11 October 1974).
[3] *Ethiopian Herald* (19 November 1974).

The war in Eritrea was to rage for another fifteen years, going through several dramatic but inconclusive phases. The Eritreans went on the offensive, and by early 1978 they controlled the entire province, save for the towns of Asmara, Massawa, Assab and Barentu. Success did not bring the rival fronts closer together. A unity agreement signed in Khartoum in 1977 was not implemented, and though active hostilities between them ceased for a time, there was no meaningful cooperation subsequently in the war against Ethiopia. Prompt Soviet Union support enabled the Dergue not only to repel the Somali invasion of 1977-1978, but also to regain lost ground in Eritrea. By mid-1978, the government army had recaptured all the towns, except Barentu in the western lowland and Nacfa in the Sahel, and the bulk of Eritrea's population came once more under Ethiopian control.

Relations between the two rival fronts deteriorated afterwards, and hostilities between them resumed at the end of the decade. The EPLF maintained a higher profile by holding on to the Sahel redoubt and the town of Nacfa, a lifeless ruin that became the symbol of continued resistance. Here, the lightly armed, youthful Eritrean fighters managed to repel a series of Ethiopian offensives. These were major military operations, enjoying complete control of the air and unimpeded access by land and sea, yet failed to capture the remote nationalist stronghold. The continued failure of the Ethiopians to eliminate the guerrilla presence kept nationalist hopes alive, and a steady stream of young recruits continued to join the rebels. Increasingly, they came from the Christian highlands of Eritrea and mostly joined the EPLF, which also developed an efficient network of support organisations abroad to gather material aid and channel it to the Sahel. By contrast, the capacity of the ELF deteriorated and by the end of the decade, the older front's active strength was estimated at one-quarter the EPLF's reported 40,000 members. A final elimination round was fought at the turn of the decade, and by 1981 the ELF had lost that struggle and was pushed out of Eritrea into Sudan. Henceforth, the EPLF had no rival in Eritrea. It withstood repeated attempts by the Ethiopian army to evict it from its base in the Sahel, and in the mid-1980s was able to go on the offensive and begin to recapture Eritrean towns.

Nation-building

Beyond the affirmation of equality, respect for all cultures and the condemnation '*Yehebereseb chiqona*' ('nationality inequality'), the soldiers-turned-politicians made no effort to define the elements of an inclusive national culture shared by all Ethiopians. They did not expressly condemn nor defend the 'Amharisation' policy of the imperial regime, and Colonel Mengistu himself cast doubt on the meaning of the term when he once said: 'In Ethiopia, the correct meaning of Amhara is highland dweller. If this is the case, who then is Amhara?'[4] Nevertheless, the Abyssinian essence

[4] Quoted in Tegegne Taka (1998: 120).

of that policy was diluted by certain developments sanctioned by his regime, not least in the field of religion. The Revolution made it possible for Islam to emerge from the shadows of the past, and for its adherents to attain equal citizenship status with Christians. Three Islamic festivals, along with five Christian, were declared public holidays. Muslim names began to appear in the lists of state, party and military officialdom, and even in the membership of the Dergue. On the other hand, the Ethiopian Orthodox Church suffered a historic reversal, losing its official status, its vast landholdings, as well as state support for the clergy and churches, a burden that now fell on its parishioners. The Dergue also installed its own Abuna (head of the Orthodox Church), having created a vacancy by murdering the previous incumbent.

There were other signs of cultural emancipation. The ban on vernaculars was lifted and some appeared in print and broadcast. Cultural diversity was celebrated, and ethnic songs and dances became a staple feature of public festivals. Ethnic cultural associations proliferated, and the first tentative steps to study the history and culture of subordinate groups were taken. It was now possible to translate the Bible into vernaculars, to invent alphabets for languages that did not have them, and to use them in religious services. In the dramatically changed political context, ethnic identity in the periphery became something of a cultural asset, and people felt the need to unearth their historical and cultural roots. A degree of recognition was accorded to the vernaculars through a massive adult literacy campaign waged in the 1980s. Fifteen languages were selected – Amharigna, Oromo, Tigrigna, Wolayta, Somali, Hadiya, Gidole, Tigre, Kambata, Sidama, Kunama, Afar, Saho, Silte and Kaffa-Mocha – whose speakers it was estimated accounted for 90% of the population. Amharigna served as the 'model language' and the Geez script was used for all. By the eleventh anniversary of the campaign in 1990, the Committee claimed to have made 18.7 million adults literate, thereby reducing the national illiteracy rate from 93 to 25%. Critics found this a gross exaggeration.

The official language spread across the highland periphery and reached even the remote corners of the lowlands. Its main carrier, the state system of education, expanded hugely during this period, particularly at the primary level where the official language was the medium of instruction. Significant growth was achieved in the secondary and tertiary levels as well, and the participation of students from the periphery was boosted by lowering the entry requirements for them. Urban growth and related economic activity strengthened the status of Amharigna as a genuine *lingua franca*. According to the 1984 census, those claiming Amhara identity numbered 29% of the population, while 67% of urban residents claimed Amharigna as the 'language usually spoken at home'.

Military service was another major venue for its promotion. The ethnic composition of the armed forces was quite heterogeneous. In the late 1970s, the composition of the enlisted ranks was about 33% Amhara, 33% Oromo and 25% Tigray, with the remainder coming from other groups. In the officer corps, 65% at the rank of lieutenant colonel and above were Amhara and 20% were Oromo; the latter having nearly doubled during that decade (Nelson & Kaplan 1981: 254-255).

Massive internal population movement and demographic change was another feature of Ethiopia under the Dergue. 'What the Ethiopian revolution actually entailed was a countlessly repeated uprooting of social relations, in thousands of local communities, in millions of lives' (Donham 1999: 35). Soldiers, cadre, state officials, students, traders and craftsmen moved around the country in unprecedented numbers and often settled far away from home. The resettlement programme relocated entire communities, and the villagisation scheme that followed brought its own unsettling consequences. This upheaval had many implications for the centre/periphery interaction. For one thing, many people found themselves in parts of the country they had never heard of, and met fellow Ethiopians whose existence they had never suspected. In one way or another, most landed elsewhere courtesy of the state, and in most cases depended on it for their survival in alien surroundings. The people in the receiving areas had the same experience of meeting fellow Ethiopians, and were perfectly aware of the state's role in their arrival. Consequently, at the end of this period it would have been hard to find many people in Ethiopia who did not know which country they lived in, or did not feel that the state had great power over their lives.

A striking phenomenon was the success of evangelisation by Protestant sects. Certainly, there were many more converts to Christianity than to scientific Marxism at this time. This was part of a noted religious revival throughout the country, presumably a reaction to the harrowing events that marked the reign of the Dergue. The ideologues who counselled the soldiers were disturbed and tried to halt the trend, playing on the Dergue's fears of subversion by sects affiliated with the West, although the Evangelical and Pentecostal congregations in Ethiopia had come under native leadership and had local resources.[5] The campaign against the 'imported religions' was led by MEISONE, whose main support base was in Wallega, and was directed mainly against the Mekane Yesus Church which was seen as a rival for local popularity. The harassment of Mekane Yesus and other churches began in 1978, and led to the confiscation of its property and the closing of the Radio Voice of the Gospel, culminating with the arrest and murder of its general secretary Gudinaa Tumsa in mid-1979. This was followed by the exodus of most foreign missionaries from Ethiopia. After MEISONE itself was crushed by the regime, the anti-religious crusade intensified and was further politicised with accusations of Protestant church links to the Oromo Liberation Front. Many churches were closed, their buildings turned into schools. Clerics were imprisoned and occasionally murdered, church elders were hounded, and people were discouraged from participating in religious activities. By the beginning of 1984, all but a handful of Mekane Yesus congregations had been closed (Eide 2000: 188). Kale Hiwot, another major Protestant church, suffered similarly.

[5] Emanuel Abraham, the long time (1963-85) president of Mekane Yesus, an Oromo, was for many years a high official and cabinet minister under Haile Selassie.

The centre divided

The perseverance of the rebellion in Eritrea owed no little to a parallel and equally determined insurgency in Tigray province on its southern border. Tigray's intense self-consciousness and historic sense of grievance against Amhara rule were noted earlier (see Chapter 1). In mid-twentieth century, there were ample reasons to reinforce such feelings. Tigray was, by any measure, the most neglected and poverty stricken province in the Abyssinian homeland. Agricultural production stagnated on a shrinking base in a region of the highlands that is the most damaged by ecological degradation. A study carried out in the mid-1970s claimed that no original topsoil remained in the central plateau and described the situation as 'critical'.[6] Peasant landholdings in Tigray were miniscule. Close to one-half were less than half a hectare and two-thirds less than one hectare. Producing one crop annually, they were barely sufficient to maintain the population at subsistence level, forcing many Tigray to migrate south in search of seasonal or permanent employment.[7] As noted earlier, there was scarcely any investment for economic development in the north under the imperial regime, and none at all in Tigray. There was not a single industrial establishment in the province; an abattoir in Makalle was the largest enterprise. The province was often ravaged by famine. Drought, followed by locust infestation caused a major famine in 1958-59, claiming the lives of an estimated 100,000 people in a population of a little more than 1.5 million. Tigray was the focal point of famine in 1972-4, and before it had time to recover the province was struck an even greater blow in the famine of the early 1980s. Not surprisingly, the people of Tigray were inclined to link the misfortunes of their homeland to its political emasculation and to blame Amhara domination for their plight.

Fiercely proud of their language, the Tigray people seethed with resentment when it was proscribed along with all other native tongues in favour of Amharigna in the 1940s. In a province where, in the mid-1970s, only 12.3% of the males claimed to know the official language and only 7.7% could read it, this created serious problems.[8] Tigray students felt at a disadvantage compared with Amharigna-speakers in clearing school examination hurdles. Only 2% of those who qualified for entry to the University in 1963-8 came from that province, while 65% came from Shoa (including Addis Ababa).[9] Those who reached the top of the education ladder were pessimistic about their future prospects in the service of a state where three-quarters of the senior officials were Shoa (Clapham 1969: 85). Not surprisingly, it was within this narrow circle, in the radical hothouse

[6] Cited in Markakis (1987: 251).
[7] Tigray accounted for 27% of all internal migrants in Ethiopia. Cited in Markakis (ibid.: 296, n.18).
[8] Cited in Markakis (ibid.: 251).
[9] Ibid.

atmosphere of the University, that the insurgency was hatched in the final days of the imperial regime.

Tigray youth were active in the Student Movement and well represented in its leadership. An association concerned with the problems of their province was formed among them in the early 1970s. An early pamphlet listing the 'Grievances of the Tigray People' was followed by one bearing the ominous title '*E tek*' ('To Arms'). At the end of the year, a group of seven militants left the capital and returned to Tigray to prepare for the armed struggle. They were the seed from which the Tigray Peoples Liberation Front (TPLF) grew, which was to seize power in Addis Ababa fourteen years later.

What form the struggle against the Dergue ought to take was the subject of fierce debate in the Student Movement (see Chapter 7). One side held the view that popular mobilisation must transcend nationality divisions and rely on class solidarity, while the opposing side argued that in certain instances nationality contradictions ought to be resolved first through a struggle of national liberation, as a prerequisite to winning the class struggle. The latter was the view taken by those who formed the TPLF. There were three significant implications in this choice, two of which were soon to become explicit. The first was that Tigray is a nation in its own right. A TPLF publication put it plainly: 'Tigreans are direct descendants of the Axumites, who once developed their own glorious civilisation which was planted on the African soil.'[10] The second was that Tigray is an oppressed nation within the Ethiopian empire, and this was likewise made explicit:

> The Tigrean people have remained distinct with their own language, culture, internally integrated economics and psychological identities...All attempts undertaken by the Amhara ruling classes to crush the Tigrean national aspirations, and even more to wipe out their cultural identity (i.e., to forcibly assimilate and Amharanize them) have been futile.[11]

Menelik was not a hero to the Tigray rebels but a villain, who in order 'to fulfil his lust for power...went as far as conspiring with the European colonialists against his African neighbours', the TPFL wrote. 'From that time onward, the national contradictions between the Amhara oppressor nation and the oppressed nations in Ethiopia, including Tigray, came on to the scene.'

As an 'oppressed nation,' Tigray was entitled to self-determination and independence. This was the third implication which, by contrast, was not made explicit. Though the TPLF proclaimed itself a nationalist movement fighting for Tigray self-determination, its position on the issue of independence was carefully hedged. Self determination, it claimed, 'could result in anything from autonomy, federation, confederation, up to and including independence.' The choice would depend on the outcome of the struggle waged by the oppressed nationalities and classes in Ethiopia. A positive outcome could result in integration within a multi-national Ethiopian

[10] *Tigray: A Nation in Struggle* 1979. (TPLF, Foreign Relations Bureau, October 1979 :4).
[11] Ibid.

state. 'Independence is taken as an alternative if, and only if, all possibilities for unity based upon equality are exhausted and it becomes impossible to live together.'[12]

Before establishing itself securely in Tigray, the TPLF had to fight off two rival movements that were also warring against the regime in Addis Ababa, albeit from opposite ends of the political spectrum. One was the Ethiopian Democratic Union (EDU), a revanchist faction led by the traditional ruler of Tigray, Ras Mangasha Seyoum, whose goal was the restoration of the *ancien régime*. TPLF propaganda branded the EDU as 'Centralist' (*teranafit*), and the two clashed violently in a series of battles at the close of 1977. At the start of the following year, the EDU was weakened by a government offensive, and was finally finished off by a TPLF assault that drove it across the border into Sudan.

The other rival was the EPRP. It had set up a base in eastern Tigray, where survivors of the Red Terror regrouped for a 'protracted armed struggle' against the regime in Addis Ababa. Both movements chose this location for its proximity to rebel held territory across the border in Eritrea, and both had members trained by the EPLF. Initial contacts between the EPRP and TPLF were friendly. Veterans of the Student Movement were in the leadership of both, and Tigray natives were prominent in the leadership of the EPRP. A series of meetings held over the next couple of years to resolve their differences revolved around the appropriate mobilisation strategy for the armed struggle against the Dergue; the old class versus nationality conundrum. The EPRP maintained that nationalism is a bourgeois concept, and the TPLF countered: 'The correct solution of the problem is a national struggle which will have a class character against Amhara chauvinism and American imperialism.'[13]

Behind this argument lay the real bone of contention. Fearing it would lead to the disintegration of Ethiopia, the EPRP opposed the proliferation of nationality based factions struggling to shake off Addis Ababa's grip, and derided TPLF's position as 'narrow nationalism'. The latter, on the other hand, had no intention of becoming a minor cog in a large multinational movement, and accused its rival of 'greater nation chauvinism'. The issue was finally settled by force. When fighting broke out in March 1978, the EPRP's untrained students proved no match for the TPLF's peasant fighters, hardened in the clashes with the EDU. They were chased out of Tigray into Eritrea, from where they made their way to Sudan and exile abroad. Trapped in Tigray, a small group of EPRP survivors surrendered to the TPLF. Taken under the latter's wing, they evolved into a valuable military ally and main political partner under the name of

[12] *Peoples Voice*. TPLF Newsletter (Vol. II, April 1981: 2. The firmness of this position was put to a test very early, when the TPLF found it had a rival called the Tigray Liberation Front (TLF), formed by a group of Tigray who had taken refuge with the ELF across the border. Presumably they held conventional nationalist views envisaging independence for their province. The difference between the two fledgling nationalist movements was resolved with ruthless determination by the TPLF, with an attack on its rival that exterminated its leadership.

[13] Programme adopted at the TPLF Second Organisational Congress, May 1983.

Ethiopian Peoples Democratic Movement (EPDM). In the early 1990s it was renamed the Amhara National Democratic Movement (ANDM) and took over the administration of the eponymous federal state.

The relationship between the rebels in the adjoining provinces of Eritrea and Tigray was close, yet fraught with tension. Tigray needed Eritrean support, and the price for it was to recognise the Eritrean struggle as a colonial issue and accept that 'the only solution to the Eritrean question is independence.' It was natural for the Tigray rebels to draw closer to the EPLF, whose leadership came from the same nationality and radical milieu as their own. By contrast, initially friendly relations with the older ELF deteriorated when the latter sought to help EPRP members, and became involved in hostilities with TPLF units pursuing them. An additional reason for tension was the ELF's presence in an enclave called Bademe on the western Tigray-Eritrea border. The ELF had been active there before the birth of the TPLF, and refused to leave. In 1981, the TPLF joined the EPLF in a coordinated attack on the ELF, and together they pushed the older Eritrean front out of its last stronghold in western lowland Eritrea. The two victors agreed to leave the question of Bademe to be settled after the conclusion of the war against the Dergue. This did not work out as expected, and Bademe was to provide the spark for an all-out war between Ethiopia and Eritrea in 1998.

With the elimination of the ELF, the distinction between the Eritrean and Tigray rebellions was blurred. Both sprung from the same blighted northernmost region of the plateau, inhabited by the Tigrigna-speaking branch of the Abyssinian family that had been separated briefly by a colonial border. The leadership of both was drawn from an even more refined stock: Tigrigna-speaking, highland Christian, educated at the same time in the same institutions, where they absorbed the same brand of Marxism. Apparent differences were mainly of an ideological nature. EPLF's bottom line for striking alliances was twofold. On one hand, it required acceptance of Eritrea's historical status as a colony and the associated unqualified right to independence. On the other, it refused to recognise the same status and right for any other nationality in Ethiopia. This required a tortuous ideological rationalisation, whereby Eritrea's situation was classified as a 'colonial issue' and all the others as 'national' issues to be resolved within the Ethiopian state. Interestingly, Eritrean nationalism did not envisage the disintegration of Ethiopia, only a change of regime in Addis Ababa. Further, the TPLF's call for self-determination of the 'Tigray nation' did not sit well with the EPLF because it could be taken to include the Tigrigna-speaking highlanders in Eritrea.

Left without a rival in its province, the TPLF faced only the threat of the Dergue. Preoccupied with the Eritreans and the Somali, the regime paid little attention to the insurrection in Tigray for some time. Reasoning that rebellion in that province would not long survive the defeat of the rebels in Eritrea, the regime concentrated on achieving that objective. In Tigray itself, it was content to keep open the two main roads leading to Eritrea and to hold on to the towns along those routes. The rebels in Tigray took advantage of the relative lull to build up their strength, improve their organisation, and to rally the peasantry to the cause through the formation of mass organisations, intensive political education, and programmes of social reform, including land reform. They harassed government convoys on their way north to Eritrea, and cleared parts of the countryside of government presence, but did not engage in major offensive operations. The Dergue changed tactics in 1988, vacating the towns in Tigray to confront the insurgents in the countryside. This proved a mistake, ending with the rout of the government forces from the province by the end of that year.

The Ethiopian Peoples Revolutionary Democratic Front (EPRDF)

At the start of 1989, as TPLF forces stood poised on the southern border of Tigray, Ethiopians wondered if the rebels would be content to rule their home province, or go on to seize power in Addis Ababa. The TPLF had confronted this issue when it was raised by its own members who wanted to know the reasons for continuing the fight outside Tigray. It was a serious matter and obliged the leadership to halt military operations for a time while it worked to persuade its fighters to carry on. They were told to consider what Tigray's prospects for peace and security would be as long as the Dergue ruled Ethiopia. Ultimately, according to a TPLF statement issued on 18 February 1989, (the 14th anniversary of Front's founding), 'having realised that there is no alternative to continuing and intensifying the struggle in order to shorten the life of the enemy, they (masses) have decided to bear their share of the brunt of the armed struggle.'

As far as the leadership was concerned the decision had been made much earlier, and the path to power in Addis Ababa had been meticulously charted. The plan was to put together a coalition of like-minded factions representing nationalities in Ethiopia, with the TPLF as *primus inter pares*. A first step was taken in 1984 with the founding of the Marxist Leninist League of Tigray (MLLT) to implement the 'maximum programme' of socialism in Ethiopia. It was expected to serve as the platform for a multi-nationality coalition. Notions of secession and independence for Tigray had faded by this time, and other internal issues had been resolved in the mid-1980s, when the TPLF went through its first internal power struggle and purge at the leadership level. The man who rose to the top was Meles Zenawi, a former medical student at Addis Ababa University, who proved himself a master political tactician. Asked by the author in an interview to explain the decision to stay in Ethiopia, Meles Zenawi was blunt: 'When we reached the borders of Tigray, we looked back and saw there was nothing there.'[14]

When the Marxist Leninist scheme made no progress, a call for a

[14] Interviewed in Addis Ababa (10 August 1993).

'united democratic front' of all movements opposed to the Dergue was sounded in 1989. The response of other insurgent movements was disappointing. Their reluctance was understandable; history had made them wary of Abyssinian political overtures. Nevertheless, the formation of the Ethiopian Peoples Revolutionary Democratic Front (EPRDF) was announced in January 1989. It consisted of the TPLF and its *protégé*, the Ethiopian Peoples Democratic Movement (EPDM). Developed under Tigray patronage, the latter had fought credibly in the neighbouring Amhara provinces of Gondar and Wollo and, following its mentor's lead, had formed its own Ethiopian Marxist Leninist Force (EMLF).

Given the refusal of other existing organisations to join the coalition, the EPRDF proceeded to produce them itself. The human material was on hand. It consisted of government soldiers taken prisoner by the insurgents. Some forty thousand of them had been captured in the first half of 1988 alone, and many nationalities were represented. Most of these men had lost faith in the Dergue, and many were favourably impressed by the humane treatment they received at the hands of their captors. They were given lectures on the EPRDF programme and its plans for Ethiopia's future, particularly concerning the 'nationality issue'. Afterwards, they had a choice of returning home, taking refuge in the Sudan, or joining the EPRDF. Those who took the last option were given further political education and trained to organise political parties and mobilise popular support. Thus, a cadre corps was being groomed for the role of subordinate elite under the EPRDF, even before it came power in Addis Ababa.

The blueprint of Ethiopia's political future was presented to the EPRDF's first congress in January 1989. Two factions had been added to the coalition – the Oromo Peoples Democratic Organisation (OPDO), and the Ethiopian Democratic Officers' Revolutionary Movement (EDORM) – this latter was never heard of again. Two others – the Gambella Peoples Liberation Movement and the Beni Shangul Liberation Movement – were invited to attend, but not to join the front. According to the resolutions of the Congress, the foundation of a restructured Ethiopian state would be a 'revolutionary democratic political system based on a multiplicity of political parties and organisations' with political rights for all. The solution to the nationality issue would 'guarantee the right of nations and nationalities to self-determination up to and including secession at all times'. This blunt statement was tempered by the stipulation that 'in a genuinely democratic state, the peoples' interests are served not by secession but by unity', and a promise that the Ethiopian state would be rebuilt 'on the basis of granting nationalities wide autonomy to administer their own internal affairs on the basis of federation or confederation'. The congress hopefully predicted that in a democratic state 'very few peoples, if any, will want to secede.' As for Eritrea, it was decided that its people would be allowed to determine their future in a referendum that might well lead to secession; 'Taking all things into consideration, this would be a lesser evil compared to the present condition of fratricidal war and unmitigated destruction', was the sensible conclusion.

Oromo nationalism

Having suffered greatly from Abyssinian rule, the Oromo peasantry and pastoralists were considered ripe for revolution long before 1974. The rebellion among the Arsi Oromo in Bale in the 1960s seemed a prelude, and a general uprising among the 'Galla', as the Abyssinians called the Oromo, was thought a distinct possibility under the imperial regime. The regime's first line of defence against this threat was the Oromo *balabbatnet* whose interest was to maintain the tribal divisions that inhibited collective Oromo action. However, the first signs of Oromo dissidence came from another direction: the emerging intelligentsia as it began to react to 'Amharisation'. In the early 1960s, in a rare concession to private initiative it soon came to regret, the imperial regime allowed the formation of voluntary associations for local development. The Matcha Tulama Association that was formed in 1962 became an immediate worry, because it aspired to develop into a pan-Oromo organisation. Its leaders addressed mass meetings in the countryside in the Oromo tongue, where taboo topics such as the issue of land were raised. Interestingly, the moving spirit of the Association was General Tadesse Birru, a thoroughly assimilated Oromo from Shoa, who was at the time head of the Territorial Army. In 1966 the Association was banned and its leaders charged with treason. General Tadesse was sentenced to death but was spared and sent to prison, a young army officer was executed, and dozens of other spent the remaining years of the imperial regime in jail. The ruthless suppression of the Matcha Tulama Association in the second half of the 1960s revealed the centre's dread of anything that might help the Oromo overcome their politically crippling divisions.

It was the vision of Oromo unity that inspired the founders of the Oromo Liberation Front (OLF) in the 1970s. The seedbed of nationalism was the budding Oromo intelligentsia that emerged in the 1960s, when limited educational opportunities became available in the highland periphery. In the early 1970s, Oromo accounted for only about 20% of the University student body (Balsvik 1979: 102). The founders of the OLF came from this group, nourished by the radicalism of the Student Movement of which they were a part. An early product of this effort was a pamphlet entitled 'The Oromo: Voice Against Tyranny' (1971: 24) which declared: 'No Oromo can rely on his ability, qualifications, or even hypocrisy to attain material wealth and self-aggrandizement because the racist regime considers him as its dangerous enemy.'

The necessity of armed struggle was an article of faith among the youthful radicals, and was fully shared by the budding Oromo nationalists. Initial moves in that direction were made at the end of the decade by small groups of Muslim Oromo from the southeast. Sheikh Hussein Sura, a merchant from Bale who had been a member of the Matcha-Tulama Association, went to Mogadisho after it was banned to join other refugees from Bale there. Impatient with the restrictions imposed by the Somali authorities, Sheikh Hussein soon made his way to Aden, where he formed a faction he named the Ethiopian National Liberation Front (ENLF), and began training young Oromo in guerrilla tactics. At the end of October 1969, about three dozen of these men landed near Berbera on their way to the Harar plateau. They were led by Abdulkarim Ibrahim Hamid, a former student from Harar, who took the *nom de guerre* of Jarra Abagada. Arrested by the Somali authorities upon landing, the would be guerrillas were kept in prison by the Siad Barre regime until 1975, during which time they had the opportunity to learn about Somali territorial claims on Ethiopia, and the extent to which they included Oromo inhabited areas.

Sheikh Hussein was not deterred by this failure. New recruits arrived in Aden, several university students among them. In June 1973, he went Addis Ababa to rally support for the ENLF. Neither the faction's name, nor Sheikh Hussein's perception of the looming struggle as a common one for all the oppressed nationalities in Ethiopia, appealed to the Oromo militants, who were by now leaning towards an independent assertion of Oromo nationalism. After he returned to Aden, Sheikh Hussein dispatched another armed group that succeeded in reaching the mountainous Chercher region west of the town of Harar. It was led by Hassan Ibrahim, a trader who took the *nom de guerre* Elemo Qiltu, and was shortly afterwards killed in a clash with soldiers. Contact was made with Oromo groups in Harar, Dire Dawa and Addis Ababa, but before more could be done, these initial Oromo stirrings were forestalled by the revolution that broke out in February 1974.

Because the Oromo peasants were arguably its main beneficiaries, the Revolution's achievements, especially land reform, took the wind out of the sails of incipient Oromo nationalism. For the time being, the Dergue enjoyed widespread support in the highland periphery, where the peasants flocked to join the *kebele*. In the towns, a cultural renaissance was in the making, with the celebration of Oromo folklore, dance and theatre, and the appearance of publications in that language. Oromo were well represented in the military, and several Oromo officers were included in the Dergue's leadership. General Tafari Bante who briefly headed the PMAC was an Oromo. If only because its founder and leader, Haile Fida, was an Oromo, MEISONE was considered an Oromo stronghold. Baro Tumsa, another prominent Oromo activist, led a faction called the Revolutionary Struggle of the Oppressed Masses of Ethiopia (acronym in Amharigna ECHAAT), which also enjoyed the regime's favour for a time. Both the EPRP and MEISONE actively sought Oromo support and sponsored Oromo affiliate groups. The youthful Oromo intelligentsia was also well represented among those appointed to office at all levels under the new regime, and the cadre ranks in the periphery were filled with Oromo who were prepared to take up the role of a subordinate elite.

For a time, the activists devoted themselves to organising Oromo cultural performances. Before long, the regime's inflexible commitment to authoritarian, centralised rule dispelled their illusions, and led them along the same path travelled simultaneously by their Tigray colleagues. A group of some thirty of them, mostly former university and secondary school students, met in Addis Ababa in mid-June 1976 to found the Oromo

Liberation Front (OLF).[15] The meeting revised a document drafted earlier, which now became the OLF official programme. It defined the Oromo position in Ethiopia as colonial, demanded the right of self determination, and called for an armed struggle as the only solution. The goal was *bilisumma* (independence) for Oromia, a state whose boundaries were drawn to include all of central and southern Ethiopia, save the Ogaden and South Omo regions; an expanse inhabited by many groups other than Oromo.

In September 1977 the OLF began to formalise its structure with the establishment of a central committee of 41 members, and the selection of a five member 'politico-military command'. Care was taken to avoid over-representation of the western Oromo region that produced the bulk of the militants, most of them the product of missionary education. Dima Nogo, who had acted as OLF chairman until then was from Illubabor; Jarra Abagada, who became military commander was from Hararghe; Magarsa Bari, who now took over as OLF chairman, was born in Bale. Of those appointed to the 'politico-military command', Demissie Teshane was born in Sidamo, Leencho Latta in Wallega, and Taha Ali in Harar.

The first OLF congress met in Chercher in April 1978. A split occurred soon after, when Jarra Abagada left the organisation with a group of Muslim Oromo followers and some time later set up the Islamic Front for the Liberation of Oromia (IFLO). This was the first in an unending series of splits in the Oromo nationalist camp. It deepened and became permanent when Jarra's group was suspected of killing Baro Tumsa, a prominent Oromo activist.[16] Jarra was replaced by Bobasa Mohammed, a former Ethiopian army officer, who also left the organisation after a while. The Somali Abo Liberation Front (SALF), a partly Oromo group was active in Bale, where the OLF was striving to mobilise support (see Chapter 9). The OLF approached SALF's leadership with a proposal for unity, and when it was rejected, it denounced SALF as a Mogadisho tool.

The OLF leadership never functioned as a unit. Dispersed inside and out of Ethiopia, its members became separately engaged in an uphill struggle to build a functioning organisation and establish a credible armed presence within the country. They faced serious obstacles from the start. Initial efforts to raise a force in the Chercher region of Hararghe province were confounded by the Somali invasion of 1977 that turned the south-eastern region into a battleground. On the one hand, this opened up opportunities for recruitment to the nascent Oromo movement in areas freed of Ethiopian control, and also provided a supply of modern weapons. On the other hand, it blurred the image the Oromo nationalists were striving to project by confusing it with pan-Somalism, as illustrated in the appearance of the Somali Abo Liberation Front under the auspices of Mogadisho. Furthermore, because they clashed with its own territorial claims in south-eastern Ethiopia, the Siad Barre

[15] Taha Ali, Baro Tumsa, Ibsa Gutema, Yohannes Lata and Makonnen Galan had joined the Matcha Tulama Association as students, and were among the founders of the OLF.

[16] It was discovered that Baro Tumsa was killed by a distraught comrade.

regime had little sympathy for Oromo nationalist aspirations. OLF territorial claims in Harar and Bale provinces overlapped significantly with those put forth by the Western Somali Liberation Front. Relations between these two insurgent movements were never good, and broke down completely in March 1980, when an OLF group headed by Magarsa Bari on its way to Mogadisho was murdered by a WSLF unit in Fiq. Subsequently, Galasa Dilbo took over as acting OLF chairman with Leenco Latta as his deputy.

The OLF had been allowed to open an office in the Somali capital in 1979, but the regime there regarded it as superfluous and pressured it to merge with the Somali Abo Liberation Front. A series of fruitless discussions ensued between the two groups. The OLF appealed to the Arsi Oromo leaders in SALF on the basis of their common Oromo identity, proof of which is the Oromo language. They replied that a common language is not sufficient proof of ethnic or political unity, citing English, Arabic and Spanish as examples to the contrary. Moreover, they listed numerous differences between themselves and other Oromo groups, including the fact that some of the latter provided the bulk of the Ethiopian soldiery. With the failure of the talks, SALF leaders pressed the Somali regime to expel the OLF, which was done in 1982. With Somalia offering neither safe haven, nor access to the sea, the OLF was never able to gain a secure foothold in south-eastern Ethiopia.[17]

The OLF had better luck in the Sudan, where it was allowed to open an office in Khartoum in 1978, and made contact with the Eritrean fronts that were well established in that country. While endorsing OLF's demand for self-determination, the EPLF did not welcome the prospect of an independent Oromia, nor did it provide the Oromo rebels with significant aid until the dying months of the military regime in Addis Ababa. It did offer to train a small number of OLF fighters, who were sent afterwards to set up bases in the Kelem and Assosa districts, a remote border region inhabited by non-Oromo groups. Contact was also established with the TPLF in Khartoum, and in 1984 a TPLF unit was sent to train OLF units on the Sudan border, but left only after a short stay.

The call of Oromo nationalism drew little response from rural Oromia. A number of reasons are cited to explain this. The most significant was the impact of the 1975 land reform on the peasantry in the highland periphery, as well as the promise of local self-administration through the peasant *kebele*. The indistinct nature of the Oromo national identity and weak political consciousness is an underlying and durable reason. According to one anthropologist, 'it is clear...that there is much that divides the numerous and far flung Oromo people: subsistence and consequent ways of life, religious belief and practice, political structure, historical experience, and many aspects of custom and practice' (H.S. Lewis, 1993: 4). Oromo traditional society was tightly integrated within the tribal framework, but lacked integrating structures above that level. The institutions that provided the sinews of unity and strength of Abyssinian society were not

[17] Although for many years it claimed to be carrying out operations there.

found among the Oromo. From the beginning of their historic migration the Oromo did not forge unity above the tribal level, nor did they ever coordinate their efforts for a common purpose. Each tribe pursued its own destiny entirely independent of the others, and inter-tribal warfare was the rule rather than the exception. In 1969, an observer in Arsi noted: 'Indeed, the pan-Oromo movement of Harar, Shoa and Wollega had, as yet, hardly stirred any interest in the local countryside ...Only a few teachers and schoolboys were eagerly curious about the Oromo movement; even the word Oromo was not much used, and the people spoke of themselves as Arssi and of their language as *afan Arssi*' (Baxter 1980: 49).

Migration dispersed the Oromo widely over the southern plateau, and memories of primordial unity were obscured by recently added layers of religious and cultural adaptation and assimilation. Accordingly, Muslim Oromo trace their origin to various revered figures of Islam, and Orthodox Christian Oromo tend to adopt the Abyssinian mythological tradition. The partial assimilation of the northernmost Oromo into Abyssinian culture, while the southernmost retained their ancestral tradition, served to dilute further the sense of common identity. Finally, as shown earlier, the relationship of the various Oromo groups with the Abyssinian state and its ruling class was far from uniform, and this was an additional factor militating against Oromo unity.

Oromo nationalism did not gather momentum until the closing years of the Dergue's reign. Lacking a broad peasant base, the insurgency flickered on and off in remote edges of the state, scarcely noticed by Addis Ababa. Its prospects improved as the 1980s wore on, and the exhausted regime in Addis Ababa was reaching the end of its tether. Its troops were massed in the northern front, leaving the periphery in the south lightly garrisoned. By this time also the regime's policies had squandered its credit with a peasantry, whose sons it had used as cannon fodder for years; whose produce it had commandeered at starvation prices; whose patience it had exhausted with disastrous scheme, such as collective farming, villagisation and resettlement, and whom it had harassed for long with demands for contributions to the war effort. *Kebele* officials could no longer meet conscription quotas, and Oromo peasant youth in the west began to drift to the OLF. So did army deserters who often brought their weapons with them.

By this time also, the call of Oromo nationalism resonated increasingly among the younger generation in the towns who had had some measure of modern education and exposure to the arbitrary violence of the regime. This was the generation from which the regime recruited the cadre corps and was meant to serve as the new peripheral elite and centre interlocutor. Ironically, this generation fell victim to the regime's dread of Oromo dissidence, an entrenched state of mind in the centre of the Ethiopian state. In the 1980s, the Oromo intelligentsia became a prime suspect of harbouring seditious nationalist sentiments. Many fell victim to spurious accusations of OLF links, not a few lost their lives, and many spend long years in prison. Many more fled abroad, reinforcing a militant Oromo nationalist diaspora.

As the grip of the regime loosened, the OLF's decade long effort began to produce results. Armed units had come into existence on the western edge of the plateau and the Chercher region of Hararghe. They had separate organisations and leadership and only tenuous contact with each other. Gradually the OLF was able to move up from the border lowlands to the western edge of the plateau in Oromo inhabited territory. Its operational front extended from Assosa to Dembidolo, covering all of western Wallega. Its units started attacking army and police posts, organising support in the villages and establishing a logistical network. The strength of the Ethiopian army in the area was low, and the OLF was able to capture and hold small towns temporarily. The area was also contested by the southern Sudanese rebels allied to the regime in Addis Ababa, and the OLF found itself involved in clashes with the SPLA.

A meeting held in Begi on the Wallega border in 1988, brought together the surviving members of the OLF leadership for the first time in ten years.[18] It chose a central committee for the western OLF, and a politbureau that included Taha Ali, Dima Noggo, Tadesse Eba and Ahmed Buna. Jamal Robleh was named military commander of a guerrilla force in the west that numbered some 3000 by this time. A similar meeting, held in east the following year, chose a central committee for the eastern OLF. Galasa Dilbo was confirmed as chairman of the united OLF. The task of organisation now proceeded smoothly; recruitment intensified, and training programmes for fighters and officers were set up. A training camp and an airstrip were built in the Didesa valley. The same year, the OLF adopted a Political Programme that included the following elastic clause: 'On the basis of the principles of representative, democratic and accountable governance, freedom and equality enunciated in this Article... an impartial referendum may resolve Oromia's participation in federal union of constituent states of Ethiopia' (art.10.6).

The OLF rejected an offer to join the EPRDF, allegedly because 'the TPLF drew up a list of conditions it demanded the Oromo Liberation Front should fulfil.' *Inter alia*, the OLF was asked to form a Marxist Leninist League of its own. Unspoken but crucial was the TPLF's rejection of what it called Oromo 'narrow nationalism' – the Oromo adoption of the colonial thesis with its implicit claim to independence. The OLF's misgivings were confirmed at the end of April 1990 with the announcement of the birth of an Oromo Peoples Democratic Organisation (OPDO) from the womb of the EPRDF. Formed by Oromo prisoners of war, the newborn entity became a member of the EPRDF. The OLF resignedly noted this was not the first time a 'subsidiary Oromo organization' had been created by the Abyssinians. In fact, this transparent ploy killed all hope that a genuine national political consensus could be reached under an EPRDF regime; and that was even before the regime had come to power.[19]

[18] Of the original politbureau members, Magarsa Bari was killed by the WSLF in 1980, Muhei Abdo was executed in Ethiopia in 1987, and Demisse Teshane was imprisoned.
[19] OLF Statement about the OPDO (15 June 1990).

Sidama dissidence

Another 'national liberation movement' appeared at this time in the highland periphery, claiming to represent the Sidama people, one of Ethiopia's largest nationalities, numbering nearly three million according to the 2007 census. A fertile, well watered region, their homeland attracted immigrants from neighbouring areas, and today is one of the most densely populated agricultural areas of Ethiopia. Traditionally subsisting on *ensete*, the Sidama were among the first to take up coffee and *chat* production. Immixgration and commercialisation enhanced the value of land and the peoples' attachment to it. While the Sidama *gabbar* welcomed the Land Reform, they were wary of other Dergue schemes such as villagisation, and strongly resented the state purchasing monopoly of agricultural produce. A trend among local communities to boycott government programmes culminated in a mass protest in 1978 in a place named Boricha. Fighting broke out when the Dergue cadre attacked the protesters who were armed, and a battle lasting twelve hours ensued. Identified as a nest of counter-revolutionaries, the area became a target for punitive measures.

It was in this climate that the Sidama Liberation Movement (SLM) emerged. It founder, Wolde Emmanuel Dubale, was the son of a former *balabbat* and one of the very few educated Sidama at the time. He had served the imperial regime as a judge and was elected to its parliament. Despite these stains to his record, the Dergue appointed him administrator of Sidama province, but a role in the subordinate elite did not suit him. With a small group of other Sidama, he crossed the border to Somalia and joined the Somali Abo Liberation Front. He left SALF in 1977 to form the SLM, which established an armed presence in three *woreda* – Arorassa, Bensa, Arbeguna – and managed to fight off the Dergue army until 1982. Much destruction was wrought in the area and on its people during that time in a conflict that one publication called 'one of the Dergue's best kept secrets' (*Human Rights Watch* 1991: 87). Eventually, the insurgents were defeated and dispersed, and the SLM leaders escaped abroad.

Summary

Its elaborate political facade and complex ideological rationalisations notwithstanding, the Dergue was a crude military dictatorship. It imposed an ever more tightly centralised administration, a 'campaign' mode of operations with defined targets, quotas and time schedules, the forced mobilisation of resources, and relied on brute force and terror as the means to the desired end. The result was the militarisation of the state, and the concentration of decision making power at the summit of the structure, ultimately in the hands of one man. The facade was impressive, prompting even an experienced observer to conclude, a bare two years before the regime fell apart, that 'Ethiopia possesses an authentic Marxist-Leninist regime, obviously copied from Soviet models, but nonetheless effective and drawing on indigenous roots' (Clapham 1988: 96).

From the perspective of nation state-building, the Revolution marks a historic rupture and opens a new stage in the process. The Dergue's grandiose projects accelerated the process of integration in various fields, reducing the distance between centre and periphery, and leaving the country far more integrated than it had been when it seized power. Even the regime's wars, it could be said, strengthened many peoples' sense of their Ethiopian identity and association with the state.

On the other hand, the Revolution gave rise to countervailing forces that strove to undo the state- building project, and the reaction of the regime succeeded only in strengthening their disintegrative potential. Although it exposed it and nailed it to its mast, the Revolution ultimately failed to resolve the 'nationality issue'. As a newspaper editorial put it, there was hope in the early days that the conflict in Eritrea could be resolved, if 'a decentralised government structure with minimum interference from the centre [were] to be introduced, and the right of self determination within a unified Ethiopia… realised.'[20] This was not to be, because Ethiopian nationalists saw the unitary centralised state as the only guarantor of sovereignty. 'Far from making concessions to the nationalities, the new state, reflecting the transition from one mode of production to another, was compelled to integrate and centralise' (Halliday & Molyneux 1981: 177).

[20] *Ethiopian Herald* (9/1/1976).

9

The Socialist State in the Periphery

Lowland experience of military rule fell into two distinct phases. The first was the initial, fleeting period of political agitation by the student *zamatcha*, and the commotion and discord it caused in some communities. The second and longer phase covered the regime's efforts to start the process of lowland integration into the renovated Ethiopian state. These had diverse effects in different regions. Areas where a degree of settlement and urbanisation had already taken place and sizeable numbers of highlanders were present, such as the Awash River Valley and the Borana Plateau, were most affected. Areas chosen for highlander resettlement, such as Gambella and Beni Shangul, were likewise impacted, as did localities where large development projects – dams, irrigation schemes, state farms – were sited. Further out, in what might be called the 'fringe periphery', barely an echo was heard of the upheaval in the highlands.

Nearly all parts of the lowland periphery experienced conflict of some sort during this period, and some communities suffered grievously as a result. Interestingly, the only note from the march of the Revolution that found a distinct echo even in the lowland periphery was 'self-determination'. Militant 'national liberation' movements mushroomed. Some fought against the regime in Addis Ababa, others supported it, and some occasionally switched sides. These conflicts spilled across borders and linked with factions waging their own political battles in neighbouring states. All of them followed the hallowed maxim, 'the enemy of my enemy is my friend', and the result was a convoluted, kaleidoscopic history of bloodshed this chapter will attempt to clarify.

The *Zalan* ('nomad') becomes *Arbto Ader* ('livestock breeder')

The 1975 Land Reform marked the first time that pastoralist rights were given legal recognition. 'Nomadic People shall have possessory rights over the lands they customarily use for grazing or other purposes related to agriculture', (Chapter 5, para. 4). The plight of the lowlanders was noted in the 1976 Programme of the National Democratic Revolution: 'Nationalities on border areas and those scattered over various regions have been subjected to special subjugation for a long time', it said, and promised that 'special attention will be given to raise the political, economic and cultural life of these nationalities. All necessary steps to equalise these nationalities with the other nationalities of Ethiopia will be taken' (Art. 5). The 1976 Settlement Authority Establishment Proclamation, which presaged a massive highlander influx in the lowlands, introduced what has been the official mantra ever since: 'It is necessary to encourage nomads to develop their present holdings into modern pastoral and arable farming.' Replacing the derogatory term *zelan* with *arbto ader* (livestock producer) was a flattering touch.

The first official study of pastoralism in Ethiopia was undertaken in the early 1980s under the auspices of the Ministry of Agriculture, and produced several well researched volumes on the *Nomadic Areas of Ethiopia* (Fekadu Gedamu et al. 1984). Settlement was a key issue the study was designed to consider, and it was expected to identify potential sites and develop models for it. Instead, the authors came to the conclusion that 'the strategy of transforming the sector into settled agriculture cannot be a proper development approach except in particular cases' (Part II: 99).

The study was funded by the United Nations Development Programme, one of several international bodies that became involved in a wide ranging effort to foster development in the pastoralist habitat. The First Livestock Development Project (LDP) (1958-63) was carried out under the imperial regime and focused on dairy development in the highlands. In 1964, the Yabelo Pilot Project was designed as an experiment in Borana. It demarcated dry season grazing areas, set limits to the number of animals allowed inside and dug water ponds. Unfortunately, it proved impossible to control livestock entry into the demarcated areas. The presence of ponds encouraged settlement in the vicinity with pasture degradation as the result, and the project was deemed a failure. The Arero Pilot Range Project launched in 1965 in another district of Borana had a similar design and met the same fate.

The famine of 1972-74 prompted the World Bank to fund four successive projects in the years that followed. The Second LDP (1973-81) was designed to link lowland pastoralist areas with markets in the highlands. It opened trek routes connecting Borana to Shoa, Jijiga to Dire Dawa, and north Afar to Asmara, with improved water sources and new abattoirs. Designed by people who had little knowledge of the lowlands, it ignored the routes used by pastoralists to reach their markets. Consequently, the new routes remained unused and the services they offered were wasted. A Borana Integrated Rehabilitation Project started as a famine relief scheme in 1981, and then shifted to rehabilitation work in 1985 to encourage herders to take up cultivation. An evaluation carried out before the project was abandoned concluded that 'the strategy of settling nomads (and turning them into farmers) which underlies the project, is not workable, considering agro-climatic, land and cultural factors' (Bassi 1997: 49). The Third LDP followed in 1988, also with the goal of improving livestock production and creating links to highland markets. Three areas were chosen for their quality of livestock breeds, proximity to highland and export markets, and access to meat packing plants: the Jijiga Plateau, the Afar region and Borana. The stated aim was 'to encourage pastoralists to limit the size of their herds to levels consistent with the carrying capacity of the ranges', in order 'to produce high quality beef cattle for the Ethiopian markets ... and help stem the flow of contraband cattle to Kenya' (SORDU n.d.: 3). Local communities were excluded from project planning and management. A technical advisor for one of the projects was of the opinion that

> ... at this stage, it is difficult to envisage pastoralist involvement at operational and executive levels...We expect them to help SORDU and cooperate in the purchasing of animals. Otherwise, the administration of the ranches should be under the control of SORDU without undue interference and impositions either from the pastoralists or other outside sources' (SORDU n.d.: 3).

A study of this project later concluded:

> There is very little evidence that previous development programs have led to any sustainable positive impact. Rather, this study revealed that the Borana pastoral system of southern Ethiopia is becoming more unstable and less reliable to sustain pastoral livelihoods. It appears that the Borana are languishing in a downward spiral of increasing poverty, chronic risk of livestock loss and food insecurity (Solomon Desta 1999: 116).

All three projects faded after 1991, leaving no trace behind.

The record of livestock development projects in the Ethiopia is one of persistent failure. Among the explanations offered, the following are worth noting. One is the remoteness of designers from their subject. Plans were drafted abroad by 'experts' who often had never set foot in Ethiopia before. Having the ranch model in the developed world in mind, the plans had a uniform design for all areas, ignoring significant differences in environment, modes of production, social structures and cultures. The fact that development interventions focused on livestock rather than people was another issue, because they failed to incorporate the knowledge of local people and to engage them in the effort. A World Bank final report acknowledged 'there was a broad cultural gap between the projects' professional staff and the traditional pastoralists. They seemed literally not to speak the same language.'[1] The large scope and highly intensive capital design of the projects put them beyond the reach not only of the target communities, but the state itself. The plans arrived in a package together with funding from abroad. Thus, serious domestic input was precluded. Moreover, the project had a termination date, beyond which no funding for its maintenance was provided, making it unlikely that it would be maintained by local communities or the state. The lowlands of Ethiopia are strewn with the wreckage of development projects that collapsed as soon as the funding dried up. Nevertheless,

[1] Cited in Hogg (1993: 31).

Addis Ababa became addicted to imported, pre-packaged models, and it is not difficult to see why. Its role is to provide the bureaucracy that absorbs the bulk of funds allotted to the project. The World Bank final report on the Rangeland Development Projects (1976-84) showed that 60% of the funds went for administration.

Afar dissidence

The 1975 land reform had little impact on the lowland periphery, where land continued to be shared as always according to custom. The exception was the Awash River Valley, where irrigated private ownership had been introduced to the cultivation of cotton. As noted earlier, among the landowners were Afar chiefs led by Sultan Ali Mirah of Aussa (see Chapter 6). Before the 1975 land reform proclamation, the wily Sultan had hastened to pledge allegiance to the new regime in Addis Ababa, and was in turn praised as a ruler who had always done the best for his people. While it did not hesitate to confiscate the plantations owned by foreign investors, the Dergue appeared reluctant to alienate the Afar traditional leaders who had grown rich in the cotton boom. Its hand was forced by the *zamatcha* students who were sent to Asayita, the Aussa capital. They brazenly agitated against the Sultan in his own capital, hoping to spark a 'class struggle' among the Afar. Ali Mirah prudently declined invitations to the capital, issuing instead his own invitation to the junta. When a group that included Dergue members and advisers arrived in Asayita to negotiate, they met with a hostile reception and were prevented by the Sultan's armed guards from addressing a mass meeting. The same evening, the Sultan's men attacked the *zamatcha* quarters, forcing a precipitate withdrawal of government officials and student campaigners from the region.

Ali Mirah fled across the border to Djibouti and thence to Saudi Arabia where he sat out the Dergue era. A government newspaper editorial saw him off: '…un réactionnaire des plus notoires, un des homes de l'ancien régime qui a beneficié de tous les titres honorifiques et honneur suprême, de créer un Etat dans l'Etat.'[2] In the following weeks, bands of armed Afar warriors interrupted traffic on the road to Assab, where Ethiopia's sole refinery was located, causing a serious shortage of fuel throughout the country. Petrol rationing was imposed and was to remain in effect permanently. Government forces soon cleared the road, but security on it was never completely restored, and traffic from then on moved in escorted convoys. Some 4,000 Afar took refuge in Djibouti in 1975, and the interior of Afar land returned to the forbidding isolation from which it had emerged only a couple of decades earlier.

Nationalisation wrecked the commercial agriculture sector that had grown under the imperial regime in the Awash Valley, and it was not until the early 1980s that the successor regime was able to turn its attention to the business of exploiting the resources of that region. Nationalised cotton

[2] *Addis Soir* (7 June 1975).

plantations became state farms, and new land was brought under cotton cultivation. A state farm (30,000ha) was set up at Dofan Boloha on the western side of the river in Dulecha *woreda* in the Middle Valley, expanding the cultivated area in the Awash Valley to 73,000ha. Large areas were appropriated at Awash Arba and elsewhere for military camps and training ranges. In the late 1980s, the Ethiopian Valleys Authority commissioned a Master Plan for the Development of Surface Water Resources in the Awash Basin (1989), which rejected the settlement programme on environmental grounds: 'It would be a short sighted and, in the long run, a self-defeating activity to move so many people into the Awash Valley, so that within the next generation population pressure on resources caused comparable environmental degradation.'[3]

Nevertheless, a settlement programme was launched to compensate the dispossessed pastoralists by turning them into cultivators, and a Public Settlement Authority was formed in 1977 to oversee it. While most of the large plantations became state farms, the farms of the Ali Mirah family and Afar chiefs were parcelled among their clansmen in plots of 2.5ha per family. By 1983 over 10,000ha were occupied by some 7,000 settlers. Considerable investment was made to provide the settlements with infrastructure and road links. The settlement farms were run by appointed managers with minimal settler participation. Many settlers worked only part time in their farms and others hired highlanders to work for them. Heavily subsidised with inputs and services, the settlement farms were far from profitable. The programme, particularly its emphasis on cultivation, was faulted by every study made of it. 'A production system totally divorced from the pastoralist traditional way of life seems to be the one major factor that has been a hindrance to its success', was the verdict of the main study. 'As it stands, it would be hard to recommend any part of it for further expansion of rainfed crop production' (Fekadu Gedamu et al.1984, Part II: 82).

Summing up the experience of the settlement policy towards the close of the Dergue era, one author described it as a 'welfare programme' (Abdulahi Bedri Kello 1989: 105). There was no lasting benefit to the region from any of the regime's development interventions. A report by the Ethiopian Red Cross noted the malaise felt by the people:

> The Afar feel their way of life has failed in terms of the viability of their pastoral economy, politically in the maintenance of their regional autonomy and in competition with their regional adversaries.... The traditionally self-reliant Afar that defied any external encroachment or subjugation now find themselves dependent and willing to receive any assistance and protection against stronger opponents (1988: 4).

*

[3] Ethiopian Valleys Authority, 1989, Volume I, Executive Summary: 6.

Its notorious isolation and xenophobia notwithstanding, the Afar region was not insulated against the currents of radicalism and exuberant political activism that swept the Horn in the 1960s and 1970s. The battles over the future of Eritrea and Djibouti – in which the Afar were hapless pawns – could not but stir the political consciousness of the nascent generation of educated Afar. A handful of youngsters had made it to the University in Addis Ababa, where they imbibed the radicalism of the Student Movement, and others had studied in Asmara and Cairo. In November 1972, a group of them in Cairo formed the Afar Koborih Angoyya (AKA) (Afar Rallying Movement). A *Mouvement Rassemblement Afar* was formed at the same time by Afar students from Djibouti. Geopolitical logic dictated that the two should remain separate and pursue distinct goals: the Djiboutians would wage an anti-colonial struggle for independence from France, while the Ethiopians would seek autonomy within the imperial state. Whatever place it may have in their hearts, pan-Afar unity is an ideal that dare not speak its name in the Horn. It is anathema to all the states that occupy their homeland.

A meeting in Berlin in mid-August 1974, a month before Haile Selassie's fall, produced an Afar Liberation Front (ALF) headed by Hanfare Ali Mirah, one of the Sultan's sons. Another son, Ahmed Ali Mirah, was chosen to lead the ALF's military wing and the search for weapons and training was on. Hanfare and AKA members travelled to Mogadisho to seek aid and contacted the Eritrean rebels for the same purpose. Although Afar putative nationalism represented a clear threat both to an independent Eritrea and a Somalia itching to annex Djibouti, both encouraged the Afar and promised them assistance. In the following months, young Afar were sent to Somalia and the ELF in Eritrea for training. An approach to Libya netted ten million dollars.

The alliance between the younger Afar generation with its radical notions and the traditional establishment led by Ali Mirah was fragile from the beginning. The AKA drafted a programme in the spirit of the time, denouncing 'the pastoral aristocrats, landed tribal chiefs and national bourgeoisie' in no uncertain terms. Further disputes emerged over leadership and tactics, and the coalition fell apart after only six months. The ALF soon became inactive, and Ali Mirah retired to Saudi Arabia with his family.

The Dergue was not without supporters among the Afar. It found them initially in the Aussa dynastic feud between the families of the late Sultan Mohammed Yayo and Ali Mirah who had replaced him in 1944. Habib Mohammed Yayo, the son of Sultan Mohammed Yayo, offered his services to the Dergue, and was appointed head of a local militia to fight against the ALF/AKA rebels.

Afar activists were dispersed and dispirited, when an opportunity for action presented itself in 1976 with the Dergue's Programme for the National Democratic Revolution and the promise of regional autonomy in 1976. Ethiopian intelligence knew that the AKA had a radical strain and was not controlled by Ali Mirah. The consulate in Assab, where an Afar naval officer, Commander Mussa Yasin, was attached, was instructed to approach them with an invitation to visit Addis Ababa.[4] Two men, Mohamood Gas and Jamal Abdelkadir Redo, were contacted and flown to Addis Ababa. Discussions in the capital convinced them of the regime's sincerity, and they took its promises at face value; no other insurgent movement did so. They went on to form the Afar National Liberation Movement (ANLM), the only ethnically based political organisation tolerated at the time. An ANLM resolution issued in 1976 stated:

> Now that the program of the Ethiopian National Democratic Revolution has recognized the inalienable right of all Ethiopians, the Afar people have resolutely joined the mainstream of the struggle of the oppressed masses and are determined to make all the sacrifices necessary in order to make the ongoing revolution total success.[5]

In mid-April 1977, the ANLM held a weeklong meeting in the town of Gewane, attended by Afar elders from all the five provinces where Afar lived, and observers from Afar political parties in Djibouti. The meeting was billed as a pan-Afar gathering and a step towards the gathering of the fragmented nation into one autonomous administrative region in Ethiopia; a promise dangled before the Afar by the Dergue. The initiative for the meeting had been taken by Lieutenant Negussie Negassa, an Oromo member of the Dergue and chairman of its political affairs committee. He was assassinated on his way back to Addis Ababa, and whatever hopes the meeting might have inspired in Afar hearts remained unfulfilled for the time being.

In the preparations for the renovated state structure unveiled in 1986, the Afar again asked that all of them be included in one administrative region. Once again they were rejected; the reason given was that such an entity would be too large to administer and impossible to develop. Meetings were held to persuade the Afar, and Colonel Mengistu himself visited Assab and Tio for this purpose. In the event, the bulk of the Afar population was included in an autonomous Assab region, and the rest were put in an Aussa district. Some Afar saw this as a positive step, and the ALF issued (and quickly retracted) a welcoming statement. Others saw it as a betrayal, resenting particularly the hiving off of Dire Dawa, a step that greatly pleased their arch enemies, the Issa Somali. The ANLF split as a result. Some of its members turned against the regime and retreated into the inaccessible salt flats of northern Afarland, where they maintained a precarious outlaw existence and later emerged as the Ugogomo (see Chapter 12).

Many prominent activists threw their lot in with the regime and became its agents. Mohamood Gas became first secretary of the Workers' Party of Ethiopia in Assab. 'I have found the right man to work for us in

[4] Commander Moussa Yasin was a member of a prominent Afar family from Tio. He went on to become Ethiopia's ambassador to Yemen and deputy ambassador to Moscow. One of his brothers, Major Mohammed Yasin was the only Afar officer in the Ethiopian army at the time and served as governor of Assab. Another brother, Yusuf Yasin, was a student radical who later became a leading member of the Afar National Liberation Movement.

[5] *ANLM Guideline*, August 1976.

Afar', Colonel Mengistu said of him.[6] Jamal Abdelkadir Redo held the same post in Aussa, Noor Murale was a member of WPE control commission, and Habib Mohamed Yayio was appointed head of the Defence Bureau in Assab. Several others were appointed *woreda* administrators: Jamal Ali Khalifa in Melka Were, Mohamood Yayio Alwan in Gewane, Omar Ali in Asbe Teferi, Mohamood Dawal in Mille and Mohamood Ahmed Shehim in Assab. Yusuf Yasin was sent to Egypt as deputy ambassador. A couple of hundred Afar joined the regime's political organisation – POMOA, WPE – to be trained as cadre.

The Dergue further disappointed the Afar by failing to support them in their feud with the Issa Somali. The road to Djibouti that traverses the Awash Valley was built in the early 1970s, when access to Assab was endangered by the rebellion in Eritrea. Until then, the only settled site on the road was Gewane, an Afar settlement dating from the Italian period. Several of the construction camps along the road evolved into hamlets providing services for the traffic. Initially employed by the German construction company, Issa clansmen settled in two of these hamlets – Gadamaitu and Adaitu – and became involved in the truck-stop economy, smuggling goods across the border with Djibouti and Somalia, as well as raising livestock in the vicinity. The Afar stayed out of these towns, while Issa herders used them as gateways to roam northwards towards the Awash River. The Issa call Gadamaitu *Garba Issa* ('shoulder of the Issa', i.e., a support to lean on).

During the Somali invasion, the Afar fought on the Ethiopian side and were pushed out of areas occupied by the Somali army. The Western Somalia Liberation Front had armed and trained Issa clansmen in preparation for a planned annexation of Djibouti, and when this plan was aborted, they participated in the invasion of Ethiopia of 1977.[7] The Afar rejoiced when the invaders were expelled, expecting the Dergue to reward them for their patriotism. The Dergue expelled the Issa from their settlements on the Assab road and demolished Gadamaitu. This proved only a temporary setback. In the late 1980s, the expelled Issa started trickling back, and soon they had re-established themselves in the Allighedi plain alongside the road to Assab. The Afar petitioned Addis Ababa in vain for help. In May 1987, Ugogomo led an attack on the Issa in the Middle Awash Valley with many casualties. The government then set up a buffer zone some 25km wide on either side of the road, and forbade armed men from crossing it on pain of being attacked by the army.

[6] Personal communication from Yusuf Yassin.

[7] The Western Somalia Liberation Front (WSLF) had several divisions, one of which, named El Tire (Revenge), was intended to occupy and annex Djibouti. El Tire was made up of Issa clansmen. The Djibouti part of the plan was abandoned after the French colony became independent in May 1977. When the invasion of Ethiopia came in June of that year, now trained and well armed, the Issa again pressed their advantage to push farther into Afar territory.

Somali irredentism

As the Dergue became embattled with the radical opposition in the centre and with the rebels in Eritrea, while at the same time losing American patronage, pressure mounted on the regime in Somalia to take advantage of what seemed a unique irredentist opportunity. The large community of refugees congregated in Mogadisho since the mid-1960s had welcomed Siad Barre's *coup d'état* in 1969 as a good omen for their cause. Emulating their counterparts in Ethiopia, students from this community demonstrated in the Somali capital, implicitly questioning the regime's nationalist credentials. The Supreme Revolutionary Council (SRC), to give the regime its formal title, had also to content with the fact that the Ogaden clan, a pillar of its political support, also provided the bulk of the Somali army, including thirteen generals and a flock of colonels. Refugee agitation confronted Siad Barre with another political problem; the refugees wanted their own armed force and freedom of action. To pre-empt this, he took the initiative to organise and control the irredentist movement. In 1970, only months after it came to power, he downgraded the Ministry of Somali Affairs to a directorate in the President's Office. From then on, the campaign for Somali unification came under the personal direction of Siad Barre, with dire consequences for all concerned.

Initially, all refugees were grouped into a United Front, commonly known as *Jebha* (Front), and Mohammed Diriye Abdi Urdoh, an Ogaden graduate of Khartoum University, was put in charge of it. Beginning in 1974, several batches of volunteers were sent to North Korea for military training, and others were trained by Somali army officers in three camps set up for this purpose in 1975. The following year it was decided to form separate organisations to represent the unredeemed territories, leading to the formation of the Western Somalia Liberation Front (WSLF) in January 1976, and the Somali Abo Liberation Front (SALF) some months later. The contested area includes Djibouti, although this enclave was represented by another faction named the Front de Liberation de la Cote Somalie (FLCS), whose members had their training camp in northern Somalia. Attended by the dictator himself, the founding meeting of the WSLF chose a central committee of twenty-five that included ten university graduates, five of them from Egyptian institutions. The majority were Ogaden clansmen, but other clans were also represented. WSLF's first secretary general, Abdulahi Hassan Mohammed, an official in the Somali Ministry of Education, was from the Bartire clan. Recently released from prison, where he was sent for agitating, Urdoh became his deputy.

SALF was born with a severe identity problem. It represented the same combination of Arsi Oromo and Somali clans that had rebelled in Bale in the 1960s, and was led by veteran warriors of that conflict, Mohammed Ali Rube as secretary general and Waqo Gutu Usu as his deputy. Choosing a name for this hybrid faction was not easy. 'Abo' is an Oromo greeting, commonly used also by bilingual Somali clans, who themselves are referred to as 'Somali Abo, to distinguish them from monolingual Somali clans who use the greeting '*wariya*'.[8] SALF had the haziest notion of the territory it claimed. Its sketchily drawn maps included the provinces of Arsi, Bale and Sidamo. Among other problems, this created a *prima facie* conflict with the WSLF, which also claimed most of Bale and southern Sidamo.

Commanded by Somali army officers, most of them from the Ogaden clan, WSLF units commenced operations inside south-eastern Ethiopia early in 1976, and SALF bands followed suit some months later in the south. SALF's theatre of operations was divided into separate provincial commands, for Bale and Sidamo, and each of these was subdivided into zones, of which Bale had two and Sidamo four. Rebellion spread rapidly among Oromo groups like the Kottu in Hararghe and the Borana and Guji in south Sidamo. The fronts had little trouble attracting recruits, and their numbers grew into thousands within months. Guerrilla operations had considerable initial success in clearing the countryside of Ethiopian forces, and by the end of the 1976 the latter had taken shelter inside a few garrison towns. The Ethiopian army was under immense pressure in Eritrea, where the insurgents were besieging the towns and were to capture most of them by the end of 1977.

Mogadisho kept the guerrilla units under tight control. The regime concealed their existence and publicly denied any involvement in events inside Ethiopia. It also kept the WSLF leadership under wraps in Mogadisho, and some of its members who protested were expelled from the central committee; including Urdoh, who was now incarcerated for the second time. There was no joint activity between the fronts in the field at any time, or even direct contact with each other. Each maintained radio contact with the Somali Ministry of Defence from where they received instructions.

Frustrated by the failure of the guerrillas to capture the main towns in the Ogaden, and impatient to score a decisive victory before the regime in Addis Ababa could regain its balance, Mogadisho opted for a full scale invasion of southeast Ethiopia. Spearheaded by a sizeable tank force, some 8,000 soldiers crossed the border in mid-June 1977, heading for the towns of Jijiga, Harar and Dire Dawa in the southeast and Gode in the south. The invasion was an initial success, making inroads in several directions, capturing Jijiga and coming close to taking both Dire Dawa and Harar. Following their initial rout, the Ethiopians poured hastily trained peasant militia units to stop the Somali drive below Harar in November 1977, where the battle line was fixed for the next few months.

For many WSLF members, the joy of victory was marred by a dawning awareness that their aspirations were not shared by their patrons in Mogadisho; in fact they were anathema to them. Among the Ogaden militants were independent spirits who hoped not only to lead the struggle against Ethiopia, but to manage the affairs of their home region afterwards without undue interference from Mogadisho. Such hopes were

[8] It was said that Siad Barre himself chose the name.

quickly and rudely dashed. No sooner had it occupied the region, than the Somali regime set about imposing its authority, brushing aside attempts by the WSLF to establish itself there. Army officers who led the WSLF guerrilla units were recalled to Somalia, where half a dozen of them were placed under arrest. The Central Committee of the WSLF was forbidden to enter Ethiopia, and its members stayed idle in the Somali capital. The WSLF leaders hoped to use the guerrilla units as the nucleus of a regional force, but these were sent instead to the front line in Harar, where they served alongside regular army units, but without pay. WSLF attempts to set up a civilian administration were blocked when Mogadisho appointed army officers as district governors under the orders of two so-called Extraordinary Commissioners, one for the Ogaden, another for Bale and Sidamo. Whether by accident or design, none of them were Ogaden clansmen. The WSLF was not even allowed to raise its own flag.

The invasion of Ethiopia proved a foolhardy adventure. Somalia's rulers had no long-range plans to secure the captured territory against the inevitable Ethiopian counterattack. They gambled on the political problems of the regime in Addis Ababa, and on Soviet aid to balance the military superiority of the enemy. In the event, neither calculation proved correct. The war was a great political boost for the Dergue, enabling it to capitalise on the patriotic fervour the invasion provoked. Instead of disintegrating, the faction headed by Major Mengistu went on to consolidate its hold on power and to put the state on a war footing. The invasion also removed Soviet inhibitions about switching support to Ethiopia and, while the United States later offered Somalia half-hearted support, it was not about to condone the dismemberment of its former client. Then and afterwards, Somali nationalists have failed to appreciate a basic geopolitical fact: both East and West oppose the break-up of the Ethiopian state. And that is because, regardless of regime, Ethiopia is bound to be at odds with its Arab neighbours, thereby spoiling their dream of turning the Red Sea into an Arab lake.

The Ethiopian counterattack was not long in coming. Soviet military hardware began to arrive at the end of 1977. Cuban soldiers followed them, and fresh peasant militia contingents were raised and trained. The Somali army, on the other hand, was running low on arms and other necessities, and Mogadisho was frantically scrounging abroad for supplies. The Ethiopian counterattack came in March 1978. Planned by Soviet officers and spearheaded by Cuban combat units, it quickly routed the invader army and regained the lost ground. Mogadisho had no choice but to sue for peace.

This marked the beginning of the end for the Siad Barre regime, and the opening of a turbulent chapter in the history of the Somali state that has yet to end. Immediately after the defeat, the Somali military was shaken by mutinies, followed by executions of suspected plotters, and the flight abroad of dissident officers who took the initiative in organising armed opposition to the regime in Mogadisho. Not surprisingly, this was built on clan foundations. The Somali National Movement (SNM) represented the Ishaq of northern Somalia, while the Somali Salvation Front was mainly Mijertein. Not surprising also, Addis Ababa welcomed both to set up bases in Ethiopia. Isolated, the dictator in Mogadisho relied increasingly on three other clans – Marehan, Ogaden and Dulbahante – with which he had blood ties. Thus, Somali nationalism dissolved into its clan components, starting the decomposition of the Somali state, the only one that had boasted a national identity in black Africa.

*

In the years that followed, the WSLF and the SALF became inactive and increasingly irrelevant in the midst of civil strife that engulfed the Somali state. With Ethiopian and Cuban troops poised on the border, Mogadisho could not afford to provoke them, and banned any guerrilla incursions into Ethiopia. In 1978, Omar Nur, a veteran guerrilla commander was released from prison and put in charge of WSLF military affairs, only to be dismissed after three month for violating this ban. The WSLF held its second congress in February 1981 in Mogadisho and adopted its first programme, which claimed its goal was self-determination and the creation of an independent Western Somali State; it mentioned the Somali republic only in passing as a 'brotherly' state. The former leader and occasional inmate of Somali prisons, Abdi Urdoh, who now became secretary general, lasted only one year, and was replaced by Abdulahi Hassan, a civil servant and later Somali ambassador to Egypt. He in turn was replaced by one of the leaders of the 1963 uprising, Abdi Nassir Sheikh Aden, a man who proved compliant enough to keep this post until the end.

In May 1982, all WSLF units were incorporated into the Somali Defence Force and stationed along the border. The WSLF budget was shifted to a new agency named the Liberation Fronts and State Relations Office. By June 1983, when the WSLF celebrated its 20th anniversary in Mogadisho, it was already a phantom organisation. SALF's leadership also underwent frequent changes reflecting tensions within the organisation. Waqo Gutu and Ali Rube alternated in the post of secretary general, the leading organs expanded and contracted in size from a few dozen members to a few hundred, and the conundrum concerning the front's name remained unresolved.[9]

The final blow to the nationalist cause was delivered by the Somali regime itself, when it entered a bargain with its counterpart in Addis Ababa. The repositioning of the superpowers in the late 1980s sounded the death knell for both regimes. Clutching at straws, the dictators sought to help each other, and in April 1988 signed a Peace Accord not to support opposition against one another. To seal the deal, Siad Barre renounced Somali claims to Western Somalia, and Mengistu Haile Mariam agreed to expel Somali opposition groups from their bases in Ethiopia. Addressing the disconsolate leadership of WSLF and SALF, Siad Barre told them that

[9] Mohammed Hadj Hassan Gababa, the Sultan of the Gerri clan, became SALF's secretary general in the mid-1980s.

Somalia's security was at stake, and forbade them to do anything that would disturb Addis Ababa; a replay of the experience they had in 1964. Addis Ababa got the better deal temporarily, being able to shift troops from the Somalia border to slow down the nationalist offensive in Eritrea. Forced out of Ethiopia, the SNM attacked the towns of Hargeisa and Burao in northern Somalia, unleashing a ferocious civil war that ended with the secession of Somaliland. The towns were levelled by Somali aircraft flown by white mercenary pilots from South Africa, and Darod clan troops committed atrocities against the Ishaq population of the former British protectorate. Another dissident movement called the United Somali Congress (USC) emerged in the central region where the Hawiye clan is dominant. The end of Siad Barre's regime came in January 1991, when the USC forced the dictator to flee the capital.

With the eruption of civil war in Somalia, the Ogaden clan found itself in a difficult position on both sides of the border. The Ishaq exploited the armed presence of the SNM, which operated with Addis Ababa's blessing, to challenge the Ogaden for control of the Haud pastureland, and also interfered with the latter's trade links to Hargeisa. When remnants of the WSLF attempted to intervene on behalf of the Ogaden, they were attacked by Ishaq herders and SNM fighters with far greater efficiency than the Ethiopian army displayed. Thus, the imperatives of pastoralism made a mockery of Somali nationalism. The Somali region in Ethiopia remained under emergency military rule until 1991, administered by the commanding general in Harar through his deputy in Kebridahar, and Cuban soldiers were stationed there for several years. Few Somali were appointed to local office in the region, and their tenure was short.

Needless to say, the impact of the socialist experiment on the Somali inhabited region of Ethiopia was devastating. The southeast was depopulated as people fled the violence of war and the anticipated retaliation of the Ethiopian regime, to languish in refugee camps in Somalia for the next ten years. Commercial farming on the Jijiga plain did not survive the political upheavals that followed the demise of the imperial regime in 1974. Highlander farmers left the area, and the dislocation of the grain market later that resulted from the influx of famine relief food forced most commercial producers to abandon the land.

The Ogaden National Liberation Front (ONLF)

Successive setbacks forced the Ogaden militants to reappraise their strategy. The twinning of WSLF with SALF was politically inept and damaging, and they tried to dissociate themselves from it; the WSLF programme adopted in 1981 did not even mention the SALF. More importantly, they realised that the identification of their movement with the Somali Republic led to its perception abroad as a feature of Somali expansionism, precluding African and international support and handing Ethiopia a propaganda advantage. Worse yet, the patronage of Siad Barre had degraded a nationalist crusade by involving it in political power struggles fought along clan lines. It had become obvious as well that that Ogaden autonomy within the Somali Republic was not to be taken for granted, but rather something for which they would have to struggle. Awareness spread that it would be politic for the WSLF to put some distance between itself and Somalia, to project the image of a genuine national liberation movement with self-determination as its goal, and to strive for self-sufficiency and a degree of independence from Mogadisho. This was the seed that produced the Ogaden National Liberation Front a few years later.

The notion to create a new organisation took hold among the younger, educated men who had served their apprenticeship in the Western Somalia Youth Union, a WSLF branch. They took the first step in mid-1980, when some of them left Mogadisho for the Ogaden to assess the local mood there. Finding their clan elders unwilling to provoke Siad Barre, they returned to the Somali capital. Wary of their restlessness, Somali security kept the youthful activists under close surveillance; not a few of them had already spent time in prison. Tension rose when the Western Somalia Youth Union published a paper denouncing the 'collapsed [WSLF] leadership who traded in the name of the people and the struggle of western Somalia.'[10] It was for their protection that Abdi Urdoh, when he served briefly as WSLF secretary general in 1981, sent several of them to represent the WSLF in the Arab region.

In 1984, six men met to form the Ogaden National Liberation Front (ONLF). Sheikh Ibrahim Abdalah Mah, a graduate of Bin Saud University in Mecca, then WSLF representative in Saudi Arabia; Abdulahi Mohamed Sadi, a merchant, member of WSLF central committee, then WSLF representative in Kuwait; Mohamed Ismail Omar, a teacher, then WSLF representative in Algiers; Abdurahman Yusuf Magan, also a teacher; Abdirahman Mahdi, another teacher, then head of WSLF Youth Union; and Abdi Gele, an engineer, then WSLF representative in Iraq. All of them were Ogaden born and educated in the Somali National University. They now formed what they called the Highest Council of the Revolution, with Abdirahman Mahdi as chairman.

Insecure in a region where Siad Barre had powerful friends, they delayed going public until March 1986, when the formation of the ONLF was announced in Kuwait. Its programme called the Ogaden an Ethiopian colony, defined the issue as 'decolonisation', and its goal 'the liberation of Ogadenia by all possible means.' It denounced the Greater Somalia concept for turning the issue into one of irredentism and secession that had cost the Ogaden African and international support. An ONLF publication named *Kaah* ('Enlightment') denounced the Mengistu Haile Mariam-Siad Barre peace accord as a 'capitulatory agreement', and charged Mogadisho with lack of 'sincerity, faithfulness, steadfastness and determination…in the cause of people's liberation.' (No. 3, 1988)

Working against the odds in the next few years, the small group of ONLF activists tried to build an organisation. WSLF leaders and Ogaden

[10] *Baraamig* (August 1984:13).

clan elders opposed the split and hampered their efforts inside the Ogaden, forcing them to work among Ogaden students in the Middle East. The hostility of regime made it dangerous to work inside Somalia. Abdirahman Mahdi himself was jailed in Mogadisho and was replaced as ONLF chairman by Abdurahman Yusuf Magan. As a result, the new organisation had scarcely a presence on the ground within Ethiopia when the political horizon widened dramatically in 1991.

The Borana

The Revolution did not impact heavily on the Borana. Land reform had little meaning in the pastoralist habitat, and the *kebele* that were formed on the basis of the *madda* made no distinction between pastoralists and cultivators. Although the *balabbat* system was abolished, the *gaada* was not attacked, and the *Gumi Guyoo* assemblies were allowed by the regime to meet for propaganda purposes. Two all-weather roads opened into Borana *awraja* ending its isolation, and in 1987 it was upgraded to an administrative region, whose territory included the mainly Somali inhabited Dolo *woreda* in the southeast corner. Some land was lost to development projects under SORDU, but there were compensations as well. Many Borana found employment in the local administration and others became political cadre. An army officer, Major Jaatani Ali, emerged as the Borana spokesman and became the chief administrator of the region, while another Borana, Godana Tunni, was WPE region representative. Both had been among the children brought to Addis Ababa by Haile Selassie from one of his visits to Borana.

The deployment of the WSLF and SALF, followed with the Somali invasion in 1977, led to a resurgence of Somali power in the region. The Somali clans were armed and reinforced by the return of many of those who had fled a decade earlier, and the Borana were forced to retreat from the contested territory ceding land and water sources. The situation was reversed with the defeat and expulsion of the Somali forces in 1978, and the garrisoning of the region afterwards and imposition of military rule. The Somali clans that had cooperated with the invaders fled once again, and were not to return until the 1990s. Having gained favour with the military regime, the Borana now recovered recently lost territory and water sources in the east. Playing the Ethiopian card proved a successful Borana strategy. 'The Borana secured state recognition and protection of their territory by adapting to the political demands of all Ethiopian regimes until 1991', noted the anthropologist (Helland 2002: 54). A Borana elder put it this way: 'It is true that both the Imperial regime and the Dergue have supported us. But that happened because we struggled for our land, and these regimes have been struggling for the borders of the empire. Therefore, our interest overlapped.'[11]

[11] Quoted in Fekadu Adugna (2004: 95).

South Omo

The experience of this region under the military regime is little known. Few anthropologists were able to work there, and those who did preferred to tread lightly on the impact of the Revolution. In the words of one: 'Much of the anthropology of the last twenty years has...paid surprisingly little attention to the impact and 'appropriation' of the Ethiopian revolution as a socio-cultural phenomenon on local societies.' (Abbink 1997: 236-7) What is presented below is the weaving together of fragments of information gathered from a variety of sources.

Only ripples of the wave that swept away the imperial regime from the highlands reached the benighted milieu of South Omo, where it appeared first in the form of a handful of intrepid *zamatcha* students who arrived there in 1975. None of them had the slightest acquaintance with the region, and all were bemused by the exotic world they encountered. Even so, they hoped to 'telescope' the process of social evolution by setting off a class struggle among the bewildered natives. They harangued them in the freshly minted Amharigna revolutionary vocabulary that reached their audience through the garbled translation of local interpreters. Emulating the Red Guards in China, they launched a frontal attack on traditional institutions and practices they condemned as 'feudal', 'oppressive', 'harmful' and 'reactionary'. The immediate targets were the local *balabbat* and they were unceremoniously booted out. The assault gathered momentum to include all figures of secular and religious authority, as well as traditional rituals, symbols and customs through which such authority was manifested. On several occasions, the campaigners laid violent hands on these, destroying shrines and demolishing ritual objects, forcing people to violate cultural taboos, and generally sowed confusion. On their departure, they left many communities divided between those who welcomed change and those who opposed it, leaving the majority agitated and perturbed.

The call of the Revolution found its loudest echo among communities on the higher elevations, where agriculture was practiced, *neftegna* landlords had settled and the *gabbar* system had been imposed. Coincidentally, these also were communities where foreign missionary work had borne fruit, and it was young Christian converts, already at odds with tradition, who welcomed the promise of radical change and became the local standard bearers of the Revolution. 'When the revolution began to promise a new beginning, local Christians, particularly the educated, entered into the work of attacking tradition as enthusiastically as Russian or Chinese revolutionaries' (Donham 1999: 178).

Such favourable conditions were ripe in the case of Maale, where a Sudan Interior Mission station had begun work in Bako in 1954.[12] In the

[12] This is the only community in South Omo whose experience during this period has been detailed by an anthropologist. See Donham (1997, 1999).

minds of the converts to Protestantism 'the Christian narrative of conversion and enlightenment was transformed into a modernist narrative of social revolution and progress' (Donham 1997: 328). Conflict over land between *gabbar* and landowners had reached the courts before the Revolution, with Christians who had learned Amharigna taking the initiative. In mid-1975, four *zamatcha* students came to Bala, deposed the Maale Kati (King) and chiefs, desecrated the venerated bones of former kings and smashed the traditional symbols of ritual authority. Excited by the land reform, the *gabbar* followed the *zamatcha* instructions to form *kebele* and exclude former landowners and 'feudal elements' from election to office. The process of grooming the local elite included military training for young men, cadre training at the Yekatit Political School in Addis Ababa, recruitment into COPWE and latter in the WPE. Eventually these people were appointed to office in the local administration. The numbers involved were minute; the WPE in Maale had no more than ten members. 'What was the main thing they taught us?' one Maale who responded to the call of the Revolution said later. 'The landowners, the big ones, the ones who made their wealth from the farmers – that way of life had to be destroyed. Everyone had to be equal. That was what we learned first. We really didn't learn much about socialism' (Donham 1997: 331).

Zamatcha agitation in Aaari, another South Omo agricultural community with a history of tension between *gabbar* and *neftegna*, exploded in violence against the *neftegna*, whose property was looted and women raped, and there was fighting with many casualties in Bio Barka. Before leaving, the campaigners managed to offend the people by forcing them to violate the taboo against Aari castes sharing a meal or having sex together; they killed an ox and forced members of different castes to eat it together. After they left, the *neftegna* and police raided the area arresting looters and confiscating animals.

By contrast, the *zamatcha* had no impact in Arbore, where no *neftegna* had settled and no missionary had put in an appearance. The people there listened to *zamatcha* speeches politely, but the only interest they evinced was in getting weapons and military training from the new regime. Afterwards, the Arbore returned to their reclusive ways and kept outsiders at bay. Only a couple of Arbore men were sent to the Yekatit School, and one was made deputy administrator of Kayfer *awraja*. One event the people here did not forgive or forget was the mindless arrest of their senior chief and the breaking of his staff (Wolde Gossa Tadesse 2002: 54); likewise with the Surma, where a handful of *zamatcha* students appeared in 1976 in Kibish. Revolutionary slogans had no meaning for them. Surma traditional authority was not affected, nor did the people respond to *zamatcha* advice to cover their nakedness, stop wearing lip-plates and settle down to cultivate. 'Suri realities did not answer to the model of an unequal, oppressive, feudalist society' and the impact of the campaign was nil (Abbink 2002: 162).

The Revolution's echo died before it could be heard in the fringe periphery, the people inhabiting the shifting, fluid ecosystem of the Omo River delta. The *zamatcha* itself collapsed before it could reach this unapproachable region and it was only years later, when the state's spreading administrative and military tentacles reached them that the people realised something was afoot. Usually this occurred when their traditional authority structure came under attack by the regime's local cadre preparing to assume the role of peripheral elite. Even the Nyangatom had their three *balabbat* supplanted by *kebele* chairmen.

Several regime initiatives boosted the process of integration of this hitherto ignored region. The reorganisation of the state in the late 1980s raised South Omo's status to administrative region. Its people were introduced to state provided education for the first time, with primary schools in many villages and a secondary school in Jinka, the regional capital. Nearly all teachers came from the highlands, but local graduates were also trained to teach, while others were employed in the local administration. A network of roads linked Jinka with district capitals, and these became arteries for the flow of local trade. Jinka got electricity and telephone connections, as well as hotels and restaurants for an expanding population of highlander civil servants, soldiers and traders. Though a measure of commercialisation was stimulated by these developments, the economy of South Omo did not rise from the basic subsistence level it has occupied since time immemorial. The regime had no policy of pastoralist development, limiting itself to occasional exhortations on behalf of agro-pastoralism. It did, however, open schools for pastoralist children in Dimeka and Kayfer.

*

The campaign of suppression waged by the radical zealots produced the first signs of disenchantment and opposition to the regime. This occurred in communities like Maale, where Protestantism had taken root. The campaign alienated Christians who initially had welcomed the Revolution. The closing of churches and schools was strongly resented and, on a few occasions, forcefully resisted. In the 1980s, the grievances of people in South Omo accumulated, and 'as the revolution wore on after the late 1970s, the state became ever more unpopular in Maale' (Donham 1997: 327). Increased and more efficiently collected taxation was a key reason. Whereas the imperial regime had levied taxes on heads of extended families, the Dergue taxed all married households. Contributions demanded by the 'call of the motherland' were an additional burden. Local officials interfered with trade, and the new road network became a venue for extortion. Transportation of certain goods – wood, hides, skins, animals, incense, sorghum – was made illegal. Vehicles were searched, identity documents checked, goods were confiscated and fines were imposed.

The reinforced presence of the state, especially the military and police, and the exertions of the new breed of political cadres, served to dampen inter-community conflict in South Omo. They followed a policy of bringing foes together in large meetings to harangue them and resolve their differences. Of course, conflict was not entirely eliminated. In a famous incident that occurred in 1984, the Hamar crossed the Segen

River to loot 18,000 Borana cattle. The regime could not control cross-border conflict, which took on new dimensions in the 1980s due to the worsening situation in Southern Sudan. Just as the war there was forcing the Nuer to cross the border into Gambella, other groups in the Ethiopia-Sudan borderland moved eastwards towards the escarpment and clashed with the local population. The Surma came under continuous pressure by the Toposa and Nyangatom who had obtained automatic weapons from the SPLA. When the Surma themselves were similarly armed, they turned the weapons against their Dizi neighbours in a relentless campaign of displacement that continues to this day. The situation deteriorated in the late 1980s as the embattled regime reduced its presence in the region, and three army posts in Surma sub-district were abandoned. When the regime collapsed, the region lapsed into anarchy.

Gambella

The impact of the socialist state on Anywaa society, an anthropologist notes, 'was profound and far reaching' (Kurimoto 1997: 799). The first shock came with the arrival of some 500 *zamacha* students who set about to convert a pre-literate society to 'scientific Marxism' with missionary zeal. Security conditions forced them to congregate in the towns of Gambella and Itang, but this did not dim their enthusiasm. The Anywaa word *agem* that signifies the deposal of a king or village headman was adopted for 'revolution;' suitably enough, because the *zamatcha* targeted Anywaa traditional leader and *balabbat* who had served under the imperial regime. Labelled 'reactionary', 'anti-revolutionary' and 'feudal', the perplexed *nyieya* and *kwaaro* were rudely removed and replaced with the chairmen of the newly formed *kebele*. 'Backward cultural practices' like bridewealth payment in beads (*dimui*), initiation scarification and witchcraft were proscribed; bridewealth payment was monetised and its price was fixed in birr. The people themselves proved less than enthusiastic to join the 'class struggle', and later tried to restore the *nyieya* and *kwaaro* to their traditional status, leading a highlander to conclude that 'although there was exploitation by indigenous *balabbat*, the broad masses were not aware of its existence.'[14]

Some sectors of Anywaa society were receptive to the reforms. While the traditional leaders and elders felt themselves under attack, youth perceived the change as progress. It appealed particularly to the first generation of missionary and government educated Anywaa who saw in it the promise of modernisation. A start was made to form mass organisations, a number of educated Anywaa joined POMOA, and a few were appointed to office in the local administration. Several were sent to Addis Ababa and Eastern Europe for political training; others joined the Ethiopian army and were sent to fight in Eritrea. A teacher training institute and twelve primary schools opened in the region, teaching in Amharigna and spread-

[14] Cited in Direje Feyisa (2003: 334).

ing the gospel of the Revolution.

Even so, the regime's officials found the Anywaa response to the Revolution lukewarm at best, and typically considered more forceful methods; as this excerpt from an official reports illustrates:

> The only way of improving this embarrassing culture [initiation and marriage practices] is through education. But until the new generation is educated with the new culture, they would still remain immersed with the old one as long as their parents continue to practice it. We told them how embarrassing and horrible their culture is for us Ethiopians and foreigners in market places and to their leaders. If it is difficult to force them directly to abandon their culture, it should still be part of the law the violation of which should entail punishment, primarily their leaders who failed to change their respective people.[15]

In the years that followed, the rude and often violent intrusion into their lives stirred resentment among the 'broad masses' leading to conflict. In 1978, a village chief chased the highland teachers from the adult education centre in Jor and burnt the books. In 1980, three highland teachers were killed in Jikaw district, and more schools were burnt. In 1979, ten militiamen were killed and seven were wounded. Rebels took control of eight villages in Jor district, made contact with the rebel Anya-nya movement in Southern Sudan, and received support from their kinsmen across the border in Pochala district.

As part of the Dergue's resettlement programme, more than 60,000 peasants from the highlands were settled in four sites in Gambella region. They came from various parts of the highlands, but became known locally as *Kambaathe* from the name of the region, Kambata, where many of them hailed. Other parts of Ethiopia were involved in this programme, but its impact was greatest in Gambella, where the proportion of settlers to natives reached 40%, the highest in the country. This massive intrusion affected the Anywaa in several ways, none of them good. To begin with, it altered the demographic pattern of the region at their expense. The size of the highlander community – settlers and immigrants – expanded dramatically and was soon to outnumber the Anywaa themselves. All four resettlement sites were located in Anywaa territory which, in some instances, the natives were obliged to vacate to make room for the settlers. As a result, the Anywaa lost valuable riverain land and fishing grounds, and the local environment suffered from widespread deforestation. With the exception of a fifth, mixed settlement that included Openo and Anywaa, the indigenous community received no benefit from the resettlement programme that absorbed generous foreign aid to subsidise the settlers.

Population transfer was not unrelated to security concerns in a region where insurgent movements thrived. The official objectives of the resettlement programme included the need 'to strengthen national unity, to defend the border regions and enhance the security arrangements'.[16] From a highlander perspective, the lowlanders were politically unreliable, a point made clear in the following comments of an official in Gambella:

[15] Ibid.: 332.
[16] Ibid.: 337.

> The people of Gambella are basically opportunistic. They stay when things are good and leave during times of difficulties. They are largely refugees. They did not do anything for the country. As Gambella is a strategically important region, enemies could easily overrun the highlands. With the safari (settlers), control could be easier. The important reason for the resettlement project is to make the people of Gambella Ethiopian. About 90% of the locals have refugee cards. Hence, they do not relate themselves to Ethiopia culturally or historically. They also admit that they are foreigners.[17]

Even more unsettling for the Anywaa was the huge influx of refugees from across the border, driven by the resumption of the civil war in Southern Sudan. Gambella in the 1980s was the reluctant host of a refugee horde that outnumbered the local inhabitants by a factor of three to one. By 1990 the number of refugees there had reached 350,000. Most of the refugees were Nuer, and most of them were settled in two huge camps at Itang and Pinyudo (Fugnido), both on Anywaa land. The camps became centres of a vast aid operation run by the UNHCR. The flood of food aid in the region for two decades was a crippling disincentive to local production. Aid goods for refugees were channelled in great quantity to the local market, where it sold for prices much lower than the same goods transported from Addis Ababa. At one point, the price of a quintal of maize fell to three birr, less than the cost of the bag itself (5 birr), forcing local producers out of the market. It was preferable for the Anywaa to purchase grain than to produce it. This was the beginning of a trend that gradually turned the Anywaa into consumers of imports, with loss of food security as the result. People abandoned the villages and drifted to the towns, where the so called 'four Ks' – hunger *(kac)*, begging *(kwac)*, prostitution *(kap)* and theft *(ku)* – unknown in traditional society, flourished (Kurimoto 1996: 7).

Gambella, Itang, Pinyudo and Abobo grew as trade centres dominated by highlander traders, an internal road network linked the refugee camps and administration centres, a 2,500 hectare state cotton farm was founded in Abobo, a dam intended for irrigation was constructed on the Alwero River, and finally a road was opened to link this lowland region with the highlands. Colonel Mengistu paid several visits to Gambella and made himself popular with the Anywaa when he ordered the building of a bridge on the Baro River that crosses the town.

The Nuer proved adept in exploiting the opportunities offered by the refugee crisis and the involvement of international aid organisations in managing it. One such opportunity was education in English offered in UNHCR operated schools inside the refugee camps. This benefited mainly Nuer youth, and produced the first shoots of a modern intelligentsia in that community. The Nuer were able to manipulate the ambiguity of their civil status. Many who were long settled in Ethiopia could pass as Sudanese refugees and benefit accordingly, and they could do the same in Southern Sudan and Kenya. 'The Nuer eat with two knives', complained the Anywaa who had less access to such opportunities. They could not pass as

[17] Ibid.: 337

refugees in Ethiopia, because they were considered Ethiopians, or in the Sudan, where they were considered Sudanese. In the 1990s, they adopted a different strategy by flocking to refugee camps in Kenya where they could pass as Sudanese. Nuer and Anywaa made their way from these refugee camps to foreign lands. About 10,000 Nuer and 1,000 Anywaa live in the United States.

In the 1980s, Gambella also hosted the rebel Sudan Peoples Liberation Army (SPLA), with which the Ethiopian regime had struck an opportunistic alliance. With its headquarters near Itang, the SPLA set up several camps in the region and a training centre in Bonga. Addis Ababa allowed the Sudanese rebels considerable freedom of action, especially in dealing with the population in the refugee camps, where the SPLA recruited youth for its guerrilla army. That army had many Nuer soldiers and commanders, and even the Murle, traditional enemies of the Anywaa, were represented in its ranks. The undisciplined behaviour of these warriors caused much grief to the Anywaa, who were victims of many incidents of looting, raping and killing. Their appeals to the Ethiopian authorities were ignored.

Relations between the Anywaa and the refugees, whom they called *Ajwili* (Dinka), were tense from the start. Things came to a head in Pinyudo refugee camp which had been set up in 1988 next to an Anywaa village by that name. On 9 September 1989, Ethiopian New Year Day, a dispute over whether the local market should close for the day escalated into violence when Anywaa militiamen fired on the refugees. Armed and supported by a local SPLA unit, the refugees then attacked Pinyudo, killing over 100 Anywaa and demolishing the village. Six days later, refugees attacked and wiped out the Anyawaa militia unit in Itang, looted shops and killed several shopkeepers. The Ethiopian authorities took no action, and no one was punished for these acts. Instead, the Anywaa militia in Gambella town was disarmed and replaced by Nuer.

The initial impact of the Revolution on the Nuer was less evident. The pastoralists lived dispersed in the remote districts of Gambella where the student *zamatcha* did not reach. Their livestock economy was not affected by the reforms enacted in Addis Ababa, nor was their highly diffused system of traditional authority disturbed. At first, the Dergue sought to maintain a balance between them and the Anywaa, neither of whom it considered capable of assuming responsibility for government. In a sort of apprentiship, an Anywaa and a Nuer were appointed deputies to the provincial administrator in 1978. As the disaffection of rural Anywaa became manifested violently in the late 1970s, the balance shifted in favour of the Nuer, who were regarded politically reliable. This became obvious when a Nuer was appointed region secretary of the Workers Party of Ethiopia (WPE) in 1984. This powerful post went to Thuat Pal, the son of a Gaajok Nuer notable and former *balabbat* from Jikaw named Pal Chay. Nuer pre-eminence was strengthened in 1987, when another Gaajok Nuer, Joshua de Luol, a former teacher and *woreda* administrator, was promoted from deputy region administrator to chief administrator of the newly established Gambella administrative region. With the top posts in the state administration and the party in their hands, Nuer identification with the regime was sealed. So was the alienation of the Anywaa, who complained: 'The Derg brought the Dinka and the Nuer on us' (Kurimoto 1993).

The Gambella Peoples Liberation Movement

In the late 1970s, Anywaa discontent gave birth to a resistance movement named Gambella Peoples Liberation Movement (GPLM). Among its founders and future leaders were members of the emerging Anywaa intelligentsia who had earlier embraced the Revolution and served the Dergue regime. Declaring its goal to be freedom for the Anywaa from highlander and Nuer domination, the GPLM became active in the second half of the 1980s. While seeking support from various quarters, it had to fend off attempts by larger groups, each with its own agenda, to absorb it. Nothing illustrates more clearly the detachment of the people in the lowland periphery from the political struggles fought on the highlands, than the perplexity felt by the Anywaa when they came to face them. A GPLM leader recalled later:

> We first approached the Sudanese government for assistance. They accepted our request but they defined us as Sudanese and asked us to join their army... Then we approached the OLF. After initial welcoming, we disagreed. They defined us as 'Black Oromo'. They said "we do not have a separate political question." Then we approached the TPLF when they came to the Sudan in order to create a united front among rebels to fight the Dergue. We also had contact with the EPLF. They said to us "the political problem in Ethiopia is Amhara colonialism," but we said our problem is with the Nuer and the *gaala*. There weren't many Amharas in Gambella, except the *safarai* [settlers] who came recently. What we know were the Oromo. Whatever happened in Gambella it happened through the Oromo. Besides, we did not make a distinction between the Amhara and the Oromo. For us they were all *gaala*... The OLF did not like our position. They said "the main issue was the political system which was created by the Amharas". For some of us it was not even clear who is Amhara and who is not.[18]

In 1986, the GPLM started operations in Gambella and Itang *woreda* and the resettlement area on the Baro River, attacking police posts and highlander state employees; six of the latter were killed and five kidnapped in Itang. In May 1987, eight of its members were captured, including Agwua Alemu, formerly a cadre sent to Cuba for training and later administrator of Jikaw *woreda*. Eighty Anywaa were executed in Gambella in reprisals, and many others were jailed and tortured. The Anywaa were now defined as *wonbede* ('outlaws'), and a wave of political repression followed. 'The main security problem in the district is the Anywaa *bihereseb* (nationality). They are now receiving military training in the Sudan. The only solution is punitive measures', an official report

[18] Ibid: 343.

recommended. The Nuer standing with the regime gained proportionately. 'According to intelligence sources the *wonbede* in the region are not ones who come from outside or even supported by neighbouring country [Sudan]...The Nuer are not part of the *wonbidine* [banditry]. The trouble makers are those who have not yet come along the revolutionary line', continued the report.[19] The highlander settlers were armed by the regime and became directly involved in the conflict. Colonel Mengistu paid a last visit to Gambella only a couple of months before his regime was toppled. Apprised of Anywaa dissidence, he is reported to have wondered aloud 'how come people who cannot even feed themselves squabble over political offices?'[20]

Conflict worsened conditions in Anywaa land. A visitor at the end of the 1980s described them as dire:

> Anywaa villages looked deserted. Young men were scarce, as they were in schools in town, being recruited to the army, or working in gold camps. Those being left were old people, women and children. They were not producing enough food for their own subsistence. Houses were poorly built and maintained. People were drinking heavily. As the indigenous political system had been abolished, village life seemed to be very much individualized... Marriage ties seemed to have become unstable. (Kurimoto 1997: 801)

Beni Shangul Gumuz

As was the case with neighbouring Gambella, Beni Shangul featured in the schemes of the military regime mainly as a suitable site for resettlement of excess population from the exhausted highlands. As noted earlier, the sparsely populated western escarpment had been the destination of a spontaneous population movement from the highland to lower elevations for a long time, displacing in the process the autochthonous Gumuz people (see Chapter 3). This continued throughout this period unopposed and sometimes facilitated by the regime. In 1979, the Beles State Farm was established on two sites in Metekel with workers brought from Gojjam and Tigray provinces. In the mid-1980s, an irrigation scheme was built in Bambasi for the use of immigrants from the highlands and became known as Gojjam *sefer*.

The highlander influx was greatly expanded by the resettlement programme of the 1980s. More than 100,000 settlers came to Metekel *awraja* and occupied two sites, Pawe and Beles. Situated in the Beles River basin crossed by several of its tributaries, and supported by the Italian government, the project earmarked around 250,000ha of what was classified 'unoccupied/uninhabited' land. Some 18,000 Gumuz living there 'were displaced, leaving their former settlement, cultivation fields, hunting and fishing areas as well as their socio-cultural space...No form of support to compensate them for their losses was extended. No effort was made to integrate them into the social development processes' (Wolde-Selassie

[19] Ibid: 341-2.
[20] Ibid: 343.

Abboute 2002: 119). Another 55 resettlement sites were located in Assosa and Bambasi *woreda*. In addition to Amhara, Tigray and Wollo from the north, Kambata, Hadiya and other nationalities from the highland periphery were also represented.

The same author noted: 'The Gumuz are critically aware of the consequences of the encroachment upon their land resources continuously pushing them further to the inaccessible peripheries throughout the different past regimes up to the present day' (ibid.: 245). As was their custom, their reaction was furtive, expressed in isolated attacks on settlements on the periphery of the projects, which forced the settlers to organised a militia to guard them.

In the 1980s, Beni Shangul was caught in a multifarious struggle waged against the regimes in Addis Ababa and Khartoum by a collection of armed movements that included the Eritrean, Tigray, Oromo and Southern Sudanese insurgents and a number of lesser rebel factions. Beni Shangul produced its own insurgency in the form of the Berta Peoples Liberation Movement (BPLM). Based inside the Sudan, it appeared to be more concerned with political events in that country, than in Ethiopia where it carried out minor raids in Assosa *woreda*. Given its proximity to Wallega and the significant number of Oromo who live in Beni Shangul, the Oromo Liberation Front saw that region as falling within its sphere of influence, and neither the Eritreans nor the Tigray rebels appeared to object. However, the BPLM fell out with the OLF over the latter's insistence that the Berta are 'black Oromo', and afterwards approached the TPLF for support. Thus the BPLM found itself invited to attend the founding of the EPRDF in 1989 but not to join it.

Summary

The 1974 Revolution brought the remote nether lands within the horizon of the Ethiopian state, and the military regime developed what was until then a nebulous connection into a closer and eventful interaction. The socialist state brought the lowland periphery under greater direct control from the centre than it had been under the previous regime. The lowlands were included into a strengthened administrative network, and an effort was made to link their economy with the national market. Unfortunately, the results were meagre and the link was not forged. It was during this period also that the lowland zone made it appearance in the national political arena and was integrated into the political edifice erected by the regime. This provided the institutional setting for the emergence of a new subordinate elite to replace the *balabbat* in the periphery. Unlike their colleagues in the highlands, however, the cadre role in the lowland periphery was negligible – not simply because their number was itself negligible, but because in the scientific Marxist scheme of things their nationalities were not considered ready to 'assume the responsibility of government'.

Enhanced control was essential for the implementation of the regime's boldest venture that affected this region's population resettlement. In the brave new world that dawned with the Revolution and the land reform, it was hoped the country's rural economy would revive and food security would be achieved. The great famine of the 1980s raised the issue of land with a new urgency. In the circumstances, the lowland zone appeared to offer an escape valve for the release of intolerable population pressure on the highlands. Apparently sparsely populated, land here could be classified 'unoccupied/uninhabited', and made available for settlement. The native population could be displaced with a minimum of political or security risk.

Enhanced control did not increase security. The politicisation of ethnic identities and dissidence elsewhere found an echo in the lowlands, and gave rise to multiple rebellions there as well. The overall result was to draw the regime into armed confrontation with insurgent movements representing lowland communities, obliging it to rely increasingly on force, making the military the state branch lowlanders were most familiar with. Although the local population could be forced to cede land for highlander settlement, it could not be persuaded to accept this loss, and most settlements did not outlive the regime that created them.

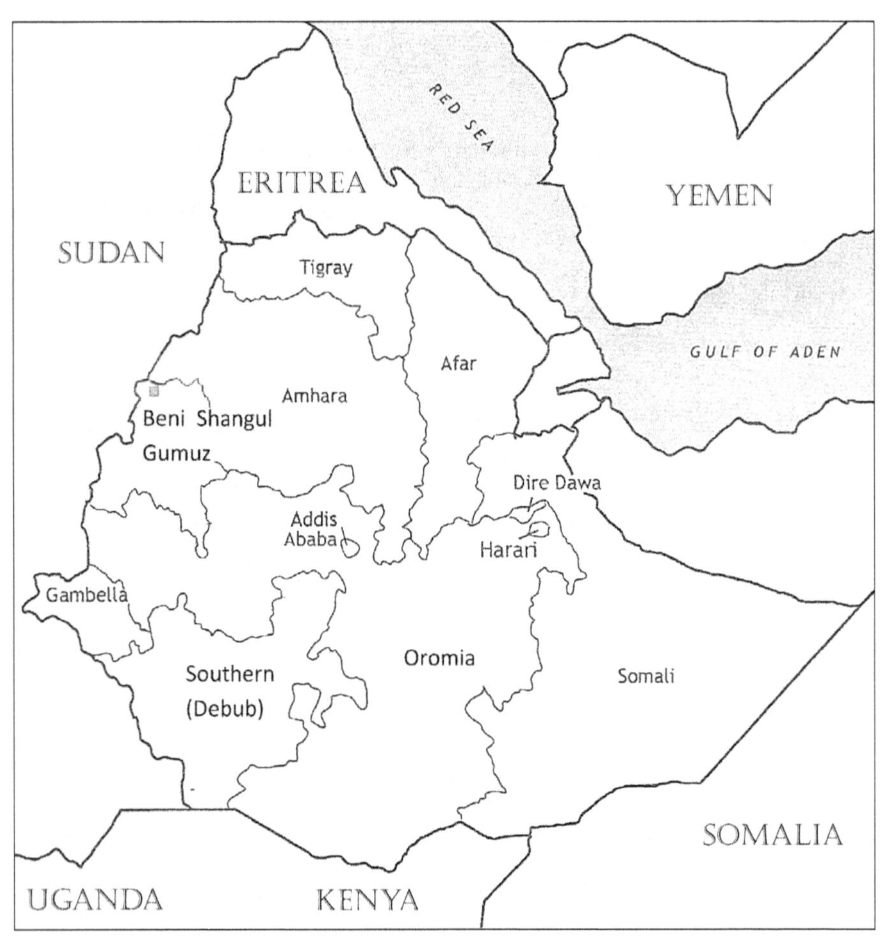

Map 6 Regional states (*kilil*)

Part IV
Rebuilding the State: The Federal Model

10

Building the Federal State
1991–1995

In the century-old life of the nation state-building project in Ethiopia, the latest phase has been the most ambitious. The reforms brought by the last rupture purported to deal with the core issue that had been ignored so far, 'the relationship between a Christian-dominated and Amharic-speaking centre and the various peripheral peoples and regions' (Clapham 1995: 117). The reforms concerned two key facets of this relationship, cultural and political. The first is the national identity of the state, an issue posed earlier in the riddle 'who is the Ethiopian?' The answer was bold and inescapably controversial: to wit, there are many Ethiopians in one state. In a pluralist society of many nationalities and cultures, the identity of the state has political, not cultural, roots, i.e., the common citizenship and loyalty of its subjects.

Centre hegemony, the cornerstone of the nationalist project, was the second issue to be addressed, and the reforms introduced in the 1990s proved bolder and even more controversial, because they reversed a century old trend of centralisation of state rule. The introduction of a decentralised federal system based on ethnic constituencies is difficult for Ethiopian nationalists to come to terms with, for it appears to reverse the process of integration and threaten the existence of the state itself. Such fears provide the soil in which the seeds of a future rupture are planted.

Implicit in the reforms is the promise that they would materialise in a political environment of the sort Ethiopians had never experienced. In a time when a 'wave of democratisation' was seen to be sweeping across Africa, this could mean only some form of democracy based on the Western model. Although the background of the reformists who seized power in 1991 was anything but promising in this respect, they appeared to have undergone a conversion on the road to power, and committed themselves to democracy with all the trimmings. Overjoyed with the coming of peace, Ethiopians took heart from this promise and the change of regime from the Dergue to the EPRDF went through unopposed.

Regime change

The reversal in the international scene with the end of the Cold War, the retrenchment of Soviet power and the entrenchment of the United States as the global hegemon, were the catalyst in the dramatic shift of political fortunes witnessed in the Horn at the close of the 20th century. The Soviet Union under Mikhail Gorbachev cut off military aid to Ethiopia, while the United States, having rediscovered an interest in its old client, cast Somalia adrift and took Ethiopia once more under its wing. The repositioning of the superpowers sounded the death knell for the military regimes in both war-torn countries. Colonel Mengistu's last speech was an abject admission of failure: 'We had numerous plans and I believe we could have realised them. They have ganged up against us particularly now, to undermine and destroy our endeavours. Hence, we could not make progress.'[1] He fled the country shortly afterwards to find refuge in Zimbabwe. It was later estimated that half a million soldiers lost their lives in the seventeen years of his rule.[2]

The collapse of the Dergue left a perilous political vacuum in the centre. The elaborate political facade it had painstakingly erected, including the Workers Party of Ethiopia, vanished instantly, and the vast war machine it had assembled fell apart. The Ethiopian army melted away overnight, leaving hundreds of thousands of soldiers to find their way home. The annihilation of the radical movement had left the centre without a single functioning political organisation. Remnants of the EPRP and MEISONE survived abroad, but ruled themselves out by refusing to collaborate with the EPRDF. In the circumstances, the latter assumed power unopposed and proceeded to implement a carefully crafted agenda without serious challenge.

There was great popular relief that the civil war over, and great hopes were pinned on the anticipated 'peace dividend'. The realisation of such hopes hinged on the willingness of other rebel movements to accept the political formula devised by the EPRDF. In March 1990, the EPRDF issued a proposal for the 'Smooth and Peaceful Transition in Ethiopia', outlining a procedure that was to be followed almost to the letter the following year. It stipulated the formation of a provisional government in which all political forces would be represented, and elections for a constituent assembly to draft a new constitution. A preliminary step was taken at a meeting held in London in the final days of the military regime, called by the Americans to secure a peaceful transfer of power in Addis Ababa. Talks with Dergue representatives broke down almost immediately, leaving the Eritrean and Tigray rebel leadership to plan the next step with Herman Cohen, the United States Assistant Secretary for African Affairs. It was decided to convene a national conference two

[1] Ethiopian Herald (16 May 1991).

[2] Siye Abraham, EPRDF Minister of Defence, *Ethiopian Information Digest* (May 1993).

months later in Addis Ababa to prepare the transitional phase. An agreement to hold a referendum on independence in Eritrea in two years' time had been agreed already.

Oromo participation was imperative for the success of the plan, yet although OLF representatives were in London they took no substantive part in the meeting. The cool reception that Oromo aspirations for independence had received from the TPLF and EPLF made the OLF wary, and the appearance of an Oromo rival in the OPDO under Abyssinian auspices reinforced age-old distrust. To make things worse, before moving on to Addis Ababa, the EPRDF forces crossed the Blue Nile and marched into Wallega, deep in Oromo territory. The move outflanked the OLF, preventing it from securing control of western Oromia. It protested vigorously but in vain: its protests were directed to the United States, which had already endorsed the transfer of power to the EPRDF.

In the manoeuvres that preceded the change of regime, the Oromo rebels came under intense pressure from several sides to accept EPRDF's terms. Caught unprepared by the rapid turn of events and with its leadership still dispersed, the OLF was unable to formulate a coherent response to EPRDF initiatives. In London, Herman Cohen urged them to cooperate, assuring them Washington would see that the EPRDF fulfilled its promises. 'No democracy, no aid', he reportedly said. The negotiations then shifted from London to Khartoum, where leaders of other rebel movements were brought to meet EPRDF leaders and had the EPRDF programme for Ethiopia's future explained to them. This involved a frantic search in the region for survivors of factions, some of which were no longer active and others that had only a nominal existence. The Sudanese regime helped in the search with intelligence and transport. In Khartoum they were presented with a National Charter, asked to subscribe to its principles, and sign it. For the aged rebels who had languished in exile for years, it was an offer they could not refuse. The EPRDF had all of them flown to Addis Ababa.

The OLF came under increased pressure in Khartoum. Its chairman, Galasa Dilbo, was abroad for medical treatment, and the man on the spot was his deputy, Leenco Leta. He accepted an Eritrean mediation offer, and with Taha Ali and Dima Nogo went to Senafe where they met Meles Zenawi in the presence of the Eritrean leader, Isayas Afeworq. Meles lectured the Oromo on the EPRDF programme, and invited comments on the National Charter. In private, Isayas himself pressed the Oromo to cooperate, assuring them he did not want Ethiopia ruled by the *Woyane*, as he always referred to the EPRDF. Anxious to have a friendly regime in Ethiopia, the Sudanese government intervened directly. It sent a blunt message from Al Bashir to the OLF team: 'Don't return to Khartoum without an agreement.'[3] The Oromo negotiators were not given time to convene the OLF central committee, or even to poll its members on the issue, before taking the decision to participate in the transitional government.

[3] Leenco Latta interviewed in Oslo, November 2008.

Having secured control of Addis Ababa, the EPRDF invited all nationalities in Ethiopia to send representatives to the July Conference. Widely publicised by the state media, it came as a surprise to most people and raised a fever of speculation. Non-ethnic organisations were not mentioned, and it soon became clear that ethnicity was to be the political order of the day. Understandably, the call found a strong echo among members of the intelligentsia from the periphery who happened to live in the capital. It was a 'magnanimous and positive gesture', thought a Hadiya academic, for the victors in the civil war to offer to share power with others.[4] A frantic scramble followed to organise before the deadline for the conference, mostly by holding *ad hoc* meetings of limited attendance in Addis Ababa. Communities that already had some form of organisation found it easier to respond, but others had to start from scratch. Meetings in the capital produced political factions to represent the Hadya, Kambata, Adari, Wollayta, Omotic, Issa and Gurgura. Some of them claimed prior existence, others posed as 'liberation fronts', and some were later rejected by the ethnic group they claimed to represent; no faction's credentials were checked.

The Democratic and Peaceful Transitional Conference of Ethiopia met during the first week of July 1991. Twenty seven delegations were present, nineteen of them ostensibly representing ethnic constituencies. The number of seats each occupied varied according to ethnic group size. Oddly, the Amhara nationality was not formally represented, because the EPDM had not yet changed its name to Amhara National Democratic Movement (ANDM); this was done in January 1994. The only Ethiopia-wide representation was provided by the trade unions and the University of Addis Ababa. Chaired by Meles Zenawi, the TPLF leader, the meeting followed the agenda prepared by it sponsors. The 'nationality issue' figured prominently in it, and a heated discussion took place on the issue of secession. Defending this pillar of EPRDF policy, Meles Zenawi had this to say: 'If you don't open the doors and windows of a house, those confined within will break the doors and walls and run out to get fresh air. So leave the doors and windows open for the people to feel free and relax inside the house.' The *de facto* acceptance of Eritrean secession – implied in the provision for a referendum on the issue limited to Eritreans – passed with only one (University) vote against and four abstentions. 'No one has said that Eritrea is an independent state', the chairman argued disingenuously. 'It cannot be until after the referendum. We are not being asked to recognise the independence of Eritrea: we are recognising only the referendum.' The EPLF sweetened the pill by offering Assab for the use of Ethiopia as a free port.

The recasting of the Ethiopian state as a federation on an ethnic basis by giving nationalities the right to 'administer their own affairs within their own defined territory', passed with a minimum of reflection. Whether the participants realised the gravity of the issue is a moot question. 'After all, what we were agreeing to was only a transitional arrangement', one

[4] Quoted in Vaughan (1994:36).

commented afterwards. Objections were brusquely overruled by the chair, and were futile, in any case, given the fact that the sponsors of the Charter – EPRDF and OLF – commanded a comfortable majority in the meeting. Masterfully stage-managed by the EPRDF, the Conference endorsed every item of a Transitional Charter. A transitional government with a two-year mandate was chosen at this meeting, representing seven political groups. The EPRDF held the office of president and prime minister, occupied by the leaders of the TPLF and EPDM respectively, as well as the ministries of defence, interior and foreign affairs. The OLF got four ministerial posts.[5] The Conference then transformed itself into a transitional council of representatives that was subsequently expanded to include representatives of thirty-two organisations. The Transitional Charter also provided for local and regional administrative councils to be elected on the basis of nationality within three months. In June 1992, the EPRDF guerrilla army was named the national defence force, a clear indication that this party was firmly in the saddle.

*

A parallel but different process of political mobilisation and state reconstruction was taking place at this time in the countryside. Former prisoners of war who had been recruited and trained by the EPRDF accompanied its units as they fanned throughout central, southern and western Ethiopia to clear out Dergue remnants and secure control. Former Dergue soldiers, now turned EPRDF cadre, returned to their home districts and set about forming ethnic political affiliates and reorganising the local administration. Following clear instructions, they focused on the rural petty intelligentsia – elementary school teachers, nurses and medical assistants, agricultural extension workers, local government clerks, secondary school dropouts – who had some education and skills, but were languishing in rural backwaters with few prospects of advancement. They eagerly grasped the opportunity offered for social mobility by climbing the political ladder thrown to them. They replaced the Derque cadre corps, whose members were now banned from political activity and state employment. The recruitment drive shunned the better educated, more prominent, urban based, and better off members of the intelligentsia – secondary school teachers, engineers, doctors, lawyers, judges, civil servants, army officers, merchants – who should have been the natural leaders of their communities. An EPRDF document for member guidance issued in 1993 divided the intelligentsia into upper and lower strata and warned: 'The upper stratum is a vacillator and could align itself with enemy forces. Members of this sector do not stand for the rights of the people.'[6]

[5] The EPRDF was given an excuse to get rid of independent political factions that had joined it in the transitional government when they took part in a meeting in Paris in 1993 with the remnants of the EPRP, MEISONE and others factions that rejected the EPRDF and all its works.

[6] 'On the Revolutionary Democratic Goals and the Next Steps'. Translated into English, excerpts of this remarkably frank document appeared in the Ethiopian Register (June, 1996).

Soon, nearly all nationalities felt the need to form their own political organisation. The EPRDF encouraged them and gathered the fledgling factions under its wing. Ethnic political mobilisation in the periphery was accompanied by a process of ethnic fission that was also encouraged by the EPRDF. Communities that were thought to have solid ethnic foundations and identities began to unravel, as clans and branches within them emerged to claim distinct identities and to demand political recognition. EPRDF policy at the time was to encourage every splinter group to form its own party. No thought seems to have been given to the consequences of this policy, which saw the emergence of a bewildering collection of miniscule political factions led by ambitious ethnic political entrepreneurs.

Local administration was rebuilt from the ground up. So-called Peace and Development Committees were set up in the beginning of June 1991 to take over the reins of local government. Promising members of these committees were selected for further training in special political schools located in Addis Ababa, for the Oromo, and Awasa for other nationalities in the periphery. After a few short months of training that included political education and party organisation, they returned to their home districts to become fully fledged EPRDF cadres and later, after the elections, local administrators. The following is a typical case:

> The EPRDF people came here in 1991 to select local people to run the administration. Thirty-three people were chosen, and four of us were teachers. We all went to Awasa for training and stayed there for a month. We studied how Ethiopia had been under the Dergue, and about the EPRDF and its policies. After one month they said to the teachers: 'You four are teachers, you got the idea, so you should go back and teach the people why the EPRDF has come to help them.' After that there was an election, and I was elected chairman of the Tepi section of the Shekisho Peoples Democratic Party.[7]

Redesigning the administration on the basis of nationality was the next task. The principles were outlined in the Proclamation to Provide for the Establishment of National/Regional Self-Government (No. 7, 1992). Ethiopia was to be divided into ethnic units, a task many would have considered impossible given the country's history of population shifts and intermingling, inter-marriage and assimilation, the paucity of reliable ethnographic and demographic data, and the lack of native expertise for this task, not to mention the notorious fluidity of ethnic identities. Such considerations did not weigh heavily on the members of the Boundaries Commission set up by the Transitional Council of Representatives, none of whom claimed relevant expertise. Stalin's stale formula, later inserted verbatim in the 1995 Ethiopian constitution, was the guideline: 'a nation, nationality or people is a group of people who have or share a large measure of common culture or similar customs, mutual intelligibility of language, belief in common or related identities, a common psychological make-up, and who inhabit an identifiable, predominantly contiguous territory' (Art. 39). The Constitution also determined *ex post facto* that the

[7] Former elementary school teacher in Tepi, Kaffa zone, Debub, interviewed in Tepi, February 2000.

regions are 'established on the basis of settlement patterns, language, identity, and consent of the people concerned' (Art. 46). In fact, the operating principle was language and the only other tools available to the Boundaries Commission for this formidable task was the rudimentary ethnographic and historical data gathered by the Institute for the Study of Ethiopian Nationalities in the 1980s.

Relying on these data, the Commission submitted a plan for discussion in the Transitional Council of Representatives in the first week of November 1991. It divided Ethiopia into fourteen regions, called *kilil,* and was proclaimed law by the end of the year. A radical departure from the past, the result was also grossly lopsided. On the one hand, it created huge units by putting all Amharigna-speaking provinces into one *kilil,* nearly all Oromo into another and the same for the Somali and Afar. On the other hand, it divided the non-Oromo areas of the south into five *kilil,* and upgraded sparsely populated former districts like Gambella and Beni Shangul to *kilil* status. Only months later, the five *kilil* in southern Ethiopia merged to form the Southern Nations, Nationalities and Peoples Region (SNPPR) commonly referred to as Debub (South). There were gross differences in land size, population and resources among the *kilil.* With one-third of Ethiopia's territory, twenty seven million inhabitants in 2007, the best watered and less densely populated land producing most of the country's commercial crops and housing the bulk of its industrial capacity, Oromia overshadowed the rest. Two *kilil* in the lowland periphery – Gambella and Beni Shangul Gumuz – were worst off in all respects. The oddest construct was the old city of Harar that became a *kilil* in its own right as the home of the miniscule Adari community, despite the fact that Oromo speakers are a majority in the *kilil* and the city itself. The town of Dire Dawa became a bone of contention between Somali and Oromo and was kept under federal jurisdiction, as was Addis Ababa. Considering its

Table 2 *Distribution of Population by Regional States (kilil), 2007*

Region	Number	Percentage of Total
Tigray	4,314,456	5.8
Afar	1,411,092	1.9
Amhara	17,214,056	23.3
Oromia	27,158,471	36.7
Somali	4,439,147	6
Beni Shangul Gumuz	670,847	0.9
SNNP (Debub)	15,042,531	20.4
Gambella	306,916	0.4
Harar	183,344	0.2
Addis Ababa	2,738,248	3.7
Dire Dawa	342,827	0.5
Special Enumeration	96,570	0.1
Country Total	73,918,505	100

momentous importance, there was surprisingly little controversy initially over this carve up. As it turned out, however, the ease and speed with which the demarcation exercise was carried out was deceptive. Controversy mounted afterwards, and many disputes have yet to be settled definitively. As a result, no official *kilil* map has been issued to this day.

Ethnic homogeneity, the goal of the exercise, proved elusive. Only the Somali *kilil* qualified in this respect. Millions of people, especially Amhara, Oromo and Gurage, now live outside their own *kilil*. The Boundaries Commission left it to the *kilil* governments to organise their domain internally into zones – the intermediate level that replaced the *awraja* – and *woreda*. Sizeable ethnic communities within a *kilil* were accommodated in 'special' zones and *woreda* with considerable autonomy to run their own affairs, including choice of language. All the *kilil*, save the Somali and Oromo, include such units. Debub *kilil* is an ethnic mosaic of its own, with more than forty-five nationalities. None of the nine zones in this *kilil* are homogeneous; most of them are ethnic mosaics themselves. Each of two 'special' zones in Amhara *kilil*, purportedly to accommodate the Agaw, had more Amharigna than Agaw speakers, while one-third of the inhabitants in the 'Oromo special zone' in the same *kilil* claimed Amharigna as their mother tongue.

The immense complexity of the country's demography, the vagueness of the criteria used, the lack of adequate preparation and hurried manner in which the scheme was implemented, as well as the political climate that encouraged political self assertion on ethnic grounds, created a prescription for conflict that has yet to run its course. It was estimated that 550 out of the 660 *woreda* had minorities.[8] Many disputes and bloody clashes followed between groups demanding their own 'special' zones and *woreda*, transfer to other units, or the status of an 'ethnic minority'. This last entitles them to a measure of representation regardless of population size. In 1994, the Council of Representatives defined 'minorities' as groups 'that are small in size compared with the size of other nationalities in a given region', and determined that minorities with ten thousand or more members should have one representative in the *kilil* assembly.

Disputes within and across *kilil* boundaries often have historical roots, as well as current concerns and calculations for the future. More often than not, they involve competition for scarce local resources, such as land and water. To these have been added new resources in the federal arrangement. *Woreda* status comes with entitlement to a secondary school, a referral hospital, as well as road, electricity and telephone facilities. A *woreda* capital is the site of local administrative institutions and line agencies of the federal and *kilil* governments. Local government creates employment, grants contracts, raises taxes, and commands other perquisites that are distributed locally. A '*woreda* empowerment' policy adopted at the beginning of this century and aiming at making it the foundation of state administration, gives *woreda* power to plan and implement their own budget. This multiplies the perquisites that go with '*woreda*' status and

[8] *Ethiopian Herald* (28 January 1994).

intensifies competition for it. The federal government left it to the *kilil* administrations to settle these disputes, even if it meant prolonged and acrimonious negotiations and occasional bloodshed. By and large, most disputes were managed peacefully, and the number of *woreda* proliferated. However, some disputes proved intractable, and require frequent federal intervention to contain them.

*

The federal structure was in place before its constitutional foundations were laid. A constitutional commission was appointed in August 1992, and the drafting process was completed in mid-1994. The draft adhered closely to the EPRDF master plan, and the Front had enough supporters among the commission's members to ensure compliance.[9] Since the structure was already in place, there was little public interest in the matter, despite the commission's efforts to promote it by inviting comments and organising public debates. Elections for a constituent assembly followed in June 1994, and the constitution of the Federal Democratic Republic of Ethiopia (FDRE) was proclaimed in August 1995.

On the face of it, this was a remarkable departure from Ethiopian political tradition. It rejected the unitary model of the state and the centralised form of government that previous regimes had struggled so hard to forge. It accepted cultural pluralism and rejected the link between culture, nationality and citizenship inherent in that model. It recognised the voluntary nature of membership in the state, as well as the right to renounce it. All in all, it seemed a reversal of direction followed in the century-old process of Ethiopian state building. To be sure, unity was still the constitutional *leitmotif.* 'Political community', 'common interests', 'common outlook', 'common destiny', 'collective promotion of our interest', were the code words in the preamble that proclaimed: 'We, the Nations, Nationalities and Peoples of Ethiopia, strongly committed, in full and free exercise of our right to self-determination, to building a political community.'

The Constitution went to great lengths to redress the iniquity inherent in centre/periphery linkage. Article 8 reads: 'All sovereign power resides in the Nations, Nationalities and Peoples of Ethiopia.' 'Nations', 'nationalities' and 'peoples' have the right 'to a full measure of self-government, which includes the right to establish institutions of government in the territory they inhabit' (Art. 39). On paper, the division of power between the federal government and the *kilil* stretched federalism to the limit. The powers of the former were limited to defence, foreign affairs, currency,

[9] The constitutional commission was chaired by Kifle Wodajo, a former Dergue foreign minister and late convert to federalism. In a paper written in 1990, he argued that 'even as an ideal, an ethnically configured African state cannot be acceptable…Africans have no alternative to accepting the prevailing nation-state system. ...The solution to the crisis of the African state lies not in its recreation along ethnic lines; it lies in its democratization at all levels.' Presented to the Centre for Northeast African Studies, Georgetown University, Washington, DC (17-18 November 1990).

inter-state transport and commerce. 'All powers not given expressly to the Federal government alone, or concurrently to the Federal Government and the States, are reserved to the States' (Art. 52). Other provisions however set limits to the initiative allowed the *kilil* in areas under their jurisdiction. A very elastic provision empowered the federal government to 'formulate and implement the country's policies, strategies and plans in respect to overall economic, social and development matters' (Art.5/2). The federal government also was given the power to 'establish and implement national standards and basic policy criteria for public health, education, science and technology, as well as for the protection and preservation of cultural and historical legacy' (Art. 5/3). Obviously, in practice the centre/*kilil* balance of power would be determined by political forces, and the way these shaped under the EPRDF left the *kilil* with scarcely any initiative.

The constitution drafting process did not raise unusual public interest, and the discussion in the Constituent Assembly brought up only a few controversial topics. By far most controversial was Article 39, which affirms the right to 'self-determination up to and including secession'. This was condemned as a reward for subversion, the gravest threat to the survival of the Ethiopian state, and a far-fetched dogmatic gesture that scarcely any group had asked for. The retention of state ownership of land was also criticised by free market advocates, and the drafting Commission was obliged to submit separate majority and minority reports on these two issues. Religion and its relationship to the state was raised in a discussion of Muslim courts, and Muslims demonstrated in Addis Ababa demanding the extension of the Sharia courts' jurisdiction to criminal matters and its application to all Muslims. The constitution deals with the thorny issue of Islamic Courts without referring to them by name. It allows 'the adjudication of disputes relating to personal and family laws in accordance with religious or customary laws, with the consent of the parties to the dispute' (Art. 34/5), and empowers the federal and *kilil* legislatures 'to establish or give official recognition to religious and customary courts' (Art.78/5).

The Constitution established a bicameral federal legislature composed of the House of Peoples Representatives and the House of the Federation. Elected by direct universal suffrage for five years, the former is the legislative body proper. The latter represents the nations, nationalities and peoples, whose members are chosen by the *kilil* legislative councils. Every ethnic group regardless of size has at least one representative, and an additional one for every million of its population. Thus, even miniscule groups have one representative at the federal level, provided they are recognised as ethnic minorities. One list shows 53 'minority' groups, represented with one seat each out of a total membership of 110. The House of the Federation acts as the interpreter of the Constitution in matters relating to the rights of nationalities, and mediates disputes between *kilil* and among nationalities within *kilil*. In the latter instance, it acts as the court of last resort.

The Constitution ordained the equality of all languages and, having made Amharigna the working language of the federal government, empowered the *kilil* to choose their own working language. The first step in linguistic indigenisation was taken by the TPLF when it adopted the Tigray tongue in the 1980s, and later encouraged its partners in the EPRDF to do the same. Anxious to boost its nationalist credentials, the OPDO followed suit in the early 1990s, taking it a step farther when it adopted the Latin alphabet instead of Geez. Other *kilil* proceeded more slowly, if only because they lacked teachers and teaching materials and, in some cases, even alphabets for ethnic vernaculars. The Somali *kilil* also adopted the Latin alphabet used across the border in Somalia, and had access to teaching materials as well as teachers from there. As a result, Ethiopia became a multi-script as well as a multi-lingual state. Multi-ethnic *kilil* – Debub, Beni Shangul Gumuz, Gambella, Harar – retained Amharigna as their working language, and left it to the zones and *woreda* to deal with the issue locally.

Not surprisingly, choice of language became a bone of contention, not least because it affects directly two areas of public life: education and state employment. According to the national curriculum, the mother tongue is the language of instruction at the primary level, with Amharigna and English taught as subjects. English becomes the language of instruction at the secondary and tertiary levels. The number of communities clamouring for their mother tongue to be used in local primary schools paralleled the mushrooming of demands for 'special' zones and *woreda*. EPRDF policy in the 1990s encouraged linguistic indigenisation. Its branches throughout the country exerted themselves to implement it, even trying to revive languages no longer spoken. By 1999, eight ethnic languages were used in education in the Debub *kilil*, some of them using the Latin and others the Geez alphabet.

Groups who had not been reached by missionaries, especially in the lowland periphery, had no alphabet of their own, or the resources to produce one. Small groups had to consider the future employment prospect of children educated in a language unknown and unused outside their own narrow world. Those with a high rate of internal migration placed high value on a *lingua franca*, particularly one they have mastered. The Gurage, for instance, a group with the highest rate of migration within Ethiopia, showed no desire to abandon Amharigna.

By the turn of the century, EPRDF policy shifted from the celebration of ethnic pluralism and cultural diversity to an emphasis on the unity and efficiency required for development. At the same time, the regime tried to raise a barrier against further fragmentation. In the words of a local official:

> In the beginning, it was a free for all for those who wanted to use their language. We gave them every freedom and allowed them to do what they wanted. Now we started raising a wall. We have criteria that must be met. We explain to people that there are complex advantages and disadvantages in using a local language.[10]

There was even an effort to reverse the trend by merging languages on the basis of affinity. Politically tainted and amateurishly done, this created its own problems.

[10] Director of Education Bureau, Debub *kilil*, interviewed in Awasa, February 2000.

The Constitution also affirms the right of the people 'to express, to develop and to promote its culture, and to preserve its history' (Art. 39/2). So far, this right has been asserted only superficially, mainly due to lack of knowledge among subordinate groups about their past, and their incapacity at present to produce such knowledge. The *kilil* depend on the federal ministry of education for teaching material, and the ministry relies for the most part on material produced by previous regimes. Neither it, nor *kilil* education bureaux have exerted much effort to insert local content.[11] The history taught today is essentially the same that children in Ethiopia have been taught for decades. While one reason for this is lack of resources needed to produce alternative versions, there is also reluctance to focus on a past that is full of discord and enmity between ethnic groups, and the fear of being labelled a 'narrow nationalist'.[12]

*

The acid test of decentralisation is whether the *kilil* are adequately resourced. The constitutional division of power between the central and regional authorities is a dead letter unless it is supported by a proportional allocation of resources. The regions must have either direct control over revenue sources commensurate with their autonomous spheres of action, or have rights to equivalent shares of centrally collected revenue. Under previous regimes, the fiscal system of Ethiopia was highly centralised. About 80% of state revenue was collected by Addis Ababa through taxes on foreign trade and excises on domestic production. The 'Sharing of Revenue between the Central Government and the National/Regional Self-Governments' was decided by Proclamation 33/1992. According to it, central government revenues comprise import/export duties, personal income tax, profit tax, sales tax from government-owned enterprises, rents from government-owned housing, and fees for licenses and services. *Kilil* government revenues comprise personal income tax from *kilil* employees, agricultural income tax, rural land use fee, profit and sales tax collected from traders, rent from properties owned by the *kilil*, sales tax collected from enterprises owned by the *kilil*, fees for licenses and services, and royalties and rent of land collected from mining activities. Joint revenue sources comprise taxes on income, profits and sales from jointly owned enterprises, and royalties on large-scale mining, gas, oil and forests. Joint taxes are collected by the central government.

The centre-region balance did not change with the change of regime.

[11] 'If you take the Sidama, for instance, all they do is translate from Amharigna and change a few pictures to make the books look appropriate.' Director, Bureau of Education, Debub, interviewed in Awasa, March 2003.

[12] There are differences in tone. In the history textbooks Abyssinia is referred to as the 'highland Christian kingdom', not Ethiopia; Menelik's conquests are called 'expansion', not unification; and the treatment of the conquered population under imperial rule is described as 'brutal.' There is also some difference in content; mention is made of the Muslim states in the Horn, and one section deals with the history of the Oromo. Ministry of Education, *History Student Text,* Grades 11 and 12 (Addis Ababa, 2006).

If anything, it became more unbalanced. Fiscal data for 1995 showed the central government received around 83.7% of all domestic revenue, and 91.13% of total revenue including external assistance. This is despite the fact that the burden for the provision of social services, including health and education, had shifted from the centre to the *kilil*. Nearly half of *kilil* spending (recurrent and capital) and less than 10% of central government spending, goes for social services. The result is that the *kilil* are able to finance less than half of their recurrent and none of their capital spending from their own resources, and are heavily dependent on subsidies from Addis Ababa.

The amount of tax revenue raised by a *kilil* is one of the variables that determines the amount of subsidy it receives from Addis Ababa, a rule intended to encourage the *kilil* to improve their revenue raising performance. However, the prospects for improvement are not promising. The bulk of *kilil* revenue (up to two-thirds) comes from direct taxes such as the personal and agricultural income tax, land use fees and trade taxes, all of which are stagnant sources with little scope for growth. By contrast, less than one-sixth of central government tax revenue comes from direct taxes. *Kilil* autonomy is further restricted by the federal government's power to determine the tax base and tax rate. Revenue raising capacity among the *kilil* varies enormously. Addis Ababa alone accounts for more than one-third of the total, while Afar, Gambella and Beni Shangul Gumuz together account for less than two per cent.

The federal subsidy is calculated on a formula that takes into account population size, level of development and revenue raising capacity. Initially, each of these variables was allocated one-third of the block grant. The formula was changed in 1997 to assign 60% to population, 25% to development and 15% to revenue, resulting in significant subsidy losses for the sparsely populated lowland *kilil*. *Kilil* budget ceilings depend on fund availability at the centre, where the federal government itself runs a chronic deficit covered with foreign aid and loans. In 1998/99, the federal subsidy amounted to 37% of the federal budget, while the federal deficit amounted to 32%.

Apart from a couple of urban regions like Addis Ababa and Dire Dawa, and certain rural districts that produce commercial crops such as coffee and chat, the *kilil* fiscal system is deficit-ridden and offers little hope for self-sufficiency, let alone development. The bulk of the recurrent budget is earmarked for salaries, an item that increased steadily in the second half of the 1990s as the *kilil* strove to develop their administrative capacity. In the case of Oromia, it rose from 522.5 million birr in 1995 to 703.7 million birr in 1999, and represented 66.6% of the total recurrent expenditure for the period. In the case of the Gurage zone in Debub, this budget item rose from 32.3 million birr in 1986 to 41.1 million birr in 1999, and represented over 80% of the total recurrent expenditure for that period.

As commonly perceived, federalism is a system that facilitates diversity in government. That is far from obvious in the case of Ethiopia, where a rigidly uniform system is imposed that does not allow the slightest departure from the prototype designed in Addis Ababa. In fact, attempts to do so are regarded as subversive. In fundamental ways, the prototype was based on the experience of the TPLF during the long years of civil war, and reflected that party's unwavering conviction that its own formula made for success. As was the case with the military regime, strict uniformity applies in all fields of state activity and all parts of the country. It is most obvious in the structure and procedures of *kilil* government. All but two *kilil* adopted constitutions that were copied from a model document distributed by the EPRDF headquarters.[13]

The party and the state

In theory, a highly decentralised federal system of government would be a serious obstacle in the path of a regime seeking to impose uniformity of rule, especially in a country as diverse as Ethiopia. The EPDRF surmounted this problem by superimposing a political system controlled and guided from the centre, which enabled the centre to retain its hegemony and the regime to impose its programme. It did so by merging party and state in the familiar 'scientific socialist' pattern, which had been tried by the TPLF in Tigray earlier and proved successful.

Born as a guerrilla band, the TPLF evolved into a political movement whose roots reached deep into peasant Tigray society. Although its founders came from the radical student milieu, they were compelled by circumstances to build on peasant foundations, for there was hardly any other suitable material in their province.[14] The 1975 Land Reform had little political impact in a region with few landlords or tenants, and the military regime got little political credit for it. In 'capturing' the peasantry and raising a guerrilla army from its youth, the TPLF founders proved themselves masterful organisers. They weaved a closely knit network of party cells in every village and hamlet that rose in a pyramid, crowned with the party leadership. Initially designed to support the armed struggle, this structure was converted later into a tool for the administration of the liberated areas. Its cornerstone was the local councils called *baito*, which were locally elected, albeit under strict TPLF supervision to ensure loyalty. The *baito* gave the peasantry a feeling of participation and a venue for expression, while also keeping the party in close touch with the people.

In line with 'scientific socialist' practice, the TPLF flanked itself with mass organisations for peasants, workers, traders, women, and youth, which functioned as party appendages for political mobilisation and indoctrination. After 1991, these became involved in reconstruction and development of their battered province. While TPLF propaganda presented them as independent bodies with elected leadership, they were party adjuncts, a link that proved politically embarrassing when the party

[13] The only known instance of policy divergence is a land redistribution carried out in Amhara *kilil* in 1997.

[14] A scholarly treatment of the TPLF story calls it a 'peasant revolution' (J. Young, 1997).

took over the reins of power in Addis Ababa. In 1997, the TPLF decided to disassociate itself from these organisations and they lost prominence thereafter, yet retained strong, unofficial ties with the ruling party.

TPLF's senior partner, the ANDM, successfully emulated the Tigray example. Initially a small fraction of EPRP survivors who attached themselves to the TPLF, it operated in the remote and impoverished Wag region and later in north Wollo. Recruitment among the prisoners taken from the Dergue army expanded its ranks in the 1980s. Modelling itself on the TPLF, the ANDM achieved organisational cohesion and effectiveness on a par with its mentor. Because the Ethiopian Peoples Democratic Movement, as it was called then, was considered a pan-Ethiopian movement, other nationalities were welcome to join it. They were obliged to leave when the EPDM turned ethnic in 1994, calling itself the Amhara Peoples Democratic Movement (ANDM).

Both the TPLF and the ANDM began as guerrilla movements and were trained to fight for power in the bush, not to compete for it in a democratic arena. Whatever changes may have affected them since they came to power, this background has a strong bearing on their political behaviour. Their unshakeable conviction carried over from a Marxist upbringing that there is only one 'correct line' and only one genuine revolutionary movement, denies a hearing to alternative points of view and any organisations that espouse them. This was amply illustrated in the fratricidal struggles of the radical movement in the 1970s, and the way the TPLF and the EPLF dealt with their rivals during the civil war. A change of tactics was required in the circumstances prevailing when they came to power, which the EPRDF felt obliged to explain to its members in the document prepared for their guidance in 1993:

> In the course of our attempts to implement our Programme, we are forced by internal and external circumstances to adjust our approach in response to these major changes...We need to make a few adjustments so that we will be able to come out victorious under the circumstances prevailing in our country and around the world.

It went on to reassure them the adjustment 'cannot and will not do away with the pillars of our Revolutionary Democracy'. Revolutionary Democracy, it explained:

> does not equally stand for the rights of both the masses and the ruling classes... Whether the rights of the ruling classes will be protected will be determined by the relevance this will have to protecting the rights of the masses...However, there are two basic reasons why it will not be possible or anymore necessary to continue indicating in our Programme that the rights of the people would continue to be respected fully and that those of the oppressor will be suppressed. In the first place, such an approach will be unacceptable in the eyes of Western Democracy and will invite the fierce opposition of imperialism...The second reason is that it is possible to ensure the human and democratic rights of the masses without suppressing all the rights of the oppressors.

An ingrained penchant for secrecy is another carry-over that rules out transparency in government. Little was known about the composition and *modus operandi* of these parties during their first decade in power. The refusal to open themselves to public scrutiny was justified on the spurious grounds that they were not part of the state, therefore, not required to make their affairs public.

Both parties strive to preserve the organisational format and operational methods that proved effective in their revolutionary past. Democratic Centralism of Leninist vintage is one of these, whose purpose, in theory, is to prevent factionalism, but in practice renders the leadership immune to challenge from within. *Gim Gima* ('self criticism') is another control mechanism designed to ensure party discipline that was perfected by the TPLF and adopted by other EPRDF branches. *Gim Gima* sessions take place periodically, where party members criticise themselves and others. It functions as a method of purging the undesirable, incompetent, corrupt, disgruntled, and dissident party members and state officials, and a very large number of them were removed in a series of purges in the second half of the 1990s, when the EPRDF unloaded much of the raw material it had recruited in the early part of that decade. Corruption (*musena*), the blanket reason invariably cited for purging was never made specific, even when the accused spent a few years in prison as a result, after which he/she is released without ever being brought to court to answer charges.[15] An exception is made for prominent personalities who are purged; some of them were dragged interminably through the courts to answer specific charges. Being 'against change' (*tsero lowt*) is another handy indictment.

The junior members of the EPRDF, the Oromo Peoples Democratic Organisation (OPDO) and the Southern Ethiopia Peoples Democratic Front (SEPDF), are pale imitations of their Abyssinian seniors. Unlike the others, the OPDO did not have the luxury of an opposition-free terrain where it can sink roots. From the beginning, it faced widespread, intense opposition and survived thanks only to the military intervention of the senior members. Opposition came from several organisations that had been fighting for Oromo political emancipation for many years. The OPDO sought to trump their nationalist appeal by raising high the banner of Oromo culture, adopting the Latin alphabet for the Oromo language, claiming Addis Ababa as the capital of Oromia, refusing to recognise ethnic minorities in the Oromo *kilil*, and intervening forcefully on behalf of Oromo minority claims in other *kilil*. The EPRDF gave it a boost by reserving the state presidency, a ceremonial post, for the Oromo.

Nevertheless, the OPDO failed to gain significant support from the Oromo intelligentsia. It is perceived as a TPLF clone, performing the historical subordinate role in the periphery for Addis Ababa. Snubbed by the EPRDF, the Oromo urban middle class has not warmed to this party either, whose reputation also suffers from charges of administrative incompetence and corruption. Haunted by the spectre of the OLF, the OPDO further alienates its constituency through a relentless campaign of harass-

[15] Used indiscriminately, 'corruption' lost its moral connotation and took on a political one instead. Asked why he had been purged, a former official replied cheerfully 'I was corrupted.'

ment, arbitrary arrests and violence against real and imagined OLF members and sympathisers, and a heavy handed reaction to frequent student demonstrations. All these have made for a poor human rights record, and encouraged defection and flight abroad that reinforced an Oromo militant nationalist diaspora.[16]

Southern Ethiopian Peoples Democratic Front (SEPDF), the EPRDF branch in Debub *kilil,* is a coalition of fourteen ethnic political factions, which underwent a bewildering process of formation and reformation, fusion and diffusion, name changes and leadership purges that is difficult to follow. Captured Dergue soldiers recruited and trained by the EPRDF accompanied its units as they moved south, and were first in place to begin the groundwork of political mobilisation and state rebuilding. The initial network of 'peace and development committees' mushroomed into a web of ethnic political factions, commonly referred to as Peoples Democratic Organisations (PDOs). Teachers, young professionals, junior government employees and recent graduates flocked to join them, and thousands of young recruits were sent for political training to a special centre in Awasa named Tatek in 1991-1992. These factions were joined together later to form the Southern Ethiopian Peoples Democratic Front (SEPDF), which became the fourth member of the EPRDF coalition in 1994. At the same time, local opposition appeared in the form of several ethnic political factions, which came together under the umbrella of the Southern Ethiopian Peoples Democratic Coalition (SEPDC).

For many years, the TPLF was the undisputed 'primus inter pares', whose senior members held the key posts in the party and the state. This position was uncontested until the dramatic split in the Tigray leadership in 2001 that left few of its founding members in power (see Chapter 11). While this obviously weakened the TPLF as a political organisation, it also crowned Meles Zenawi as the unchallenged ruler of party and state. He became chairman of the executive committees of both the TPLF and the EPRF and prime minister of Ethiopia, whose authority is unchallenged. The historical pattern, whereby regimes come to power in Addis Ababa in a collegiate form and end up as personalised autocracies, was repeated.

The administrative edifice of the reconstructed Ethiopian state rests on the *woreda.* The ideal size of this unit was set at 100,000 inhabitants. In practice it varies widely, from more than twice as large to far smaller. The level where all state agencies – federal, regional, zonal – are represented, and where their functions are coordinated, the *woreda* is well placed to play an effective role in local self-government. Government authority at this level is invested in the *woreda* council elected for two years, and is exercised by its executive committee. The council itself meets three to four times annually for three to four days to hear executive committee reports and approve the budget.

[16] 'Hundreds of people were detained without charge for supposed involvement with the OLF and the ONLF.' *Country Reports on Human Rights Practices* (Washington: Department of State, 2001).

Since the EPRDF made a clean sweep of the first three local government elections, it was no surprise that virtually all elected officials at this level were party members, or joined soon after election. Candidate lists are drawn by the party, and people know it would be self-defeating to choose anyone who is unacceptable to the party. This produced a party-state merger that compensated for the centrifugal tendencies of federalism, and afforded the regime effective control to impose its policies throughout the country without variation. Policy directives came from Addis Ababa to be discussed by party committees before being taken up formally by the elected bodies and endorsed as a matter of course. All matters administrative and political were first discussed and decided at party meetings before reaching the elected councils. It is no wonder that Ethiopians see no difference between party and state. Such a complete overlap became an embarrassment to the regime itself, and a revision of the *kilil* constitutions was ordered in 2001 'to ensure that constitutional provisions for independence as well as for checks and balances between the executive, legislature and judiciary are fully realised in practice'. Since then, the *woreda* party chairman may not concurrently become chairman of the *woreda* executive committee, and the same applies to all levels, from *kebele* to *kilil*.

In the original design of regional government – *kilil*, zone, *woreda*, *kebele* – the zone, although it had no elected component, was the key planning, coordinating and fiscal level with supervising authority over the *woreda*. Administrative, technical and clerical expertise was concentrated here, where requests and plans from the *woreda* were scrutinised, modified, approved or rejected. *Woreda* budgets were subject to the same procedure, and funds were doled out to them from the zonal finance bureau. After a decade of disappointing performance, the federal government unveiled a '*woreda* empowerment' plan to make this level the fulcrum of all government activities, on the premise that it was closest to the people. Identified as a bottleneck, the zone was to be shorn of most of its functions and its skilled staff shared among the *woreda*. Promoted as the ideal instrument for good governance, '*woreda* empowerment' was ordained throughout the country; with the exception of 'special zones' wherever they were found.

It was not a popular plan among officials. *Kilil* administrators and politicians were not pleased to have their powers curtailed, especially over the budget that the plan proposed to transfer *en bloc* directly to the *woreda*. Skilled staff remain unwilling to live in remote *woreda* capitals bereft of basic amenities, including housing. Many ways have been devised to evade the regulations and stall the plan's implementation. Its fundamental weakness, however, has been the lack of resources for the *woreda* to perform their envisaged role. In addition to physical isolation and scarcity of skilled manpower, the lack of adequate funding has hampered what was conceptually a sound plan. *Woreda* budgets are consumed by current expenditure, often months before the end of the fiscal year. More often than not, what passes for development initiatives at this level are shoddy buildings intended for schoolrooms and health stations that stand empty for lack of equipment and staff.

The *kebele* is the level where the state actually touches the people. The population size of this unit varies widely and can reach several thousands. The *kebele* has its own elected council and executive committee, and elects three representatives to the *woreda* council. The party-state merger functions here as well, turning this base unit of administration into an appendage of the ruling party. Its role in managing peoples' lives cannot be exaggerated. The *kebele* has its own militia unit, court and prison to enforce state-party dictates covering a wide spectrum of activities. Tax collection is a familiar function entrusted to the *kebele*, and is diligently pursued as always. Defaulters are summarily thrown in prison for as long as needed, and ultimately are compelled to sell animals and other possessions to meet this obligation. Credit received by the peasantry for fertiliser is guaranteed by the *kebele*, which is subsequently saddled with the task of recovering the money from indebted peasants.

Another state function entrusted to the *kebele* is the identification, registration and surveillance of its members. The *kebele* issues identity cards, and provides recommendation letters for people applying for public services such as utilities, medical treatment, education and state employment. The distribution of food aid, participation in food-for-work projects, and access to other giveaways are *kebele* responsibility. The management of scarce resources enhances the *kebele's* capacity for population control. To begin with, it controls the land and its distribution among its members. Young people planning to marry have to ask the *kebele* for a share of land, as outsiders who move into its area also have to do. Increasing demand for land from agri-business puts *kebele* officials in a mediating and potentially lucrative position. This became obvious in peri-urban areas, especially around Addis Ababa, where agricultural land is in demand for middle class housing. The urban *kebele* also administer low cost housing for which there is an extraordinary demand.

The state-party tentacles reach below this level. The *kebele* itself is subdivided into *nus-kebele* (sub-kebele) sections and, further down, into clusters of households known as *mengistawi budin* (government groups) of up to fifty households and *lemat budin* (development groups) of ten to fifteen households. Introduced by the TPLF in Tigray, it was recommended to all EPRDF members. *Mengistawi budin* are supposed to mobilise people for the implementation of government policy at the grass roots, while *lemat budin* are expected to plan and implement small local development projects. The task of managing this micro level fell largely on a corps of agricultural development agents, many thousands of whom were dispersed throughout the countryside after a brief course of training.

Popular versus liberal democracy

As the administrative net was drawn ever more tightly, a parallel process was shrinking the space for political competition that was thrown wide open initially with the invitation in 1991 to all and sundry to participate. Aspiring rivals for power at the centre who responded to the invitation fell into two categories. The first was a collection of nationality based political organisations/national liberation fronts, most of them older than the EPRDF. With the exception of the OLF, none of the others competed for power at the centre. They challenged the EPRDF in the periphery, where they had taken root earlier and could easily outbid the patchwork of recently created PDOs for popular support. The older among them were included in the transitional government with seats in the legislative council, and a few were found deserving of ministerial posts.

As it turned out, this was a brief period of political grace. Ironically, it was the introduction of democratic elections, an unfamiliar experience for Ethiopians, which brought it to an end. The challenge to the EPRDF was openly manifested and its reaction was decisive. It expelled these factions from the transitional government at the centre, and eventually from the political arena by making it impossible for them to function at any level. In the end, none remained active in the political process, most of them fell apart, and a few resumed the armed struggle in the bush.

The second category of aspiring contestants for power comprised political organisations that appeared with the change of regime, but resisted coming under the mantle of the EPRDF. Most of them, including the EPDM, claimed, or were compelled to claim, an ethnic identity and constituency. Nevertheless, led by young, sophisticated, albeit neophyte politicians, they posed a serious challenge in the urban sector and a potential alternative to the regime. For reasons of history and ideology, the EPRDF had not thought it necessary to win over the townsfolk of Ethiopia, a political sin of omission it was to regret. Its roots lay in the history of the TPLF. Unlike its ideological kin, EPRP and MEISONE and the rest of the radical cohort whose contact with the peasantry was notional, the TPLF's formative experience determined a political outlook in which the peasantry occupied the central position. The TPLF credited its success in the struggle against the military regime entirely on its strategy of peasant mobilisation and political education, and believed it could repeat this feat on an Ethiopia-wide front.

It did not change this strategy after coming to power; it made it the guiding principle of all the initiatives launched by the EPRDF, from ethnic federalism to social and economic development. It is perfectly logical in a country whose peasant sector encompasses over 80% of its population to see peasant mobilisation as imperative for success in any government endeavour. According to the document for EPRDF member guidance,

> ...this class is the pillar of Revolutionary Democracy. Just as the centre of our economic development program is the rural part of the country, so, too, the focus of our political work is the peasantry...We should mobilize its members through social, political and economic organisations of its own...We should identify and transform into our strong cadres those prominent peasants who have earned the respect of their communities.

Meles Zenawi spelled it out in his address to the House of Peoples Representatives in 1995: 'Let the peasants never be disaffected. Once they are disaffected, it will be the end of the world. But whatever happens, with the support of the peasantry, we may stagger, but we would surely make it.'[17]

The corollary of this peasant-focused strategy is an aloofness within the urban milieu, and a reluctance to engage with the intelligentsia and middle class that dominate it. Urbanisation made no progress in Tigray, hence the TPLF did not have to accommodate it. It is different in other parts of Ethiopia, where towns have grown and townsmen are politically conscious. Furthermore, their experience with the EPRP and MEISONE has given the Tigray rebels a dim view of the Amhara dominated urban sector, particularly the capital city of Addis Ababa. 'Addis Ababa is not Ethiopia', Meles Zenawi declared in 1991. 'Its population was fed on Dergue propaganda...It is where all the Dergue supporters fled to as the country was liberated.'[18] Since the towns became opposition strongholds, he was proved right, and EPRDF's misgivings about the 'bourgeois elements' that dominate town life were confirmed.

The ideological focus on the peasantry illuminates the concept of 'revolutionary democracy' or 'popular democracy', which presumably defines EPRDF philosophy and political practice. Following the land reform and other 'levelling' measures, the Ethiopian peasantry was seen as a homogenous class with common needs, interests and political outlook. Therefore, it could be approached from a class perspective. Political participation in this context presumes a commonality of interests that makes political pluralism irrelevant and competition harmful. Pluralism reflects class divisions that are not present in peasant society. Consequently, there was no need for more than one venue (party) for political participation in popular democracy. Confirmed by the TPLF's experience in Tigray, this became the political compass of the EPRDF. It redoubled its efforts to 'capture' the peasantry and secure an impregnable political base in the countryside from where it could rule the country. It made an extraordinary effort to achieve this, lavishing time, energy and resources, while virtually ignoring the towns.

Needless to say, 'popular democracy' runs contrary to 'liberal democracy'. In the Marxist logic followed by the EPRDF, liberal bourgeois democracy is the political superstructure of mature capitalism, and has no place in Ethiopia where capitalism is neither present nor welcome. 'The Basic Questions of Democracy in Ethiopia', a tract reportedly written by Meles Zenawi and issued in 2001, made this clear: 'Liberal democracy has no social base in Ethiopia...As long as democracy is an instrument in the hands of the few it cannot strike roots. For our democracy to be guaranteed and to strike roots it should be based upon the all inclusive participation of the people.'

Although 'popular democracy' conveys politically correct notions of inclusiveness, direct participation, and accountability, it sets clear limits to pluralism in political life. If the EPRDF had its way, only ethnic based political organisations would be legal. The Popular Registration Act compelled all Ethiopians to declare a nationality that was shown in their

[17] *Parliament* (Vol. 1, No. 1: 9).

[18] Press interview, *Ethiopian Herald* (15 June 1991).

identity card. Declaring oneself 'Ethiopian' was not acceptable. Starting with the July 1991 Conference, the regime regarded efforts to organise on an Ethiopia-wide basis as subversive. Furthermore, while it supported the right of ethnic groups to political representation, it also rejected pluralism on that level, because it reflects class divisions that are of no importance in a peasant society. Accordingly, it sponsored only one political organisation per nationality, forcing local rivals to join the opposition.

EPRDF political intolerance is evident in its unwillingness to engage with alternative political points of view. Despite the fact that it has had to discard most of its ideological and programmatic baggage on the road to power, the ruling party remains firmly convinced of own infallibility. A common accusation against the opposition is that it 'does not have a programme, only a lust for power'. The opposition is routinely accused of collaboration with foreign interests seeking to dominate Ethiopia. Opposition leaders are ridiculed for allegedly making the rounds of foreign embassies asking for money and intervention in Ethiopia's domestic affairs.

These affectations serve to rationalise the regime's refusal to distinguish among shades of opposition, and its rejection of those that conceivably could be its natural allies in transforming the centre/periphery relationship. Among these are the nationality based factions in Debub that came together in the Southern Ethiopian Peoples Democratic Coalition (SEPDC), the Oromo National Congress, as well as a couple of other small factions belonging to the so-called 'legal opposition'. They are in basic agreement with the federal redesign of the state and support state ownership of land. Meles Zenawi slammed the door in their faces saying in a 1994 interview: 'We don't seek to get other groups to join us, for it would require the EPRDF to change and dilute its programme in order to accommodate them.'[19]

In practice, the EPRDF's contempt for its political opponents translates into denying them the space needed to function effectively. The ruling front makes full use of the state machinery and resources, including its monopoly of mass media and instruments of repression, to relentlessly and ruthlessly harass them. The party-state apparatus is fully engaged mobilising support for the regime using the carrot, and to discourage opposition using the stick. The carrot represents all the benefits local officials can dispense and they are many, while the stick represents all the services, licenses, permissions and endorsements they can refuse, plus the fines and jail terms they mete out to the non-cooperative. Local officials wield great power over the peasants, power that is often self-serving, arbitrary, biased and abused. They herd people into endless meetings to be harangued by higher officials, they ensure that party rallies and demonstrations are well attended, that visiting dignitaries are received with singing and dancing in traditional dress, and that people troop to the polls on election day to vote for ruling party candidates. At the same time, everything possible is done to snuff out opposition, making life unbearable for the hardy souls who dare identify with opposition parties.

[19] Ethiopian Herald (20 September 1944).

Physical violence against opponents was routine throughout the first decade of EPRDF rule, costing many lives. An ineffectual Elections Board ran by EPRDF minions turned a blind eye. Understandably, a series of elections held under these conditions were boycotted by the 'legal' opposition and were swept by the regime.

The state and civil society

Intolerance of competition extends well beyond the political arena to a budding civil society that made a timid appearance after 1991. Freedom of association is enshrined in the 1995 Constitution (Art. 31), along with a list of forty-four articles devoted to the protection of citizens' rights – human, social, civil, political – including 'the right to a clean and healthy environment' (Art. 44/1). Early on, the EPRDF was justly praised for opening space for civil society to function, yet it remained wary of institutions aspiring to play a public role but not affiliated or accountable to it. Referring to 'the so-called civil society', the ruling front appeared to question its legitimacy, and before long it moved to suppress or supplant its most important members.

This was the fate of the small but intrepid labour movement which, having been born under the imperial regime as CELU and reborn under the Dergue as AETU, went through a third rebirth and political trial by fire under the EPRDF to become the Confederation of Ethiopian Trade Unions (CETU). The new regime's strategy in this field was outlined in the 1993 document for member guidance: 'We should encourage trade unions, but without compromising their organisation, we should try to control and lead them through indirect organisational links.' It wasn't easy. A so-called Proletarian Branch of the EPRDF started organising workers at plant level and prepared to form a national organisation. A meeting called in early June 1993 in Addis Ababa brought together some three hundred delegates of plant unions. They were surprised to see four members of the transitional legislative assembly appointed by that body to represent workers take the platform. The meeting challenged their credentials, and after a heated discussion they were obliged to leave. The meeting then chose a committee to form a national body named the Confederation of Ethiopian Trade Unions (CETU), and an executive committee of seven to direct it. Of the twenty-nine organising committee members, eleven were associated with the EPRDF.

Relations with the government became strained before long. From the workers' point of view, ethnic federalism divided and weakened their movement, and syndicalists made this clear in public statements. CETU also opposed the sale of state enterprises to private capital that invariably brought mass worker dismissals in their wake. The inevitable confrontation occurred in 1994 when, worried about job losses, CETU's leaders condemned the structural adjustment programme imposed by the World Bank, which the Ethiopia was obliged to accept in order to remain eligible for loans. The regime's reaction followed a script that became standard procedure in confronting resistance to its policies. A campaign of denunciation and harassment against CETU's leadership ensued, and a pro-government 'splinter group' emerged within CETU's executive committee to challenge the leadership, giving the Ministry of Labour and Social Affairs an opening to intervene. Alleging that the organisation was paralysed by an internal power struggle, the Ministry cancelled its registration and closed it down. A legal farce followed when the courts twice upheld CETU's appeals against the Ministry, only to have their rulings ignored. A third ruling reversed the position and found for the government. In the aftermath, CETU's secretary general went into exile, and the organisation was taken over by the faction allied with the EPRDF.[20]

A similar fate befell the Ethiopian Teachers Association (ETA), another institution with a history of resistance under previous regimes. Its view of ethnic federalism was similar to labour's. Having trained to teach elementary school in Amharigna, teachers resented the EPRDF's Education and Training Policy that promoted the use of ethnic languages at that level, and ETA made its opposition clear. A campaign to defame its leadership followed, implying subversive motives and links with insurgent groups. When ETA complained to the International Labour Office in 1995, its office in Addis Ababa was closed. Two years later, an ETA official was shot dead by the police, and a year after that its offices were closed again. In 1999 its chairman was convicted of treason and sentenced to 15 years imprisonment. Subsequently, the EPRDF produced its own teachers' association.

Founded by Addis Ababa University staff members in 1991, the Ethiopian Human Rights Council (EHRCO) was soon involved in confrontation with the EPRDF. It was refused registration for years on the grounds that it was a political organisation, and its bank account was blocked until 1999. Its chairman was arrested in 2001 accused of inciting students to riot. Another group, the Human Rights League, founded in 1996 in Oromia, was also harassed and accused of having links with the OLF.[21] The same was the fate of the Ogaden Human Rights Committee. In 2000, the regime announced plans to set up its own Human Rights Commission and Ombudsman, and they materialised in 2007.

Immediately after it came to power, the EPRDF issued a declaration on the freedom of the press, an unheard of luxury in this country that was subsequently enshrined in the 1955 Constitution. The response was exhilarating, spawning a stream of publications in the form of weekly and monthly newspapers and periodicals, whose number exceeded one hundred by the middle of the decade. The EPRDF had its own publications, a government owned press, plus radio and television channels, and ambitious plans to dominate the media sector, as shown in the 1993 document for its members' guidance:

> Apart from the newspapers, radio and television, theatre and cinema houses controlled by the State should also be reorganised and their practices reoriented

[20] Dawi Ibrahim, former CETU secretary general, interviewed in The Hague, January1998.
[21] In May 2001, eight founding members were acquitted in court after spending three-and-a-half years in detention.

to serve as useful propaganda tools… But since the State media is poorly staffed and organised, and not up to the job, Revolutionary democracy's own media should be modernized and expanded to control the market.

The private press was almost unanimously and aggressively critical, all too eager to find fault with the regime, and their relationship was frosty from the start. Predisposed to detect political motives behind any criticism, the regime cut off communication with the independent media. They were excluded from official functions and interviews, and were not informed of government announcements and plans. Inexperience and political passion on the part of the private press led to exaggeration and misinformation, giving the regime reason to crack down with fines and imprisonment of journalists for 'dissemination of false information', or 'inciting people against the government', followed by closure of publications.

The Ethiopian Free Press Journalist Association (EFPJA) was formed in 1993, in opposition to the Ethiopian Journalists Association (EJA) that was controlled by the editors of the state owned media. Not surprisingly, it came in for heavy handed government harassment. Many of its members landed in prison, and its president was convicted six times in the next ten years for fabricating information against the state and spreading information that 'upset the public.' During the same time, some 200 journalists spend time in prison, and Ethiopia ranked high on the list of countries with imprisoned journalists. Under the circumstances, the number of independent publications shrank quickly, and by the beginning of the new century there were less than a dozen that preserved a circumspect presence. It was not until 2007 that the first private radio station was licensed. A long debated media code of practice enacted at this time was roundly denounced as attack on the freedom of the press.

Non-governmental organisations (NGOs) were another component of civil society to run afoul of the regime because of their claim to independence. Their presence in Ethiopia dated from the mid-1970s, when foreign NGOs took up the task of famine relief that neither the imperial regime nor its successor could handle. The TPLF itself was the beneficiary of NGO assistance that brought food across the border from Sudan into liberated areas during the famine of the 1980s. This so-called 'cross-border' operation violated sundry international and national laws, and made the TPLF wary of western NGO assertiveness and financial clout. The number of international NGOs in Ethiopia increased greatly after 1991, and was supplemented by domestic organisations that were, more often than not, affiliated with, or at least funded by, organisations abroad. The EPRDF was anxious to manage the flow of aid funds itself, rather than share it with independent NGOs. It was also legitimately concerned with rationalising NGO activities to limit duplication and waste.

More than anything, however, the ruling front had political concerns mentioned in the 1993 document for its members' guidance: 'We should not try to bring in outsiders to lead the peasants. In the rural areas, there are an increasing number of governmental and non-governmental development workers. These lower-level members of the intelligentsia can undermine our influence and development program if they oppose our political line.' Its concern was heightened when international NGOs, following the lead of donor governments, took up the 'advocacy' of human rights, governance and peacemaking, areas in which the regime was attracting criticism from abroad. NGO eagerness to become involved in the preparation and monitoring of the disastrous 2005 elections, finally forced its hand. Until then, it had endeavoured to control the NGOs using the power of registration. Meddlesome ones were denied it, or had their registration revoked without opportunity of appeal. It took decisive action in 2009 by barring foreign organisations from involvement in the fields of human rights and conflict. By defining any NGO receiving more than ten percent of its funds from abroad, or having non-citizens on its board of directors, as 'foreign', it effectively excluded domestic organisations as well. A Charities and Societies Agency was established to police the field.

Summary

The operation of the federal system over two decades (1991-2010) revealed two powerful trends working against it. The first was inspired by Ethiopian nationalism and was most powerfully manifested in the centre as a rejection of 'ethnic federalism', believing that it foments political fragmentation and incubates secession. This belief brought together a coalition of disparate factions into a widening opposition to the EPRDF, which threatened not only its hold on power, but the future of the federal experiment as well. The ruling party's refusal to engage with the opposition showed that the promise of democracy is hollow and limited to the familiar institutional and procedural facade for authoritarian rule.

Federalism and cultural emancipation were welcomed throughout the periphery, earning the EPRDF significant support. The long subordinate nationalities are now administered by their own people, their cultures and languages enjoy recognition and a chance of revival, and a multitude of their young men and women joined the new corps of peripheral elite brought into being with remarkable speed by the new regime. However, the passing of the years revealed a second powerful trend working against federalism under EPRDF auspices. It emerged in the periphery, when it became clear that the political process fabricated by the EPRDF negates the promise of equitable centre/periphery power sharing. The party-state merger reproduced the old iniquitous relationship, albeit under a dense camouflage of institutional trappings. This puts the EPRDF initiative in a different light, revealing that it did not truly depart from the century old Ethiopian nationalist project. It simply pursues the same end through different, subtler means.

11

Ruling the Federal State
1995–2010

When the EPRDF came to power in 1991, it found the country's economy in 'a coma'.[1] Its strategy for economic recovery focused on rapid growth in agricultural production to feed the population and provide raw material for industrialisation, and depended on the use of inputs, whose cost the producer had to bear regardless of results. Because generally the results did not justify the cost, the strategy failed. The regime then shifted its focus from the peasant to the land itself, and adopted the simple method of exploiting this resource by leasing it to private capital for large scale, commercial cultivation. The fact that the land put up for leasing was almost exclusively located in the lowland periphery added an explosive political dimension to this strategy of development.

Obliged to liberalise the rest the economy, the EPRDF retained a significant share under state ownership, transferred another share to its member parties, and kept the private sector at arm's length. While noticeable progress was made in the early years with significant growth rates in the GDP and currency stability, the failure to develop agriculture kept purchasing power at low levels and restrained growth elsewhere in the economy. During the few years of peace in the 1990s, Ethiopia demilitarised and hopes for a peace dividend flourished. They were dashed when once more it became mired in conflict with Eritrea and Somalia.

Also obliged to undertake political reform, in its first decade of power the EPRDF was able to preserve a democratic facade against a disparate and ineffectual opposition by stage managing and winning a series of elections. The turn of the century saw a great improvement in opposition performance. Taking advantage of widespread popular disillusionment with the ruling front, the opposition came close to ending the regime's exclusive hold on power. The latter's reaction was to rip off the facade of democratisation, making it clear that it had no intention of surrendering power. Once more, conflict over power divided the centre, raising the spectre of another historic rupture in the process of state-building.

[1] Mekonnen Manyawazal interviewed in Addis Ababa, July1999.

Land and the peasant

The economy's comatose state was recorded in the following statistics: the GDP at constant prices showed negative growth in 1988-1992, and per capita income had declined by 3.7% during the same period. The agricultural production rate of growth had averaged 0.7% for the previous seventeen years, when the population grew at the rate of 3 per cent. The overall balance of payments had declined steadily since 1986, and export earnings were 21% of imports. Current account deficit equalled 12.3% of GDP, and the foreign exchange reserves were nil. The deficit was covered by grants and loans, and the new regime started its reign heavily dependent on foreign aid, a position that has not changed to this day. There were less than 100,000 workers in industrial enterprises employing more than ten persons, and a huge pool of unemployed people was swollen by the disbanding of the Dergue army of some 500,000 soldiers.

The resolutions of the first EPRDF congress in 1989 envisaged an economy in which the commanding role of the state differed little from what it was under the Dergue. However, its leaders discovered very soon that 'this situation is not acceptable in current global economic thinking', and conversion to the free market was among the adjustments they had to make upon coming to power. It was not heartfelt or complete. As the EPRDF document for the guidance of its members explained in 1993, 'key industrial and agricultural enterprises...could still be controlled by the State', while other important sectors could be taken over by 'various revolutionary democratic associations, organizations, and individuals who can be involved in investment'. A dim view was taken of foreign investment. 'If foreign investors want to be involved...they should be denied the necessary incentives and pressurized by legal instruments to toe the line.'

Land was one area where pressure for privatisation was firmly resisted, and state ownership was enshrined in the 1955 Constitution. Modest changes were made to meet cogent criticisms of the existing system. One of these concerned security of tenure, the lack of which presumably deprived the peasant of incentive to invest in improvements needed to increase production. The Constitution decreed:

> Every Ethiopian shall have the full right to the immovable property he builds and to the permanent improvements he brings about on the land by his labour or capital. This shall include the right to alienate, to bequeath, and where the right of use expires, to remove his property, transfer his title, or claim compensation for it. (Art. 40/7)

Plans were made to bolster the feeling of security by issuing land use certificates to the peasants. Provisions for leasing land to encourage agro-industry were also made. The old system banned renting of land, except for those who could not work it themselves: the old, the sick and widowed women. The 1975 land reform also banned hired labour, and limited household holdings to a maximum of ten hectares. None of these restrictions appeared in the new legislation governing land. The Constitution gave the authority to administer land to the *kilil*, provided they acted in accordance with federal law, and the Federal Rural Land Administration Proclamation (89/1997) gave authority for land administration to the *kilil*, including the 'assignment of holding rights and the execution of distribution of holdings', but ruled out mortgaging or selling land.

Constitutional and political prescriptions notwithstanding, land privatisation was well under way in many parts of Ethiopia in the first decade of the 21st century. It began with the most valuable land surrounding the fast expanding towns and *kilil* capitals. The most spectacular sellout was in Addis Ababa, where high quality housing complexes, complete with swimming pools and tennis courts, mushroomed to serve a growing middle class joined by returnees from the diaspora. Land was acquired cheaply from Oromo peasants, who were allowed to rent half their holding; a form of disguised sale.[2] The centre of Addis Ababa itself was transformed from an antique conurbation, where rich and poor lived cheek by jowl in amicably shared squalor, into a modern concrete and glass city with clearly marked class distinctions. Ironically, it was the 1975 land reform that deprived the mass of the capital's inhabitants of their legal rights to the land they occupied, and made it possible for a massive urban clearance to move them into housing projects in the outskirts, leaving the town centre to glitzy hotels, banks and high-rise buildings rented to foreigners. Not surprisingly, the urban poor were the losers in this process. A report on land use administration in 2009 found that 'access to land by the poor in most cities and towns has been deteriorating over the years.' In Addis Ababa and other cities, 'weak law enforcement, poor land administration, the high price of land, allocation procedures which favoured the elite, bad governance and corruption and the limited capacity of local government were found to be the principal reason for failure to reduce urban poverty and to improve living conditions.'[3]

*

Ethiopia has the smallest urban sector (17%) in sub-Saharan Africa (average 34%). Agriculture feeds its people and provides nearly all its exports, as well as the bulk of the raw material used in domestic manufacturing. Appropriately, the main goal of the EPRDF's economic policy was to raise agricultural productivity and attain food security, a welcome shift from the emphasis on export crop production under previous regimes. The much-touted Sasakawa Global 2000 formula (fertilizer + improved seeds + pesticides + improved cultivation practices) was launched in the early 1990s with great fanfare. Consistent with its political instincts, the EPRDF turned it into a mass campaign, mobilising the party-state appara-

[2] Oromia *kilil* Directive, No.3/1995.

[3] SIDA Report, 2009. (p. ix).

tus for this purpose. Also consistent with EPRDF practice, the same formula was applied indiscriminately everywhere, ignoring the country's highly diverse rural ecology. Credit was provided by EPRDF-affiliated microfinance agencies, and was pressed unrelentingly on a peasant sector that was not yet fully monetised. The *kebele* were mobilised to coerce their members to join the scheme and afterwards to pay their debts, threatening to deprive them of state provided services if they did not.

The programme met with initial success, reaching a participation rate of 2.8 million households – about one quarter of the total – by the end of the decade. Yield increases for maize rose from 1,200 kg per hectare to 4,700 kg, and for wheat from 860 to 2,930 kg. The benefit was obvious in parts of the country, such as Gojjam, where flat grain-producing areas were mechanically cultivated. Relatively good weather also helped. Elsewhere, where land size and shape, the crops planted, or the cultivation techniques were not suitable, the results did not justify the expense. Initially subsidised, the inputs were later sold at market prices. Finally, with debt default mounting and peasant participation declining, the project was abandoned.

The next nostrum purveyed by the World Bank in Africa was the Sustainable Development and Poverty Reduction Strategy, whose goal was to fund safety nets to catch the casualties of its earlier Structural Adjustment Programme. In Addis Ababa, the money was welcome, the programme was adopted with a great deal of official fanfare, and no more was heard of it afterwards. It was followed by the announcement of a Food Security Strategy that likewise faded away without further mention. The next addition to the growing list of failed development strategies, a so-called 'Agriculture Led Industrial Development' announced at the start of the new century, appeared to take peasant resistance into account, as well as the need for a flexible approach to meet rural diversity. In his address to Parliament (30 January 2002), Meles Zenawi promised 'an assortment of packages compatible with a given environment, from among which the farmer may select a package or packages best suited to him'. It was followed by latest World Bank palliative called the Accelerated and Sustainable Development to End Poverty Programme (2006/7-2010/11).

The 1991 EPRDF statement on economic policy cancelled the resettlement and villagisation programmes of the military regime 'until conditions are ripe for such programmes'. Conditions apparently ripened by the beginning of the 21st century, when a three-year voluntary resettlement programme aiming to move 2.2 million people was announced. This time, political considerations ruled out shifting people across *kilil* boundaries, and the programme was carried out within *kilil* in Amhara, Tigray, Oromia and Debub. About 180,000 households were resettled in more than 100 villages by the beginning of 2005. A study of several resettlement cites reported that people were enticed to move with promises of good land, housing and food rations for up to three years.[4]

[4] 'Understanding the Dynamics of Resettlement in Ethiopia', (2005) (Addis Ababa: Forum for Social Studies).

None of these efforts managed to set in motion the process of structural change needed in an economy that remains heavily dependent on a subsistence-oriented, smallholder sector, whose rate of growth in the past decade was 2, 27% per annum, an improvement on past performance, yet still below the population rate of growth of around 3%. Per capita landholding was reduced from 0.28ha in 1960 to 0.10 ha in 1990.[5] Food production remained entirely dependent on rain, with dramatic shifts from one year to the next, and was seldom sufficient to feed the burgeoning population. The shortfall amounted to an average of 10% of annual cereal production. An average of 700,000 metric tons of food was imported every year. Agriculture did not perform well even as a rural 'subsistence' economy. The per capita annual food deficit in the rural sector had grown from 83kg in the imperial era to 119kg in the mid-1990s. No less than 52% of the rural population was poor in that sense, compared with 37% of the urban population. Famine was a frequent visitor in rural Ethiopia, and hardly a year went by without government appeals for international food aid.[6]

Production flourished in one area without benefit of government intervention: chat. The appeal of this drug spread from its native region in the eastern highlands of Ethiopia to the entire region of the Horn and across the sea to Arabia. Its cultivation spread to all the coffee-producing areas of the country, where it competed with Ethiopia's main export. Chat was exported by air to Djibouti, Hargeisa in Somaliland and Bossasso in Somalia, and from there to Aden and Yemen. Dried chat was shipped to Europe and North America. The export trade was licensed and regulated by the state to ensure receipt of foreign currency through the banking system.

Land to the investor

Another opportunity to break the shackles of subsistence agriculture appeared in the first decade of the 21st century, when the world economy was alerted to a looming global food crisis resulting from increasing land and water scarcity, and a concomitant energy crisis due to the lack of ecologically sustainable sources. Food importing rich countries looked abroad for opportunities to invest in food production, and sparsely populated, capital-starved sub-Saharan Africa was a prime choice. Energy producing countries were also attracted to the region for investment in crop production for conversion to bio-fuels. Low production costs in Africa and high consumer prices in rich countries made for large profits and lured capital investment from many parts of the world, including Asia, the Middle East, Europe and the United States, in a massive trend

[5] Central Statistical Agency, *Annual Agricultural Sample Surveys*.

[6] During 1994-2003, an average of five million people needed food aid. During 1998-2005, the numbers fluctuated between five and fourteen million (IDS, Sussex, 2006). In 2009, the figure given by the government was six million.

that critics called an international 'land grab' and the 'second scramble for Africa'.

By this time, the EPRDF appeared to have lost faith in peasant agriculture, and in what amounted to a vote of no confidence in the peasantry, chose to promote large scale commercial agriculture in partnership with foreign capital. This policy was in force for several years before it was announced officially in mid-2009. By this time, Ethiopia was already a leader among African states offering land to international capital for production of food and bio-fuels. An Agricultural Investment Support Agency was set up to expedite the process. According to its director, there is no limit to the amount of land available for leasing in Ethiopia. 'We have 74.5 million hectares of cultivable land of which only about 15 million is cultivated by small scale farmers', he said. 'Two million hectares were already leased by 2009 and three million more were available for investment in the following two years.'[7]

The regime's shyness about what promised to be the most significant development in the rural economy during its reign was understandable given the explosive political potential of issues concerning land in Ethiopia. The new policy touched on many of these. First and foremost, the process of leasing land touched the very core of the federal arrangement, since the main advantage of decentralisation from the viewpoint of the periphery was to give its communities a measure of control over their land, and to prevent its being taken over by Addis Ababa fiat as in the past. As noted earlier, according to the Constitution, authority to administer land belongs to the *kilil*. As it turned out, the federal government took the initiative, and it is hard to see how the policy could be implemented otherwise. Ethiopia has no land use policy at the national or *kilil* levels; the need for it received perfunctory recognition with the establishment of Land Administration and Use Teams, staffed with a few untrained civil servants. Early on, aspiring investors were directed to the *kilil* investment bureaux, but after a period of confusion and indecision, the process was taken in hand by the Natural Resources Management branch of the Ministry of Agriculture and Rural Development, whose own capacity for the task was assessed as 'very limited'.[8] Much of the potentially cultivable land came under federal jurisdiction anyway, and its administration has been entrusted to the Ethiopian River Basins Development Authority.

Land offered for leasing is classified as 'available' because it is 'idle' or 'wasteland', which implies it neither belongs to, nor is used, by anyone. Accordingly, there is no obligation on the part of the government or the investor to pay compensation to anyone. The classification criteria take us back to an earlier era, when little was known about the extensive use of land in shifting cultivation and mobile pastoralism. The auctioning of land targets the sparsely populated lowlands that are presumed to have large swathes of 'unused' land. This is where marginalised communities of

[7] Reuters Report, Addis Ababa (6 November 2009).
[8] SIDA report, p. 8.

traditional cultivators and pastoralists face the threat of losing their land, their livelihood, and even their way of life. The best they can hope for is seasonal plantation work for pitiful wages. Needless to say, traditional cultivators and pastoralists live on the margins of society, and are least able to defend their rights against the combined weight of the state and foreign capital. From producers of food they will become consumers, in a country that is already facing a severe problem of food deficit. Although much of the investment in agri-business is planned for food production, it is not food that local people eat or can afford to buy; it is for export. The consequences for the land itself can be catastrophic. Large scale, mechanised monoculture cultivation is known to have a devastating impact on the environment – land, water and biodiversity. In the words of one critic:

> Outsourcing food production will ensure food security for investing countries but would leave behind a trail of hunger, starvation and food scarcities for local populations...The environmental tab of highly intensive farming – devastated soils, dry aquifers and ruined ecology from chemical infestation – will be left for the host country to pick up.[9]

Leases are granted from thirty to ninety years, with fees set very low – three to ten US dollars per year. The government offers inducements such as low taxation of profits – twenty dollars per hectare per year – initially suspended for a number of years. Land fees and other monetary transfers are not the main anticipated benefits for the recipient country: these are the anticipated investment in production with the promise of employment creation and infrastructural development. Normally investors are required to commit themselves to targets in these areas, but experience shows that such commitments are vaguely framed, difficult to enforce, and often wholly or partially evaded.

The rapid growth of the flower industry in the centre of the country since 2000 could be a harbinger of things to come. Starting that year from zero, this sector numbered more than one-hundred firms by 2009 and made Ethiopia the second (after Kenya) largest cut-flower exporter in Africa. Not a few firms shifted operations from Kenya for economic reasons. These include cheap land at an average annual lease rate of two-hundred dollars per hectare; free ground water; cheap labour whose cost amounted to less than 6% of the total cost of production; duty free exports, and many other inducements. Located mostly within a radius of 50km from Addis Ababa, the industry engaged a workforce of about 50,000, of which 70% were women earning one dollar per day – less than the cost of a single flower in the Amsterdam market.

The environmental cost is easy to observe and has been reported in the local and international media. Floriculture depends heavily on fertilisers, pesticides and insecticides, 128 types of which are imported in Ethiopia, with some of them known carcinogenics. Ground water in the region, including the Akaki River and Lake Koka, is heavily polluted, and the local population faces a severe shortage of safe water for drinking. The

[9] *The Guardian* (4 July 2009).

flower plantations used to operate without even nominal state supervision, and it was only when the trade unions and NGOs became involved that a beginning was made to adopt safeguards, on a voluntary basis.

The party and the market

Privatisation of the state-owned sector was the first commitment that the incoming regime had to make to the international financial institutions, foreign governments and donors, whose support was and remains essential. Even though the World Bank and the IMF took an active role in the process, progress in the Public Enterprises Reform Programme was slow. The Ethiopian Privatisation Agency (EPA) was set up at the beginning of 1994, but it was not properly staffed and the task proved beyond its capacity. When a law decreed the restitution of 'illegally confiscated' properties under the military regime in 1966, the EPA was inundated with applications in the tens of thousands, and the process ground to a halt. Foreign capital has showed little interest in Ethiopia, and substantial assets remain in the state sector. According to EPA reports, only 200 state enterprises were privatised in the first seven years. It was officially admitted that privatisation failed 'to generate revenue required for financing development activities undertaken by the government', (Proclamation 146/1998).

Doubts concerning the regime's conversion to the free market were reinforced by its refusal to privatise key sectors of the economy, including telecommunications, mining, airlines and arms production. 'The government's commitment to opening up the economy is questionable', sniffed *The Economist.*[10] The EPRDF's lukewarm approach to the free market notwithstanding, its economic performance was judged satisfactory. It accepted the structural adjustment programme, deregulated trade, removed price controls and taxes on exports other than coffee, deregulated the labour market, reduced state expenditure and the budget deficit, shifted investment from defence to the social sector, improved the balance of payments, and devalued and floated the currency. All this was accomplished without appreciable inflation in the first decade. The GDP scored spectacular gains in the mid-1990s, leading the regime to set a goal of 7-10% growth for the second half of the decade. As a 'severely indebted' state, Ethiopia had 50% of its debt cancelled by the Paris Club and the rest rescheduled for 25 years. The GDP continued to show a steady increase in the new century, reaching 8.5% in 2007-8; supported by several years of growth in agricultural production; a boom in the urban construction industry; state investment in infrastructure, and high prices of coffee, oil seeds, leather and gold. Growth lacked balance, however, and this affected how people experienced it. One indicator was soaring inflation that passed 40% on a year-on-year basis in 2008. Despite several years of good harvests, food inflation rose to nearly 30%, putting a heavy

[10] *Economist, Country Report, 4th Quarter 1997* (London 1997: 11).

burden on the urban population, which the regime sought to ease by suspending the value-added tax of 15% and the turnover tax for grains, flour, cooking oil and the surtax on soap.[11] Another indicator was currency devaluation. The birr that had floated for years at 9 to the US dollar, slipped to nearly 12.5 in 2009.

The retreat of the state created the space for a private sector that has since provided nearly all the new capital investment, most of it going to services, construction, banking, insurance and transport. This did not earn it praise from the regime. On the contrary, the EPRDF made it plain from the outset that it had no more faith in the private sector's capacity to promote development, than it had in the political opposition to promote democracy. In its view, the private sector lacked the capacity 'to respond efficiently to opportunities created in the economy'.[12] Meles Zenawi was given to drawing distinctions between 'productive' and 'parasitic' private enterprise. He never appointed a businessman to high office, and did not deign to meet with representatives of the private sector until 2002. Apparently seen to belong the 'productive' category, a fast expanding conglomerate named Midroc has become by far the biggest private investor in the country, amassing manufacturing assets, leasing vast tracts of land for commercial farming, leading the urban construction sector, and operating gold mines. Midroc is controlled by Sheikh Al-Mudi, an entrepreneur of mixed Ethiopian-Yemeni parentage and strong Saudi Arabian financial connections, who enjoys the regime's favour and a Midas-like status among the people.

Denationalisation did not necessarily mean privatisation. The 1993 document for EPRDF member guidance foresaw a role 'revolutionary democratic forces' could play in the economy. That is how the EPRDF member parties and affiliates came to acquire denationalised assets ranging from banks and industrial plants to commercial farms, transport firms and travel agencies. The lead was taken by the TPLF, when it embarked on a major drive to reconstruct its war-torn home province of Tigray. A conglomerate named the Endowment Fund for the Rehabilitation of Tigray (EFFORT) was set up in 1995 as a holding company for an expanding group of industrial, financial and service enterprises that soon dominated the local economy. TPLF's example was followed by its partners, the ANDM in the Amhara *kilil* with an endowment called Endeavour, the OPDO in Oromia with the DINSHO Trading House, and the SEPDF in Debub with Wondo Trading House.

Militarisation

Nothing illustrates the extent of militarisation of Ethiopian society in the 1980s better than the fact that the combined strength of insurgent groups was more than twice the size of the armed forces under the imperial

[11] The Economist Intelligence Unit (2008) *Country Report: Ethiopia.*

[12] Country Presentation to United Nations Conference, May 2001.

regime. It was estimated the EPRDF itself had about 100,000 fighters, the bulk of them belonging to the TPLF. The programme endorsed by the first EPRDF National Congress in 1991 promised to dismantle the Dergue army, and reflecting the people's yearning for peace, its leader struck a pacific pose. 'There is no need for a large army', said Meles Zenawi in an interview. 'We don't need Africa's biggest army. There are no problems concerning our borders.'[13]

The 1993 EPRDF document for member guidance outlined its plans for the country's defence: 'Under a multi-party system the Defence Force cannot continue as the army of the EPRDF – it has to become the army of the State. Nobody will accept its continuation as EPRDF's army in the context of a free competition. Such a condition will invite the opposition of imperialism.' Nevertheless, a politically neutered army was not part of the plan. 'Severing its direct link with the EPRDF does not mean abandoning its revolutionary democratic character...Although it becomes free and neutral in appearance, the army will be revolutionary democratic in content and will protect the constitution and the rights of the masses.' Speaking some years later, the army chief of staff clarified the issue when he was reported as saying: '...the most important aspect of the army is not its national composition but its political character.'[14] The EPRDF army became the national defence force in January 1992, and leading TPLF figures took over the top defence and security posts in the government.

The renaming exercise that turned an ethnic guerrilla force into a national army was received with understandable scepticism by the emerging opposition, and was loudly criticised in the fledgling news media. The EPRDF then announced the demobilisation of its own soldiers, and the recruitment of other nationalities to make the military genuinely pan-Ethiopian. In 1994, the TPLF formally disbanded its armed force, and the other EPRDF members followed suit. All insurgent groups in the periphery were compelled to disband, including Oromo, Somali, Afar and Sidama. With the exception of the OLF, these were small and did not present a military challenge. However, their presence in their home territory was an obstacle to the EPRDF's plan to secure exclusive political control in the periphery. No official figure was ever put on this process, but various sources estimated the number of demobilised fighters at between 20,000 and 30,000. In an interview given in May 1966, the Minister of Defence claimed that 'the task of setting up a fairly representative defence force has been successfully accomplished. Thousands of EPRDF troops have been demobilised and replaced by new recruits belonging to various nations and nationalities including those from Somali, Gambella, Beni Shangul Gumuz and Afar regions.'[15] The fact that the military was rebuilt in the image of the EPRDF had negative political side effects. 'It is impossible to believe that the Ethiopian army,

[13] *Ethiopia Herald* (7 June 1991).
[14] *Addis Tribune* (4 May1995).
[15] *Ethiopian Information Digest* (25 May 1996).

in view of the situation it is in, is currently free of political partisanship and treats the ruling party and opposition parties equally as well as impartially', was how an independent newspaper editorial saw it.[16]

Upgrading the quality of the military was EPRDF policy until the outbreak of war with Eritrea in 1998. The rebuilding of the air force, the creation of engineering capacity, the reorganisation of armament production, and the establishment of specialist paratrooper and commando units were part of the process. Upgrading involved formalising the hierarchy of ranks with uniforms and insignia which the guerrilla army had done without until that time. Top EPRDF military leaders were given general rank, and some 500 senior officers, 1,000 junior officers, and 3,000 non-commissioned officers were promoted. A militia force was revived, based at the *kebele* level, with members recruited according to a quota system.

Foreign assistance was essential for this task, and the United States happily resumed its role as Ethiopia's armourer. The 1990s had opened on a note of great expectations in the Horn. The coming to power in Ethiopia and Eritrea of a new political generation tempered in the fires of civil war and avowedly committed to peace, raised hopes that harmony would prevail in the war-ravaged region. An unprecedented era of regional concord seemed to have dawned in the Horn, and bold words were spoken of abolishing border controls and trade restrictions between Ethiopia, Eritrea and Sudan. Washington led the welcoming chorus with promises of generous assistance to regimes that it planned to take under its wing. Early on, mindful of the popular yearning for peace, and unwilling to alarm Ethiopia's neighbours, it put limits on the size of the military aid programme and restrictions on the use of the equipment it provided; 'non-offensive weapons' was the operative word.

At war once more

The raging civil war in Somalia cast a long shadow in the troubled region, and the peaceful interlude proved all too brief. The first warning was the appearance of Al Itihad Al Islami (Islamic Union) in 1991, a branch of an international movement devoted to the dissemination of Wahabbism, the school of Islam promoted by the regime in Saudi Arabia. Unlike conventional Islamic groups in Somalia, Al Itihad had an effective organisation with a disciplined core of younger men educated in the Arab region, a following among the urban youth, and ample funding from religious foundations in the Middle East. What distinguished Al Itihad most from other Islamic factions was its declared mission to gain political power through the armed struggle, and a territorial agenda that included the Somali- inhabited territory of Ethiopia. Its refusal to deal with the EPRDF made it inevitable that it would clash with the new regime in Addis Ababa.

Al Itihad came to prominence in 1991, when its militia forces launched a campaign to take control of Somali seaports on the Indian Ocean.

[16] *The Reporter* (18 April 2001).

Ephemerally successful, they were soon chased away by other Somali factions. Retreating from the coast, they moved to the Gedo, Bakol and Bay area alongside the border with Ethiopia, from where they ran raids into Ethiopian territory. Al Itihad also claimed credit for a string of terrorist attacks in Addis Ababa and Dire Dawa, including the attempted assassination of a prominent Ethiopian Somali politician and federal minister, Abdul Majid Hussein. The result of such provocation was to draw Addis Ababa into the Somali civil war.

In August 1996, Ethiopian army units crossed the Somali border and occupied several border towns, including Luq, Al Itihad's main base. The latter got the worse of some heavy fighting, and the following month announced a retreat from the border region. Sometime later, it declared it was abandoning the pursuit of power through military means, and limited its activities to Somalia proper. 'From now on, the Islamic Union movement has been transformed into a political organisation that seeks to hold power in Somalia, but our target is not only power, but to work towards the attainment of a Muslim president to run the country based on the Sharia', it declared.

Two years later, Ethiopia was at war again with Eritrea. Until then, relations between the two states appeared to be at their best. Eritreans had no reason to resent a regime that supported their bid for independence, earning the virulent hatred of Ethiopian nationalists. Close ties between Asmara and Addis Ababa were established; official hopes for full economic integration were voiced; border controls were curtailed allowing free movement of people and goods; Eritrea continued to use the Ethiopian currency, and several joint committees were set up to implement these plans. Limited progress was made along these lines in the following years. Yet signs of disenchantment appeared on both sides. Asmara wanted permission for its citizens to work, invest and trade in Ethiopia, and accused Addis Ababa of protectionism. For its part, the latter believed Eritrea was exploiting the customs union by exporting abroad goods produced in Ethiopia, and re-exporting to Ethiopia goods imported from abroad through its ports. When Eritrea introduced its own currency (*nakfa*) in 1997, it wanted it to be freely exchangeable in both countries at equal value, something Ethiopia refused categorically, insisting instead that trade between the two countries be done in hard currency. When this measure took effect, the price of *teff* in Eritrea imported from Ethiopia trebled. Relations between the two regimes had cooled significantly by this time, but the war that followed in 1998 was wholly unexpected.

The invoked *casus belli* for the war, the region of Bademe in the northwest border, had figured as a bone of contention years earlier between the ELF and the TPLF (see Chapter 8). The issue was revived in 1997, when the two governments established a joint commission to resolve outstanding boundary issues. Until that time, the border had little meaning for the people who live on either side and moved across it without ceremony. The formation of the commission and the prospect of negotiations, however, galvanised local officials on both sides to assert the respective claims of their states by enforcing border controls and increasing the number of armed frontier guards. In anticipation of a final settlement, the Tigray *kilil* administration published a map showing Bademe as inside Ethiopia's northwest border. A clash was inevitable and it took place in the first week of May 1998, when the Eritreans attacked and pushed the Ethiopians back, taking control of Bademe, with a few casualties on both sides.

Asmara appeared to regard the incident as a trifling matter to be settled by the joint commission scheduled to meet a couple of days later in Addis Ababa; hence the latter's response must have come as a shock. When its demand for an immediate Eritrean withdrawal was rejected, Ethiopia declared war. In the months that followed, the size of the Ethiopian armed forces multiplied to reach the levels of the 1980s. Demobilised members of the EPRDF guerrilla arms were recalled to arms. Large numbers of *kilil* militia were inducted into the army, as were policemen. Thousands of Dergue army veterans were recruited to fight the Eritreans once more. The bulk of the soldiery came from the peasant youth recruited through the rural and urban *kebele* that were given quotas to fill. Ethiopians throughout the country rose to the challenge, and there was no need to resort to conscription. Instead, the government offered generous wages for recruits of 450 birr per month, and considerably more for volunteers with technical skills. Since the strength of the expanded force was not disclosed, speculation about it ranged from 350,000 to half-a-million.

In the weeks that followed, fighting spread eastwards into the Afar lowlands, with heavy casualties among soldiers and civilians and the displacement of a large population from the war zone. No significant gains were made on the ground by either side. After a lull in the fighting, an Ethiopian offensive in February 1999 recaptured Bademe, and afterwards the war settled down to old-fashioned trench warfare, involving hundreds of thousands of soldiers and heavy weaponry, while the international community busied itself with mediation efforts under the aegis of the OAU and UN. The stalemate lasted until May 2000, when the Ethiopians attacked along the entire front and pushed the outnumbered Eritreans deep into their own territory. A truce was called the following month, when a Cessation of Hostilities Agreement was brokered by the OAU.

While the truce held, the issues underlying the conflict were not resolved, and ten years later the two countries remain on war footing, glaring at each other across a buffer zone held by soldiers of a United Nations Peace Mission. Both accepted the establishment of a Boundary Commission to settle the territorial claims, and pledged to accept its findings as final and binding. Yet, when the Commission assigned most of the Bademe region to Eritrea, Ethiopia stalled the process with various objections. Ten years on, the conflict is still unresolved, and the atmosphere remains charged with the risk of renewed fighting. While holding off from that option, both regimes are busy working to undermine each other by befriending each other's enemies. Asmara plays host to the leaders of insurgent movements operating in Ethiopia, and Addis Ababa sponsors a dozen factions hostile to the regime in Eritrea. Though none of them present a serious threat to the regime in either country, this time honoured practice ensures that rebel movements can survive indefinitely regardless of innate potential. Furthermore both regimes became involved at cross purposes in the Somali quagmire, and in 2009 the United Nations Security Council imposed sanctions on Eritrea for providing weapons to the Islamist foes of a tottering Transitional Federal Government in Mogadisho that was being propped up by Ethiopia.

The consequences of the war were grave for both countries. Some 80,000 soldiers lost their lives, many civilians in the border areas were killed and maimed, and many more lost their homes and possessions. Eritreans living in Ethiopia suffered a particularly harsh collective punishment, when they were deported *en masse* to Eritrea at the start of the war on the grounds that they represented a security threat. Eritrea retaliated by expelling Ethiopians still living there.

The material cost of the war was crippling for countries already deeply impoverished. Because the United States suspended military aid for the duration of the war, Ethiopia had to pay for weaponry it bought in vast quantities during that period. Economic aid was also suspended for the same period. The World Bank estimated that Ethiopian 'defence spending, which had fallen to 2.5 percent of GDP in 1996-97, rose to 8.7 percent in 1998-99 and as high as 13.3 percent in 1999-00.'[17] The budget for non-military allocations was cut to the bone, and whatever plans and projects Ethiopia had for development were shelved. The much touted *woreda* empowerment project was undermined from the start, when the promised capital budget did not materialise, and even the current budget failed to meet expenditure. In addition to shifting funds to defence and collecting contributions from the people, public debt increase enabled the government to survive the crisis without printing money or devaluing the currency.

The dawn of the 21st century found Ethiopia once more armed to the teeth, and the military restored to its traditional elite position in the state. The number of officers with general rank rose from ten to forty. Since the problem with Eritrea was not resolved, there was no prospect of the armed forces being cut down in size. Prime Minister Meles made this clear in a briefing he gave to foreign diplomats on May 31, 2000: 'The troop levels of the Ethiopian army are not going to go back to pre-1998 circumstance. We have learnt that lesson and we are not going to forget that lesson any time soon. And so we will have a robust defence capability even after the end of this war.[18] The point was amplified by the Chief of Staff, General Tsadkan Gebretensay, in a speech in January 2001, when he was reported to have said: 'Ethiopia should make adequate preparations during times of peace to ward off repeated attacks from

[17] World Bank Report No. T7405-ET: (11 September 2000: 7).
[18] *Ethiopian Herald* (2 June 2000).

foreign aggressors. Ethiopia should build an accomplished military force to defend its sovereignty and people at all times in the Horn of Africa, a region which is plagued by a lack of peace and stability.'[19]

*

Whether the world's poorest country can maintain a garrison state was a question the regime in Addis Ababa was not called upon to answer. The launching of the 'war on terror' by the United States in 2001 changed the situation dramatically, raising the stakes and the benefits of American patronage. In the perception of the United States, the lowlands of the Horn with their footloose, unruly, devoutly Muslim pastoralist population are a likely breeding ground of Islamist terrorism. These fears are played upon by every regime in the region vying for American patronage. Seeing an additional opportunity for domestic political profit as well, they wasted little time discovering 'terrorists' lurking among their opponents at home, hoping to see them listed in Washington's index of proscribed 'terrorist organizations'. Al Itihad was among the first to be listed. Ethiopia was increasingly drawn into this new global confrontation, and the United States generously provided the military hardware. The distinction between 'offensive' and 'non-offensive' weapons was dropped.

Concern with China's growing involvement in Africa reinforced US anxiety. A Combined Joint Task Force-Horn of Africa was set up in 2002. The regime in Djibouti outbid its neighbours to become the base for American troops and a multinational naval force patrolling the Red Sea, the Gulf of Aden and the Indian Ocean. In 2007, the formation of an Africa Command (Africom) was formed 'to work in concert with...African partners for a more stable environment in which political and economic growth can take place'. Many projects were planned for the continent, including equipping and training African soldiers at home and African officers in the US, joint military exercises, unloading obsolete weaponry in Africa, renting land for bases in Africa, and an African Centre for Strategic Studies with an annex in Addis Ababa. A search for an African state to host Africom's headquarters had not produced results as the first decade of the 21st century neared its end.

By the turn of the century, the ascendancy of the Union of Islamic Courts (UIC) in war-torn Somalia came to confirm Washington's worst fears for the Horn. The Islamic Courts had wrested control over large areas of the country from the warlords, tamed the outlaw gangs that preyed on the people, cleared the roads of bandits and self-appointed tax collectors, and brought a degree of security to the country unknown since 1991. They also imposed Sharia law and proposed to erect an Islamic state on the ruins of the failed republic. Overweening confidence born of success led them to make imprudent threats of *jihad* against Ethiopia, which the latter took all too seriously. Accordingly, Addis Ababa joined an international coalition to dislodge the Islamic Courts,

19 Radio Ethiopia (Amharigna) 1700 GMT (18 January 2001).

despite the fact that they offered the only hope of stability in the war ravaged country. After several false starts, this effort produced a Transitional Federal Government (TFG) in 2004, and Ethiopia became its staunchest supporter in the region.

The first step was to move the TFG inside the country it was supposed to govern. Prodded by the US, the UN Security Council promised international support, but passed the task to the African Union, and Uganda sent a small military contingent to Mogadisho in 2006. When no other African state offered to help, Ethiopia sent a large force backed with heavy weaponry at the end of that year. A foolhardy attempt by the Islamic Courts to resist with untrained mobs of civilians and light weapons ended within a week with heavy Somali casualties. Their fighters routed, the leadership of the UIC went into hiding, and the Ethiopians occupied the Somali capital to make it safe for the TFG. The idea of ruling Somalia on the back of Ethiopian military support was preposterous, and the besieged TFG never exercised real authority even in Mogadisho. Two factions emerged from the ashes of the UIC – Al Shabab and Hizb al Islam – and joined forces against the TFG. For the next two and a half years, the Ethiopian soldiers came under unrelenting attack from a resurgent Islamist force fighting a murderous urban guerrilla battle. Relying on heavy weapons, the Ethiopian took a heavy toll among civilians and levelled what was left standing in the devastated town. In the face of a unanimous refusal of African states to become involved, the Ethiopians finally pulled out in the summer of 2009. Questioned in the House of Peoples Representatives later about Ethiopian casualties in that operation, Meles Zenawi told the peoples' representatives they were not entitled to that information.

The centre divides

As the 1993 EPRDF document explained to its members, popular democracy did not mean sharing power with others, let along surrendering power to them:

> We can attain our objectives and goals only if Revolutionary Democracy becomes the governing outlook in our society, and only by winning the elections successively and holding power without let up can we securely establish the hegemony of Revolutionary Democracy. If we lose in the elections even once, we will encounter a great danger. So, in order to permanently establish this hegemony, we should win in the initial elections and then create a conducive situation that will ensure the establishment of this hegemony. In the subsequent elections, too, we should be able to with without interruption...We have military and political superiority, as well as considerable accumulated material resources.

Not many Ethiopians read this document, and many threw themselves enthusiastically into the narrow space for political competition that opened in 1991. A report of the Transitional Legislative Council in mid-1992 listed some 90 political organisations. The majority were EPRDF ethnic affiliates (PDOs), and only three claimed a pan-Ethiopia constituency. The first election round, for *kebele* and *woreda* officials, was held in mid-1992 before the emerging opposition could prepare for it, and the EPRDF claimed 96.5% of the votes. Despite calls for postponement from the opposition, including the OLF, elections for *kilil* officials followed, and the opposition parties boycotted them. Recently elected local officials, most of them EPRDF members or aspiring members, saw it as their duty to stifle any opposition, and made it very difficult for opposition activists to rent offices, to hold rallies and canvass support. Not a few were imprisoned, and there were many allegations of violence. As a result, EPRDF candidates ran unopposed in most districts. A team of Norwegian observers reported: 'Only in a few places were there competitive and genuine multi-party elections.'

The first show of militant opposition came suitably from the University of Addis Ababa. Given its experience with the radical movement in the 1970s, the TPLF leadership took a dim view of the university community in Addis Ababa, the movement's birthplace. Meles Zenawi complained: 'University students today are not like their predecessors in the student movement. The latter fought for self-determination, the former are against it.'[20] Taking advantage of a visit by the United Nations Secretary General Boutros Boutros Ghali in January 1993, the students demonstrated against Eritrea's independence and chanted anti-government slogans. They were attacked by the police and one was reportedly killed. The consequences for the University of Addis Ababa were harsh. Its top officials were fired, its staff lost their tenure, forty-five senior academics were later dismissed, and the University grounds were put under police guard. Subsequent student disturbances brought mass dismissals, and for the time being the University community was cowed. The regime allowed the country's prime educational institution to stagnate, while it put resources into a new Civil Service College to train the new corps of peripheral elite, and later founded higher education institutions in every *kilil*.

The first important opposition party to emerge, the All-Amhara Peoples Organisation (AAPO), made its appearance in 1994. Its name indicated a claim to represent Amhara wherever they live in the country. Its first leader was a University professor, Asrat Woldeyes, who had cast the sole negative vote on the issue of Eritrea in the July 1991 Conference. As was expected, his party condemned Eritrea's secession, opposed ethnic federalism, demanded the denationalisation of land and the return of properties nationalised by the Dergue, and supported the free market. The party's programme was unambiguous. Ethnic federalism, it declared 'is a conspiracy between our foreign enemies and the *banda* (Ethiopians who collaborate with the country's enemies) to divide the country by highlighting differences.' In a fair contest, the AAPO posed a serious challenge to the ANDM in the Amhara *kilil*, and consequently became the target of sustained harassment. Asrat Woldeyes was sent to prison in

[20] Press interview (30 January 1992).

1994, from where he emerged two years later to die of illness. Subsequently, his party disintegrated.

For the rest of the decade, the EPRDF went on to sweep elections with huge margins, not difficult to do since most of them were boycotted by the opposition. Complaints of irregularities were legion, and even a government newspaper once published a critical report from Oromia *kilil*: 'At the polling station of Hasenge farmers' association the reporter witnessed children lining up to vote carrying registration cards. Election executives deployed by the National Elections Board were absent from the place, and observers sent by political parties other than OPDO were forced to flee.'[21]

In advance of the 2000 elections, the disparate opposition made an effort to coordinate activities through *ad hoc* consultations among the leaders of the larger parties, but was distracted almost as soon as it had began by a split in the AAPO, whose youth wing broke off to form another party with a strong Ethiopian nationalist agenda. At any rate, there was little common ground between the Amhara politicians in the centre who were virulently opposed to federalism and the parties from the periphery that favoured it, other than their mutual opposition to the EPRDF. Fifty political parties took part in 2000 with more than seven hundred candidates and over four hundred independents. Even then, nearly half the seats for the federal legislature, most of them in rural districts, were not contested. The EPRDF once more swept the field, taking 481 out of 546 seats in the House of Peoples Representatives. Despite the fact that many incidents of intimidation and fraud were reported and six people were killed in Debub *kilil*, observers found the election generally free and fair. More to the point was the conclusion reached by a team of foreign observers: 'When all resources and means of communication, control, administration, distribution and taxation are in the hands of the ruling party through the government, there is little room for free and fair competition.'[22]

University students in Addis Ababa challenged the regime again in April 2001. Ostensibly they were protesting against the ban on student organisations and the stationing of police on campus, although hostility against the regime, especially among Oromo and Amhara students, was palpable. A class boycott started on 11 April and continued for a week, accompanied by demonstrations on campus and inconclusive negotiations with officials. On 17 April, thousands of university and high school students marched through the city, attracting rowdy support from the crowds of unemployed men that gather in the streets of the capital and vagabonds who found an opportunity for looting. The demonstration turned into a riot in several parts of the city that lasted for two days, during which the police killed over thirty persons and injured more than two hundred. Several thousands were arrested, including students and teachers, opposition party leaders and members.

[21] *Ethiopian Herald* (19 June 1995).
[22] Pausewang et al., (2002: 241).

*

Among the victims of the Ethiopian-Eritrean war were the ruling parties in both countries. They suffered crippling splits in their leadership, precipitated if not caused by the war, which essentially neutralised their political effectiveness. The splits occurred simultaneously and were wholly unanticipated. In the case of the TPLF, the crisis was attributed solely to disagreement over the conduct of the war.[23] A rift emerged when a feeling spread at the top that the war was not being 'prosecuted resolutely', because of United States' pressure to conclude 'peace at any cost', and Meles Zenawi was believed to be susceptible to it. The breaking point was reached with the signing of a so-called Technical Agreement in December 2000. Dictated by the United States, it called for a truce and obliged both countries to submit their differences to international arbitration. Given Ethiopia's decisive military advantage in the field, the dissident faction saw it as a humiliating concession and challenged the Prime Minister in the TPLF councils. The depth of feeling was shown in a statement issued later by the dissidents: 'On our part', it said, 'right from the downfall of the Dergue, we had a stand that Eritrea was our strategic enemy.'[24] In the debate that followed, the disagreement widened to cover the overall posture of the government in its relationship with foreign donors, which the dissidents condemned as servile. In another statement one of the dissidents declared: 'I believe that the major challenge to our system and the TPLF is submissiveness.'[25]

The Prime Minister's opponents naively believed they could resolve the dispute within the party councils, where they believed they had a majority, and by following party procedures. They made a tactical error when they withdrew from a central committee meeting, leaving the floor to the Prime Minister's faction, who then went on to take severe measures against them. While going through the motions of following party procedure, Meles Zenawi relied essentially on the state apparatus to isolate his opponents and expel them from their posts in the party and government. In March 2001, twelve members of the TPLF central committee, five of them members of its Politbureau, were expelled.[26] They represented the core of the party's leadership and some of the regime's best known figures. If they had expected support from the other parties in the EPRDF, they were disappointed. One notable exception was the then President of Ethiopia, Negaso Gidada, an OPDO leader, who resigned blaming Meles Zenawi for acting like a dictator.

While the war with Eritrea was the catalyst in the crisis, it was certainly not the only or sufficient cause of it. The slipping of the TPLF's ideological anchor and the drifting away from its ideals under Meles

[23] Former members of the TPLF Central Committee – Gebru Asrat, Tewolde Wolde Mariam, Aregash Adane - interviewed in Addis Ababa in 2004.

[24] *The Reporter* (25/4/01).

[25] Gebru Asrat in *The Reporter* (25/4/01).

[26] Two of them recanted and were readmitted to the party.

Zenawi was a contributing factor. 'A difference arose on how the people could be the beneficiary of capitalist development and democracy. How could we ensure that our policy did not only benefit the few?' was how one of the dissidents put it.[27] The root cause undoubtedly was the unravelling of the traditional TPLF collegiate system of leadership, and the increasing autonomy of Meles Zenawi. The failure of the challenge against him bolstered his position immensely, and a widespread purge that followed removed actual and potential dissidents from EPRDF ranks, the military and the state apparatus. By portraying his opponents as hard-core radicals, he also raised his status as a moderate with the international community. Surrounded by technocrats bereft of political stature, the Prime Minister emerged the undisputed master of the country. This time it had taken ten years for personalised authoritarian rule to be re-established in Addis Ababa. It was a personal triumph for Meles Zenawi, but a political disaster for the regime he headed. The magnitude of it was soon made obvious in the 2005 elections.

Relatively few of the TPLF dissidents suffered anything worse than expulsion from the party and loss of state office. A few seniors were imprisoned with the all-purpose charge of 'corruption' and were dragged through the courts for several years before they were released. This was nothing compared to the fate of those who sought to challenge the Eritrean president Isayas Afeworq. In the wake of the disastrous war with Ethiopia, a dozen of the most senior members of the former EPLF and Isaya's lifelong comrades declared publicly that it was time to introduce a competitive political process in Eritrea, with parties and democratic elections. Like their counterparts in Ethiopia, they naively relied on party instruments to curtail the power of the President who ruled Eritrea like an oriental satrap. Like Meles Zenawi in Ethiopia, Isayas used the state apparatus to crush his opponents, but then exacted vicious vengeance on his former comrades. A dozen of them were arrested and disappeared from sight, and have remained so ever since. They were never brought to trial, their place of detention is kept secret, and no one knows whether they are alive or dead. Severe political repression followed as the country sank deeper into poverty and, once more, many Eritreans were forced to flee abroad. The fact that not a few sought political refuge in Ethiopia was one of history's ironies.

*

The 2005 election was the turning point in the brief history of democratisation in Ethiopia. Emboldened by the split in the TPLF, the opposition mounted a campaign without parallel in terms of organisation, public relations and effectiveness. A concerted effort was made to achieve a degree of coordination of opposition forces, resulting in two blocs that broadly represented the centre and the periphery. Formed around the remnants of the All Amhara Peoples Organisation, now renamed the All

[27] Abaye Tsehay, open letter, *The Reporter* (18/4/01).

Ethiopia Unity Party (AEUP), a Coalition for Unity and Democracy (CUD) emerged the standard bearer of traditional Ethiopian nationalism and contemporary liberalism. It opposed federalism, the right to secession and state ownership of land, and supported a liberalised economy and the free market. The United Ethiopian Democratic Forces (UEDF) brought together the opposition representing the periphery, comprising mainly the Oromo National Congress and the Southern Ethiopia Peoples Democratic Coalition representing Debub. Understandably, it accepted the federal system, but opposed the EPRDF's authoritarian way of running it. Interestingly, nearly all prominent opposition party leaders were university teachers. Support came from the Ethiopian diaspora that had previously opposed engagement, but now provided funds, advice and some skilled political operators. Under international scrutiny, the regime was obliged to make a number of concessions, such as state funding for all political parties, greater access to state controlled media, permission to hold mass rallies, and allowed Ethiopians living abroad to vote.

The subsequent exuberant campaign was avidly followed by a people fascinated with the unprecedented spectacle of an incumbent regime excoriated in public by its opponents. Becoming increasingly bolder, the opposition did not refrain from raising the issue of Tigray primacy in the national government, and predicted its end was near. This provoked the wrath of the EPRDF which lashed out at the CUD, labelling it the party of the Amhara *neftegna* bent on provoking ethnic conflict. Such bitter exchanges reached a crescendo in mass rallies aimed at whipping up supporter enthusiasm. One result was to stir up anti-Tigray sentiment in the towns, and to raise genuine fear that defeat for the EPRDF would have serious consequences for that nationality.

The elections of 15 May 2005 went without reports of major incidents or infractions. This was partly due to the sizeable presence of observers from home and abroad. A desire to make a good appearance, supplemented by confidence in its popularity with the peasantry, prompted the EPRDF to instruct its members and local officials to avoid embarrassing incidents. An astounding 90% voter participation was announced by the National Elections Board the next day. What followed showed that the ruling party's calculations had gone badly wrong. Before the vote count even started, an emergency situation was declared, the Prime Minister announced a month long ban on demonstrations and public meetings, and took personal command of the police and security forces in the capital. The next day, the government press claimed another sweeping victory for the EPRDF. Yet, when the final results were released months later, in September, they gave the opposition at least one third of the seats, with a clean sweep of the votes in the urban sector. In the capital itself, the ruling party had failed to get a single seat.

The opposition unanimously refused to accept the results, alleging fraud and claiming to have won the election outright. Its position was strengthened by observer reports – one of them from a European Union team – of fraud committed during the long period of vote counting. Opposition leaders did not mince their words; the government accused them of inciting rebellion and threatened to charge them with treason. In the volatile situation that emerged, the rivals were unable to negotiate directly, and a bizarre scenario evolved with a miscellaneous team of foreign diplomats and international figures engaging in a lengthy mediation process that ultimately led nowhere. By the time the new parliament convened on 11 October 2005, the opposition had splintered hopelessly over the issue of participation. In the event, few CUD members took their seats, while most UEDF members did. The CUD also boycotted the Addis Ababa municipal council, where it had won all but one of the seats.

Having ridden the storm, the regime went on to ensure that it would not happen again. One of the first acts of the new House of Peoples Representatives was to lift the immunity of opposition members who failed to take their seats. This was the prelude to the ruthless persecution of those who had taken this stand. Tension increased when spontaneous protests were staged in Addis Ababa and other towns in early November, for which members of CUD's central committee were blamed and arrested. When the protests spread and turned violent, the regime faced the threat of an urban uprising. Its response was characteristically harsh. Over two days of indiscriminate shooting, the police and security forces killed 193 and injured over 700 Ethiopians in the capital. Seven security members were also killed. A roundup of thousands of youths, journalists, civil society activists, opposition party members and leaders followed. In December 2005, 131 of them, including all CUD prominent figures still in the country, were charged with treason, genocide and incitement to violence. For the next eighteen months, they were forced to participate in a long drawn out, judicial charade with a predictable end. They played their part badly, first refusing to recognise the authority of the court, then deciding to defend themselves and finally, having been sentenced to long terms of imprisonment, they wrote a letter admitting mistakes and accepted a pardon. Afterwards, many of them went abroad.

Having demolished the opposition, the regime took additional measures to discourage other actors in civil society from daring to criticise or embarrass it. Newspapers and periodicals were closed; journalists and editors were imprisoned and dragged through the courts to face outlandish charges such as 'committing outrage against the constitutional order'. A long delayed Mass Media and Freedom of Information Proclamation finally materialised to add further restrictions on the much abused independent media. A Charities and Societies law came in force, banning NGOs from advocacy activities (particularly concerning human rights and conflict) and to cripple the indigenous NGOs by banning funding from abroad. The legal profession, whose members had defended the opposition leaders in court, received a clear warning when the Ministry of Justice issued a code of sanctions for the profession, and questioned the status of the Ethiopian Legal Professionals Association.

As the 2010 national elections approached, the regime went to great lengths to prevent a repetition of the 2005 fiasco. The EPRDF launched a massive recruitment drive that raised its membership fivefold to a staggering five million. The party-state apparatus was mobilised to prevent any opposition from getting a hearing in rural Ethiopia, and this time it surpassed itself. The climate of intimidation that existed since 2005 was reinforced when the regime discovered a plot to overthrow it, allegedly hatched by army officers and some of the most important figures of the opposition who had fled abroad. All of them were sentenced to death in November 2009. A few months before, the regime had returned a prominent CUD to prison on the grounds that she had violated the conditions of her pardon. The opposition engaged in an endless process of fission and fusion until it became impossible to distinguish who was who among the fragments, or even where they stood vis à vis the EPRDF; a number of them entered into a coalition with the ruling party. Knowing that this was the event where the issue would be finally decided, Negaso Gidada, the former president of Ethiopia, who had left the EPRDF in 2001 and later joined the opposition, predicted in 2009: 'My general conclusion is that unless the situation changes dramatically in the next few months, I do not expect the 2010 election will be fair, free or democratic.'

That was putting it mildly. This time the EPRDF stopped toying with the opposition and declared a 99.6% victory. Only one token opposition candidate was allowed in the House of Peoples Representatives with its 547 members, and only one other was included in the combined 1900 membership of the *kilil* assemblies. Such brazen tokenism showed the regime's disregard of public opinion, nationally and internationally. Washington contented itself with mildly disapproving murmurs about the elections not meeting 'international standards'. Thus the curtain fell on the parody of democracy enacted for two decades in this troubled country.

Summary

Whatever ideas the EPRDF leaders might have had about economic recovery, they had to abandon them and were obliged instead to experiment with a mixed bag of schemes formulated and funded by foreign donors, none of which had significant impact. Among them was the shift from peasant food production to large scale, commercial production for export, based on foreign capital and technology. This raised once more the issue of land, and made land alienation on a very large scale inevitable. This process was disguised by the practice of leasing land while retaining notional state ownership. The manoeuvre meant little to the indigenous cultivators who were barred from using leased land for generations to come. Lack of transparency meant that once more the status of land was being changed by the elite in the centre, this time by stealth. A double political risk was involved in this policy: one was the undermining of food production by displacing food producers from the land and turning them into consumers. The other derived from the fact that this policy was applied almost exclusively to the lowland periphery, where it was certain to further aggravate an already volatile relationship with the centre.

Prospects for economic recovery were not improved when Ethiopia found itself fighting the same wars it had fought on and off for nearly half-a-century without conclusion. The state-building project was still contested within the country and outside it by neighbours pursuing their own projects. Inevitably, this led to another round of militarisation. Hopes for political stability were also disappointed when the democratic experiment turned into a farce. The regime's unwillingness to share, let alone surrender power had several implications. The most important was the continuity of centre domination over the periphery, federalism notwithstanding. Deriving from that was the failure to advance towards political integration, an indispensable step in the nation state-building project. Crossing this political frontier requires a system of rule that enjoys legitimacy and citizen support throughout the country. The failure to achieve an orderly transfer of power has divided the centre, creating the possibility of yet another rupture with unforeseeable consequences.

Part V
The Federal State in the Periphery

12

The Highland Periphery & the Lowland Afar

Regime change marked a major shift in the centre/periphery interaction, which now proceeded under a new political order and new perspectives. Federalism offered the opportunity to remove two features of this relationship that had disrupted and threatened to derail the process of state-building. The introduction of a decentralised federal system of government promised to end the centre's historical monopoly of ruling power, while the reformulation of Ethiopia's national identity on the basis of cultural pluralism lifted the burden of cultural inferiority from the periphery and the threat of forced assimilation. This was a fundamental shift that opened new and hopeful perspectives for the country's future. In stark contrast to the scepticism that this development met with in the centre, it gave rise to great expectations in the periphery. In the long run, its success would depend on the extent to which periphery expectations are realised and if the elite in the centre accept the consequences. Two decades on is long enough to make the preliminary assessment offered in this and the following two chapters. Again, since the experience of high and low lands in the periphery has differed over this period, they are treated separately. Once more, the highland periphery is treated in summary form, while the rest of this chapter and those that follow are devoted to a detailed treatment of the lowlands.

The highlands

Of the two important initiatives credited to the new regime – power sharing in a federal system and the multicultural definition of Ethiopia's national identity – the latter was the boldest. Rather than seeking to suppress cultural diversity, the EPRDF celebrated it. In the words of its leader:

> Diversity must not be wished away, camouflaged, suppressed. It must be embraced as it is, it must be allowed free expression...It must be possible for people to assert their own national and cultural identity...within the context of their

> common Ethiopian identity...We believe there is no incompatibility, no inherent conflict in being at the same time an Amhara and an Ethiopian, an Oromo and an Ethiopian...and so on.

Although this was a vision whose substance remained quite vague, it was an unambiguous break with the past and was universally welcomed in the periphery.

It was presumed that this vision would be realised through the process of education, that the new regime made a concerted effort to expand. This was reflected in budget allocations that rose annually from 9% in 1990 to 16.7% in 2005/6. From the launch in 1997/8 of an Education Sector Development Programme hundreds of schools have been built annually, with the goal of universal primary education by 2015. Accordingly, half of the budget has been allocated to the primary level. State efforts were supplemented by the private sector. Nationalised by the Dergue, private schools made a vigorous comeback in the 1990s, spurred by demand for a better quality of education than that provided in the hugely overcrowded state sector, and covering the entire span, from kindergarten to university. Overall enrolment at the primary level (grades 1-8) has increased at an average rate of 13.4% per annum, and enrolled 80% of the relevant age group in 2007/8. Enrolment at the secondary level has expanded slowly, and stood at 13.8% of the relevant age groups in grades 9-10, and 5.8 in grades 10-11. Higher education has lagged far behind; there were less than 300,000 students at this level in state and private institutions in 2008.[1]

Growth was achieved at a considerable cost to quality. Poor facilities and inadequate teaching have been the rule. Less than half of secondary school teachers are certified. Teacher/student ratio at primary level is above sixty. The dropout rate is dramatic, with some 20% leaving after the first grade and less than half surviving to grade five. Marked disparities remain in the education system. Most striking is the concentration of secondary school facilities (90%) in the urban sector. Gender disparity begins at the secondary level and progresses into higher education, where female participation is less than 25 per cent. In 2007, only 20% of higher education graduates were female. Regional disparities are also striking, with Addis Ababa having the lion's share of student participation at all levels, in facilities, certified teachers, and other indicators while the lowland *kilil* is falling far behind. As in the past, the focus of education is on academic training. Formerly, graduates were absorbed mainly into an expanding state sector. With that sector now contracting and the private sector stagnating, the employment prospects of school leavers are uncertain. According to one assessment, 'the educational system...is a major source of the unemployed and unemployable people.'[2]

Seen as proof that 'Amharisation' is no longer the goal of national integration, the hallmark of cultural pluralism is the validation of vernaculars. These have been widely introduced in primary education in

[1] All figures for education are taken from the *Education Statistics Annual Abstract, 2007/08*.

[2] Ethiopian Economics Association, *Annual Report of the Ethiopian Economy* (Addis Ababa, 1999/2000: 113).

the periphery, but beyond that hardly anything has changed in the content of education. Identical textbooks are used throughout the country, making no concession to its diversity. Despite the upgraded status of the vernaculars, Amharigna continues to gain ground as the *lingua franca*, due to a new surge of urbanisation. This is most impressive in the north where, in addition to Addis Ababa, Makale, the capital of Tigray, and Bahir Dar, capital of Amhara, have been transformed from provincial backwaters to modern cities. Awasa, the capital of Debub, is undergoing a similar transformation. All *kilil* capitals have experienced growth in size and improvement in urban facilities. Among the latter are higher education institutions that have multiplied in number, albeit with grossly inadequate facilities. Higher education is a federal responsibility, and students are assigned to institutions by the federal Ministry of Education, so that the student body in each represents a cross section of Ethiopian society. Thus, young Ethiopians are given the opportunity to get to know their fellow countrymen from other regions and to learn other Ethiopian languages.

Nearly all parts of the country are now served through a vigorous road construction programme that has absorbed the bulk of aid coming from the European Union. In 1992, Ethiopia had 19,000km of all-weather roads, although only 20% of them in good condition. By 2007, the network had reached 44,000km. Similar advances were made in communications. The country is linked with radio and television coverage which, although allowing space for vernaculars and local content, is mainly a vehicle for Amharigna and national affairs. Finally, a mobile telephone network covers even the remotest parts.

Self-administration has been a major step forward in the periphery. Two benefits have derived directly from it. One is the engagement of a large segment of the intelligentsia in the affairs of local government, with the accompanying perquisites of power, social status and economic privilege. Another is generous federal assistance in terms of budget subsidies, and a package of development programmes in education, health, energy, transport and communication; all of which have improved facilities and provided employment for the local population. The *kilil* subsidies in the 2009/10 budget amounted to one-third of the national budget. Oromia took the lion's share with nearly 31%, while Harar got only 0.84%. However, the subsidies barely cover the *kilil* budget deficit, and go mostly to cover current expenditure. For example, Debub was allocated 19% of the federal subsidy in 2008/9, but the head of its administration wondered 'if the subsidies will cover the salaries we pay'.[3]

Oromo nationalism

Federalism provided an institutional base for the new class of subordinate elite, who were assigned greater responsibilities and corresponding power than was the case under previous regimes. Even so, this class does not have

[3] *Capital* Newspaper, Addis Ababa (17 May 2009).

a greater input in the centre where national issues are decided than its predecessors enjoyed. The elite in the centre continue to rule; the elite in the periphery continue to administer. Federalism does not entail equitable sharing of power and did not end the historical hegemony of the centre. This remains the structural fault that continues to destabilise the nation state-building project.

Failure to advance towards political integration by redressing the historical imbalance in the centre/periphery relationship provides the regime's opponents in the periphery with their most persuasive argument. Opposition has come in two forms, so-called 'legal' and 'illegal.' The first represents parties that accept ethnic federalism but challenge the EPRDF monopoly of power, and yet participate in the political process described in the preceding chapter.[4] 'Illegal' opposition represents movements which, having tried the 'legal' route found it futile and turned to rebellion. It is not only the means chosen to wage the political battle that distinguish 'legal' from 'illegal'. It is also the aims of the latter that leave open the option of secession. Given its claim to represent the largest by far nationality in the country, the Oromo Liberation Front is clearly the most important party in the 'illegal' opposition. Mindful of this fact, the architects of the federal project sought to involve the OLF in the design stage, and succeeded in securing its participation in the transitional government (see Chapter 10). What happened afterwards is described below in some detail, because it illustrates the *modus operandi* of the EPRDF and its impact on Oromo political aspirations.

There was euphoria when OLF units entered western Oromia from the Sudan to be greeted with jubilation by the people, and saw their ranks swell with youthful volunteers. Even so, its military limitations prevented the OLF from taking full advantage of the power vacuum that prevailed in many Oromo areas in the wake of the Dergue's collapse. It managed to gain control in south-western Wallega around Dembidolo and in some areas in eastern Ethiopia, but failed to take control in Illubabor, Jimma and Hararge, where the EPRDF arrived first. The first disappointment for the OLF was to find EPRDF units deployed throughout Oromia, and the OPDO cadre hastily laying the foundations for the party-state under TPLF protection. When the OLF protested, it got the standard EPRDF response: in a democratic system everyone has the right to organise and compete for popular support. The fact that no such competition was countenanced in Tigray or Amhara was ignored. After establishing its headquarters in Addis Ababa, the OLF opened branch offices in many towns of Oromia and began to recruit members.

The OPDO, whose armed strength at the time did not exceed 2,000, was not the only rival the OLF had to contend with in Oromia. The EPRDF had made certain that all other Oromo factions were represented in the July 1991 Conference and in the transitional legislative council where the OLF had twelve seats. The Islamic Front for the Liberation of Oromia (IFLO) led by Abdulkarim Ibrahim Jarra Abagada had three

[4] For a statement of this viewpoint see Merara Gudina (2002).

seats, while two factions that had emerged from the dissolution of the hybrid Somali Abo Liberation Front (SALF) each merited one seat. A bizarre situation developed in the months that followed, which found the OLF embroiled in violent clashes in the countryside with the EPRDF/OPDO and feuding with other Oromo factions, while at the same time holding four ministerial posts in the transitional government. Strenuous efforts were made by Oromo elders and notables to forge unity among the factions. None were fruitful, and Oromo political unity remained a chimaera.

The rivalry between the OLF and the OPDO in Oromia reached fever pitch and turned violent. In September 1991, the OLF complained of attacks on its supporters, the closure of its offices, and demanded the EPRDF army leave Oromia. Numerous clashes followed between EPRDF/OPDO forces and armed contingents of the OLF and IFLO with hundreds of casualties. To make matters worse, there was an outbreak of fighting between nationalities throughout the periphery, a common sequel to the breakdown of central authority. Attacks on Amhara in Arsi took many lives; Oromo were slaughtered in Hararghe, while Oromo and Somali fought along their common border from Dire Dawa to Moyale. The EPRDF and the OLF engaged in a war or words, accusing each other of fomenting ethnic cleansing. At the beginning of 1992, the EPRDF Southern Command launched a pacification campaign against 'anti-peace' elements, which the OLF claimed targeted its supporters. With all-out civil war threatening, pressure from the United States in the early part of 1992 produced a series of negotiations, with the Eritreans in the role of mediators. The Americans promised the Oromo that they would have fair treatment in a democratic Ethiopia. 'We hoped the involvement of the US Government would be a sufficient deterrent to the TPLF's propensity to dominance and exclusiveness.'[5] In mid-April, an agreement was reached to cease hostilities, and all armed units were restricted to camps. Proceeding on the assumption that the agreement applied to the EPRDF forces as well, the OLF complied. The size of its force gathered in eight camps in Oromia was about 20,000.

Hostilities resumed almost immediately afterwards. When the OLF realised that the EPRDF had no intention of restricting its army, which was now recognised as the national defence force, it withdrew its own units from the camps only days before the June elections for local government. Also realising that it had little chance in the circumstances of winning the elections, it called for their postponement. When this call was not heeded, it withdrew from the transitional government.[6] The EPRDF moved swiftly to surround and disarm the OLF units and put them in prison camps.[7] By October 1992, the OLF was militarily neutralised and the Oromo

[5] Statement of the Secretary General on the State of the Oromo Peoples Struggle, 1 March 1993. Isayas Afeworq assured them he did not want Ethiopia ruled solely by the 'Woyane'

[6] Waqo Gutu and Sheikh Jarra kept their seats in the transitional assembly for a while, and then both returned to the bush.

[7] They were put through a programme of re-education and released.

nationalist cause had suffered a major setback. Nevertheless, the forceful assertion of Oromo power in Ethiopia, brief and ill managed though it was, had enormous impact. It won over the younger generation to Oromo nationalism. No mean feat, this is believed by Oromo nationalists to have ensured the eventual triumph of their cause. By what means, and in what form this would come about became the bone of contention that was to sow perennial dissension and disarray in the nationalist camp in the years to come.

OLF units regrouped in the bush and the insurgency resumed soon afterwards. The OLF leadership dispersed abroad once more, and strove to rebuild the organisation's fighting capacity, while also lobbying for foreign intervention. Petitions were routinely addressed to Washington. Given their experience with the United States' promises in the past, the Oromo rebels' expectations are naïve and, of course, futile. OLF efforts to escalate the insurgency inside Ethiopia have been hampered by the old problem of not having a base across the border in a neighbouring state. A breakthrough occurred when a pact was made with the Somali warlord, Hussein Aideed, when he fell out with Addis Ababa because it intervened in the Somali civil war on the side of his enemies. The OLF found a welcome in Mogadisho, where it held its second national congress in 1998. Galasa Dilbo was re-elected secretary general, with Daud Ibsa Gudina, a Christian from Wallega, as his deputy. Changes were made to the OLF programme at this meeting, the most significant being to accept a referendum on self-determination. At the same time, the OLF was able to establish a presence in northern Kenya on territory inhabited by the Borana. From there, it launched a series of raids into southern Ethiopia that kept government forces occupied and made the news. However, this opening was closed when Addis Ababa delivered an ultimatum to Hussein Aideed and also persuaded the Kenyan government to expel the OLF from its territory.

The resumption of conflict between Eritrea and Ethiopia in 1998 opened new possibilities. The OLF found welcome in Asmara, where it held its third national congress in December 2004. Galasa Dilbo resigned in 2003, pleading personal reasons, and was replaced by Daud Ibsa. The first of a series of splits at the top occurred when a number of central committee members refused to acknowledge the new leadership, claiming that Galasa Dilbo had been forced out illegally. In a meeting held in Bergen soon afterwards, several central committee members reportedly called for an end to the armed struggle and for OLF participation in the 2005 elections in Ethiopia. This became the defining issue in the internal dispute that left the Oromo movement leaderless. After the two decades that the OLF have spent in the wilderness, the classic formula of a protracted armed struggle appears increasingly unviable, and the goal of independence unrealistic, if not undesirable. Nonetheless, the OLF has found it impossible to adjust its sights to bring reality into sharper focus. Renouncing the goal of independence became the issue whose name could not be pronounced. Instead, it became a term of abuse in the interminable leadership squabbles that have all but paralysed the organisation in recent years.

A faction around Daud Ibsa allegedly leaned towards compromise and negotiations with the EPRDF, while a hard-line faction led by Galasa Dilbo, calling itself OLF Transitional, opposed any compromise. A third faction emerged in 2008, led by General Kamal Geltchu Dove who defected from the Ethiopian army in 2006 taking a number of Oromo soldiers with him. Calling itself the OLF Committee for Reform, it accused the other two factions of incompetence and failure. The rival factions expelled each other from the organisation, and one went to court in the United States to claim ownership of the name Oromo Liberation Front.[8]

In the meantime, the banner of Oromo political aspirations was taken up by other groups that emerged to join the 'legal' opposition to the EPRDF. Led by Merara Gudina, a university professor, the Oromo National Congress (ONC) was formed in 1996, 'because of the divisive role of the OLF leadership that created a condition where the Oromo forces could not come together'.[9] The Oromo Federalist Democratic Movement (OFDM) was founded by Bultcha Demeksa, a former minister in the imperial government. The initial OLF reaction to these initiatives was to denounce them as EPRDF stooges, but subsequently it moderated its tone in the name of political pluralism. Making no distinction between those who accept federalism and those vowing to dismantle it, the EPRDF's reaction to the ONC and OFDM was consistently and vehemently hostile. It hindered their operation with every imaginable obstacle, so that the few seats they managed to gain in elections provided no indication of their popular support. Both parties won several seats in the 2005 elections and entered the House of Peoples Representatives. They were wiped out in the 2010 elections along with the rest of the opposition.

Sidama dissidence

The experience of the Sidama Liberation Movement in the 1990s was similar to that of other groups that sought to challenge the EPRDF. Invited to attend the July 1991 Conference, the SLM was represented by its founder, Wolde Emanuel Dubale, and was allocated two seats in the transitional assembly. Any hopes that its members had of leading their community in the federal era were frustrated by the appearance of a Sidama PDO, headed by a former Dergue soldier, Abate Kisho, who went on to become the president of Debub *kilil*. Political authority in Debub was in the hands of Bitew Belay, a TPLF central committee member with

[8] In a forlorn effort to put the pieces together, Eritrea promoted yet another faction called the 'United Liberation Forces of Oromia', where the venerable rebel chieftains Wako Gutu and Sheikh Jarra resurfaced as chairman and vice chairman respectively, Galasa Dilbo as Secretary General and Daud Ibsa as vice chairman. In 2006, Jarra dropped the religious tag of his organisation, renaming it the Front for Independent Democratic Oromia (FIDO).

[9] Political Programme of the Oromo National Congress (23 April 1996).

experience in mass organisations, who exercised his influence from Awasa until 1998 when he was made head of the regional affairs department in the Prime Minister's Office.

This was a period of widespread violent conflict in the region, as nationalities fought over territory and membership in *woreda*, zones and *kilil* of their choice. Fierce fighting took place during 1991-1993 between the Sidama, Gedeo and Guji in the process of settling administrative boundaries. The SLM followed the OLF when it left the transitional government, and its armed band of some 500 was disarmed and detained. Accused of having committed crimes under the Dergue, Wolde Emanuel and other SLM leaders escaped abroad. Sidama region became a zone in Debub *kilil*, but the peoples' aspirations were for a *kilil* of their own with Awasa as its capital. Sidama resentment was fed by a widespread feeling of having lost territory and status in the federal carve up, and the fact that with a population nearly as large as Tigray, the subsidy for Sidama zone was only a fraction of the former's. Trouble broke out in 2002, when it was rumoured that the fast growing town of Awasa, which served both as Sidama Zone and Debub *kilil* capital was to be detached from Sidama zone. A demonstration against the alleged plan on 24 March 2002 was suppressed, with the loss of tens of lives, followed by a wave of mass arrests.

'Legal' opposition made a strong showing within the Hadiya nationality in Debub – the only instance where local opposition seriously threatened the ruling front. The Hadiya PDO formed by the EPRDF was challenged by the National Hadiya Democratic Organisation (NHDO), led by Beyene Petros, a university professor and architect of the Southern Ethiopia Peoples Democratic Coalition (SEPDC). Formed in 1992, this was an umbrella organisation of fifteen opposition ethnic political parties. The coalition participated in the transitional government and its leader served in the cabinet. It was expelled in 1993, and went on to become the pre-eminent opposition to the EPRDF in the highland periphery, and its leader, Beyene Petros, a prominent political figure.

The Hadiya opposition showed extraordinary tenacity in the face of harsh measures taken by the local EPRDF officialdom to obstruct their activities and intimidate their supporters. They gamely fought most elections and achieved the highest results in 2000. The national and *kilil* elections in that year were fought amidst great tension and violence in Hadiya zone; five people were killed there on that occasion. Even so, the opposition won outright in several constituencies and contested the results in several more. It won all but one of the latter in the rerun. Repression and intimidation redoubled in the run-up to the 2001 local government elections. Tension reached a level where it was considered unsafe for the Hadiya's leader to visit the area, forcing his party to withdraw. In the 2005 elections, the United Ethiopian Democratic Forces (UEDF), of which the Hadiya party was a member, won many seats in Debub *kilil* and its successful candidates took their seats in the House of Peoples Representatives. The UEDF suffered the same fate as the rest of the 'legal' opposition in 2010.

The lowlands

Federalism raised the profile of the lowlanders. For the first time, communities were congregated in their own *kilil*, zone or *woreda*, with a degree of self-administration and recognition of their distinct identity and way of life. Self-administration restored some of the autonomy they had lost, and the recognition of their languages was the first step towards restoring the dignity of their cultures. These were major and quite unanticipated gains, for which the lowlanders were beholden to the new regime. Federalism also produced resources allocated to the *kilil* by the federal government, and these became the object of competition among local elite factions and the substance of lowland politics. It was not surprising that politics here were ruled by the clan formula rather than the guidelines issued by the EPRDF, or that the results were political chaos, administrative paralysis and a total waste of resources.

The EPRDF had scarce knowledge of the lowlands when it came to power. Meles Zenawi admitted later, 'we went in there blind'. An EPRDF official explained: 'These are clan based societies, unlike our peasantry, and we did not know if our political experience suited them.'[10] There had been few lowlanders in the Dergue army, and hardly any were taken prisoner by the EPRDF for political grooming. There had been tenuous contact with a couple of lowland factions that applied to the TPLF for support and were considered allies in the struggle against the Dergue. Although none of them were regarded as sufficiently politically mature for membership in the EPRDF, they were prime candidates for power and the ruling party had to deal with them in order to gain a measure of control over the unruly lowlanders.

In so doing, the EPRDF showed a lack of imagination that contrasted sharply with the talent for political inventiveness it displayed elsewhere. Overcoming an initial wariness of clan-based societies, it resorted to the same political formula used in the highlands. A bewildering series of PDOs (Peoples Democratic Organisations) were formed, reformed, merged and split, and changed names and leaders in the years that followed. These were shells inside which the lowlanders carried on with their clan and ethnic feuds. They produced neither political stability nor administrative effectiveness, and failed to make the best use of the federal subsidy – the carrot the regime offered them. Alternatively, the EPRDF wielded the stick with the all-purpose charge of corruption that had lowland officialdom rotating between office and prison. It also began the process of grooming a corps of lowland peripheral elite individuals called 'regional intellectuals'. Young people with secondary education were sent to the Civil Service College in Addis Ababa and to institutions of higher education elsewhere in Ethiopia and abroad, from where they returned on graduation to be appointed to senior positions in the *kilil* administration.

[10] Bitew Belay, interviewed in Addis Ababa, 4 February 2007.

More often than not, these novices with degrees were backed by highlander deputies with the required skills and experience.

The lowlands and the NGOs

The resolutions of the July 1991 Conference committed the transitional government to 'give special consideration to hitherto neglected and forgotten areas', (Art. 16), and the 1995 Constitution required both the federal and *kilil* governments 'to provide special assistance to nations, nationalities and peoples least advantaged in economic and social development' (Art. 89/4). Pastoralist rights to land for grazing and cultivation as well as the right 'not to be displaced from their own lands' were also enshrined in the Constitution (Art. 40/5). The lowlands were included in the early Emergency Recovery and Reconstruction Programme but, given the dire state of transport and communications in that region, the administrative disarray and prevailing conflict, little was done.

In 1997 it was reported that the four lowland *kilil* – Afar, Somali, Gambella, Beni Shangul Gumuz – now dubbed 'emerging regions', had requested federal technical assistance in terms of skilled manpower, training and equipment. Technical and managerial assistance teams of federal civil servants were dispatched by the Prime Minister's Office, while secondary school graduates and *kilil* civil servants *were* given fast-track training in the Civil Service College in Addis Ababa. At the same time, the EPRDF intervened to stabilise the political process through the single party formula, and the Ministry of Federal Affairs was created to take the 'emerging regions' under its wing. The EPRDF's initial Statement on Economic policy referred to nomadic regions as areas with special problems, and promised 'to issue policies based on studies in order to alleviate the particular problems of these regions' (TGE 1991: 23). No studies or policies were produced, and the issue was not mentioned again, save for a brief Statement on Pastoral Development Policy issued by the Ministry of Federal Affairs a dozen years later, which referred vaguely to sedentarisation and agro-pastoralism.[11]

The Statement invited the NGO sector to participate, provided it 'worked in line with government policies' (p.13). In the absence of such policies, the NGOs were left to improvise with only nominal state supervision. The *woreda* empowerment scheme assigned responsibility for development to that level, and it was here that the NGO sector was supposed to link with the state. However, since the *woreda* budget for capital expenditure is insignificant, nearly all development interventions in the lowlands are funded and implemented by NGOs. In most cases, the NGOs form a nominal partnership with the *woreda* administration to secure permission and local official cooperation.

The first years of the 21st century witnessed a remarkable upsurge of interest in pastoralism internationally. Leading funding organisations –

[11] Ministry of Federal Affairs, March 2002.

World Bank, UNDP, FAO, USAID, GTZ, DFID – 'discovered' the plight of traditional livestock producers and espoused their cause with the zeal of the convert. Presumably this was linked to concerns over environmental degradation for which pastoralists are held partly responsible. The Global Environment Facility (GEF), set up in 1991 to combat land degradation, cited overgrazing as one of the main causes. The UNDP launched a Global Drylands Imperative programme, whose initial concern was to show that 'mobility is an ecological necessity and that mobile pastoralism is often the best way to manage dry environments sustainably' (UNDP 2004). Increased funding for development in the pastoralist zone is channelled through major international aid consortia – OXFAM, MSF, SCF, CARE – which then distribute funds to subcontractor NGOs for project implementation in the lowlands of Africa. The Horn took a major share of the funds, and saw a mushrooming of NGOs, both local and international, to compete furiously for it.

NGOs activities cover a very wide range: famine relief, support of vulnerable groups, such as children, women, the old and the disabled, health care, vocational education, employment creation and many others. The main strategy follows the guidelines set by orthodox development theory, which focuses on promoting agro-pastoralism through sedentarisation and crop cultivation, improved livestock quality and access to the national market, and natural resource conservation through water harvesting, fodder production, and similar activities. This strategy for pastoralist development is found wanting on several grounds. It ignores the laws of nature in the arid region that make regular cultivation unsustainable and unfit, without other resources to support human existence. Sedentarisation ignores the fact that livestock production in the ecological niche has to be mobile, and that traditional pastoralism is not a mode of production for the market; although herders engage in market transactions, they do not primarily produce livestock for the market. It also ignores the fact that traditional pastoralism is not just a mode of production, but a way of life, with its own social organisation and culture that are based on movement. Settlement and commercialisation would affect not only the pastoralist economy; they would irreparably damage an ancient way of life. From the state's point of view, the logic in this outsourcing of development activities in the lowland periphery is clear. In promoting sedentarisation and commercialisation of pastoralism, NGOs are implementing state policy.

The crucial flaw in NGO activity is lack of continuity. NGO discourse has an anthology of concepts purporting to ensure 'sustainability', 'community ownership', 'recipient empowerment', 'stakeholder participation', and so on, implying that communities and local government can shoulder the burden of project maintenance after NGO departure. The truth is that despite an emphasis on labour intensive intermediate technologies, the maintenance costs of the average NGO project are beyond the financial and technical capacity of communities and local governments. NGO projects have finite duration. Once the cash flow stops, they fold. The lowlands in the Horn are littered with their remains:

> It is a common characteristic of development projects generally to fail to consider in any detail the financial ability of government (at various levels) or other organisations, to carry on the activities of the project once the phase financed by external donors is finished. The consequence is that they are seldom sustained, and the marginal political position of pastoralists tends to lead to a greater failure to sustain services to them than to other more influential sectors of the population.[12]

*

The coming of federalism did not reduce the frequency or the intensity of conflict in the lowlands. Managing it became a problem that confounded the combined efforts of the federal and *kilil* governments that were supplemented by NGOs until recently. Initially, the Department of Regional Affairs in the Prime Minister's Office, formed in 1995, kept a distant watch over developments in the periphery, while army commanders and security officials stationed in the lowlands were responsible for keeping the peace. The Ministry of Federal Affairs (MoFA) was created in 2001 to take the 'emerging regions' under its wing. In addition to the Department of Regional Affairs, the Ministry's portfolio included the Federal Police and Prison Service. For a long time, MoFA was seriously understaffed and its activities were limited. In terms of conflict management its role, as one Minister put it, was that of a 'fire brigade'. In 2009, the Ministry was considerably strengthened with the addition of new staff.

The federal government's policy has been to pass the burden of conflict management to the *kilil* administrators, backed by the federal police force and, when necessary, the army. Having initially shunned traditional authorities as a 'feudal class', the EPRDF later sought their involvement in this effort, and now uses them as mediators alongside civil and military officials. Councils of Elders with an advisory role were formed at the woreda, zone and *kilil* level. Elders are widely sought also by NGOs, churches and voluntary associations concerned with managing conflict in their communities. Their effectiveness in performing this traditional function depends on several factors. The main one is the degree to which traditional culture still rules society and customary authority retains its traditional status. While this varies from one community to another, tradition and customary authority generally have lost ground everywhere. A familiar sign of this is the readiness of young warriors to disregard and bypass their elders. Elder status is further undermined by the summary way in which state officials often treat them; throwing them into prison for non-compliance is routine. Elder influence is also limited by the fact that often they instigate conflict themselves. Finally, elder influence is nil when the resources in dispute are externally generated and beyond community control.

In the early years of the new century, 'conflict vulnerability' studies became mandatory and 'conflict resolution' components were added to

[12] Stephen Sanford (2005: 7).

every development project. The conjunction of development and peace-making was greatly reinforced with the launching of the 'War on Terror' and the perception of the Horn as a battleground. Money was no problem and NGOs, carried away with the cash flow, scrambled to add peace-making to their agenda. Their approach is guided by the belief that conflict is caused by misunderstanding and a breakdown of communication between hostile groups. 'They see conflict as at root dysfunctional, as an aberration, even when in part it arises from resistance to human rights abuses or intervention or defence against violent attack.'[13] Accordingly, their efforts concentrate on promoting dialogue and understanding, and rely heavily on elders to bring rival groups together for that purpose. In this area also, NGOs promote state policy in stifling conflict whatever the cause. Even so, the EPRDF became concerned with the unwelcome publicity that NGO exertions brought to this issue and the government's inability to deal with it. Legislation passed in 2009 banned NGO involvement in conflict prevention activities.

*

As the first decade of the 21st century wore on, the lowlands acquired priority status in Ethiopia's search for a way out of the country's economic predicament. Drilling for petroleum, pursued by previous regimes, was revived in spectacular fashion.[14] In 1994, the World Bank extended a loan of 74 million dollars to Ethiopia for the development of gas deposits discovered in the Somali *kilil* in the 1980s. Since that time, about a dozen agreements have been signed with foreign companies and consortia – Chinese, Malaysian, Russian, American, Arab – for exploration and exploitation, none of which have come to fruition. The appearance of Malaysia on the scene, seconded by China, revived Addis Ababa's hopes. Malaysia's PETRONAS company, one of the top ten international oil firms, became the latest to sign an exploration agreement in 2003, and the following year, it subcontracted the Chinese company Zhongyuan Petroleum Exploration Bureau (ZPEB), a subsidiary of China Petrochemical Corporation (SINOPEC), to commence exploration in Gambella. In 2005 the same consortium began exploration work also in the Somali *kilil*.

The lowlands have also figured prominently in the new strategy of agro-industrial development on leased land. Nearly all the land earmarked for

[13] Allen (1996: 4).

[14] Exploration started in the mid-1940s, when the Sinclair Oil Company began drilling in the Somali inhabited south-eastern region, but was abandoned after the 1963 Ogaden uprising. Texaco took over in the early 1970s, only to give up after the 1974 revolution. Tenneco discovered gas in the southeast in 1973, where the Soviet Exploration Enterprise made a similar discovery later. The Soviets worked there for eleven years without reaching production stage when the military regime fell in 1991 and they left Ethiopia. Having discovered oil in the Sudan in the early 1970s, Chevron stared exploration in Ethiopia's southwest and identified significant petroleum possibilities in Gambella, before its activities were interrupted by regime change in 1974. Resumed in the 1980s by Soviet companies, exploration in that area was interrupted in 1991 by another change of regime.

agro-industry is in the lowland belt, especially in Afar, Gambella and Beni Shangul Gumuz. This sparsely populated terrain holds vast stretches of land that can conceivably be described as barren and unused. It is also here that popular resistance to land alienation can be more easily overcome with the collaboration of the peripheral elite, who have nominal authority to administer land. Addis Ababa had already taken care to exclude *kilil* governments from the management of the most valuable land resource – areas that are irrigable – by giving that responsibility to the federal Ethiopian River Basins Authority. The leasing process for the so-called 'marginal' lands is also centrally handled. The first stop for a potential investor is the federal Ministry of Agriculture where the seriousness of the application is evaluated, before the aspiring investor is forwarded to the relevant *kilil* investment bureau.

Land alienation on such levels is bound to have manifold consequences for the lowlanders, most of who survive on some form of agro-pastoralism. One thing it is unlikely to do is to bring them closer to the centre. It is more likely to alienate them further and thereby boost the potential of insurgent movements already active in the borderlands. These were quick to grasp the opportunity to denounce the policy as 'neo *gabbar*'. An OLF statement in September 2009 stated: 'the current Oromo farmland transaction between the TPLF regime and third parties is a continuation of the serfdom you have been subjected to for more than a hundred years.'

The federal state and the Afar

Unlike other lowlanders, the Afar were not an unknown quantity to the EPRDF. North-western Afarland had been part of Tigray province until the late 1980s. The salt trade that continues to this day is an ancient link between the two regions. Northern Afar was a traditional refuge for Tigray outlaws and rebels, a tradition followed by the TPLF in the 1970s and 1980s. The latter had recognised the Afar as one of five nationalities in Tigray, and set up a Tigray Afar Democratic Organisation to represent them. It established bases in the Afar Depression and sought to recruit fighters from the local population, but Afar chiefs did not welcome outsiders setting up bases in their territory and opposed the recruitment of young Afar men. In 1978, TPLF units were refused passage through Berahale district, and many Afar were killed in a clash that followed and is recalled as the 'Wednesday War.'

A split in the ANLM in 1979 produced a Northern Afar Liberation Front, later renamed the Afar National Liberation Front, which struck an alliance with the EPLF and the TPLF against the common enemy in Addis Ababa. It proved short lived, because the ANLF opposed the presence of TPLF units in Afar land and Eritrean claims to Afar territory. Afar resistance to highlander intrusion in their homeland crystallised in the appearance of bands of outlaws who led a shadowy existence in the depths of the Afar Depression, and fought any and all intruders. They called themselves Ugogomo, a newly-coined word meaning 'revolution'.

The Afar were represented in the July 1991 Conference by the Afar Liberation Front (ALF) with three seats, occupied by the octogenarian Sultan Ali Mirah, recently returned from exile in Saudi Arabia, and two of his sons. Though long inactive, the ALF claimed to have 2,500 fighters, and was in a position to play a dominant role in Afar affairs. United for the first time in a *kilil* of their own and with a measure of self-government, the Afar had much to be grateful for to the EPRDF. The loss of part of their homeland to Eritrea was taken in stride. Keeping to the accustomed role of subordinate elite, Ali Mirah and sons raised no objection, and the family was amply rewarded. Ali Mirah had 12 sons and 10 daughters from four wives, and was able to choose from among them those who were appointed to ministerial and ambassadorial posts. He was given a government villa in the capital, and 10,000ha of land in Aussa that had been nationalised by the Dergue were returned to him.

Wary of alienating the Ali Mirah clan, the EPRDF did not move immediately to sideline the ALF, which went on to win the 1992 *woreda* and *kilil* elections, and Hanfare Ali Mirah became the first head of the Afar *kilil*. The EPRDF rounded up most of the leading cadre of the Afar National Liberation Movement who had worked with the Dergue and kept them in prison for a decade. After their release, most of them found employment in the Afar *kilil* administration. In the chaotic early days of the new regime, the ALF clashed with the TPLF in Gewani town in September 1991, in a battle that lasted four days and left hundreds of Afar dead and wounded. This marked the beginning of the political decline of the Ali Mirah dynasty and the eventual dismantlement of the ALF. Miffed by Addis Ababa's support for his opponents at home, the Sultan took himself off to Saudi Arabia once more, and from there denounced his son, Hanfare, for collaborating with the EPRDF. Hanfare Ali Mirah lasted only a few months in office. A split in the family and in the ALF followed, when another son, Omer, formed the Afar National Liberation Front (ANLF) in 1994. Yet another faction, the Afar National Democratic Movement (ANDM), was founded the same year by the descendants of the Sultan of Birou, Ahmed M. Ahaw.

While the ALF, the only faction with an independent political base in Afar was unravelling, the EPRDF engineered a merger of five minor groups to produce an Afar PDO. This party took the field in the 1995 elections, winning twenty-three out of forty-eight seats in the *kilil* assembly, while the ALF got only eleven. The elections were such a farce that even the government press could not take them seriously. In Assaita, one newspaper reported, 'voters had virtually no idea how to cast ballots, election officials in the area were either just as ignorant or not willing to explain the process, ten to twelve year old teenagers were voting, and officials harassed press people when asked for an explanation.'[15] In one *woreda*, half a dozen polling stations were closed soon after opening because no voters showed up, causing the administrator in all seriousness to complain: 'it was unfair to

[15] *Ethiopian Herald* (19 June 1995).

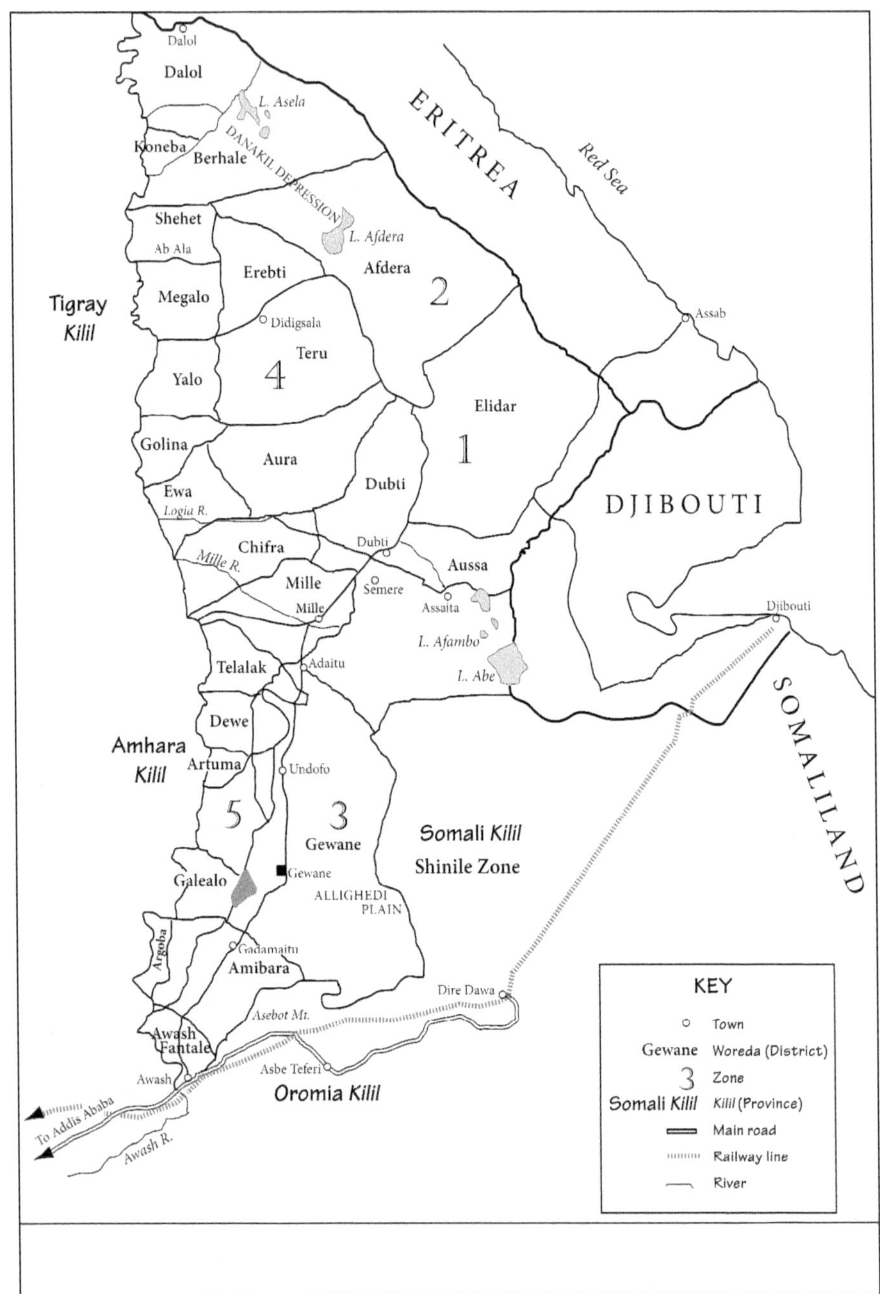

Map 7 Afar *kilil*: zones & *woreda*

usurp peoples' right to elect, on the mere pretext that they were not around.'[16]

Hanfare was once again chosen *kilil* president, and again lasted only a few months. While out of the country, he was dismissed by the *kilil* assembly and replaced by the leader of the PDO, Ismail Ali Siro.

Whatever its demerits, the 1995 election installed an Afar PDO in power in Assaita, and repeat performances in the elections that followed have kept it there until now. These were conducted virtually without opposition, save for the odd independent candidate. Factions that made an occasional appearance were induced to join the PDO in a renamed Afar National Democratic Party (ANDP). The Afar *kilil* became a model of political stability and continuity in the turbulent lowlands, without a significant change in the political leadership since 1995. Once more, Addis Ababa found the right man to manage this part of the periphery. Ismail Ali Siro, a farmer's son from northern Afar, joined the TPLF in the 1980s, having completed fourth grade. He was still *kilil* president in 2010, having set a national record for peripheral elite longevity in office.

Detached from the political rivalry for control of the Afar *kilil* administration and the sharing out of the federal subsidy, Ugogomo armed bands maintained a shadowy existence in the northern badlands of Zone 2, making their presence felt occasionally with sensational acts of banditry. The Berahale *woreda* in Zone 2 with its salt mines became the Ugogomo stronghold, where it collects taxes from the salt trade. In 1991, a former leading ANLM cadre who had fled to Britain, Mohamooda Gas, announced the formation of the Afar Revolutionary Democratic Union (ARDU) as a political vehicle for Ugogomo. A couple of years later, it was joined by other Afar factions in exile and renamed the Afar Revolutionary Democratic Unity Front (ARDUF). ARDUF's distinction lay in the fact that it firmly opposed the cession of Afar land to Eritrea, and set as its main objective 'to unite all the territories inhabited by the Afar people in Ethiopia proper and to attain a federal or confederate political status for this administrative unity of the Afar people.'[17] In this quest for pan-Afar unity ARDUF made an exception of Djibouti, 'because the international community recognized a sovereign status for the French Territory of the Afar and Issa.'[18]

In the following years, Addis Ababa and Asmara played a cat and mouse game with Ugogomo, while also keeping a wary eye on each other in northern Afar. They tried separately and jointly but failed to eliminate Ugogomo, whose strength did not exceed a few hundred fighters. In April 1995, nine Italian tourists were abducted by Ugogomo and had to be ransomed. The EPRDF had some success with its technique of splitting the opposition. When a former ANLM leader who later joined Ugogomo, Muhedin Miftah, was captured in Djibouti and turned over to Ethiopia, he was persuaded to form a faction he named Ugogomo Proper and

[16] *Ethiopian Herald* (21 June 1995).

[17] Mohamooda Ahmed Gas interview in *Ethiopian Review*, (September 1993:15).

[18] Ibid.: p.16.

joined the Afar PDO. He was rewarded with the job of director of the bureau of sports, while his followers were taken into the Afar police force and the Ethiopian army.

A thaw in the relations between the EPRDF and the Afar opposition came with the outbreak of the war with Eritrea in 1998. Ali Mirah returned to make a patriotic appeal on television. His son Hanfare, who had been accused of corruption and fled abroad, also returned. He was now sent to represent Ethiopia in Kuwait, and another relative, Kadafo Ali Mirah, became ambassador to Sudan. Only one son of Ali Mirah, Omar, sided with Eritrea and went to Asmara. On its part, ARDUF 'placing the national duty over and above political differences,' declared a ceasefire and 'aligned itself on the side of the Ethiopian peoples and government.' Negotiations to bring this dissident faction into the fold had the expected outcome of splitting ARDUF. With the end of the war, ARDUF announced it was abandoning the armed struggle as well as its claim to Afar land in Eritrea, opting instead for peaceful political activity.[19] A strongly worded refutation issued a month later by a faction claiming to represent ARDUF, denounced Mohamooda and his deals. Nevertheless, the latter managed to bring a group of Ugogomo members out of the bush, and was rewarded with a vice-ministerial post in the Ministry of Youth and Sports.

This rapprochement notwithstanding, Ugogomo resumed its nefarious activities in 2007 by abducting a group of British diplomats who had blundered into the Berahale badlands along with a large group of Ethiopian assistants. They were taken across the border into Eritrea, and kept for five weeks before the foreigners were ransomed through the mediation of Afar elders. The Ethiopians were kept for another month, before a hugely embarrassed Ethiopian government could negotiate their release. To cover its embarrassment, Addis Ababa sought to pin the blame on Asmara.

The construction of a modern administration system in the Afar *kilil* started late and faced immense difficulties. These had to do mostly with the problems of distance, transport and communications common to the lowland periphery. Assaita, the old capital, remained a decrepit backwater bereft of urban facilities, and was not even connected with a paved road to the main Addis Ababa – Djibouti artery passing only a few kilometres away. At the turn of the century, the capital was moved to the newly built town of Semera on the road to Djibouti. Also common to the lowlands, but severe in the case of the Afar, was the lack of educated and skilled manpower for the administration. Highlanders were recruited to fill this gap, and Afar secondary school graduates were sent for training to the Civil Service College in Addis Ababa. As a rule, youthful, inexperienced Afar were appointed to head all *kilil* departments, where the work was done by highlanders. Not surprisingly, such appointments often were the result of nepotism and political patronage. Prior to a purge carried out in 1997, a *kilil* official complained that 'all key offices were occupied by

[19] Central Committee Endorsed Political Transformation of ARDUF (11 December 2002).

siblings and kinsmen of the leaders in disregard of their qualifications and competence.'[20]

The coming of federalism marked an abrupt change in the traditional Afar system of government which never had a unified structure or a single ruler to represent the nation. A centralised system of decision making represented by the *kilil* was now imposed on people whose affairs seldom extended beyond the local community and were managed by their elders. The absence of customary figures of authority at *kilil* level meant that the Afar chiefs are totally excluded form that level of government, and have no appreciable influence in the new political process. The situation is different at the local level, where the new government structures were late in emerging and have yet to take root two decades later. Traditional authority remained indispensable in the management of local community affairs, particularly in matters concerning land and justice. Speaking of this, Ali Mirah was categorical: 'It [*kilil* government] does not interfere in the affairs that are the jurisdiction of the traditional authorities' (Aramis, 2007).

Land to the investor

The plantation economy in the Awash Valley that had flourished in the late imperial era and expanded under the Dergue collapsed entirely in the 1990s. State farms, settlement schemes, community projects and other ventures dependent on state management simply dissolved. Widespread looting of machinery and destruction of facilities led to abandonment of cultivation, while the suspension of canal maintenance and dredging operations in subsequent years brought uncontrolled flooding and river diversion with serious consequences for pastoralists and cultivators alike. Faced with the collapse of state plantations in the region, the federal government chose to return part of the land to local communities. Having no plans of its own to exploit the resources of the Awash Valley, it passed this burden on to two groups of outsiders. The first group were the so-called 'investors' in agri-business, attracted to the area by the profit making potential of irrigated cultivation, utilising the cheapest land, water and labour available anywhere, plus tax holidays and other inducements. The *kilil* administration actively encouraged investment, but it was the clan elders who were the agents in this process. Neither the federal government nor the Afar *kilil* administration produced a land use policy, and investors were left to decide the use they make of leased land regardless of consequences. Environmental damage due to mismanagement of irrigation was one consequence that was observed. 'Neither the private nor the state farms are using modern irrigation management practices, which is the major reason for wastage of water and causes severe salinity problems in the area.' (Lijalem & Moltot 2003: 12) Thousands of hectares were

[20] Mohammed Seid Meki, Secretary of Afar Kilil Council (*Ethiopian Herald* 7 December 1997).

abandoned because poor drainage allowed the water table to rise close to the surface, ruling out desalinisation through sub-surface flushing.

As practiced, land leasing is at variance with both national and customary law. While the authority to administer land belongs to the *kilil* administration, the main agents in this process are Afar chiefs and elders, who themselves are not authorised under national legislation to administer land. The customary law that gave them such authority stipulates that all clan members have equal rights of access to clan land. Leasing also contravenes custom because it excludes clan members from access to land leased to outsiders. Afar elders understandably prefer leasing land to investors for immediate financial returns, rather than encourage young herdsmen to take up cultivation. The system leaves open the possibility of exploitation for personal gain. Some elders accept money from investors to expedite the process, others become overseers on leased land, and others still become farmers themselves. One report noted 'a trend towards the marginalisation of the poor.' Clansmen who wanted to cultivate were pushed towards less valuable sites. Another trend was the hardening of *khida* claims on land with cultivation potential, and increased conflict among Afar as a result.[21] The second group to which the government entrusted the task of development are NGOs. While their efforts should not be unappreciated, they could not be relied upon to make an appreciable impact on the dire situation of the Afar people.

These desultory efforts were overtaken by the EPRDF's latest and most ambitious scheme to capture the Valley's resources. The Tendaho Dam and Sugar Project conceived in the first years of the 21st century is designed to occupy nearly all the irrigable land in the Middle and Lower valleys for sugar production. Three existing plants in Ethiopia produce some 267,000 tons of sugar, and the country's domestic consumption is predicted to reach 400,000 tons annually by 2010. The projected output of the new scheme is expected to meet domestic demand and export sugar in the Horn. To reach this goal, the scheme covers 85,000ha in the Middle and Lower valleys, 65,000ha for cultivation and rest for infrastructure, factories and supporting services.

This expanse includes not only the land of existing state cotton plantations in the Valley and vast grazing areas, but – inconsistently, given the regime's penchant for agro-pastoralism – all the land cultivated by Afar for centuries in Aussa. Four *woreda* – Afambo, Assaita, Dubti, Mille – are the most immediately affected. According to the report of the Indian firm of consultants who prepared the feasibility study, 'the irrigation scheme will therefore occupy much of the most productive grazing in Afambo, Assaita and Dubti districts.'[22] Construction of a giant dam began in 2007 near Logia town to harness Awash River water for irrigation. Its reservoir alone

[21] Werer Annual Report (n. d., p. 22).

[22] Draft Final Report: 'Sugarcane Production Agronomy and Farm Machinery.' (Section 007), Addis Ababa, June 2005. Prepared by Water Works Design & Supervision Enterprise and Water Power Consultancy Service (India) LTD, and Hora Agroindustry PLC. (Addis Ababa, 2005: 105).

will inundate 17,000ha. A canal will carry water to plantations starting 18km down from the dam and extend for 70km along both sides of the Awash River to its terminal lakes of Gamari, Afambo and Abbe. A similar but smaller project is under construction in the southwest with a dam on the Kessem River, a tributary of Awash River.

The devastating implications for the ecology of the Valley and its inhabitant were bluntly stated in the feasibility study. It acknowledged that in this desiccated and denuded land 'a forested area of 15,000ha will be cleared, plus 19,000ha of bush and shrub land' (ibid: 23). An accompanying environmental impact assessment made the following chilling predictions: 'The impact of the project on the existing wildlife species is significant because most of the land in the area will be allotted to the irrigation scheme and vegetation will be cleared…It is not simple to suggest a solution to this problem...The project site is in one of the most malarial parts of the region…malaria is and will be the major cause of death in the project area... The dam poses a vital threat to the lakes that form the Awash River inland delta, and unless adequate amount of water is released to the lakes, they will dry out.' Moreover, it acknowledged that 'the Dam and Reservoir site is located in the most seismic area of the country.'[23] The area to be occupied by the dam and reservoir is described as 'desert area and has no significant cultural, economic & agricultural importance to the Afar community'. Even the loss of pastureland is not deemed harmful. 'Even though a big area of pasture land will be expropriated for irrigation development, the conditions for livestock appreciably will be improved due to the irrigated pasture, range improvement and services provided to the pastoralists.' To compensate the herders for this massive dispossession it recommends a mere 1,800ha be allotted for 'pastoralist development.'[24]

The report does not attempt to veil the fact that the scheme spells death for the Afar economy and way of life. It does put the familiar gloss on it, in terms of the benefits it would bring to the people of the region:

> Prior to the implementation of Tendaho Dam and Sugar Project some major social, cultural and economic changes are envisaged in the Afar…Training will provide the guarantee of smooth integration of the Afar into the Tendaho project. Without it, the majority of them will not be able to understand or benefit from the project.

In the meantime, the mass of displaced and stockless people would be gathered in resettlement camps. 'Resettlement sites to be provided with access roads, schools, health units, mosques, veterinary health posts, flour-mills, watering points, etc., before displacement'; all familiar promises routinely made and unfailingly reneged by previous regimes in Addis Ababa. The enormity of the task was seen as 'challenging,' yet it was cheerfully assumed that it would be made possible by 'efficient management and perfect planning'. Neither 'efficient management nor perfect planning' prevented the project from hitting a series of obstacles, and full

[23] 'Interim report: Environmental Impact Assessment', (Addis Ababa, 2005: 29).

[24] 'Interim Report: Livestock', Section 010, (Addis Ababa, May 2005).

implementation was still a distant goal by the end of the decade. Nevertheless, the fate of the Afar people is sealed. Their future lies in seasonal work at starvation wages in the sugarcane fields.

Remarkably, no Afar voice was raised to criticise the project. A series of public meetings addressed by top federal officials were convened in the *kilil* to list the benefits that will accrue to the region, and Meles Zenawi himself visited the area twice for this purpose. The consent of the Afar intelligentsia is not surprising, since this group is certain to benefit from the project. The acquiescence of the Afar elders is partly explained by their lack of influence in the *kilil* administration, and a feeling of resignation born of bitter experience that opposition is futile.

Afar and their neighbours

The history of Afar relations with their neighbours is a litany of hostility and violent conflict. They call their borderlands with the Somali, Oromo, Tigray, Argoba and Wajirat the 'land of fear' (*doka'a*), and the Afar homeland the 'land of light' (*la'o*). Unlike intra-Afar conflict which is regulated by customary law, conflict with outsiders is often violent and far more difficult to resolve. Such conflict is common along the western periphery of the Afar *kilil*, in the escarpment interface between Afar and highlanders in Tigray and Amhara *kilil*. Zone 5 that runs along the escarpment is the smallest in territory and largest in population in the Afar *kilil*, with a density of ninety-four inhabitants per square kilometre compared to seventy-seven for Zone 2. In this relatively crowded space, the Afar are threatened by the inexorable descent of highland cultivators down the escarpment due to the increasing shortage of land on the plateau. 'As soon as they see us starting to engage in agriculture,' the Afar complain, 'they come and take that land for themselves.'[25]

There was tension in the Afar-Tigray border when the boundary between the two *kilil* was drawn. Afar settlements found themselves on the Tigray side and had to relocate across the boundary. Borderline clashes required the intervention of the military in 1996. Subsequently, the situation improved considerably thanks to the efforts of local officials on both sides. By contrast, Afar-Amhara relations along their common border are marred by frequent violence. Two marketplaces on the escarpment – Senbetie and Shoa Robit – are the flashpoints of conflict. In November 2002, a group of thirty-eight Afar women and children were killed on their way back from the market. A survey conducted jointly by the two *kilil* administrations in 2004 showed that 174 people had been killed and another 75 wounded between 1995 and 2003. It was based on police data, and presumably the actual figures were higher.

In the southern periphery of the Awash Valley, the Afar frequently clash with several of their neighbours, the Karrayu, Ittu and Nole Oromo agro-pastoralists and the Issa Somali pastoralists. The area of conflict with

[25] Interview, Megale *woreda* official, (November 2004).

the Karrayu and Ittu is the border zone between the Upper and Middle Awash valleys, which includes the Awash National Park and Mt. Fantale, and encompasses the Fantale *woreda* of Oromia *kilil* and the Awash Fantale *woreda* of Afar *kilil*. The Afar and Nole meet farther south on the foothills of Mt. Asebot. The resources of this border zone became increasingly important for both groups in recent years, particularly as the Afar were displaced from the rangelands west of the Awash River by the Issa. Drought in the early 2000s aggravated the situation. In January 2003, a clash between Afar and Kereyu inside the Awash National Park left 40 dead.[26]

*

The Afar dispute with the Issa Somali is of a different order. For the Afar it is a struggle for survival, for the federal government it is a vexing problem with regional implications. Certain developments added to the complexity of the dispute in the 1990s. Federalism exacerbated claims over territory, especially in the lowlands where large tracts of sparsely inhabited land are open to competing claims. Unlike the past, when Addis Ababa could alter administrative boundaries at will, it is now assumed that once drawn *kilil* boundaries are final. Consequently it is crucial to secure a favourable settlement now, because it would not be possible to change it in the future. Loss of access to the port of Assab as a result of the Ethiopia-Eritrea war, and the consequent heightened importance of the road to Djibouti that crosses the Awash Valley, was another factor. After 1998, traffic on this road multiplied, the truck-stop hamlets became hives of commercial activity that attracted highlanders, and the road emerged as a new and valuable source of wealth in the midst of a deprived region. The collapse of border controls between Ethiopia, Somaliland and Somalia in the 1990s gave contraband trade, an old pastoralist avocation, new dimensions. A veritable common market emerged along the eastern and southern sections of the Ethiopian periphery, where people and goods moved freely without benefit of passports, visas, or customs controls. Contraband trade flourished, bringing manufactured goods from many parts of the world, especially China, through the ports of Djibouti, Berbera in Somaliland, and Bossaso in Puntland.

Not surprisingly, it was the Issa that came to dominate this trade, since they could move freely among their own clan kin throughout the region. They control the camel caravan trade, renting animals and providing services as guides, porters and guards, to bring smuggled goods to the hamlets on the Addis Ababa–Djibouti road, from where they are channelled to the highlands by motor vehicle and the railway. Dikhil and Balbala are staging areas in Djibouti, from where goods are brought to staging points on the Ethiopian side – Gadamaitou, Adaitou, and a third hamlet, Undofo, that emerged at the turn of the century. The three towns are controlled by Issa and highlanders, many of them from Tigray, who

[26] IRIN (8 January 2003).

collaborate in the trade. No Afar live there. It is widely believed that a silent third party in this trade is the army stationed in the area, whose job is to prevent it.

The Afar remain aloof and realise scant benefit from activities, licit or illicit, on the road that crosses their territory. Nevertheless, they became increasingly concerned about the tightening Issa grip on the three hamlets, and Issa incursions west of the road towards the Awash River. This led to increasingly frequent clashes between Afar and Issa herdsmen over waterholes, a resource that is becoming scarcer with time, and clashes became deadlier through the use of automatic weapons. There is no traditional conflict resolution mechanism between the two groups, and the efforts of local officialdom were ineffective. As a result, grievances accumulated on both sides and tension rose steadily during the 1990s.

The civil war in Djibouti in the early 1990s was another contributing factor. On one level, this was a power struggle between Afar and Issa urban elites in the enclave. On another level, it was an extension of the ongoing Afar-Issa struggle inside Ethiopia, where it raised tensions further, as each side accused the other of getting support from their kinsmen in Djibouti. The Ethiopian-Eritrean war (1998-2001) was fought partly in northern Afar and caused havoc among the population, many of who had to abandon their land and move south with their animals, increasing the burden on already congested pasturelands. In 2000, Saudi Arabia imposed a ban on animal imports from the Horn – the second in recent years – due to the outbreak of Rift Valley fever. The ban hit the Issa particularly hard, because they are major exporters of sheep and goats to the Arabian market. The ban caused overstocking and overgrazing in Shinille zone, and forced Issa herders to range deeper into Afar territory towards the Awash River, where they met an increasingly hostile reception from the Afar. Finally, the drought of 2002-3, one of the worst in memory, hit both groups severely, intensifying their desperate struggle over water sources.

The war with Eritrea and the loss of Assab port in 1998 turned the road and railway to Djibouti into lifelines for Ethiopia, and it was only then that the federal government turned its attention to the problem. It appealed to both sides to refrain from hostilities, promising a resolution of the issue after the end of the war. Conferences were held and an agreement was reached to maintain the status quo until the end of the war. In 1999 the Office of Regional Affairs in the Prime Minister's Office formed a committee of four academics from Addis Ababa University to report on the issue. The committee studied the record, visited the region to interview both sides, and submitted a report at the end of that year. It recommended further study of the competing claims, and recognising that resource scarcity was the root cause of the conflict, it recommended carrying out a land use survey to be followed by a programme of livestock development and planned settlement.[27] None of these were done, and the problem was allowed to fester. When the war ended, the federal government was distracted by the split in the TPLF, and no action was taken until serious

[27] Seyoum G/Sellasie *et al.*, (1999).

bloodshed led to the closing of the road to Djibouti. In May 2000, Neina Tahiro, a popular Afar politician elected to the federal legislature, was murdered on the road. The Issa were blamed, and the Afar went on a murderous spree in Gadamaitu and Gewane killing nineteen Issa.

The Afar *kilil* administration came under increasing pressure from two sides to act. On one side, the federal government demanded it put a stop to the violence and reach an agreement with its Somali counterpart. The main problem was the demarcation of the border between the two *kilil*. When the federation was formed in the mid-1990s, the territory of each *kilil* was roughly, but neither precisely nor officially delineated. As elsewhere in Ethiopia, it was left for the *kilil* themselves to settle. On the other side, the Afar administrators came under local pressure to expel the Issa from Afar land and the three hamlets on the road. The Afar based their case on history, claiming land occupied by Issa had been theirs until recently. The Somali countered with a demand for a referendum, obviously expecting that the three Issa inhabited hamlets would become part of their *kilil*. They moved to pre-empt the issue by integrating them administratively into Shinile zone, although they lay inside Zone 3 in Afar *kilil*.

In order to strengthen their position on the road and to checkmate the Issa by blocking their access to the Awash River, the Afar responded by moving some *woreda* centres in Zone 3 from the vicinity of the Awash River on to the Djibouti road. Borimadaitu *woreda* centre was moved from the marshland near the river to a site on the road near Galaelu, a seasonal stream that provides water from shallow holes in the dry season, and also supports a well with a permanent supply of water. Galaelu is a few kilometres from Gadamaitu, and the Issa leaders of the town protested what they considered a violation of the agreement to maintain the status quo. The Afar gathered a force of about thirty warriors to protect the site. Asked afterwards why this task was not given to the police, the Borimadaitu *woreda* administrator said this was an 'affair of the people' not of the administration.[28] On 23 March 2002 at dawn, a group of about 50 Issa arrived at the site and fell into a well prepared ambush, suffering thirteen killed and ten wounded before the battle ended several hours later. The Afar acknowledged having sought assistance from Ugogomo. Afar youth had been trained in the north, and had returned along with members of that organisation to Zone 3 to train others.

Following the battle of Galaelu, the road to Djibouti was closed on several occasions, and at least one truck driver was reported killed, prompting his colleagues to stage a strike that caused a shortage of fuel in Addis Ababa. This moved the federal government to action. It ordered the formation of so-called 'Integrated Security and Peace Committees' at *woreda*, zone and *kilil* levels involving administrators and elders from both sides, as well as security officials and military officers. Replica committees were set up to administer the hamlets of Gadamaitu, Undofo and Adaitu. The committees were tasked with bringing criminals to justice and arranging for compensation payment and the return of looted livestock. It

[28] Interviewed in Galaelu, January 2004.

was agreed that both Afar and Issa should have open access to the Allighedi plain until the *kilil* borders were finally demarcated. In the following years the committees met many times and arranged for the return of looted animals and the arrest of some culprits. Even so, each side continued to accuse the other of not fulfilling its obligations.

A long series of meetings were held subsequently in Addis Ababa under the chairmanship of the Prime Minister, and in Awash, Dire Dawa and Jijiga under the Minister of Federal Affairs, in a continuous and ultimately futile effort to resolve the festering conflict. Neither side would compromise. The Afar demanded the return of lost territory and a final demarcation of the boundary. 'When two people fight, first they have to be separated before they reconcile', they said. They wanted the federal government to draw the boundary, so it would have the responsibility of enforcing it. Basing their claim on current political practice, the Somali wanted a referendum to decide the status of the contested territory. The federal government faced a dilemma. A return to the territorial status *quo ante* would alienate the Somali, while a referendum would further upset the Afar. And there the matter rests.

Violence continued to claim lives in the meantime. In the four months that followed the battle of Galaelu, the Shinile Zone administration recorded some fifty Issa deaths and many more wounded. To keep the road to Djibouti open, the federal government banned anyone carrying arms to come near it, and ordered the army to enforce this measure. Instead of easing up, Issa pressure intensified, and a fourth hamlet named Ammuli appeared on the road to service the contraband trade. In 2007 the federal government launched a major operation to stamp out this trade along the eastern border with Djibouti and Somaliland. The army raided smuggler haunts, confiscated goods and vehicles, set up mobile patrol units to control smuggler routes and, as a result, dislocated the local economy founded on smuggling. Ammuli, the latest addition to the Issa strongholds on the road to Djibouti, fell victim to this clean-up effort, when the military ordered its inhabitants to vacate it and then burned it down. The Afar were not spared. Eighteen of them were killed by soldiers in August 2008.

Summary

The litmus test of ethnic federalism in Ethiopia is the experience of the periphery during the two decades under this system of government. Federalism was introduced in Ethiopia as the solution to widespread, prolonged and violent political conflict that had brought the state to the brink of collapse. This is a political formula, and it is in political terms that it is evaluated by its proponents and opponents alike. The former argue that the changes federalism brought are momentous and for the process of nation-building positive. The highland periphery is the main beneficiary, and the gap that separates it from the centre has narrowed as a result. The latter argue that the working of the system under the EPRDF preserves the hegemony of the centre, albeit with a new structures and corps of centre and peripheral elite. Data presented in this study shows that the latter are essentially right.

The experience of the Afar under EPRDF rule demonstrates the extent that decision making power is retained by the centre and is wielded over the periphery. It also illustrates the grim consequences of exclusion from power for the people in the periphery. The trappings of self-administration notwithstanding, the Afar are the hapless subjects of decisions that vitally affect them, but are taken over their heads with scarce consideration for their welfare. This is a repeat of the experience these people had under previous regimes, and shows that the process of resource appropriation in the periphery introduced by the empire builders continues. The rulers in Addis Ababa can rightly argue that the resources of the Awash Valley belong to the nation, and not only to the Afar. They cannot argue, however, that the decisions they've taken have benefitted the Afar. The conclusion is that no significant progress was made under federalism towards political integration, the last frontier that needs to be crossed in the nation state-building process, and more battles will have to be fought in this front.

13

The Somali

An auspicious start

The readiness of the Somali rebels to accept the EPRDF offer was a welcome surprise for the incoming regime. 'We never expected the Somali to take part in the July conference and to change their minds about joining Somalia', said Meles Zenawi.[1] In the preparations for the July 1991 Addis Ababa conference, the EPRDF searched for representatives of Somali organisations that had long been inactive and whose leadership was not easy to locate. With Sudanese assistance, they found the remnants of the WSLF leadership hiding in a Mogadisho cellar to escape Hawiye vengeance. They were brought to Khartoum with their leader, Abdinassir Sheikh Aden, and were easily persuaded to accept the EPRDF Charter. 'After all', one of them reasoned, 'this is what we have fought for.'[2] They were required to change the name of their organisation, which became the Western Somali Democratic Party (WSDP) and was allocated two seats in the July Conference. It took a little longer to deal with the leadership of the Somali Abo Liberation Front, who baulked at the demand to dissolve the front into separate ethnic organisations. Eventually they were persuaded, and a United Oromo Peoples Liberation Front (UOPLF) was formed under Wako Gutu Usu, and an Oromo Abo Liberation Movement (OALM) led by his old comrade-in-arms Mohammed Siraj.[3]

The ONLF proved much harder to win over. It leadership was dispersed, with its acting chairman Sheikh Ibrahim Abdallah Mah in Saudi Arabia, its foreign spokesman Abdulahi Mohammed Sadi in Scandinavia, and Mohammed Sirad Dolal in London. The EPRDF initiative caught them off guard, and it took them some time to prepare a coherent

[1] Interviewed in Addis Ababa, 10 August 1993.

[2] Mohamed Ugas Abdi interviewed in Addis Ababa, July 1993.

[3] Wako broke with the EPRDF in 1992 and went abroad. When he died in 2006, the OPDO honoured him as an Oromo hero. His body was flown to Addis Ababa to be met at the airport by OPDO leaders and was ceremoniously buried at Meda Walabu.

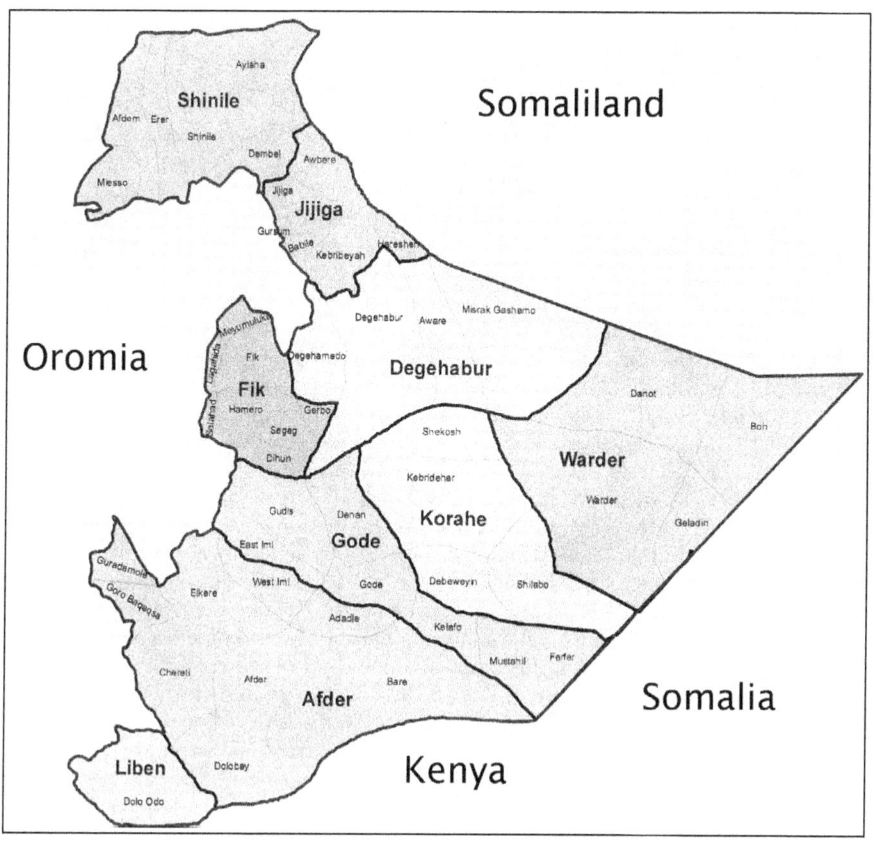

Map 8 Somali *kilil*: zones & *woreda*

response. Sheikh Ibrahim Abdallah and a couple of his colleagues were among those invited to Khartoum to be briefed and the only ones who refused to sign the Charter. They claimed the right to administer the Ogaden and asked the EPRDF to stay out of it. Consequently, they were not invited to attend the July 1991 conference in Addis Ababa.

The Somali nationality was allocated four seats in the conference. Two seats were earmarked for the WSDP, and the other two for the Issa and Gurgura Liberation Movement, a recent entry in the field. Because the Gurgura have their own distinct language, they were told to form a separate organisation: they named their new one Horyal and took one seat in the July Conference, while the fourth seat went to the Issa. This set off a scramble to form clan-based political organisations, and soon there were as many as there are Somali clans in Ethiopia; thirteen to be exact.

The Somali had every reason to be gratified by the *kilil* demarcation that followed. Their own included all the Somali speakers in Ethiopia, and was the second largest (after Oromia), of the nine *kilil*, covering about one-quarter of the country's total area of 1.2 million square kilometres. It included the Liben district between the Genale and Dawa rivers in the southwest, long fought over by the Gerri and the Borana, which thus became the scene of bloody clashes that continue to this day. Marking the ethnic divide between Oromo and Somali in the east also proved a protracted, painful process yet to be fully resolved.

The EPRDF had no plans for a political transition in a region that had been under military rule for more than two decades. Nor were the aged WSLF veterans who returned home capable of providing leadership. Into this vacuum stepped the untried ONLF, whose leadership had a change of heart and decided to put federalism to the test. Abdilahi Mohamed Sadi, its foreign spokesman, arrived in Ethiopia in February 1992. In a statement he made upon arrival in Addis Ababa, he endorsed the Charter, but pointedly refused to renounce secession as a future option.[4] In return, the ONLF was assigned one of the four Somali seats in the transitional assembly.

It was a half-hearted change. The ONLF leaders made their way to the Ogaden, where the organisation held its first national congress in January 1992, in the hamlet of Garbo in Fiq Zone. It chose a central committee of 45 members and Sheikh Ibrahim to be its chairman. A teacher by profession, educated in Islamic jurisprudence in Riyad University in Saudi Arabia, where he had lived for many years, he was reputedly a man of strong religious convictions who opposed the rapprochement with Ethiopia. He made his headquarters in Garbo, his birthplace, and travelled in and out of Ethiopia through Somalia, avoiding Addis Ababa and contact with the EPRDF. Abdilahi Mohammed Sadi supported participation in the federal experiment as a strategy that would give the ONLF the opportunity to test the promise of federalism as well as time to prepare for a military option, should that be needed.

The approach of the 1992 elections exposed the structural fault lines in the Somali body politic: clanism. Fundamental was the split between the Ogaden and other Somali clans that live within Ethiopia's borders. An intense rivalry over control of the Somali *kilil* broke out from the start, pitting the Ogaden against the rest, remaining a destabilising factor in the politics of that region to this day. In a matter of months, no less than thirteen political organisations emerged to represent an equal number of clans. Aware that fragmentation gave an advantage to the Ogaden, the others sought to unite in opposition, but failed to produce a result before the elections.

The ONLF had a rival within the Ogaden clan led by veterans of the WSLF, now regrouped as the WSDP. The ONLF campaigned energetically to mobilise support, while the elderly Abdinassir Sheikh Aden relied on the record of the WSLF and his personal reputation. The elections for *woreda* and *kilil* officials were postponed three times in the Somali region, setting a precedent for every subsequent election, and were finally held in

[4] *Ethiopian Herald* 22 February 1992.

January 1993. It was not a smooth affair. Out of forty-eight *woreda*, the process was completed in thirty-seven. Even so, the EPRDF did not interfere, and the results were a fair reflection of local realities. The records of the neophyte National Elections Board gave the ONLF the largest vote and seventy-nine seats in the *kilil* assembly of 111 seats. The WSDP came a poor second with only nine seats.

The elected representatives attended a seminar organised by the federal government in Dire Dawa to learn the rudiments of parliamentary procedure, and the clan bargaining for office began. The inaugural session of the *kilil* assembly took place in Dire Dawa at the end of January 1993, and was addressed by then Prime Minister Tamrat Layne, who told its members they were proof 'that Ethiopian Somalis are Ethiopian citizens of Somali stock.'[5] The region that was previously known as the Ogaden was officially named the Somali Regional State. From a shortlist of three towns – Dire Dawa, Gode, Degehabur – for *kilil* capital (Jijiga was not listed) they chose Dire Dawa, a town also claimed by the Oromo. For that reason, the federal government vetoed this choice, and the Somali *kilil* administration moved to Gode, a remote backwater in the heart of the Ogaden clan homeland. In an audaciously provocative gesture, the flag of the Somali *kilil* was graced with the five pointed star, the symbol of Somali nationalism.

The assembly elected an executive council of nineteen, in which the Ogaden clan was represented by at least fifteen members belonging to three parties (ONLF 12, WSDP 2, Tadamun), while the Issa clan had only one representative.[6] Abdilahi Mohamed Sadi was elected chairman of the executive council, that is, as head of the *kilil* administration. Abdilahi's deputy was Siad Badrie Mohammed (ONLF), and the assembly secretary was Mahdi Ahmad Warsame (Horyal). This untried administration faced the daunting task of establishing a government in a region that had been under military rule for decades. The few civil servants that worked in the region were highlanders, most of whom left when the regime in Addis Ababa changed, leaving a skeleton staff of about 100 employees. Movable state assets in the region had been thoroughly looted, buildings were burned and records destroyed. Insecurity reigned in many parts, especially along the contested borders with Oromia and Afar. Abdilahi and members of the executive council spent months in Addis Ababa recruiting Somali staff and searching for assets assigned to the region under the previous regime. They were dumbfounded to find records showing a wealth of assets that had never been delivered, and state posts that were budgeted for but never filled. They began recruiting Somali professionals – policemen, teachers, medics, technicians, clerks – to staff the administration. The federal government gave an initial grant of six million birr, most of which went for hotel and other expenses in Addis Ababa.

Meanwhile, the other clans were mobilising to depose the Ogaden dominated administration. The move was coordinated in Addis Ababa by

[5] *Ethiopian Herald* 26 January 1993.

[6] Tadamun was a religious party founded by Suleiman Ahmed, a Gadabursi, who later founded Amud University in Borama, Somaliland.

a cabal of Somali who held important posts in the federal government. It included Abdul Majid Hussein (Ishaq), Minister of Economic Development and Cooperation, Samsudin Ahmed (Gadabursi), Vice Minister of Mineral Resources and Energy, and Abdi Aden Mohamed (Ogaden), Vice Minister of Health.

Abdilahi, who did not speak Amharigna, did little to gain the trust of the EPRDF. He kept harping on the right to self-determination and the possibility of secession, refused to drop the 'liberation' tag from the ONLF name, to change its name from Ogaden to Somali, or to change the Front into a party. At the same time, he was losing support from the hardliners in the ONLF led by Sheikh Ibrahim Abdallah. Intra-Ogaden clan rivalries also played a role in his downfall. When he was accused, along with the secretary of the Executive Council of embezzlement – issuing trading licenses illegally and for personal profit – thirteen members of his executive council turned against him and resigned. Abdilahi was removed in August after seven months in office. He was arrested in October 1993, brought to Addis Ababa and kept in prison until June 1994, when he was released and went abroad.

The fate of the first administration set a pattern that has been followed faithfully ever since and left the Somali *kilil* in limbo without real governance for two decades. Delayed, incomplete and disorderly elections produced contested results and short-lived administrations that collapsed amidst charges of embezzlement and criminal behaviour, the incarceration of leading officials and their subsequent release without benefit of judicial process – an experience that did not prevent some of them returning to office at a later time. In the process, the region gained an unenviable reputation for swallowing federal subsidies that vanished without a trace; for its unwillingness to follow national policies and guidelines set by the EPRDF; and its inability to promote meaningful development in any field.

A new *kilil* executive was chosen in August 1993, headed by Hassan Jire Qalinle (Aulihan/Ogaden), a former pilot in the air wing of the police force in Somalia. He had been elected in Gode as a member of the WSDP and then switched to the ONLF. Ahmed Ali Dahir (Rer Ishaq/Ogaden), former head of finance in the national police force of Somalia, became vice chairman, and Eiid Tahir Farah (Ishaq), who had been a member of the SNM in Somaliland, became secretary of the executive council. The new leadership set about staffing the administration and the local school system. Following federal government directives, it appointed the same number of teachers in every zone, regardless of the number of schools in existence. Thus, Fik Zone with only one school in operation got the same number as Jijiga Zone with its 53 schools. Most of the teachers were unqualified. In 1996, all of them were re-examined and many were dismissed.

Constitution-making for the *kilil* took place in 1994, and the right of secession was the hottest issue debated. The ONLF decided it was time to put the issue to the test. It issued a declaration in late January in favour of self-determination for 'Ogadenia', and asked for a meeting of the *kilil* assembly to discuss it. A week later, ten other Somali organisations denounced the declaration, attributing it to Al Itihad Al Islami. The ONLF central committee responded with a statement in support of its confrontational policy.[7] Thus, early in the life of the new regime, the issue of secession emerged as the litmus test of the Somali political mind-set in Ethiopia, and Addis Ababa's criterion for assessing subordinate elite reliability in that region.

Rising tension over this issue soon led to violence. The federal security branch had not relaxed its vigilance in a region where it had long exercised joint control with the military. The activities of local politicians were closely monitored, and army units were posted throughout the Somali *kilil* ready to intervene. On 22 February 1994, ONLF chairman, Sheikh Ibrahim Abdallah was in Warder to address a political rally, when an attempt was made by soldiers to detain him. Fighting broke out and dozens of people were killed, including senior ONLF officials. Sheikh Ibrahim escaped and went into hiding. The rift within the ONLF between those who favoured working with the EPRDF and those who opted for secession now widened rapidly amid bloodshed. Several prominent Ogaden politicians were killed by federal forces in 1994, including the *woreda* administrator of Kebridehar, Mohamed Omar Tubee, his deputy, Deq Mohamud Arab, the deputy zone administrator of Kebridehar, Abdulahi Qani, the mayor of Gode, Mirad Leyli Sigale, his deputy, Mukhtar Aden Geedan, and the president of the Degehabur zonal court, Dhuux Ziyad Hassan.

The situation was spinning out of control as the *kilil* assembly, meeting temporarily in Jijiga on 24 March 1994, discussed a proposal asking for a referendum on secession. Those who opposed the move abstained for fear of offending Somali opinion, and the assembly resolved to form a committee to negotiate self-determination with the federal government. A letter was sent to inform Addis Ababa, whose reaction was swift. The *kilil* president was summoned to the capital; he was dismissed by the same *kilil* assembly in Gode on 30 April 1994. 'Preventing the people of the region from enjoying the benefits of the transitional period', was the stated cause.[8] After nine months in office, Hassan Jire Qalinle went straight to prison, accompanied by his deputy and eight members of the *kilil* assembly, including Sheikh Abdinassir and the mayor of Gode, Shukriya Yasin.

Hassan Jire was succeeded in July 1994 by Abdurahman Ugas Mohammed Qani, who had no party affiliation. Ahmed Makahil Hussein (ONLF) was his deputy, and Eiid Tahir Farah (Ishaq) stayed on as secretary of the executive council. Pressure was building on the administration from the non-Ogaden clans to move the capital to Jijiga. Abdurahman Ugas opposed moving the capital outside the Ogaden clan homeland, and in a radio interview denied that such a move was being considered. Pressure for the move came from the Prime Minister's Office, with a threat to split the Somali *kilil* in two separate regions. At

[7] *Ethiopian Herald* 25 March 1994.
[8] *Ethiopian Herald* 9 April 1994.

the end of the year, all *kilil* bureau heads were dismissed by the executive council for 'corruption', and Abdurahman himself was sacked for being 'an obstacle to carrying out development projects'.[9] He had lasted five months, and while in office lost several members of his family in clashes with soldiers in Gode. He avoided imprisonment by going into hiding.

The Ethiopian Somali Democratic League (ESDL)

The EPRDF had already taken the first step to forge unity among the non-Ogaden clans in order to counter the ONLF. The man chosen for this task was Abdul Majid Hussein (Ishaq), a former student activist and long time international civil servant, who was then serving as federal Minister of Economic Development and Cooperation. He had no prior involvement in Somali politics, but with Addis Ababa's backing he became the leading Somali politician in Ethiopia.

Somali politicians and elders were summoned to a meeting in Harar during the first week of February 1994 to be addressed by the then President Meles Zenawi. He pointedly told them that the right of self-determination is 'exercised by the people and the nation, not a political party or a clan'; the standard response whenever this issue is raised in Ethiopia. At the conclusion of the meeting in Harar, the politicians and elders were bussed to the Hurso military base near Dire Dawa where, to the surprise of many, the ESDL held its founding congress, an event attended by Prime Minister Tamrat Layne.[10] Abdul Majid became chairman of the new party. The ESDL was conceived as the merger of eleven clan factions, represented in its central committee according to clan size.

Worried by the political divisions in their clan, manifested in the rivalry between the WSDP, ONLF and Al Itihad Al Islami, and also by the widening confrontation with the federal government, Ogaden elders convened a 'Peace and Unity Conference of the Somali Nation' in Kebridehar, in January 1994. The elders sought to lay down rules that would guide political activity in the approach to the 1995 elections. They told Al Itihad Al Islami to sever relations with its parent movement in Somalia, to expel all outsiders from its ranks and to disarm. Likewise, the ONLF was told to disarm and to change its name according to EPRDF directives. ONLF leadership was characteristically divided. Two members of its central committee, Abdirazak Tibba and Bashir Abdi Hassen, spoke in favour of participation in the elections and were expelled from the organisation. Days later, the ONLF announced its decision to take part in the elections, but asked for a postponement, international supervision, release of political prisoners, and a ten kilometre buffer zone between its own and government forces. The EPRDF countered with two demands: the ONLF should declare publicly that its members were Ethiopians and

[9] *Ethiopian Herald* 6 December 1994.

[10] 'League' was a reference to the Somali Youth League, the first Somali nationalist organization.

send its fighters to designated camps.

The split in the ONLF was made official soon afterwards, when the secessionist wing led by Sheikh Ibrahim Abdallah announced a resumption of the armed struggle. Sheikh Ibrahim himself returned to Saudi Arabia, and other leaders dispersed abroad. The following year, the ONLF burned its political bridges by signing agreements with the Oromo Liberation Front, the Islamic Front for the Liberation of Oromia and Al Itihad Al Islami, to work together for the overthrow of the regime in Addis Ababa. A so-called 'legal wing' comprising those who still thought it possible to work with the EPRDF remained in the region. At a meeting in Harar held in May 1995, the ONLF 'legal wing' dismissed the leadership in exile for 'provoking conflict', and formed a new central committee of forty-seven members. Bashir Abdi Hassan became chairman, Khadar Mualim his deputy and Adan Osman secretary. When Bashir went abroad soon afterwards, the leadership fell to Khadar.

After two postponements in the Somali *kilil*, national elections were held in June 1995. The ESDL enjoyed the full backing of Addis Ababa, and financial support – government and private – from Djibouti. The 'legal wing' of the ONLF complained repeatedly of harassment, and the National Elections Board twice warned *kilil* officials not to obstruct the registration of its candidates. The announcement of the results was delayed for more than a month. The results were challenged in four constituencies, and invalidated in several polling stations where the ballot boxes had arrived full before voting started, or had disappeared after the event. Confusion was compounded when the ESDL claimed victory before the official results were declared, and rushed to call a meeting of the new *kilil* assembly in Jijiga. Later, the National Elections Board annulled the results in four districts, three of which had been won by ESDL. When the dust finally settled, the 'legal wing' of the ONLF held 30 seats in the *kilil* assembly whose size had been enlarged to 139, and only one seat in the executive council. Ahmed Makahil Hussein (Reere Amaadin/Ogaden), who had been acting *kilil* chairman since the dismissal of Abdurahman Ugas Mohammed Qani in December 1994, refused to recognise the election results, to vacate his office, or to move the *kilil* capital to Jijiga. Arrested for 'carrying arms', he was sentenced to seven years. His stint in office had lasted some fifteen months.

The next *kilil* chairman was Eiid Tahir Farah (Ishaq), who had served as secretary of the *kilil* executive council under the two previous administrations, before participating in the founding of the ESDL. Abdilahi Hassen Mohammed 'Luqubuur' (Ogaden, ESDL) was vice chairman, and Mohammed Aden Bille was secretary of the executive council. The capital was moved to Jijiga at last, where the new assembly met in March 1996 to adopt a constitution; a copy of the draft prepared by the EPRDF and adopted by all *kilil* in the country. Article 11 which ordained the separation of church and state caused a stir, but was approved.

The ESDL proved to be a fragile clan coalition kept together mainly by its chairman, Abdul Majid Hussein, whose close ties with the EPRDF leadership gave him high stature among Somali politicians. Even so, for fear of providing a venue for factionalism, the League did not hold a congress for more than two years after its founding, and there were few central committee meetings at that time. In August 1995, three central committee members were dismissed for 'making statements contrary to the League's stand'.[11] In December 1996, the vice chairman of the *kilil*, Abdilahi Hassen Mohammed 'Luqubuur', was dismissed 'for failing to discharge his responsibilities, for inclination towards clannishness, and for obstructing the close working relationship between the *kilil* administration and the national defence force.'[12] The security situation deteriorated markedly in 1996-7. A series of bomb attacks on hotels in Addis Ababa for which Al Itihad Al Islami claimed credit peaked with the attempted assassination of Abdul Majid Hussein in Addis Ababa in July 1996; miraculously he survived six bullet wounds. A series of arrests of Somali political figures accused of complicity in this crime followed, including members of the *kilil* assembly and the hapless Abdinassir Sheikh Aden once more.

A move to oust Eiid Tahir, allegedly instigated by his deputy, Mahdi Ayub Guled, occurred in October 1997, when fourteen members of the executive council voted to remove him. This occurred while Abdul Majid was abroad, and was sanctioned by the Secretary of the ESDL, Ahmed Samsudin. Upon his return, Abdul Majid denounced the 'coup', and called successive meetings of the League's central committee and the *kilil* assembly, but was unable to reverse the decision. Pressure from Addis Ababa and complex manoeuvres then succeeded in compelling the *kilil* assembly to lift the immunity of the fourteen dissidents, thirteen of who were arrested, while one fled abroad. The thirteen were kept in prison for two and a half years. In December 1997, sixteen ESDL members, including the party's Secretary, Shamsudin Ahmed, then Ethiopia's ambassador to Djibouti, were dismissed from the central committee for 'acts against the democratic system', and Eiid Tahir and his deputy were removed from their posts. Eiid's tenure had lasted nearly two years. Afterwards, he too was accused of corruption and sent to prison.

The Somali Peoples Democratic Party (SPDP)

In June 1998, the ONLF 'legal wing' merged with the ESDL to form the Somali Peoples Democratic Party (SPDP), with Abdul Majid Hussein as chairman and Khadar Mualim (ONLF) as vice chairman. Both factions were required to undergo purification through self-criticism (*gim gima*), and hundreds of their members were purged as a result. A reshuffled executive council elected Khadar Mualim to succeed Eiid Tahir as chairman of the *kilil*, Riyaleh Hamud (Issa) as his deputy, and Sultan Ibrahim (Garire) as secretary. Although his relationship with the federal government was not without problems, Khadar was to last longer in office than any of his predecessors – from October 1997 to September 2000. Khadar's father, a

[11] *Ethiopian Herald* 2 August 1995.

[12] Ethiopian News Agency 12 April 1996.

well-known religious teacher, had been killed and his mother shot and crippled by Haile Selassie's soldiers. Given his ONLF background, he was distrusted by the EPRDF, and he repeatedly clashed with its representatives who acted as political and technical advisers to the *kilil* administration. In the approach to the 2000 elections, he was involved in a public row with Addis Ababa over the under-representation of the Somali in the federal legislature. With the same population size, Tigray had thirty eight and the Somali twenty-three seats. In the 2000 elections, the SPDP took all but a dozen seats in the *kilil* assembly.[13]

The following years witnessed the unravelling of the SPDP, and the complete collapse of government in the Somali *kilil.* Several factors contributed to this denouement. One was the absence at the helm of Abdul Majid Hussein, who was sent to represent Ethiopia in the United Nations. Mohamud Dirir Geddi, then federal Minister of Transport and Communications, was chosen to succeed him as party leader. An Issa from the town of Aishia on the Addis Ababa–Djibouti rail line, he had lost his father in the massacre of the townspeople carried out by the Imperial Bodyguard in 1960, and had been a member of the WSLF in the late 1970s. A three-way leadership split now paralysed the SPDP, pitting rival factions led by Mohamud Dirir, Khadar Mualim and Abdirashid Dulune Rafle in a public struggle for power, which saw unprecedented public demonstrations in Jijiga. Khadar Mualim lost the battle, the *kilil* chairmanship, and spent time in prison, resurfacing in 2007 as state minister in the Ministry of Labour. He was replaced in September 2000 by Abdirashid Dulune Rafle (Rer Makahil/Ogaden), then federal vice-minister of Water Resources. His father, Dulune Rafle Guled had spent many years in prison and internal exile under the imperial regime. Abdi Jibril Abubakar (Issa) became vice-chairman, a post that had become an Issa prerogative.

During 2001-2002, SPDP leaders spent months in Addis Ababa undergoing self-criticism and listening to lectures by high officials, including Meles Zenawi. An immediate result was the expulsion of eight SPDP central committee members, including Khadar Mualim. In the spring of 2002, the central committee was enlarged from twenty-nine to forty-five members to bring in new blood. A third factor was the determination of the federal government to push through reforms that the Somali politicians were reluctant or unable to implement.

Abdirashid's tenure in office lasted two and three-quarter years, before he was accused of having links with 'anti-peace elements' and ousted in July 2003. More fortunate than his predecessors, he was not imprisoned, but returned to his previous post as federal vice minister of Water Resources, and was later sent to Japan as ambassador. Vice-chairman Abdi Jibril Abubakar became acting president, a post he retained until September 2005. This was a veritable political *saison morte* in the Somali *kilil*, when neither party nor government functioned in a meaningful sense. Symbolically, a chain was drawn across the entrance to the administration compound in Jijiga to keep vagrants from squatting in the buildings.

[13] Four women were candidates and two were elected.

*

In 2003, a team from the federal Anti-Corruption Commission sent to investigate the administration was astonished with the state of the accounts, but even more with the nonchalant attitude of the officials responsible for keeping them. 'Elsewhere they skim from the top, here they take the lot', remarked one team member. Embezzlement was the standard accusation against officials prior to their removal from office and sojourn in prison. Life in Jijiga prison, otherwise known as 'Ogaden prison' because so many members of that clan passed through its gates, was no great hardship. Former officials-turned-prison-inmates still commanded influence and respect, because it was always possible they could make a political comeback. Consequently, they enjoyed relative comfort and privileges, including a supply of chat and access to wives and family.

The pastoralist perspective concerning public funds is quite different from that of the highlanders. Respect for property in the lowlands is sanctioned by customary law and enforced by the threat of reprisal. Property outside the clan boundaries falls outside the scope of customary law and is not protected. The state is an alien institution, and its assets are not seen as protected property, since the pastoralists have no experience of commonality on that level, particularly when assets are not raised locally through taxation, but come in the form of subsidies from the federal government. The proper way to handle them is equitable distribution among the clans, and officials at every level come under intolerable pressure to conform to the pastoralist ethic.

'*Shehad*' is the traditional Somali practice of asking for money from a clansman who is in a position to give it. Neither embezzling nor begging, *shehad* is a reciprocal obligation. Elders are entitled to demand money and favours from officials whom they help put in office. A person who does not give *shehad* to his clan kin is called disdainfully '*faroud*' ('empty pockets'). If an official refuses *shehad* to an elder, the latter will declare 'this person does not belong to our clan anymore, he must be replaced.'

The ease with which Somali have always moved about in the Horn of Africa, making use of clan links rather than passports, and the effortless way that they take up government posts in the states of the region is legendary. The family of Sheikh Hassan Nuriye, a Gadabursi merchant from Dire Dawa, three of whose sons served in the 1980s as ambassadors of Ethiopia, Djibouti and Somalia respectively, is an often cited as an example.[14] The Somali refugee influx into Ethiopia in the early 1990s

[14] Sheikh Hassen Nuriye, a wealthy merchant of the Makahil/Rer Ugas/Gadabursi clan, married four women from different clans and fathered 13 sons and 6 daughters, who were born in various parts of the eastern Horn. Several sons were educated in Borama, Berbera and Dire Dawa, some went abroad for higher education and subsequently made careers in different states in the Horn. Adan Sheikh Hassen Nuriye served as Djibouti's Ambassador in the Middle East and in 2008 was an adviser to the president of Djibouti. Ismail Sheikh Hassen Nuriye joined the Ministry of Foreign Affairs in Ethiopia under Haile Selassie, and served as Ethiopia's Ambassador to Sudan and Libya under the Dergue. Mohammed

included many former officials of the Siad Barre regime. Not a few of the 'colonels', as they were dubbed locally, had found positions in the Somali *kilil* administration. When a law was passed giving Ethiopians in the diaspora the right to vote but not to stand for office, a further limitation was added in the Somali *kilil* for those who had served in the Siad Barre regime. In May 2003, fifty-two *kilil* assembly members were listed as such, but ultimately, only fourteen were suspended.

*

Officials in the newly established Ministry of Federal Affairs became exasperated with the failure of the Somali to implement the *woreda* empowerment programme. In contrast to the rest of the federation, the Somali had yet to establish an elected *woreda* administrative structure: lack of infrastructure and skilled manpower for an effective local administration was given as the reason. Federal officials suspected the real reason was the politicians' unwillingness to lose control of the *kilil* budget. SPDP leaders and cadre were summoned repeatedly to the national capital and federal officials commuted to Jijiga. Matters reached a point in 2004 where the federal government had the House of the Federation pass a resolution threatening to invoke Article 62 of the federal constitution, which sanctions federal intervention 'if any state, in violation of this Constitution, endangers the constitutional order'. The resolution accused the Somali administration of having 'never shown any commitment to solve the longstanding problems of the region...So far there is no bureaucratic setup and elected legitimate government at *woreda* level.' The Ministry of Federal Affairs raised the threat of installing 'a provisional leadership…capable of ensuring peace, justice and development…as the last alternative to the crisis'.[15]

The first step was to hold elections for *woreda* officials, and these were held for the first time in January 2004. There was inevitable confusion and conflict over the results. Even the number of *woreda* was in dispute. The National Elections Board recognised forty-nine and conducted elections in forty-six, while the *kilil* administration recognised fifty-one *woreda*. No matter: 'the discrepancy did not cause any significant problem', according to a paper released by a relieved Ministry of Federal Affairs.

National elections followed in May 2005. Once more, they were delayed in the Somali *kilil* until mid-August. The sensational gains scored by the opposition parties on that occasion put the EPRDF on the defensive, and gave the delayed Somali election unusual importance for the ruling Front. By this time, the regime had come to appreciate the political importance of traditional authority in the pastoralist zone and sought to enlist elder support. The traditional Somali council of elders, the *Guurti*, was introduced at the end of 1999. A hierarchy of advisory *Guurti* councils

[14] (cont.) Sheikh Hassen Nuriye worked in the Ministry of Planning and Foreign Affairs in Somalia under Siad Barre, and served as Somalia's ambassador in several countries in the second half of the 1980s. In 2008, he was Somaliland's Liaison Officer in Addis Ababa.

[15] *Meleekte Federal*, Journal of the Ministry of Federal Affairs. (1 July 2004: 38).

was established to parallel the administrative hierarchy from *woreda* to *kilil;* members are chosen by the elders themselves with proportional clan representation.

In June Somali elders were invited for the first time to meet with Prime Minister Meles Zenawi in Addis Ababa to express their views. They did not mince their words. 'We are happy the opposition has the EPRDF by the throat,' one of them said, 'but we don't want it dead', meaning they appreciated the fact that the ruling party needed Somali support. 'A dog barks not only to defend his master but himself as well', said another, meaning Somali support of EPRDF was not without self interest. Others complained of heavy-handed federal interference in their region. 'We want a government chosen by us, not one chosen by you', was their succinct demand.

The SPDP was in total disarray as elections approached. The frequent changes of leadership had earned it popular contempt. In a meeting for the women of Jijiga Zone held by the SPDP, the male zonal administrator was berated by the audience. 'Dogs who fight among themselves, cannot defend themselves against hyenas', quoted one woman. 'Why should I talk to you now?' said another: 'You will not be here tomorrow.'[16] A report on another meeting noted:

> Undoubtedly, governance was the low point of the discussions at the meeting. A public outcry echoed from the walls of the meeting hall whenever governance came up. The highlights of the public discontent levelled at the regional administration were poor service delivery, shameless corruption, abuse of power, misappropriation of the fiscal budgets, lack of transparency and accountability, indifference to regional security and clan conflicts, and arrogance and irresponsiveness to the concerns of the citizens.[17]

Officials from the Ministry of Federal Affairs, SPDP leaders and prominent Somali elders gathered in Dire Dawa at the end of July 2005 to prepare for the elections. The first task was to draw a list of candidates that would have general acceptance, in other words, clan support. In Somali political practice, this requires striking a fine balance among clans and sub-clans to ensure fair representation for the greater number. This avoids the threat of independent candidates, more than 500 of whom had appeared in the *woreda* elections the previous year. In addition to the clan calculus, certain criteria imposed by the EPRDF had to be accommodated. The list for the *kilil* assembly had to include diploma holders (50%), elders (25%), women (15%), and SPDP cadres (10%). Provision also had to be made for a dozen so-called 'minority' clans.

The election results showed the clan formula had worked to near perfection. All twenty-three seats in the federal House of Peoples Representatives went to the SPDP, and the size of the winners' vote proved the success of the formula. No less than 14 of them received more than 90% of the votes cast, and only one fell below 70 per cent. The SPDP also

[16] Attended by the author 17 March 2002.

[17] 'Report of Regional Consultation', July, 2005. Jijiga: Bureau of Finance and Economic Development. (p.10).

swept the *kilil* assembly seats, save for nine that went to independents. The voting pattern reflected the arrangement reached at clan level prior to the elections. In most districts, all of the SPDP candidates received roughly the same number of votes. Hudet district in Liben Zone was typical. It is home to four Gerri sub-clans: Adola, Furkesa, Ali, and Aser. They split the four *kilil* assembly seats assigned to the district among themselves, and the votes received by each candidate ranged from 36,083 and 36,223. Likewise the number of votes for the five winning candidates in Shinile district ranged from 28,645 to 28,910. Conversely, success for independent candidates indicated instances where the clan formula did not work, due to local disagreements.

The clan formula was used also to allocate posts at the *woreda* administration level, and here it served to compensate smaller clans for losing out at the higher levels of political office. Twenty Gerri clans living in Moyale *woreda* are divided into two sections, Tuff and Quran. Tuff has eleven subsections, of which two, Ali and Adola, are dominant. Likewise, Quran has nine sub-sections, of which two, Asher and Furkesa, are dominant. Moyale *woreda* is part of Filtu electoral district, which sends one representative to the House of Peoples Representatives in Addis Ababa. The SPDP candidate, Issak Ibrahim Ajei 'Hashi', a Tuff, took no less than 99.37 percent of the votes. Moyale *woreda* sends six representatives to the *kilil* assembly in Jijiga. Of these, Tuff got three, Kuran two, and the Gabbra got one. To compensate the Kuran for having less in the *kilil* assembly, a Furkesa/Kuran was made zonal administrator, and an Adola/Tuff became his deputy. Likewise, the *woreda* council speakership went to an Ali/Tuff, and the deputy speakership to an Asher/Quran.

The next task was to reorganise the SPDP. Politicians and elders gathered in Jijiga during the last week of September 2005 for this purpose, under the watchful eyes of officials from the Ministry of Federal Affairs. The reorganisation of the party was done in exemplary fashion, once more using the clan formula. Every *woreda* branch was asked to propose five to seven persons, including women, for the central committee. A list of five criteria was issued which included 'fair clan distribution.' A meeting of some 600 persons chose the membership of the central committee from the list of submitted names. Its 75 members (the old one had 45 members) included ten women and twelve representatives of minority clans. The central committee then elected an expanded executive committee of 21 (the old one had 11 members), comprising two representatives from each of the region's nine zones, plus three women. Several former leaders were readmitted to the party and elected to the central committee, but none made it to the executive committee, which met on the last day in closed session to choose the party chairman.

Ali Abdi Shaqah (Gursum/Ishaq) was the new SPDP chairman. A university graduate who had worked in Asmara and spoke Tigrigna, he had been onetime head of the *kilil* bureau of Finance and Planning, from where he had been dismissed and sent to prison in 2002, staying nearly three years before emerging in time for the 2005 elections. He was flanked by two Civil Service College graduates: Daud Mohammed Ali (Makahil/

Ogaden) who became party vice chairman, and Ahmed Shide (Gurrah) who became secretary. The SPDP congress ended with the election of the *kilil* administration. The top posts went to veteran politicians. Abdilahi Hassen Mohammed 'Luqubuur' (Bah Gerri/Ogaden) was chosen to head the regional administration. A former journalist and speaker of Arabic, with a Tigray wife, he had served as *kilil* deputy chairman in the first ESDL administration, and had been dismissed in 1996. Abdi Jibril Abubaker (Issa) retained the vice chairmanship. Ali Mohammed 'Kunaye' (Gerri) was chosen speaker of the regional assembly, with Sultan Abdurahman Bede (Abaskul) a former assembly speaker as his deputy. The following day, the *kilil* assembly met in a brief session to endorse the party choices.

The painstaking arrangements that went in sharing out offices among the clans in the wake of the 2005 elections did not bring stability to the administration of the Somali *kilil*. In fact, the circulation of the elite resumed immediately thereafter. SPDP chairman Abdi Ali Shaqah was the first to go in 2007, and was succeeded by Daud Mohamed who departed a year later to be replaced by Ali Abdufatah Sheikh Abdulahi (Abaskul). Daud took over the chairmanship of the *kilil* administration, a position vacated by Abdilahi Hassen Mohammed 'Luqubuur' who had been wounded in an assassination attempt in May 2007. Daud lasted in that position until 2009, and was succeeded by Abdi Mohammed Omer (Ogaden) until then bureau head of justice, security and administration. Most posts in the *kilil* administration also changed hands. First to go was Mahdi Ayoub, the security chief who was removed in 2006 and imprisoned on charges of 'having links with anti-peace elements.' Ali Kounaye, speaker of the *kilil* assembly, was accused of corruption and fled the country, leaving his wife in prison. The Auditor General was replaced, the head of the HIV/AIDS bureau was arrested for allegedly attempting to bribe the *kilil* chairman, and several *woreda* administrators were accused of sundry infractions and removed.

The achievements of self government in the Somali *kilil* were definitely modest. A number of institutions were founded, including a teacher training institute, a health college and a management institute. The University of Jijiga opened in 2007. Of the 750 students admitted that year, only three were Somali. This reflected both the fact that the *kilil* had only one functioning secondary school, and the federal policy of mixing nationalities in higher education. Jijiga was graced with a new airport, and the 100km road linking it to Harar was finally paved. In contrast with the Afar, no land was commandeered in the Somali *kilil* by the federal or *kilil* administration. Land for the airport and the university had to be bought from the local Bartire clan, who put a price on every chat tree planted on it. The *woreda* empowerment programme was supported by the UNDP with a three-year pilot project in three *woreda* including Jijiga. Here it ran into the familiar problem of the unaccountability of disbursed funds, leading to the dismissal of the entire Jijiga *woreda* administrative council and several officials in Gode *woreda* in 2007.

Return of the ONLF

For a decade after the break with the EPRDF in 1994, little was heard of the ONLF. It was in 1998 that the leadership gathered for a meeting and formalised its organisation. Central and executive committees were selected, and Mohamed Omar Osman, replaced Sheikh Abdallah Mah as ONLF chairman. He had had military training in Egypt and the Soviet Union, and had been a member of the central committee of Siad Barre's Somali Nationalist Party, before becoming head of the Somali Republic's navy. Little was known about the ONLF's structure in the field, if only because that was rudimentary and informal. Manpower and logistical support was provided by the Ogaden clan, and the fighters were mostly pastoralist youth who harassed the Ethiopian army as a part-time activity, without abandoning care of their herds. What contact they had with the dispersed ONLF leadership abroad was tenuous. Only one of its members, Mohammed Abdi Yassin, stayed in the Ogaden during this period.

The leadership of the ONLF, most of whose members resided in London, concentrated its efforts on raising its profile internationally. To do this, they had to disentangle themselves from parallel rebellions with overlapping constituencies in the region. Firstly, they had to distance their cause from the quest of pan-Somalism, because 'interference from Somali regimes and Ethiopian propaganda helped the misconception of the international community which considers the Ogaden as a disputed territory between Somalia and Ethiopia.'[18] Secondly, they had to distance the ONLF from Islamist movements in the Horn that had become the target of the West's 'war on terror'. Addis Ababa deliberately confused the ONLF with Al Itihad Al Islami, in order to include it in the wider context of the Islamist threat to Ethiopia. 'The ONLF is a national secular organisation', an ONLF message sent to the Department of State in Washington avowed. 'It was never supported by certain organisations because they accused us of "secularism" (*cilmaani*). ONLF has no links to al-Qaida, nor does it intend to establish any because it is not fighting a religious war.'[19] Thirdly, they had to refute the accusation that it represented only the Ogaden clan. An ONLF document submitted to the European Union declared: 'ONLF rejects tribalism and strongly believes that clannish forms of organisation that have become the bane of the Somali nation are not in the interest of the Ogaden Somalis, and rejects outright any attempt to portray the ONLF in terms of clan politics.'[20]

Even so, the refusal to drop the 'Ogaden' tag from its name made it practically impossible for the ONLF to shed its clan image. If nothing else, it seriously limited its appeal to other clans whose young men might

[18] 'ONLF Position Paper' 9 June 1995. See also Abdi M. Abdullahi (2007).
[19] Dated 29 April 2007.
[20] Dated 15 December 2007.

otherwise be tempted to join it. The other clans accused it of seeking to impose Ogaden clan rule, and Addis Ababa capitalised on this by recruiting clan militias to fight the rebels. The reasoning given by the ONLF is legalistic. Ogaden, they argue, is the name of a territory that has been the subject of international treaties; therefore, it has recognised status in international law as a colonial issue. A change of name would annul this status, and undermine the effectiveness of its appeal to international institutions and world powers. In private, they add that their strategy is to seek a referendum that would lead, after a transition period, to unification with Somalia. In that wider context there could be no question of Ogaden domination.[21]

Gradually the ONLF force in the field acquired a rudimentary organisation with the rebel units grouped into four territorial divisions. The Gorgon (Eagles) division operates north of Fiq, the Dufan (Storm) in the Jarer region south of Degehabur, the Danab (Lightning) in the south between Warder and Chilabo, and the Hangan (Struggle) in the southwest as far as Moyale. Insurgent activity is most intense in five *woreda* – Degehabur, Fik, Gode, Korahe, and Warder – where the Ogaden clan is dominant. The rebels claim their basic needs are provided willingly by the population, and their weapons are captured from government forces. A field operation in 2007 did more than anything else to raise the ONLF's profile. This was a daring attack on a petroleum exploration site operated by a Chinese company. Sited near a village called Obolo in Degehabur district, it was guarded by Ethiopian soldiers when it was attacked by the Dufan division with a large force, at dawn, on 24 April 2007. The attack killed sixty-five Ethiopians and nine Chinese. Seven Chinese and a number of Ethiopians were taken captive, and were later released through the mediation of elders.[22]

The affair won the ONLF international publicity and name recognition. Foreign newsmen made their way undercover to the region, while reports and films of the insurgents surfaced on the Internet. The frantic reaction of the federal government kept the story going. It closed off the area below Jijiga, stopping transport, trade and communications, and ordered all foreign organisations and personnel out of it.

Past experience shows the behaviour of the Ethiopian soldiers is calculated to exacerbate rebellion rather than quell it. Surprisingly, given the experience and political sophistication of the EPRDF, little has changed in this respect. The Somali are continuously harassed by interrogations, searches, and army raids in pursuit of elusive insurgents. They are routinely imprisoned on suspicion and sometimes tortured to extract information. In instances where the rebels inflict casualties, the soldiers take savage revenge on the local population. Reports of atrocities and near famine in the isolated area circulated worldwide, and persuaded the

[21] Abdirahman Mahdi, ONLF foreign spokesman interviewed in Exeter and London in 2009.

[22] Thirty-two of the civilians killed were Somali

United Nations to send an official to investigate.[23] The government began sponsoring clan militias called *tadaki* to combat the insurgents, and forced local officials and civil servants to prove their loyalty by taking part in counter-insurgency operations. Thus, war once more claimed this region, as it had under previous Ethiopian regimes.

More than two decades after its formation, the founders of the ONLF retain the top leadership posts under Mohamed Omar Osman. Mohamed Ismail Omar and Abdulkadir Hassan Hirmoge were the two vice-chairmen and Abdirahman Mahdi was foreign spokesman. In 2006, a faction led by Mohamed Sirad Dolal broke away. Dolal had been the public face of the ONLF in London for years and also managed the movement's radio station named Horiyo in Germany. Fifteen members of the central committee, including Dolal, were dismissed. Dolal went inside the Ogaden afterwards where he was killed, reportedly by Ethiopian soldiers.

Somali and their neighours

The Somali border with Afar and Oromia forms a huge arc along which conflict was endemic long before federalism was instituted in Ethiopia. The arc marks the geographical meeting point of three pastoralist nations – Somali, Oromo, Afar – which historically pushed against one another in a perennial quest for territory containing pasture and water. Bigger, stronger and more aggressive, the Oromo and Somali eventually squeezed the Afar into the arid depths of the Rift Valley, then fought each other to a standstill approximately where their common border rests today. However, perennial warfare could not be sustained even in the pastoralist habitat, and the frontier communities often worked out symbiotic arrangements that allowed them to live together. A degree of assimilation often followed, with inter-marriage, multi-lingualism and cultural borrowing. The result in many areas was cultural blending and identity ambivalence. People did not think of themselves as Somali or Oromo, if only because the issue had not arisen nor the question asked.

The issue was raised suddenly and the question posed with great urgency, when it came to demarcate *kilil* boundaries in the federal state. Now people were asked to declare their 'nationality', and a great deal hung on the answer they gave because it could affect their rights to land. Generally, language was taken as the identity marker and it worked fairly well among sedentary communities. On the other hand, it posed serious problems among pastoralist groups with hybrid cultures and ambivalent identities occupying the interface between the Somali, Oromo and Afar. Here, language was not the only, or even the most salient, identity marker

[23] 'From information gathered, it was apparent to the mission that the human rights and protection situation for the civilian population in the areas of military operation is alarming and requires urgent attention.' 'Report on the findings from the United Nations Humanitarian Assessment Mission to the Somali Region, Ethiopia' (30 August–5 September 2007).

since bilingualism is common. 'When discussing linguistic categories one has to resist the temptation...to equate languages with people,' (Schlee & Shongolo 1995: 9). This was borne out by the example of the Gerri pastoralists who live on the junction of the Ethiopian, Somali and Kenyan borders and claim land in all three states. Some of them use the dialect spoken by their Borana neighbours to the west, others speak the language of the Rahanweyn clan, their neighbours to the south, and others yet speak Gerri Kofar, a language distinct but very close to Rahanweyn. It is not surprising that the Gerri were caught in a vicious conflict over identity and territory that has yet to be resolved.

The conjunction of language, nationality identity and territory made for an explosive compound when it was politicised and used to determine citizenship and rights to land. Before the EPRDF had time to consolidate its control, a host of armed factions converged in the lowlands to seize territories they claimed belonged to nationalities they represented. It was here that great pressure was put on people to declare themselves Somali, Oromo or Afar, a distinction that had not concerned them till then. Most had no perception of identity that transcended the local territorial and clan boundaries. As Schlee and Shongolo remarked of one area, 'the term Oromo was simply unknown to many ordinary people. One was Borana or Gerri or Gabbra' (ibid.: 11). 'The question of whether one is Oromo or Somali now has a political significance which it never had in the past… Numerous small groups who are Oromo by one set of criteria (language, former political affiliation) and Somali by another (clanship, religion) are now forced to identify with one or another. Definitions are no longer scholarly exercises, but instruments of inclusion and exclusion with consequences like expulsion and killing' (Schlee & Shongolo 1995: 8-9).

A prime bone of contention was Dire Dawa, the second largest city in the country (2007 pop. 232,000) and the meeting point of three nationalities – Somali, Afar, Oromo – all of which claimed the city as their own. In recent decades, the Afar were displaced from the area by the Issa Somali, and their claim lapsed. The Issa make up the bulk of the population in Shinile Zone adjacent to the town, and they spill into Dire Dawa itself. The same is true of the Gurgura, a clan that speaks Oromo but claims to be Somali. In 1991, before the EPRDF forces gained effective control of the eastern region, rival armed movements fought for control inside and around the town. With EPRDF backing, the OPDO was first to arrive and to claim it for the Oromo *kilil*, while the Somali initially chose it as capital for their *kilil*, a choice that was vetoed by the federal government. To pre-empt inter-*kilil* conflict, the EPRDF placed Dire Dawa under federal jurisdiction, and the town was administered by a five member appointed council; two members nominated by the OPDO, two by the SPDP, and one by the Amhara National Democratic Movement (ANDM) that represents a sizeable community of highlanders resident in the town. Later, the town was granted autonomy and has an elected administration.

The district and town of Babile (2007 pop. 17,000) on the Harar–Jijiga road was another flashpoint. The district is inhabited by several bilingual communities that speak Oromo and Somali and intermingled easily and extensively in the past. The OPDO appeared first to set up its own administration in Babile town, and was challenged by the ONLF and Al Itihad Al Islami on one side, and the IFLO on the other. The district's Hawiye Somali majority organised a militia of its own and a multi-sided clash ensued. The EPRDF supplied the Hawiye with weapons to fight off the IFLO, and later allowed them to set up their own separate town administration. Thus, Babile district emerged with a dual – Oromo, Somali – administration, each catering to each own constituency, a situation that created tension and occasional violence in the town, as well as insecurity on the Harar-Jijiga road that crosses the district. In 1994, the Regional Affairs Department in the Prime Minister's Office conducted an investigation polling people at the *kebele* level, and apportioned eight of the disputed *kebele* south of the town to the Somali *kilil*, and another thirty-four *kebele* plus Babile town itself to Oromia *kilil*. The Somali refused to accept the decision and continue to maintain their own separate administration in Babile,.

Miesso district was a third flashpoint in the inter-*kilil* boundary dispute. Located 215 km from Dire Dawa, it is crossed by both the railway line to Djibouti and the main road artery from Dire Dawa to Addis Ababa. Located on the edge of the Rift Valley, the district is inhabited by Oromo (Ittu, Alla, Noole, Obor) cultivators and agro-pastoralists, Somali (Hawiye, Jarso) agro-pastoralists on higher ground, and Issa Somali pastoralists on the lowland. Hawiye, the dominant group, lived peaceably among the Oromo whose language they speak in addition to Somali. Conflict was not unknown in the past, but was mostly between cultivators and pastoralists without ethnic connotations.

External intervention drove a wedge between these communities, beginning with the appearance of the WSLF and the subsequent Somali invasion in the 1970s. Anti-Somali hostility among the Oromo was directed against their Hawiye neighbours, group relations were strained and they began to draw apart. A Hawiye elder recalled:

> We lost our pasture land to farmers expanding into our areas between Mulu, Bordede and Miesso areas. Our grazing land was distributed to Oromo farmers by the Dergue government in line with the implementation of the agrarian reform and 'land to the tiller' proclamation.[24]

The Issa retaliated, expelling the Oromo, and forced the military regime to garrison the area. A battle between the army and the Issa in 1986 took the lives of fifty herders and thirty soldiers. Afterwards, many Issa left the area and moved close to the Djibouti border.

They returned after 1991 thirsting for revenge, and together with the Hawiye fought the Oromo along the length of the road from Afdem to Korra. Entire communities were displaced and refugees flocked to the town of Mieso. 'It used to be farmers expanding toward pastoral grazing areas, but our case in relation to Issa is different', complained an Oromo

[24] Cited in Ahmed Shide (n.d.: 33).

elder. 'We have lost our farm land to Issa pastoralists by force, and now they have changed it into grazing land...We have lost whole *kebele* areas to them.'[25] It took the federal government sometime to restore order in the area. By then, the dividing lines between ethnic groups were beginning to emerge, though they had yet to harden and divide them. Hawiye and Oromo continued to live together in hamlets like Asebot and Bordede. Like Babile, Miesso town had two rival – Oromo, Somali – administrations.

From Dire Dawa to Miesso the railway crosses the Shinile Zone of the Somali *kilil*, and all the railway stop towns – Hurso, Erer Gota, Bike, Afdem, Mulu – are inhabited by Issa Somali. From Miesso to Awash, a distance of 77km, the railway and road run parallel, and the towns – Asebot, Daima, Kora, Bordede – were inhabited by Hawiye Somali and Oromo and also attracted Issa pastoralists to their markets. The towns on the Miesso-Arba stretch of the road had significant economic potential as trade and transport centres. It was here that tensions reached a peak and resulted in bloodshed on several occasions in the beginning of the 21st century. In June 2001, Oromo raided Issa cattle when it crossed the Arba River between Bordede and Korra towns, and killed two Issa youths. In response, the Issa invaded Daima the same month and killed thirty-nine Oromo.

Community relations now became very strained, and the dividing line between Somali and Oromo widened. Pressure on people to declare an identity along 'nationality' lines became irresistible. Those who could not, or would not, risked becoming targets for both sides with no one to defend them. People who shared the same villages grew suspicious of each other, and many felt compelled to leave before they were attacked. Thus, a process of ethnic separation was well under way before the referendum in October 2004. Conditions were worse along the western boundary of the Somalil *kilil* and Oromia, from Fik to Moyale, where violent conflict was triggered by the collapse of the Dergue and continued intermittently for two decades. This is mainly pastoralist habitat occupied by Oromo groups – Arsi, Guji, Borana, Gabbra – and several Somali clans, including the Gerri. The border town of Moyale is the flashpoint here.

As a rule, the federal government encouraged the *kilil* administrations to resolve the thorny issue of boundary demarcation themselves. Where they proved unable to do so, it favoured the use of the referendum as the most democratic and effective method, and had the National Elections Board organise it. The process covered *kebele* located along the contested boundary and involved asking people to declare their 'nationality'. The choice of the majority decided which *kilil* the *kebele* would join, and the minority had to decide whether to accept the choice or to leave, relinquishing its rights to the land. In this sense, the referendum was the latest episode in an age old struggle over land, as a Somali elder pointed out: 'Now a permanent struggle over land ownership and its control is the biggest problem between Hawiye Somali and Oromo clans in the district. Previously we were living together' (Ahmed Shide n.d.: 37). The referen-

[25] Cited in Ahmed Shide (n.d.: 32).

dum took place in October 2004. It covered 424 *kebelle* located on the border from Babile to Moyale, of which Oromia took more than 350 and the Somali the rest. Oromia also took the towns of Babile and Miesso, while the referendum in Moyale was aborted. The first attempt at voter registration there was blatantly manipulated by the officials of both regions, and was declared invalid by the National Elections Board. A second attempt was also discounted, because each side tried to flood the town with voters from the surrounding areas. In the end, the attempt to hold a referendum was abandoned and the town remains divided. There are two Moyale *woreda*; one that belongs to Liben Zone in the Somali *kilil*, and another that belongs to Borana Zone in Oromia.

This was not the end of the story. On 7 July 2005, Somali warriors raided Miesso and clashed with Oromo policemen. Thirty people were killed and considerable damage was caused to property before the Somali were expelled. One day later, people who had chosen the Somali identity in the referendum were attacked and expelled from Assebot, some 3km from Miesso, by their Oromo neighbours; their huts were burned and their animals looted. A month later, fighting broke out over a lucrative customs checkpoint near the town, following which the Oromo invaded a Hawiye neighbourhood in Hardim and burned a hundred houses. A dozen people were killed, and the Hawiye fled to the Afar region, but returned to burn an Oromo hamlet near Bordede. The federal army intervened to quell the violence for a time, but the day after it withdrew fighting broke out in Bordede town between Hawiye and Oromo. The Oromo majority there was incensed when several hundred of their Hawiye neighbours declared themselves Somali in the referendum. Houses were burned, shops looted, a dozen people died, and the Hawiye fled abandoning their homes, fields and livestock. While Somali were being pushed out of the roadside towns and villages, Oromo were fleeing from the railway stop towns of Bike, Afdem and Mulu in Shinile Zone to congregate in Miesso.

The events following the referendum showed that the flashpoints of conflict are areas crossed by major transport routes lined with settlements, market centres and larger towns, where the contenders are neither peasants nor pastoralists, but the emerging urban strata involved in trade and the service sector whose material interests are linked with local administration.

> Local elites emerged on both sides that controlled the newly formed local government and instrumentalised the conflict for their elite interests...Both are now more interested in the control of the urban settlements and associated revenue raising opportunities, namely tax and customs. The boundary dispute became the focus for this conflict' (Ahmed Shide, n.d.: 36).

Summary

The relationship of the Ethiopian state with its Somali subjects under ethnic federalism is as volatile as it has been since the making of the empire. Unlike the Afar, where the EPRDF has been able to rely on a subservient and reliable local elite, the opposite is true of the Somali. The

Somali 'regional intellectuals' proved neither subservient nor reliable, or able to run the *kilil* administration. The *modus operandi* of administration in the Somali *kilil* is best described as the 'circulation of the elite'. The top post there changed hands no less than eleven times between 1992-2009, and nearly all *kilil* presidents exchanged office for a prison cell, from where they sometimes returned to office.

As the first decade of the 21st century wore on, signs of increasing activity by the ONLF spread a cloud of suspicion over all Somali in Ethiopia. Lurking in the minds of most highlanders is the suspicion that secession is dear to the hearts of these people, the local political class included. Most of them come from families with a history of Somali nationalist activity; many were members of the WSLF or ONLF at one time, and many lived, educated and worked in Somalia and still have close family connections there. The Somali are aware that Addis Ababa mistrusts and expects them to demonstrate faithfulness to the regime and loyalty to the state. Those who fail this test are given short shrift: '*Korka laga wattaa*' ('He was pushed from above') it is said, when someone is booted out of office. 'Having links with anti-peace elements' is the all-purpose accusation that lands many in prison. Despite the EPRDF's bold distinction between culture, nationality and citizenship, the Somali know that to qualify as 'Ethiopians' they must renounce the ties that bind them to their brothers across the border; for them something unimaginable. Recent cosmetic changes, for example, dropping the five pointed star from the *kilil* flag, making Sunday the weekly day of rest, and adding 'Ethiopian' to the name of the party, (now the Ethiopian Somali Peoples Democratic Party), do little to mask reality. The resumption of war against Islamists across the border and ONLF secessionism within, brought the southeast lowlands again under military rule, eliminating any vestige of autonomy that region may have gained earlier. The reversion to the *status quo ante* shows that federalism has not advanced the integration of the Somali into the Ethiopian state.

14

Borana, South Omo, Gambella & Beni Shangul Gumuz

The southern and western borderlands are the remotest and least known parts of Ethiopia. Managing federalism in this immensely complex and challenging setting would have been extremely difficult under any circumstances. The EPRDF did not make it easier by failing to depart from the rigid formula used to administer the highland periphery, that is, the 'Peoples Democratic Organisation', the vehicle steered by 'regional intellectuals'. The problem here is the sheer inadequacy of this vehicle, which made centre intervention all the more necessary and obvious. Save in the most superficial sense, decentralisation has been a failure: in reality, the result was to bring the borderlands under tighter central control than ever before.

The Borana

As described in the preceding chapter, the early 1990s were a period of intense Oromo-Somali conflict along the entire length of their common border in Ethiopia. Nowhere was this more violent and intractable than in the Liben region, where the Borana had managed to halt the Somali advance earlier with the help of the Dergue. The collapse of that regime signalled the start of a new phase in the old conflict, in which the Borana found themselves losing more ground, including valuable water sources and ancient ritual sites. Federalism did not make the situation easier to manage. Rather, it made it more difficult because it appeared to legitimise this loss and make it permanent.

Following the collapse of the Siad Barre regime in Somalia, a flood of humanity poured across the south-eastern border into Ethiopia. It included 'returnees' – that is, former refugees – who were returning to their homes, and 'refugees' who were escaping the mayhem of civil war in Somalia. Many had spent up to three decades in Somalia, and were to spend more time in refugee camps in Ethiopia. They belonged to many clans, some of

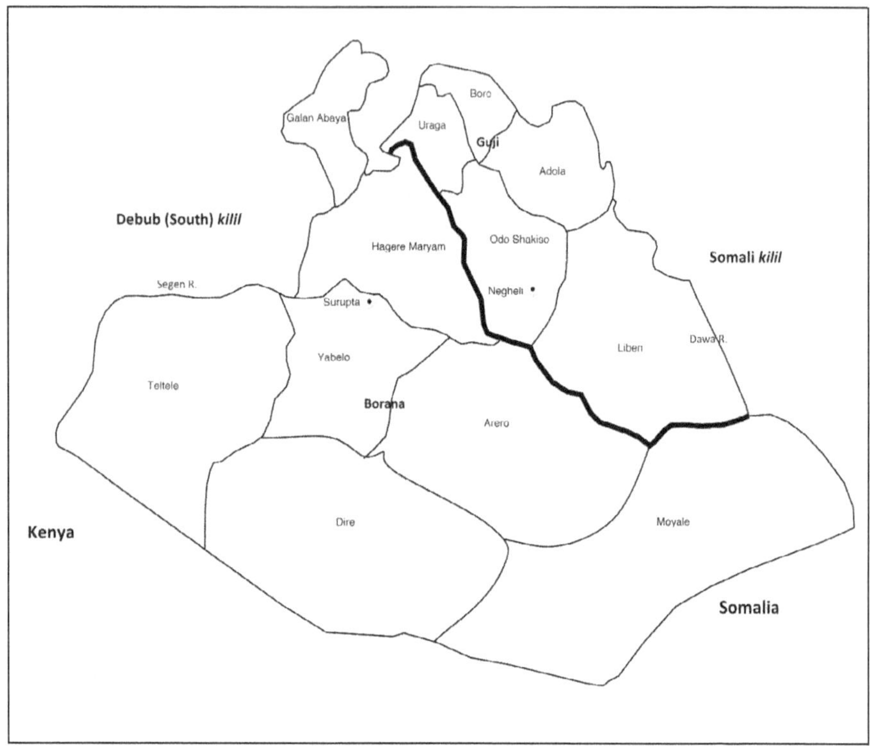

Map 9 Borana & Guji: zones & *woreda*

them well established inside Ethiopia, and others that had no earlier connection with this country. Some found land and shelter in territories controlled by their clans; some reasserted claims on territories now occupied by other clans, and others still sought to clear land for themselves by displacing the current occupants. A large number of them made their way to Liben district, the battlefront in the enduring struggle between Somali and Borana, which now entered a new phase, more complicated and violent than before

The complexity and violence of the conflict was aggravated by the involvement of new political actors and issues. They included several competing Oromo political factions – the Oromo Liberation Front (OLF), the Islamic Front for the Liberation of Oromia (IFLO), the United Oromo Peoples Liberation Front (UOPLF), and the Oromo Peoples Democratic Organisation (OPDO) – who supported the Borana. On the Somali side were the remnants of the Western Somalia Liberation Front (WSLF), the Oromo Abo Liberation Front (OALF), and the Ogaden National Liberation Front (ONLF). EPRDF forces appeared in the southern borderland in November 1991, five months after the collapse of the Dergue. In the meantime, rival Somali and Oromo factions had established themselves in Moyale and lesser towns in the region, and had begun organising ethnic support for the confrontation that was to come. Their work was made difficult by the demographic complexity of the region, where groups intermingled and blended and had never before identified themselves as Somali or Oromo. Such was the prevailing confusion that the Gerri Sultan, Mohammed Hajj Hassan Gababa, was sent as OLF representative to the transitional legislative council in Addis Ababa. He had been chairman of the Somali Abo Liberation Front (SALF) and, after its dissolution, a prominent figure in the Oromo Abo Liberation Front (OALF). Learning of this, Borana elders travelled to the OLF headquarters in Addis Ababa to protest. 'This man is a Gerri, not an Oromo. He speaks our language because he has none of his own. He lives in our land because he has none of his own' (Schlee & Shongolo, 1995: 11).

The Marehan Somali clan was the first to clash with the Borana. Siad Barre's clan, it had prospered during his reign, but was now without land or allies in Liben district, where it claimed territory it allegedly had possessed under the Italians, and from where it had been evicted by the Dergue. The Borana objected, citing their own historical claims. After all efforts to mediate failed, the two sides fought a three day battle in September 1991 that took seventy lives and ended with a Marehan defeat. The remnants of their camel herds were soon afterwards looted by the Digodia.[1] What the Borana call the 'First War' started in November 1991, when they attacked the Gabbra in Yabelo and forced them to flee north to Fincha on the border with the Guji who, in turn joined the conflict on the Gabbra side. The Borana also attacked the Gerri and Migo Gabbra in Moyale district, thousands of whom sought refuge in Kenya and were later brought back by the UNHCR.

The Gerri now returned to the region from Somalia and Kenya and fighting broke out with the Borana almost immediately, and has continued intermittently until the present day. A permanent state of war reigned in the area crossed by the road from Moyale to Negheli, which forms a sort of a border between the Oromo and Somali *kilil*. The so-called Second War was fought in 1997-8, when the Gerri attacked the Borana in Liben and took control of the well clusters in that district. Understandably, the Borana developed a siege mentality, as the following comment by one elder illustrates.

> A flooded river is crossed at three stages; at knee depth, at waist and at neck. When at knee, you wade into it, at waist it shakes you, and at neck it takes your life. The Somali are like a flooded river. Now they are at our knee, we can say no. When they are at our waist, it costs us fighting, and when they are at our neck, they remove us and take our land. [2]

The Borana also found themselves out of favour with the new regime in Addis Ababa. Signs of OLF activity in the borderland worried the

[1] Years later the Marehan dropped their claim to land ownership and were allowed by the Borana to graze their herds in the district.

[2] Cited in Fekadu Adugna (2004: 102). See also Boku Tache and Gufu Oba (2009).

EPRDF, and as the relationship of these two Fronts deteriorated, so did the fortunes of the Borana in the region. Matters were made worse when Major Ali Jataani, who had risen to local prominence under the Dergue, fled to Kenya and declared war on the EPRDF.[3] On one occasion, the Abba Gaada hoisted the OLF flag at a public ceremony, a gesture that was taken as a confirmation of Borana support of Oromo nationalism. This worried the Borana elders, and in the 1996 *Gumi Gayyo* Assembly, they presented a petition to the presidents of Ethiopia and the Oromia *kilil* who were present that said:

> It is an understandable fact that after the demise of the previous regime there have been vital misunderstandings between the Borana community and the present regime...In our opinion, the very root cause of the conflict is that the government believed and considered the community of the Borana as being OLF fighters and more precisely, identified us as a whole anti EPRDF.[4]

The decline in Borana fortunes was dramatically illustrated when the *kilil* boundaries were drawn in the early 1990s, and Borana became a zone in Oromia *kilil.* The much fought over region between the Genale and Dawa rivers was taken by the Somali *kilil.* The loss of the historic Liben inter-riverain region shocked the Borana, who firmly believed they were being penalised for their earlier closeness to the Dergue. The lost land includes the wells at Hudet, Gadaduma, Wachille, Lei, Gof and Moyale, which have been the bone of contention for Borana and Somali pastoralists for decades. Moreover, it includes ritual sites where *gaada* ceremonies are traditionally held. A new *gaada* was initiated in 2000, and tradition requires that a grand assembly (*Gumi El Dalloo*) should meet in its third year at a shrine located near the town of Filtu, inside Liben *woreda* of the Somali *kilil.* When the grand assembly travelled there in 2003, it had a military escort and stayed only for one day. The *Gumy Gayoo* assembly that took place the following year in Dire *woreda* in Borana Zone was attended by some 5,000 people. They included the Oromia *kilil* president and other high OPDO officials, who took the opportunity to condemn the OLF as well as the 'legal' opposition to the EPRDF. When the conflict with the Somali was raised, one elder addressed the OPDO officials bluntly: 'We in fact know that you do not have the real authority to solve our problems. In that case, better allow us to go directly to your masters so that we can tell them our problems ourselves.' (Ibrahim Amae Elemo 2005: 47)

*

The pastoralist economy of the Borana was devastated by drought on three occasions, losing up to 70% of livestock in 1991-2, more in 1999-2000, and up to 80% in 2005-6 (ILRI 2006b). Resort to cultivation in order to supplement food requirements continued, further limiting pasture availability. Traditionally, every village had enclosed land (*Kaloo*) reserved for calves and other uses. Now this term came to refer to private land

[3] He was murdered in Nairobi in July 1992, allegedly the victim of political assassination.
[4] Fekadu Adugna (2004: 75).

enclosure. The *Kaloo* issue was discussed at the *Gumi Gayoo* (August 1996) where it was resolved that no one should enclose pastureland as private property or restrict livestock passage through it. This resolution had no effect on an expanding process promoted by the proliferation of *birked* water storage tanks that require fencing, continuing land enclosure for forage production, expanding cultivation in valley floors, and leasing land for commercial agriculture.

The result is a marked decline in both quantity and quality of pasture. Population and herd growth in a decreasing area of land has meant that 'Borana resources are being exploited at a much higher rate now than before.' (Helland 2001: 75) Perhaps most important was the loss of autonomy for Borana society to devise and implement measures to deal with these problems. One observer points to an institutional crisis

> ...characterised by the failure of Borana institutions to come to grips with developments and trends in Borana society over the past few decades... For many years the Borana have been disenfranchised on their own land by government and non-government organisation alike, in most matters including those which matter most to the Borana...All the fundamental decisions mediating and structuring relations between the Borana and the state have been made without involving the Borana. (Helland 2001: 75-77)

Proof of the decline of the traditional economy is the fact that famine relief that started in the mid-1970s has continued without interruption ever since.

Numerous NGOs were active in Borana Zone in the first decade of the 21st century. Improved water provision for livestock was a major component of their work, and that meant constructing more water points and *birked* storage tanks. *Birked* owners sold water, a practice known as *aadmale* (outside Borana custom). Water provision has two aims; to increase livestock production and to promote cultivation. Increased livestock production by itself does little to improve peoples' welfare, and has a negative environmental impact unless it is channelled to the market. Accordingly, market integration is a major concern for most NGOs working in Borana. The usual strategy is to establish ties between local producers and livestock traders in the main highland market towns, the assumption being that the missing link is contact between those two. This ignores the fact that the Borana trade most profitably across the border in Kenya, where demand and price are highest.

Like all pastoralist regions in Ethiopia, the Borana plateau lags far behind the rest of the country in terms of modern development. This remote region suffered from near total isolation until it was linked to the national road network in the 1980s. Hundreds of kilometres of rural roads constructed by SORDU were not maintained and are no longer functional. Today, Borana Zone is still without an adequate internal road network, and during the rainy season large parts of it are cut off. Likewise, the region was quite neglected in the fields of education and health. Progress in education was inordinately slow before 1991. An informal census of elders gathered in the *Gumi El Daloo* assembly of 2003 discovered only two who could read and write. In 1985 there was only one primary school with 79 students in Arero *woreda*. Significant progress was made under the EPRDF. In 2005 there were fifteen primary schools with 3,673 students in Arero woreda.

In the Borana Zone administration, human resources are severely limited, and staff levels fall far short of requirements. In 2007 the personnel of the capacity building department in the zone consisted of a deputy administrator and one staff member, neither with relevant qualifications. The staff turnover was strikingly high, partly due to the *woreda* empowerment programme that required the transfer of staff from zone to *woreda* level. The reform was undermined because it proved impossible to retain skilled staff at *woreda* level. Many sought transfer back to zone level citing personal reasons and, if they were refused, transferred to other departments or other zones.

Borana and their Oromo neighbours

In the beginning of the 21st century, the Borana lost more land, this time to the Guji, their Oromo kinsmen. In the internal administrative demarcation of Oromia, Guji and Oromo were put together in Borana Zone with its capital in Neghele town. The Guji complained that the vast size of Borana Zone made it difficult to administer, and lobbied the *kilil* administration for their own zone. In 2002 the zone was divided in two to create a Guji Zone, with its capital in Neghele, incorporating most of the highland *woreda* inhabited by Guji – Adola, Odo Shakiso, Bore, Uraga – plus the lowland Borana inhabited Liben *woreda*. Most of the lowland *woreda* inhabited by Borana – Arero, Yabelo, Teltele, Dire and Moyale – and two districts inhabited by Guji – Hagere Mariam and Galana Abaya – remained in the reduced Borana Zone with its capital now in Yabelo. No attempt was made to clearly separate the two Oromo groups at this time, and soon the Guji began agitating for a second zone of their own to 'bring all the Guji together'.

Tension in the area mounted in anticipation of where the boundaries of yet another Guji Zone would be drawn, when a third group, the Gabbra, became involved. Claimed by both the Oromo and the Somali as part of their nationality, this bilingual marginalised community responded opportunistically without compromising its own integrity. A meeting of elders representing Gabbra clans in Moyale in 1996 chose Hassen Kala from the Dolio clan as *Talia* ('first among equals'). He claimed his people were Somali, and they are represented as a minority clan in the Somali *kilil* assembly. In the conflicts of the early 1990s, the Gabbra fought on the side of the Somali and most of them were expelled to Kenya by the Borana. One Gabbra group fled northwards to Surupta, on what is the border between Borana and Guji zones, 35km south of Fincha town. Surupta hamlet is the centre of three *kebele* that have Borana and Guji cultivators as well as a large number of Gabbra camel herders. Because of increasing land enclosure by cultivators and the occupation of a large track of land by a firm that uses it as holding ground for livestock, the herders have found it increasingly difficult to maintain their herds, and relations with their neighbours deteriorated.

Both Guji and Borana were indignant when the Gabbra in Surupta asked for their own separate *kebele*, hoping to have exclusive access to its land. The spark that set off the conflict in the spring of 2005 was the killing of a Guji woman by Gabbra. Both communities mobilised and drew apart as Guji and Gabbra left the sites they occupied jointly. Finchaa town was evacuated when the Guji fled to Hagere Mariam, and issued the traditional call for mobilisation that all males must obey by rushing armed to the scene. There they chose an Abaa Dula and attacked the Gabbra in March 2005. Fighting lasted a few days and some sixty people were killed, allegedly quite a few of them by the military who arrived to stop the fighting. Hundreds of Gabbra homes were burned, thousands of their livestock were looted, and many people fled to Moyale. There was no mechanism of conflict resolution between Guji and Gabbra because, as they said, they had 'never fought before'.

When the Guji retreated north of Fincha during this conflict, abandoning land south of the town, the Borana promptly moved into it. In the summer of 2006, after the Guji-Gabbra conflict subsided and the Guji began drifting back to reclaim their land, they met Borana resistance, and the two clashed heavily over several weeks with the loss of many lives. The road to Moyale was blocked and federal military intervention was required to open it. A meeting held in Yabelo in June 2006 attended by the Guji and Borana Aba Gaada and state officials arranged a ceasefire but did not resolve the conflict.

The three Oromo groups clashed with extraordinary violence in northern Kenya a few months later. On 12 July 2005, in the Didigalgalo-Turbi area, 130 km from Marsabit town, some 1000 heavily armed raiders attacked the Gabbra town of Turbi, killing 76 people, including 22 primary schoolchildren, destroying schools and shops, and looting thousands of livestock. Although the slaughter continued for a whole day, the Kenyan security forces did not appear until it was over. The raiders were said to be Borana and Guji from Ethiopia supported by the Oromo Liberation Front.

South Omo

During crises in the centre, state power in the periphery reaches low ebb, and violence claims the lowlands as communities seize the opportunity to settle accounts with their neighbours over accumulated grievances. The collapse of state authority in 1991 was the signal for a free-for-all among groups in South Omo, just as the region was flooded with automatic weapons left by the dismantled Dergue army. Dergue officials fled to Kenya, leaving arms depots to be emptied by youths who sold weapons to the rural people. Police stations were looted, prison guards fled and prisoners escaped, and Jinka was left without telephone and radio links with the rest of the country for some time. The Borana were immediately attacked by a coalition of Konso, Hamar, Arbore, Tsemay and Bana. An

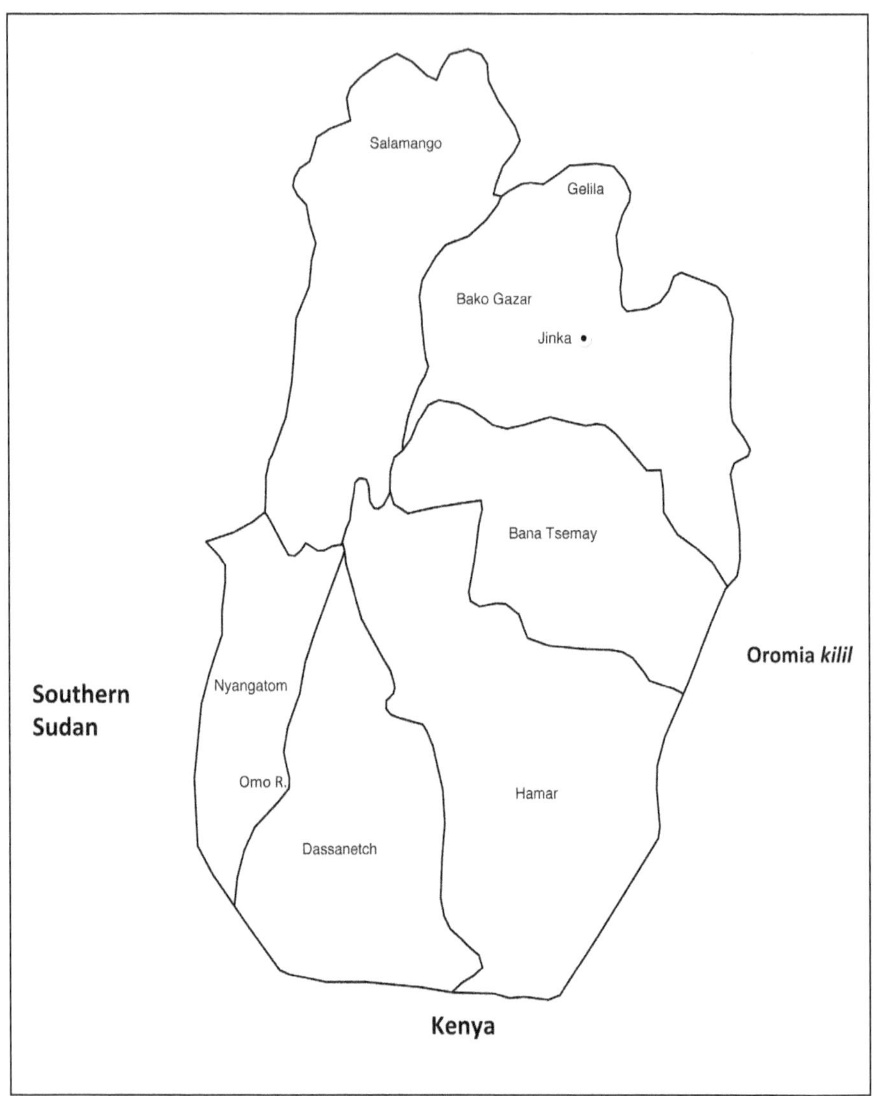

Map 10 South Omo: zones & *woreda*

ill-timed Borana retaliatory attack against the Arbore left 400 of the attackers dead. The mayhem continued until early 1993, when elders of twelve communities reached an agreement that secured the peace until 1997. Land use rights were the focal point of the agreement. It was stipulated that rights over land concern use not ownership, and all groups and their animals have the right to survival. Accordingly, the Borana agreed to allow access to their territory for a limited number of their neighbours' livestock after harvest time.

The EPRDF army arrived in the autumn of 1991 to set up bases in Jinka and Kara (70km from Jinka). With the exception of a handful of former Aari soldiers who had joined it, there were no natives of South Omo in its ranks, and the initiative to represent that region was taken by a handful of educated natives who found themselves in Addis Ababa at the time. A group of them put together an Omotic Peoples Democratic Front, and two – Makonnen Dori and Assefa Chabo – were seated in the July 1991 Conference. In 1992 a rival Omo Peoples Democratic Union appeared to represent the descendants of the Amhara settlers in the Omo region. Neither of these was acceptable to the EPRDF, and a third party whose title listed the names of nearly all communities in the Omo region appeared with its blessing. This party took most of the seats in the 1992 local elections and then proceeded to lose most of them to challenges and reruns. A fourth entry named the South Omo Peoples Democratic Movement came first in the 1995 elections.

In the federal arrangement South Omo became a zone in Debub *kilil* and was subdivided into *woreda*, whose number increased steadily as most ethnic groups in the zone demanded to have their own. Larger groups were given a *woreda*, and an effort was made to accommodate smaller groups in their own *kebele*. The political status of the descendants of the *neftegna* who had long dominated the region was a controversial issue at the time. The EPRDF insisted on inclusiveness and fair representation, and the first administration of South Omo Zone was headed by an Aari teacher, Getahun Goitang, whose deputy was a Gurage, Yaqob Dembel. The principle of inclusiveness applied also in the *woreda* and *kebele* councils by giving every group fair representation.

Federalism shifted the task of administration to local people. This was a great advance on the past, if only because it brought government closer to the population and opened the possibility of gaining their trust. Unfortunately, local government did not have the means to carry out the tasks assigned to it. Due to severe shortages of human and material resources, the *woreda* empowerment programme ran into serious difficulty. There are not enough educated natives to staff the administration, and few non-natives are willing to work in the primitive hamlets that serve as *woreda* centres, despite a bonus offered for this purpose. The *kilil* budget assigned 61% of the total to *woreda*, yet this proved inadequate to meet even staff salaries. In 2006, South Omo Zone was 2.2 million birr in the red, and most *woreda* had not paid staff salaries for months. Needless to say, the zone's revenue capacity is nil, and it depends entirely on federal subsidies.

*

A painfully slow start was made in the first years of this century to raise the capacity of the indigenous communities in South Omo for self-administration. A network of elementary schools brought modern education to this borderland for the first time, and a beginning was made to accommodate pastoralist youth in boarding schools. Jinka began to acquire a modicum of urban facilities and was linked by air with Addis Ababa. A road connection through Konso to Borana was started, but the zone still lacks a direct connection to the national network. The economy of South Omo remains purely subsistence. There is no market in it even for livestock, its major resource. It has not attracted investment save for a private cotton plantation at Birale that had been established before 1991 on land taken from the Tsamako community without permission or compensation.[5]

The exceptional physical setting of the Omo River Valley attracted interest as a potential tourist area. A major portion of it had already been reserved under previous regimes for national parks, wildlife reserves and controlled hunting. The reserved area amounted to more than 18,000 km^2 in South Omo Zone whose total area is 22,360 km^2, that is, over three-quarters. Its potential for tourism could be exploited only if herders and livestock were excluded from the designated areas, or their activities restricted. Mago National Park was established in 1978 in an area covered 2,200 km^2. An area twice as large was later designated as the Omo National Park, but neither was demarcated or gazetted. Both are in Salamago *woreda*. The Park is regularly grazed by Hamar and Bana herds from the south and Mursi herds from the north, and all depend on the waters of the Mago and Omo rivers in the dry season. The Mursi also cultivate the banks of the Mago River in the south, while the Aari cultivate higher land in the north. The history of Mago National Park is one of continuous confrontation with the local people. In 2002 the Park Warden and two policemen were killed in a Bana village. Park employees are intimidated by the herders: 'They are armed and they see us as the enemy', one said. Prudently, they did not attempt to expel the herders from the Park.[6]

In 2005, the Wildlife Department of Debub *kilil* carried out a demarcation of the Omo and Mago parks. This was prompted by a proposal from a Dutch enterprise, the Stichting African Parks Foundation, to take over their management. It had already secured a contract for the management of Nech Sar National Park in neighbouring Gemu Gofa Zone. Drafted by the Foundation, the agreement put heavy emphasis on banning hunting by the local people, calling it 'poaching'. 'It is most essential that poaching is stopped', it stated, and made plans for 'a highly mechanised scout unit, with airplane, radio, binoculars and 80 motorcycles. It is predicted that

[5] A confrontation between the Tsamako and the plantation owners in 1995 led to military intervention and the killing of nine Tsamako men.

[6] Interview with Getu Wolde, Warden of Mago National Park, Mago Park, (27 January 2006).

nearly all poaching will have ceased in year three', it confidently predicted.

The people who used the land had other ideas and were given a chance to voice them in a meeting organised locally by the UNDP.[7] 'This demarcation is like itching. It is really itching us, really very tough', complained a Nyangatom elder:

> We know the wildlife, they are our resources. It is our wealth, like our domestic animals. We need to balance wildlife and animals. If we give a large portion of grazing land to the wildlife, what about the domestic animals? If this demarcation happens in this place, it is really, really better for us to die.

Another elder added: 'We will never agree that we will never hunt anymore. In our culture it is really very difficult because when a new bride comes she cannot be married until an animal is killed and a skin is prepared for her to wear.' A third accused the authorities: 'The land is being privatised without telling the people.'[8] Local resistance led the Foundation to reconsider, and following the death of its owner, it pulled out of South Omo and Nech Sar.

The rivers that cross the zone are another resource with potential for development to which Addis Ababa has turned its attention in recent years. The focus is the Omo-Gibe basin, whose hydroelectric energy potential is second only to that of the Blue Nile. The country's biggest supplier of electricity, fed from a dam known as Gilgil Gibe I, it began operations in 2004. Known as Gibe II, a second power plant fed from this dam was nearing completion in 2010. Neither of these is thought to have a significant impact on the hydrology of the lower Omo. By contrast, a third project known as Gibe III, sited on the Omo River 300km southwest of Addis Ababa, has raised great concern in that respect. Gibe III, whose construction began in 2006, is advertised as the second largest dam in Africa and expected to double Ethiopia's generating capacity. Up to 50% of its output will be exported to neighbouring countries. The Italian government provided part of the funding for the project, the contract for which was awarded to an Italian company without bidding, as was the contract for the initial ecological impact assessment that made no mention of the dam's potential impact on the ecology of the Omo River flood plain.

Concern voiced abroad prompted Ethiopia's Environmental Protection Authority to carry out its own assessment two years after construction began. Referring to the lower Omo, it recommended the annual release of 'controlled flood' over a ten day period 'to fully compensate all adverse effects'. This assessment was roundly condemned abroad as 'grossly inadequate'.[9] The African Development Bank, which had provided part of the initial funding and was considering additional support, was then obliged to produce its own assessment. Critics abroad found this one 'fatally flawed in terms of its logic, in terms of its thoroughness, in terms of

[7] Global Pastoralist Gathering organised by the UNDP at Turmi, South Omo, 9 January 2005 – 2 February 2005.

[8] The organisers published a newsletter (*Turmi Morning Herald* 29 January–2 February 2005) from where the statements cited here are taken.

[9] International Rivers Press Release, (23 July 2009).

its conclusions'.[10] Nevertheless, a Chinese firm was awarded the contract for a fourth dam on the Omo River, 100 km to the south on the northern end of South Omo zone.

Those who know the area warn of a potentially devastating impact on people whose livelihood depends entirely on the river's floodwaters. Seasonal flooding sustains pastures for their livestock and prepares the land for crops that make up a good portion of their diet. Already significantly reduced, Lake Turkana, which is fed by the Omo River, is threatened with extinction, as are the people who live on its shore. The intrusion of agri-business based on irrigation is another development prospect seen as beneficial for the area because it would provide employment for the local population as well as improved infrastructure. It began with the acquisition of 30,000ha by an Italian 'alternative energy company' for oil palm and jatropha cultivation. Undoubtedly, there would be gains for the state from this development. If the experience of the Afar in the Awash Valley is any guide, however, there will be little gain and possibly great loss for the people of South Omo.

Conflict in South Omo

Federalism had no dampening effect on conflict in South Omo, where it remains endemic and irrepressible. According to the records of the Justice and Security Bureau of South Omo Zone, 204 people were killed in 2000-2005. Since not all incidents are reported to the police, this was an understatement. With a zone population of some 450,000 at the time, the incidence of violence might not seem alarmingly high. The picture changes when the spatial distribution of this phenomenon *is* considered. All the incidents cited in the report took place in four *woreda* – Nyangatom, Dassanetch, Hamar, Salamago – inhabited by herders and agro-pastoralists. Nyangatom and Dassanetch *woreda* together held the zonal record with 171 deaths during that period. Hamar came second with 29 deaths, and Salamago a distant third with 5 deaths. There were no reports of violent deaths in the other *woreda* of the zone. A follow up report for January-April 2006 that listed 17 deaths – including five women and four children – described this period as 'relatively peaceful' (CEWARN July 2006).

The extent of the problem is magnified by the fact that the area and population involved include adjacent areas and kindred populations in Northern Kenya and Southern Sudan. Dassanetch and Nyangatom are found also in Kenya's Turkana District, while Nyangatom and Murle live also in Eastern Equatoria and Jonglei provinces respectively in Southern Sudan. The border is neither garrisoned nor patrolled. A thriving trade in automatic weapons and ammunition is conducted across it and livestock raiding, another cross-border activity, flourishes. Nearly all males are

[10] Richard Leakey interview, BBC Amharic Service, (14 April 2009).

armed and carry their weapons everywhere, except inside Jinka town. Asked why they need weapons, they invariably reply 'for self-defence'.

Indeed, the imperative of self-defence that prevailed in the pastoralist habitat in the past remains valid in the beginning of the 21st century. Although the lowland periphery was brought under the Ethiopian flag over a century ago, succeeding regimes have done little to provide security for its inhabitants. The police force for the entire South Omo zone numbered less than 500 in 2007 and was supported by a militia of one dozen men in each *kebelle*. The police are stationed mainly in *woreda* capitals and a handful of other posts. Without vehicles, the police is effectively immobilised and is no match for raiders who move swiftly even when driving looted livestock. The police have a mixture of automatic weapons, M1 rifles and carbines of WWII vintage. *Kebele* militias have only a few weapons they use on a shift basis.[11] By contrast, there must many thousands of automatic weapons in the hands of the population.

An advantage of local self-government is the fact that local officials are cognizant of peoples' need for self defence and their own limitations in providing security. Wisely, they refrain from aggravating the situation with coercive measures. Instead, the preferred approach is negotiation and conciliation with the aim of containing conflict. Officials become involved only when an act of violence is reported to the police, which is not always the case, or when they are warned of impending serious conflict between groups. Their first concern is to prevent conflict from spreading. This requires convincing the victim's kinsmen not to retaliate until the elders complete negotiations for blood compensation and the return of stolen property, and persuading the guilty party to surrender and be taken to prison for his own protection. 'We go to the site of a crime to make peace, not to make arrests', one official explained.[12] Punishment is a secondary consideration, subject to lengthy negotiations between the authorities, the elders and the culprits themselves, and seldom reaches the state courts.

Gambella

The chaotic interval that followed the overthrow of the military regime in 1991 was particularly violent in Gambella, where it is remembered as *girgir* ('turmoil'). When the Dergue soldiers abandoned the area, pent up Anywaa resentment of highlander settlement in their midst found immediate release through attacks on settler villages. The initial incident was an assault on the village of Ukuna that had a mixed population of some 3,000 settlers and 770 Anywaa. The village was burned down and as many as 100 highlanders lost their lives. This signalled the start of an exodus of settlers that eventually left only a small number behind in Gambella.

[11] Interview with Getachew Toronche, Head of Justice & Security Bureau, South Omo Zone, Jinka, (25 January 2006).

[12] Interview with Moluka Wubneh, Bako Gazar Woreda Administrator, Jinka, (24 January 2006).

The Anywaa then turned on the Nuer who had gained local ascendancy under the Dergue. Nuer who had served under the Dergue fled to Sudan, followed by Nuer from the refugee camps in Itang and Pignyudo. The SPLA also moved its troops across the border. With EPRDF blessing, the Gambella Peoples Liberation Movement (GPLM) took charge of the region and installed an all-Anywaa administration headed by Agwua Alemu. He was killed a few months later in a clash with GPLM fighters inside Gambella town. For the next few years, the Anywaa held a monopoly of power, and used it to reverse Nuer territorial gains made under the Dergue.

In 1991-92, the Anywaa attacked the Nuer in Gambella town and Itang district, killing people and burning villages. The followers of a Nuer prophet called Wutnyang Gatkek retaliated with an attack in Itang, killing a number of highlander traders as well as looting their shops. Among the dead were the entire EPRDF military unit stationed in Itang. Wutnyang then led a Nuer band towards Gambella town, but was intercepted by the government army and annihilated, though the prophet himself managed to escape to Sudan. The Nuer regrouped across the border in Nasir and fought back in the Jikaw and Itang districts. Supported by the Nasir faction of the SPLA, they raided Anywaa territory, burning villages and looting livestock and crops. The fighting left few villages, Anywaa or Nuer, untouched, it halted agricultural production, dislocated trade and demolished the rural economy.

The GPLM fell out with the EPRDF when it refused to demobilise its force of some 1,200 fighters, and in August 1992 it fought a pitched battle with the army inside Gambella town that left several soldiers and many more civilians dead. The GPLM fighters then fled across the border to Pochalla in Southern Sudan, where they stayed for a few months before returning to be demobilised. Afterwards most of them were integrated into the federal army and sent to other regions. Obliged to change its name in 1995, the GPLM was renamed Gambella Peoples Liberation Party (GPLP). The *kilil* administration that was formed in 1992 excluded the Nuer by not including representatives from the *woreda* where they were the majority. Three representatives were chosen from each of four Anywaa *woreda*, and they selected a regional council of seven Anywaa, three Majangir, one Komo and one highlander. Ukeelo Uman had succeeded Agwuwa Alemu as GPLM leader, and now became head of the *kilil* administration, with an Anywaa deputy and a highlander as secretary.

It did not take long for the Nuer to rally and challenge Anywaa monopoly of power. The Gambella Peoples Democratic Party (GPDP), formed by Nuer students in Addis Ababa in 1992, was recognised by the National Election Board the same year. It was not welcomed by Anywaa politicians, who did all they could to obstruct it, raising the familiar argument that the Nuer are Sudanese. Nevertheless, prodded by the EPRDF, the GPLM and GPDUP agreed in 1993 to bring the inter-community conflict to an end, and a period of relative peace followed. The administrative structure of the *kilil* was redrawn in 1995, when it was divided into two nationality zones. Zone 1 grouped five Anywaa-inhabited *woreda* along

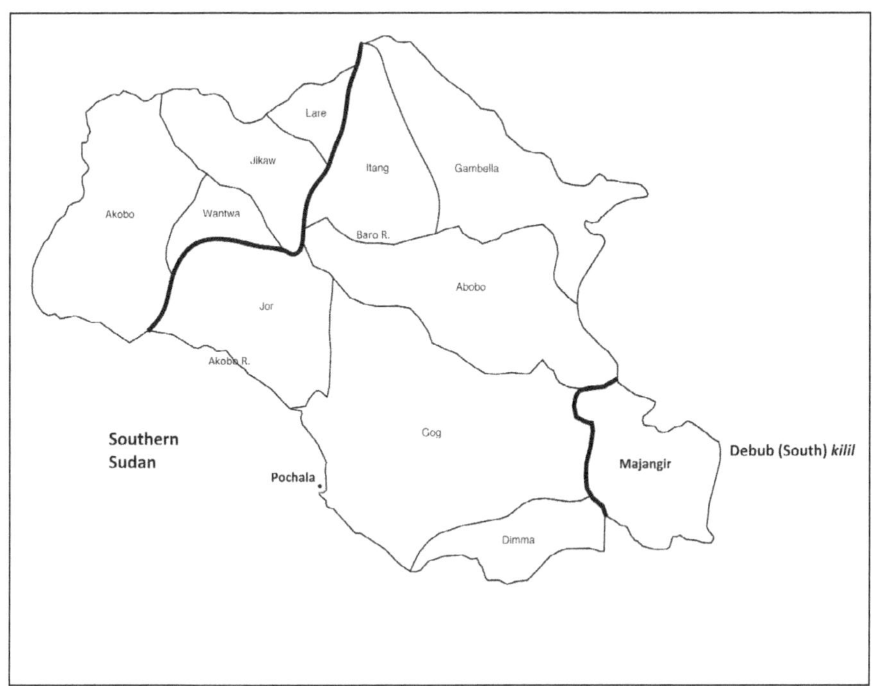

Map 11 Gambella *kilil*: zones & *woreda*

the Baro and Akobo rivers – Gambella, Itang, Abobo, Gog, Jor – with Itang town as its centre. Zone 2 consisted of three Nuer inhabited *woreda* – Akobo, Jikaw, Lare – with its centre at Pignyudo. This made the Anywaa a political majority in the *kilil*, because they controlled five out of eight *woreda*. When Dimma *woreda* with its Anywaa majority was transferred from Debub *kilil* to Gambella in 1996, the Anywaa came to control six out of nine *woreda*. Nuer demands for more *woreda* in their zone were rejected by the Anywaa administration.

The 1995 *kilil* elections were won by the Anywaa GPLP, but the Nuer GPDUP took 10 of the 42 seats in the *kilil* council and was allocated the office of vice-president. Accused of corruption in connection with a road building project, Ukeelo Uman and his Anywaa team were removed in 1997. Ukeelo was sentenced to six years' imprisonment, and several members of his administration were also jailed. Ukeelo Nigelo, another Anywaa former elementary schoolteacher, became *kilil* president, with a Nuer, Ket Touach, as deputy and a Majangir as secretary. The Nuer remained dissatisfied with their share of power which was grossly disproportionate with their share of the population as shown in the 1994 census.

The period of relative peace that lasted some five years ended in January 1998, when fighting broke out again between Anywaa and Nuer on the banks of the Baro River in Itang *woreda* and went on for six months.

Many villages on both sides were burned, about 60 people were killed and some 3,000 were displaced. Both Anywaa and Nuer policemen were implicated in distributing weapons to their respective sides and taking part in the fighting. The conflict ended in June 1998 after a state of emergency was declared and the federal army intervened. Soon afterwards, the EPRDF applied the standard political formula by merging the GPLP and the GPDUP into the Gambella Peoples Democratic Front (GPDF). It won the 2000 elections, and the Nuer increased their representation in the *kilil* council to nineteen, compared to twenty-nine for the Anywaa.

Another round of inter-community conflict started after the elections. In July of that year, Nuer attacked Itang's police station killing many Anywaa policemen. When the *kilil* president called a meeting of Anywaa leaders, he was accused of conspiring to massacre Nuer. He and forty-four other Anywaa were arrested and kept in prison without trial until December 2005.[13] At the end of the year, simmering tension between Anywaa villagers and Nuer refugees in Pignyudo led the former to demand the UNHCR move the refugee camp out of their area. They were ignored, and on 2 December 2002 they attacked the camp, killing thirty-three Nuer refugees. The UNHCR then decided to move the camp and chose a site in Odier village, 265 miles from Pignyudo, near the Sudan border in Anywaa territory.

Further political engineering took place in the wake of this violence. The GPDF was dissolved and replaced by another coalition, the Gambella Peoples Democratic Movement (GPDM) comprising three nationality-based parties: the Anywaa Peoples Democratic Organisation (APDO), the Nuer Peoples Democratic Organisation (NPDO) and the Majangir Peoples Democratic Party (MPDP). A Majangir Zone had been formed in 2002 with a single *woreda*, Godere. A share-out of posts was agreed among them. The *kilil* presidency was reserved for the Anywaa, the vice presidency for the Nuer, the office of speaker of the Regional Assembly for the Majangir, the deputy speaker for the Komo, the office of Supreme Court president for the Nuer and deputy president for the Anywaa. Ukeelo Akway Ochalla, an Anywaa former nurse became *kilil* president, with Ket Touach, a Nuer, as his deputy.

On November 17, 2003, five highlanders working on a road building project outside Abobo, 40km south of Gambella town, were ambushed and killed. Anywaa were blamed, although no one was arrested. On 13 December 2003, a group of eight highlanders employed by the federal Administration of Refugee Affairs were ambushed and killed, along with their Anywaa driver outside Gambella town. Because of earlier attacks on highlanders for which the Anywaa were blamed, tension between the two communities was high, and a mob of highlanders gathered at the administration headquarters when the bodies were brought to Gambella town. It turned on Anywaa bystanders killing indiscriminately then, reinforced by highlander soldiers and policemen, rampaged through the Anywaa quarter, burning houses and massacring the inhabitants. The federal government put the death toll at sixty-five, including two high-

[13] Six of them had died in prison. Interview with Ukeelo Nigelo, Gambella, (1 March 2006).

landers, while local sources and human rights organisations estimated the number of victims at more than 400. Six soldiers and several highlander civilians were charged with involvement in the massacre and jailed, but were never brought to trial. A number of Anywaa were also jailed on suspicion of involvement, prompting the *kilil* president to flee abroad, followed by many people who fled their villages to join their Anywaa kinsmen in Pochalla and Otalo in Southern Sudan, while others went to Kenya.

The GPDM coalition won the 2005 elections. The Anywaa and Nuer parties now had parity of representation in the *kilil* assembly with 34 seats each, and the Majangir had 11 seats. Omot Obong Ogom, an Anywaa Civil Service College graduate and former head of the *kilil* security bureau, became president in September 2005. Guen Yer Suor, a Nuer, became vice president, and Wanido Abera, a Majangir former elementary schoolteacher, became speaker of the *kilil* council with a Komo deputy. In 2007, the twenty member *kilil* executive council included eight Anywaa, eight Nuer, and four Majangir. The quota system for sharing office applied also to the branches of each ethnic community.[14]

*

There was little change in Gambella under federalism. With Anywaa food production declining steadily and Nuer livestock production constrained by a shortage of land, the rural economy stagnated. About one-fifth of the population depended regularly on food aid.[15] Although giant dams were built in the highlands, the dam built by the Dergue on the Alwero River remained unused. Outsiders were beginning to move into the region to exploit available resources. Highlanders started clearing the land for coffee farms and timber production in the Majangir forest region. The Gambella plain, with its many rivers, was beginning to attract attention and investors eager to open the land to commercial exploitation were lining up with applications in hand. The first was the MIDROC conglomerate with plans for half-a-million hectares. A start was made in rice production on 10,000ha on the banks of the Alwero River. An Indian-owned oil seed project on 300,000ha was unveiled in 2009 on the Baro River. The ninety-year lease gave the Karuturi Global company free land for six years, after which it would pay 15 birr ($1.18) per hectare annually. Local labour cost $50 per month, while the company's projected profit per year over ten years was $100,000. 'This strategy will build capitalism', boasted Omot Obot Ogom, the *kilil* president. The search was on for another valuable resource, petroleum. The Malaysian Petronas company was the latest to sign an exploration agreement, in April 2003. The Gambella concession that covered 19,600km of land was an extension of the Melut Basin in

[14] The 34 seats allocated to the Nuer in the *kilil* assembly were divided among the three Jikany sections: Gaajak, Gaajok and Gaaguang. In turn, the Gaajak quota was divided among its own five sections: Wau, Nyajani, Rieng, Cany, and Thiang.
[15] According to the DPPC office in Gambella town.

Southern Sudan known for its huge oil reserves. Sub-contracted by Petronas, a Chinese company began drilling in 2006.

In common with all lowland *kilil*, Gambella lags behind in education. There were only twelve primary schools in the region under the Dergue. Rapid expansion occurred after 1991, and in 2005 there were 131 primary schools – not all of them complete – with about 62,500 students. Reflecting the distribution of political power within the *kilil*, the distribution of educational facilities among zones was grossly uneven. Anywaa Zone with 27% of the region's population had more than half of the primary schools and nearly half the students, as well as three out of the five secondary schools with more than half the students. By contrast, the Nuer zone with 40% of the population had a quarter of the region's primary schools and about the same number of students, and one secondary school with a little more than 1,000 students. Health facilities were scarce. There was one state hospital with 96 beds for a population of over 300,000. There was no asphalt road and few all-weather roads in the *kilil* in 2009.

A remarkable phenomenon of this period was the massive conversion of the indigenous population to Protestant sects. According to the 2007 census, their followers accounted for 70% of the population. The Ethiopian Orthodox Church claimed a mere 16% presumably most of them highlanders, Islam 5% and Catholics numbered less than 3 per cent. The leader in the field was the Ethiopian Evangelical Mekane Yesus church. Because initially this church was dominated by the Anywaa, the Nuer formed their own branch, the Western Gambella Bethel Synod, and afterwards outstripped the Anywaa in conversion rates. Given the segmentation of Nuer society, it was not surprising that conversion was followed by fission and church proliferation. An anthropologist counted ten churches in a Nuer village of about 200 households, and some churches in Fugnido refugee camp consisting of a single family (Falge 2005: 186-190).

Conflict in Gambella: the Nuer

While conflict within the Anywaa community was reduced to insignificance, conflict among the Nuer on both sides of the border remained endemic and more violent than ever. The long civil war in Southern Sudan pushed successive waves of Nuer pastoralists across the border into Gambella, increasing pressure on local resources and generating conflict between Nuer latecomers and Nuer who had settled there earlier. An enduring intra-Nuer feud that transcended the Ethiopia-Sudan border involved the Lou and Jikany sections, who clashed when the Lou crossed the border to enter territory settled earlier by the Gaajok Jikany. In the early 1990s, the larger and militarily superior Lou defeated the Gaajok, who survived thanks to the timely intervention of the Ethiopian army. In 2001 hostilities broke out again, and again the Gaajok had to appeal to Addis Ababa for support, claiming the Lou were Sudanese invaders. The Lou responded by applying for Ethiopian citizenship. The federal government held a series of meetings with Gaajak and Lou leaders in 2004, and set up a peace committee of elders from both groups. A new Nuer *woreda*, Wantua, was established as an inducement. The conflict resumed in 2006, and the Gaajak elders appealed directly to the Prime Minister in Addis Ababa, who instructed the army to order the Lou to vacate Gaajak land.

There was intense rivalry and frequent conflict also among the five sections that comprise the Jikany Gaajak group; particularly between the Thiang and the other four sections: Reng, Waw, Nyajani, Cany. Earlier, the mobile Thiang led and other sections followed. This strategy worked as long as the Nuer were not in competition among themselves for land, and scarcity was addressed by continual eastward expansion into Anywaa territory. As pastoral mobility was reduced and population pressure on land increased, more Nuer groups shifted to agro-pastoralism and the Thiang took up cultivation in the best part of the rangeland between Itang and Jikaw districts. Permanent settlement by the Thiang blocked other Gaajak sections from their traditional avenues of expansion and gave rise to conflict.

Conflict in Gambella: 'Blacks' versus 'Reds'

The pattern of inter-community conflict in Gambella has another dimension, the confrontation between the indigenous 'Black' population and the 'Reds' who have come from the highlands during the past century. While most highlanders brought by the resettlement programme in the 1980s departed in the early 1990s, others were attracted by economic opportunities in the urban sector, especially trade and construction, a demand from the expanding state sector for skilled manpower provided by highlanders working under indigenous officials, as well as employment opportunities in the NGO sector. Thus, the number and economic power of the highlanders increased significantly after 1991. However, their position under federalism is quite anomalous, because they are politically disenfranchised. Although the official language of the *kilil* is Amharigna, the indigenous elite, with EPRDF tacit support, managed to exclude the 'Reds' from political office. Though the highlanders constitute nearly one-quarter of the region's population and control its economy, they are not recognised as a political constituency and are not represented in the *kilil* administration. This has produced a strong feeling of insecurity in this community that was manifested in the violent incidents of 2003, and was reinforced by events that followed.

On 30 October 2005, a daring attack took place on the prison in Gambella town. The attackers killed twelve Anywaa policemen and the Anywaa *kilil* police commissioner, and freed sixty-three inmates, including a few highlanders. Responsibility for the attack was claimed by the Gambella Liberation Front (GLF), a previously unknown organisation said to have been formed in 2004. It identified itself as a member of a so-called 'coalition of armed groups', together with the OLF and the Ethiopian Patriotic United Front (EPUF), a Nuer organisation led by Thuat Pal, the leading politician in Gambella under the Dergue, now living in Southern Sudan. Another raid on a police station in Abobo town took place the following month. Unlike previous attacks that targeted highlanders randomly, these raids were selective; government personnel, including Anywaa, were targeted. In June 2006, a bus on route from Addis Ababa was attacked near Bonga, 35km east of Gambella town: twenty-five persons were killed and many more were wounded. Subsequently, strict security measures were imposed. Travel within the *kilil* was restricted to certain days of the week and then only with military escort; even the short journey from the airport to Gambella town was thus conducted.

Beni Shangul Gumuz

The change of regime in Addis Ababa was greeted in the region with a spasm of violence, as the Gumuz in Metekel gave vent to their hatred of the resettlement programme by attacking settler villages and killing scores of highlanders. The main settlement site, Beles State Farm, was thoroughly looted, the settlers fled, and the scheme stopped functioning. While the EPRDF was securing control over the rest of the country, it was the OLF that took control of Beni Shangul in 1991. It faced opposition by the Berta Peoples Liberation Movement (BPLM), which had represented the region in the July 1991 Conference and occupied two seats in the Transitional Assembly. The two groups clashed violently, and the BPLM was forced out of the region, only to return in 1992 after the OLF left the transitional government.

The Beni Shangul *kilil* (Gumuz was added to its name in 1995) was formed by joining the *awraja* of Assosa in former Wallega province south of the Blue Nile River with Metekel *awraja* in former Gojjam province north of the river. Following EPRDF policy, the other three indigenous groups soon produced their own factions to compete with the Berta. A Gumuz Peoples Liberation Movement (GPLM) was formed in 1992, a Shinasha Peoples Democratic Movement (SPDM) followed, and even the miniscule Komo and Mao communities were likewise organised. An attempt at rationalisation of the political mosaic the following year clustered all the factions in a coalition hopefully dubbed the Democratic Unity Party, and a Berta, Atom Mustapha, became *kilil* president. In September 1993, the Gumuz once again attacked highlander settler villages around Pawe, provoking settler counterattacks, and the conflict escalated when federal troops clashed with Gumuz militiamen with many casualties on both sides. In the aftermath, the *kilil* capital was transferred to Assosa, and a special *woreda* was formed for highlanders in Pawe (renamed Gilgil Beles) with representation in the *kilil* assembly.

The Democratic Unity Party proved anything but united. The Berta elite itself was riven with factionalism, partly derived from the old antagonism between the Arabised upper layer known as Alhamer (Red) and the commoners known as Undulu (Black). Atom Mustapha, an Undulu, was deposed and sent to prison after only three months in office. His successor,

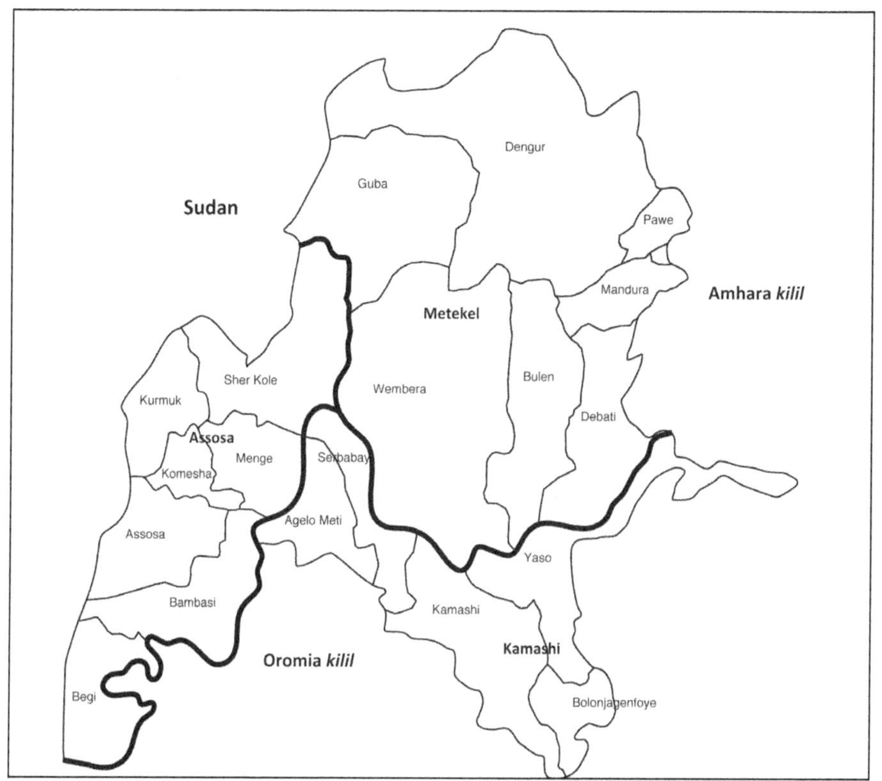

Map 12 Beni Shangul Gumuz *kilil*: zones & *woreda*

another Berta named Atieb Ahmed, lasted nine months before taking his turn in prison, and the third *kilil* president, Abdu Mohammed, stayed in office until the 1995 elections.

Before the elections that year, the EPRDF tried again to bring political order in the *kilil*. Its attitude towards the Berta politicians was coloured by Addis Ababa's fluctuating relations with the Islamist regime in Khartoum. An initial thaw in relations in the early 1990s ended as Addis Ababa fell in line with Washington's desire to isolate Sudan internationally, and relations broke down completely with the attempt to assassinate Egypt's president Hosni Mubarak in the Ethiopian capital in 1995. The Ethiopian government tried to pin the blame for this action on Khartoum. The Berta elite took pride in their Sudanese connection, and the BPLM had close links with the National Islamic Front in the Sudan during the insurgency against the Dergue. When its armed unit was disbanded, some of its members took to the bush as Jihadists (*Kawarja*). This core Berta Islamist faction based in Sudan surfaced occasionally over the years with attacks on Ethiopian police posts. Its activities provoked characteristically heavy handed security crackdowns and arrests of suspected supporters.[16] Wary of Islamist infiltration in the western borderland, Addis Ababa regarded the Berta as a potential Trojan Horse, and they were keenly aware of it. 'Living in a border area is very problematic for our people', acknowledged a Berta elder. 'Both governments have suspicions on us and always want to divide and rule us. For the Sudan government we are Ethiopians, for the Ethiopian government we are Sudanese, for the SPLA we are Muslims.'[17]

The issue was highlighted in 1995, when the deputy Prime Minister, Tamrat Layne, chaired a so-called Peace, Democracy and Development Conference in Assosa. This preceded a massive purge that swept into prison the entire executive council of the *kilil*, except its president, followed by more than one-hundred lesser officials. The bulk of the *kilil* police force was also dismissed. Tamrat Layne did not mince words in making clear Addis Ababa's security concerns. He denounced 'narrow nationalists and agents of foreign powers,' and warned local politicians to choose between their 'Ethiopia-ness and Sudan-ness.'[18] Thoroughly purged and chastened, the BPLM was renamed the Ethiopian Berta Peoples Democratic Organisation, and was pressed into another coalition named the Democratic Unity Front. The rise to the *kilil* presidency of a Gumuz, Yarekal Aysheshin, was another sign of Addis Ababa's exasperation with the fractious Berta elite, as was the addition of Gumuz to the name of the *kilil*. In Yarekal, a former elementary school teacher, Addis Ababa had found its man. He was to last a remarkable thirteen years in office, a record surpassed only by his Afar colleague, Ismail Ali Siro. Another ingredient in the volatile political mix of this area was Addis Ababa's wariness of support for the OLF among the Oromo in this area. Frequent reports of OLF activities were followed by security crackdowns and arrests of suspected dissidents. The *kilil* was perfunctorily policed by a force that numbered less than 1,000 in 2007, supported by an unpaid and untrained militia force of 2,500.

The Democratic Unity Front won the elections in 2000, and promptly fell apart over the sharing of offices. A Berta demand for the *kilil* presidency was rejected, and with Addis Ababa's backing Yarekal was re-elected for a second term. The Berta then withdrew from the coalition and the *kilil* administration, demanding a *kilil* of their own. The EPRDF rejected this out of hand with the standard formula it uses when such issues arise: it is the people, not political parties, who are entitled to raise them. It then sent the case for arbitration to the House of the Federation, where a power sharing agreement was reached on the basis of population size that increased Berta representation in the *kilil* administration. The Democratic Unity Front swept the 2005 elections, taking 85 out of 99 seats in the *kilil* assembly, and Yarekal Aysheshin was re-elected to a third term.

[16] The federal government offered amnesty on several occasions to former BPLM militants turned Jihadist rebels.
[17] Cited in Asnake Kefale (2009:108).
[18] Ibid.: 249.

Such lively competition among the indigenous groups over the spoils of political office overshadowed a simmering conflict with the highlanders over land and political power. The latter account for close to 30% of the *kilil*'s inhabitants and are congregated in Metekel Zone making up half its population, and in Assosa Zone where they make up 43 per cent. At the same time, the highlander community is steadily reinforced by the arrival of land hungry peasants from Amhara in the west and Oromia in the south.[19] This is illegal but unstoppable, despite the protests of local politicians and the occasional violent outburst of the indigenous population. The Amhara and Oromia *kilil* administrations do nothing to stop it, and the federal government refuses to intervene on the grounds that it is a spontaneous, not state sponsored, movement.

The issue of highlander political representation arose in the 2000 elections, when the Democratic Unity Front itself sponsored several settler candidates. Invoking the electoral law that required candidates to speak the language of the district they seek to represent, the Berta complained to the National Elections Board and the highlander candidates were disqualified. The issue was brought to the House of the Federation which produced a Solomonic verdict: it upheld the electoral law, but rejected its application in the case of candidates for the federal legislature, since the official language of Beni Shangul Gumuz is Amharigna. The *kilil* constitution was also amended afterwards to eliminate the language requirement for *kilil* office, and an agreement was reached to give the highlanders nine of the 100 seats in the *kilil* assembly, where the Berta have forty, the Gumuz thirty-five, the Shinasha eleven, and the Mao and Komo together five. A token solution, nevertheless it was recognition of a potentially serious political problem, something not addressed in similar circumstances in Gambella.

*

The economy of Beni Shangul Gumuz made little progress under ethnic federalism. Subsistence agriculture retained its bimodal form, with plough cultivation practised by the highlanders and shifting cultivation by the indigenous people. There was no sign of alternative economic activity. One small state bank and two petrol stations were the only new establishments in Assosa town in 1999 (J. Young 1999:338), and little else had been added a decade later. There is still no market integration within the *kilil*. Metekel Zone is linked to markets on the highland and Assosa Zone to markets in the Sudan. This is hardly surprising, since there is no road connection between the two zones separated by the Blue Nile River. The nearest bridge over the river lies far to the east in Oromia, and to reach Metekel from Assosa requires travelling over 1,148km of unpaved road through Wallega and Gojjam. Assosa town is connected by air to Addis Ababa, but is inaccessible from most parts of the *kilil*.

The *kilil*'s manpower capacity is very low. It is the only one in the

[19] There were as many Amhara (142,557) as Gumuz (141,645) in 2007.

lowlands with highlanders in charge of administration bureaux rather than deputies. The highlander presence distorts education statistics, because they do not discriminate between the indigenous population and the rest. For example, in 2005 Beni Shangul Gumuz had a higher rate of primary school net attendance (49.7%) than the national rate (42%).[20] This was certainly not the case for the indigenous groups. In 1999, of 300 students in Assosa secondary school, only twenty were indigenous, and only three were girls. An analogous situation existed in the Teacher Training Institute and Health Professionals School in Metekel, and the Small Scale Enterprise Training Centre in Kamashi.

As the first decade of the 21st century came to a close, it appeared that the future of the *kilil*'s economy was going to be decided by Addis Ababa's policy of leasing land to investors for biofuel production. This has the support of the local political elite. 'The Region has huge available plots', enthused Yaregal Aysheshin.[21] An early start was made in Metekel zone by investors from the highlands who leased land for commercial farms and mining ventures. By 2001, eleven such enterprises were listed with a total of 38,000ha.[22] This was a trifle compared with the vast tracts of land being considered for leasing to foreign investors at the end of the decade. MIDROC alone was asking for 100,000ha.

Protestant missionaries made an appearance in the region at the start of the new century. They made early inroads among the Oromo in southern Beni Shangul Gumuz, where they claimed some 90,000 adherents according to the 2007 census. Amhara and Tigray immigrants remained faithful to the Ethiopian Orthodox Church whose flock numbered about 221,000 according to the same source. With over 300,000 faithful, Islam outnumbered both of them, while some 40,000, mostly Gumuz, held on to their traditional faith. It was the latter who became the target of the Blair Foundation, an American mission offering to build a hospital and an orphanage in Kamashi. By 2009, it claimed to have 'planted' 1,131 churches among the Gumuz, a good start towards its proclaimed goal: 'the planting of Christian churches in an area previously controlled spiritually by witchdoctors and Islamic fundamentalists'.[23]

Conflict in Beni Shangul Gumuz

Conflict had simmered for a long time in the southern border of Beni Shangul Gumuz with Oromia's Eastern Wallega Zone. Oromo peasants long descended the western escarpment into the lowland valleys, pushing the Gumuz into what became Kamashi Zone. This incursion slowed down when the *kilil* boundaries were drawn but did not stop, and met increasingly militant resistance from the Gumuz, who now could rely on

[20] Ministry of Education, *Annual Abstract, 2005.*

[21] *Addis Fortune* (28 January 2008).

[22] Wolde Selassie Aboute Deboch (2002:121).

[23] *Blair Foundation Newsletter.*

support from their own *kilil* administration and militia. In mid-May 2008, a large, well armed force of Gumuz crossed the border into Eastern Wallega to attack Oromo villages. The raid lasted two days and left scores of Oromo peasants dead, many villages burned and thousands displaced. This was by far the worst inter-community violence in recent years, and it ended Yarekal Aysheshin's record run in office.

Summary

It was only at the turn of the 21st century that Addis Ababa began to reach out to the southern and western borderlands with an eye to closing the integration gap, beginning the process literally from the ground up by linking the fringe periphery to the the rest of the country with transport and communication services. An effort to groom a subordinate corps of 'regional intellectuals' produced meagre results, obliging the federal government not to let the reins of administration slip from its grasp. The EPRDF proved wholly lacking in imagination when it repeated the same PDO formula in an attempt to bring a modicum of stability to the indigenous communities. The fusion and diffusion of parties with ever-changing names was a threadbare facade for small cliques of officeholders and office seekers competing for Addis Ababa's favour. Party membership consisted solely of actual and aspiring candidates for state employment, who were obliged to register as party members and pay fees. State offices changed hands not through elections – since it was inconceivable that the incumbents would lose – but only when Addis Ababa withdrew its favour. If such play acting had any effect, it would be to debase the idea of democracy in the minds of the people.

Keeping a tight rein suited the regime as the potential of resource appropriation in the lowland periphery emerged in dramatic fashion at the turn of the century. Resources such as land and water for agro-industry, hydroelectric energy and mineral wealth, flora and fauna for tourism, were coming within exploitation range with the help of foreign capital. The exploitation of lowland resources was perceived on a grand scale and was bound to have a momentous impact on the lives of the area's communities and on their relationship with the centre. This would be no time for the centre to relax its control over the region.

Conclusion

Nation building was the lodestar of African nationalism in the heady days of decolonisation half a century ago, and it was in keeping with the times that Ethiopian nationalists launched their own project. Universally regarded as the political hallmark of modernisation, nation building acquired an aura of predetermination and inevitability derived from this connection; since modernisation is inevitable, so is the success of the project. Encouraged by social scientists who confidently predicted the passing of traditional society (Lerner 1958), this teleological perspective illuminated the nationalist mindset in the early post-colonial era.

It took the experience of a few decades to shatter 'the illusion that national integration is a historically-ordained destiny' (C. Young 1982: 164). Initial concepts of 'political development' with their intrinsic optimism soon lost their lustre to be replaced by others steeped in pessimism. At least one scholar saw the flaw in the theory early on. 'Theories of "nation-building" have tended to either ignore the question of ethnic diversity or to treat the matter of ethnic identity superficially as merely one of a number of minor impediments to effective state-integration', he wrote. To the contrary, he argued, modernisation tends to heighten ethnic consciousness and to politicise ethnic identities that resist state-promoted schemes of integration (Connor, 1972: 319). Most scholars now agree that there was 'a misreading of the historical relationship between modernization and cultural consciousness' (C. Young 1982: 169).

Connor also drew attention to the fact that the twin of nation-building is 'nation-destroying', given that every nationalist project entails the suppression and eradication of rival identities and cultures. C. Young adds: 'The nation-building idea is likely to be most mischievous in centre-periphery cultural polities. The historical association of the state with the core culture means that the nation is inevitably identified with the dominant group. The imperative of nation-building then means the imposition of the core culture upon the periphery. …Nation-building as a moral cloak for intensified domination is a dangerous doctrine' he warns, citing Ethiopia as an example (ibid.: 175).

Even so, social scientists continue to make qualitative distinctions between the nation building efforts of dominant groups, which they attribute to 'nationalism', and similar efforts of subordinate groups which they attribute to 'ethnicity'. In his influential work, *Nationalism and the State*, John Breuilly avoids the confusion resulting from this play of words: 'Nationalism is, above all else, about politics and politics is about power. Power, in the modern world, is principally about the control of the state. The central task, therefore, is to relate nationalism to the objective of obtaining and using state power' (1993: 1). Breuilly highlights the similarity of goals by those who engage in struggles for state power and the common resort to nationalism as the preferred ideology. What is the goal of 'ethnic' political movements other than gaining power in an existing state or a new state of their own?

The notion of 'negotiated statehood' challenges another assumption that state builders share, that the end product of their efforts will be the one they have in mind. It draws attention to the contested nature of the project and the multitude of variables that interact and influence its course. Every step of that course is negotiated rather than dictated; consequently the final outcome is neither predetermined nor predictable (Doornbos, 2010). The present study traced the process of contestation and negotiation that marks the course of state-building in Ethiopia over a century. Certain conclusions can be drawn from it. The main one is that the project is far from completion and its end cannot be predicted. The analysis of succeeding crises along the route highlights the structural fault in its design, which is the centre's monopoly of power. In the nationalist mindset this is non-negotiable, because to relinquish it would be to remove the linchpin that keeps the state structure intact. This attitude is typical in a region where 'national self-determination' is the catalyst of political mobilisation and where no self-respecting nationality is without its 'national liberation front'. Rational as this feeling of insecurity might be, it is also a measure of how far the nationalist project is from completion. For Ethiopian nationalists, the loss of Eritrea is a recent bitter lesson, and the loss of access to the sea an open wound. Above all, however, it is the cloud of Oromo nationalism that darkens the horizon of their country's future. However feeble its presence may have been in the past, there is no doubt that it has a future, and given the weight of the Oromo nation in the scale of things, it will play a crucial role in determining Ethiopia's future.

There is a second conclusion to be drawn from the study of the past. The strain of maintaining centre hegemony in the face of persistent, militant opposition from subordinate groups has divided the centre itself twice in the past, leading to as many ruptures and changes of regime. Each of the latter sought to relieve the strain by modifying the centre/periphery relationship without, however, relaxing the centre's grip on power, and the first two went down defending it. The present regime is engaged in the same struggle on two fronts. Compelled to concede the loss of Eritrea, it is fighting off secessionist threats in other parts of the periphery. At the same time it has to defend itself against mounting opposition within the centre itself, a threat that it has managed so far to suppress at the cost of derailing a tentative experiment in democratisation which it had itself introduced. The conclusion is that the political rift in the centre foreshadows another rupture with unforeseeable consequences.

What could be expected from another rupture and change of regime in Addis Ababa? Of course, that will depend on the nature of the successor regime. Assuming that it would rise from the ashes of the so called 'legal' opposition to the EPRDF, certain of its features can be discerned and may serve as harbingers of the future. Incoherent as the 'legal' opposition may have seemed, it is clear that it is dominated by nationalist factions viscerally hostile to 'ethnic' federalism and committed to reversing the process of state decentralisation, to reassert full centre control over the periphery, and to curtail the administrative autonomy now enjoyed by the *kilil*. This, of course, is anathema to the factions that represent the periphery in the ephemeral, brittle coalitions they formed with the hard core nationalists on the eve of elections.

The real issue behind the debate on federalism, which ostensibly focuses on power sharing between centre and periphery, is the perennial concern with access to land. Land scarcity in the Abyssinian homeland has not diminished; it has worsened, and no alternative means of livelihood have emerged to absorb the excess population. Giving the *kilil* the authority to administer land was necessary to relieve the political pressure that had accumulated over a century by the expropriation of land in the highland periphery. This, in effect, shut off the safety valve which in the past released pressure in the north by allowing population shifts southwards to the highland periphery. With population growth remaining high and agricultural production stuck at subsistence level, it is inevitable that mounting pressure in the north will force the opening of this safety valve. A start in that direction has already been made, with the federal government taking the initiative in the land leasing programme that has so far affected mainly the lowlands. The decisive moment will come when it proves imperative to open the highland periphery to land-starved Abyssinian peasants from the north. Then the modicum of self-administration allowed to the periphery at present will be revoked, and the centre/periphery relationship will revert to its historical form.

Land is also a ripening political issue in the lowlands. In the past, this region did not offer readily exploitable resources, and the centre was content with a token state presence in it. The resource equation changed at the start of the 21st century, and the centre shook off its complacency, joining hands with capitalist enterprise in an effort to turn the sun-baked, infertile lowlands into an efficient area of production for food and sources of energy. Employment creation is advertised as an immediate benefit for the local population, but experience shows that pastoralists are unlikely to become plantation workers; consequently the work force is likely to consist of peasants emigrating from the highlands. Experience shows also that this will exacerbate tensions with indigenous communities in a region already tormented by conflict which the state is unable to manage. Securing the means of production – land and labour – for the new strategy of agricultural development will oblige the centre to reinforce the shaky hold it has at present over the region. The failure to exploit existing mineral resources in the Somali *kilil* decades after discovery illustrates this point.

Land, the catalyst in the political process, is another issue that divides the 'legal' opposition in the centre. Because of its incendiary potential, the issue is avoided in political debate, save for arguments over state versus private ownership. Privatisation is advocated by the nationalist factions that oppose 'ethnic federalism' implying, without saying so, that access to land should be determined by market forces. Factions of the 'legal opposition' representing the periphery are haunted by the prospect of another Abyssinian invasion of their homelands driven by market forces, and oppose any reform touching the land that is decided at the centre where the periphery is not fairly represented. It is no surprise therefore that the 'legal opposition' was unable to come up with even a hint of a common programme beyond plaintive appeals for more democracy. Consequently, a credible successor to the EPRDF that blends both these political currents is unlikely.

A worrisome contradiction lay in this juxtaposition of incompatible goals and the yearning for democracy manifested by Ethiopian nationalists. The return to the *status quo ante* of a centralised state under centre control that they advocate can only be imposed on the periphery with greater exertion and force than ever. If this were to happen, it would condemn yet another generation of Ethiopians to authoritarian rule and civil strife, without guaranteeing the ultimate survival of the state. It would greatly improve the prospects of 'illegal' opposition movements and the mortal threat they represent to the state-building project.

Ethiopia's rulers face a genuine dilemma, a choice between two risky alternatives. One would be to cross the political frontier, make a clean break with the past, renounce centre hegemony and accept equitable power sharing with the periphery. The result could be a genuine multinational, multi-cultural, decentralised state. Of course, there would be a price to pay. The loss of the Somali region would be one part of it. Another would be the political downgrading of the Abyssinian core, and the loss of the centre's prerogative to determine the distribution of national resources – land being the most important of these. The alternative is not to enter into this uncharted terrain, to hold tight to the reins of power at the centre and rely on the collaboration of the subordinate elite to help control the periphery, while pressing on with efforts to improve peoples' welfare and for the regime to earn their trust and the state their loyalty. As far as the incumbent regime is concerned, however, the die has been cast.

*

The state-building project is faced with additional problems in the lowlands. The process of integration there lags behind by a century compared to the rest of the country. None of the developments that brought regions, communities and social classes closer to the centre and to the state over the same period touched the lives of people in the lowlands in a way that would encourage them to turn their sights towards the centre, or to pin their hopes for betterment on the regimes that followed one another in Addis Ababa. Remote, uninformed and uninterested, lowlanders are scarcely aware of, and quite detached from, the power struggles in the centre. They are painfully aware that they are powerless and have no say in these matters. In the meeting organised by the UNDP in 2005, a Mursi elder put it succinctly: 'We understand the problem is that we have no person who can make appeals on our behalf to the government or someone who works for the government,' he said.

The problems the elder referred to are existential and focus on access to land and water to produce food and ward off famine. These are the same problems that Ethiopia's rulers have wrestled with for decades. However, there is a crucial difference between their respective world views within which these problems are perceived and solutions envisaged. The Mursi view of the world is admittedly narrow, and looks to solutions within the traditional mode of production and through their own efforts. The world view of Ethiopia's rulers encompasses a nation-state in which the Mursi are invisible. The former have tried and failed to break the shackles of a stagnating agriculture, and in the process lost faith in their peoples' ability to do so. Now they have put their faith in external intervention as the way to spark off an agricultural revolution.

Neglected for an entire century, this region is now emerging as a bright hope in Ethiopia's search for an escape from poverty. The lowlands' resources – land, water, minerals – are expected to play a primary role in this latest effort. In addition to converting marginal lands to commercial cultivation, the search is on for mineral energy sources in an area of the Horn where important discoveries have been already made. If the search bears fruit, the lowlands will become the unlikely catalyst for economic development for the country at large. The effect this will have on the lowlanders and their relationship with the centre will influence the direction of the state-building process for the foreseeable future.

Undoubtedly, the world view of the state builders will prevail, and the Mursi world is destined for extinction. This would be a matter of regret for many reasons, but it is not a feeling one could reasonably expect Ethiopian nationalists to share. On the other hand, there is little doubt that this latest expropriation of indigenous resources will prove an additional destabilising factor in the lowlands. The Mursi will not feature prominently in what follows, but others – Afar, Somali, Borana, Anywaa, Nuer, Gumuz – certainly will. Keeping them pliant to the spoliation of their habitat and the destruction of their world will take far more investment in the application of force than the centre has been able to make so far. The danger is that reliance on force to cross this frontier, in order to genuinely integrate the lowlands into the Ethiopian state, will prove to be just as unsuccessful as it was in the past.

The fact that nationalists continue to regard centre hegemony essential for their project, and the likelihood of far greater force to maintain it in the future, is of vital concern for all Ethiopians. As an instrument of social and political control, force is inept and indiscriminate; its malignant impact is catholic. No one enjoys freedom, security, and human or political rights under authoritarian rule, neither in the periphery nor at the centre. Generations of Ethiopians have paid a heavy price for misgovernment. Their lives were blighted by endless conflict and their country reduced to abject poverty. There is no point in asking nationalists whether the end justifies such means. However, one can ask whether in the 21st century these means are the only, or the best suited, for the accomplishment of their cherished goal.

Selected Bibliography

Abbreviations

CSA: Central Statistical Agency
DFID: Department for International Development, UK.
ESUNA: Ethiopian Students Union of North America.
ICARA: International Conference for Assistance to Refugees in Africa
ICES: International Conference of Ethiopian Studies.
ILCA: International Livestock Centre for Africa.
ILRI: International Livestock Research Institute.
ISEN: Institute for the Study of Ethiopian Nationalities.
OSSREA: Organisation for Social Science Research in East Africa.
PCDP: Pastoralist Communication Development Programme.
ROAPE: Review of African Political Economy.

Abdi M. Abdullahi. 2007. 'The Ogaden National Liberation Front: The Dilemma of its Struggle in Ethiopia', *Review of African Political Economy*, 34: 113.

Abdi Umar, Hassan Ahmed, Taufik Adan. 2002. 'Herders with no Herds: Displaced pastoralists in Fik Zone, Somali National Regional State, Ethiopia', Jijiga: SCF-UK

Abdussamad H. Ahmad. 1995. 'The Gumuz of the Lowlands of West Gojjam: The Frontier in History, 1900-1935', *Africa* 50: 1.

——. 1999. 'Trading in Slaves in Bela-Shangul and Gumuz, Ethiopia: Border Enclaves in History, 1897-1938', *Journal of African History*, 40: 3.

Abbink, J. 1997. 'Territory, Space and State among the Suri: Changes in an Ethiopian Periphery, 1977-1997', Presented to the 13th ICES. Kyoto.

——. 1998. 'Ritual and Political Forms of Violence', *Cahiers d'Etudes Africaines*, 150/152, 38.

——. 2000. 'Violence and the Crisis of Conciliation: Suri, Dizi and the State in South-West Ethiopia', *Africa*, 70, 4.

——. 2002. 'Paradoxes of Power and Culture in an Old Periphery: Surma, 1974-98', in *Remapping Ethiopia: Socialism and After*, edited by W. James, D.L. Donham, E. Kurimoto, A. Triulzi, London: James Currey.

Abdulahi A. Shongolo. 1994. 'The Gumi Gaayo Assembly of the Borana: A traditional legislative organ and its relationship to the Ethiopian state and a modernising world', *Zeitschrift fur Ethnologie*. 119.

Abdulhamid Bedre Kello. 1989. 'Settling Semi-nomadic Pastoralists in the Awash Valley', *Ethiopian Journal of Development Research*. 11, 1.

Abir, M. 1965. 'The Emergence and Consolidation of the Monarchies of Enarea and Jimma in the first half of the Nineteenth Century', *Journal of African History*, 6, 2.

——. 1968. *Ethiopia: The Era of the Princes*, New York: Praeger.

——. 1970. 'Southern Ethiopia', in *Pre-Colonial African Trade in Central and Eastern Africa*, edited by R. Gray & D. Birmingham. Oxford: Oxford University Press.

Abraham Demoz. 1995. 'State Policy and the Medium of Expression', in *Silence is not Golden: A Critical Anthology of Ethiopian Literature*, edited by Tadesse Adera & Ali Jimale Ahmed. Lawrenceville, NJ: Red Sea Press.

Addis Hiwet. 1971. 'The Ethiopian Student Movement: Some Critical Remarks', *Struggle*. Addis Ababa, June.

——. 1975. *Ethiopia: From Autocracy to Revolution*, Sheffield: *ROAPE*.

——. 1976. *Ethiopia: From Autocracy to Bourgeois Dictatorship*, London: (self-published).

——. 1987. 'A Certain Political Vocation: Reflections on the Ethiopian Intelligentsia', Presented to the Conference on the Ethiopian Left and the Revolution. New School of Social Research, New York, 29-30 May.

Afar National Regional State. 1999. 'Short Description about the Afar Administrative Region', Presented to the Investment Workshop for Afar, Somali, Gambella, Beni Shangul Gumuz. Addis Ababa, May 1999.

——. 2003. 'Regional Public Sector Capacity Building Program. Justice System Reform Program Action-Plan, FY 2004-2008'. Semera: Capacity Building Co-ordination Bureau.

Aguilar, M. 1998. *Being Oromo in Kenya*, Trenton NJ: Red Sea Press.

Ahmed Hassen Omer. 1997. 'State and Ethnic Relations in North-eastern Shewa (Ethiopia), 1912-1935', Presented to the 13th ICES. Kyoto.

——. 2002. 'Emperor Menelik's Attempts towards Political Integration: Case Study from North-Eastern Shoa (Ethiopia), 1889-1906', *Annales d'Ethiopie*, 18.

Ahmed Yusuf Farah. 1997. 'Gadabursi Clans of Northern Somalia and South-East Ethiopia', in *Pastoralism, Ethnicity and the State in Ethiopia*, edited by R. Hogg. London: Haan Associates.

Ahmed Shide (n.d.). 'Conflict is Everyday Business: Changing Nature of Local Conflict in Federal Ethiopia: The Case Study of Ma'eso District', (Typescript).

Aijmer, G. & J. Abbink, (eds). 2000. *Meanings of Violence*, Oxford: Berg.

Ajit Kumar Chose. 1985. 'Transforming Feudal Agriculture: Agrarian Change in Ethiopia since 1974', *The Journal of Development Studies*, 22, 1.

Aklilu Abraham, Asnake Kefale, Hussein Jamma, Tafesse Olika. 2000. 'Conflict and Conflict Mitigation Mechanisms in Dollo Ado and Dollo Bay Woreda of the Somali Regional State', Addis Ababa: Report to SCF/USA.

Allen, C. 1996. 'The Cunning of Conflict', *ROAPE*, 23, 67.

Almagor, U. 1978. *Pastoral Partners: Affinity and Bond Partnership among the Dassanetch of Southwest Ethiopia*, Manchester: Manchester University Press.

——. 1986. 'Institutionalising a fringe periphery: Dassanetch-Amhara relations', in *The Southern Marches of Imperial Ethiopia. Essays in History and Social Anthropology*, edited by D. L. Donham & W. James. Oxford: James Currey.

Almeida, M. 1954. 'The History of High Ethiopia or Abassia', in *Some Records of Ethiopia: 1593-1646*, edited by C.F. Beckingham & G.W.B. Huntingford. London: The Hakluyt Society.

Alvares, F. 1954. *The Prester John of the Indies*, edited by C.F. Beckingham & G.W.B. Huntingford, London: The Hakluyt Society.

Amanuel Sahle. 1982. 'Tigrigna: Recent History and Development', Presented to the 7th ICES, Lund.

Amman, C. 2005. 'Review of Food Aid Delivery in the Somali Region of Ethiopia, 1984-2004', Addis Ababa: UN-OCHOA.

Andargachew Tiruneh. 1993. *The Ethiopian Revolution*, Cambridge: Cambridge University Press.

Anderson, B. 1983. *Imagined Communities: Reflections on the Origin and Spread of Nationalism*, London: Verso.

Anderson, D. 1986. 'Stock Theft and Moral Economy in Colonial Kenya', *Africa*, 56, 4.

Andreas Eshete. 1970. 'The Problem of Regionalism and Religion: Some Theoretical Considerations', ESUNA.

Aneesa Kassam. 1995. *Gabra*, New York: Rosen Publishing Group.

Anouar Abdel-Malek. 1981. *Nation and Revolution: Social Dialectics*, New York: State University of New York.

Aramis Houmed Soule. 2005. *Deux Vies dans L'Afrique: Mahamad Hanfare (1861- 1902) et Ali Mirah Hanfare (1944-), Sultans Afars*, Addis Ababa: Centre Français des Etudes Ethiopiennes.

Asafa Jalata. 1993. *Oromia & Ethiopia: State Formation and Ethnonational Conflict, 1868-1992*, Denver: Lynn Rienner.

——. (ed.). 1998. *Oromo Nationalism and the Ethiopian Discourse: The Search for Freedom and Democracy*, Lawrenceville, NJ: Red Sea Press.

Asfa Yilma. 1936. *Haile Selassie, Emperor of Ethiopia*. London.

Asmarom Legesse. 1963. 'Class Systems Based on Time', *Journal of Ethiopian Studies*, 1, 2.

——. 1973. *Gadda: Three Approaches to the Study of an African Society*, New York: Free Press.

——. 2000. *Oromo Democracy: An Indigenous African Political System*, Lawrenceville, NJ: Red Sea Press.

Asme Giyorgis. (n.d.) *Ya-Galla Tariq*, (Amharigna), Addis Ababa University, Institute of Ethiopian Studies.

Austin, H. H. 1902. 'Survey of the Sobat Region', *Geographical Journal*. 17.

Ayele Gebre. 2001. *Pastoralism under Pressure: Land Alienation and PastoralTransformation among the Karrayu of Eastern Ethiopia*, Maastricht: Shaker Publishing.

Ayele Solomon, Assegid Workalemahu, M. A. Jabbar, Ahmed M. M, Belachew Hurrisa. 2003. 'Livestock Marketing in Ethiopia: A review of structure, performance and development initiatives', Nairobi: ILRI.

Azarya, V. 1996. *Nomads and the State in Africa: The Political Roots of Marginality*, Aldershot: Ashgate Publishing.

Badie, B. 2000. *The Imported State: The Westernization of the Political Order*, Stanford: Stanford University Press.

Baer, G. W. 1967. *The Coming of the Italian-Ethiopian War*, Cambridge MA: Harvard University Press.

Bahrey. 1954. 'History of the Galla' in *Some Records of Ethiopia 1593-1646*, edited by C. F. Beckingham & G.W. B. Huntingford. London: Hakluyt Society.

Bahru Zewde. 1983. *Economic origins of the absolutist state in Ethiopia (1916-1935)*.

——. 1987. An Overview and Assessment of Gambella Trade (1904-1935)', *The International Journal of African Historical Studies*. 20. 1.

——. 1991. *A History of Modern Ethiopia, 1855-1991*, London: James Currey.

——. 2002. *Pioneers of Change in Ethiopia*, Oxford: James Currey.

Barnes, C. 2000. 'The Ethiopian State and its Somali Periphery circa 1888-1948', Ph.D. dissertation,, University of Cambridge.

Bartels, L. 1983. *Oromo Religion*, Berlin: Dietrich Reimer Verlag.

Barth, F. 1973. 'A General Perspective on Nomad-Sedentary Relations', in *The Desert and the Sown*, edited by C. Nelson. Berkeley CA: University of California.

Bassi, M. 1997. 'Returnees in Moyale District, Southern Ethiopia: New Means for an Old Inter-Ethnic Game', in *Pastoralists, Ethnicity and the State in Ethiopia*, edited by R. Hogg. London: Haan Associates.

——. 2005. *Decisions in the Shade: Political and Juridical Processes among the Oromo-Borana*, Trenton, New Jersey: Red Sea Press.

Baxter, P. T. W. & U. Almagor. 1978. *Age, Generation and Time: Some Features of East African Age Organisation*, London: Hurst.

——. 1980. 'Always on the outside looking in. A view of the 1969 Ethiopian election from a rural constituency', *Ethnos*. 1-2.

——. 1991. '"Big Men" and Cattle Licks in Oromoland', in *When the Grass is Gone'*, edited by P. T. W. Baxter. Uppsala: Scandinavian Institute of African Studies.

——. 1994. 'The Creation and Constitution of the Oromo Nationality', in *Ethnicity and Conflict in the Horn of Africa*, edited by K. Fukui & J. Markakis. London: James Currey.

——. & J. Hultin, A. Triulzi (eds). 1996. *Being and Becoming Oromo: Historical and Anthropological Enquiries*, Lawrenceville, NJ: Red Sea Press.

Bayne, E. A. 1965. *Four Ways of Politics. State and Nation in Italy, Somalia, Israel, Iran*, New York:

American Universities Field Staff.

Beachey, R. W. 1962. 'The Arms Trade in East Africa in the late Nineteenth Century', *The Journal of African History*. 3, 3.

Beckingham, C. F. & Huntingford, G. W. B. (eds). 1954. *Some Records of Ethiopia: 1593-1646*, London: The Hakluyt Society.

Belachew Hurissa & Jemberu Eshetu. 2002. 'Challenges and opportunities of livestock trade in Ethiopia', Presented to the 10th annual conference of the Ethiopian Society of Animal Production in Addis Ababa.

Bender, M. L. 1976. *Language in Ethiopia*, Oxford: Oxford University Press.

Berhanou Abebe. 1971. 'Evolution de la propriétée foncière au Choa (Ethiopie) du règne de Menelik à la constitution de 1931', Ph.D. dissertation, University of Sorbonne.

Berihun Mebratie. 2004. 'The Past in the Present: The Dynamics of Identity and Otherness among the Gumuz of Ethiopia', Ph.D. dissertation, Norwegian University of Science and Technology.

Bestemann, C. & L. V. Cassanelli. 2000. *The Struggle for Land in Southern Somalia: The War Behind the War*, London: Haan Associates.

Boku Tache. 2000. 'Changing Patterns of Resource Control among the Borana Pastoralists of Southern Ethiopia,' in *Pastoralists and Environment: Experience from the Greater Horn of Africa*, edited by L. Manger & Abdel Ghafar M. Ahmed. Addis Ababa: OSSREA.

Boone, C. 2003. *Political Topographies of the African State*. Cambridge: Cambridge University Press.

Bourdieu, P. 1994. 'Rethinking the state: genesis and structure of the bureaucratic field', *Sociological Theory*, 12, 1.

Borelli, J. 1890. *Ethiopie Meridionale: Journale de mon voyage aux pays Amhara, Oromo, et Sidama, September 1885 a November 1888*, Paris.

Boserup, E. 1981. *Population and Technology*, Oxford: Blackwell.

Braukamper, U. 1977. 'La Conquête and l'Administration Ethiopienne du Kambata au temps du Menilek II', Presented to the 5th ICES. Nice.

——. 1980. 'Oromo country of origin: a reconsideration of a hypothesis', Presented to the 6th ICES. Tel Aviv.

Broch-Due, V. (ed.) 2005. *Violence and Belonging: The Quest for Identity in Post Colonial Africa*, London: Routledge.

Brooke, J. W. 1905. 'A journey west and north of Lake Rudolf', *Geographical Journal*, 25.

Bruce, J. 1972. 'A Preliminary Consideration of the Legal Status of Nomadic Lands', Report to the Land Tenure Division, Ministry of Land and Administration. Addis Ababa.

Bulatovich, A. 2000. *Ethiopia Through Russian Eyes: country in transition, 1896-1898)*, edited by R. Seltzer. Lawrenceville, NJ: Red Sea Press.

Burton, R. 1856. *First Footsteps in East Africa*, London: Longman.

Bustorf, D. 1997. 'Imam Sugato Zayni, A war-lord of the Selt'e Gogot', Presented to the 13th ICES. 1997, Kyoto.

Butzer, K. W. 1961. 'Climatic Changes in Arid Regions since the Pliocene', *Arid Zones Research*, 17.

——. 1971. 'Recent history of an Ethiopian Delta. The Omo river and the level of Lake Rudolf', University of Chicago, Department of Geography Research.

Carlyle, T. 1841. *On Heroes, Hero-Worship and the Heroic in History*.

Cerulli, E. 1933. *Etiopia occidentale (dallo Scioa alla frontiera del Sudan: Note del viaggio 1927-1928*. Rome.

Clapham, C. 1969. *Haile Selassie's Government*, London: Longman.

——. 1988. *Transformation and Continuity in Revolutionary Ethiopia*, Cambridge: Cambridge University Press.

——.1995. 'The Politics of Post-Insurgency', in *Democracy and Political Change in Sub-Saharan Africa*, edited by J. A. Wiseman. London: Routlege.

——. 2000. 'War and state formation in Ethiopia and Eritrea', University of Sussex: The Global Site.

——. 2002. 'Rewriting Ethiopian History', *Annales d'Ethiopie*. 18.

Claude, I. L. 1986. 'Myths about the state', *Review of International Studies*, 12, 1.

Cohen, J. M. & N. I. Isaksson. 1987. 'Villagisation in Ethiopia's Arsi Region'. *The Journal of Modern African Studies*, 25, 3.

——. & D. Weintraub. 1975. *Land and Peasants in Imperial Ethiopia*, Assen: Van Gorcum B.V.

Cohen, R. 1984. 'Warfare and state formation: wars make states and states make war', in *Warfare, Culture, and Environment*, edited by R. B. Ferguson. New York: Academic Press.

Collins, R. O. 1971. *Land Beyond the Rivers: The Southern Sudan, 1898-1918*, New Haven: Yale University Press.

Consozione Turistica Italiana. 1936. *Guida Dell'Africa Orientale Italiana*, Rome.

Conzelman, W. E. (ed). 1895. *Chronique de Galawdewos (Claudius)*, Paris.

Cooper, R. L. 1976. 'Government Language Policy', in *Language in Ethiopia*, edited by M. L. Bender. Oxford: Oxford University Press.

——. & M. King. 1976. 'Language and University Students', in *Language in Ethiopia*, edited by M. L. Bender. Oxford: Oxford University Press.

——. & R. J. Horvath. 1976. 'Language, Migration and Urbanisation', in *Language in Ethiopia*, edited by M. L. Bender. Oxford: Oxford University Press.

Cossins, N. J. 1971. 'A Study of the Somali Clans in the Jijiga Area of Ethiopia', Addis Ababa: Livestock & Meat Board.

——. 1973. 'Green Heart of a Dying Land: A Study of the New Cotton Wealth of the Old Afar Sultanate of Aussa', Report for Hunting Technical Services. Addis Ababa.

——. 1981. 'New Ways for Old Worlds: Development and Research. A New Approach to the Ethiopian Rangeland Development Project', Addis Ababa: Third Livestock Development Project (TLDP).

Crummey, D. 1980. 'Abyssinian Feudalism', *Past & Present*, 89.

——. 1990. 'Society, State and Nationality in the recent historiography of Ethiopia', *Journal of African History*, 31.

Dahl, G. & A. Hjort. 1976. *Having Herds: Pastoral Herd Growth and Household Economy*, Stockholm: University of Stockholm.

Darkwah, R. H. K. 1975. *Shewa, Menelik and the Ethiopian Empire*, London: Heinemann.

David, R. 1967. *Le Droit de la famille dans le code civil ethiopien*, Milano: Universita degli studi di camerino, instituto giuridico.

Davidson, B. 1982. *The Black Man's Burden: Africa and the Curse of the Nation-State,*, London: James Currey.

Deflem, M. 1999. 'Warfare, Political Leadership, and State Formation: The Case of the Zulu Kingdom, 1808-1879', *Ethnology* 38, 4.

De Haven King, L. 2006. *Africa and the Nation-State: State Formation and Identity in Ancient Egypt, Hausaland and Southern Africa*, Lewiston, NY: Edwin Mellen Press.

Dessalegn Rahmato. 1988. 'Settlement and Resettlement in Mettekel, Western Ethiopia', *Africa* (Rome) 43, 1.

Deutsch, K.W. 1966. *Nationalism and Social Communications*, Cambridge MA: Cambridge University Press.

Direje Feyisa. 2003. 'Ethnic Groups and Conflict: The Case of Anywaa-Nuer Relations in the Gambella Region', Ph.D. dissertation, Martin Luther University.

Dolal, S. M. 1990. 'Development Prospects for Pastoralism in the Horn of Africa: A Study of Pastoralist Farming Systems in Ogadenia', Ph.D. dissertation, University of Leeds.

Donham, D.L. 1985. *Work and Power in Maale, Ethiopia*, Ann Arbor, Michigan: University of Michigan.

——. & W. James. (eds)1986. *The Southern Marches of Imperial Ethiopia: Essays in History and Social Anthropology*, Oxford: James Currey.

——. 1986. 'Old Abyssinia and the new Ethiopian empire: themes in social history', in *The Southern Marches of Imperial Ethiopia: Essays in History and Social Anthropology*, edited by D. L. Donham & W. James. Oxford: James Currey.

——. 1997. 'The Increasing Penetration of the Revolutionary State in Maale Life, 1977-1987', Presented to the 13th ICES. Kyoto.

——. 1999. *Marxist Modern: an Ethnographic History of the Ethiopian Revolution*, Los Angeles: University of California Press.

Doornbos, M. 2010. 'Negotiating African Statehood: Dynamics: Negotiability and its Limits',

Development and Change. 41, 4.
Dyson-Hudson, N. 1985. 'Pastoral Production Systems and Livestock Development Projects: An East African Perspective', in *Putting People First*, edited by M. M. Cerea. Oxford: Oxford University Press.
Eide, M.O. 2000. *Revolution and Religion in Ethiopia, 1974-1985*, London: James Currey.
Emanuel Abraham. 1995. *Reminiscences of my Life*, Oslo: Lunde Forlag.
Eisenstadt, S.N. 1963. *Political Systems of Empires*, Glencoe, Ill.: Free Press of Glencoe.
Epple, E. S. 2005. 'Missionary work and cultural change among the Banna and Bashada of southern Ethiopia: an emic perspective', in *Ethiopia and the Missions: Historical and Anthropological Insights*, edited by V. Boll *et al.*, Munster: LIT Verlag.
Erlich, H. 1984. 'Tigre in Modern Ethiopian History', Presented to the 6th ICES. Lund.
——. 1986. *Ethiopia and the Challenge of Independence*, Boulder CO: Lynn Rienner.
Ertman, T. 1997. *Birth of the Leviathan: Building States and Regimes in Medieval and Early Modern Europe*, Cambridge University Press.
ESUNA 1976. 'The National Question in Ethiopia: Proletarian Internationalism or Bourgeois Nationalism'.
Ethiopia, 1969. *Report on Land Tenure Survey of Tigre Province*, Addis Ababa: Ministry of Land Reform and Administration.
——. 1970. *Report on Land Tenure Survey of Begemdir and Semien Province*, Addis Ababa: Ministry of Land Reform and Administration.
——. 1974. 'A Ten Year Plan for the Controlled Expansion of Ethiopian Education', Addis Ababa: Long Term Planning Committee, Ministry of Education and Fine Arts.
——. 1979. 'Class Struggle and the Problem of Eritrea', Addis Ababa: COPWE.
——. 1984. 'Instructions given to the Nationalities Affairs Unit of the Central Committee of the Workers Party of Ethiopia and to Officials of the Institute for the Study of Ethiopian Nationalities by President Mengistu Haile Mariam. Addis Ababa: ISEN (Amharigna).
——. 1984. 'A Report of a Discussion on the Institute for the Study of Ethiopian Nationalities', Addis Ababa: ISEN (Amharigna)
——. 1984. 'Excerpts from documents of the Founding Congress of the Workers Party of Ethiopia', Addis Ababa: ISEN.
——. (n.d.). *Basic Documents*, Addis Ababa: ISEN.
——. 1986. *A Brief Almanak of Ethiopian Nationalities*, Addis Ababa: ISEN.
——. 2001. 'Report on Large and Medium Scale Manufacturing and Electricity Industries Survey', Addis Ababa. CSA.
——. 2002. *Statement on Pastoral Development Policy*. Addis Ababa: Ministry of Federal Affairs.
——. 2002. *Water Sector Development Programme, 2002-2016 Main Report*, Addis Ababa. Ministry of Water Resources.
——. 2004. 'Welfare Monitoring Survey: Statistical Report', Addis Ababa: CSA
——. 2004. 'Welfare Monitoring Survey: Analytical Report', Addis Ababa: CSA
Ethiopian Red Cross. 1988. 'Even after good rains, Afar pastoralists remain vulnerable', Addis Ababa.
Evans-Pritchard, E. E. 1940. *The Nuer*, Oxford: Oxford University Press.
——. 1941. *The Political System of the Anuak of the Anglo-Egyptian Sudan*, London: London School of Economics and Political Science.
——. & M. Fortes. (eds) 1940. *African Political Systems*,, Oxford: Oxford University Press.
Ezekiel Gebissa. 2002. 'The Italian Invasion, the Ethiopian Empire, and Oromo Nationalism: The Significance of the Western Oromo Confederation of 1936', *Northeast African Studies*, 9, 3.
Falge, C. 2005. 'The Ethiopianisation of the eastern Jikany Nuer from a religious perspective', in *Ethiopia and the Missions*, edited by V. Boll. Munster: LIT Verlag.
Fekade Azeze. 2002. 'Mengistulore. Oral Literatures Depicting the Man, His Regime, Officials and Proclamations', in *Ethiopia: The Challenge of Democracy from Below*, edited by Bahru Zewde and S. Pausewang. Uppsala: Scandinavian Institute of African Studies.
Fekadu Adugna. 2004. 'Inter-Ethnic Relations between the Oromo and Somali: the Case of Borana, Digodia and Marehan', M.A. Thesis, School of Graduate Studies, Addis Ababa University.

Fekadu Gedamua et al. 1984. *The Nomadic Areas of Ethiopia*, Addis Ababa: Ministry of Agriculture and UNDP.
Ferguson, R. B. & N. L. Whitehead (eds), 1992. *State and War in the Tribal Zone*, Santa Fe, New Mexico: School of American Research Press.
Fetha Nagast (Law of the Kings), (n.d.). Law Faculty, Addis Ababa University.
Friedrich, C. S. 1963. *Man and His Government: An Empirical Theory of Politics*, New York: McGraw Hill.
Galaty, J. G. & D.L. Johnson. 1990. 'Pastoral Systems in Global Perspectives', in *The World of Pastoralism*, edited by J. G. Galaty & D. L. Johnson, New York: Guildford Press.
Galtung, J. 1971. 'A Structural Theory of Imperialism', *Journal of Peace Research* 8, 2.
Gardner, J & J. El Bushra (eds). 2004. *Somalia, The Untold Story: The war through the eyes of Somali women*, London: Pluto.
Garretson, P.P. 1980. '*Manjil* Hamdan Abu Shok (1898-1938) and the Administration of Gubba', Presented to 5th ICES, 1977, Nice.
——. 2002. 'Vicious cycles: ivory, slaves, and arms on the new Maji frontier', in *Remapping Ethiopia: Socialism and After*, edited by W. James, D.L. Donham, E. Kurimoto, A. Triulzi, London: James Currey.
Gellner, E. 1964. *Thought and Change*, Chicago: Chicago University Press.
Getachew Haile, 1986. 'The unity and territorial integrity of Ethiopia', *Journal of Modern African Studies*, 24, 3.
Getachew Kassa Negussie. 1997a. 'A Case Study of the Afar in the Middle Awash, North-Eastern Ethiopia ', Presented to the 13th ICES, Kyoto.
——. 1997b. 'Tradition, Continuity and Socio-Economic Change Among the Pastoral Afar of the Middle Awash Region, North-Eastern Ethiopia', Ph.D. dissertation, School of Oriental and African Studies, University of London.
——. 1983. 'A Short History of the Garri of Southern Ethiopia up to 1941', Addis Ababa: Department of History, Addis Ababa University.
——. 2004. 'An Overview of Root Causes of Problems that Currently Affect Borana Pastoralists of Southern Ethiopia', in *Resource Alienation, Militarization and Development: Case Studies from East African Drylands*, edited by Mustafa Babiker. Addis Ababa: OSSREA.
Gezahegn Petros. 1994. 'The Karo of the Lower Omo Valley: Subsistence, social organization and relations with neighbouring groups', M.A. Thesis, Addis Ababa University.
Gilkes, P. 1975. *The Dying Lion: Feudalism and Modernisation in Ethiopia*, London: St. Martin.
Gilkes, P. 1999. *Ethiopia: Perspectives of Conflict, 1991-1999*, Bern: Swiss Peace Foundation.
Girma Negash. 1982. 'Language and Politics. A Comparative Analysis of Revolutionary Rhetoric of Regime Leaders and Power Contenders in Ethiopia between 1974 and 1977', Ph.D. dissertation,, University of Colorado.
Greenfield, R. 1965. *Ethiopia: A New Political History*, London: Pall Mall.
Griffiths, J. F. 1972. 'The Horn of Africa', in *Climates of Africa*, edited by J. F. Griffiths. Amsterdam: Elsevier.
Guebre Selassie. 1931. *Chronique du Règne de Menelik II*, Paris.
Haberland von, E. 1963. *Galla Sud-Athiopiens*, Stuttgart: W. Kohlhammer Verlag.
Hagmann, T. & D. Plecard. 2010. 'Negotiating Statehood. Dynamics of Power and Domination in Post-Colonial Africa', *Development and Change.*
Haile Mariam Larebo. 1994. *The Building of an Empire: Italian Land Policy and Practice in Ethiopia, 1935-1941*, Oxford: Clarendon Press.
Haile Selassie I. 1976. *Autobiography of Emperor Haile Selassie I: My Life and Ethiopia's Progress*, Oxford: Oxford University Press.
Halliday, F. & M. Molyneux. 1981. *The Ethiopian Revolution*, London: Verso.
Halpike, C. R. 1972. *The Konso of Ethiopia*, Oxford: Clarendon.
Hardin, G. 1968. 'The Tragedy of the Commons', *Science*, 162.
Helland, J. 1997. 'Development Interventions and Pastoral Dynamics in Southern Ethiopia', in *Pastoralists, Ethnicity and the State in Ethiopia*, edited by R. Hogg, London: Haan Associates.
——. 2002. 'Land Alienation in Borana: Some Land Tenure Issues in a Pastoral Context in Ethiopia', in *Resource Alienation, Militarization and Development: Case Studies from East African Drylands*, edited by Mustafa Babiker, Addis Ababa: OSSREA.

Heran Sereke Berhan. 1994. 'Ethiopia: A Historical Consideration of Amhara Ethnicity', Presented to the 12th ICES, East Lansing.
Herbst, J. 2000. *State and Power in Africa*, Princeton, NJ: Princeton University Press.
Herskovitz, M. J. 1926. 'The Cattle Complex in East Africa', *Anthropologist*, 28.
Herui Wolde Sellassie. 1930. *Biographie de Sa Majesté Haile Selassie Premier, Empereur d'Ethiopie*, Addis Ababa.
Hiroshi Matsuda. 1994. 'Annexation and assimilation: Koegu and their neighbours', in *Ethnicity and Conflict in the Horn of Africa*, edited by K. Fukui & J. Markakis, Oxford: James Currey.
——. 2002. 'Political Visibility & Automatic Rifles: The Muguji in the 1990s', in *Remapping Ethiopia: Socialism and After*, edited by W. James, D.L. Donham, E. Kurimoto, A. Triulzi, London: James Currey.
Hess, R. 1970. *Ethiopia: The Modernisation of Autocracy*, Ithaca NY: Cornell University Press.
Hinnant, J. T. 1977. 'The Gada System of the Guji of Southern Ethiopia', Ph.D. dissertation, University of Chicago.
Hoben, A. 1973. *Land Tenure among the Amhara of Ethiopia*, Chicago: University of Chicago Press.
Hogg, R. 1993. 'Continuity and Change among the Borana of Ethiopia', in *Conflict and the Decline of Pastoralism in the Horn of Africa*, edited by J. Markakis. London: Macmillan.
——. 1997. 'Changing Land Use and Resource Conflict Among Somali Pastoralists in the Haud of South-East Ethiopia', in *Pastoralism, Ethnicity and the State in Ethiopia*, edited by R. Hogg. London: Haan Publishing.
Holcomb, B. K. & Sisai Ibssa. 1990. *The Invention of Ethiopia*, Lawrenceville NJ: Red Sea Press.
Human Rights Watch. 1991. *Evil Days: Thirty Years of War and Famine in Ethiopia*, New York.
Huntingford, G. W. B. 1955. *The Galla of Ethiopia: The Kingdoms of Kaffa and Janjero*, London: International African Institute.
——. 1993. *History of the Galla (Oromo) of Ethiopia*, Oakland: African Sun Publishing.
Hutchinson, S. E. 1996. *Nuer Dillemas: Coping with Money, War and the State*, Berkeley: University of California Press.
Ibrahim Amae Elemo. 2005. *The Roles of Traditional Institutions Among the Borana Oromo, Southern Ethiopia*, Addis Ababa: Artistic Printing Enterprise.
Jama Sugule & R. Walker 1998. 'Changing Pastoralism in the Ethiopian Somali National Regional State' Addis Ababa: UNDP-EUE.
Jennings, J. W. 1905. *With the Abyssinians in Somaliland*, London: Hodder & Stoughton.
James, W. 1986. 'Lifelines: Exchange Marriage among the Gumuz', in *The Southern Marches of Imperial Ethiopia. Essays in History and Social Anthropology*, edited by D. Donham & W. James. Oxford: James Currey.
——. 1997. 'Local Centres on the Western Frontier, 1974-97: A Case Study of Kurmuk', Presented to 13th ICES, Kyoto.
——. D.L. Donham, E. Kurimoto, A. Triulzi (eds) 2002 *Remapping Ethiopia: Socialism and After*, London: James Currey.
Jesman, C. 1958. *The Russians in Ethiopia*, London: Chatto & Windus.
Jordan Gebre Medhin. 1989. *Peasants and Nationalism in Eritrea: A Critique of Ethiopian Studies*, Trenton, NJ: Red Sea Press.
Juniac de, G. 1979. *Le Dernier Roi des Rois: L'Ethiopie de Haile Selassie*, Paris: Plon.
Kassim Shehim. 1982. 'The Influence of Islam on the Afar', Ph.D. dissertation, University of Washington.
Kelemework Tafere. 2001. 'The Afar in Aba'Ala: Modes of Livelihood and Relations with Tigrean Highlanders' in 'Dryland Husbandry in Ethiopia', edited by Mitiku Haile, Addis Ababa: OSSREA.
——. (n.d.) 'Indigenous Institutions of Conflict Resolution among the Ab'ala Afar of North-eastern Ethiopia', M.A. thesis. School of Graduate Studies, Addis Ababa University.
Keller, E. J. 1988. *Revolutionary Ethiopia: From Empire to People's Republic*, Bloomington: Indiana University Press.
Khazanov, A. M. 1983. *Nomads and the Outside World*, Cambridge: Cambridge University Press.

Kiflemariam Melake. 1997. 'Eco-Physiological Memorrhage of Traditional Agroeconomic Systems in Ethiopia', Presented to the 13th ICES, Kyoto.

Kloos, H. & Aynelem Adugna. 1989. 'The Ethiopian Population: Growth and Distribution', *The Geographical Journal.* 155, 1.

Kluckholm, R. 1962. 'The Konso Economy of Southern Ethiopia,' in *Markets in Africa*, edited by P. Bohannan & G. Dalton. Evanston: Northwestern University.

Knutsson, K. E. 1967. *Authority and Change: A Study of the Kallu Institution among the Macha Galla of Ethiopia*, Gotenborg: Ethnographiska Museet.

Kofi Darkwah, R. H. 1975. *Shewa, Menilek and the Ethiopian Empire: 1813-1889*, London: Heinemann.

Korn, D. 1986. *Ethiopia, the US. And the Soviet Union*, London: Groom Helm.

Kurimoto, E. 1992. 'Natives and Outsiders: The Historical Experience of the Anywaa of Western Ethiopia'. *Journal of Asian and African Studies*, Tokyo.

——. 1993. 'The Dergue Brought the Dinka and the Nuer on Us', Presented at the Workshop on the Sudanese Civil War.

——. 1996. 'People of the River: Subsistence Economy of the Anywaa of Western Ethiopia.' In *Essays in Northeast African Studies*, edited by Shun Sato and Eisei Kurimoto. Osaka: National Museum of Ethnology.

——. 1997. 'Politicization of Ethnicity in Gambella Region', Presented to the 13th ICES, Kyoto.

——. 1998. & S. Simonse. *Conflict, Age and Power in North East Africa*, Oxford: James Currey.

Langmuir, C. R. & Getachew W. Selassie. 1968. 'Technical Memorandum 1968-2', Addis Ababa: Haile Selassie I University.

Laremont, R.R. 2005. 'Borders, States and Nationalism', in R.R. Laremont (ed.) *Borders, States and Nationalism*, Boulder, CO: Lynne Rienner.

Leenco Lata. 1999. *The Ethiopian State at the Crossroads*, Lawrenceville, NJ: Red Sea Press.

——. 2004. *The Horn of Africa as a Common Homeland*, Waterloo: Wilfrid Laurier University Press.

——. 2009. 'Peacekeeping as State Building: The Challenge in the Horn of Africa' Unpublished MS.

Lefort, R. 1983. *Ethiopia: A Heretical Revolution?* London: Zed Books.

Lerner, D. 1958. *The Passing of Traditional Society: Modernising the Middle East*, New York: MacMillan.

Leontieff de, N. 1900. 'Explorations des provinces équatoriales d'Abissinie', *La Geographie*, 2.

Le Sage, A. 2005. 'Stateless Justice in Somalia: Formal and Informal Rule of Law Initiatives', UNDP, Somalia.

Levine, D. N. 1965. *Wax and Gold: Tradition and Innovation in Ethiopian Culture*, Chicago: Chicago University Press.

——. 2000. *Greater Ethiopia: The Evolution of a Multiethnic Society*. Chicago: Chicago University Press.

Lewis, H. S. 1965. *A Galla Monarchy: Jimma Abba Jifar, Ethiopia 1830-1932*, Madison: University of Wisconsin Press.

——. 1993. 'Oromo Political Culture and Ethiopia's Future', Presented to the Symposium on the Making of a New Ethiopian Constitution', Addis Ababa, 17-21 May.

Lewis, I. M. 1958. 'Modern Political Movements in Somaliland', *Africa*, 3/4, 28.

——. 1961. 'Notes on the social organisation of the Ise Somali', *Rassegna di studi Etiopici*, 17.

——.1994. *Blood and Bone: The Call of Kinship in Somali Society*, Lawrenceville, NJ: Red Sea Press.

Lichtheim, G. 1971. *Imperialism*, New York: Praeger.

Lienhardt, G. 1957. 'Annuak village headmen', *Africa*. 27/ 28.

Lijalem Zeray & Moltot Zewdie. 2003. 'Agricultural Water Management in Zone 3 of the Afar Region, Ethiopia: Potential, Constraints and Intervention Options', Werer Agricultural Research Centre.

Lipsky, G. A. 1962. *Ethiopia*, New Haven: HRAF Press.

Little, P. D. 2003. *Somalia: Economy Without a State*, Oxford: James Currey.

Luckham, R. & Dawit Bekele. 1984. 'Foreign Powers and Militarism in the Horn of Africa', *ROAPE*, 29/30.

Lundestad, G. 1990. *The American Empire*, Oslo: Norwegian University Press.

Luttwak, E. N. 1999. 'Give War a Chance', *Foreign Affairs*, 78, 4.

Lydall, J. & I. Strecker. 1979. *The Hamar of Southern Ethiopia*, Hohenschaftlarn: Renner Verlag.

McCann, J. 1987. *From Poverty to Famine in Northeast Ethiopia*, Philadelphia: University of Pennsylvania.

McClellan, C. 1984. 'State Transformation and Social Reconstruction in Ethiopia: The Allure of the South', *International Journal of African Historical Studies*, 17, 4.

Mahteme Selassie Wolde Maskal. 1966. 'Portrait de l'éthiopien typique', Presented to the 3rd ICES. Addis Ababa.

Maknun Gamaledin. 1993. 'The Decline of Afar Pastoralism', in *Conflict and the Decline of Pastoralism in the Horn of Africa*, edited by J. Markakis, London: Macmillan.

Mamdani, M. 1996. *Citizen and Subject.* Princeton, NJ: Princeton University Press.

Mantel-Niecko, J. 1980. *The Role of Land Tenure in the System of Ethiopian Imperial Government in Modern Times.* Warsaw: University of Warsaw.

Marcus, H. 1969a. 'Imperialism and Expansionism in Ethiopia from 1865-1900', in *Colonialism in Africa, 1870-1960*, edited by L. H. Gann & P. Duignan, Cambridge: Cambridge University Press.

——. 1969b. 'Imperialism and Expansion in Ethiopia from 1865 to 1900', in *The History and Politics of Colonialism, 1870 – 1914*, edited by L. H. Gann & P. Duignan, Cambridge: Cambridge University Press.

——. 1975. *The Life and Times of Menelik II: Ethiopia 1844-1913*, Oxford: Clarendon Press.

——. 1987. *Haile Selassie I: The Formative Years, 1892-1936*, Berkeley: University of California.

Markakis, J. 1974. *Ethiopia: Anatomy of a Traditional Polity*, Oxford: Clarendon Press.

——. & Nega Ayele. 1978. *Class and Revolution in Ethiopia*, Nottingham: Spokesman.

——. 1987 *National and Class Conflict in the Horn of Africa*, Cambridge: Cambridge University Press.

——. (ed.). 1993. *Conflict and the Decline of Pastoralism in the Horn of Africa*, London: MacMillan.

——. edited with K. Fukui (1994). *Ethnicity and Conflict in the Horn of Africa*, Oxford: James Currey.

——. 1994. 'The Somali in the New Political Order of Ethiopia', *ROAPE*, 59.

——. 2004. *Pastoralism on the Margin*, London: Minority Rights Group.

Mekonnen Manyawazal. 1994. 'Perspectives on the Sequencing and Speed of Economic Reform in Ethiopia,' in *The Ethiopian Economy: Problems of Adjustment*, Proceedings of the second annual conference on the Ethiopian Economy. Addis Ababa.

Melesse Getu. 1997. 'Local Versus Outsider Forms of Natural Resource Use and Management: The Tsamako Experience in Southwestern Ethiopia', Presented to the 13th ICES. Kyoto.

Mesfin Wolde Mariam. 1986. *Rural Vulnerability to Famine in Ethiopia, 1958-1977*, London: Intermediate Technology Publications.

——. 1999. *The Horn of Africa: Conflict and Poverty*, Addis Ababa Commercial Printing Press.

Minear, L. 2001. 'Pastoralist Community Harmonization in the Karamoja Cluster', Medford MA: Tufts University.

Mkutu. K. A. 2008. *Guns and Governance in the Rift Valley: Pastoralist Conflict and Small Arms*, Oxford: James Currey.

Mohamed Abdi Mohamed. 1997. 'Somalia: Kinship and Relationships Derived from it', in *Mending Rips in the Sky: Options for Somali Communities in the 21st Century*, edited by Hussein M. Adam & R. Ford, Lawrenceville, NJ: Red Sea Press.

Mohammed Hassen. 1994. *The Oromo of Ethiopia: A History, 570-1860*, Trenton, NJ: Red Sea Press.

Mosley, L. 1964. *Haile Selassie: The Conquering Lion*, New Jersey: Prentice Hall.

Motyl, A. J. 1999. *Revolutions, Nations, Empires: Conceptual limits and theoretical possibilities*, New York: Columbia University Press.

Muhereza, F. 2004. 'The Economic Contribution of Pastoralism in Uganda: An Assessment'. Kampala: Centre for Basic Research.

Naty, A. 1992. 'The culture of powerlessness and the spirit of rebellion among the Aari people of southwest Ethiopia', Ph.D. dissertation, Stanford University.

——. 1994. 'From Independent chiefdoms to Abyssinian subjects: the Aari interpretation of conquest and colonization', *Africa*, Rome. 49, 4.
——. 2002. Memory & the Humiliation of Men: The Revolution in Aari', in *Remapping Ethiopia: Socialism and After*, edited by W. James *et al.*, London: James Currey.
Negussie Tilahun. 1983. 'Livestock Marketing in Eastern Ethiopia', Joint Ethiopian Pastoral Systems Study. Addis Ababa: ILCA.
Nelson, C. (ed.). 1973. *The Desert and the Sown*, Berkeley: University of California.
Nelson, H. D. & I. Kaplan. 1981. *Ethiopia: A Country Study*, Washington: Department of the Army.
Nene Mburu. 2005. *Bandits on the Border: The Last Frontier in the Search for Somali Unity*, Oxford: James Currey.
Nesbitt, L. M. 1934. *Desert and Forest: First Journey through the Danakil Country of Eastern Abyssinia*, London: Jonathan Cape.
——. 1935. *Hell-Hole of Creation: The Exploration of the Abyssinian Danakil*, New York: Knopf.
Oberle, P. 1971. 'Afars et Somalis; le Dossier de Djibouti', *Presence Africaine*, 24, 2.
Paulos Milkias. 2006. *Haile Selassie, Modern Education and Political Revolution in Ethiopia*, Amherst, NY: Cambria Press.
Pankhurst, R. (1964) *The Great Ethiopian Famine* (Mimeo: H.S.U library)
——. 1965. 'The Trade of Southern and Western Ethiopia and the Indian Ocean Ports in the Nineteenth and Early Twentieth Centuries', *Journal of Ethiopian Studies*, 3, 2.
——. 1968. *Economic History of Ethiopia: 1800-1935*, Addis Ababa: Haile Selassie I University.
——. 1977. 'The Secret History of the Italian Fascist Occupation of Ethiopia, 1935-1941', *Africa Quarterly*. 16. 4.
Parker, E. 1971. 'Afar Stories, Riddles and Proverbs,' *Journal of Ethiopian Studies*, 9,2.
Pausewang, S., K. Tromvoll, L. Aalen. (eds), 2002. *Ethiopia Since the Derg: A decade of democratic pretension and performance*, London: Zed Books.
Perham, M. 1948. *The Government of Ethiopia*, London: Faber & Faber.
Perner, C. 1997. *The Anyuak – Living on earth in the Sky, The Human Territory*, Basel: Helbing & Lichtenhahn.
Raikes, P. 1981. *Livestock Development and Policy in East Africa*, Uppsala: Scandinavian Institute of African Studies.
Reid, R. 2007. *War in Pre-Colonial Eastern Africa*, Oxford: James Currey.
Robinson, P. W. 1985. 'Gabra Nomadic Pastoralism in the 19th and 20th Century Northern Kenya. Strategies for Survival in a Marginal Environment', Ph.D. dissertation, Northwestern University.
Roth, E. A. 1994. 'Demographic Systems' in *African Pastoralist Systems: An Integrated Approach*, edited by E. Fratkin, K. A. Galvin, E.A. Roth, Boulder CO: Lynne Rienner.
Roundy, R. W. 1976. 'Altitudinal Mobility and Disease Hazards for Ethiopian Populations', *Economic Geography*. 52, 2.
Rubenson, S. 1966. *King of Kings Tewodros of Ethiopia*, Addis Ababa: Haile Selassie I University.
Said S. Samatar. 1982. *Oral Poetry and Somali Nationalism: The Case of Sayyid Mohammed Abdille Hasan*, Cambridge: Cambridge University Press.
Salviak de, M. 1905. *Une Peuple antique au pays de Ménélik: les galla, grande nation.*
Sandford, S. & Yohannes Habtu. 2002. 'Report of the Pastoral Appraisal Team', Addis Ababa, DFID.
——. 2005. 'Evaluation report of Save the Children US projects in Filtu and Liben woreda of Somali kilil', Addis Ababa.
Sbacchi, A. 1985. *Ethiopia under Mussolini: Fascism and the Colonial Experience*. London: Zed Press.
Schlee, G. 1992. 'Ritual Topography and Ecological Use: The Gabbra of the Kenyan/ Ethiopian Borderlands' in *Bush base: forest farm*, edited by E. Croll & D. Parkin, London: Routledge.
——. & Abdulahi A. Shongolo. 1995. 'Local War and its Impact on Ethnic and Religious Identification in Southern Ethiopia', *GeoJournal*, 36, 1.
——. 2002 'Regularity in Chaos: The Politics of Difference in the Recent History of Somali', in *Imagined Differences: Hatred and the Construction of Identity*, edited by G. Schlee, New York: Palgrave.

Schuiver, J. M. 1996. in *Schuiver's Travels in North East Africa, 1880-1883*, edited by W. James, G. Baumann, D. Johnson, London: Hakluyt Society.

Schwab, P. 1972. *Decision-Making in Ethiopia*, London: Hurst.

Scott, J. C. 1998. *Seeing Like a State*, New Haven: Yale University Press.

Sibson, V. 2004. 'Findings of a Nutrition Survey, Zone 3, Afar Region', Addis Ababa: GOAL.

Sihab ad-Din. 2003. *Futuh al-Habasa: The Conquest of Abyssinia (16th Century)*, Holywood: Tsehai Publishers.

Smith, A. D. 1987. *The Ethnic Origins of Nations*, Oxford: Blackwell.

——. 1993. *National Identity (Ethnonationalism in Comparative Perspective*, Reno: University of Nevada Press.

Solomon Desta. 1999. 'Diversification of Livestock Assets for Risk Management in the Borana Pastoral System of Southern Ethiopian', Ph.D. dissertation, Utah State University.

Somali National Regional State. 1999. 'Livestock Development Program for Jijiga Zone'. Jijiga: Bureau of Finance and Economic Development.

——. 2000. 'Resource Potential Assessment and Project Identification Study of the Somali Region', Jijiga: Industrial Projects Services.

——. 2002. 'Capacity Building for District Level Decentralisation Program for Somali State', Addis Ababa.

——. 2005a. 'Woreda Budget Sharing Grant Formula', Jijiga: Bureau of Finance and Economic Development.

——. 2005b. 'Regional Consultation Outcome for the Formulation of Ethiopia's Second Sustainable Development and Poverty Reduction Program', Jijiga: Bureau of Finance & Economic Development.

Sorenson, J. 1993. *Imagining Ethiopia: Struggles for History and Identity in the Horn of Africa*, New Brunswick, NJ: Rutgers University Press.

Spencer, J. H. 1984. *Ethiopia at Bay. A Personal Account*, Algonac, Michigan: Reference Publications.

Stalin, J. 1936. *Marxism and the National and Colonial Questions*, London: Lawrence and Wishart.

Stauder, J. 1971. *The Majangir: Ecology and Society of a Southwest Ethiopian People*, Cambridge: Cambridge University Press.

Strecker, I. (n.d.). 'The Temptation of War and the Struggle for Peace Among the Hamar of Southern Ethiopia', *Sociologus*. Berlin.

——. 1990. 'Political Discourse among the Hamar of Southern Ethiopia', Proceedings of the First National Conference of Ethiopian Studies, Addis Ababa.

——. 2006. 'Cultural variations in the concept of face', in *The Perils of Face: Essays on cultural contact, respect and self-esteem in southern Ethiopia*, edited by I. Strecker & J. Lydall, Berlin: Lit Verlag.

Swedish International Development Cooperation Agency. 2009. 'Ethiopia: Study on Institutional Structure and Human Resource Development Needs in the Sector of Land Administration in Ethiopia', (Framework Agreement on Public Sector Development 2007-000832) Final Report. 31 January 2009. ORGUT.

Tablino, P. 1999. *The Gabra Camel Nomads of Northern Kenya*, Nairobi: Kolbe Press.

Tadesse Berisso. 1991. 'Warfare among the Guji Oromo of Southern Ethiopia', Presented to the 11th ICES. Addis Ababa.

——. 2002. 'Modernist Dreams & Human Suffering: Villagisation among the Guji Oromo', in *Remapping Ethiopia: Socialism and After*, edited by W. James *et al.*, Oxford: James Currey.

——. 2006. 'The Pride of the Guji-Oromo: An essay on cultural contact and self-esteem', In *The Perils of Face: Essays on cultural contact, respect and self-esteem in southern Ethiopia*, edited by I. Strecker & J. Lydall, Berlin: Lit Verlag.

Teferra Haile Selassie. 1997. *The Ethiopian Revolution*, London: Keegan Paul.

Tegegne Taka. 1998. 'Amhara Ethnicity in the Making', in *Ethnicity and the State in Eastern Africa*, edited by M.A. Mohamed Salih & J. Markakis, Uppsala: Scandinavian Institute of African Studies.

Tesema Ta'a. 2007. 'Defying the System: The Forgotten Rebellion of Abaa Xoonee in

Wallaga', Presented to the 13th ICES, 1997, Kyoto.
Teshale Tibebu. 1996. 'Ethiopia: The "Anomaly" and "Paradox" of Africa', *Journal of Black Studies*. 26, 4.
Tesfaye Shewaye & C. Taylor. 1976. 'Language Curricula', in *Language in Ethiopia*, edited by M. L Bender, Oxford: Oxford University Press.
Thesiger, W. 1935. 'The Awash River and the Aussa Sultanate', *Geographical Journal*, lxxxv.
Tilahun Sinehaw. 1994. 'A Critical Examination of the 1979-1991 Ethiopian National Literacy Campaign', Presented to the 12th ICES, East Lansing.
Tilly, C. 1975. 'Introduction', in *The Formation of Nation States in Western Europe*, edited by C. Tilly, Princeton: Princeton University Press.
——. 1985. 'War Making and State Making as Organized Crime', in *Bringing the State Back In*, edited by P. Evans, D. Rueschemeyer, T. Skocpol, Cambridge: Cambridge University Press.
——. 1990. *Coercion, Capital and European States, AD 990-1990*, Oxford: Blackwell.
Tivey, L. 1981. *The Nation-State-The Formation of Modern Politics*, New York: St. Martin's Press.
Tornay, S. A. M. 1979. 'Armed Conflict in the Lower Omo Valley, 1970-1976,' in *Warfare among East African Herders*, edited by K. Fukui & D. Turton, Osaka: National Museum of Ethnology.
——. 1981. 'The Nyangatom: An Outline of their Ecology and Social Organisation', in *Peoples and Cultures of the Ethio-Sudan Borderlands*, edited by M. L. Bender, East Lansing: Michigan State University.
——. 1989. 'Un Système Générationnel: les Nyangatom du Sud-ouest de l'Ethiopie et les Peuples Apparentes', Thèse d'Etat, Université de Paris X Nanterre.
Torry, W. 1978. 'Gabbra Age Organisation and Ecology', in *Age, Generation and Time*, edited by P.T.W. Baxter & U. Almagor, London: Hurst.
Touval, S. 1963. *Somali Nationalism: International Politics and the Drive for Unity in the Horn of Africa*, Cambridge, MA: Harvard University Press.
Trewartha, G. T. 1961. *The Earth's Problem Climates*, Madison: University to Wisconsin Press.
Trimingham, J. S. 1952. *Islam in Ethiopia*, London: Oxford University Press.
Triulzi, A. 1973. 'The Background to Ras Gobana's Expedition to Western Wallega in 1886-1888', in Marcus, H. (ed.) Proceedings of the 1st ICES Addis Ababa.
——. 1977. 'Social Protest and Rebellion in Some Gabbar Songs from Qellam in Wallaga', Presented to 5th ICES. Nice.
——. 1981. *Salt, Gold and Legitimacy*, Napoli: Instituto Universitario Orientale.
——. 1984. 'Center-Periphery Relations in Ethiopian Studies: Reflections on Ten Years of Research on Wellega History', Presented to 5th ICES. East Lansing.
——. 2002. Battling with the Past: New Frameworks for Ethiopian Historiography', in *Remapping Ethiopia: Socialism and After*, edited by W. James *et al.*, London: James Currey.
Tronvoll, K. 2001. 'Voting, violence and violations: peasant voices on the flawed elections in Hadiya, Southern Ethiopia', *Journal of Modern African Studies*. 39. 4.
——. 2009. *War and the Politics of Identity in Ethiopia*, Oxford: James Currey.
Tsegaye Tegenu. 1997. 'Ethiopia: What's in a Name?' Presented to the 13th ICES. Kyoto.
Turton, D. 1973. 'The social organization of the Mursi, a pastoral tribe of the lower Omo valley', Ph.D. dissertation, London School of Economics and Political Science.
——. 1985. 'Mursi Response to Drought: Some Lessons for Relief and Rehabilitation', *African Affairs*, 84, 336.
——. 1986. 'A problem of domination in the periphery: The Kwegu and the Mursi', in *The Southern Marches of Imperial Ethiopia. Essays in History and Social Anthropology*, edited by D.L. Donham & W. James. Oxford: James Currey.
——. 1994. 'Mursi Political Identity and Warfare: The Survival of an Idea', in *Ethnicity and Conflict in the Horn of Africa*, edited by K. Fukui & J. Markakis, London: James Currey.
——. 2002. 'The Same only Different: War and Duelling as Boundary Marking Rituals in Mursiland, Southwestern Ethiopia', in *War and Games*, edited by T. J. Cornell & T. B. Allen. Woodbridge Suffolk: The Boydell Press.
——. 2003. The Politician, the Priest and the Anthropologist: Living Beyond Conflict in Southwestern Ethiopia', *Ethnos*, 68, 1.

——. (ed.). 2006. *Ethnic Federalism: The Ethiopian Experience in Comparative Perspective*, Oxford: James Currey.

Ullendorff, E. 1965. *The Ethiopians*, Oxford: Oxford University Press.

UNDP/ECA. 1998. 'Jijiga Zone, Jijiga Woreda (Project ETH 94/001/01/99)', Addis Ababa: Woreda Agriculture and Rural Development Integrated Services.

UNDP. 2003. 'Integrated Biodiversity Management in and Around Yangudi Rassa National Part, Mid and Northern Afar Region, Ethiopia', Addis Ababa: Project Document.

UNHCR. 1992. 'Socio-Economic Survey of the Refugee Population in Somalia', Mogadisho. April.

Vaughan, S. 1994. 'The Addis Ababa Transitional Conference of July 1991', Edinburgh University, Centre of African Studies.

——. 2003. 'Ethnicity and Power in Ethiopia', Ph.D. dissertation, University of Edinburgh.

Van der Loo, J. 1991. *Guji Oromo Culture in Southern Ethiopia*, Berlin: Reimer.

Werer Agricultural Research Centre (WARC). [2003]. 'Rain Deficiency According to the Data at Werer Meteorological Station Data. 1970-2003', Afar National Regional State.

——. [n.d. (b.)]. 'Crop Production,' Afar National Regional State.

——. [n.d. (c)]. 'Annual Report of Socio-Economic Impact of Commercial Agriculture on Pastoralists', Afar Regional State.

Wellby, M. S. 1901. *Twixt Sirdar and Menelik*, London: Harper and Brothers.

Wesson, R. 1967. *The Imperial Order*, Berkeley: University of California Press.

Wistanley, D. 1973. 'Rainfall Patterns and General Atmospheric Circulation', *Nature*, 245, 5422.

Wolde Gossa Tadesse. 1997. 'Cowrie Belts and Kalashnikovs', Presented to 13th ICES. Kyoto.

——. 2002. 'Evading the Revolutionary State: The Hor under the Derg', in *Remapping Ethiopia: Socialism and After*, edited by W. James *et al.*, London: James Currey.

——. 2006. 'Having friends everywhere. The case of the Gamo and the Hor', in *The Perils of Face: Essays on cultural contact, respect and self-esteem in southern Ethiopia*, edited by I. Strecker & J. Lydall, Berlin: Lit Verlag.

Wolde Selassie Abboute Deboch. 2002. 'Gumuz and Highland Resettlers: Differing Strategies of Livelihood and Ethnic Relations in Metekel, Northwestern Ethiopia', Ph.D. dissertation, University of Göttingen.

——. 2004. *Gumuz and Highlander Resettlers: Differing Strategies of Livelihood and Ethnic Relations in Metekel, Northwestern Ethiopia*, Berlin: Lit Verlag.

Wood, J. 1999. *When Men are Women: Manhood among the Gabra nomads of East Africa*, Madison: University of Wisconsin Press.

World Bank/PCDP. 2005. 'Baseline Survey Report for Oromia Region, Borana Zone, Arero Woreda', Addis Ababa.

Ydibli, M. 2006. *With Ethiopian Rulers: A Biography of Ydibli*, Addis Ababa University Press.

Young, C. 1982. 'Nationalising the Third World State: Categorical Imperative or Mission Impossible', *Polity*. 15, 2.

Young, J. 1996. 'The Tigray and Eritrean Peoples Liberation Fronts: A History of Tensions and Pragmatism', *The Journal of Modern African Studies*, 34, 1.

——. 1997. *Peasant Revolution in Ethiopia: The Tigray Peoples Liberation Front, 1975-91*, Cambridge: Cambridge University Press.

Yukio Miyawaki. 1994. 'Demographic Composition and Kinship Structure of the Village of the Tsamai Chief, South-Western Ethiopia', Presented to the 11th ICES, Addis Ababa.

——. 2006. 'Hor memory of Sidaama conquest', in *The Perils of Face: Essays on cultural contact, respect and self-esteem in southern Ethiopia*, edited by I. Strecker & J. Lydall, Berlin: Lit Verlag.

Zewde Gebre Selassie. 1975. *Yohaness IV of Ethiopia: A Political Biography*, Oxford: Clarendon Press.

Index